HUMPHREY BOGART

Humphrey Bogart c. 1942. *Courtesy of Photofest*.

HUMPHREY BOGART
A Bio-Bibliography

Gerald Duchovnay

Popular Culture Bio-Bibliographies
M. Thomas Inge, Series Editor

Greenwood Press
Westport, Connecticut • London

Library of Congress Cataloging-in-Publication Data

Duchovnay, Gerald, 1944–
    Humphrey Bogart : a bio-bibliography / by Gerald Duchovnay.
        p. cm.—(Popular culture bio-bibliographies, ISSN
    0193–6891)
        Discography: p.
        Filmography: p.
        Includes bibliographical references and index.
        ISBN 0–313–22338–6 (alk. paper)
        1. Bogart, Humphrey, 1899–1957. 2. Bogart, Humphrey, 1899–1957.—
    Bibliography. 3. Motion picture actors and actresses—United
    States—Biography. I. Title. II. Series.
    PN2287.B48D83   1999
    791.43'028'092—dc21
    [B]   98–26538

British Library Cataloguing in Publication Data is available.

Copyright © 1999 by Gerald Duchovnay

All rights reserved. No portion of this book may be
reproduced, by any process or technique, without the
express written consent of the publisher.

Library of Congress Catalog Card Number: 98–26538
ISBN: 0–313–22338–6
ISSN: 0193–6891

First published in 1999

Greenwood Press, 88 Post Road West, Westport, CT 06881
An imprint of Greenwood Publishing Group, Inc.

Printed in the United States of America

The paper used in this book complies with the
Permanent Paper Standard issued by the National
Information Standards Organization (Z39.48–1984).

10 9 8 7 6 5 4 3 2 1

Copyright Acknowledgments

The author and publisher are grateful to the following for granting permission to reprint from their materials:

Bogart, Humphrey. "Censorship." *Hollywood Reporter*, 11th Anniversary Issue (October 31, 1941). In *The Hollywood Reporter: The Golden Years*. Ed. Tichi Wilkerson and Marcia Borie. New York: Coward-McCann, 1984: 140–41.

Bogart, Humphrey. "I Stuck My Neck Out." *The Saturday Evening Post* (February 10, 1945). Reprinted from *The Saturday Evening Post*. © 1945 The Curtis Publishing Company.

Bogart, Humphrey. "Bogart on Hollywood." *Look* 20 (August 21, 1956): 96–98, 100–101. Reprinted with permission from H & C Communications, Inc.

Hover, Helen. "Popping Questions at Humphrey Bogart." *Motion Picture* (December 1943): 38–39, 55–59.

Every reasonable effort has been made to trace the owners of copyright materials in this book, but in some instances this has proven impossible. The author and publisher will be glad to receive information leading to more complete acknowledgments in subsequent printings of the book and in the meantime extend their apologies for any omissions.

CONTENTS

Preface ix

The Bio-bibliography

1. **Biography** 1

2. **Humphrey Bogart's Impact on Popular Culture** 45

3. **Interviews** 87

4. **Bibliographical Essay** 115
   Biographies and Career Overviews 115
   Films 148

5. **Bibliographical Checklists of Humphrey Bogart Sources** 243
   Biographical and Critical Studies 243
   Films 247

   Appendixes
   I. Chronological Biography 277
   II. Theatrical Performances 283
   III. Filmography 285
   IV. Radio and Television Appearances 315

V. Discography	319
VI. Broadcasts and/or Videos about Humphrey Bogart	321
VII. Internet	323
Index	325

PREFACE

He was a personality, a star, and a professional. Within a decade after his death, he became a legend. More than forty years later, to his fans and film historians he remains a symbol of the Golden Age of Hollywood, the star system, and an iconoclast within that system. Whether we are attracted to him through his movies or are reminded of him via screen look-alikes, the French praise of *l'existentialisme de Bogart*, the influence of filmmakers such as Jean-Luc Godard and Woody Allen, restaurants and bars, or the repetition of phrases such as, "I stick my neck out for nobody," or "Here's looking at you, kid," Humphrey Bogart remains an integral part of our social consciousness. His role as a Hollywood icon, regular reference to such films as *Casablanca, The Maltese Falcon*, and *The Big Sleep*, and audience identification with the actor or his roles are a highly visible part of the fabric of our culture. Jack Nicholson, Clint Eastwood, Mel Gibson, and Harrison Ford may create a more contemporary take on his image, but there remains one Bogart. The very multiplicity of associations suggests that while a critic or fan may focus on one or two aspects of the actor or his persona as touchstones to an understanding of Bogart, it is his life and films, and especially his life on films, that will continue to sustain us as time goes by.

Humphrey Bogart: A Bio-Bibliography provides an overview of the actor's life, an extensive survey of the scholarly and popular articles about Bogart and his films, and a review of his impact on American popular culture. Also included are representative interviews, comments from one of his B-film directors, a filmography, listings of theater, radio, and television appearances, a discography, a videography, and selected web sites.

The completion of the research on this book has involved the assistance of many individuals on several continents over more years than I care to remember.

To those who offered support, new leads, observations, and bits of information, I will forever be indebted. They are, however, blameless for any oversights, inconsistencies, omissions, or errors that may have found their way into the text. Robert Armour introduced me to the idea for this project, and to him and Tom Inge, the series editor, I will always be grateful. At Greenwood Press, I thank Alicia Merritt and Pamela St. Clair for their patience and support, and Terry Park and Beverly Miller for their excellent editorial assistance.

Marty Sugden and Anna Large of Jacksonville University were instrumental early on in locating some of the sources that helped initiate this project. Friends and colleagues at Jacksonville University who shared Bogart references include Robert Waxman, Mary May, George Hallam, Pat McLeod, Dedra Torelli, Joan Carver, and Fran Kinne. I thank Jacksonville University's Research and Development Committee for awarding me a grant to defray partially my initial research at the Warner Bros. Archives at the State Historical Society of Wisconsin. Adrienne Reep, George Lucas, John Byron, and Sean Kelley were students (and later friends) who offered insightful suggestions about Bogart and his appeal. To Michele Lellouche, who has shared many of her Bogart memories and associations related to popular culture and web site discoveries, I owe special thanks.

One of the main problems confronting those interested in researching Humphrey Bogart and his films is the lack of a comprehensive bibliography of available reference materials and depositories of materials. For this study I visited numerous archives, film centers, and research libraries and corresponded with individuals too numerous to name who assisted in countless ways. I especially thank Maxine Fleckner Ducey and the staff at the Wisconsin Center for Film and Theater Research, located in the State Historical Society of Wisconsin. I remember fondly my visits to the center and the support of those who work there, as well as the many kindnesses of staff personnel in the various University of Wisconsin libraries in Madison. I also was assisted by the staffs at the Princeton University Library, which for a time housed some Warner Bros. documents; the Special Collection in Cinema at the Doheny Memorial Library of the University of Southern California; the Theatre Arts Library at the University of California, Los Angeles; the Margaret Herrick Library of the Academy of Motion Picture Arts and Sciences; the American Film Institute libraries in Washington, D.C., and Los Angeles; the Motion Picture, Broadcasting, and Sound Division of the Library of Congress; the UCLA Radio Archives; the Billy Rose Theatre Collection at the New York Public Library for the Performing Arts; and the Dallas Public Library.

The Graduate School at Texas A&M University-Commerce (formerly East Texas State University) provided me with a mini-grant, which permitted me to continue aspects of my research. Scott Downing, Diane Downing, Shannon Ashbaugh, Patti Towne, Mary Brunz, Chess Johnson, Penny Dooley, Elaine Fahrenkamp, James W. Byrd, James A. Grimshaw, Jr., Maria dos Santos, Bill McCarron, Brenda Bell, Bob Houston, and Steve Razniak contributed in a myriad of ways to this work. Alicia Alderman supplied information about Bogart and CMG Worldwide, Ken Harris of Imperial Film Services (Burbank) offered information on the Bold Venture radio shows, Ida Jeter shared little-known information on *Black Legion*, Bill Holodnak and the staff at the Brattle Theatre in Cambridge, Massachusetts, provided background information on Bogart festivals, Robert Sacchi was kind enough to provide me with information on his uses of the Bogart persona, and Vincent Sherman was most generous with his time when I interviewed him on Humphrey Bogart. I am also most appreciative of the assistance of Sarah J. Davis, who shared clippings related to Bogart and information about the Bogart and Bacall fan club, which she founded. In addition, a work of this nature builds on the previous commentaries of Humphrey Bogart's family, friends (and enemies), colleagues, fans, film critics and scholars. Without them, this book would not exist.

For their encouragement and support during the research and writing of this work, I thank Jay Telotte, Wade Jennings, and the late Ted Ross. A special thanks to Judy Riggin for her numerous forays into the Library of Congress, and most especially for her friendship and good humor.

My deepest appreciation is to my family, who has been there in good and bad times, contributing to the many essences of this work. I am deeply indebted to my deceased father who taught me the joy of learning, my mother who is always there with her support and the latest Bogart reference, my brother who introduced me to the complexities of filmmaking and film viewing, and to Brian and Bram, who have given me greater joy than any movie possibly could.

1

BIOGRAPHY

THE EARLY YEARS

Some of the facts and most of the fictions that helped generate the legend of Humphrey Bogart are traceable to his actions, studio press releases, articles by or about him, and a number of biographies. When an individual becomes a legend, it is sometimes difficult to trace the facts because they have been woven into the cloth of numerous retellings. When faced with printing the truth or continuing the legend, the newspaper editor in John Ford's *The Man Who Shot Liberty Valance* (1962) remarks, "When the legend becomes fact, print the legend." Such seems to be the case with some parts of Bogart's life.

The obfuscation starts with something as simple as Humphrey Bogart's birthdate. Some of his biographers are at odds as to when to begin. As early as September 7, 1924, a biographical blurb in the *New York Times* says he was born in 1900. Other accounts, including studio files and some press releases, as well as some fan magazines in 1936 and 1937, specifically give Christmas Day 1900, at Sloan's Maternity Hospital in upper Manhattan. Sources as late as the mid-1930s, including *Current Biography*, different studio press releases, and *Who's Who*, indicate the actor was born on January 23, 1899. The obituary in the *London Times* gives the date as June 23, 1899, as does *Who Was Who in the Theatre: 1912–1976*.[1] One biographer, David Hanna, says the actor was born January 23, 1889—nine years before the actor's parents were married—and in an otherwise accurate story about Bogart's breakup with his third wife, Louella Parsons gives the date as Christmas Day 1894.[2]

Some of the confusion may be intentional, if Bogart, or his press agent, ever aware of the benefits of an appealing story and the need to create memorable publicity, and never wasting an opportunity to hype his client, tried to romanticize his image. As a Hollywood heavy, he could achieve greater mileage by giving out that he was a Christmas present from his parents to the screen. Published reports in the 1940s indicate that he celebrated his birthday on Christmas and occasionally lamented the loss of presents. Lauren Bacall says they always celebrated his birthday on Christmas Day, and Stephen Bogart's book on his father also gives a Christmas birthdate, while CMG, the licensing agent for all things related to the Bogart name and image, oddly gives the date as January 23, 1899, on one page of its Internet site, and December 25, 1899, on another page. Jonathan Coe takes the middle road, giving both December and January dates as possibilities. Ezra Goodman, who did a cover story for *Time* and later a biography on Bogart, reports that over lunch at Romanoff's, Bogart told him that he was born on December 25, 1899.

Many recent biographers or editors, including Nathaniel Benchley, Otto Friedrich, Jeffrey Meyers, and A. M. Sperber and Eric Lax, agree on December 25, 1899.[3] One fan of Bogart, Robert Young, claims on a Bogart web site to have a copy of the marriage license application from the Richland County, Ohio, Probate Court Records Office on which December 25, 1899, is listed as Bogart's date of birth. In Bogart's FBI file there is a personnel security questionnaire completed for his participation in USO camp shows that lists his birthdate as December 25, 1899. The application is typed and not signed (and misspells his father's middle name as "De Forist"), so there is no evidence that Bogart, rather than the USO Camp Shows Inc. or some other group or individual, typed up the form. The report attached to this application, which reports on his loyalty and character, says that his birthdate in New York City was not confirmed. This may explain why I was denied confirmation of the exact date by the vital statistics section of the Public Health Department in New York City, and why A. M. Sperber notes that the actual certificate is "lost." Sperber, though, in an outstanding bit of sleuthing, was able to track down a birth announcement in the January 10, 1900, issue of the *Ontario County Times*, which announces the birth on December 25, 1899.[4] This paper printed news of the "region's notables"; the Bogarts, well known and well connected, had a summer home in upstate New York. I suggest that some of the confusion surrounding the January 23 date may be attributed to Bogart's second marriage to Mary Philips, who was born on January 23, 1901.[5] Might someone early on have confused her birthdate with his?

Humphrey Bogart's parents spared no expense in rearing their son, and later his two younger sisters, Frances and Kay (Catharine). His father, Belmont DeForest Bogart, was a young and up-and-coming physician. His mother, Maud Humphrey, was a famous illustrator and author of children's stories. Both could trace their ancestry as far back as 1500, including royalty. Prior to the wedding of Prince Charles and Lady Diana Spencer, Hugh Peskett, the senior genealogist of *Debrett's Guide to the Aristocracy*, and David Williamson, senior editor of *Burke's Peerage*, announced that Lady Diana was Humphrey Bogart's seventh cousin on his mother's side, linked through two daughters of Joseph Morgan, a New England farmer who died in 1704.[6]

With money that he inherited and income from his wife's job, the young couple established their residence in a four-story brownstone at 245 West 103rd Street, near Riverside Drive. Dr. Bogart's office was located on the first floor, where he treated fashionable, upper-class patients. Maud Humphrey had a studio on the top floor, where she secluded herself from the daily maintenance of the home to write children's books, work on illustrations, or suffer from frequent migraine headaches.

Several months after her son was born, Maud Humphrey brought her cherub-faced offspring up to her studio to use as a model. Of the various drawings and illustrations she made for children's stories, advertisements, and numerous magazines, including *Delineator*, the sketch of baby Humphrey was to become the most recognized. Mellins Baby Food Co. purchased it for use in advertisements and on labels for its baby food. By the age of one, the face of Humphrey Bogart was already well known as "the original Maud Humphrey Baby."[7] He was to remain a model for years to come, including as a frontispiece for George MacDonald's *The Light Princess* at age eight. Later in life he tried to conceal from his schoolmates that it was his likeness on those labels and in the books; by the mid-forties that face, this time with its weary, pained expressions, had become a visual touchstone for decades to come.

An early advocate for women's rights, Maud Humphrey gave top priority to her career. As her son remembers her, "She was essentially a woman who loved work, loved *her* work, to the exclusion of everything else. I doubt that she read very much. I know that she never played any games. She went to no parties, gave none. Actually I can't remember that she even had any friends, until she was a very old woman—and then she had only one. She had a few acquaintances who were mostly male artists. . . . But she never had a confidante, never was truly intimate with anyone and, I am certain, never wanted to be."[8]

Dr. Bogart often took off from work for up to three months, retreating to Willow Brook, the family resort home at Seneca Point on Canandaigua Lake, one of the Finger Lakes in upstate New York. He would fish, hunt, and motor around the lake. Dr. Bogart's love of boating was shared by his son. Later in his life, being at the helm of his boat became Humphrey Bogart's main solace and only peace during the difficult periods in his life. When the family did get together, the atmosphere frequently was charged. Those traits that attracted the young medical student to his future bride—her imposing demeanor, elegant manners, and sharp, often sarcastic tongue—were the same ones that created a rift in the household. The battles were verbal rather than physical, and they seemed to have helped shape aspects of Bogart's character, choice of wives, and later screen image.

The Bogarts, members of Dau's *New York Blue Book*, the social register for the respected and fashionable, generally were too busy to attend to their son's needs, and the young Humphrey saw very little of them. Being a two-income family, with income well exceeding $50,000 per year, an amount that Maud herself was bringing in as early as 1895,[9] the Bogarts could easily afford to send their son to the best private schools. For his early years they chose Delancey School, where the emphasis was on discipline. Each day a nurse or other servant escorted him to and from school and catered to his wants at home. Starting in the fifth grade, he attended Trinity School, on 91st Street between Columbus and Amsterdam, for seven years.[10] These schools had programs rigorous enough to satisfy his parents, both of whom expected their son to attend Yale or Columbia. However, he was somewhat withdrawn and apparently lacking social graces, and classmates do not recall his bringing any girls to the dances. Although the school taught dancing, he "could dance, but not well," and with little interest in sports, he had a rough time there. Doug Storer, a classmate, says that "he was always afraid of getting hurt," and Eric Hodgins remembers him as wearing a black derby to school and being somewhat distant. Trying to overcome his isolation, each spring he entertained his classmates at his home for lunch and a trip to the circus.

Outings aside, his peers did not much take to him: "Bogart's good looks, his tidiness ('one of the best-groomed youngsters in the school'), his 'sissy' name (we always called him Humphrey and never thought to give him the solace of a nickname) were all against him. Added to this was our knowledge that as a baby he had posed for his mother's 'pretty picture.' The fact that his mother was Maude [sic] Humphrey, the most famous woman illustrator of her day, impressed us not at all; the fact that Humphrey had been a model, however, seemed hilarious."[11]

With grades mostly in the fifties and sixties and a repetition of eleventh grade, he showed little promise of becoming the surgeon his parents wanted. In an effort to prep his son for some kind of a career, Dr. Bogart wrote to a former classmate and then headmaster at Phillips Academy, in Andover, Massachusetts, Dr. Alfred E. Stearns, requesting admission for his son. He informed Dr. Stearns that Humphrey was most likely not going on to college, but that he needed the year of schooling.

Young Bogart was admitted in 1917, but he disliked Phillips and rarely studied. His indifference to academics resulted in a series of warnings from the school's administration and his parents, but to little avail. By May 1918, after a series of probations and the loss of out-of-town and evening rights, Humphrey Bogart packed his bags, turned his back on school, and headed for New York.[12] Years later Bogart spoke favorably of Phillips, and his widow, Lauren Bacall, sent their son, Stephen, there to continue the Bogart family tradition.

When Humphrey Bogart returned from school, both parents were disappointed. His failure only served to heighten the family's sudden decline in fortune. Dr. Bogart's purchase of Michigan timberland had proved to be a poor investment, and the family was forced to sell their home at Lake Canandaigua. Realizing that to remain at home would lead only to continual harassment and with no career plans, Bogart turned to the military. Friends were joining the army, but his love of sailing and a chance to travel convinced him that the navy was the route to take. At approximately age eighteen, with a war raging on foreign shores, what danger did he face? Years later Bogart said, "The war was a big joke, . . . Death? What does death mean to a kid of eighteen? . . . At eighteen war was great stuff. Paris! French girls! Hot damn!"[13] This response could easily be a part of Bogart's tough yet innocent image that he later tried to foist on his viewing public. In this same interview, Bogart tells fans that his records were lost, for months he was considered a deserter, and that he got his scar from a piece of wood that splintered off a beam and lodged in his lip during a shelling. As Nathaniel Benchley has noted, by the time Bogart saw active duty on the troopship USS *Leviathan*, the war had been over for sixteen days.

Another alleged scenario for the scar and lisp was a result of Bogart's graciousness or naiveté. While transporting a prisoner to the brig, Bogart struck a match to allow the prisoner a smoke. Not unlike some of the action seen in *The Last Detail* (1973), his captive turned, swung at him with his handcuffs, hit him on the mouth, and fled. As the story goes, Bogart prevented the prisoner's escape by shooting, but not killing, the man. Sperber and Lax maintain there was "no definite cause" to the scar.[14] Whatever the circumstances, the scar and a controlled lisp remained to contribute to his later screen persona. Bogart finished out his tour on the USS *Santa Olivia*. Except for a short term in the brig for missing a sailing, he was given a good evaluation on his honorable discharge on June 18, 1919. Years later when asked about his military career, he described it as "completely undistinguished."[15]

When he returned home, job prospects were no brighter than before he enlisted. Seeking the aid of his friends and parents, he was able to secure a series of odd jobs, including a clerk's position for the Pennsylvania Railroad and serving as a runner for a Wall Street brokerage firm. Much of his spare time he devoted to carousing with John Cromwell, Kenneth MacKenna, Bill Brady, Jr., and Stuart Rose, who later married his sister, Frances ("Pat"). It was through the offices of the Brady family that the dissatisfied young man found the first job that he liked. Harrison Ford, who has been linked to the Bogart persona for his roles in the Indiana Jones films, sounds almost as if he is speaking for Bogart when he tells Tom Seligson, "Acting was a way out at first. A way out of not knowing what to do, a way of focusing ambitions. And the ambition wasn't for fame. The ambition was to do an interesting job. After I did it for a while, I realized that this would be a wonderful way to spend a life. I thought of it like being in the Navy. I would travel around and meet interesting people. But I wouldn't have to kill them."[16] Leonard Nimoy explains why he turned to acting: "I was trying to understand my frustrations. What was I going to do with my life? I didn't enjoy academics or school. I was not athletically oriented. I wanted to attach myself to something, give myself a sense of focus. I, too, was floundering, floundering. I became attached to the theater. It made great sense to me. Eventually, I realized that I could move sideways and play people other than those my own age. And this stubbornness drove me on. Once I set a goal for myself, I don't like to admit defeat. My goal was to be accepted as a professional, to be part of the body of work when work was scarce, when there was not enough work to go around. It was persistence. I decided to do it in spite of any difficulties."[17] The sentiments of Ford and Nimoy could well serve as glosses for Bogart's decision to become part of the theatrical world.

The Brady family lived around the corner from the Bogarts. William Brady, Sr., produced plays, many of them starring his second wife, Grace George. His daughter by his first marriage was Alice Brady. A well-established actress, she was the original Lavinia Mannon in Eugene O'Neill's *Mourning Becomes Electra* (1931) and later a hit in Gregory La Cava's *My Man Godfrey* (1936). Alice Brady took a professional interest in her brother's friend and suggested that he take acting lessons.[18] Later she asked her father to employ Bogart. Brady did, first as an office boy and then, after dismissing Travers Vale as director on his film *Life*, as a movie director. This effort was short-lived. The office-boy-as-director was dismissed, forcing Brady to try to salvage the disaster. Shortly after Alice Brady asked him if he would be the road manager for *Experience* (1920). Needing a job, wanting theater experience, hoping to travel and at the same time remain close to a friend, Bogart accepted.

For the first time, Humphrey Bogart was not locked into a boring, stifling position. Although ultimately accountable to the Bradys, he was giving, not taking, orders and managing company details. His next job was as company manager for the touring company of *The "Ruined" Lady*, for which he was paid fifty dollars per week and was responsible for detail work and making sure that all aspects of preproduction ran smoothly. At the end of the run, Neil Hamilton, tired of hearing Bogart taunt the actors about how soft a job they had, let Bogart take his place. One biography maintains that he never got past the Saturday rehearsal; Alice Brady became ill, thus forcing the closing of the show. Another contends that Bogart was terrified and thankful when the curtain came down. *Who's Who in the Theatre* (1939) states that the role of Bill Bruce was his first stage appearance.[19] Why should he continue to appear on the boards when he could work behind the scenes? Money. As the elder Brady told him, actors made good money. It was a job, and it paid well; the idea of having enough money to control his own life was ever-present to Bogart. To Richard Schickel, "There was no conviction in the decision, certainly no grand passion. Nor did he appear to have an abounding natural gift." Schickel notes that the only way film director Raoul Walsh could "lure Bogart out of his blackness was to remind him of how good the money was in the movies as opposed to any other line of endeavor he might reasonably have undertaken."[20] It was also an "easy" profession. In a conversation with Stig Björkman, Woody Allen says (of *Play It Again, Sam*): "Once the play opened it was a very easy job. There is no easier job than being in a play. I mean, you have the whole day off and you do whatever you want. You can write, you can relax, whatever you want. You just drop over to the theatre at eight o'clock.... There's no nervous tension. The play is running. You're on stage with your friends. Curtain goes up.

You play it. It's about an hour and a half. And two hours later you're in a restaurant having dinner with your friends. It's the easiest job in the world!''[21]

Alice Brady subsequently got Bogart a part in the melodrama *Drifting* (1922), in which she was starring. The play ran sixty-three performances. Bogart played the role of Ernie Crockett and possibly two other parts.[22] The *New York Times* review makes no mention of the calibre of his performance, and if his next few roles were any indication of his talent, he was fortunate that he was ignored. Eminently forgettable on most accounts, *Drifting* was the vehicle by which Bogart met Helen Menken (1901–1966), his first wife.[23] According to reports, Alice Brady was pregnant during the run, and one evening she was rushed off to deliver her child. Her replacement was Helen Menken, and it was Bogart's responsibility to prep her for her performance. All went well until the show began. When the sets collapsed on her, she ranted and raved at Bogart, who was doubling as stage manager. They went at each other until, reportedly, he kicked her in the rump and she punched him. Such was the start of their romance. Within weeks the *New York Times* carried an announcement of their engagement, one that was to last four years.

Bogart's subsequent minor theatrical roles included *The Teaser, The Nest, Mary the Third*, and *Steve* (in Chicago). John Cromwell recalls: "He used to hang around the Playhouse Theatre with young Bill Brady and another kid named 'Bull' Durham; they sat in on rehearsals just from interest, and a situation came up with one of those comedies when a part is underwritten and you can't get a good boy to do it so you compromise. That's what this was: somebody thought of Bogart, who at that time was the most responsible, the most charming ... the best of the three kids. He was of course goggle-eyed to do it.''[24] *Swifty* (1922), which starred Hale Hamilton and was directed by John Cromwell, had its script doctored by Ring Lardner, but to little avail. New York critics panned the production. Alan Dale of the *American* said Bogart and a fellow actor "gave some rather trenchant exhibitions of bad acting.'' Bogart, playing Tom Proctor, a roué who seduces the young heroine, was singled out by *Herald* critic Alexander Woollcott: "The young man who embodies the aforesaid sprig was what might mercifully be described as inadequate.'' At one point in the production, his mouth was so dry that he walked offstage to get a glass of water and left the players to ad-lib until he returned.[25]

Stung by Woollcott's criticism, the young actor clipped the comment and carried it around in his wallet as a reminder of his inadequacy and what lay before him. To a less determined actor, the devastating criticism might have ended a career. Bogart could have easily returned to being a stage manager for Brady's productions. Instead, he decided that acting was to be his life and that he would stick with his career choice. He wanted to prove the critics wrong, and he liked earning money in what he found to be a lucrative and not especially demanding profession. Events were to prove him right, but for the next dozen years, he had to satisfy himself with a small measure of critical success, bills, and two marriages.

Following *Swifty* he appeared with Mary Boland and Clifton Webb in *Meet the Wife* (1923). This time the critic for the *World* gave him his first good notice as "a handsome and nicely mannered reporter, which is refreshing." He appeared subsequently in *Nerves* (1924), which Heywood Broun did not like but tipped his hat to Bogart, who "gives the most effective performance," followed by *Hell's Bells* (1925) with Shirley Booth, *Cradle Snatchers* (1925), *Baby Mine* (1927), *Saturday's Children* (1928), *A Most Immoral Lady* (1928), *The Skyrocket* (1929), and *It's a Wise Child* (1929). In most of these he dressed in white duck trousers and sport coat or tie and tails. Robert Garland says of his role in *The Skyrocket*, "Mr. Bogart does as well as could be expected. If Vic Ewing never manages to appear either interesting or alive the fault is not Mr. Bogart's. With pleated pants and a pleasant smile, he manages to carry on from act to act with his chin up."[26]

Generally he played a juvenile, a young sprig—to use Woollcott's term—more intent on bedding than wedding. The casting came naturally. While most film fans remember him as Duke Mantee, Sam Spade, Rick Blaine, Charlie Allnut, or Captain Queeg, in the 1920s, Bogart cut a gallant, debonair figure in tails. An offspring of one of the top families in the city, his breeding, good looks—scar notwithstanding—and demeanor made him eminently suitable as a man about town. In an article first published in French and then translated in the film journal *Sight and Sound*, Louise Brooks recalls the Bogart of 1924 as a "slim boy with charming manners, who was extraordinarily quiet for an actor. His handsome face was made extraordinary by a most beautiful mouth. It was very full, rosy, and perfectly modelled."[27]

To Joe Hyams, Bogart was merely playing onstage a role that he carried off outside the theater: "A routine evening's entertainment for Humphrey and his friends was dinner after the show at a conservative hotel, restaurant, or speakeasy. That was followed by a tour of the night spots, ending at dawn in some hot and low-down saloon. Then to bed—if one was fortunate, and Bogart usually was—in some warmhearted lady's hideaway provided by a rich butter-and-egg man." Of such are legends made. But a woman who dated Bogart and later wrote about him for fan magazines found him attractive but not very popular. He would join his cronies for slumming in the Village or attending masquerades, but he was generally very proper when with women.[28] David Hanna finds Bogart "very much the nineteenth century man when it came to women," but the situation and the woman he was escorting determined his behavior. He could be courteous, flippant, or obnoxious, as the situation and woman demanded: "They tittered and laughed appropriately—just as they were expected to. When it came to his leading ladies, Bogie would needle on a wider scale—but that was gamesmanship—having nothing to do with his basic decency and old-fashioned respect for women. Bogie's vocabulary was extensive enough—and sharp enough—that it needed only a handful of four-letter words to hold its own at a truck driver's convention. Instinctively, he held back when women were around. There was nothing vulgar about Bogart—in his language or his actions."²⁹

In the 1920s, Bogart thrived on his work. Several of the plays had fairly substantial runs (*Meet the Wife*, 232 performances; *Hell's Bells*, 120 performances; *Cradle Snatchers*, 332 performances), and he was honing his skills by working with talented actors (Clifton Webb, Shirley Booth, Mary Boland, and others). Unlike the shy, quiet loner of Trinity and Phillips Andover, who shirked school work, Bogart met the challenge of improving his acting skills. Within a year of Woollcott's barb, a notice in the *World* described him as "a handsome and nicely mannered reporter, which is refreshing." Such occasional plaudits for performances in weak shows became commonplace for the young actor. By the time of *Cradle Snatchers* in 1925, Woollcott found Bogart competent. Chicago critic Amy Leslie marveled: "As young and handsome as Valentine, as dexterous and elegant in comedy as E. H. Southern, and as graceful as any of our best romantic actors." A correspondent for the *New York Times* saw him as one who "rapidly covered the distance that leads from the obscurity of the struggling thousands to the comparative serenity of a definite place in the knowledge of theatrical managers and observers."³⁰

With some favorable critical notices in hand and a career that was beginning to take shape, Bogart was hesitant to take on a wife. He and Helen Menken had been engaged since 1922, and he needed to decide if he was ready for marriage. On the stage since 1906, established and wielding some influence on critics, even with Bogart's nemesis Woollcott, Menken would be a great asset, or so his friends suggested. Like Maud Humphrey, Menken was a career woman. She, as well as his future wives, had traits not unlike Maud Humphrey: attractive, strong-willed, vocal, and determined to get what she wanted. And Humphrey Bogart was what she wanted. The ceremony, attended by a sizable press contingent, theatrical friends, and some family, was performed on May 20, 1926, in Helen Menken's apartment at the Gramercy Park Hotel. It was an Episcopal service that, for the benefit of the bride's parents, who were deaf and mute, was conducted in sign language. The marriage lasted eighteen months. Menken filed for divorce in Chicago, where Bogart was appearing in *Saturday's Children*. She told the judge she was willing to give up her career to keep her marriage, but claimed neglect, cruelty, and physical abuse and that Bogart owed her $2,300, an amount he did not contest. In one of her brief statements, she said, "He regarded his career as of far more importance than married life." But she gave a fuller answer to the *New York Herald*: "I tried to make my marriage the paramount interest of my life. Although my career was a success, I was willing to give it up and concentrate my interests on a home. I was deeply interested in acting, but I felt that the managing of a home was something greater. I had planned to make a home for my husband, but he did not want a home. He regarded his career as of far more importance than married life."³¹ In an interview with Grace Mack in 1937, Bogart described the two of them as "volcanoes." Bogart did not contest the divorce, and the decree was finalized on

November 18, 1927, in Chicago. Years later, Lauren Bacall recounts meeting Menken at a party for wounded soldiers and Menken's telling her that it was her fault that the marriage failed.[32]

Not one to be long without a woman's companionship, Bogart renewed his friendship with Mary Philips, with whom he had appeared in *Meet the Wife* and *Nerves*. After a brief courtship, they married on April 3, 1928, in Hartford, Connecticut. Like Helen Menken, Mary Philips wanted to continue her career, but she was supportive of her husband's desire to improve his acting skills.[33] They lived comfortably in Connecticut on their combined salaries, his being as much as $500 per week and hers somewhat less. But with the stock market crash the next year, the theaters attracted smaller and smaller audiences. Bogart looked to Hollywood, which was heavily recruiting stage actors for the talking pictures as actors or voice coaches. Stuart Rose, his brother-in-law by now, was story editor at Fox Studios. At his suggestion, Al Lewis, head of the New York office, tested Bogart for a role in *The Man Who Came Back*. When Fox offered him a contract for $750 per week, Mary told him to take it, but that she wanted to remain in New York for a current production. They agreed that their careers were the top priority, even if it meant long separations. When Bogart arrived in Los Angeles, two of his friends, Bobby Ames and Kenneth MacKenna, met him and let it be known that they too were recruited for the same part. Eventually it went to Charles Farrell, and Bogart, like other Broadway actors before him, found himself behind the scenes, serving as Farrell's voice coach.

While most filmographies say that Bogart's first film was *Broadway's Like That* (1930), a ten-minute short for the Vitaphone Corporation used to showcase new talent, Jonathan Coe claims Bogart made a two-reeler with Helen Hayes in 1928, *The Dancing Town*, for Paramount.[34] In *Broadway's Like That*, Bogart plays a young sprig, this time courting Ruth Etting over lunch at a Chinese restaurant. Also in this short were Joan Blondell and Mary Philips, who had joined her husband for a short time in Hollywood. Bogart's roles did not get much better, only somewhat longer. In 1930 and 1931 he made five films for Fox and one on loan-out for Universal.

A Devil with Women (1930), starring Victor McLaglen, found him cast as a juvenile again. His next film was *Up the River* (1930), a prison comedy occasionally shown in film retrospectives because it was directed by John Ford and was Spencer Tracy's first film. Of the very early films, his role as a convict jailed for an accidental murder is his most substantial part and earned him a little recognition in the reviews. There followed in short order *Body and Soul* (1930), *Bad Sister* (1931), *Women of All Nations* (1931), and *A Holy Terror* (1931). Minor roles all, but they gave Bogart a taste of Hollywood and the opportunity to gain experience and work with Tracy and Ford, Bette Davis, Sidney Fox, Zasu Pitts, Myrna Loy, Victor McLaglen, Charles Farrell, and Raoul Walsh. After extended periods without Mary, who had returned to New York and the theater, and dissatisfied with Hollywood, Bogart packed his bags and returned to her and the theater.

BROADWAY BECKONS BUT HOLLYWOOD PAYS

In New York, Humphrey Bogart secured a role in *After All* (1931), starring Helen Haye. The show ran only twelve performances and closed before Christmas. His new year's present was a request from Harry Cohn to return to Hollywood for a six-month contract at Columbia. His first substantial part since *Up the River* was the lead in *Love Affair* (1932), opposite the popular Dorothy MacKaill. It won him recognition at Warner Brothers, to whom he was loaned out for *Big City Blues* (1932). Working in the first of several feature pictures with Joan Blondell, Bogart demonstrated signs of what he could do in anger as he engaged in a fistfight with Lyle Talbot. Years later, Blondell described her costar as one who "stood apart" and kept to himself. He was "legit" before he was a star.[35] His next part, again on loan to Warners, was as a hoodlum in *Three on a Match* (1932). Working with Blondell and Davis again, though, was not enough to keep him in Hollywood.

He returned to New York, where he and Mary shared an apartment at 434 East 52nd Street. This time he was closer to the theater and his family, who by now had moved from 103rd Street to a brownstone at 79 East 56th Street. Dr. Bogart had retired from his practice and was in ill health. Unconfirmed reports claim that in his despondency over family misfortunes, he turned to alcohol and drugs, but others suggest that his addiction was ongoing.[36] The actor's sister, Frances, was hospitalized frequently for depression, and his other sister Kay, a model, developed a fondness for drink. It was left to Maud Humphrey to tend to her husband's basic needs and maintain some semblance of stability. She may not have been an affectionate woman, but her sense of duty and responsibility to family never wavered. Her son was of little financial help. He had parts in *I Love You Wednesday* (1932), *Chrysalis* (1932), *Our Wife* (1933), and *The Mask and the Face* (1933), but his longest run was with *I Love You Wednesday* (1932), and only for sixty-three performances. Hard times set in, and Bogart was reduced to playing chess, a favorite hobby he learned from his father, for up to a dollar a game to help support himself and his wife. It was during one of these games that he was notified of his father's hospitalization. A few days later, on September 8, 1934, Dr. Bogart died in Manhattan's Hospital for the Ruptured and Crippled. He left debts amounting to about $10,000, which his son was determined to pay off. There were also about three times the debt amount in uncollected fees and a ruby ring that Bogart wore the rest of his life.

Bringing home barely enough money to eat, and with family obligations and his father's death weighing heavily on his mind, Humphrey Bogart was at the low point of his career. When Charles Erskine approached him about playing in *Midnight* (1934), a gangster film for Universal to be shot in New York, he accepted. He was not enthusiastic about making another movie, but he needed the money and the change from what has been called his "Tennis, anyone?" roles.[37] At the end of the film, his scorned lover (Sidney Fox) shoots him, and for the first time Humphrey Bogart dies in a movie.

Bogart returned to the stage to play another heavy in Rufus King's *Invitation to Murder* (1934),[38] a mystery melodrama that ran for a month. One of the performances was seen and remembered by Arthur Hopkins, a producer and director who was casting *The Petrified Forest*, a new play by Robert E. Sherwood. At the age of thirty-five, after a fifteen-year apprenticeship, with billings anywhere from twelfth to the lead in *Love Affair*, Humphrey Bogart got his first major break. At the point of becoming "an aged juvenile," visited by the ennui of critics and public alike, Bogart, by this time an alcoholic and beaten down by events, had the kind of physical appearance described by Sherwood.[39]

Supposedly what most impressed Hopkins was Bogart's voice. It had the flat sound he needed for one of the characters. When Hopkins told Sherwood that Bogart was going to test for the role of Duke Mantee, Sherwood argued against it. Except for *Invitation to a Murder* and *Three on a Match*, Bogart's previous roles suggested he would be miscast. The part of Boze Hertzlinger, the doltish Romeo, would be more suitable for Bogart. Over Sherwood's objections, Bogart tested for and won the role of Duke Mantee.

A murderer on the run, Mantee hides out in the Last Chance Fill Up on the edge of the Petrified Forest. In this last outpost of civilization, Anderson places a variety of social types, all dying in one way or another. Alan Squier (Leslie Howard) is a cold, world-weary existentialist and vagrant writer who wants to drown himself in the Pacific; Gabrielle Maple (Betty Conklin), the stifled daughter of the proprietor, reads François Villon's poetry when she is not preparing hamburgers or fending off the advances of her suitor; Boze (Frank Milan), an ex-football star, lives in the past, and his only wish is to marry Gabrielle; Gramps Maple, an old codger, will not allow his granddaughter the freedom she desperately seeks; Jason Maple, her father, is off with the Black Vigilantes, looking for the killer who has, unknown to him, invaded his diner; and the Chisolms, members of the respected middle class, are dying from a passionless marriage.

The play had its first tryout in Hartford, Connecticut, in mid-December, followed by one in Boston beginning Christmas Eve. It opened on Broadway at the Broadhurst Theatre on January 7, 1935. From its first rehearsal, Bogart worked to polish the role, and this paid off handsomely. The audiences gasped when, with a two-day growth, the disheveled, Dillinger look-alike ambled onstage. Robert Garland said that "Humphrey Bogart is gangster Mantee to the tip of his sawed-off shotgun," and Brooks Atkinson commented that Bogart did "the best work of his career as the motorized guerilla." The play ran until the end of June, when Leslie Howard tired of the role and would not allow his understudy, and Bogart's friend, Kenneth MacKenna, to replace him. Warner Bros. had purchased the screen rights to it, with the understanding that Howard was to reprise his stage role. So taken by Bogart's performance was Howard that he promised the actor that no one else would play Mantee on the screen. Jack Warner, though, was of another mind and cast Edward G. Robinson as Mantee. Robinson was already under contract, and Bogart's last stint at the studio had not left much of an impression. Howard, true to his word, said that he would not recreate his stage role without Bogart. After much wrangling back and forth, Howard prevailed, and Bogart, after working summer stock in Maine, headed west again, this time assured of a substantial part, and forever indebted to Leslie Howard.[40]

Shortly after his move to California, his sister Frances, who had been unwell since she had endured a twenty-seven-hour delivery in 1930, divorced her husband, Stuart Rose, and was hospitalized in California. She was in and out of mental institutions for the rest of her life, and her brother took total responsibility for her. His other sister, Kay, six years younger than her brother, died from peritonitis in 1937 after suffering a ruptured appendix.[41]

The Petrified Forest was the beginning of a long, and often unhappy, contractural agreement between Bogart and Warner Bros. that was to last until 1953. But in 1935, for an actor who a year earlier had been battling to stay afloat financially, the success of the play and a film contract for forty weeks were a welcome change. From *The Petrified Forest* he now had enough money to pay off his and his father's debts and establish the Humphrey Bogart F. Y. Fund, to be used when he wanted to refuse a role or had contractual differences with the studio hierarchy. The fund was to be put to good use later.[42] Although he was well off as a child, his own hand-to-mouth existence in New York, his father's death and debts, and his subsequent support of his mother and two sisters scarred him and always left him concerned about financial security. Although he was not happy about it, he was willing for a time to take second-rate roles if he had that weekly paycheck.

The Hollywood cliché is that you are as good as your last film; if you played a gangster and the film was a financial success for the studio, your next film most likely would find you cast in the same type role. Warner produced films like Ford produced cars, and a contract player might find himself in as many as seven or eight films a year. Early on, Bogart did not mind this; he liked to work and wanted the money. In his next picture for Warner, *Bullets or Ballots*, he was cast as Bugs Fenner, a gangster and killer. Joining Warner's Murderers Row, or the Rogue's Gallery of gangsters and tough guys, Bogart made gangster or prison films in the next two years: *Kid Galahad, San Quentin*, and *Dead End* (on loan-out to Samuel Goldwyn). But there were eight others in 1936 and 1937 that were somewhat different and expanded the Bogart screen image. In *Black Legion* and *The Great O'Malley* he played a "good Joe" driven by prejudice or circumstances to engage in criminal activity. In *Isle of Fury*, wearing a mustache for the first time in his film career, he was a newlywed thought to be an escaped murderer. *China Clipper* found him piloting an airplane across the Pacific in its first trans-Pacific flight; in *Marked Woman* and *Two Against the World* he crusaded against evil; and in *Stand-In*, reunited with Leslie Howard, he played an alcoholic producer who sobered up in time to save a languishing film company. Portrayed by colleagues and some newspaper stories as a drinker and carouser, Bogart in these years was a workaholic: he made five films in 1936, six in 1937, and five in 1938, but was not considered a leading man in the industry.[43]

Bogart's contracts with Warner Bros. showed an increasingly astute businessman negotiating for fine points. The contract signed on December 10, 1935, was the standard Warner document, giving the actor $550 per week for twenty-six weeks, with an option for another twenty-six weeks at $600 per week. His contract could be sold to any other major studio, a change from the usual phrase of "reputable" studio, and allowed Bogart a small amount of leverage. And instead of agreeing to the usual screen credit and publicity accorded his performance, he requested and received "featured screen credit." By December 1936, he was receiving $650 per week, and by the end of the next year, his contract called for a weekly salary of $1,100. The options were such that by the end of the seventh year, if this contract remained in force, he was to receive $2,000 per week. In comparison, an actor such as Donald Briggs was receiving $250 per week, and Edward G. Robinson was making several thousand dollars more than Bogart.

Bogart's importance to the studio was being championed by others. His agent, Noll Gurney, in correspondence with Jack Warner in mid-April 1937, encouraged Warner to adjust Bogart's salary for personal (his sister's medical care) and professional reasons. Gurney noted that after eight or nine less than stellar pictures following *Petrified Forest*, Bogart's performance in *Black Legion* showed that he should be in "more important pictures."[44] Gurney noted that even when Bogart was not on the payroll, he was working with the publicity department and doing radio spots to enhance the studio image.

Bogart was no longer financially strapped. Now, though he was somewhat secure about his place in Hollywood, he was having domestic problems. Mary had been to Hollywood in 1930, did not like it, and returned to New York for a part in a play. Returning to California near his birthday in 1935 and after he signed his Warner Bros. contract, Philips spent most of her time catering to Bogart and his friends. When Mary said she wanted to return to New York to continue her career, Bogart was upset. He was now able to support her and knew a separation would create a strain on their marriage. Previous separations had done just that; the need to pursue two professional careers had led to his first divorce. When he had returned to New York in 1932 after his unsuccessful stint in Hollywood, Mary had confessed that she was in love with another man.[45] They were able to patch up their marriage, but Bogart feared another separation. Mary left anyway when she was offered a role in *The Postman Always Rings Twice*. When she next returned to Hollywood, she found her husband in the company of Mayo Methot. The numerous separations caused great stress, and while Bogart tried to keep the bond alive and work out their marriage, the situation became untenable. After a seven-month separation, both decided to end the marriage. In Los Angeles on July 21, 1937, Mary Philips Bogart received an interlocutory decree. The actual divorce itself did not take place until the decree was picked up by Mary Baker for Philips in early August 1938, shortly before Mary's marriage to Kenneth MacKenna, Bogart's old buddy and Leslie Howard's understudy in *The Petrified Forest*. A week later, on August 20, 1938, Humphrey Bogart married the woman he had been seeing for many months.

THE BATTLING BOGARTS

Bogart and Mayo Methot had known each other as actors in New York. Born in Portland, Oregon, Mayo had started out there in the Baker Stock Company. Early roles included a part in *Sappho* (playing a little boy) and *The Littlest Rebel*. She moved to New York in 1922, and after less than a year she had a substantive role in George M. Cohan's *The Song and Dance Man* (1923). In his review, Brooks Atkinson remarked, "Mayo Methot gives a splendid performance—vivid in composition, sincere in feeling." Unlike Bogart, whose early stage roles as a juvenile resulted in little positive recognition, Mayo had a fairly distinguished career on Broadway, appearing in such plays as *The Mad Honeymoon* (1922), *What Ann Brought Home* (1927), Vincent Youman's *Great Day* (1929), Sidney Howard's *Half Gods* (1929), *All the King's Men* (1929), *Now-a-Days*, and *Torch Song* (1930).

Like so many of her peers, Methot moved to Hollywood to try her hand at films. Although she did not receive the plaudits in Hollywood that she had on Broadway,[46] Mayo did have relatively steady work, appearing in such films as *Virtue, Vanity Street, Harold Teen, Mr. Deed Goes to Town, Corsair, The Night Club Lady* (lead), *Lilly Turner, Women in Prison, Dr. Socrates, Unexpected Father, A Woman Is the Judge, The Case of the Curious Bride*, and *Brother Rat and the Baby*. Like Bogart, she had been married twice. She divorced her first husband, John M. Lamond of New York, in 1927. She married Percy T. Morgan, Jr., of Portland, Oregon in 1931; they were divorced in 1937. About the time their marriages were disintegrating, Bogart saw her at a Screen Actor's Guild Ball. He obviously had improved his dancing since his years at Trinity. When he and Mayo renewed acquaintances, they found themselves attracted to one another's humor and zest for life. Their romance continued when both were cast in *Marked Woman*. To Bogart, Mayo was a "regular guy": she loved the sea, could hold her own when drinking, and was capable of physically and verbally abusing anyone who crossed her. She was the right match for Bogart's image of the perfect woman.

As Bogart told one writer, "I hate women who are spineless, brainless clinging vines, who open their eyes wide and their mouths still wider and sigh, 'Oh, you great big wonderful man,' all the time fluttering their eyelashes at some helpless, captivated male." In the same article he described the kind of woman he liked, a description that fit Mayo: "I adore women who do things, who have guts, who can stand up to a man and say, 'You're wrong' when he is wrong, who like to stand on their own two feet, who pack a good wallop and in case of an emergency know when and how to apply it."[47] Another view was advanced by Louise Brooks: "He found her at a time of lethargy and loneliness, when he might have gone on playing secondary gangster parts at Warner Brothers for years and then been out. But he met Mayo and she set fire to him. Those passions—envy, hatred, and violence, which were essential to the "Bogey" character, which had been simmering beneath his failure for so many years—she brought to a boil, blowing the lid off all his inhibitions forever."[48]

They married on August 20, 1938, and after a honeymoon in Seattle settled into a life of domestic strife. Both Lauren Bacall and Mary Baker, a lifelong friend, claim that Bogart was not anxious to marry Mayo, but he thought it was the gentlemanly thing to do—what was expected of him after living with her after Mary moved out.[49] Both had been through two previous marriages. This time Bogart wanted someone to be at home. Early on, Mayo accepted Bogart as the main attraction. Subordinating her career to marriage, and eventually giving it up entirely, Mayo was a devoted and dedicated wife. Streetwise and a product of the Warner Bros. system, she encouraged and supported her husband in his ever-increasing conflicts with the studio, pushed him to get better and more diversified roles, including romantic leads, and traveled with him whenever possible to locations or on USO tours around the world. Mayo once described Bogart as "fun, essentially honest, good natured. I married a man who behaves like a man, who offers some excitement as well as security and fun along with my food."[50]

The fan magazines of the late 1930s and early 1940s played up Bogart's domestic image, showing him tending his garden, enjoying his dogs, cruising on his boat the *Sluggy* (named after Mayo), partying with Mayo, and caring for her.[51] But she was often envious and insecure, and as his flame burned brighter, she was always in the shadows. Jealously often led to rage. During the course of this marriage, Bogart's reputation as a brawler was firmly established. Known as the "Battling Bogarts," their fights, both public and private, became Hollywood legends. If Bogart even so much as looked at another woman, Mayo would slug him. Frequently her rage was channeled into a fusillade of ashtrays, dishes, and sharp instruments. Anita Loos, a neighbor of the Bogarts, recalls, "First came curses, then crashing glass, screams, and eventually moans of passionate reconciliation."[52] Ironically, Mayo's push to have the studio give him romantic roles led to more intense battles when he finally got that kind of role. When he played opposite Ingrid Bergman in *Casablanca*, Mayo was livid. Friends who had boats anchored near the *Sluggy* tell of the noises, cries, and banging that could be heard at all hours. Sometimes the fights were staged: two actors having a good time putting on a show for friends or any other available audience. Occasionally their friends would join the charade. Broderick Crawford and Robert Benchley, for example, staged mock battles with Bogart and Mayo. But most often the domestic squabbles were real. Left more and more to herself while her husband was at the studio, Mayo turned increasingly to drink. When Bogart returned to "Sluggy Hollow," their aptly named home, she would needle him about almost anything, but especially his star status and his female costars.

The stress with Mayo may have been a partial cause for Bogart's complaints at the studio and on location. Raoul Walsh recalls that Bogart, who by this time had earned the nickname "Bogey the Beefer," would rail about what an actor had to do to make a movie: "They get you up before daybreak and work your ass off all day until sundown. In the theater I went to work at eight in the morning and was through by eleven; all the rest of the night and next day to play and catch up with my drinking. Working in pictures is for the birds." While making *High Sierra* he complained about the food and the accommodations: "I'll take a parlor, bedroom, and bath any time. When you think what an actor has to do to earn his salary in this goddamn business. That crumby, two-bit hotel last night."[53] Walsh would frequently remind him of the money he was making, which tended to moderate Bogart's outrage for a time.

Bogart's career flourished as a result of his films, and his much publicized domestic squabbles plus the less public complaints on the set, gave credence to the tough guy image. Although the studio chiefs often tried to quash negative publicity, at times it enhanced Bogart's image. For other actors and in other times, this might have tarnished their fan appeal, but as with contemporary stars,[54] the bravado and the fights with Mayo that made it into public view endeared him to some of his public. The tough guy on the screen was a tough guy with women in real life, and the Battling Bogarts made good copy. As early as 1939, after a vicious battle at the Algonquin, James Thurber portrayed their fisticuffs in his cartoon "Jolly Times—1939." The bill for the hotel damage and Thurber's cartoon, badges of honor and much humor, were framed and hung over their fireplace.[55] The screen persona was slipping over into real life, or so the tabloids and gossip columnists intimated.

Some fans wrote recommending that he apply himself to other than gangster roles. As he told a writer for the *New York Times*, "Those letters always strike me funny . . . because in the theater I was the harmless collegiate with the slick haircomb, the spotless white flannels and the tennis racquet who ran out on the stage just before the curtain was run down." Bogart himself enjoyed playing these roles, but as he noted in the same interview, he too wanted "action roles consisting of something more than just a one-dimensional character. You know, a role that you could get the feel of and actually do something with."[56] In discussing the way the studio treated Bogart, James Cagney tells how by the time of *The Oklahoma Kid*, "he'd become entirely disillusioned with the picture business. Endlessly the studio required him to show up without his even knowing what the script was, what his dialogue was, what the picture was about. On top of this he would be doing two or three pictures at a time. That's how much they appreciated him." Both actors did what they had to to meet the obligations of their contracts: "We shared the same attitudes: when there's a job to be done, you do it. New acting talent would come along, and the studio's idea of building them up was simply to throw them into one picture after another as quickly as possible. In this sink-or-swim situation, the ones who survived were the ones with natural durability. Bogie had that kind of durability. Albeit he was a tremendous personality, the studio didn't do anything about him until fortuitous circumstances put him opposite Ingrid Bergman. . . . The studio had no thought of using him to the fullest, indeed of using anyone to the fullest bent of their talent. The policy toward talent was simplistic: just throw them in, then throw them out. Talent was not nurtured, it was simply consumed."[57]

In "Tattle Tales," a retrospective publicity piece in the Warner Bros. files, Robert S. Taplinger, director of publicity, wrote that Bogart dated his film career to *The Petrified Forest*, saw no difference between stage and screen acting, and professed his dislike for dressing up and a preference for rough, tweedy clothes. Other personality traits included his aversion to attending movies, his lack of interest in food, and his preference not to handle money. One area that studios tended to shy away from was mentioning religion. In this piece Bogart described himself as a "personal-religionist," who was raised in and still attended the Episcopal church. Taplinger described Bogart as a "good talker," with a sense of humor but often sulky.

Later the actor was to describe himself as an "arguer and lover, not a fighter." He loved to test people's mettle and enjoyed attacking pompous people. Most of the time Bogart was a fighter when it came to defending his own character. In a prelude to events that were to follow seven years later, a former "chief functionary" of the Communist party, John L. Leech, testified before a grand jury and named Bogart and several other notables, including Franchot Tone, James Cagney, Frederick March, and Jean Muir, as members of the party. A front page story in the *New York Times* on August 15, 1940, reported accusations leveled against Bogart for attending study groups and contributing $150 per month to the cause. Bogart issued a denial printed with the story:

I have never contributed money to a political organization of any form. That includes Republican, Democratic, Hollywood Anti-Nazi League or the Communist Party. Furthermore, I have never attended the school mentioned nor do I know what school that may be.

I dare the men who are attempting this investigation to call me to the stand. I want to face them myself and not by a proxy to whom I am only a name.[58]

Within the week, Congressman Martin Dies of Texas traveled to Hollywood to meet with industry personnel, including Bogart. Satisfied with the answers he got, he exonerated Bogart and others, calling them patriotic Americans. He also said that "numerous actors and screen people, out of humane motives, . . . have made their contributions to, and let their names be used by certain organizations which the Dies committee has unanimously found to be organized under Communist leadership."[59] In his FBI file, a summary report of November 24, 1947, Dies indicated that Leech was a "pathological liar" and that Bogart's supposed link to the Communist party "did not appear to be founded on fact." After the dust settled, Bogart turned his attention to studio projects and to Mayo.

Studio correspondence four months later indicates that Bogart was battling on all fronts.[60] Scheduled to appear at the Earle Theatre in Philadelphia in the first week of January 1941, the studio wanted a completed soundtrack to *High Sierra*. Bogart had been in New York, appearing at the Strand with Mayo (December 6–19), and was to head to Philadelphia for an appearance at the Earle Theater as an employee of Warner Bros. If Bogart was not willing to comply by inconveniencing himself "a little" with their request, they were willing to suspend him as of December 29 and cut off the income (about $3,000) from the appearance at the Earle. The glitch was worked out, because Bogart appeared at the Earle and also the Strand in Camden, but the pressures at home and from the studio continued. The battles with Jack Warner were constant. Archive material of transcribed conversations and telegrams between Warner, studio personnel, and Bogart shows that the actor retained his sense of worth and constantly guarded his career. In 1940, Sam Jaffe telegrammed Jack Warner asking to permit Bogart to do a series of radio broadcasts for the Chase and Sanborn coffee company opposite Elsa Lancaster. Jaffe thought the broadcasts would establish a new kind of character for Bogart. Bogart was willing to donate 50 percent of his salary to charity, but Warner would not let him do it. To Bogart either the parts were not good enough, the studio was not recognizing his talents, he was not being paid adequately, or he did not have the freedom to earn money without the studio's approval. Typical of Bogart's exchange with the studio about this time was a brief memo in which he told Steve Trilling that since Lupino and Raft were casting pictures (Lupino chose Garfield over Bogart for *Out of the Fog*), maybe he could have the opportunity as well. Later in the year, there were more laments about still doing roles that George Raft was turning down.[61] A few years later, trying to avoid a personal battle with Warner, Bogart argued with Jack Warner that *Conflict* was not for him. He said he had done many things for the studio, but this particular picture not ready and he was unwilling to take a suspension rather than make it.[62] Warner, always one to know what was best for his employees and the studio, urged Bogart to do it. Warner won out.

Bogart never forgot the debts he assumed when his father died, and over the years he was gratified that his salary was going up. In 1941, he earned about $96,000, and in 1942, when he made *Casablanca, Across the Pacific*, and *All Through the Night*, he received in the neighborhood of $114,000. Other actors, though, including Gable, Cooper, and Cagney, were making several times more. At this time Bogart was more worried by domestic matters than financial ones. Another much less publicized way that Bogart may have sought solace from these pressures was with other women. One relationship story of uncertain veracity is the one with Verita Thompson. Introduced to Bogart by Ann Sheridan in 1942, Thompson later became the actor's hair stylist and was in charge of his toupees. She frequently traveled with him and was introduced playfully by Bogart as his "executive secretary and mistress." According to Thompson, the friendship lasted fifteen years and their intimate relationship about a decade.[63]

The flip side of Bogart's appeal as a brawler and tough guy were being transformed to a kind of existential lover, first by *The Maltese Falcon* and then

Casablanca. These roles complicated his domestic life. Forever concerned about his fidelity to her, Mayo went so far as to slash her wrists in a supposed suicide attempt while Bogart was making *Casablanca*. To Bogart, the jealousy was fueled by Mayo's playing the only role she had: "My wife's an actress. She's a clever actress. It just so happens that she's not working right now. But even when an actress isn't working, she's got to have scenes to play. And in this case I've got to give her the cues."[64]

In a piece for *Silver Screen* in late 1943, Bogart detailed to Jack Holland ten ways on "How to Keep Your Marriage Alive"—for example: argue and keep on arguing, but don't take yourself seriously; compromise; keep friends around; be an optimist; avoid separations; don't try to dominate the other; and avoid jealousy. In the article Mayo said she was jealous; Bogart said jealousy was okay as long as it did not become obsessive.[65] But it did. Mayo's constant harassing calls to the set, generally triggered by her jealousy of his leading ladies, her constant abuse at home, including attacking her husband with a penknife; and her inability to control her drinking took their toll. To Richard Schickel, "Theirs was the story of two alcoholics locked in a punishing and dismal mutual dependency. Their screams at each other were screams for help."[66] It may not have been the primary cause, but these fights seemed to enhance his screen persona as it weakened his resolution to do battle. If one is to believe Bogart's statements about his propensity to nineteenth-century values, the marriage might have survived had it not been for Mayo's violent, insane jealousy combined with her excessive drinking. Bogart's main solace from battles at home, exhaustive shooting schedules at Warner, and fights with studio chiefs was his boat.

After a number of layoffs, including a forty-two-day suspension for not appearing in *Bad Men of Missouri*, and a loan-out to Columbia for *Sahara*, Warner asked him to report to the studio to star in a film version of Hemingway's *To Have and Have Not*, with a screenplay by William Faulkner and Jules Furthman, to be directed by Howard Hawks. With his career at its height and his personal life in shambles, Bogart was about to enter a relationship that was to give him the personal stability and security that he never had before.

BACALL AND AFTER

Howard Hawks had his wife, Slim, to thank for spotting Lauren Bacall on the March 1943 cover of *Harper's Bazaar*[67] and challenging him to "make her a star" by using her in one of his films. At a time when Bacall was entertaining several possible jobs, she accepted Hawks's offer of an option. Known for portraying women as strong, masculine types, with strength of character and verbal insolence, Hawks tested her and signed Bacall to a seven-year contract with Hawks-Feldman Productions. When he chose his new protégée, he had no idea that he would ignite a sizzling romance, both on and off the screen.

Bacall first met Bogart late in 1943 on the set of *Passage to Marseille*. Hawks took her there to give him an opportunity to "look her over" and see if she might be suitable for his next picture. After finishing *Passage to Marseille*, Bogart and Methot, along with Don Cumming and Ralph Hark, two New York entertainers, left to entertain the troops on a 35,000-mile, three-month tour of the Mediterranean and African theaters.[68] For the Bogarts, not unlike John Barrymore and Elaine Barry, their battles across Europe were mirror images of those at home.

When they returned, Bogart met with Hawks to view Bacall's screen test and talk about the film. On leaving the director's office, he bumped into Bacall, complimented her on her screen test, and casually remarked, "We'll have a lot of fun together."[69] Little did he know. Shooting began in February 1944. Six months earlier, Bogart told Maude Cheatham, "An actor interprets love scenes according to directions, just the same as any other scene the script calls for; and of course, like everything you do, the more experience you have the better you will do it. But I say, when it comes to playing love scenes, you're talking to the wrong fellow. I don't live 'em, I just work at 'em. In the movies, I mean!"[70]

From Bacall's account, Bogart was always the professional, "meticulous about not being too personal, [and] known for never fooling around with women at work or anywhere else."[71] Two or three years after publishing her autobiography, Bacall, trying to get out of the shadow of the man who helped shape her career, and possibly stung by Thompson's book about the alleged affair, refused for a time to talk about Bogart. As late as 1981, she told Earl Wilson she preferred not to be questioned about Bogart again (*Beverly Hills Courier*, November 27, 1981, 5). She has had little to say about the affair, but in a Liz Smith column she remarked that an *ET* television segment on Bogart was "sleazy." Of the reputed relationship with Verita Thompson, she said, "I think I knew Bogie better than his hairdresser, or better than anyone for that matter. And everything she proclaims about him, I consider to be her fantasy. She worked for him and was crazy about him. O.K. But Bogie was the least likely man ever to have had such an affair while he was married to me because he didn't believe in that. . . . My interest is only in defending Bogie's reputation and the feelings of our children and grandchildren" (*Los Angeles Times*, September 13, 1991, F2).

With a few exceptions, most of the early accounts of Bogart's private affairs while married paint him as committed to each of his wives. An obituary in the *New York Herald Tribune*, for example, reports, "One of his major prides was that tempestuous as his marriages might have been, he was never involved in a domestic scandal nor was his name linked with that of another woman other than his current wife during his marriages" (January 15, 1957, 2:10). To David Niven, on Bogart's marriage to Betty Bacall, "He was, above all, proud of the fact that he had a partner with whom he could share everything good or bad. He never looked at another woman" (*Bring on the Empty Horses* [New York: Putnam, 1975], 251). Alistair Cooke, who found Bogart a "complex private man" (*Six Men* 188), says that the actor considered fidelity "a married man's duty" (202). When Bogart learned that the Democrats were going to make public a letter about Eisenhower's infidelities if Joe McCarthy delivered a planned speech in Chicago, Cooke found Bogart "genuinely shocked" by the charge of adultery. "That moment of shock on the train was the first hint I had that what we were dealing with here were two characters, one fictional, the other private" (187).

Working and living at a time when private affairs were most often private, Bogart was not the subject for sexual dalliances. Before Thompson, the most public comments about his sexuality were by Kenneth Anger, in his sleazy and gossip-filled *Hollywood Babylon* (San Francisco: Straight Arrow Books, 1975), and by Louise Brooks. To Anger, when it came to talk about sex organs, Bogart and Chaplin were considered "well-endowed" (171). Louise Brooks, in her generally scathing portrait of Bogart, his acting, and his cult status remarks that "it was security in sex that preserved Humphrey's ego for success after he had endured, three times longer than any actor known to history, the bitterest humiliation, ridicule and failure." She claims he knew he was attractive to women, and "when a woman appealed to him, he waited for her like the flame waits for the moth" (*Sight and Sound* 22).

Another view comes from Joshua Logan's description of how in 1936 he invited Bogart to a party to entertain models for the movie *Vogues of 1938* (a.k.a. *Vogues*). Told by Walter Wanger to invite men of class—gentlemen such as Henry Fonda and Jimmy Stewart—he invited Bogart, "a world symbol of the killer, especially for the ladies. He was the best bad man around—the best looking, the most virile. In short, a star of the highest power." From Logan's perspective, "Bogey shone when surrounded by girls. Men liked him, but women had him for breakfast." During the party he and the other male guests were total gentlemen: "It was perhaps the most innocent evening any of us had spent since we were adolescents" (*Movie Stars, Real People, and Me* [New York: Delacorte, 1978], 24, 26).

Bacall herself has said that he liked and thought about sex a great deal. In an interview in 1970 with some members of the Bogart cult, Bacall said, "Mr. Bogart was interested in sex 24 hours a day" (Christopher Hart and Douglas Kenny, "The Bogie Gap," *Movie*, January 23, 1970, M35). In an assessment of his career, Molly Haskell refers to Bacall's comments and herself talks about the actor's sex appeal and how he had "a decidedly lecherous streak" in his films (*GQ* 58 [January 1988]: 161). In a journal entry for December 11, 1977, Nicholas Ray, who was very close to Bogart in his later years, says, while comparing his ex-wife Gloria Grahame to Lauren Bacall: "Both were talented actresses who worried about the same wrinkles, the twenties wrinkles. Each was promiscuous, Gloria by far the more offensively so. Each had her own style, but Bacall's was elegant, and she was the more intelligent of the two" (Nicholas Ray, in *I Was Interrupted: Nicholas Ray on Making Movies*, ed. Susan Ray [Berkeley: University of California Press, 1993], 159). Even in *By Myself*, Bacall mentions times when Bogart was jealous of her infatuations with Adlai Stevenson, Leonard Bernstein, and others. Others, such as Joe Hyams, quote Swifty Lazar on Bogart's faithfulness, while Sheila Graham, in *Hollywood Revisited: A Fiftieth Anniversary Celebration* (New York: St. Martin's Press, 1985), says he flirted with her and with other women (39). When asked directly by Harvard students in 1970 if she thought Bogart was faithful to her, she replied, "Oh I know it. Absolutely know it. I'll show you how extreme a man he was—his feeling was that if you even thought about it, it was already wrong. He used to say to me, 'Look, if you ever meet a guy and you want to take off with him, you come to me and tell me before. Introduce me to him and if I think he'll take care of you, I'll wish you luck' " (M35).

But even his son admits that prior to his two divorces, he was already in relationships with his spouses-to-be. Stephen Bogart says that while it was possible, given all the women Bogart met, Verita Thompson was an unlikely candidate for his attention, and certainly after the marriage to Bacall it was even less likely that he wandered outside the home (249–250). But the suggestion is present in some of the comments that there may be more to the story of Bogart's "private" life. Of the two recent biographies of Bogart, Jeffrey Meyers, after quoting Nathaniel Benchley on Bogart's fidelity, says this "shows how well they kept their liaison hidden" (94). Sperber and Lax take a middle road, with phrasing such as "whether or not the relationship with Thompson was intimate" (223); they summarize Thompson's account and interview Bogart's friends and acquaintances, but remain neutral about the matter. However, in the course of their describing Bogart's stormy relationship with Mayo, they were the first to report that on occasion he sought solace from his disintegrating and destructive marriage in the arms of his former wife, Helen Menken: "Helen Menken, lovely as ever, was a sometime visitor in Los Angeles and a welcoming friend in New York" (168). If he did have a relationship with Thompson and an occasional dalliance with Menken, to Stephen Humphrey Bogart it only reinforces the idea that his father was "imperfect" (249–250).

On the set in 1944, aware that Bacall was an actor new to movies, and recalling some of his own experiences, he went out of his way to assist her with their scenes together. As the shooting progressed, so did the courtship. Innocent of the Hollywood scene, Bacall thought nothing of meeting Bogart for lunch or joking around on the set. Mary Murphy noted, "Despite the danger, romance on the set is one of Hollywood's most powerful drugs. Strangers suddenly become magnetically connected. There is instant intimacy. It becomes the ultimate shipboard romance. Rationally it makes no sense, but emotionally it is hypnotic. But it can also tear a set apart, destroy careers and ruin marriages."[72] At first Hawks tried to dissuade Bacall from getting involved with an established star twenty-five years her senior. He had numerous conversations with both of them, warning Bogart of his marital status and alerting Bacall to the possible damage to her career. He even threatened to bury her in B-pictures by selling her contract to Monogram Studios. Hawks's protestations were to no purpose.[73]

After the first weeks of shooting, the two were in love. Bacall was compassionate, understanding, loving, innocent, and fun to be with—everything Mayo Methot was not. They met in restaurants, on the set, after he finished his once-a-week patrols for the Coast Guard, aboard friends' boats, at all hours of the day and night, anywhere and anytime they could without Mayo's finding out. To some, Bogart was being unfaithful to his wife and damaging his career. Bacall later said that Bogart told her, "Never damage your own character. To have a love affair breaks a bond between husband and wife—and even if your partner doesn't know it, the relationship must be less open, so something very important will never be the same."[74] With little more than harassing phone calls on the set and drunken battles at home, Bogart was at the end of his third marriage. Bacall was his salvation. Still, he was also very much aware of his commitment to Mayo. She had promised to conquer her drinking problem, and it was his duty to stand by her, as his mother had done with his father during his illness. But Methot had seen *To Have and Have Not*, and, according to one source, she knew the marriage was over: "He never played love scenes like that before.... This has to be the real thing."[75] Without much success, the studio tried to downplay the disintegration of the Bogart-Methot relationship, but later used the May–December romance (he was forty-four, she nineteen) to generate interest in the couple's "celluloid relationship."[76]

With limited communication from him after *To Have and Have Not*, Bacall was frustrated. But her mentor, Howard Hawks, for all his earlier protestations, served as cupid again. Based on their screen electricity, head of publicity Charlie Einfeld's description of them as "one of the biggest and hottest attractions we have ever had,"[77] and the response to the early screenings of their screen presence, Hawks knew he had something special in the pair and wanted them for *The Big Sleep*. Shooting began in October 1944. Again, they spent as much time together as possible. Home life was no better for Bogart, and periodically he would stay at the Beverly Hills Hotel. Eventually he moved to the Garden of Allah.

With pressures from all sides, Bogart found keeping his volatile marriage alive more difficult than managing his career. The marriage had endured his most productive period, August 1938 through May 1945. The twenty-nine films he made during this period included those that solidified his position at the studio: *High Sierra, The Maltese Falcon, Casablanca*, and *To Have and Have Not*. He had been taken out of, declined, or did not get roles in *Valley of the Giants* (put in *Racket Busters*), *Of Mice and Men* (put in *Roaring Twenties*), *House Across the Bay, My Little Chickadee*, with Mae West and W. C. Fields, and *This Gun for Hire*.[78]

One of his most often reprised scenes from *Casablanca* combines real-life trauma with fine acting. Alone in Rick's Café, glass in hand, bottle nearby, wearing a worn and weary expression, Bogart-Rick portrays the essence of living anguish.[79] What kept Bogart going was his work. But studio personnel were very concerned about Bogart's heavy drinking and how his mental turmoil was affecting the making of *The Big Sleep*.[80] Try as he might, publicly and privately, by late 1944, after several violent tiffs, aborted attempts by Mayo to control her drinking, reconciliations, and splits, the marriage was over. By Christmas both retained lawyers, who began negotiating a settlement. Absent from the set of *The Big Sleep* on December 26,[81] he was found at Mayo's in a drunken stupor, one of only a few times that he absented himself from shooting caused by a hangover.

After some delays, Methot eventually spent the necessary six weeks to get a divorce in Las Vegas. Bogart had Lloyd Wright represent him, and Mayo used Jerry Giesler and later Paul Ralli at her Las Vegas divorce, where she charged extreme cruelty, great mental suffering, and impairment of physical health. The divorce was granted on May 10, 1945. On May 21, 1945, Bogart and Bacall were married in a private, three-minute ceremony, performed by Judge Shettler at the farm of Bogart's friend Louis Bromfield in Mansfield, Ohio. The next day, they headed back to California so that he could finish *The Two Mrs. Carrolls*[82] and Bacall could begin work on *Confidential Agent*. They had purchased a three-level house on King's Road in Hollywood Hills, but resided in the Garden of Allah until the house was ready for the newlyweds and their cook, gardener, secretary, and business manager.[83] The monthly and weekly fan magazines and the daily newspapers gobbled up what they could about the private wedding and played the story for all it was worth: the forty-five-year-old, cynical, tough-mannered star marrying the twenty-year-old starlet. Many thought it would not last, but as David Niven observes, "In spite of her extreme youth, she had a mountain of common sense and the guts to put it to work. She never kowtowed to Bogie. She never nagged him, and above all, she truly admired him as a man and as an actor. For his part he adored her and was proud of her looks, her honesty, and her spirit."[84]

Bacall gave up what could have been a flourishing career to keep her marriage on terra firma and later to have children. After *Confidential Agent*, her next three pictures—*The Big Sleep, Dark Passage,* and *Key Largo*—were with Bogart. They also did several radio broadcasts together and for the most part accompanied one another on location or relaxed aboard their new boat, *Santana*, a fifty-five-foot ketch that Bogart purchased from Dick Powell. Bogart's work, friends, wife, and later family kept him busy, but there was always time for sailing. From those early days when he had spent time with his father in their upstate New York vacation home, he had loved the water. Whether it was on the *Sluggy*, when married to Mayo Methot, or now, aboard the *Santana*, whenever he was on a forced layoff or a vacation, spending a weekend with friends, satisfying a need to be by himself, or competing in a sailboat race, Bogart was a frequent sight at the Newport marina. And he often measured his friends by their acumen at sailing or at the chess board: "His theory was simple—if a man could handle a boat in rough weather or be a good shipmate in days of calm, he should be awarded one star like a reliable restaurant in the *Guide Michelin*. If in addition, he proved to have interests, experience, and curiosity outside the small world of filmmaking and enjoyed a game of chess, he might receive a higher rating."[85] Near the end of his life, during his battle with cancer, "the boat was his health, his safety."[86]

Bacall offered Bogart the camaraderie of a buddy, the warmth and love of a woman, and the stability he sought but could not find in his three previous marriages. Never one to spend much time with other actors and directors (there are some exceptions, such as John Huston), with Bacall his demeanor was more relaxed and expansive. Unlike the previous year or two, when friends tended to stay away due to the uncertainty of Mayo's welcome, they now found an open door. Playwrights, novelists, composers, singers, journalists, and an occasional actor or director would socialize at the Bogarts'. With a happy home life, there was also a noticeable lessening of filmmaking. No longer did he have to prove himself and make five or six pictures a year. For all the hype in the fan magazines and the press about brawls in clubs and arguments with the studio, when the day's shoot was over, Bogart preferred life away from the spotlight. He enjoyed being with friends, "liberal thinkers, writers, newspapermen, intellectuals, men who talk and argue" about such things as politics and playwrighting,[87] having a meal at one of his favorite bistros, playing chess, sailing aboard the *Santana*, and spending time with Bacall. When something riled him, when something did not meet his standards, he spoke up. But like other actors, he sought privacy. He wanted to give the fans a good screen performance but not his private life. As he said to Virginia McPherson, "I don't owe my public anything except a good performance. That's what they pay for and, if they get it, we're even-Stephen."[88]

Charles Samuels noted that in 1943 and 1944, Bogart was in seventh place in the Box Office Champion lists, and in 1945 he moved to sixth place (tied with Gary Cooper), and that the only other "toughie" close to him was Alan Ladd at fifteenth. These three years saw the release of *Casablanca, Action in the North Atlantic, Sahara, Passage to Marseille, To Have and Have Not*, and *Conflict*. He remained on the list through 1949, being as high as fifth (1947) and as low as ninth (1949).[89] Bogart was making more money for the studios than Flynn or Davis, and his box office appeal rested with his "instinctive flair for endowing a picture with suspense. Watch him on the screen, in any shot of any film, and you'll discover you never know what he is going to do or say next."[90]

On August 21, 1946, at about the time of the release of *The Big Sleep*, Bogart's hand- and footprints were immortalized in the forecourt of the Chinese Theatre. Four months later, as a top money producer for the studio, he renegotiated his contract with Jack Warner. The new agreement, for a previously unheard-of fifteen years, required that he make only one picture a year for the studio and could star in one outside production. According to his contract, his commitment to the studio was for the first six months of each year, and the minimum budget for the studio production was $900,000.[91] He had approval of the director, but agreed to work with five directors at any time: Delmer Daves, Howard Hawks, John Cromwell, John Huston, and Michael Curtiz.[92] He also had script approval and was required to do no more than one radio or television broadcast for each movie. As he told Jack Holland on the set of *Dark Passage*, "It took me a long time to get what I wanted in the way of roles, and after I'd been in Hollywood for a while I came very near to chucking the whole thing overboard. I'm an impatient guy. I wanted things to happen right away. So—maybe if I could relive my career, I'd be a little less impulsive, more patient of the usual delays and frustrations. The picture business can be awfully tough on a guy with a temperament like mine, for three-fourths of it is waiting. But I guess it all pays off in the end."[93] While he was making *Dark Passage* Bogart's hair began falling out in clumps. He hated doctors, but he went and was diagnosed as having alopecia areata, for which he had to take shots of B_{12} and eat a greater variety of foods, and drink less alcohol.[94] Slowly some of his hair began to return but thereafter wore a hairpiece for his films.

The next two years saw the release of *Dead Reckoning* (for Columbia), *The Two Mrs. Carrolls*, *Dark Passage*, *The Treasure of the Sierra Madre*, and *Key Largo*. On April 7, 1948,[95] he formed his own company, Santana Pictures Corporation, along with Robert Lord, a producer and former writer at Warner Bros., who served as vice president, and A. Morgan Maree, his business manager. Originally Bogart was to work with his good friend Mark Hellinger, who had his own company. Hellinger was working on a deal with Harry Cohn to make pictures with Bogart for Columbia when he died suddenly on December 21, 1947. Bogart subsequently formed Santana and worked out an agreement with Columbia to rent production facilities for $225,000 per picture and then release the film through Columbia. He told the *New York Herald-Tribune*'s Otis L. Guernsey, Jr., that he would buy only scripts he could use immediately, that he they did not have big dollars for stars or the flexibility of the big studios, and most of the supporting actors were freelancers.[96] Dana Polan notes that Bogart, as the highest-paid star in Hollywood by 1949, may have formed the company more for tax purposes than as a show of independence, but as tax laws changed and the films were not as successful as they might have been, being an independent may have lost some of its appeal to Bogart.[97]

The company's first production was *Knock on Any Door*, directed by Nicholas Ray, and starring Bogart and John Derek. In the next few years he was to make four additional pictures for Santana, taking roles in each of them (*Tokyo Joe*, *In a Lonely Place*, *Sirocco*, and *Beat the Devil*), while working for other studios on *Chain Lightning*, *The Enforcer*, *The African Queen*, *Deadline—U.S.A.*, *Battle Circus*, *The Caine Mutiny*, *Sabrina*, *The Barefoot Contessa*, *We're No Angels*, *The Left Hand of God*, *The Desperate Hours*, and *The Harder They Fall*. As president of the company, Bogart, for the first time in his career, was able to control his roles and property, and he enjoyed being his own boss. At the urging of Howard Thompson of the *New York Times*, Bogart assessed Santana's success: " ' "Knock on Any Door," ' he recalled, 'was good, could have been better and set us up on our feet because it made money. We made it for $900,000, plus 25 percent overhead, but I could afford that now. "Tokyo Joe" made money too.' He shrugs. ' "Sirocco" was one we had to do, and it stank, of course.' "[98] He had limited success with his productions, but he was able to sell the company in 1953, before *Beat the Devil* opened, and accomplished what he wanted: financial security for his family and control over his film career. The profit from the sale of the company to Columbia, reported to be between $750,000 and $1 million,[99] assuaged Bogart's financial concerns for his family's immediate future. Always remembering what happened to his father, Bogart wanted enough money to be able to tell others to get out of his life. "The only reason to have money is to tell any s.o.b. in the world to go to hell."[100]

The press found Bogart good copy, but except for his divorces, battles with Jack Warner, and business ventures, he tended to stay away from the legal system. One case that required a court appearance focused on the much-heralded great panda furor at El Morocco in New York in 1949. After a night on the town with Bacall and some of his drinking buddies, Bogart and Billy Seaman went to the Stork Club, where each purchased a huge stuffed panda. With twenty-pound pandas in tow, they continued their celebration at El Morocco, where actress Robin Roberts, "a dark-haired and lush model,"[101] tried to take Bogart's away from him. He defended his own property, she fell or was pushed down, and she filed suit. She lost the case (September 1949), but gained publicity for her career. Bogart, confident that he would win the case, was not concerned about the publicity. Outside the courtroom, his fans cheered, and his friends in Hollywood sent telegrams of support and congratulations.[102] He was subsequently banned from the club, and the next year, after a shouting match with Sherman Billingsley, he was also banned from the Stork Club. Of the panda incident and scandal in general, Bogart told Ezra Goodman: "I don't think such things as getting loaded or the panda incident hurt me. I'm established in the public mind as a rather rough, tough character. It would hurt Jimmy Stewart, the all-American boy. I'm lucky enough to get away with all this stuff. For a man who has lived in a glass house for some 30 odd years, I've done pretty well. My life, I'd say, is a kind of an open book. None of the scandal I've been involved in has been disastrous. There is not any that I'm ashamed of."[103] The press seemed to agree.[104]

Except for remarks Bogart made to S. R. Mooks (*Screenland*, 1941) warning actors to focus on entertainment and stay off political committees,[105] he was never shy about speaking his mind. By the late forties, more sure of himself and influenced in part by Bacall's enthusiasm for certain causes and political candidates, Bogart became more visible and vocal on the political front. Never one to mince words or be silenced, he ignored Warner's threats that his actors stay out of politics unless, of course, they were supportive of Jack Warner's views.[106] When Warner subtly threatened studio employees who supported FDR, Bogart openly voiced his support. In 1944, one unpopular position he took was challenged by the union for the Federated Motion Picture Crafts when it asked its members to boycott pictures of certain actors, including Bogart, who did not support their picket lines.[107] This was a surprising tack against an actor voted the year before as one of Hollywood's most cooperative stars. A few years later, in 1947, Bogart was present at the birth of the Committee for the First Amendment. Organized by Huston, Wyler, Billy Wilder, and screenwriter Philip Dunne, this group sent a petition with approximately 500 signatures to New Jersey Republican J. Parnell Thomas in support of freedom of expression. "Our object was to exert our influence in defense of a principle—the principle that no man should be forced to tell what political party he belongs to.... We weren't protesting Congress's right to hold such an investigation. We were only protesting, as individuals, the manner in which it was conducted."[108] On November 23, 1947, Ed Sullivan of the *New York Post*, saying he did not want to be conned by Bogart, questioned J. Edgar Hoover's aide Clyde Tolson about Bogart's sympathies.[109] Although Sullivan said he did not think there was anything "sinister" about Bogart, he was concerned that he received a lot of mail complaining that he besmirched Hoover's name when he ran in one of his columns Bogart's statement that "I am about as much a Communist as J. Edgar Hoover."[110]

During the hearings of the House of Un-American Activities probe of communists in Hollywood, Bogart, along with a number of other Hollywood actors, directors, and writers (Bacall, Marsha Hunt, Richard Conte, June Havoc, John and Evelyn Keyes, John Huston, Paul Henreid, Sterling Hayden, Danny Kaye, Sheppard Strudwick, Jane Wyatt, and Geraldine Brooks), rented a plane from Howard Hughes and flew to Washington to attend the hearings. Bogart said the abuse of civil liberties and loss of civil rights were the reason he went. This time he paid a price for his activities. He was soon to view the trip as ill advised. Alistair Cooke notes that Bogart "was aghast to discover that several of them were down-the-line-Communists coolly exploiting the protection of the First and Fifth Amendments to the Constitution. He had thought they were just freewheeling anarchists, like himself." Bogart said, "We turned out to be lousy politicians, but we muddled through and got some attention for our point of view." And as Sidney Olson notes, the committee had "more of an eye on sensation than on justice or fact-finding."[111] Subsequently Bogart, in what Coe and others have called a "graceless and unnecessary" recanting of his position, declared he detested "Communism just as any decent American does." As reported in *Newsweek*, Bogart said, "We went green and they beat our brains out."[112] And he was not happy when his picture appeared on the front page of the *Daily Worker*. He protested he was not a communist and that he had been "foolish and impetuous." These events, especially his protests on how he had been duped, cast a shadow over Bogart's image, but his experiences did not dissuade him from future involvement in politics, especially in 1952, when, with Bacall's prodding, he was won over from the Eisenhower camp and campaigned for Adlai Stevenson.[113] Even when he was dying of cancer, Bogart was concerned with the proposed amendment to the Constitution to limit a president to two terms.[114]

Between the HUAC hearings and the 1952 political campaign, Bogart lost his good friend, writer Mark Hellinger (December 21, 1947), formed his own production company (Santana, April 7, 1948), traveled to Africa to work with Katharine Hepburn and John Huston, and saw the release of a number of his films, including *Treasure of the Sierra Madre* and *Key Largo* with Bacall, *Knock on Any Door, In a Lonely Place,* and *The African Queen.* More significant than any of those events, though, were the births of their two children: a son, Stephen, on January 6, 1949, and a daughter, Leslie, on August 23, 1952. Fatherhood was a new role for the outspoken, gun-toting gangster and cynical, world-weary adventurer, but Bogart prospered as a family man.[115]

At the same time, he continued to nurture his image as a nonconformist. The Bogarts launched the Holmby Hills Rat Pack, a group of "adult delinquents" known for their carousing together. Membership included Mike Romanoff, Judy Garland, Sid Luft, David Niven, Frank Sinatra, and agent Swifty Lazar. On numerous occasions Bogart played up his dislike of actors. He told Virginia MacPherson that he considered New York "a fun town," but in Hollywood, "you see the same dull crowd at night spots. They sit in the same seats with the same people . . . bored with everything—including themselves."[116] But Bogart and the Rat Pack would occasionally take out ads in the trade papers defending someone who was getting unfair publicity or being attacked by the establishment. The group would assist one another in small ways as well. Bogart, for example, as a good-luck token for a film comeback for Garland, shouted "Sing Melancholy Baby!" during the "Born in a Trunk" number of *A Star Is Born.*[117]

On November 28, 1950, Bogart had his Warner Bros. contract amended from a weekly salary to a flat $160,00 for the first picture and $150,00 for any subsequent picture in the same year. Bogart's concern with financial stability for his wife and children was reflected in another effort of his, this one in concert with Bacall. In April 1951 he and Bacall initiated "Bold Venture," a Frederic W. Ziv Co. production of radio shows. Bogart played Slate Shannon, a proprietor of a small hotel in Havana, and Bacall was Sailor Duval, Shannon's "ward." *Bold Venture* was Shannon's boat. Marrying elements of *To Have and Have Not* and *Casablanca,* the show, broadcast over 423 stations, earned the Bogarts about $4,000 a week. By the time they were off to Africa for the making of *The African Queen,* they had completed thirty-eight of the shows.[118]

Shortly before going to Africa, Bogart was at home with Bacall and Richard Brooks and his wife decorating a Christmas tree. Lillian Ross recounts that Bogart, who was finishing *Sirocco* for Santana Productions, lamented about business matters: " 'Too many business worries. . . . The role [in *Sirocco*] is a cinch. The role doesn't bother me. I've been doing the role for years. I've worn that trench coat of mine in half the pictures I've been in. What I don't like is business worries. I like to work with John [Huston]. The monster is stimulating. Offbeat kind of mind. Off center. He's brilliant and unpredictable. Never dull. When I work with John, I think about acting, I don't worry about business. With Santana, I'm bowed down with business worries.' " He also lamented that of the eleven writers he had on *Sirocco,* not one had an ending for the picture.[119]

The filming of *The African Queen* gave the Bogarts an opportunity to travel overseas together. Not especially fond of traveling, Bogart nevertheless was willing to go almost anywhere to make a film with Huston, and this was an opportunity to work with Katharine Hepburn. Somewhat distraught about leaving her young son for the first time, Bacall knew how much Bogart did not want to be separated from her for any length of time; such separations had contributed to previous divorces. Prior to their ship's departure for Europe, they received notification that Steve's nurse had a stroke and died. That did not prevent them from continuing. After London, Paris, and Rome, including a visit with the pope, they found the location shooting in Africa difficult, the accommodations less than ideal, the food barely passable, and the infections debilitating. Of all the cast and crew, Bogart seemed to have come out of the ordeal with the least physical damage. He jokingly claimed that the bugs stayed away from him because of the high level of alcohol in his blood.[120]

Not unlike contemporary actors such as Dustin Hoffman, Bogart did not believe that actors should compete with one another for awards. He made his views known as early as 1937, when he debunked Hollywood awards by giving Asta a *Skippy*, a silver statuette for best animal performance of the year. He had told Virginia MacPherson his first commandment as a performer: "I don't owe my public anything except a good performance. That's what they pay for, and if they get it, we're even-Stephen."[121] Thirteen years after the "Skippy affair," Bogart published "The Oscar Myth" in *Cosmopolitan* in which he decried the Academy Awards as a "publicity stunt" and blasted the rating of film stars as "ridiculous." Nominated himself in 1943 for best actor for *Casablanca*, Bogart saw movie acting, unlike acting on the stage, as "strictly piecework." To him, some award-winning performances belonged more to the editor, cinematographer, or director. While analyzing how the membership votes and the lack of winners for comic rather than dramatic roles, Bogart remarked that for all its hype, the award was the kiss of death for some actors. Although not unreceptive to receiving an Oscar, he trivialized what he would do with the award if he ever received it.[122]

Hollywood has a long memory for those who attack the establishment, but two years later Bogart was nominated for his serio-comic performance of Charlie Allnut in *The African Queen*. For all the public veneer about the Oscars, Nunnally Johnson remarked, "To hear Betty [Bacall] talk, you'd think they were headed for the White House.... The truth is, the man [Bogart] is promising anything to anybody." That year Marlon Brando was odds-on favorite for his performance in *A Streetcar Named Desire*, but as Johnson noted in a letter to Thornton Delehanty, although Brando might have had the edge on the performance, Bogart was "more popular."[123] As the evening progressed and Kim Hunter and Karl Malden won as supporting actors and Vivian Leigh won for best actress, the audience anticipated a Brando win and a sweep in the acting awards for *Streetcar*. Prior to the ceremony, and later at a press conference, Bogart said that he too thought Brando would win. When Greer Garson announced Bogart's name, there was a collective gasp of surprise, followed by a standing ovation. As happens with the Oscars, the performance may have won it for him, or it may well have been "a cumulative tribute, an acknowledgment of his enduring presence and influence."[124]

Like so many of his contemporaries, Bogart had entered films reluctantly. He was an actor on the legitimate stage, and his roots were in New York. Although a legion of people were his "friends," he kept a small circle of close associates. Whenever he went to New York, he spent time with writers and journalists and with friends from the theater. Except for his immediate family, he was never concerned with winning the love of others. He did not always believe that he was well liked in Hollywood, nor did he really care about it, but the standing ovation he received for his Oscar win told him otherwise. For all his put-downs of the Oscar, he was humbled (at least momentarily) to win. Bogart accepted graciously, saying how it was "nicer" to be at the Plantages Theatre than in the Belgian Congo. Later he thanked those who helped give him his start: William A. Brady, who gave him his start on Broadway; Winnie Sheehan, who gave him his first substantive film role in *Up the River*; Arthur Hopkins, who selected him for Sherwood's *The Petrified Forest* and convinced Sherwood and Gilbert Miller to let him play the role and whom Bogart credited as being "the one who changed me from Joe College to Trigger Joe"; and Leslie Howard, who insisted he play the film version of Sherwood's play. Returning to reality later that evening, he told the press that he still stood by his earlier remarks: "This Oscar doesn't prove I was the best actor of the year. The only honest way would be to let everybody play Hamlet and let the best man win." A realist, he knew the award could have been based on factors other than artistic merit.[125] Then he went to Romanoff's to celebrate. As Bacall comments on this time in his life, "Bogie had everything now—a happy marriage, a son, another child on the way, an ocean racing yawl, *Santana*, success, and the peak of recognition in his work."[126]

After having slowed down in the late 1940s and early 1950s, from his earlier frenetic pace, with a growing family to support, Bogart returned to the studios to make *Deadline—U.S.A., Battle Circus, Beat the Devil, The Caine Mutiny, Sabrina, The Barefoot Contessa, We're No Angels, The Left Hand of God, The Desperate Hours,* and *The Harder They Fall*. For all his box office clout, Bogart still battled Jack Warner. In 1952, as part of their ongoing conflict, Warner told Bogart that he was a lucky fellow because the studio was going to have to pay him a lot of money and keep him in pictures even when he lost his teeth and had no hair,[127] and that Warner Bros. was responsible for making him what he was. Warner was right about that, but Bogart had not made a film for the Warner logo since *The Enforcer* (1951). Earlier in his career Bogart said, "We'd all like to have new faces. I'll trade mine in any day but producers will have to come up with something better than this new crop—these guys with fancy names all look alike. I can't tell them apart and I'm in the business. How in hell is the public supposed to know?"[128] On September 21, 1953, Bogart enjoyed one of the happiest days of his career when he signed the release from his fifteen-year contract with Warner Bros. Following on the heels of a financial and professional hardship, the making of *Beat the Devil*, Bogart returned to playing Captain Queeg, a suspicious, "sick man" who lived "a life of frustrations and insecurity."[129] This character was not unlike two of his finest roles: Dobbs in *The Treasure of the Sierra Madre* and Dixon Steele in *In a Lonely Place*.

He worked on *Sabrina* next, and supposedly took the role at the urging of Swifty Lazar, who, a friend of both Billy Wilder and Bogart, thought Bogart should be playing high comedy. Bogart felt uncomfortable from the start, especially since Wilder had wanted Cary Grant for Bogart's role. Relations with everyone on the set were strained, and the fights on the set were legendary. Maurice Zolotow, in his biography of Billy Wilder, reports that "Bogart ridiculed every aspect of the screenplay and his costume" and that "perhaps Bogart identified too strongly with Queeg while filming *The Caine Mutiny*. He had gone straight from that picture to *Sabrina*. His delusions of persecution seized on anything."[130] Bogart abused the director on the set and in the media. He told *Time*: "He's the type of director I don't like to work with. This picture *Sabrina* is a crock of shit anyway."[131] Wilder vowed never to work with Bogart again.

After the disaster of *Sabrina*, the film that he most wanted to work on was *The Desperate Hours*, provided he could team with his good friend Spencer Tracy. They had not worked together since 1930, and they had talked on numerous occasions about the "dream-casting,"[132] but supposedly Bogart's (or Tracy's) unwillingness to take second billing prevented it from happening. Sperber and Lax quote Phil Gersh as saying that Bogart offered Tracy top billing,[133] but the pairing never happened. When asked if he would do television, Bogart, who at one time considered setting up a company with Bacall, told Dave Kaufman, "I won't go into TV unless I feel myself slipping."[134] Although he had numerous offers from producers, he restricted himself to very few guest appearances. A little over a year later, he made his dramatic debut on May 30, 1955, in a very well-received *The Petrified Forest* for Producer's Showcase. It was directed by Delbert Mann and starred Henry Fonda, Lauren Bacall, and Bogart, reprising his role as Duke Mantee. He claimed he did it for nostalgic reasons only. To Bogart the two media were distinct: "A man can't work in both mediums at the same time, and I am a motion picture man."[135] Up to that time, he had appeared only on Jack Benny's show, in an interview with Edward R. Murrow, and as a host presenter of Academy Award telecasts.

Anyone who has seen a Bogart movie knows that he could have been a walking advertisement for cigarettes. There is even a phrase to describe how to hold a cigarette, named after him: "to Bogie a joint." His incessant smoking led to cancer of the esophagus. At work on *The Harder They Fall* in 1955, he began noticing minor signs of physical exhaustion. He was tired, had less energy, and coughed frequently. In late 1956, while lunching at Romanoff's, Bogart had a coughing fit and complained that he was having a hard time swallowing. He was also losing weight. One visit to Dr. Maynard Brandsma, a doctor recommended to him by Greer Garson, resulted in several tests during the next few weeks. Bogart continued having difficulty swallowing. One of the tests showed a cancerous polyp on his esophagus. (Maud Humphrey had died of cancer at the age of seventy.) Bogart wanted to delay the operation to remove the polyp so that he could complete *Melville Goodwin, USA*, with Bacall, their first picture together in almost a decade. The doctor recommended immediate surgery. The following week, on March 1, 1956, the surgeon, Dr. John Jones, found that the cancer had spread to Bogart's lymph nodes, two of which were removed. The nine-hour operation involved altering his digestive system by relocating his stomach. Recovering slowly, he had emergency surgery a few days later to stitch up his abdominal incision, which had opened from his coughing. The anticipated healing process took weeks, and the biopsy of the lymph nodes indicated that radiation was necessary. The eight weeks of radiation left him sick and weak, with little appetite.

Numerous friends visited Bogart in the hospital and at home for the next several months, with each recounting Bogart's mood and positive attitude. There was little talk of *Melville Goodwin, USA*, but Bogart was always concerned about whether Harry Cohn at Columbia would hold another project, *The Good Shepherd*, for him.[136] By the end of the summer Bogart was gaining back some strength, and his family life was taking on some sense of normalcy. He tried to spend time on the *Santana*.[137] The press, with which he had a good working relationship throughout his career, respected Bogart's need for privacy and said little about him or his health. An exception was Dorothy Kilgallen, who, never much liked by Bogart, reported in the *Journal-American* that he was "fighting for his life."

Bogart was furious. Venting his rage, he called her paper and complained. Then he took action. In 1939 he told Jack Holland that he would "rather have my own harmless versions of my doings plastered across the newspaper than those of someone else who might get unduly excited when he hears a rumor and reports me dead."[138] Bogart sent Louella Parsons a telegram, which she printed, saying that he was doing fine. He also called his friend and columnist Joe Hyams and asked him to print "An Open Letter to the Working Press" about his "reported demise." Not unlike Swift's "Verses on the Death of Dr. Swift" in which the speaker imagines public reation to his death, Bogart related that it was not time yet to write him off: "I have been greatly disturbed lately at the many unchecked and baseless rumors being tossed to the people regarding the state of my health. Just to set the record straight, as they say in Washington (and I have as much right to this as anybody else in Washington has), a great deal of what has been printed has had nothing to do with the true facts. It may be even necessary for me to send out a Truth Team to follow you all around." Continuing for several paragraphs, Bogart described aspects of the operation, his weight loss, and the need for reporters to verify his condition—"I'm in the book."[139]

Anxious to get back to work, he had problems gaining back the 30 pounds he had lost from his 155-pound frame. He also wanted to get back to sailing and to share with his son his love of the sea. A year earlier he had won the 300-mile Channel Yacht Cup with the *Santana*. Always at ease on the sea, even if he could not sail, gave Bogart comfort. Then he had problems in his shoulder, which the doctors called a pinched nerve caused by the healing process, but it required nitrogen mustard treatment.

Bogart rarely voiced his pain and tried to be as upbeat as possible, more concerned with how friends and family who visited daily would view his frailty. Seemingly aware of what was about to happen, but never pushing the issue or speaking about it openly, Bogart made it through his fifty-seventh birthday, struggling valiantly to be at his best when friends visited. Those close to him could see and knew what was happening. The doctors told Bacall that death was imminent. On Sunday, January 13, 1957, Bogart lapsed into a coma, and at 2:10 A.M., on January 14, 1957, he died.

Lauren Bacall called Joe Hyams, Bogart's spokeman to the newspapers, and asked him to notify the news services. Headlines for news stories and features the next few days tried to capture the essence of the Bogart persona: "Bogey Died as He Lived—Bravely," "Lust, Hard-Drinking Bogey Hated Phonies," "It Took Death to Shatter Legend of Tough Bogart," "Bogart, B.O. Star and Copy, Dies," and "Saga of a Tough Guy—That Was Bogie to the Very Last."

The funeral services were conducted by the Reverend Kermit Castellanos at All Saints Episcopal Church and held at 12:30 P.M., on January 17, 1957. Several studios in Hollywood, including Warner Bros. and Twentieth Century Fox, observed a minute of silence. Newspapers reported that nearly 3,000 people lined the streets outside All Saints. Attendees included Gregory Peck, Gary Cooper, Marlene Dietrich, Katharine Hepburn, Spencer Tracy, Danny Kaye, Jack L. Warner, David O. Selznick, Jennifer Jones, Billy Wilder, Harry Cohn, Charles Brackett, Mike Romanoff, Ronald Reagan, and Ida Lupino. The ushers, who reflected Bogart's varied interests and friendships, were actor David Niven, writer and director Nunnally Johnson, restaurateur Mike Romanoff, producer Leland Hayward, agent Irving Paul ("Swifty") Lazar, and yachtsman Larry Dudley. Castellanos recited the Ten Commandments, "because Bogie had believed in them and lived by them," the Twenty-third Psalm, and Tennyson's "Crossing the Bar." On the altar was a model of the *Santana*, Bogart's fifty-five-foot yawl. John Huston delivered the eulogy. Brief but pointed, Huston spoke of the importance of Bogart's family, his work, his friends, and his boat. Of his attitude toward his profession, Huston said:

With the years he had become increasingly aware of the dignity of his profession—Actor, not Star: Actor. Himself, he never took too seriously—his work most seriously. He regarded the somewhat gaudy figure of Bogart, the star, with an amused cynicism;

Bogart, the actor, he held in deep respect. Those who did not know him well, who never worked with him, who were not of the small circle of his close friends, had another completely different idea of the man than the few who were so privileged. I suppose the ones who knew him but slightly were at the greatest disadvantage, particularly if they were the least bit solemn about their own importance. Bigwigs have been known to stay away from the brilliant Hollywood occasion rather than expose their swelling neck muscles to Bogart's banderillas.[140]

While the service was being conducted, Humphrey Bogart was cremated at Forest Lawn.

In Bogart's will of June 6, 1956, he made modest bequests to two employees (Kay Smith and Kathryn Sloan); he left all his personal possessions to Bacall, one-half of his residuary estate to her, and the rest in trust for his children until they reached the age of forty-five. The trusts were to be used for the education of Stephen and Leslie and at the trustee's discretion. If the Humphrey Bogart Foundation came into property, he requested that his estate establish a corporation to donate the funds to distribute grants for medical research, in particular cancer research, and to various charities.[141]

In writing about Bogart years after his death, Bacall said he had many layers, some of which she still was not aware of. He grew up in a family of means, only to see his family disintegrate and the means disappear. His father died and left his son his love of the sea, his ring, and numerous debts; he took financial responsibility for his sister, Pat, who was institutionalized off and on; his relationship with his mother was reserved at best; his first two marriages broke apart because of career pressures and personal differences; his marriage to Mayo Methot was one battle after another, at a time when he had his share of run-ins with Jack Warner. He drank too much, followed daily rituals regarding meals and drinks, shamelessly needled others to get a rise out of them, loved sailing and being on his boat, was willing to give of his time for causes he found just,[142] came to fatherhood late in life and found it scary. He was dedicated to the well-being of his children.

For all his rough edges, he was especially committed to those who were struggling to make it. Remembering his own difficulties, he was a friend of the "regular Joe" and less concerned with the big shots and stars. When the Newport Yacht Club asked the skipper of the *Santana* to have his cook leave the club because he was not of the calibre of the guests, Bogart gave them his resignation from the club on the back of the check. Other members sided with Bogart, and the board was forced to refuse his resignation.[143] When neighbors of Bogart and Mayo Methot learned that Lena Horne was living in the house across from the Bogarts, the neighbors began action to evict her; when the Bogarts found out, they let it be known that Lena Horne was to be left alone.[144] Florence Pritchett, who met Bogart in 1947, when she was writing for *Movie Show*, recalls that "not everyone thought highly of Bogart as a person or an actor: There are those who don't like him for the obvious reasons of jealousy and envy. They, therefore, magnify the natural outbursts of his personality. Straightforwardness can often be termed abrupt, brusque and rough. Honesty can often be interpreted as unkindness and tastelessness." Bogart told her to call him any time she was short on money and needed a story. She was impressed by his lack of pretension and high standards: "It's a unique thing in Hollywood to see a star of prominence remain a man who can live by his own standards, mind his own business and still have a group of friends, male and female, who would swear by him."[145]

To Bacall, Bogart was her teacher: "He taught me his philosophy of life. He taught me the rules of the Hollywood game. He taught me the usage and abusage of actors, called stars by the press, which couldn't have cared less what happened to any of us. It was good copy, true or not, that mattered most. We were expendable—he taught me that too. He taught me about standards and the price one must pay to keep those standards high. He taught me about the value of work and the importance of truth and character."[146]

David Niven, who came to know him fairly well because of their many trips aboard *Santana*, observed, "Things to Bogie were either black or white; he had little patience with the grays. To sort people out quickly, he used the shock technique. Early on in an acquaintanceship he would say or do something completely outrageous, and the reaction of the other person told Bogie most of what he wanted to know. People in movie theaters saw him as the personification of the tough and the sardonic, and up to a point they were not far wrong. He gamely presented the same facade in real life, but my own theory was that he worked to maintain it and had a difficult time covering up the fact that he was really kind, generous, highly intelligent, and deeply sentimental."[147]

Alistair Cooke has summarized nicely the contrasting views of Bogart:

In Bogart, the contradictions were evidently so gross that people who loathed him could never credit how much anyone could love him. And vice versa. Some people saw nothing but a moody drunk, a barfly given to random practical jokes and spasms of sadism, a cynic with more than a touch of paranoia leading to tasteless verbal assaults on anyone who conveyed a hint of pomp or authority or the lacier attributes of homosexuality. Others, who knew him well, found him gentle, gallant, modest, full of an indulgent or rueful humor, courteous with strangers, quietly and acutely sensitive to the plight of guests who were shy or being left out. [As an actor, he was] . . . a much more intelligent man than most of his trade, or several others, a touchy man who found the world more corrupt than he had hoped; a man with a tough shell hiding a fine core. He had transmuted his own character into a film persona and imposed it on a world impatient of men more obviously good. By showily neglecting the outward forms of grace, he kept inferior men at a distance. For he lived in a town crowded with malign flatterers, hypocrites and poseurs, fake ascetics, studio panders, and the pimps of the press. From all of them he was determined to keep his secret: the rather shameful secret in the realistic world we inhabit, of being an incurable puritan, gentle at bottom and afraid to say so.[148]

NOTES

1. *Who Was Who in the Theatre: 1912–1976* (Detroit: Gale Research, 1978), 1:235. David Hanna, *Bogart* (New York: Leisure Books, 1976), 29. Hanna's may have been a typographical error.

2. "The Bewildering Bogarts,"*Photoplay* 26 (February 1945): 92.

3. The book-length biographies of Bogart include those by Richard Gehman, Ezra Goodman, Joe Hyams (one on Bogart and a reworking of the material for one on Bogart and Bacall), Jonah Ruddy and Jonathan Hill, David Hanna, Howard Greenberger (on Bogart and Bacall), Lauren Bacall (an autobiography, *By Myself*, and the follow-up *Now*, which deals primarily with her current feelings), Jonathan Coe, Stephen Bogart, Jeffrey Meyers, and A. M. Sperber and Eric Lax. Unless otherwise noted, all references to Bacall are to *By Myself*. For complete citations, see Chapter 4. For a discussion of these and other biographical works, see Chapter 4.

4. Sperber and Lax 13.

5. *Who's Who in the Theatre*, 9th ed. rev., ed. John Parker (New York: Pittman, 1939), 1159.

6. *Florida Times Union*, July 16, 1981, A9.

7. Bogart's poster image for Mellins Baby Food appears in *Hello, Dolly!* (1969).

8. *McCall's* (July 1949); rpt. *McCall's*. 103 (April 1976): 41.

9. Hyams 21; Sperber and Lax 13.

10. Hyams and Charles Francisco mistakenly say that he entered Episcopal Trinity at age fourteen.

11. Doug Storer, "Amazing But True," *St. Petersburg* (Fla.) *Independent*, August 20, 1979. See also Gehman 83 and Hyams 25. A picture in the clipping file of the Wisconsin Center for Film and Theater Research at the University of Wisconsin shows Bogart taking a rhumba lesson from Barry Norman during the filming of *Casablanca*. The photograph is reprinted in Harmetz, *Round Up the Usual Suspects* (171), with a comment that Bogart was "uncomfortable" dancing the rhumba. For the information from Hodgins, see Hyams 28.

12. Apocryphal stories tell of Bogart's pushing a teacher into a fountain or being caught in bed with a girl as the reason for his departure, but the facts support academic failure as the reason.

13. Katharine Albert, "Meet Humphrey Bogart," *Photoplay* 51 (July 1937): 44. Repeated in Hyams 32.

14. Sperber and Lax 27.

15. "Tough Guy! Humphrey Bogart's Real Life Movie," 1943 or 1944, clipping file, Wisconsin Center for Film and Theater Research.

16. "What Harrison Ford Learned About Success," *Parade Magazine* (December 25, 1988): 9.

17. Marian Christy, "In Search of...Leonard Nimoy," *Boston Globe* (June 15, 1982): 23.

18. Storer, "Amazing But True," n.p.

19. Hyams 36; Benchley 25; *Who's Who in the Theatre*, 1159.

20. "Bogart," *Film Comment* 22 (May–June 1966): 36, 38.

21. Woody Allen, *Woody Allen on Woody Allen: In Conversation with Stig Björkman* (New York: Grove Press, 1993), 48.

22. *New York Times* (September 7, 1924): 2, C7.

23. Menken had a long and distinguished career in the theater as an actress and later as producer. *Who Was Who in the Theatre* cites one of her two favorite parts as Cassie Cook in *Drifting*.

24. Coe 16.

25. Madeline Glass, "Strong, But Not Silent," *Screenland* (January 1937): 92.

26. Benchley 30, 32; Kay Proctor, "You Can't Insult Me!" *Stardom* (September 1943): 21. In *Skyrocket* Mary Philips plays Del Ewing, his wife.

27. "Humphrey and Bogey," *Sight and Sound* (winter 1966–1967): 19. This article was translated from *Positif*. Its content appeared in Brooks's subsequent *Lulu in Hollywood* (New York: Knopf, 1982), 59–67.

28. Hyams 39; Ruth Rankin, "Humphrey's Halycon Days," *Modern Screen* (December 1936): 34–35. For other comments by Rankin, see Hyams 34–35.

29. Hanna 45.

30. Benchley 30; Gehman 98; "Who's Who" (on Humphrey Bogart), *New York Times* (September 7, 1924): 7.

31. Hanna 49; Robert Williams, "The Bogart Story, Part III," *New York Post* (January 17, 1957): 5.

32. Quoted in Alan Frank, *Humphrey Bogart* (New York: Optimum, 1982) 13; Bacall 145.

33. Many biographies and stories about Bogart spell Mary's last name with two lls. In an interview in 1937, Bogart recounts that he studied the books and papers of Edwin Booth, whose materials were available to him through his first wife, Helen Menken, a direct descendant of Booth. He realized from studying the papers that to play Shakespeare would take a great deal of "thought, analysis, and dissection" and that Shakespeare, which requires minute research and a "natural capacity for that sort of portrayal," was not his strength (Glass 93).

34. Coe (20) says the film was made for Paramount, and all subsequent references to the film say the same thing. There has been no discussion of this film, nor has anyone written about it being extant. I found a reference to *The Dancing Town* in the Universal, not Paramount, film archives at the Billy Rose Theatre Collection, New York Public Library at Lincoln Center, but the folder was missing. The library had no information as to what might have been in the folder, although these Universal archives folders supposedly had stills from films.

35. Blondell previously acted with him in the short *Broadway's Like That; Bogart*, dir.: Martin Flamm, ABC documentary, 1967.

36. For a discussion of Dr. Bogart's drug addiction, see Sperber and Lax's *Bogart* (1–25), and passim.

37. The line was a device used by scriptwriters and directors to clear the stage of unwanted players.

38. Goodman (31) calls this play "Murder by the Clock," his first role as a villain.

39. Benchley 54; Coe 24, 29.

40. Bogart recreated the role for television on May 30, 1955, with Bacall and Henry Fonda.

41. Gehman 79; Benchley 49.

42. In an interview with Katharine Albert, "Meet Humphrey Bogart," *Photoplay* 51 (July 1937):45, Bogart said he had $1,000 left over.

43. The January issue of the *1937 Academy Players Directory Bulletin*, its first (rpt.

Beverly Hills: Academy of Motion Picture Arts and Sciences, 1981), lists him under "Characters and Comedians" (130).

44. Warner Bros. correspondence, University of Southern California (USC), April 13, 1947.

45. Hyams (48) says it was Roland Young; Bacall (106) says it happened in 1936 or 1937, but there were different times and different circumstances.

46. An "accomplished actress, with a splendid stage presence," according to one reviewer in an item in the clipping files at the Wisconsin State Historical Society.

47. Dora Albert, "Happy Though Married," *Movie Mirror* (1939/1940?), n.p., clipping file, Wisconsin Center for Film and Theater Research.

48. *Lulu in Hollywood* (New York: Knopf, 1982), 66.

49. Bacall 106; Sperber and Lax, 85.

50. Robert Williams, "The Bogart Story, Part I," *New York Post* (January 15, 1957): 5.

51. Ruth Rankin, "Battling Bogarts," *Photoplay* 52 (September 1938): 22, 84, and Kay Proctor, "Happy Ending for a Villain," *Movie Mirror* (January 1939): 52, 81–82.

52. Gary Carey, *Anita Loos* (New York: Knopf, 1988), 159.

53. *Each Man in His Time: The Life Story of a Director* (New York: Farrar, Straus and Giroux, 1974), 302, 307.

54. In July 1995 English actor Hugh Grant, a media darling of sorts, saw his popularity with fans skyrocket after a much-publicized encounter with a prostitute in Hollywood.

55. Hyams 71. Also, Thornton Delahanty, "The Battling Bogarts," *Photoplay* (March 1943): 30–32, 82.

56. "The Art of Mr. Bogart," *New York Times* (February 19, 1939): 9:4.

57. *Cagney by Cagney* (New York: Pocket Books, 1977), 99–100.

58. *New York Times* (August 15, 1940): 1, 22 (for denial).

59. *New York Times*; see also Otto Friedrich, *City of Nets: A Portrait of Hollywood in the Forties* (New York: Harper & Row, 1986), 52–53.

60. R. J. Obringer to Sam Schneider, December 16, 1940, Warner Bros. Archives, USC.

61. Bogart to Trilling, March 17, 1941; Sam Jaffe to Steve Trilling, August 4, 1941, Warner Bros. Archives, USC.

62. May 6, 1943, correspondence, Warner Bros. Archives, USC.

63. As a result of thinning hair, Bogart grudgingly accepted a hair stylist. In 1947, during the filming of *Dark Passage*, he began to take hormone pills to make him more fertile, which resulted in even more hair loss. The studio made a cast of Bogart's head for shaping hairpieces and wigs. Some hair came back, but he continued to have a receding hairline. Generally Bogart was against any softening of his image. After seeing studio photos by Hurrell, who had softened the lines around his mouth and eyes and moved his hairline down, Bogart had the photos destroyed, according to Thomas Wood's "Menace as Usual," a 1942 unpublished article, written about the time of release of *Action in the North Atlantic*, in Academy of Motion Pictures Arts & Sciences files (3). For Thompson's full account of the relationship with Bogart, see *Bogie and Me* (New York: St. Martin's Press, 1982).

64. Hyams 82.

65. Humphrey Bogart as told to Jack Holland, "How to Keep Your Marriage Alive," *Silver Screen* 14 (November 1943): 30–31, 68–70.

66. "Bogart," *Film Comment* 22 (May–June 1986): 38.

67. She had appeared in the magazine in January, February, March, April, and May 1943.

68. German radio announced that troop "morale was so low that a notorious gangster had been sent out to entertain the troops." Barry Norman, *The Hollywood Greats* (New York: Franklin Watts, 1980), 130.

69. Bacall 101.

70. *Screenland* (September 1943): 60.

71. Bacall 105.

72. *TV Guide* 33 (August 3, 1985): 4.

73. Bacall 107; *Now* 179. Hawks sold 50 percent of her contract to Warners, and later Warner Bros. bought out Hawks-Feldman Productions, including the remaining 50 percent of Bacall's contract.

74. Bacall 170–171.

75. Hanna 96.

76. Bacall 113.

77. Bacall 117.

78. Walter Wanger wanted him for this, correspondence July 6, 1939; October 19, 24, 1939, Mr. Wallis to Mr. Trilling, said that this was only a temporary script; August 21, 1941, correspondence said they were considering Bogart or Garfield, and that Bogart often fought roles such as *Brother Orchid* with Edward G. Robinson.

79. Otto Friedrich in *City of Nets* says that the drinking and violence are seen in his portrayal of Sam Spade in *The Maltese Falcon*: "It was the portrait of a man who had been up all night, a man with both a hangover and a determination to get a day's work done, a man whose wife had stabbed him in the back and might do so again" (84).

80. Eric Stacey to T. C. Wright, December 26, 1944, and T. C. Wright to Obringer and Dick Pease, December 26, 1944, Warner Bros. Archives, USC.

81. Eric Stacey to T. C. Wright, production memo, December 26, 1944, Warner Bros. Files, USC.

82. Not released until 1947, the film is about a painter who murders his first wife and plots to kill his second wife so that he can run off with his neighbor.

83. Bacall, *Now*, 83.

84. Niven, *Bring on the Empty Horses*, 244.

85. Niven 245.

86. Bacall 261.

87. Cameron Shipp, "Bogey Is the Gentlest," *Movie Stars Parade* (March 1946): 83.

88. "Bogie the 'Playboy,'" *Los Angeles Evening Herald and Express* (November 10, 1949): A11. He repeated this idea to Earl Wilson and others in subsequent interviews.

89. Samuels 88; Cobbett S. Steinberg, *Film Facts* (New York: Facts on File, 1980) 58.

90. Samuels 88.

91. Contract, 7–8, Warner Bros. Files, Wisconsin Center for Film and Theater Research.

92. In his recent study, Coe mistakenly says the directors were Huston, Wyler, Ford, Wilder, and Dmytryk (110). This is probably based on a comment made by Hyams naming these five in his book (120) as he lists the ten good directors with whom Bogart would work.

93. Jack Holland, "Mellow Merchant of Menace," *Movie Show* (June 1947): 33.
94. Bacall 166.
95. Coe says April 7 (137); McCarty in *Bogey: The Films of Humphrey Bogart* gives the year as 1947 (148): Polan gives April 7, 1948.
96. "Mr. Bogart Enjoys the Producer's Life," *New York Herald Tribune* (March 6, 1949): 1–2.
97. Dana Polan, *In a Lonely Place* (London: BFI, 1993), 47–49.
98. *New York Times* (March 2, 1952): 2:5. In "How Are Bogie's Heirs Managing," *LA Calendar* (August 17, 1997), Irene Lacher reports that the two children are currently earning less than a half million dollars a year from royalties for the use of their father's image on products (79).
99. The $1 million cited in Bob Thomas, *King Cohn* (New York: Putnam's, 1967), 279.
100. Robert Williams, "The Bogart Story, Part I," *New York Post* (January 15, 1957): 5.
101. *Newsweek* 32 (October 10, 1949): 22.
102. Bacall 193–194.
103. Goodman, *Bogart*, 25.
104. A second model, Peggy Rabe, also tried to get involved in the fracas, but with less attention. *Newsweek* 32 (October 10, 1949): 22.
105. "Humphrey Bogart's Warning to Hollywood Actors," *Screenland* (May 1941): 56–57, 80–81.
106. See Hanna 99 and others on how studios tried to muzzle their actors and keep them from voicing socially conscious ideas.
107. Hanna 101.
108. "The Playbill: Citizen Bogart in Defense of a Principle," *New York Herald Tribune* (November 23, 1947): 5:1.
109. The name was supplied in a column by Jack Anderson, "Long Distance Audits," *St. Petersburg Times* (April 16, 1980): 15A.
110. Official memorandum, FBI Files, Washington, D.C., November 24, 1947.
111. Alistair Cooke, "Humphrey Bogart: Epitaph for a Tough Guy," in *Six Men* (New York: Knopf, 1977), 186; "The Playbill: Citizen Bogart in Defense of a Principle," *New York Herald Tribune* (November 23, 1947): 5:1; "The Movie Hearings," *Life* (November 24, 1947): 148.
112. Coe 132; "Bogart's Regret," *Newsweek* (December 15, 1947): 23.
113. Bacall was originally a supporter of Eisenhower, but after being prodded by Mildred Jaffe, wife of Bogart's agent and friend, to listen to Stevenson, she became a convert to the Stevenson camp (*Now* 154). In *By Myself*, Bacall implies she was always a supporter of Stevenson (219).
114. Hyams, January 15, 1957; "Bogart's Death—He Was Game to the End," *New York Herald Tribune* (January 15, 1957): 14.
115. On elections, politics, and children, see Hyams 97.
116. "Bogie the 'Playboy,'" *Los Angeles Evening Herald and Express* (November 10, 1949): A11.
117. Benchley 169–170; Eyles 127.
118. "The Bogarts' Venture," *Newsweek* (April 9, 1941): 48.
119. Lillian Ross, *Picture* (New York: Limelight, 1984), 127.
120. For the many stories coming out of the making of this film, see Bacall's *By Myself*, Hepburn's *The Making of the African Queen*, and Peter Viertel's 1953 novelization of the making of the film, *White Hunter, Black Heart* (1953), which was

made into a film of the same name, directed by and starring Clint Eastwood, released in 1990.

121. "Bogie the 'Playboy,'" *Los Angeles Evening Herald and Express* (November 10, 1949): A11.

122. "The Oscar Myth," *Cosmopolitan* (March 1950): 165.

123. *The Letters of Nunnally Johnson*, ed. Dorris Johnson and Ellen Leventhal (New York: Knopf, 1981), 75.

124. Coe 158.

125. He confided to Ed Sullivan that winning could have been based on popularity, sympathy, or studio pressure. "Little Old New York," *Sunday News* (March 30, 1957): II:4; "The Oscar Myth," 165.

126. Bacall 216.

127. Hedda Hopper, *Los Angeles Times* (May 19, 1952). Letter, July 7, 1952, Warner Bros. Archives, USC.

128. "New Faces—Hard-Drinking Bogey Hated Phonies," clipping file, Warner Bros. Archives, Wisconsin State Historical Society and Wisconsin Center for Film and Theater Research (January 14, 1957): 13.

129. H. Bogart, "The Way I See Queeg," *American Weekly* (June 27, 1954): 9.

130. Maurice Zolotow, *Billy Wilder in Hollywood* (New York: Proscenium, 1987), 251, 252, 254.

131. Zolotow 188.

132. Niven 249.

133. Sperber and Lax 501.

134. "On All Channels," *Variety* (April 23, 1954): 14; also, "Bogart's on Television—But Not for Long," *TV Guide* (May 28, 1955): 7–9.

135. "Bogart's on Television," 7.

136. In her autobiography, Bacall recounts a letter she received from Cohn telling how he would not allow anyone to discuss the project except for changing the anticipated start date out of respect for Bogart and to preclude newspaper stories: " 'It was the least we could do for Humphrey Bogart—would we had been able to do more' " (297).

137. In *Now* Bacall says that she did like being on the boat, and for Bogart, "the boat was there, and expensive, and the only place other than home that Bogie really wanted to be" (33).

138. "Everything Happens to Humphrey," *Silver Screen* (December 1939): 64.

139. Quoted in Bacall 267–268.

140. Bacall 294.

141. See Herbert E. Nass, *Wills of the Rich and Famous* (New York: Warner Books, 1991), 33–36. According to Maree in a newspaper clipping, part of Bogart's estate was to establish the Humphrey Bogart Foundation to dispense money to various charities.

142. For example, he helped to establish the Permanent Charities Organization. Jill Brook, CNN Entertainment, January 31, 1995.

143. Hyams, "Bogart's Death—He Was Game to the End"; also Cooke, "Epitaph for a Tough Guy," *Six Men*, 195.

144. Harmetz 244.

145. Florence Pritchett, "Completely Amazing Guy," *Movie Show* (January 1948): 69.

146. Bacall, *Now*, 5.

147 Nivens, *Bring on the Empty Horses*, 246.

148. Cooke, *Six Men*, 201, 205.

2

HUMPHREY BOGART'S IMPACT ON POPULAR CULTURE

In the academic world, film and cultural studies, especially the study of the impact of stars on our culture, remain a somewhat marginalized field. Dean, Monroe, Presley, Madonna, and other stars are forever influencing our cultural perceptions. Yet not too long ago, after a call for papers was sent out for a conference on Marilyn Monroe and Elvis Presley, the conference sponsors received telephone calls asking if it was indeed an academic conference.[1] And in August 1996, the provost of the University of Mississippi at Oxford, where there is an annual William Faulkner conference, announced that the university would no longer host future Presley conferences.[2] Despite the reservations about figures of contemporary culture, the past two decades have seen a steady increase of discourse relating to movie stars as icons and as reflections of ideology, spectatorship, and performance. In addition, some media studies have analyzed our culture's historical consciousness through its "mediated" or intertextual links; in so doing, when we view stars and their films, we bring "all kinds of relationships with anonymous or absent others."[3] One of these others is often the movie star, and one actor whose image and movies continue to evoke passion, mystery, power, and intertextual and intercultural references is Humphrey Bogart.

Bogart's influence on the various texts of American popular culture is as varied as the audiences who see his films. Young or old, male or female, blue collar or professional, there is something in those films that touches a common nerve. Some of his seventy-five feature films have as much appeal today as they did during the three decades of his filmmaking career. Revival houses continue to have Bogart festivals; film series focusing on specific types of films, whether they be gangster, romance, spy, horror, western, adventure, films from novels, or classics, often include at least one film with Bogart; television stations continue to satisfy audience preferences by showing Bogart films, often in prime time; and surveys in publications in the United States have placed him at the top or near the top of polls of favorite stars.

If the merchandising of an actor's image is any indication of that actor's impact on a culture, then Bogart's has been long lasting and ubiquitous, more so than even the images of Charlie Chaplin or John Wayne, and less intense than that surrounding Marilyn Monroe and Elvis Presley. Bogart has been the subject of plays, films, novels, and poems; his image has appeared on postal cards, buttons, and greeting cards; impressionists have mimicked his voice and appearance, and publications have parodied his films and persona; restaurants, lounges, and bars have been named after Bogart or roles that he has played, as have food and drinks; apartment complexes have been named after his films; record companies continue to sell scores from the films and radio broadcasts, and a best-selling record featured the Bogart persona; poster companies and auction companies continue to do a steady business selling the Bogart image; the United States Postal Service issued a Humphrey Bogart stamp on July 31, 1997; publishers of video and film magazines, as well as prestigious publications, such as the *Wall Street Journal*, use the Bogart name or image to help sell their products; quotations from his films appear in cards, on mugs, as titles and subtitles of books and articles; there have been Humphrey Bogart fan clubs; and there are numerous web sites and collectors of Bogart memorabilia. All of these exist in addition to histories of American film, with their many references to his various performances. More focused books target such topics as classic, cult, romance, spy, adventure, western, horror, or gangster films. Often sections of books are devoted to his life or screen career. His acting and films have been the subject of numerous fan magazine and scholarly articles. And even his name has influenced our language.

The first example of the Bogart image's receiving national recognition appeared about a year after he was born. Maud Humphrey, Bogart's mother and a well-known illustrator, used her cherub-faced offspring as a model for some sketches. The sketch of young Humphrey, purchased by Mellins Baby Food Co. and used on labels for its baby food, became famous. By the age of one, the face of Humphrey Bogart was already well known as "the original Maud Humphrey Baby."

Bogart was a relatively handsome young actor. On Broadway he was cast frequently in what others have termed "Tennis, anyone?" roles. His various early pictures generated a fair amount of fan mail, some of it romantic, but it was not until he played Duke Mantee on stage in *The Petrified Forest* (1935), and then later reprised his role on film (1936), that the Bogart image began to be remembered. By the mid- to late 1940s, his expressive face, cutting repartee, and the angst and ennui displayed by his characters started to shape what would become visual and cultural touchstones for the generations that followed.

FILM FESTIVALS AND FILM TRENDS

It was not until the early 1960s that the Bogart appeal and its subsequent merchandising took off. Triggered in part by packed houses for Bogart films starting in 1957, followed by the success of Jean-Luc Godard's *Breathless* (1959), with its classic, romanticized gangster hero who idolizes Bogie, the Brattle Theatre in Cambridge, Massachusetts, began to run Humphrey Bogart film festivals. The festival, which showed as many as fourteen of his films,[4] continued into the early 1980s, often around final examination time at Harvard, drawing large audiences, many of whom knew the dialogue verbatim.[5] This festival was only one of many that has occurred over the years across the nation's campuses, in art museums, and in commercial and revival houses here and abroad. As Gerald Weales noted during the mid-1960s, "Hardly a week goes by without at least one Bogart film available at some time of day or night in every viewing area."[6] In London the Classic Cinema ran a fortnight of Bogart films (1971), with lines as long as those found in front of box offices of hit first-run plays. A short time later when another series played at the National Film Theatre, hundreds of young hopefuls "queued up for nearly six hours until the midnight commencement on the off-chance of a few tickets being returned."[7] In 1983 *Casablanca* topped the list of the fiftieth anniversary poll of the British Film Institute membership.

In 1980 Swedish television ran six of Bogart's films in their fall schedule. WTBS and TNT have run Bogart films over a series of weeks, and another major independent station, WGN in Chicago, has run a "Here's Looking at You, Kid" Theatre during a Saturday night slot. WNFT, a Jacksonville, Florida, station, ran a Humphrey Bogart week (1987), and my own random review of weekly listings in 1993, 1994, and 1995 turned up several Bogart films in a given week or month. For example, the line-up for commercial and cable television in Dallas, Texas, during the week of November 1, 1993, listed a number of Bogart films: Cinemax was showing *Action in the North Atlantic* and *Battle Circus*; Showtime was airing *Black Legion* and *Bullets or Ballots*; KERA, one of two PBS stations, had *To Have and Have Not* and the fiftieth anniversary special on *Casablanca; High Sierra* was on the Movie Channel; *Key Largo* and *To Have and Have Not* on WGN in Chicago; *Chain Lightning* was on Fort Worth independent station KTXA, Channel 21; and a Bogart take-off, *The Cheap Detective*, was airing on HBO. The week of August 11, 1996, in Dallas, Texas, found Robert Mitchum's *The Big Sleep* (1978) on Showtime, as well as *Key Largo* and *To Have and Have Not*, and *Stand-In, Dead End*, and *The Left Hand of God* on AMC.

Program directors for local television stations have indicated that Bogart continues to draw audiences. These directors often track their area to see what movies are held over in the theaters and they try to measure star value. And it is not uncommon to find a Bogart film or two (almost always *Casablanca*) being broadcast by the independent stations during ratings week. Charles Francisco reports that WPIX-TV in New York ran it twice a week at key ratings times.[8] While some movies and stars such as Elvis Presley, John Wayne, or Burt Reynolds may draw better in particular regions of the country, often depending on the star or the type of film (e.g., *Smokey and the Bandit* used to do exceptionally well in the sun belt because of the appeal of Reynolds and the type of picture it was), one *TV Guide* survey covering the late 1970s and early 1980s indicated that Bogart was the top draw in terms of star appeal.[9] The American Film Institute's (AFI) 1976 poll of top films found *Casablanca* third, behind *Gone with the Wind* and *Citizen Kane*. The next year, a *TV Guide* poll placed the film at the top of the most popular and most watched films.[10] This popularity might explain why when *Casablanca* was shown in Jacksonville, Florida, in prime time on a Friday evening in October 1979, people who had never seen the film and others who had seen it as many as thirteen times watched. Still, it is not uncommon to find arts organizations using *Casablanca* as a major fund raiser, as occurred, for example, in Jacksonville, Florida, in the late 1980s. For its fiftieth anniversary of the Inwood Theatre in Dallas, Texas, on May 17, 1997, Landmark Theatres and the USA Film Festival began festivities with a showing of *Dead Reckoning*. The colorization of black and white films has sparked much debate and drawn additional attention to *Casablanca, The Maltese Falcon*, and other Bogart films, most notably those directed by John Huston.[11] A colorized version of *Casablanca* aired on Ted Turner's TBS Superstation on November 9, 1988.

In the past decade, the addition of color to several films, both televised and in the video rental market, has attracted a new audience, according to Ted Turner and others responsible for the process. Today most of Bogart's post-1941 movies are available in video stores, but such was not always the case. In 1973 Warner Brothers announced that three of Bogart's films—*Casablanca, The Maltese Falcon*, and *The Treasure of the Sierra Madre*—were first, second and fifth respectively, on an all-time-favorites list.[12] Although some of his lesser-known films played on television, there was little stampede to get the bulk of his seventy-five films into the hands of viewers once the video boom began. In 1982, Harvey Elliott notes, only six of his films were available in stores—and this for the individual whom, according to Elliott, "really started this whole thing—watching old movies again and again."[13] Within a year of his article, an additional twelve films made it to the shelves. As studios and other copyright holders saw video stores as a source of revenue, they have gone to their vaults for some of his lesser-known films.

In 1980 the Los Angeles County Museum of Art had a John Huston film festival that included six of Bogart's films. In the same year it ran another series on best-selling twentieth-century novels, which included *To Have and Have Not* and *High Sierra*. In 1980 the University of North Florida ran a week-long series of Bogart films. Students had quite strong feelings about which actors they wanted to see, and they chose Bogart. In a special advertising supplement directed to college students, *Newsweek*'s "Campus Film Trends" for spring 1981 indicated that *Casablanca*, along with *Harold and Maude* and *10*, was one of the three most popular films on college campuses. The following year, the fall 1982 issue of *Nutshell*, a publication distributed nationwide on college campuses, indicated that *Casablanca* was one of the top four favorites. A little over a decade later, Bogart was the cover of *Entertainment Weekly*. In the accompanying article, the editors explained that they "set out to pick the 30 greatest stars of all time—not actors, not sex symbols, but stars, with all the charisma, appeal, and influence that the word brings with it." Bogart was the number one favorite in their poll.[14] More recently, in a fall 1996 special collector's issue of *Entertainment Weekly* devoted to "The 100 Greatest Movie Stars of All Time," Bogart is considered "the biggest star of all."[15] Rounding out the top ten are Katharine Hepburn, James Stewart, Marilyn Monroe, John Wayne, Cary Grant, Marlon Brando, Clark Gable, Charlie Chaplin, and Bette Davis. On July 20, 1996, the closing event of UCLA's Festival of Preservation was a showing of the rarely seen 1945 version of the *The Big Sleep*. This version had narrative exposition that made a somewhat confusing film less confusing; the footage had been removed in part to make way for the sexual repartee between Bacall and Bogart that Hawks added after the box office success of *To Have and Have Not* and the Bogart-Bacall wedding. A random check of the World Wide Web for October 1996 came up with thirteen movies and a biographical documentary on cable channels (TV Now).

The international homage continues. In Madrid, Spain, for example, there is a Cine Bogart in his honor. And in the United States, Ted Turner's Turner Classic Movies ran a "Bogie Week" (January 6–12, 1997), in which more than fifty of his features and short clips were aired twenty-four hours a day. This was preceded the day before (January 5, 1997) by a new documentary, *Bogart: The Untold Story*, narrated by Stephen Bogart and aired on TNT. The documentary was followed by a showing of *Casablanca*. During the marathon, TCM also aired "Becoming Attractions: The Trailers of Humphrey Bogart," an overview of his changing image as seen through movie trailers. Most recently, Laemmle's Sunset 5 Theatres in West Hollywood and Laemmle's Monica 4 in Santa Monica have run a "Play It Again: The Best of Bogart" series, with fifteen of his films playing between May 24 and September 9, 1997.

Bogart's films and his screen persona continue to draw large audiences and evoke "iconic moments"[16] and intertextualities to viewers of all ages and nationalities. This appeal of Bogart's persona, or personae, and the multiple readings of his films and iconography are most apparent in the numerous uses of the actor's name or image or references to his films in novels, plays, television productions, advertisements, lounges, and restaurants.

LOUNGES AND RESTAURANTS

The pervasiveness of Bogart film festivals is almost matched by the presence of restaurants, lounges, and bars throughout the United States and overseas that have played on Bogart associations. Of all the films, *Casablanca* has had the greatest impact. As Gary Taylor notes, the stimuli from *Casablanca* are based on episodic rather than semantic memory: once you experience the film, its characters or music, you are bound to the film emotionally.[17]

There are or have been hundreds of clubs, lounges, and bars named after some aspect of the film. In San Francisco, one could dine at Casablanca on Polk Street, and listen to piano music and the whir of ceiling fans, in the tradition of Bogart and Bergman. On the water at Marina Pacifica, in Long Beach, California, you could dine in the Casablanca room to the mellow sounds of a pianist. If one prefers to drink only, there are or have been the café-cabaret decors of Casablanca bar in Atlantic Beach, Florida; Rick's American Bar in Austin, Texas; Rick's American Cafe, in East Lansing, Michigan; Rick's lounge at the Jacksonville Airport Hilton. In Chicago, another watering spot was at North Lake Shore and East Ontario, where one could listen to jazz in a relaxed, neo-Casablanca atmosphere. If one likes to dance, there is the Casablanca Club in Winston-Salem, North Carolina. Working out of the same address is the Casablanca Booking Agency. Aljean Harmetz has spotted a southern California establishment, Casablanca Restaurant, that tries to replicate Rick's Café.[18] In Philadelphia, there has been a Bogart's restaurant, with ceiling fans and pictures relating to the actor and his films. There have been a Bogart's in Gainesville, Florida, and a Bogie's in Orlando, Florida; in Madison, Wisconsin, you could dine, dance, or watch free Bogart movies in the restaurant's theater, and in Seattle there are Bogey's Sports Bar and Grill and a Bogart's on Second. One cinema and suds establishment in Florida had a "Bogart" on the sandwich menu. New York's Taft Hotel for several years had the Bogey Bar, with rattan chairs, slow-moving ceiling fans, and bamboo tables. Cincinnati has had a Bogart's, and in Washington, D.C., one could go to Bogart's for a haircut and a shave amid a 1930s decor. In Vail, Colorado, there was Bogart's, with a 1930s atmosphere. At Debbie Reynolds' hotel and movie museum in Las Vegas, there is a Bogie's Bar, with walls decorated with visuals of Bogart and a piano for playing nostalgic songs. If solving mysteries is your forte, then you might have enjoyed Bogie's, a mystery-oriented restaurant run by Bill and Karen Palmer. This New York restaurant hosted a variety of organizations, such as the Mystery Writers of America and the Maltese Falcon Society. According to the Palmers' web site,[19] the restaurant and its owners have appeared in "over thirty-five mystery novels." They now host Bogie's Mystery Tours and began Bogie's Mystery Book imprint for PaperJacks.

If one prefers more distant retreats, there is Rick's Bar in the Hyatt Regency in Casablanca, Morocco, which has had several rooms adorned with black and white pictures and a variety of posters from the film. A little closer to the United States is Rick's Café in Negril, Jamaica. In Cancun, Mexico, the "most expensive and talked-about restaurant in town"[20] is Bogart's, on the Paseo Kukulcán. With lots of movie memorabilia, wicker chairs, Persian rugs, ceiling fans, and a white piano, this restaurant has kin in Ixtapa, Mexico, where there is another exotic and expensive restaurant with a Moorish fountain, piano music, and movie-related decorations.

CEILING FANS

With the trend to conserve energy and seek alternatives to costly air-conditioning, American consumers have turned to ceiling fans. Fan companies and the stores have capitalized on the consumers' associations with Humphrey Bogart movies, especially *Casablanca*, to market their product. A visible example of the Bogart link to fan companies was Ceiling Fan Sales Company in Louisville, Kentucky. Before entering the store, one was greeted by a painted portrait of Bogart and Bergman on an exterior wall of the building. Once inside this or other fan stores, one might find a selection from the CasaBlanca Fan Company or the Key Largo Fan Co. Emerson Electric has had at least three different models with the name *Casablanca*; Hunter advertised its fan as "the original, authentic ceiling fan, the one shipped to India, Africa and the rest of the world at the turn of the century, and the kind that cooled Rick's Cafe in *Casablanca*." And Leslie-Locke has had a "Play It Again Sam" collection of ceiling fans.

Selling the Bogart association to customers is part of the marketing strategy of these companies, and it is big business. Jim Northcutt, of Encon Industries Inc. of Fort Worth, believes it is as much nostalgia and intertextuality as energy costs. When home owners come to his company, they often ask, "Where's Bogey?" According to Northcutt, "Most of them come in because they remember it from when they were growing up, or from Humphrey Bogart movies."[21] In addition to conjuring up images of rumpled white linen suits and Humphrey Bogart and Sydney Greenstreet, several of the fan companies for a time were dealing with litigation as to who had the right to the name *Casablanca* for their fans.

RECORDS AND MUSIC

Other products merchandised by entrepreneurs cashing in on nostalgia and the appeal of Bogart include movie posters, stills, and records. Flipping through a record catalog, one is likely to spot advertisements for radio broadcasts of *The Maltese Falcon, The Enforcer*, and *The African Queen*, or packaged sets such as "Hollywood's Heroes on the Air" (Bogart and *Maltese*). RCA, under its Red Seal label, issued *Casablanca: Classic Film Scores for Humphrey Bogart*, which includes music from several of Bogart's films. It was not until late in 1997 that Turner Classic Movies and Rhino Movie Music released a 20-track *Casablanca* CD with the original soundtrack album, plus a song that did not make it into the film and some dialogue from the movie.

The link between records and music is not as extensive as, say, literary and filmic intertextuality. The connections are in part attributable to nostalgia, fan adoration, and having a gimmick. As early as 1949, Betty Garrett recorded the Humphrey Bogart Rumba. Although there has been no resurgence of this dance, several decades later Little Feat recorded "Don't Bogart That Joint," a version of which was sung as "Don't Bogart Me" by Fraternity of Man in *Easy Rider* (1969). In 1981, Bill Lowery Production and Kat Family Records released "Key Largo," by Bertie Higgins and Sonny Limbo, as a single and as part of the album, *Just Another Day in Paradise* (1981). The love song, which champions the Bogie-Bacall love affair and was one of the top forty songs in 1982, continues to receive occasional radio air time. For those who are having a hard time tracking down records of the 1940s and 1950s, one location to try is Bogart's in Oxford, England.

The song most frequently associated with Humphrey Bogart, and often used in advertisements or as a theme song, is "As Time Goes By." Charles Revson used a version of the song as background music for one of its 1979 commercials for Ciara perfume to evoke romance, and in 1994 it was used for a television commercial for a Cadillac DeVille lease program in Dallas, Texas. At a regional conference held in Cincinnati during March 1981, the Sweet Adelines, a nonprofit organization of women devoted to making the public aware of the art of barbershop singing, and whose motto is "Harmonize the World," used *Casablanca* and "Play It Again, Sam" as motifs of their Region 4 Convention. The ushers wore trench coats, hats, and carried cigars or wore Lauren Bacall scarfs. The gift shop was appropriately named Bogie's Boutique. On February 11, 1991, Ted Turner's TNT presented a special, *Kisses*. Hosted by Lauren Bacall, the show's theme song was "As Time Goes By" and featured a history of on-screen kissing, including, of course, Bogart and Bacall. (A book version of the show is available.)

A number of book distributors and stores, such as Publishers Central and Barnes & Noble, as well as a variety of record stores, offer original radio broadcasts. Included are such items as Bogart in the Lux Radio Theatre Treasure of *The Treasure of the Sierra Madre*, Bogart and Bacall in *To Have and Have Not*, Bogart in *The Enforcer*, and Bogart, Sidney Greenstreet, and Mary Astor in *The Maltese Falcon*. Sometimes readings are included in multirecord sets, such as *Hollywood's Heroes on the Air*. Sometimes companies such as Nostalgia Lane repackage the broadcasts into cassettes. Bogart's *Maltese* is in "Here's lookin' at You kid." Heywood Hale Broun cassettes include nearly sixty minutes of excerpts of Nathaniel Benchley's biography of the actor.

In 1974 the late Neil Bogart, who had changed his name to Bogart from Bogats, after a stint as wunderkid of Buddha Records, capitalized on his name ("Bogart belongs in Casablanca") and established Casablanca Records. He later worked with Peter Gruber to create Casablanca Record and FilmWorks, which was subsequently purchased by the PolyGram Group. And if you want to attend a concert, you could attend a show at Bogart's Concert Venue in Long Beach, California.

In addition to music, Bogart is on disc with the Lux Radio Theatre (Radiola

MR-1007), presenting *To Have and Have Not*, as a gangster in *Love's Lady Counterfeit* (Radio MR-1061), a reading of *The Maltese Falcon* on Lady Esther Screen Guild Players and Academy Award Theatre (Radiola MR-1091), an abridged version of *Casablanca* with the Screen Guild Players (Radiola MR-1099), *The Treasure of the Sierra Madre* (Mark 56 Records No. 610), a reading from *Bold Venture* (Command Performance Records LP-4), and *50 Years of Film* (Warner Bros. Records 3XX2737), with selections from several of Bogart's films.[22]

STILLS AND POSTERS

A number of stores throughout the nation have done a brisk business in selling Bogart stills. As one might expect, many are clustered in New York and California. Several of the research centers and film archives provide stills, but theirs is primarily a service to researchers, authors, and publishers.

Film stills are no longer the domain of fans, buffs, and collectors. Elias Fellus, of Graphics East, a gallery in Washington, D.C., notes that photographs from films should be viewed as a fine art that captures the essence of a time as well as documenting a film.[23] The distributors for these stills-as-art are also selling poster enlargements of the stills, with the date and locations of the gallery shows. Sotheby's and Christie's in New York City regularly auction off the works of Hollywood master photographers. Butterfield and Butterfield in Beverly Hills has sales of photography and memorabilia, and Christie's in London had an auction celebrating one hundred years of cinema in 1995.[24]

The selling of movie photographs, or stills, as art is relatively new, but the poster business has been a lucrative field, and one of the biggest sellers over the years has been Bogart posters. Ira Kaplan of Ira Roberts, Inc., a publisher of fine art prints, posters, stationery, and related products, notes that into the early 1980s, "of all the 24 movie posters [Ira Roberts] publish and distribute, the *Casablanca* piece remains [their] best seller at a rate of 3 or 4 to 1 over all others' movie posters."[25] Their *Maltese Falcon* poster remained a "medium to good seller" into the 1980s. Seattle Cinematic Productions has marketed a *Casablanca* poster, as have other companies, posters from Bogart's films, and a six-foot poster of Bogie in trench coat and hat.

There are composite posters of stills from Bogart's many films, posters made from lobby cards advertising his various films, as well as many of just Bogart. Artist Monte Dolack produced a six-color lithograph of Bogart facing Bacall, with a bottle and drinks on a table with a fan above and ferns and palm leaves to the side, as an advertisement for the Crystal Theatre in Missoula, Montana.[26] The poster of Bogart and Bergman, cheek to cheek, remains the best seller, and its cult status may have something to do with its exceptional longevity and sales interest. A lobby card of the same image might bring as much as $5,000 or more.[27]

In the early 1980s, Anthony Slide noted that "Humphrey Bogart posters vary tremendously in value. Better titles sell for $500 or more, while it is still possible to find one-sheet posters from Bogart 'B' pictures for as little as $50 each."[28] In less than two decades, the rush for movie memorabilia has pushed prices up astronomically. When Christie's had an auction of film and television memorabilia on June 28, 1995, an original Italian poster for *The Oklahoma Kid* (1939) was expected to sell for $1,400 to $1,800. It brought $3,220. A 22- by 14-inch lobby card from *The Maltese Falcon* (estimated at $1,600 to $2,200) brought $4,205. In May 1996 and again in November, Butterfield and Butterfield in Los Angeles auctioned off vintage Hollywood movie posters and memorabilia, including a number of Bogart-related items. At the May sale, prices ranged from $230 for a pressbook from *Angels with Dirty Faces* to $19,550 for a one sheet (poster) in mint condition from *The Petrified Forest* of Davis, Howard, and Bogart (used as the illustration for the catalog cover). Other prices paid were $16,100 for a lobby card set in mint or near-mint condition for *Casablanca*; a one sheet from *Angels with Dirty Faces* with Cagney, O'Brien, Bogart, and the Dead End Kids ($6,325); a poster and lobby card set from *High Sierra* ($3,162.50); and a *King of the Underworld* poster ($1,495) and lobby card set ($1,495). Also in this sale were items from *Marked Woman, Dark Victory, Oklahoma Kid, Key Largo, Kid Galahad,* and *The Maltese Falcon*. The November sale included posters for *The Big Shot, Casablanca, High Sierra,* and *The Maltese Falcon,* and the prices ranged from $805 (*The Maltese Falcon*) to $1,265 (*The Big Shot*). The visuals in these posters were fairly bland and no doubt contributed to the lower prices. A movie poster sale at Sotheby's on December 14, 1996, brought in $2,760 for a poster for *The African Queen,* and one for *The Maltese Falcon* was purchased for $4,600.[29] Other items are selling as well. As Dana Hawkes, director of Sotheby's Department of Collectibles, has noted recently, "Movie posters have been collected for decades and there are dealers all over the country who specialize in them. But when the auction houses got involved with movie posters, as they did 10 years ago, it became a very public matter and people who didn't know the market existed began buying them, so prices went up considerably." The appeal is greatest for posters with Bogart, Dietrich, and Garbo, but "those stars have to be on the poster for it to be valuable."[30]

Photographic portraits are also becoming big business. George Hurrell considers his photographic portraits of movie stars to be "luminous triumphs of black and white portraiture from the glamorous decade of the '30's, when Hollywood beauty inspired the world," and recent auctions would suggest that such items would go for considerably more today. The Humphrey Bogart photographic portrait was selling for $3,000 in 1983 and with appreciation much more today. On June 7, 1997, Christie's in Beverly Hills sold in tandem two pictures, one an undated, eight-by-ten inch, signed picture of Bogart and a signed Bacall photo for $1,610. For a series of photographs of current stars posing against murals of former Warner Bros. stars, Roddy McDowell shot Lauren Bacall next to a life-size image of Bogart.[31] Sebastian Krüger's caricature of Humphrey

Bogart, hanging in 1998 in the Galerie Morpheus in Beverly Hills, is selling for $7,500. For those looking for less expensive memorabilia, there have been and are places such as Cooney Art Studio, in Moline, Illinois, that specialize in movie star portraits at more modest sums, and there have been countless books that are mainly collections of portraits of celebrities, sometimes with brief biographies or commentaries, such as Nickolas Murray and Paul Gallico's *The Revealing Eye: Personalities of the Twenties* (New York: Atheneum, 1967) and Brad Benedict's *Fame: Portraits of Celebrated People* (New York: Harmony, 1980), a collection of graphics of star artists in caricature. The *Chateau Marmont Hollywood Handbook* (New York: Universe/Rizzoli, 1996) lovingly details and illustrates how an exclusive apartment house became a chic Hollywood hotel, with photographs of the famous who stayed there, including a 1930s photograph of Bogart tending a garden. With more attention to Hollywood photography, there have been more exhibitions, such as the recent one of "John Engstead: Photographer," one of Hollywood's most prominent portrait photographers. Held at the Academy of Motion Picture Arts and Sciences (April 25–June 29, 1997), the exhibit prominently displayed images of Bogart and Bacall and other Hollywood celebrities in a collection of sixty-four large-format portraits and thirty vintage prints.

If the Bogart image might help to sell a product or attract a customer into a shop, a poster is one form of inexpensive advertising. In Greenville, Texas, the Texan Theatre, closed for more than a decade and turned into a mini-mall, still has a poster of Bogart encased in glass in front of the theater, a lasting statement of his legendary status and an appeal to those who might shop in the mall. William Morrow Publishers made up a poster of its cover photograph of Bogart for John Kobal's book of portraits of actors. More than a decade ago Gordon Gin Co. and Renfield Imports, Ltd. distributed a poster of a Bogart look-alike, surrounded by crates of Gordon Gin, aboard a boat that viewers are to assume is the *African Queen*. To advertise its wares, Cine Monde, a store that specializes in rare, original photos, soundtracks, and lobby cards, used as many as half of its ad illustrations from Bogart movies,[32] and a Bogart-Bergman shot from *Casablanca* is part of a two-page spread, along with shots from four other classic films, used to advertise the Turner Classic Movies channel (TCM).[33]

Marketing specialists have used and continue to use the Bogart image, voice, or name to sell their products. The Hamilton Collection sells porcelains based on original works by Maud Humphrey by reminding readers that she was the mother of the actor and by saying the works are by Maud Humphrey Bogart, even though the artist always went by her maiden name. Numerous books and games use pictures of Bogart on their cover or inside it, seemingly trying to say to the prospective purchaser or reader, "This book or game is about the movies," and what better way to indicate it than with an image of Bogart, often in white dinner jacket and in front of Rick's Café Américain—an immediately recognizable icon—or with Ingrid Bergman? The first picture in *The New York Times at the Movies* (New York: Arno, 1979), a collection of movie reviews, is of Bogart in front of Rick's. The cover of Richard Lawton's *A World of Movies: 70 Years of Film History* (New York: Dell, 1974) is of Bogart and Bergman, as is the cover of the recent *American Cinema: One Hundred Years of Filmmaking* by Jeanine Basinger (New York: Rizzoli, 1994), a book that accompanies the PBS series on American movies. Frank Sacks's *The Movie Game* (Los Angeles, 1981) includes Bogart on the cover, along with other celebrities. Armand Deutsch calls his book *Me and Bogie: And Other Friends and Acquaintances from a Life in Hollywood and Beyond* (New York: Putnam's, 1991), although the discussion of his interaction with Bogart covers but four pages in a work that deals more with other friends and acquaintances in Hollywood. Another case in point is Robert A. and Gwendolyn Nowland's *Film Quotations* (Jefferson, N.C.: McFarland, 1994). Within a year, the title was changed to *"We'll Always Have Paris"* (New York: Perennial, 1995) to increase its mass market appeal. In addition, the publishers put a picture of Bogart and Bergman on the cover. So why Bogie or Bogie associations in the title? Might it be to sell a book by association that might otherwise have an extremely limited circulation? Many other books include sections on Bogart or Bogart and Bacall to attract readers.[34]

LITERARY INFLUENCES

Humphrey Bogart's influence on literature, like his influence on film, often takes the form of homage, imitation, parody, or an attempt to recapture the aura of an era via nostalgia. In 1947 *Good Housekeeping* published Mignon McLaughlin's "The Woman Who Dreamed About Humphrey Bogart," a short story about Hilda and Warren Parrish, who had been married for twelve "comfortable, companionable, quietly happy years,"[35] when she begins dreaming of Humphrey Bogart. They are violent lovers, and then Bogart alerts her to a wayward husband. Dream becomes reality: the husband confesses his flirtation with a young artist. Hilda then has her last dream: she and Bogart in a nightclub where he, "ruthless and implacable," confronts Warren with his young redhead and pummels him into submission.

Although it never came to fruition, Alan J. Lerner and Frederick Loewe had discussed turning *Casablanca* into a musical in the early 1950s.[36] In one of his first Broadway roles, Paul Newman appeared in a stage version of *The Desperate Hours* (directed by Robert Montgomery). The play *Bogart Slept Here*, directed by Mike Nichols, presented an off-Broadway actor who gets lucky and becomes a Hollywood star. The title refers to a New York hotel where Bogart may have stayed during his career. The play was to star Robert DeNiro and Marsha Mason, but the play folded after DeNiro was fired (May 1977) by Nichols. Another play about Bogart appeared in the same year and opened at the Los Angeles Actors' Theatre Playwrights' Workshop Festival. Sean Michael Rice's *When Bogart Was* presented two hoboes, one young and one old, who are waiting for an A train. This on-the-road vignette dealt with the drifter's fantasizing about carousing with Bogart on Mexican locations for *The Treasure of the Sierra Madre*. Paul Foster's comedy *A Kiss Is Just a Kiss* played off-Broadway in June 1983 and starred Kevin O'Connor, who had the lead in the made-for-television movie *Bogie* three years earlier. The play, about a woman's infatuation with the screen persona, introduces the audience to Bogart's wives (especially Helen Menken and Mayo Methot) and his early stage and film career through *Casablanca*. About eighteen months later, Mike Hood and John Close's *Bogart: The Good Bad Guy* opened at the Canal Cafe Theatre, a new café-theater venue in London (December 1984). The revue-style musical focuses on the life and loves of the actor, with Steve May as Ezra Goodman, the narrator-biographer and real-life author of the biography on which the play was based.

The most famous of the Bogart-related plays is Woody Allen's *Play It Again, Sam* (1969), produced by David Merrick. The play starred Diane Keaton, Jerry Lacy, and Woody Allen as Allen Felix, a young film critic struggling to find himself and his way with women after his wife leaves him. Counseled by Humphrey Bogart throughout, Felix falls in love with his best friend's wife, only to cut their ties via the Bogart farewell speech to Bergman at the end of *Casablanca*. By the time he becomes more comfortable with women (his fantasy date with Sharon at the end of the play), Bogart bids him adieu, telling Felix that he cannot teach him anything more. The play was set in New York.

Because of a film technicians strike, the movie *Play It Again, Sam* uses San Francisco as its locale. Directed by Herbert Ross, it has Allen, Keaton, and Lacy reprising their stage roles. As Maurice Yacowar notes, "Everything about romantic and free San Francisco emphasizes Felix's personal failure."[37] There are more references to *Casablanca* in the movie, and the use of Bogart movies-within-a-movie on the big screen instead of the stage version using a small television adds greater power to the Bogart influence. Allen says he wrote *Play It Again, Sam* "to honor Bogart for at least giving me a few months of smooth sailing, and also to get even with a certain girl (or a particular sex that gives me trouble, to tell the truth)."[38] To Herbert Ross, "what the movie is about, in a strange way, is outgrowing Bogart, outgrowing a childhood fantasy."[39] The Woody Allen–Humphrey Bogart liaison is played for laughs at Allen's expense on the British television show *Spitting Image*. In one segment of this satirical series, Bogart and Allen (puppets) are sitting at a table in a club, like *Casablanca*, and Bogart asks Allen why, of all the daughters in the world, he had to sleep with his own.[40] The American Playhouse televised *Overdrawn at the Memory Bank* (February 4, 1985), which has allusions to *Casablanca* throughout the play.

A number of fictional works play on aspects of the Sam Spade or Philip Marlowe aspects of the Bogart persona. In John Stanley and Ken Davis's *Bogart '48* (New York: Dell, 1979), the film star is the hero of a murder mystery, as Stanley and Davis use biographical information about Bogart to ground the story in reality. Stuart Kaminsky's *Bullet for a Star* (New York: St. Martin's Press, 1977) has as its gimmick a detective in Hollywood who meets Bogart while the latter is making a movie. This work is one in a series of Toby Peters mysteries. Gore Vidal refers to Bogart in *Myra Breckinridge* (Boston: Little, Brown, 1968) as a world-weary lover who is past his prime. In Andrew Bergman's *Hollywood and LeVine* (New York: Holt, Rinehart, 1975), Bergman uses his Spade-like detective, Jack LeVine, to battle overzealous communist hunters in Hollywood. Le Vine deals with FBI agents and a freshman congressman named Nixon, and at the climax is involved in a midnight auto chase along a two-lane coast highway with Humphrey Bogart as his chauffeur. Andrew J. Fenady's *The Man with Bogart's Face* (Chicago: H. Regnery, 1977) is a mystery-comedy about a man who has plastic surgery to make him look like Humphrey Bogart. Thereafter he becomes Sam Marlow, an embodiment of integrity, fortitude, and justice in a world of hypocrisy, pretension, and injustice. This novel later became a feature film (1980), starring Robert Sacchi as Sam Marlow.

A novel that has little to do with Humphrey Bogart, except for the main character's being a loner, but one that uses his name in its title, is Adam Kennedy's *Just Like Humphrey Bogart* (New York: Viking, 1978). Edwin Corley's *Shadows* (New York: Stein and Day, 1975) is show business fiction that weaves Bogart, Flynn, Gable, and others into its plot. Bogart turns down an offer to do a film for screenwriter Mitch Gardner because he is working on *High Sierra* and anticipates work with Huston on *The Maltese Falcon*. The two talk about the sea, Mark Hellinger, and Mayo, and Gardner rushes Bogart to a doctor after Mayo stabs him. Film critic David Thomson uses Captain Renault's famous line, "Round up the usual suspects," as the first of his memorable quotations in *Suspects* (New York: Knopf, 1985). Thomson weaves together into a metafilm fiction a number of capsule biographies from movies, including Ilsa and Victor (*Casablanca*), Dickson [*sic*] Steele and Laurel Gray (*In a Lonely Place*), Roy Earle and Marie Garson (*High Sierra*) and Vivian Sternwood (*The Big Sleep*), showing how they might have crossed paths. We learn from Thomson that the marriage of Ilsa and Victor was a ploy to smuggle Victor to safety and that Rick had been a labor leader in America who enjoyed reading Trotsky, Marx, and John Reed. Robert Coover's *A Night at the Movies* (Fresno, Calif.: Linden, 1986) plays on Hollywood conventions, including a steamy love scene between Rick and Ilsa that would never have found its way into *Casablanca* in the 1940s. Aljean Harmetz uses "Round Up the Usual Suspects" as the title of her excellent book on the making of *Casablanca* (New York: Hyperion, 1992).

Play It Again (New York: Forge, 1995) is a thriller written by Stephen Bogart. The detective in this novel, R. J. Brooks, is the son of a legendary movie tough guy and a sultry leading lady. Trying to escape from his father's image, R. J. leaves Hollywood and becomes a matrimonial detective in New York. His mother lives there, and when she is murdered, he goes on a quest through family history and Hollywood connections to find the killer. With echoes of family autobiography, Bogart-type films, and other noir films, such as *Chinatown*, the novel opens:

There was a bullet hole in his windshield, courtesy of a Tong hothead down in Chinatown, just so nobody forgot he was in a serious trade. His business card read:
R. J. Brooks
Matrimonial Detective
It was the lowest form of sleuthing. His clients—mostly bluestocking lawyers from Manhattan law firms—generally used slimeball types for this kind of work, but R. J. had a reputation. He was reliable and effective.

This novel, along with his recent autobiography, *Bogart: In Search of My Father*, is Stephen Bogart's attempt to come to terms with his own identity and a past burdened by being the son of a legend.

Another recent mystery is Lawrence Block's homage to the actor, *The Burglar Who Thought He Was Bogart* (New York: Dutton, 1995). Part of a series of Bernie Rhodenbarr mysteries, this novel has a protagonist who is a bookseller and part-time burglar. Asked by Hugo Candlemas to steal a portfolio from an East Side townhouse, Rhodenbarr is interrupted in his mission, Candlemas disappears, and there is a relationship with the alluring Ilona, who, of all the bookstores in the world, walks into his looking for Bogart books. Like Bernie, Ilona reads everything she can on Bogart and spends her evenings going to Bogart movies. As the situations play themselves out, Bernie is always wondering what Bogart would do in his situation. During the course of the novel, mention is made of nearly all of Bogart's films, Bernie speaks like Bogart ("We'll always have Paris"), and the situations and dialogue are often echoes of Bogart films. The farewell between Bernie and Ilona, who is to return to her country to fulfill her obligations at the side of another man, plays with our intertextual consciousness:

I shook my head. "It wouldn't work, sweetheart. The hopes and dreams of a couple of little people like you and me don't add up to a hill of beans next to the cause you and Michael are fighting for...."
"Bear-naard, I have tears in my eyes."
"I'd kiss them away," I said, "but I wouldn't be able to stop. So long, sweetheart. I'll miss you."
"I'll never forget you," she said. "I'll never forget Twenty-fifth Street."
"Neither will I." I took her arm, eased her out the door. "And why should you? We'll always have Twenty-fifth Street." (284)

George Baxt's *The Humphrey Bogart Murder Case* (New York: St. Martin's Press, 1995) is the tenth in a series of celebrity mysteries, including ones on Bette Davis, Mae West, and Marlene Dietrich. This one is set in 1941, prior to the filming of *The Maltese Falcon*. Bogart and his wife, Mayo, find their home burglarized. It seems that someone is trying to find a cornucopia that Mayo's father once owned. Three murders, studio personalities, and aspects of *The Maltese Falcon* are woven into the mystery that Detective Herb Villon and his girlfriend-assistant must solve. Another mystery that uses associations with *The*

Maltese Falcon to entice readers is Robert J. Randishi's *Eye in the Ring* (Toronto: PaperJacks, 1987). A Miles Jacoby "hard-boiled boxing mystery" in the Hammett vein, the publishers use "Bogie's Restaurant" and a small falcon logo as part of its front and back cover design.

There has been verse about Bogart, including Margaret Boe Birns's "Heaven," in which Bogart and Bacall are dancing to "you're too marvelous for words";[41] Charles Bukowski's "Bogart in the World of the Dead"; John Berryman's ninth "Dream Song," with its references to Roy Earle's death in *High Sierra*; and "Bogart Dies" by J. Sewell, which focuses on meeting Betty Bacall Bogart at 4 A.M. and Bogart's death.[42] David Halliday's *The Black Bird* (Erin, Ontario: Porcupine's Quill and Firefly Books, 1985) is a collection of poems about Humphrey Bogart and *The Maltese Falcon*. The *Faber Book of Movie Verse* includes Nicholas Flocos's "Bogart," which deals with the actor's grandeur and how his eyes communicated the idea of "To Have and Have Not"; Norman Rosten's "Nobody Dies Like Humphrey Bogart" (originally published in *Thrive Upon the Rock*, Trident, 1965); and Lee L. Berkson's "Bogey," a reverie of Bogart images.[43]

Literary parodies of Bogart, his films, or aspects of his persona include Christopher Leopold's *Casablack* (Garden City, N.Y.: Doubleday, 1979), a World War II thriller dedicated to the cast of *Casablanca* and those at Warner Bros. who helped make the film. A syndicated columnist, Nad Klaf, knows the "real" story and gives us an account of Steve Wagner, the real Rick Blaine, a worn-out adventurer, and his love, a hooker. Gerald Sussman produced "The Maltese Canary" for *National Lampoon* (March–April 1982), in which the hero spends too much time reading about the detective's being the last American hero and winds up giving up his license and taking a job as a security guard in a housing project. Thomas Meehan's "Goodbye Sam Spade, Hello Stephen Foster" is a parody of the cult worship of Bogart, using Don Ameche as the foil.[44] Another playful glance at the detective role Bogart made famous is Richard Brautigan's *Dreaming of Babylon: A Private Eye Novel, 1942* (New York: Delacorte, 1977). The protagonist, C. Card (a play on S. Spade), is a nebbish continually threatened by his overbearing mother. An inversion of the strength and masculinity of the Bogart persona, Card has the makings of a Woody Allen antihero. David Geherin's *Son of Sam Spade: The Private-Eye Novel in the 70s* (New York: Ungar, 1980) details several of the parodies and changes in the genre in three contemporary writers. And Thomas Pynchon's *Vineland* (Boston: Little, Brown, 1990) plays with numerous movie references, including *The Maltese Falcon* ("Mall Tease Flacon").

There is a comic book out of Scotland called *The Bogie Man*, published by the Fat Man Press (1990), as well as *Bogie*, a comic-style biography of Bogart, published originally in France in 1984 and translated and published in the United States in 1989.

Even textbooks are not free of the Bogart persona. In the Heath *Life Science* book for seventh graders (1984), there is a segment on the scene from *The*

African Queen when Bogart finds the bloodsuckers all over his body and growls, "If there's anything in the world I hate, it's leeches." The text goes on to discuss the worthiness of leeches for laboratory study.

In Richard Bach's short story "Budgie Zerbie, Where Are You?" (*Family Circle*, February 1973), a young boy becomes friends with Bogart and Bacall because his family had a boat in a slip next to the Bogarts. Jean Van Leeuwen's *The Great Cheese Conspiracy* parodies the gangster films of the 1930s and 1940s, as three mice, fed up with their domestic food source—a movie theater—decide to rob a new target: a cheese store. Merciless Marvin, the wily gang leader, tells his cronies, " 'The joint is a cinch to knock over,' I finish, borrowing a line from an old Humphrey Bogart movie I've seen a few times."[45] V. S. Naipaul's "Bogart," in *Miguel Street* (1959), details how Bogart influenced young men in Port of Spain. In E. L. Doctorow's *The Book of Daniel*, we learn that "if you recognize a Humphrey Bogart movie for the cheap trash it was, you had culture."[46] In Douglas Adams's *The Hitchhiker's Guide to the Galaxy*, after traveling through hyperspace Arthur realizes that "every Bogart movie had been wiped out . . . and that gave him a nasty knock."[47]

In addition to the resonance of Bogart's words, at least one of his gestures, the way he holds a cigarette, has contributed to our slang. The term is "to bogart," as in "to bogart a joint."[48] Clouds of cigarette smoke were part of the romantic aura of Hollywood films, and Bogart, with cigarette dangling from his lip, was its icon. Recent articles on a tentative settlement between the tobacco companies and the attorneys general from numerous states refer to Bogart with "smoke in hand" or how his image (along with others) helped promote cigarette smoking as a "cool vice."[49] The stigma of cigarette smoking and the increased death rate from cancer has changed that image in viewers today, but less so with filmmakers. A 1994 study in the *American Journal of Health* found 785 references to tobacco or tobacco use in sixty-two films, and 78 percent of the time it was on-camera use.[50] But retro is hip in some circles, and as Randi Hutter Epstein notes, "Many of the newly popular cigar and martini bars are reminiscent of Humphrey Bogart films: Men wear hats and hold a martini in one hand, a cigar in the other. Except this time around, women are smoking cigars too."[51]

A wire service item from Gainesville, Florida, reports that "Bogart" means more than the actor; it also has come to mean a cheapskate or pennypincher, and "to bogart" or "to bogue" means to steal, hoard, or to borrow without asking.[52] This may have originated in Milos Forman's *Taking Off* (1971), when one of the characters is warned not to "bogart the roach." An example of the use of the latter appeared in Robb Armstrong's cartoon "Jump Start," when the husband asks his wife, "OK, so you're gonna Bogart the remote too, huh?" (December 12, 1993). It may also have been derived from comments about Bogart by friends who recount how he lamented the money Bacall spent and how he would often arrange it so that when dining out, others would get the bill.

WAX MUSEUMS

Life-size images of the actor can be found in wax museums throughout the world. Madame Tussaud's in London, for example, has Bogart in trench coat and hat and has sold an oversized poster of the actor's image with the line, "Here's looking at me, kid." The Hollywood Wax Museum had an image of Bogart; the former Six Flags' Stars Hall of Fame in Orlando, Florida, had used Bogart's image on its admission ticket and a four-color poster, had a restaurant called "Bogey's," and an *African Queen* set with Bogart and Hepburn. The set was chosen because it allowed the museum to include Hepburn and provided "an opportunity to create what certainly is one of the most dramatic, colorful and popular sets in the museum."[53] Movieland Wax Museum, the Hall of Fame's sister museum in Buena Park, California, had a Bogart figure in a similar setting.

MOVIES

Humphrey Bogart's continuing appeal as a star, legend, and persona has led to intertextual references to him or his films throughout the cinema history of the past four decades. As Roger Copeland noted about this quoting of other films, "The result is often a film about other films, a film which doesn't deal directly with 'the world,' but rather gives us a world 'mediated' through other movies."[54]

A number of films and television shows have used images from Bogart films or played off his character or were remakes or variations on a theme. In *Never Say Goodbye* (1946), Errol Flynn does an imitation of Bogart, using Bogart's dubbed voice,[55] and in the same year we had the Marx Brothers in *A Night in Casablanca*. Warner Bros. wanted to make a sequel to *Casablanca* called *Brazzaville* and had a ten-page synopsis, but the plan was nixed by David O. Selznick, who did not want Bergman in a sequel. And while Geraldine Fitzgerald was mentioned as a possible replacement, the project died.[56] Steven G. Kellman claims that it is possible that several films—*A Night in Casablanca* (1946), *Rope of Sand* (1949), *The Happy Ending* (1969), *The Projectionist* (1971), and *Play It Again, Sam* (1972)—might not have been produced had it not been for *Casablanca*.[57] Miller reminds us that Hal Wallis used some of the cast members in *Rope of Sand* to capture a flavor of the Curtiz film, not unlike what was done five years earlier in *The Conspirators* (1944), with Hedy Lamarr and Lorre, Henreid, and Greenstreet.[58] In the 1952 *Life with Buster Keaton*, a scene from a 1951 television episode of the *Buster Keaton Show* has Keaton playing a store clerk trying to become a private eye like Sam Spade. As the parody continues, Keaton falls asleep and dreams he is Sam Keaton in quest of the Yellow Canary Café.[59] Jack Palance starred as a wanted criminal in a remake of *High Sierra* in *I Died a Thousand Times* (1955). As Kenneth Alley notes, in *Save the Tiger* (1972), "When Jack Lemmon and Jack Gilford enter a bar midway in the film,

High Sierra is being telecast over the bar's TV set, and the scene we see is Bogart leaning down from a park bench to pick up the children's ball. Thus, when Lemmon performs a similar action in the final scene of *Save the Tiger* and is told by one of the boys that he can't play with them, both *High Sierra* and *Save the Tiger* are enriched by making us aware of the universal thread of continuity that runs between the late-Depression gangster and the contemporary unethical businessman. Both of these outcasts have been stranded upon the beach of time and change."[60]

In Alain Resnais's *Hiroshima, Mon Amour* (1959), the club that Nevers goes to in her last night in town is Casablanca, an allusion to film, love, and the past. The most famous early film homage to Bogart is Jean-Luc Godard's *Breathless* (1959), with Michel Poiccard (Jean-Paul Belmondo) as an inner-directed French gangster who likes Bogart. Copeland remarks that Godard's film is "in large part an essay about the way in which the character played by Jean-Paul Belmondo had adopted certain postures, attitudes and mannerisms from American films—specifically those of Humphrey Bogart."[61] This film triggered the Bogart vogue and was followed by Truffaut's *Shoot the Piano Player* (1960), which conveys an intellectual's version of the Bogart persona, and Godard's *Alphaville* (1965), which links science fiction with *film noir* as Lemmy Caution travels to Alphaville to investigate the disappearance of Henri Dickson. Philippe Labro's *Without Apparent Motive* (1972), a tale of corruption and murder set in Nice, France, and based on an Ed McBain story, is presented as an homage to Bogart and Bacall in *To Have and Have Not* and *The Big Sleep*.[62] Barbra Streisand and Ryan O'Neal play off *Casablanca* dialogue, and she teases him with "A Kiss Is Just a Kiss" in *What's Up, Doc?* (1972), and most studio histories of Warner Bros. devote significant space or footage to the film. The film documentary *Here's Looking at You, Warner Bros.*, for example, pays homage through its title, then begins with clips from *Casablanca* and comes to closure with stars and former employees entering Rick's Café Américain, amid references to the film, as all the guests begin a celebration of the 1990 renaming of the Burbank studio.[63] In *Gremlins 2: The New Batch* (1990), the filmmakers have a bit of pointed fun when they have Danny Glover, who plays a Ted Turner–Donald Trump type of entrepreneur, announce a showing of *Casablanca* "in full color and with a happy ending."

Years earlier Harrison Ford as Hans Solo in *Star Wars* (1977) reprised with variations the Bogart roles in *Casablanca* and *Across the Pacific*, and Steven Spielberg's Indiana Jones series (film and television) continued the trend. *Raiders of the Lost Ark* (1981), for example, pays homage to Bogart via Indiana Jones's dress, the time of the action (during World War II), the fight against Nazis, a bar in Nepal, the toughness conveyed by Indiana and Marion Ravenwood, and encounters with menacing characters. Links in other films abound. Paul Newman's role in *Harper* (1966) is related to *The Big Sleep*, and Albert Finney imitates Bogart's waiting for a car ride in *Two for the Road* (1967). *The Maltese Bippy* (1969) spoofs the horror venue, and in *Gumshoe* (1971), directed by Stephen Frears, Albert Finney is a vaudevillian who becomes a would-be Sam Spade in this crime-comedy homage to *film noir* and the private eye genre. *Play It Again, Sam* (1972), directed by Herbert Ross, is based on Woody Allen's play, with its self-reflexive, intertextual techniques that focus on Bogart's persona and the culture forces in the United States, while at the same time serving as a reflection of Allen's own preoccupations and his main character's sense of insecurity. A TV movie of the same year, *Goodnight My Love*, has clear echoes of *The Maltese Falcon*. In *The Long Goodbye* (1973), a Robert Altman film scripted by Leigh Brackett, who co-scripted *The Big Sleep*, Elliott Gould plays a run-down Philip Marlowe. Following Altman's playfulness is Alain Robbe-Grillet's 1974 *Glissements progressifs du plaisir* (*Slow Slide into Pleasure*, 1974), which has the detective dressing like Bogart in trench coat and fedora (although he has glasses and wears a moustache) and asking inane questions. After he sees a dead girl, he asks, "Do you like eggs? Can you swim? Do you know a man named Boris?" The same year saw *Chinatown*, Roman Polanski's famous homage to *film noir* and Bogart. In *Farewell My Lovely* (1975), Moose Malloy hires Philip Marlowe (Robert Mitchum) to find his long-lost girlfriend, Velma. In a film strong on atmosphere and locale, Mitchum gives a first-rate performance as the world-weary detective. *Dynamite Chicken* (1971), directed and written by Ernie Pintoff, with its cinematic collage of interviews, film clips, and parodies of television commercials with Bogart, Monroe, Cagney, O'Brien and others is another tongue-in-cheek salute to the actor.

The comedy-melodrama *The Black Bird* (1975) plays off elements of Bogart's character and *The Maltese Falcon*, as Sam Spade, Jr. (George Segal), inherits his father's detective agency and a dusty falcon. He pawns it, later learns of its value, and begins a bumbling search to retrieve the black bird. *I Wonder Who's Killing Her Now* (1976), written by Woody Allen's one-time co-writer Mickey Rose, is about a husband who is trying to get someone to kill his wife for insurance money, who then tries to have the murder stopped. It is a satire on movies, marriage, murder tales, doctors, and Bogart. Another play on the genre is Neil Simon's *The Cheap Detective* (1978), which brings together Peter Falk, Dom DeLuise, John Houseman, Paul Williams, Madeline Kahn, and Marsha Mason as characters from *The Maltese Falcon*; Nicol Williamson, James Coco, Louise Fletcher, and Fernando Lamas for the *Casablanca* send-up; and Ann-Margret and Sid Caesar for *The Big Sleep* segment. Some of Clint Eastwood's films, such as *The Enforcer* (1976), the third of the Dirty Harry films, were influenced by Bogart. In court Eastwood convinced a jury that the name of his movie came from the title of Humphrey Bogart's film, not from a paperback adventure series by Andy Sugar that featured a character called the Enforcer.[64] In *The Goodbye Girl* (1977), Richard Dreyfuss is in a tuxedo on the roof of the building with Marsha Mason, using something of a Bogart accent. Robert Benton's *The Late Show* (1977) plays on Chandler, Hammett, and the Bogart image as Art Carney portrays a worn-out, aging detective trying to solve the murder of his partner with the assistance of a young woman (Lily Tomlin).

Other films with intertextual references include *Take Off* (1978), a porno film based on the idea of Dorian Gray, directed by Armand Weston. Darrin, a sex star from the 1920s, uses old movie clips to show his aging life of film as he remains youthful in real life. In part the film spoofs Bogart, Cagney, and Brando. Jean Paul Barbet (Jack Lenoir) is a chauffeur outside the Regina Hotel and drives for Wayne Rogers, a Hollywood screenwriter who comes to Paris to work on a script and falls in love in *Once in Paris* (1978). Lenoir tells other drivers that he wrote all the Bogart films. In *A Little Romance* (1979), we encounter a love affair between thirteen-year-old Daniel, who spends all his time in the movies where he learns his English, and thirteen-year-old Lauren, the daughter of an American jet-setter who does not want her daughter to spend time with Daniel. In this Romeo and Juliet story, Daniel tells Lauren to "Call me Bogie."

Echoes of the Bogart persona and playful intertextual phrasing are found in a number of the James Bond films. In *Moonraker* (1979), for example, Roger Moore pushes an adversary through a stained glass church window that holds a clock. When he lands head first in a piano below the window that is there for a recital, Moore looks out the window and says, "Play it again, Sam." *Caboblanco* (1980) is a reworking of *Casablanca* with Charles Bronson running a bar in Peru. Jason Robards plays a Nazi, Fernando Rey is a police captain, and Dominique Sanda is a French woman trying to find her lover. *The Man with Bogart's Face* (1980), directed by Robert Day, stars Robert Sacchi as Sam Marlow, who, as a result of plastic surgery, lives his fantasy as a hard-boiled 1940s detective in present-day Hollywood. With echoes of *The Maltese Falcon*, the film includes George Raft and Yvonne De Carlo in yet another spoof of Bogart's image. A superficial treatment of the actor's life, based on Daniel Taradash's adaptation of Joe Hyam's biography and directed by Vincent Sherman and starring Kevin O'Connor, is *Bogie*, which aired on CBS on March 4, 1980. Carl Reiner and Steve Martin pay tribute to *film noir* in *Dead Men Don't Wear Plaid* (1982), as they use movie footage from films of the 1940s and 1950s, with Steve Martin as the private eye Rigby Reardon, hired by Rachel Ward to investigate the death of her father. Reardon gets help from his mentor Bogart via clips from *The Big Sleep, Dark Passage,* and *In a Lonely Place*, as the film both parodies and uses clips to move the narrative along. Lina Wertmuller's *Sotto, Sotto* (1984) opens in the bedroom of Oscar (Enrico Montesano) and Ester (Veronica Lario) as *Casablanca* plays on the television. Ester's view of the world is colored by her love of old romantic films. Her husband, jealous of her fantasies, says that since Bogart did not go with Bergman and chose instead to walk off into the fog with Claude Rains, Bogart must be gay. In *When Harry Met Sally* (1989), the Bergman-Bogart love affair serves as a touchstone for Harry and Sally, as they argue about why Ilsa leaves Rick. To Sally, Ilsa is a practical woman who does not want to spend the rest of her life married to a bar owner. Later in their lives, after Harry and Sally reconnect, there is a split-screen segment in which while watching *Casablanca* in separate apartments, Harry explains how Ilsa is a "low-maintenance" woman, while Sally, who wants everything her way, is "high maintenance." More recently there has been *Sirocco* (1995), a sexual fantasy about homosexuality that uses the same name as a Bogart film. One of 1995's surprise hits was Bryan Singer's *The Usual Suspects*, the title of which screenwriter Christopher McQuarrie borrowed from Captain Renault's refrain in *Casablanca*. In *Big Night* (1996), a tale of two immigrant brothers who try to keep their Paradise Restaurant open in the face of philistine customers, a friendly competitor, Pascal (Ian Holm), invites Secondo Pilaggi (Stanley Tucci) to his office to explain how surviving involves salesmanship. Pascal has Secondo look at the pictures on his wall, especially the one with Bogart, and explains how he was able to lure the big star to his restaurant. Kevin Spacey's *Albino Alligator* (1996) is a *noir*-inspired caper film whose posters of Bogart and other gangsters over the Dino's Last Chance bar serve not only as decoration but as a subtext for this brooding film.

And if there are not direct references to Bogart and his films, film reviews often link Bogart or his films to other releases. Representative of one of hundreds is Roger Ebert's review of *The Third Man* in his syndicated "The Great Movies" series. In discussing Carol Reed's film, Ebert compares this film to *Casablanca* when he says, " 'The Third Man' is like the exhausted aftermath of 'Casablanca.' Both have heroes who are American exiles, awash in a world of treachery and black market intrigue. Both heroes love a woman battered by the war. But 'Casablanca' is bathed in the hope of victory, while 'The Third Man' already reflects the Cold War years of paranoia, betrayal, and the Bomb. The hero doesn't get the girl in either movie."[65]

In *Last Man Standing* (1996), Walter Hill uses Akira Kurosawa's *Yojimbo* as a model, with Bruce Willis playing a tough, hard-boiled character based on the "hard characters" played by Bogart and Mitchum.[66] *Barb Wire* (1996) has Pamela Anderson Lee running the Hammerhead Bar and Grille in Steel Harbor, the only neutral city in an America that is undergoing a civil war. Into the bar comes a resistance leader, whom she hides, as she battles with evil forces. In *The Glimmer Man* (1996), hard-boiled detective Jim Campbell (Keenen Ivory Wayans) is all business in his hunt for a ritual killer who crucifies his victims. He is brought to tears, however, reading Ilsa's farewell note to Rick in the train station in *Casablanca*. When questioned by his colleague Lt. Cole (Steven Seagal) about his emotions, he denies he was crying. In 1996 *The English Patient* was nominated for twelve Oscars and as a wartime romance was frequently compared to *Casablanca*, as seen in the "Oscar Special" of the *Los Angeles Times* "Calendar," which linked the two films and ran pictures of Bogart with Bergman, Mayo Methot, and others under the heading "Let's Play it Again."[67]

Michael Walsh is currently at work on a screenplay and novel tentatively entitled *As Time Goes By*; in a conversation with Liz Smith of *Newsday* early in July 1997, Walsh, who will have no voice in the casting, said he would like to see Sean Penn as Rick, Ray Fiennes as Laszlo, and Julia Roberts as Ilsa. Warner Bros. is interested in making a miniseries or movie from the novel, which Maureen Egen, Warner Books's president, says is "not a sequel. It's a prequel, the current story (the movie) and a sequel, the whole story of *Casablanca.*"[68]

Television has had its share of Bogart spoofs, parodies, and pseudo-imitators, including the early *Buster Keaton Show* and Bogart's appearance on the *Jack Benny Show* in 1953. ABC broadcast *Casablanca* during the 1955–1956 season. Starring Charles McGraw as Rick Jason, Marcel Dalio as Captain Renault, and Dan Seymour as Ferrari, this triweekly series, part of the rotating *Warner Brothers Presents*, tried to capture some of the romance and adventure of the original—with little success.[69] Peter Falk played a trench-coat variation in the 1968 TV movie *Prescription: Murder.* Three years later there was another Columbo TV movie, which served as lead-in to the series *Columbo* (1971–1978), and subsequent TV movies (the latest being *A Trace of Murder*, May 1997).

Kermit the Frog, also in trench coat, was a star in *The Muppet Movie* (1979), as well as in segments of the television success, *The Muppet Show*. It was not uncommon to have Kermit dress as Rick, in trench coat and fedora. A TV special, *Muppets Go to the Movies: Play It Again*, on May 20, 1981, included a spoof of the airport scene in *Casablanca* with Miss Piggy playing Ilsa and Kermit as Rick. Because of gusts of wind, Miss Piggy's being pulled by the airplane, and the noise of the propeller blades, she can hardly discern Kermit's (Rick's) farewell lines. An episode of *The Love Boat* (April 26, 1981) had one of the men in love with a model aboard ship; he dreamed of himself as Bogart in trench coat and at the plane in *Casablanca* and the girl was Bergman.

Around this same time, Nardo, the Super Sleuth on the television show *Letter People*, solves cases with vowels and consonants. Dressed in a raincoat, with Bogart's voice, we hear such things as, "You're sharp, real sharp" (July 1981). Other imitators included Rich Little's *A Christmas Carol* (December 1979), in which Little was dressed in trench coat and fedora, with a cigarette in hand, and remarked, "With all the places, I have to come here." Don Adams as Maxwell Smart, in the series *Get Smart*, played a Bogart-type figure. The opening episode of *Remington Steele* (October 1982) had Steele with six different passports, all in the name of Humphrey Bogart characters. He quoted or cited lines from *The Maltese Falcon* and other Bogart films. One thing we learn about his identity is that "he likes Bogart." In one episode of the show, Steele, on Malta, goes after the Maltese falcon. The *A-Team* had an episode called "The Maltese Cow," in which Murdoch wore a fedora and had a cigarette dangling from his lip. The Team was after a cheap plaster cow figurine, "the Maltese cow," that held microfilm evidence of a mobster's activities. *Feel the Heat*, a pilot for the 1983 ABC season, tried to bring together elements from *Key Largo* and *Casablanca*. The setting was Key Blanco, an island off Florida, where gamblers played poker at Rick's Place. Nick Mancuso played the Bogart role, with Lisa Eichorn as an attorney. David Wolper tried without success to capitalize on the Bogart popularity by creating a *Casablanca* TV series for NBC (1983), with David Soul as Rick Blaine and Hector Elizondo as Captain Renault. One of the *Sledgehammer* episodes (ABC, October 1, 1987) was a spoof of 1940s detective movies. Bogart came back as a ghost to help Sledgehammer, who had become a private eye. Away from earth, we find an episode of *Star Trek: The Next Generation* entitled "We'll Always Have Paris" with a plot similar to *Casablanca*: Picard left the girl in Paris, and the next time he saw her she was married to a scientist. One of Kurt Browning's 1993–1994 ice-skating routines was set to music from *Casablanca*, and he skated it in a white dinner jacket, as if he were Rick.[70]

The thirty-minute season finale for HBO's *Tales from the Crypt* for 1995 (air date February 16, 1995), directed by Robert Zemeckis and casting by Victoria Burrows, opened with a cadaverous Forrest Gump chatting with Hitchcock, offering him candy, as part of the introduction to "You, Murderer," with John Lithgow, Isabella Rossellini, Sherilynn Fenn, and Robert Sacchi. Bogart's character, Louis Spinelli, has had plastic surgery to prevent being identified by the police and his wife, Betty (Isabella Rossellini). Oscar (John Lithgow) has been Betty's lover for a year, and the two conspire to kill Lou and make it look like suicide. Events conspire against the faked suicide, Betty is forced to kill Lou, and Oscar and Betty try to bury him, only to be interrupted by Erika (Sherilynn Fenn), a faithful employee and Lou's lover. Taking its cue from the opening of *Dark Passage*, with clips and images the viewer sees Bogart-Spinelli only in mirrors, and hears him (alive and deceased) via voice-over narrative and commentary. Zemeckis uses clips and images from *Dark Passage, The Maltese Falcon, Conflict, All Through the Night*, and *Key Largo*.

ANIMATED CARTOONS

Until the past decade or so, animated cartoons have been a marginalized aspect of Hollywood creativity. Some of that changed with the full-scale retrospective at the Museum of Modern Art in 1985. One thread that runs through the cartoons is how animators at Warner Bros. and other studios intertextualized their cartoons by playing with images or phrasing based on well-known feature films or star personae.

There are at least five Warner Bros. cartoons with Bogart associations. *She Was an Acrobat's Daughter* (1937) includes a segment on "The Petrified Florist" with caricatures of Leslie Howard and Bette Davis (but no Humphrey Bogart). *Hollywood Steps Out* (1941) has movie stars attending a glitzy Hollywood party at which they dance and tell jokes. In one scene Bogart, Raft, and Cagney pitch pennies. In *Slick Hare* (1947), Humphrey Bogart orders rabbit for dinner and tells Elmer Fudd he has but twenty minutes to present it. Bugs tells Elmer, "If he wants me, all he has to do is whistle." There is some slapstick in the restaurant and references to "Baby," who gets her own treatment in *Bacall to Arms* (1946), featuring Bogey Gocart and Laurie Becool in "To Have . . . To Have . . . To Have." A wolf in the audience pays little attention to what is on the screen until Bacall appears. When she kisses Bogart, he kisses the person in front of him, and when Bacall flips her cigarette off the screen, the wolf chases after the memento, only to be shot by Bogart. When he picks up the butt to smoke it, it explodes, creating a Bogart in blackface. He imitates Rochester and says he can work for Mr. Benny. In *8 Ball Bunny* (1950), Bugs is responsible for getting a penguin to its home at the South Pole. As Bugs travels south, he encounters in Martinique and elsewhere a Bogart–Fred C. Dobbs character who asks, "Could you help out a fellow American who's down on his luck?" With his last appearance, Bugs turns the table on Bogie and asks him to help out a fellow American and gives him the penguin. In Paramount's *Candy Cabaret* (1952) a piece of candy is caricatured as Bogart, who gets up on the dance floor and says, "All right, lolly, drop that gum." In a summer 1995 release that was given fairly extensive newspaper ad space, Warner Bros. featured Bugs Bunny in *Carrotblanca*, an animated short in which Bugs Bunny plays Rick.

MEMORABILIA

The boat the *African Queen* continues to draw attention. It remained in Uganda until 1968, when it was auctioned off to Fred Reeve, a San Francisco restaurateur. Reeve later sold it to Hal Bailey, who used it as an attraction on Oregon's Sun River, before moving it to Ocala, Florida. Bailey sold it to Jim Hendricks, a retired attorney, in 1982 for $65,000, and Hendricks anchored it at the Key Largo Holiday Inn on U.S. 1. In 1984, still sporting its original metal hull and weather-beaten mahogany decks, the *African Queen* was on display at the Louisiana World's Fair, and subsequent to that time it has been anchored again at the Key Largo Holiday Inn. During part of 1995 and again during the summer of 1996, the *African Queen* was used for tours and for teaching boating safety in the Hartford, Connecticut, area. In 1995, Hendricks brought it north for tours from Hartford to the Long Island Sound. He liked the area, and in concert with Ben Clarkson, director of the River School, a nonprofit organization dedicated to teaching about the history of the Connecticut River, river safety, traditional boating, and boat restoration, brought it to the area for river rides out of the River Landing Marina in Saybrook, Connecticut, from June to October 1996.[71]

In 1988 movie memorabilia collector Gary Milan had Sotheby's auction off one of the two green upright pianos from *Casablanca*. At the sale price of $154,000, the piano was purchased by C. Itoh & Co., a Japanese trading firm.[72] One of these two pianos that Dooley Wilson played in *Casablanca* was on display at MGM Studios in Orlando in 1990, before being sold at auction. And now some of the memorabilia from *Casablanca*, including one the pianos, clothes worn by Rick and Ilsa and Laszlo, and documents from and relating to the film, and other Warner Bros. films, can be viewed at the Warner Bros. Museum in Burbank, California, which opened on June 13, 1996. In December 1994, Christie's auctioned Howard Koch's Oscar for Best Screenplay (*Casablanca*) for $184,000.[73]

Imagine the studio dismay when Tom Alderman of Chicago wrote requesting a replica of *The Maltese Falcon* and was accidently sent one of the "real" statuettes.[74] Subsequently recovered, this is only one of two statues known to have been made. It was exhibited at Disney-MGM Studios for several months in 1994. Items from the various Bogart films, including one of the Maltese falcons, remain much in demand and command outstanding prices. At an auction of television and movie memorabilia in December 1994, Christie's East (in New York City) auctioned a brown cane chair, with a red painted wood seat upholstered in red, white, and blue cotton and used in Rick's Café; a passport issued to Victor Laszlo; a set of entrance doors to Rick's Café that separated the gambling room from the main area; and one of the forty-five-pound, bronze patina statues in the image of a falcon. Christie's expected to get from $3,000 to $4,000 for the chair, $5,000 to $7,000 for the passport, $20,000 to $30,000 for the doors, and $30,000 to $50,000 for the falcon. The chair sold for $5,980, the passport for $9,775, the doors for $20,700, and the falcon for $398,500 to Harry Winston, a well-known New York jeweler.[75] Six months later, on June 28, 1995, Christie's had another auction of film and television memorabilia. Bogart-related items included an agreement with many signatures (including Bogart's) for dissolution of Capricorn Oil Company, a limited partnership; the 1940 Buick Phaeton used in *Casablanca*; an original Italian poster for *The Oklahoma Kid* (1939); and a twenty-two- by fourteen-inch window card from *The Maltese Falcon*. The agreement, expected to bring $1,000 to $1,500, sold for $1,150. The Buick (estimated at $60,000 to $80,000) sold for $211,500.[76] On June 7, 1997, a red Moroccan armchair from *The Maltese Falcon* sold at Christie's in Beverly Hills for $32,200.

Garnering less lofty prices, but still appreciating faster than the stock market, is Bogart's autograph. In an essay for *Autograph Collectors* (November 1994), George and Helen Sanders note that in 1991 his signature was valued at $600, and by 1994 it was worth $1,000.[77] What the signature is on may increase the price manyfold. Book City Collectibles was selling a personally autographed, original, vintage eight- by ten-inch sepia portrait photograph of Bogart and one of Bacall for $4,000, matted and framed together. Aljean Harmetz, in her study of the making of *Casablanca*, notes that a postal card with one of Bogart's chess moves in a game he was playing simultaneously with Irving Kovner and in *Casablanca* sold for $1,750.[78]

DOUBLES AND BOGART'S IMAGE

The demand for doubles in advertising, films, and public affairs for a time spawned a number of companies, such as Ron Smith's Celebrity-Look-Alikes. And since Bogart was not available, the company for a time used Jerry Lacy or Robert Sacchi, who have made careers out of being Bogart look-alikes in the United States. In France Eric Losfeld has done the same kind of work. Lacy remarks that he never intended to make a career of playing Bogart until he played a role as a gangster in a play at Los Angeles City College. After one of the performances, a member of the audience remarked to him how much he looked like Bogart. After that, he began working on imitating Bogart's speech, and when he heard about Bogart's being a character in Woody Allen's play, *Play It Again, Sam*, he got the role after reading for it. He has since appeared in advertisements, movies, and television spots as Bogart, although he once told Rebecca Morehouse, "I'd never thought of myself as looking like Bogart and I still don't. But as I grow older the resemblance grows stronger."[79]

Robert Sacchi has been playing Humphrey Bogart for more than thirty-five years. A New Yorker who started his acting career in college and continued in off-Broadway and touring productions, Sacchi has appeared in *Play It Again, Sam*, starred in *The Man with Bogart's Face* (1980), and has been in more than one hundred Bogart-related commercials or industrial films for such firms as Ford Motor Co., Gillette, Mobil Oil and Chemical, Ryder Truck, Busch Gardens, Casablanca Ceiling Fans, London Fog Trenchcoats, and Big A Auto Parts. He has toured college campuses with his one-man show, *Bogey's Back: An Evening with Humphrey Bogart*.[80] He played in "You, Murderer," the much publicized 1995 season finale for HBO's *Tales from the Crypt*.

Sacchi remarked to Vernon Scott of UPI, " 'I've looked like Bogart since I was a kid. When I was in high school, the other kids never let me forget it. I'd rather have looked like Paul Newman or Robert Redford.' "[81] In addition to facial similarity, Sacchi's voice and mannerisms reproduce Bogart's. Lauren Bacall is irritated whenever she sees or hears of Bogart impressionists, but Sacchi, who considers himself an actor, not an impersonator,[82] never does anything to offend the memory of Bogart: "I admire him as a man and actor."[83] A decade earlier, Bacall had lamented to Bob Thomas that "every s.o.b. and his brother is trying to make a buck from Bogie,"[84] and although she thought Woody Allen had a "creative" idea for *Play It Again, Sam*, "it was a tasteless idea on film. Why? Because film lasts; plays don't."[85]

In his own lifetime Humphrey Bogart allowed his name or image to be used to advertise a limited number of products. In 1946 he (or Warner Bros. for him) allowed Brown and Williamson Tobacco Co. to use his name, signature, and photographs for Raleigh cigarettes in newspaper, magazine, and radio advertisements that said that the cigarettes were low in nicotine, had "less throat irritants," and were safer for individuals to smoke.[86] Another advertisement was for Whitman's Sampler in 1954.

After Bogart's death, Lauren Bacall decried the use of her husband's image to sell products or services, and for a time, she threatened to instigate litigation to have the offending companies cease and desist. In 1971, for example, Pan American World Airways advertised flights to Casablanca, featuring a photograph of Humphrey Bogart and the line, "Play it again, Sam." Although Pan Am had gotten the okay from holders of the copyright on *Casablanca*, Bacall urged J. Walter Thompson, the agency for Pan Am, to stop the campaign.[87] When a made-for-television film on Bogart's life was announced, Bacall unleashed a barrage of protests, but eventually dropped her suit against the producers of *Bogie*.[88] After calling the movie "a bunch of crap" and lamenting how "people will do anything for money," she suggested that "actors should have copyrights on their personas."[89] Bacall's voice has been heard.

The marketing of images has taken on legal ramifications as numerous court cases dealing with proprietary rights have resulted in the use of an actor's image. In mid-January 1984, for example, Manhattan judge Edward J. Greenfield ruled that model Barbara Reynolds was to stop appearing in advertisements in which she masqueraded as Jacqueline Kennedy Onassis. Citing the civil rights law that forbids the use of someone's "name, portrait or picture ... for purposes of trade" without the approval of the party, Judge Greenfield said, "No one has an inherent or constitutional right to pass himself off for what he is not."[90] The preliminary ruling focused on one advertisement for one plaintiff who was alive. In 1985 California enacted the California Celebrity Rights Act, which gave "celebrity's heirs exclusive licensing rights for fifty years after the star's death. At least 11 other states now have laws protecting heirs."[91] This law prevents unauthorized use of the celebrity's name, voice, signature, photograph, or likeness. The judge's ruling has been upheld in other courts, and individuals and estates work with licensing agents for permission to use images. In 1986 Woody Allen won a $425,000 settlement against Woody Allen look-alike Phil Boroff.[92]

CMG Worldwide, the company that now markets the use of the Bogart image with the approval of Stephen and Leslie Bogart, has been aggressive in the licensing of its uses and filing suit against those who use the likeness without permission. In 1992 the actor's children sued a jeans manufacturer for marketing Bogart jeans,[93] and when *Rendezvous à Montreal*, a short film with a computer-generated image of Marilyn Monroe, was shown, it "drew complaints from lawyers for Humphrey Bogart's estate," who may have been concerned with others profiting from use of his likeness.[94]

With digitized computer technology, or "humanoid technologies," the issue has become even more complex and controversial.[95] Starting in late 1996, the use of *Forrest Gump*–type promotions has become more common. For the first time since 1976, John Wayne's family permitted use of the star's likeness in a 1996 commercial.[96] Mercedes Benz has used images of Bing Crosby and Clark Gable, and in 1997 Service Merchandise used Lucille Ball and Jack Webb in digitized commercials. About the same time, Fred Astaire has been seen dancing with a Dirt Devil vacuum cleaner in computer-enhanced images from *Easter Parade* and *Royal Wedding*. After the appearance of a Diet Coke commercial with Bogart, Cagney, and Louis Armstrong in a nightclub scene, *TV Guide* editorialized, "There's something unconscionable about using the dearly-departed to promote a product they were never associated with in their lifetimes."[97] More recently Stephen Bogart has said he thought a Diet Coke segment with Humphrey Bogart and Paula Abdul was "fun" and that he "enjoyed it," which means he approved the commercial (and the fee).[98] Bogart's image also has been used for television commercials and magazine advertisements for Sara Lee layer cake. In one there is a shot from *Casablanca* where Bogart turns to Sam and asks how he could forget the woman who left him with the other brand of layer cake.[99]

FASHIONS

Bogart's name appears in fashion articles, which is strange considering his preference for one or two comfortable jackets and baggy pants. In fact, except for his dress in such films as *To Have and Have Not, The Treasure of the Sierra Madre, Key Largo*, and *The African Queen*, when he wears casual clothes or open-collared shirts, he appears out of keeping with his image and persona. With their emphasis on the preppy look, manufacturers and image makers have tapped Bogart's early years, his films, the way he delivers his lines, his attitude, and his dress.[100]

In the mid-1980s, with the success of the television series *Miami Vice*, and in particular the unshaven, rugged, masculine look of Don Johnson, the two-day growth that Bogart made famous in *The Petrified Forest* (and later by Marlon Brando, Montgomery Clift, and Dustin Hoffman) was back in fashion for a time.[101] As a tie-in to an article by Molly Haskell on Bogart's screen appeal and an opportunity to generate advertising revenue, *Gentleman's Quarterly* ran a six-page spread, "The Bogie Look: This Is the Stuff That Personal Style Is Made Of," in which *GQ* chose comparable contemporary fashions from *The Maltese Falcon, Casablanca, To Have and Have Not*, and *Sabrina*. The magazine tells us that not only does the image endure, so, too, do the clothes: "Bogart's look was as much a part of his style as were his prickly persona and that smoky voice. And like the legend of Bogie himself, the era of Hollywood high style endures in these contemporary counterparts of those Forties classics."[102]

One of the items of clothing most associated with Bogart is the trench coat. Belmondo in *Breathless* wears one, it is part of the iconography of Peter Falk in his television series *Colombo*, and part of the dialogue in *The Onion Field* (1979) has someone refer to a character wearing "a Humphrey Bogart trench coat." In the last few years French manufacturer Jean-Paul Senejoux was selling knock-offs of Bogart's *Casablanca* trench coat for $700.[103] Casa Blanca, a store in Madrid, Spain, sells stylish men's attire. The House of Fragrances, Inc., distributes Bogart Eau de Toilette, a perfume by Jacques Bogart that benefits from the name association. In keeping with his generally casual attire off screen, Bogart's picture with the caption "Bogart wore khakis" (October 1993) was included in a series of national advertisements for the Gap stores. In an article in a Beverly Hills publication, Gary Amo notes that Bogart was one of many luminaries who purchased clothing at the haberdasher who "has always had a reputation for style."[104]

CARTOONS

Cartoonists love Bogart. Two fairly well-known early cartoons were the 1935 *New Yorker* caricature (by Frueh) of Bogart and Leslie Howard and Peggy Conklin in the stage version of *The Petrified Forest*, and James Thurber's "Jolly Times" (1939), which portrayed the "Battling Bogarts." Considerably more recent is Gary Larson's Weiner dog art scene from a classic nature film in which the lithsome snake asks the smoking private eye, "You know how to kill a pig, don't you, Steve? . . . You just put your coils together and squeeeeze" (May 3, 1988). Charles Schultz uses "The Stuff That Dreams Are Made Of" as part of an entire *Peanuts* strip related to the falcon (February 19, 1995). Influenced no doubt by Ted Turner's penchant for colorizing black and white films, Tom Wilson's *Ziggy* says, "Colorizing 'The Maltese Falcon' is enough to make Humphrey Bogart blush" (March 30, 1991). Another *Ziggy* cartoon has him tell his parrot (dressed in fedora and cigarette dangling from its beak), "I'll sure be glad when you're off your Bogart kick!" (September 10, 1986).

Tom Armstrong has had several segments of *Marvin* devoted to Sam Pulp, Private Eye. In one he uses a dialogue box at the top of each segment to serve as a voice-over that counters the dialogue (April 7, 1985), and in another, Marvin wears a fedora and trench coat and has a cigarette dangling from his lip as he sits by his girl drinking formula. When he says, "Here's looking at you, Kid," she hits him over the head with her bottle of formula. Marvin is left to reflect on the modern woman (April 12, 1995).

In a somewhat morbid cartoon, *Bloom County* refers to Bogart and his smoking (June 21, 1988), and Crock uses the line, "Just like a 'Bogart' movie, huh?" for part of a strip (June 24, 1980). Garfield meets a young thing and invites her to Rick's Café Américain, but unfortunately, as he says, "Here's lookin' at you, Sweetheart" and smacks her on the chin, he knocks her out (November 4, 1984). Doug Marlette's *Kudzu* has a series of lines from Bogart's films, including *The Maltese Falcon* and *Casablanca*, with his main figure's closer being, "Sometimes my Bogart is so good it scares me" (April 24, 1983). The *New Yorker* ran an S. Hunt cartoon of a husband returning from work saying, "Well, you know Jessica, it's still the same old story. A fight for love and glory, a case of do or die" (October 19, 1981). In a *Funky Winkerbean* strip, after the male is told by his love that she has to stay in Paris until her contract is finished, he retorts, "No matter what happens sweetheart . . . we'll always have Paris!" (August 18, 1995).

The Chronicle of Higher Education ran Carol Cable's portrait of Rick holding Ilsa with the caption, "Rick was moved to Ilsa's plea for viable constructs for the referentially challenged."[105] A syndicated political cartoon by Gary Brookins in the *Richmond Times-Dispatch* has Uncle Sam pulling the *African Queen*, which is named here *Zaire Mission*, through the infested river, with President Clinton looking over the bow and saying, "Don't worry, if it starts to look dangerous, I'll let you know."[106]

MEMORABLE DIALOGUE AND ITS USES

Several of Bogart's most famous lines of dialogue have become a part of Americana, incorporated into everyday speech and by advertisers and writers as a hook. Except for Clark Gable and his line in *Gone with the Wind*, "Frankly, my dear, I don't give a damn," probably no other actor has had his film lines quoted more often than Bogart. The most memorable are: "Here's looking at you, kid"; "I'm going to send you over"; "It's the stuff that dreams are made of"; "You're good, you're very good"; and "Play it, Sam."

The *Wall Street Journal*, for example, in a letter to prospective student subscribers, began, "As Humphrey Bogart said to Claude Rains at the end of *Casablanca*, 'This looks like the beginning of a beautiful relationship'" [*sic*]. There are numerous references to "play it again" in articles, as titles to essays in advertisements, in reviews,[107] and sprinkled in everyday conversation.

"Here's looking at you kid" can be seen on mugs, countless greetings cards, posters, and in various advertising. Sam Spade's comment on the Maltese falcon, "It's the stuff that dreams are made of," has been used by G. D. Ritzes, an ice cream chain, to the effect that its product is "truly the ice cream that dreams are made of." It was also part of a headline detailing a U.S. Customs Service auction featuring "stuff dreams are made of," including thirty-three colored diamonds.[108]

Memorable lines or parts of lines or scenes from movies are ubiquitous in our culture. Imitapes has made a line called Phonies, which are imitations or impressions of famous personalities to use in telephone answering machines. Two of its Bogart tapes are "Whistle" and "Sweetheart." Nostalgia Lane, one of numerous suppliers of mugs, has had a series of famous mugs with the likenesses of movie stars, including Gable, Monroe, Wayne, and Bogart. The one of Bogart is an image of Bogart with a soft-brim hat and a cigarette dangling from his lip on one side and the words, "Here's lookin' at you, Kid" on the other. Art Buchwald made the newsmaker columns when he toasted Katharine Graham on her seventieth birthday celebration with the same phrase.[109] The same phrase was used as a subtitle for a Valentine's Day story, "Cinematic Cooing: Here's Looking at You, Kid," distributed by the *New York Times*,[110] and the title of a documentary by William E. Cohen shown at the New York Film Festival in 1980. The documentary is a series of interviews with a ten-year-old burn victim and his mother.

"Play it again" is also ubiquitous. The 3M Company used figures dressed like Rick and Sam in *Casablanca* to tell us to "Play It Again on Scotch Video Tape."[111] The Texas Lottery has used it in an advertisement for its trivia contest.[112] The Horseshoe Casino and Hotel in Bossier, Louisiana, was running for a time in 1997 a television advertisement with the phrasing, "Of all the joints in the world, you had to walk into the Horseshoe. Play it again."[113] Motorola recalled Bogart as part of its promotion of cellular phones.[114]

Often newspaper and magazine writers allude to Bogart to get the reader's attention or to evoke a feeling. Glen Meade, for example, titled his travel piece "Casablanca after Bogart."[115] Henry R. Breck's "Maltese Falcon of Foreign Debt" for the *Wall Street Journal*[116] uses Bogart allusions to help us better understand the U.S. debt crisis. Breck recommends familiarity with Shirley Jackson's "The Lottery" and Hammett's *The Maltese Falcon*, in particular the scene with Lorre, Greenstreet, Bogart, and Elisha Cook, Jr., in which the Fat Man says that Wilmer (Cook) is like a son to him. After that Lorre whispers in Greenstreet's ear, and Bogart says to Wilmer, "Two to one they're selling you out, son." To Breck, "That's just what the current villains are going to do to the U.S. commercial banks.... The U.S. banks are going to take the fall.' " Jeff Greenfield in a syndicated column on Calvin Klein ads opens his piece with, "Like the police inspector in *Casablanca*, the Calvin Klein company is shocked—."[117] In a similar opening to a story on international espionage, Russell Watson says, "Like the sly police chief in the movie classic 'Casablanca,' French interior Minister Charles Pasqua was shocked—*shocked*—to learn that the CIA had been spying on the French industry."[118] Aljean Harmetz notes that as an example of hypocrisy, there are "nearly one hundred references in 1990 and 1991, from the *New Republic, Newsday*, the *Washington Post*, and *Daily Variety* to the business and sports pages of the *Los Angeles Times* and the Op-Ed columnists of the *New York Times*."[119] And of course, there are numerous references on television. One fairly recent closer that referred to Rick and Ilsa was ABC's *Prime Time Live* piece on how our biological clocks work (July 26, 1995).

The Home Club in 1991 used a Bogart look-alike dressed as a membership card. The scenario included the card/Bogart discussing the cessation of certain membership rights as in the final scene from *Casablanca*.[120] In 1992 Taster's Choice ran the advertisement, "Casablanca and Taster's Choice: This could be the beginning of a beautiful friendship," in the movie review section of *Newsweek* with the shot of Bogart and Bergman looking at one another at the airport, juxtaposed to a contemporary couple looking at one another and holding between them a jar of the coffee (November 23, 1992). And a play on the romance between Bogart and Bergman was used in a commercial spot shown on Dallas television for a florist (June 1995).

Boxed-In is one of numerous companies that produce or have produced Bogart buttons. A variety of postal cards, including photographs by Philippe Halsman and Scotty Wellbourne, a caricature by David Levine that appeared in the *New York Review of Books*, and a picture of Bogart's foot and hand prints and the line, "Sid, may you never die till I kill you," in the forecourt of the Chinese Theatre in Hollywood, are popular, as are lines of note and greeting cards marketed by Paper Moon Graphics, Portal Publications, Midnight Movies, and MJK Illustrations in Canada.

Cardesign, a manufacturer of greeting cards, has a card cut-out of Bogart with smoking cigarette and in trench coat and hat, and a car in the background, reminiscent of the end of *Casablanca*. There is a Bogey Bank that plays "As

Time Goes By," as smoke trails from Bogie's cigarette when a coin is inserted. For those who prefer stuffed images, Barbara Isenberg's North American Bear Co. makes Humphrey Beargart, a stuffed bear twenty inches tall, wearing a fedora, trench coat, and pants, and a Lauren Bearcall.

A recent advertisement for Lux toilet soap foregrounds a bar of soap with the words, "Of all the bars in the world." In the center of the advertisement is a woman in a 1940s hairdo, sitting behind what might be a piano, in a setting not unlike Rick's Café. Andrew Tolson notes the advertisement might work for a reader unfamiliar with *Casablanca*, but only when the readers decode it on several levels: the soap, the references to *Casablanca* and Hollywood mythology, and the notion of illusions. We fully appreciate the advertisement when we see how the "intertextual reference transforms the meaning of the advert as a whole" and how this advertisement "relies on the reader's ability to perceive this cleverness." The advertisement becomes more interesting as the reader-viewer becomes involved with Hollywood mythologies and Hollywood stardom as the advertisement and bar of soap enter the "knowing" consumer's home.[121] Tolson's reading of these intertextual references could be applied in one way or another to many of the other products and advertisements associated with Bogart.

OTHER REFERENCES: A MISCELLANY

References to Bogart can be found in unanticipated places. In *Near Mint*, a fanzine for old movie and comic book art, W. Parke Johnson uses a series of images of Bogart with a machine gun taken from *Passage from Marseille* to illustrate technique.[122] A drawing by Bush of Bogart in a pose from *The Treasure of the Sierra Madre* adorns the cover of issue number 12 (1982) of the legendary 'zine *Witzend*, a collection of "heavy metal" stories.

Larry Evans, in a syndicated chess column (September 25, 1983), recounts how Bogart, known for spending his off-screen time playing chess, challenged Dr. Paul Limbos to a series of games when Bogart was in Stanleyville, working on *The African Queen*. The column includes one of the games and the information that Bogart usually played the Italian or Scotch openings as white, and when black, the French Defense.

Two female dolphins, named Bogie and Bacall, made the news when they were being moved from their home in the Florida Keys to the Sugarloaf Dolphin Sanctuary before being released into the wild.[123] Travelers were recently lured by a punfilled Bogey and Bacall golf package to Scotland. There has been a shuttle bus on the Berkeley campus called the Humphrey Go Bart. Celebrity Window Wavers has marketed a full-color, lifelike image of Bogart that attaches to a car's back window; the car's motion makes the hand wave. In one of the issues of the newsletter from the now-defunct Slim and Steve: The Bogart and Bacall Fan Club, a collector advertised a miscellany of items including a Bogart doll, statue, golfball, pins, mask, puzzles, bank, calendar, handpainted shirt, pencil sharpener, collectible plates, cartoon book, sheet music, and a one-of-a-kind watch.

A November 30, 1995, showing of NBC's *Frasier*, starring Kelsey Grammer, showed a clip from the 1953 *Jack Benny Show* that included Bogart as "Baby Face." An undated four-page brochure on a master's in American studies at the University of Alcalá in Spain uses an image of Bogart in fedora and overcoat and "bogarting" a cigarette on its cover (fall 1995). Lots of magazines and books that feature "great love teams" use Bogart and Bacall to sell their product. In its Academy Awards edition, *Architectural Digest* reprinted an earlier piece by Michael Frank on Bogart and Bacall and the home that they purchased from Hedy Lamarr in Benedict Canyon.[124]

A more recent example is *People* magazine's cover story, "The Greatest Love Stories of the Century," which included a picture of Bogart and Bacall among the eight other couples.[125] In addition to showing Bogart films such as *Casablanca* for fund raisers, some organizations use images from his films as gifts for their contributors, and sometimes with distinction. The American Film Institute acknowledged contributions of more than $100 in 1994 with a memento of three frames from *Casablanca* embedded in a cylindrical piece of lucite, and a message of thanks on its base. This item won a CLIO Award for creative excellence and innovative design in the specialty advertising category.

Bogart's picture and name are more readily recognized than those of many leading politicians and cabinet members and have been given even greater recognition with the issuance of a collectible that everyone can afford—a thirty-two cent stamp issued July 31, 1997, by the United States Postal Service as part of the Legends of Hollywood series. The Bogart stamp, following ones in honor of Marilyn Monroe and James Dean, is based on a poster image from *The Big Sleep*. More serious collectors could buy matted sheets, first-day issues and first-day covers, a souvenir book, and a variety of other formats ranging in price from thirty-two cents to a signed uncut press sheet for $125. John's Grill in San Francisco, the locale for an early scene in *The Maltese Falcon*, had festivities honoring the issuance of the stamp, including men and women dressing up as Sam or Brigid.[126] At the ceremony honoring the release of the stamp at the Chinese Theatre in Hollywood, Lauren Bacall said that even though Bogart was not much for awards, he would have been truly moved by this honor. She also noted how amazed she was that his appeal has continued for so long.

In *The Casablanca File*, Colin McArthur traces *Casablanca*'s intertextuality in advertisements and images worldwide and finds the film "the most prolific generator of secondary texts in the field of popular culture." Additional secondary texts to *Casablanca*, as noted by McArthur, include stills, subsequent Bogart movies, sheet music from other songs in the film, belts ("This is a hold-up"), headlines, an episode of *Moonlighting*, a quit-smoking poster, Austria's Casablanca brand cigarettes, the many articles on the fifty-year anniversary of *Casablanca*, the staging of the original play in London in 1991 ("Rick's Bar Casablanca"), stores and restaurants and bars in Toronto, Brussels, and Waldshut

(Germany), travel brochures, and a British board game named after the movie. Wolfgang Fuchs notes other uses of Bogart's likeness or name in Europe in a Samson cigarette advertisement, a venetian blind advertisement in *Der Spiegel*, as a character in the comic strip *Yellow Bugi Bugk*, and as the detective Sorrow for the magazine *Albo TV*.[127]

Companies or individuals that use likenesses of stars or their name for logos or to promote their commercial products must secure the approval of licensing agents. For those who want to produce or manufacture an item with a Bogart image, all uses of the image or property must be approved by Stephen and Leslie Bogart through Curtis Management Group in Indianapolis. CMG has licensed the Humphrey Bogart likeness, name, or associated phrasing for a cut-out, a cookbook, a sculpture, prints, T-shirts, nesting dolls, a teddy bear, posters, signs, hats and caps, neckties, a die-cast vehicle, apron, boxer shorts, giftwrap, a coaster set, greeting cards, calendars, portfolio of prints, postcard book, note-cards, optical frames, bag, belt, music box, jogging suits, sports shirt, sweatshirt, seriographs, and magnets.[128] Stephen Bogart has indicated that about 75 percent of the requests are approved, but "they nix advertisements promoting alcohol (unless they include a disclaimer about drinking and driving) or his trademark cigarettes.... Even ads for other products using the star's image must have any cigarette cropped out."[129]

FAN CLUBS

As of July 1998, there were no active Humphrey Bogart Fan Clubs on record, but the Internet has spawned a number of sites that serve a similar function. For a number of years, Chaw Mank ran a "Lest We Forget Fan Club" that included Bogart and other stars. At the time the club existed, the primary focus was to keep Bogart's memory alive, especially with shut-ins, and to generate letters, exchanges, and newsletters among those interested in the actor. Mank would send postal cards with pictures of Bogart, news sheets, and the like. When I asked him in 1982 why he had the fan club, he said that he liked the Bogart roles, the way he presented himself on the screen, and his "finished" acting style.

More recently Sarah Davis was president of the Slim and Steve: Bogart and Bacall Fan Club. The club existed for a number of years in the late 1980s, but ended by 1992. Started because of her interest in Bacall, Davis reports that most of the members were interested in Bogart. Davis says that to her, Bogart is a symbol of the "old movies," a "classic" who never goes out of style. Still perceived by fans as a "bad ass," he was tough under pressure, did not take any nonsense from others, and was down to earth and straight with his friends and family.[130]

CONCLUSION

Humphrey Bogart has been the subject of plays, films, novels, and poems; his image or his words have appeared on postage stamps, postal cards, buttons, greeting cards, and in cartoons; impressionists have mimicked his voice and appearance, and publications have parodied his films and persona; restaurants, lounges, and bars have been named after Bogart or roles that he has played, as have food and drinks. There is even a *Casablanca* cookbook. Apartment complexes have been named after his films; record companies continue to sell scores from the films and radio broadcasts, and a frequently played record featured the Bogart-Bacall love affair; poster companies continue to do well selling the Bogart image; publishers of video and film magazines, as well as prestigious publications such as the *Wall Street Journal* and *Esquire*, have used the Bogart name or image to help sell their products; quotations from his films appear on greeting and postal cards, on mugs, and as titles and subtitles of books and articles; there are web sites devoted to the actor and his films, and there have been Humphrey Bogart fan clubs. Numerous collectors are willing to pay royal sums for Bogart memorabilia. All these exist in addition to histories of American film, discussions of specific genre films, and sections of books devoted to his life or screen career. Bogart's acting and films, except for *High Sierra, The Maltese Falcon, Casablanca, The Big Sleep, To Have and Have Not*, and to a lesser degree another four or five films, have received surprisingly little scholarly attention in the United States.

Whether we are reminded of Bogart via screen look-alikes, the French praise of *l'existentialisme de Bogart*, the influence of filmmakers such as Jean-Luc Godard (*Breathless*), Woody Allen (*Play It Again, Sam*), François Truffaut (*Shoot the Piano Player*), George Roy Hill (*A Little Romance*), Robert Day (*The Man with Bogart's Face*), or remakes (*Sahara* with Jim Belushi, Showtime, 1995; Sydney Pollack's *Sabrina* with Harrison Ford, 1995), neologisms (''Don't Bogart that joint, my friend''—*Easy Rider*), designer fragrances (''Bogart for Men''), restaurants and bars (Bogart's, Rick's Cafe, The Blue Parrot), or the repetition of phrases such as ''I stick my neck out for nobody,'' or ''Here's looking at you, kid,'' Humphrey Bogart remains an integral part of our social conscience and popular culture. As Tom Maurstad remarks, ''It is no coincidence that this post-death revival is occurring at precisely the moment when baby boomers are reaching their mid-40s and early 50s.'' To Maurstad this attempt to reach what advertisers call ''pulse points'' by using past icons ''can be seen as the first of many responses as boomers, a demographic juggernaut nostalgic for the glories of their youth, confront their looming mortality.''[131] True, but for Humphrey Bogart, this power of nostalgia—his role as a Hollywood icon and audience identification with the actor or his roles—has been at play for the four decades since his death and for the better part of the previous two decades. References to Bogart and his films, especially *Casablanca, The Maltese Falcon*, and *The Big Sleep*, are a highly visible part of the fabric of our culture. Jack Nicholson, Clint Eastwood, Mel Gibson, and Harrison Ford may create a more contemporary take on his image, but there remains only one Bogart. The very multiplicity of associations suggests that while a critic or fan may focus on one or two aspects of the actor or his persona as touchstones to an understanding of Bogart, his life and films, and especially his life on films, will continue to sustain us.

NOTES

1. Sandy Fernandez, "The Iconography of Elvis and Marilyn," *Chronicle of Higher Education* (May 4, 1994): A10.

2. *Dallas Morning News* (August 5, 1996): C6.

3. Andrew Tolson, *Mediations: Text and Discourse in Media Studies* (London: Arnold, 1996), xi; see also Jackie Stacey, "Hollywood Memories," *Screen* 35.4 (winter 1994): 317–335, on women's memories of movies. Also see Barbara Deming's *Running Away from Myself: A Dream Portrait Drawn from the Films of the Forties* (New York: Grossman, 1969).

4. J. Hoberman and Jonathan Rosenbaum, *Midnight Movies* (New York: Da Capo, 1991), 28.

5. According to Bryan How, telephone interview, Brattle Theatre, January 5, 1997, the annual Bogart festival stopped in the early 1980s.

6. "The Bogart Vogue: Character and Cult," *Commonweal* (March 11, 1966): 664.

7. Terence Pettigrew, *Bogart: A Definitive Study of His Film Career*, rev. ed. (London and New York: Proteus, 1981), 5.

8. Charles Francisco, *You Must Remember This* . . . (Englewood Cliffs, N.J.: Prentice Hall, 1980), 3.

9. Stan Franklin, "How They Choose Movies That Go on TV," *Florida Times Union* (March 6, 1981): D1.

10. Frank Miller, *Casablanca: As Time Goes By* (Atlanta: Turner Publishing, 1992), 184. More currently, the American Film Institute's list of "Top 100 U.S. Movies" (released June 16, 1998) had *Casablanca* in second place, *The African Queen* at seventeen, *The Maltese Falcon* at twenty-three, and *The Treasure of the Sierra Madre* at thirty. Two months later, *TV Guide*'s issue featuring the "50 Greatest Movies on TV and Video" (August 8–14, 1998) also had *Casablanca* in second place and *The African Queen* at thirty-five.

11. For an account of Huston's attack on colorization, see Lawrence Grobel, *The Hustons*, (New York: Avon, 1989), 772–773.

12. Francisco 3.

13. "Here's Looking at You, Bogie," *Video*, 5.12 (March 1982): 66–67, 98–101.

14. Ty Burr, "Oeuvre Achievers: 30 Stars Who Made the Movies Matter," *Entertainment Weekly* (August 13, 1993): 18–30, 33–34, 37–38, 40, 45–47, 49–51; Steve Daly, "Humphrey Bogart," 21. In direct conflict to the *EW* survey is a 1995 Harris Poll asking, "Who is your favorite star?" As Garry Wills notes in "John Wayne's Body," *New Yorker* (August 19, 1996): 39–49, only one dead actor, John Wayne, was ranked, and he was number one (39). Wills's article serves as a prologue to *John Wayne's America: The Politics of Celebrity* (New York: Simon & Schuster, 1997), in which he explains that Wayne is the number 1 movie star in the United States because he "embodies the American myth."

15. "The 100 Greatest Movie Stars of All Time," *Entertainment Weekly* (Fall 1996): 41.

16. Jackie Stacey, "Hollywood Memories," *Screen* 35.4 (Winter 1994): 317.

17. *Cultural Selection: Why Some Achievements Survive the Test of Time—And Others Don't* (New York: Basic Books, 1996), 23–42.

18. *Round Up the Usual Suspects: The Making of Casablanca—Bogart, Bergman, and World War II* (New York: Hyperion, 1992), 81.

19. www.concentric.net/~Bogies1/bio.html.

20. *Fodor's 97: Mexico*, ed. Edie Jarolim (New York: Fodor's Travel, 1996), 468.

21. Ray Huard, "High Energy Costs Make Fans of Fans," *Florida Times Union* (March 27, 1980): A14.

22. Wolfgang Fuchs, *Humphrey Bogart: Cult Star, A Documentation*, trans. Richard Leigh (Berlin: Taco Verlagsgesellschaft und Agenture, 1987), 124–125.

23. Personal interview, July 23, 1983.

24. For a general discussion of "Hollywood Glamour" through photography, see *American Photo* 6.3 (May–June 1995), an issue devoted to the topic.

25. Personal correspondence, July 24, 1981.

26. *Film Comment* (May–June 1980): 10.

27. See John Kobal and V. A. Wilson, *Foyer Pleasure: The Golden Age of Cinema Lobby Cards* (N.p.: Album Press, 1982).

28. Anthony Slide, *A Collector's Guide to Movie Memorabilia with Prices* (Des Moines, Iowa: Wallace-Homestead, 1983), 84.

29. "Auction Results," Sotheby's sale number 6934, December 20, 1996.

30. *Los Angeles Times Calendar* (December 6, 1996): F1, F10.

31. Flyer on Hurrell distributed at showings at Atlas Savings and Loan of San Francisco and Harcourt Gallery, in the same city, March 1983; *People* (February 2, 1998): 96–98.

32. *Film Comment* (January–February 1980): 53.

33. *Film Comment* 30.3 (May–June 1994): 4–5.

34. These include but are not limited to: *Bettina*, London, 1963; *Sheilah Graham's Hollywood Revisited: A Fiftieth Celebration* (New York: St. Martin's Press, 1985); Charles Hamblett's *The Hollywood Cage* (New York: Hart, 1969); Radie Harris's *Radie's World* (New York: Putnam, 1975); Joe Hyams's *Mislaid in Hollywood* (New York: Wyden, 1973); George Jessel's *Halo over Hollywood* (Van Nuys, Calif.: Toastmaster, 1961); Garson Kanin's *Together Again!*; Dick Kleiner's *Hollywood's Greatest Love Stories* (New York: Pocket Books, 1976); and Barry Norman's *The Hollywood Greats* (New York: Franklin Watts, 1980).

35. Mignon McLaughlin, "The Woman Who Dreamed of Humphrey Bogart," *Good Housekeeping* 125 (October 1947): 47.

36. Francisco 205.

37. Maurice Yacowar, *Loser Take All: The Comic Art of Woody Allen*, exp. ed. (New York: Continuum, 1991), 57.

38. Woody Allen, "How Bogart Made Me the Superb Lover I Am Today," *Life* (March 21, 1969): 66.

39. *Woody Allen's* Play It Again, Sam, ed. Richard Anobile (New York: Grosset and Dunlap, 1977), 9.

40. Segment shown on *60 Minutes*, CBS, spring 1996.

41. *Journal of Popular Film and Television* 8.2 (1980): 27.

42. *Poetry Review* 78.3 (autumn 1988): 45.

43. (Boston: Faber and Faber, 1993), 198–200.
44. *Saturday Evening Post* (March 12, 1966): 16.
45. (New York: Random House, 1969), 17.
46. (New York: Signet, 1972), 43.
47. (New York: Pocket Books, 1981), 61.
48. J. Weberman, "How to Bogart a Joint," *Stone Age Magazine* (summer–fall 1979).
49. Bill Minutaglio, "A Long Love Affair Smolders," *Dallas Morning News* (June 22, 1997): A1, A28; Andrew Ferguson, "Pardon Me If I (Still) Smoke: For Some It's a Badge of Honor—A Refusal to Give In," *Time* (June 30, 1997): 32.
50. Lauran Neergaard, "Cigs and Celluloid," *Dallas Morning News* (June 24, 1995): 29A.
51. "Is There a Backlash Against Healthy Living?" *Washington Post* (January 7, 1997): Z12. Of course Bogart was not a cigar smoker, and although he did drink martinis, his preferred drink was scotch.
52. AP, September 17, 1983.
53. Truman "Duffy" Myers, director of public relations, July 9, 1981, personal correspondence.
54. "When Films 'Quote' Films, They Create a New Mythology," *New York Times* (September 25, 1977): 2:1.
55. James Robert Parish and Don E. Stanke, *The Swashbucklers* (New Rochelle, N.Y.: Arlington House, 1976), 306.
56. Miller 182.
57. "Everybody Comes to Roquentin's *La Nausee* and *Casablanca*," *Mosaic* 16.1–2 (winter–spring 1983): 103–112.
58. Miller 182.
59. Joanna E. Rapf and Gary L. Green, *Buster Keaton: A Bio-Bibliography* (Westport, Conn.: Greenwood Press, 1995), 202.
60. "*High Sierra*: Swan Song for an Era," *Journal of Popular Film*, 5.3–4 (1976): 261–262.
61. "When Films 'Quote' Films," 2:24.
62. Pauline Kael, *Deeper into Movies* (Boston: Little, Brown, 1973), 413–415.
63. Robert Guenette Production, 1991; Warners Home Video, 1993.
64. *Miami Herald* (June 7, 1980): A2.
65. "Roger Ebert's The Great Movies: '*The Third Man*,' " *Beverly Hills Courier* (December 13, 1996): 31.
66. Marilyn Beck and Stacy Jewel Smith, "From Hollywood," *Beverly Hills Courier* (August 23, 1996): 14. One of the movie reviewers and columnist for the *Dallas Morning News* offered readers the opportunity to suggest the cast for a talked-about remake of *Casablanca*: Jane Sumner, " 'Casablanca' Casting Call," *Dallas Morning News* (July 28, 1997): C5.
67. *Los Angeles Times* (March 23, 1997): 14.
68. Jeannie Williams, "News and Views," *USA Today* (May 28, 1997): D2.
69. *Complete Directory of Prime Time Shows, 1946–Present* (New York: Ballantine, 1979), 108.
70. Michele Lellouche, personal correspondence, July 22, 23, 1996, called my attention to the *A-Team*, *Star Trek*, and *Power Rangers* episodes, and the Kurt Browning program, and refreshed my memory about the *Remington Steele* premiere.
71. Telephone interview, July 10, 1996, Tom Barnett, executive director, Saybrook,

Connecticut, Chamber of Commerce. A spokesperson for the chamber of commerce indicated that mechanical difficulties prevented the *African Queen* from visiting in 1997 (telephone conversation, October 20, 1997).

72. Nikki Fine, "Eager Collectors Paying Big Bucks for Film Mementos," *Florida Times Union* (December 25, 1988): D6, and Miller 188.

73. Scott Huver, "Spielberg Gives Gift of Gable's Golden Glory," *Beverly Hills Courier* (December 20, 1996): 1, 42. Included in this article is information on Koch's Oscar for *Casablanca*.

74. *St. Petersburg Times* (January 26, 1976).

75. Sale No. 7639, Price List, December 6, 1994.

76. Sale 7741, Christie's *Price List*, June 28, 1995.

77. "Humphrey Bogart: 'The Bold, the Bad, the Bogey,' " 66.

78. "The Santana Times," 3.2 (fall 1991): 17; Harmetz 205.

79. *Washington, D.C., Sunday Star* (December 7, 1969), AFI Clipping File, np.

80. Personal correspondence, August 16, 1980.

81. *Washington Post* (June 20, 1979).

82. *Family Week* (July 31, 1983): 14.

83. *Washington Post* (June 20, 1979).

84. *St. Petersburg Times* (December 19, 1974), clipping file.

85. *St. Petersburg Times* (December 19, 1974), clipping file.

86. Clipping files, USC.

87. *St. Petersburg Times* (March 3, 1971); *St. Petersburg Independent* (March 2, 1971).

88. *St. Petersburg Times* (February 16, 1980).

89. *Los Angeles Times* (August 22, 1979): IV:18.

90. *Florida Times Union* (January 13, 1984): A6. One of the matters arising from the tragic death of Princess Diana (August 31, 1997) is how different countries have privacy rules about what images may be published. In France, for example, each person owns the right to her or his private image, but that does not prevent photographers from selling pictures to publications in other countries.

91. Joshua Hammer and Karen Springer, "They Are Hip, Hot—and Dead," *Newsweek* (July 10, 1989): 34.

92. *Newsweek* (October 6, 1986): 81. For a more recent discussion, see Steve Ditlea, June 19, 1996, "Virtual Humans Raise Legal Issues and Primal Fears," n.p. Online. Available: http://www.search.nytimes.com/search/daily.

93. *Daily Variety* (September 22, 1992).

94. Ditlea, " 'Virtual Humans' Raise Legal Issues and Primal Fears." "Cyber-Times," *New York Times* (June 19, 1996). http://www.search.nytimes.com/search/daily.

95. See, for example, "Ghosts in the Commercials," *Time* (December 23, 1991): 56.

96. *USA Today* (May 21, 1996): 48.

97. "Ghoulish New Diet Coke Commercial," *TV Guide* 39.52 (December 28, 1991): 23.

98. Irene Lacher, "How Are Bogie's Heirs Managing," *Los Angeles Times, Calendar* (August 17, 1997): 79.

99. *People* (September 30, 1996): [10].

100. *Florida Times Union* (February 1, 1981): G6.

101. *Newsweek* (December 9, 1985): 62.

102. *Gentleman's Quarterly* 58.1 (January 1988): 162–167.

103. "Raves of Christmas," *American Way* (December 1993): 30.

104. "Neal Fox: Celebrating a Century of Style at Sulka," *Beverly Hills* (July 31, 1996): 7.

105. *Chronicle of Higher Education* (May 12, 1995): B4.

106. *Richmond Times*, rpt. *Commerce [Texas] Journal* (December 4, 1996): A5.

107. For example, *Passages: The Magazine of Northwest Orient Airlines* ran "Play It Again, Sam," by Colin Covert, on changes in video recorders and videodisc machines (May 1980): n.p.; Datsun Focus '81 contest for college students (letter, fall 1980); Charles Champlin, "Play It Again Hollywood" for *KCET Magazine* (March 1988): 25–28.

108. October 1983, radio ad, Jacksonville, Florida; Ralph Blumenthal, "Customs auction to feature stuff dreams are made of," *Dallas Morning News* (April 12, 1998).

109. "A Grand Celebration," *Newsweek* (July 13, 1987): 37.

110. *Dallas Morning News* (February 13, 1995): C1.

111. *Video* 5.12 (March 1982): inside back cover.

112. *Dallas Morning News* (July 9, 1995): C10.

113. KXAS, Channel 5, Dallas, Texas, March 7, 1996.

114. *Newsweek* (July 10, 1989): 34.

115. *World Press Review* 31 (August 1984): 62.

116. *Wall Street Journal* (February 3, 1987).

117. "Calvin Klein Ads Are Worse Than Porn," *Dallas Morning News* (August 25, 1995): 29A.

118. "Trade Spies: The CIA Takes Off the Gloves," *Newsweek* (March 6, 1995): 36.

119. Harmetz 309–310.

120. *The Santana News* 3.1 (spring 1991): [8].

121. Andrew Tolson, *Mediations: Text and Discourse in Media Studies* (London: Arnold, 1996), 12–13.

122. *Near Mint*, no. 3, (n.d.).

123. *Newsweek* (January 8, 1996): 8; *Best Fares Discount Travel Magazine* 16:2 (February 1998): 38.

124. *Architectural Digest* (April 1990): 272–274.

125. "Humphrey Bogart and Lauren Bacall," *People* (February 12, 1996): 140–141.

126. John Anders, "Fans of 'Falcon' Gather to Honor Bogey Man," *Dallas Morning News* (August 13, 1997): C1.

127. London: Half Brick Images, 1992. Back cover of *Humphrey Bogart: Cult Star*, trans. Richard Leigh (Berlin: Taco, 1987), 122–123.

128. Alicia Alderman, CMG Worldwide, personal correspondence, July 14, 1995.

129. Irene Lacher, "How Are Bogie's Heirs Managing," *Los Angeles Times, Calendar* (August 17, 1997): 79.

130. Telephone interview, July 14, 1995.

131. "Behold the Might of the Living Dead," *Dallas Morning News* (November 26, 1995): C8.

3

INTERVIEWS

There have been many fan magazine articles, based on interviews or studio publicity, and a number of articles ascribed to Bogart, but not much that peels away the facade. To some, there may not be a facade. What you see, and what you hear, is Bogart.

For all the good copy Bogart provided reporters and writers, there are surprisingly few substantive or extended interviews. As he told Helen Hover at the end of the long interview (1943), he did not like talking about himself, and he found boring those people who do. His most public interview was on *Person-to-Person*, with Edward R. Murrow, on Labor Day weekend, 1954. Informal and rambling, the questions and answers covered such topics as the nature of the weather in Los Angeles, whether Bacall and Bogart missed New York (she did; he did not), Bogart's loss of enthusiasm for doing a Broadway show, Alexander Woollcott's early and biting criticism of one of his theatrical "performances," Bacall's best picture and her famous photograph on Harry Truman's piano, the possibility of Bogart's working with Huston on *The Man Who Would Be King*, and an introduction to their son, Steve.

Always enamored of writers, Bogart, unlike many other actors, probably penned many of the essays attributed to him. Included in this section are two of them. The first, "Censorship," conveys his ideas about how "movies don't cause crime any more than prison wardens cause crime." Speaking about censorship in areas that he knew best, Bogart stressed that incursions on freedom of the press, radio, and movies must be stopped. Of all the essays attributed to Bogart, this one most sounds as if it came from the hands of a studio publicist. One of the telling signs is how so many of the Bogart essays contain personal observations that are accurate. Except when he was playing games with his interviewer (usually the fluffy fan magazine pieces), there is little that is fabricated or dishonest. This essay says he went to college, which is not accurate. In contrast, in "I Stuck My Head Out" Bogart defends his right to endorse a candidate for political office. His announced support of FDR on radio riled many of his fans. He defends his action, claiming that actors must do more than celebrate their latest movie or speak out on the merits of certain products. To Bogart, actors are no different from lawyers, doctors, business executives, or other citizens: they have the right to make their choices known. To maintain our democracy, all citizens, including actors, must speak out. His actions in 1947 and in 1952 echo his sentiments in this commentary.

Helen Hover's "Popping Questions at Humphrey Bogart" is an extended interview in question and answer format. While there is a fair amount of fluff in the give-and-take (Bogart as a dancer, his worst fault is eating walnuts in the living room), behind the humor there are responses that get at his essential nature and attitudes: hating phonies, playing love scenes, method actors, clothes, kids, the traits of a meaningful relationship, smoking, speaking his mind, and his fondness for chess, writers, and especially the sea. His exchange with young actors published in *Look* in 1956 captures some of his lasting attitudes toward Hollywood, acting, the star system, and the press.

The interview with Vincent Sherman, conducted in 1990 and published here for the first time, is a view of Bogart from a director who worked with him just as he was about to hit it big. Sherman worked as a writer on *Crime School* (1938), and later directed Bogart in *The Return of Dr. X* (1939) and *All Through the Night* (1942), and completed the final scene of John Huston's *Across the Pacific* (1942). Years later he was to direct *Bogie* (1980), a made-for-television biography of the actor. In this interview Sherman reflects on Bogart's professionalism, the influence of the theatre on his tolerance of poor roles and approach to acting, and his realistic and cynical persona.

"Censorship"
Humphrey Bogart
Hollywood Reporter
65.25 Sec 2. October 31, 1941

The blanket of censorship covers practically every country in the world these days except our own. And, judging from the editorials whenever the threat of censorship rears its head in this country, most of us seem agreed it is the No. 1 enemy of a free democracy.

This is where my pet peeve comes in. While people are always quick to take up the cudgels against censorship of the press or radio, any crackpot can advocate new forms of censorship for the movies, and not a voice is lifted in protest. There's something illogical about this indifference to censorship of the movies. After all, it's just as much a medium of public expression as are the radio and newspapers.

My own type of film has shown me how wrong and unfair advocates of censorship can be. For several years now, various groups have urged the banning of crime pictures on the ground that they influence youths to turn to crime. When Jimmy Walker was minority leader of the New York State Legislature there was a censorship fight on the floor of the House. A powerful group of pious bluenoses wanted to bar from circulation good books that dared to mention certain well-known facts of life. The bluenoses said the books were indecent, bawdy, lascivious, and would lead their young and innocent daughters astray. Jimmy stood the debate as long as he could, then he said, "I have been around a good deal, but I have never heard of a woman's being seduced by a book." That killed the censorship bill.

I have never heard of any youngster going wrong, turning to crime, because of the movies. It simply isn't possible. Our relation to crime is, in a sense, the same as the prison warden's. We don't create it. We deal with it after it has happened, and we always make the criminal look bad.

When I went to college, I studied under a professor of geology who wanted to make us understand how the different peoples of the world got the way they are, their racial tendencies and characteristics, dark-skinned Africans and fair-haired Swedes. He cited geography and climate and food and opportunities, and he summed it all up with the phrase: "We are what we are largely because we are where we are."

The proof of that argument can be found in the Uniform Crime Reports and the Department of Justice. The spot maps of cities show it. Not so long ago, I examined some maps showing juvenile delinquency, diphtheria, tuberculosis and murder quotients in a number of cities from New Orleans to Los Angeles. The maps all looked alike. Disease, crime and delinquency were invariably grouped in the same parts of the cities—in the slum districts. That is the cause of crime, not the motion picture.

About ten years ago, I was a guest at a little dinner party in Hollywood, and my hostess' son, a boy of about nine, sat across the table from me. He was an obnoxious little brat. His manners were very bad. He was hard-boiled, truculent and talked out of the side of his mouth. His mother finally whispered to me "Don't pay any attention to him now, but he is your greatest admirer. He thinks you are wonderful, sees all your pictures, and he's acting for you."

That didn't make me happy. I made friends with the boy and took him over to the studio one day. We rode along in silence for a little while, and then he said, "Say, Bogey, are you bad in this new picture?" I had a good part in the film, so I replied, "Why, no, as a matter of fact, I think I'm pretty good." "Aw, nuts," said the kid. "Dontcha smack anybody down?"

He felt better when I admitted I did put a couple of guys on the spot, and his next suggestion was that we ought to stick up the First National Bank, and when he grew tired of that we talked about baseball. The boy turned out all right, in spite of me and my bad acting. He came from the right kind of home, had the right kind of parents, and he attended the right kind of school. His environment was right, and no amount of motion pictures could have made a criminal of that boy. He could take the Cagneys and the Rafts and Bogey, or leave them alone. (He'd better not miss my latest epic, "The Gent From Frisco.")

Movies don't cause crime any more than prison wardens cause crime. It has been charged against the motion picture industry that we take a sympathetic attitude toward gangsters, thugs, racketeers and criminals. I deny that. After the things that have happened to me and my fellow screen heavies, I don't see how they can say that. So many criminals get killed in "The Maltese Falcon" that there's a special announcement at the end of the film saying, "If any persons are alive in this picture, it is purely coincidental."

There are groups that would like us to show the criminal always outmatched, poorly armed, and all policemen a good six inches taller, armed with tear gas and tommy guns, while the poor, dear, miserable rat of a gangster has to fight it out alone with only one measly little pistol. The object would be to deglamorize the gangster.

That's all right, but it seems to me they are asking us to go about it in the wrong way. It seems to me that disarming the gangster tends to add glamour rather than to remove it, and in some instances even make him seem gallant. What these critics forget is that the sympathies of the crowd are always with the underdog.

It is better, I think, to deglamorize His Excellency the Rat as we do it at Warners, by showing him well-armed, with an up-to-date arsenal, with smokescreen for his automobile, expensive short-wave radios, and other good equipment for the art of murder and arson. When we show a criminal on the screen like that, there is no doubt in the mind of the weakest low-grade moron who the hero is. The hero is unquestionably your friend and mine, the cop.

I have dealt with only one phase of the attempt to impose censorship on the movies. It is the phase with which I am most familiar. But there are men who advocate even more dangerous types of film censorship, and if America is to continue to have freedom of the press and radio, as well as every other type of freedom, these insidious enemies of freedom must be emphatically discouraged. Because once the movies are gagged, these men will move on to the other mediums of public expression. We have seen it happen in other countries, and it can happen here.

Copyright: *The Hollywood Reporter*

"I Stuck My Neck Out"
Humphrey Bogart
Saturday Evening Post
(February 10, 1945): 19, 87–88

On the evening of November 6, 1944, I exercised the privilege granted me by the Constitution of the United States and guaranteed by the Bill of Rights. I voiced my choice for the presidency. Right out loud and over the radio, I said I hoped F.D.R. would be elected.

In doing so, it seems, I stuck my neck out. In the weeks since I exercised that simple and fundamental prerogative of American citizenship, my mail has increased tremendously and my lexicon of epithets has grown accordingly. A great many of the letters have been complimentary. After all, there were enough Democrats in the country to win the election. An equal number—and they haven't all come from Republicans—are decidedly not the kind of letters friendly fans write to their favorite screen actors. They've taken me apart more violently than the filmscript writers did when I was playing gangster roles. And not being bound by the Hays-office censorship, they've called me names the scenarists couldn't use.

I may be as stupid as the more unflattering letters say, because I don't quite get it. I fail to see why I should be either praised or damned for doing no more, nor less, than millions of my fellow Americans did—and, in my humble opinion, should have done.

My political neck extending had one result for which I'm grateful. It brought letters from two or three thousand persons who'd never written me before, and that's more than my acting accomplished. Maybe it will take them to see my pictures, if only to hiss, and that will be fine. A lot of actors have won fortunes from hisses.

In searching through the denunciatory letters for a possible clue to my sin, I am forced to the conclusion that it lies solely in being an actor. Actors, many of the writers seem to believe, should be seen and heard only on the screen or stage. When they voice opinions on subjects more vital than love, swimming pools and the kind of breakfast food they prefer, they're stepping out of bounds.

"Take my advice, Mr. Bogart," wrote one of the more temperate of my critics, "stick to picture making and save your personal opinions under your hat. You'll stay in pictures longer and lose fewer fans."

"You cheap sissy—portrayer of gangster parts, have the asinine impudence to attempt to tell your superiors how to vote!" exploded a more agitated correspondent. "You of the celluloid, stay in your filmy field!"

Both of those letters were signed Anonymous.

Another Mr. Anonymous expressed pain that an "ignorant Hunky" like myself "could have come to this country to contaminate the air of free America." He also scolded me for changing my name and not having the courage to leave it the Bohunski or Bohinski he surmised it must have been originally.

THE RIGHTS OF ACTORS

For the record, I must say that I do not know how my parental ancestors acquired the name Bogart. I do know it has been in the family a great many generations—just as the family has been in this country for generations—and that I came by it through right of descent. I even acquired the Humphrey through the dual process of family possession and christening. It happens to have been my mother's maiden name. Incidentally, she did very well by it. A great many persons remember Maud Humphrey, artist and illustrator. My father also did very well by the name Bogart. He was a successful surgeon. So it happens, I'm proud of my name, and not because of any accomplishment of my own. Nevertheless, I have no quarrel with anybody changing his name, so long as he doesn't change it to Anonymous.

Getting back to the "original sin" of being an actor who has the stupidity or public interest—take your choice—to express honest opinions concerning his country's welfare—just how serious is it? The founders of our republic didn't seem to worry about it. But, of course, there wasn't a Hollywood when they drafted the Declaration of Independence, the Constitution and the Bill of Rights.

I've made myself tolerably familiar with those great documents. In none of them can I find a clause prohibiting actors from exercising any of the rights or privileges they affirm and guarantee. I do find in them ringing affirmations of the equal rights of all men.

"All men," I take it, includes actors, along with industrialists and laborers, conservatives and liberals, blacks and whites, Christians and Jews, Protestants and Catholics.

Actors and actresses happen to be men and women who earn their living practicing a highly specialized profession which requires, for success, years of hard study, experience and a reasonable amount of talent. In that respect, they differ no whit from physicians, lawyers, business executives, artisans—and politicians.

Most motion-picture actors and actresses own homes and property, which gives them a material as well as spiritual stake in their country. They even pay taxes. All of which, to my possibly biased way of thinking, qualifies them for all the rights of free expression enjoyed by their fellow citizens.

I hesitate to inject this note, but if it will help allay any fears about the possible evil effects of actors participating in politics, I think it belongs. An impartial examination of the collective and individual records of my profession will reveal that actors and actresses are doing their full, unstinting share in the nation's war effort. On the battlefields, behind the lines, on the camp-show tours, in the bond drives and on the home front, they are far more active than they are ever likely to be in political campaigns.

After some of the letters I have received, I frequently wonder why the recruiting officer didn't ask me if I was an actor, or intended to become one, when I enlisted in the Navy in 1917. He didn't. But he did ask me about my United States citizenship before he passed me on to the medics for examination. They didn't detect any signs of future antisocial tendencies, so the Navy took me. At that time I was just out of Phillips Andover Academy and hadn't the slightest idea of what profession I intended to follow. I did know I was a United States citizen and intended to remain one.

Later on, when I gravitated into acting, I had no idea I ever would be called upon, even by a vociferous minority, to renounce any of the simple rights of citizenship I thought I'd earned. But let's skip the earning business. In this country of ours, a person isn't required to earn citizenship privileges. He can be born into them—as I was—or acquire them through simple processes of law. We are given a priceless "free ride" on the liberty earned by the blood and courage of our forebears.

Only I don't believe in free rides, and that is why I am likely to have a permanently sore neck. I believe we must pay our freight in this democracy by working with all our intelligence, to keep it a living, vital force. That, to my way of reasoning, includes voicing our considered opinions on issues of the day, even on who we think should be our next President—be that individual Democrat or Republican.

The less caustic of my "stay in your filmy field" correspondents have softened their verbal shots with the explanation that actors shouldn't express political opinions because they exercise considerable influence upon the public. Let's give ourselves the break and say we have some influence. That doesn't give us an edge on the family physician, the parish pastor, the local newspaper and national magazine editor or any other individual who pulls his weight in society. And most of whom had their political says during the late campaign.

I'd hate to think that an ailing Democrat would cancel an appendectomy at the operating table because he suddenly discovered his surgeon was a Republican who'd spoken for Dewey. Or that a Republican housewife would struggle along with a plugged kitchen sink rather than call in a Roosevelt Democrat plumber. From my viewpoint, either of those acts would be as reasonable as boycotting an actor's pictures because of his political beliefs.

Personally, I've never known of honest political opinions affecting a surgeon's skill, poisoning a farmer's vegetables or influencing an actor's performance.

Hitler's Nazis, it is true, have some novel ideas along that line. They've banned much of the finest German music because the composers were something less than 100 per cent Aryan. They've burned the paintings and books of many of their greatest masters because the artists and authors did not agree with the Nazi political philosophy. They've even banned some actors for similar reasons.

My most impassioned correspondents will, I believe, agree that such ideas are best left in Germany.

Had all the critical letters come from the Anonymous fraternity, I'd have been glad to draw in my neck and let it heal for the next campaign. Fun is fun and I wouldn't want to deprive anybody of harmless and possibly educational literary exercise.

Many of them, however, came from serious, sober citizens who sounded sincere in their expressed beliefs that actors should wear political muzzles. Furthermore, this issue has had repercussions beyond the letter-writing circles.

When the "treat 'em nice so long as they stay in their sound-stage cages and perform entertaining tricks, but rap their noses when they come out of them" school of thought finds a champion in a Hollywood motion-picture trade paper, I think it is time for one of the "menagerie" to speak up.

Well, that happened during the last campaign. In its editorial column, this trade publication expressed the opinion that actors and actresses should keep out of political discussions, on the purely commercial grounds that, by voicing their views, they were bound to offend some of their fans, hurt their draw at the box office and thus bring in fewer dollars for this reasonably well-nourished motion-picture industry.

I've never had an aversion to money. I'm downright fond of the stuff. But not fond enough to earn it by keeping my mouth shut when I want to express my honest convictions.

Indicating the seriousness of this business and the extent to which it may go is the statement attributed to a young actor during the campaign. This chap apparently feared that the motion-picture producers were on the side of those who'd like to muzzle actors during political campaigns. He was quoted as saying that he probably was jeopardizing his career in pictures by speaking out for Tom Dewey.

Somebody either misquoted that young man or fed him some hot misinformation. If he'd been reading the newspapers or keeping up with his Hollywood contemporaries, he'd have known that a lot of them were speaking out for Dewey without the slightest fear of losing their careers or even their contract options.

I can name one because she happens to be one of the biggest stars of our own studio. She's Ann Sheridan, who was as keen for Dewey as I was for F.D.R.

Ann wired to J. L. Warner, our mutual boss, and a Roosevelt man if there ever was one, asking that she be permitted to linger on in New York a few weeks to do some campaigning for Dewey.

J. L. wired her back the permission and a bossly blessing to the effect: "Isn't this a wonderful country where we can campaign for different men and still remain friends?"

I'd like to add a couple of amens to that, along with the statement that if any actors think they can't express their political opinions freely and keep their jobs, they're either seeing bogymen or have the wrong kind of bosses. I'm inclined to think it is the former.

It may be a moot question what good, except to their own souls, actors, painters, musicians and members of kindred artistic professions may accomplish by participating in politics. We may be giddy dopes or impractical dreamers incapable of coping with down-to-earth problems of governing ourselves. Only I seem to recall a distinguished gentleman by the name of Ignace Paderewski, who not only was the world's greatest concert pianist but a great enough patriot—and politician—to serve with distinction as prime minister and minister of foreign affairs of his native Poland.

History records Benvenuto Cellini as one of the greatest artists of all time.

Less brilliantly, but still brightly, it records the activities of this same genius as a defender of Rome in the year 1527. Because of his political activities, Cellini's life became one banishment and restoration after another. It didn't seem to affect the quality of his craftsmanship.

What, no actors yet? Well, I'll give you one. Name of François Joseph Talma. No Paderewski or Cellini, I'll grant you, but he was good enough to be one of the Emperor Napoleon's intimate friends and closest political advisers. He died in 1826. Give us time, and we may produce a prime minister or president yet.

Winston Churchill, whose voice and dramatic delivery qualify him for stardom in almost any acting role, is listed in his current biography as an author. He seems to have done all right in politics.

Our own Paul Revere, research informs us, was better known in his own time for engraving and silver and gold smithing than he was for horseback riding. And Thomas Jefferson was a right smart violin player.

There may possibly be a few die hards who still insist the country would be better off had Jefferson stuck to his fiddle playing, but I doubt any American can be found who wishes Paul Revere hadn't left his engraving to gallop around the countryside yelling that the redcoats were coming.

I'm not trying to compare any of the present generation of actors with those legendary gentlemen. I'm merely trying to point out that you can't tell under what professional or artistic exterior political talent and patriotic sentiments may lurk.

George Washington was a country farmer and surveyor, before he became the father of this country. Benjamin Franklin was printer, author and scientist. Benjamin Rush, one of the signers of the Declaration of Independence, was a physician.

If that doesn't exactly make a case for actors, it does make a case for equal opportunities and equal rights of citizenship. All we actors want is our share of them.

We don't think it is right or American to be threatened with boycott of our screen performances because we spoke out for Franklin Roosevelt or Tom Dewey any more than we think it is right for German composers and painters to have their works destroyed because they don't believe in Hitler's Nazi philosophy.

That's so simple it may sound absurd. If it is absurd, it is equally serious for members of my profession. We are receiving such threats, get them in every mail. Our right to livelihood is threatened if we persist in exercising our right of citizenship. But while we don't like them, I'm quite sure none of us is taking those threats too seriously or is actually fearing the slow starvation some of my new mail acquaintances are promising me. We have altogether too much confidence in the good common sense of the overwhelming majority of the American people.

Personally, I'm going to keep right on sticking my neck out, without worrying about its possible effect upon my career. I love doing it. You may meet so many interesting people that way.

Copyright: *Saturday Evening Post* 1945

"Popping Questions at Humphrey Bogart"
Motion Picture (December 1943): 38–40, 56, 58
By Helen Hover

Q. What do the make-up men do to make you prettier for the screen?

A. They just spray a little Flit on me and say, "Get going." In *Maltese Falcon* and *Conflict* they did tack a carpet on my head—hairpiece, to you—thinking it might make me look a bit more romantic. That taught them a lesson!

Q. What is your pet gripe in women's clothes?

A. Those hats that look like a well-kept grave. Tight fitting slacks on girls with Model T figures. Those wedgies that make their feet look like Japanese toe dancers.

Q. How do you keep fit?

A. I'm either working or sailing, so I never have time to keep fit. Golf is my favorite game. I've been known to play a hot set of croquet, but the way I play it my opponent almost lost a leg.

Q. How are you and your wife, Mayo, most alike?

A. We both hate phonies. Actors with a message give us a laugh. We've never been in the social register and live in constant fear that it could happen—but we doubt it. We love "characters"—wonderful guys like Louis Bromfield [author and friend].

Q. How are you two most unlike?

A. Mayo looks better in shorts.

Q. What do you notice first in a woman?

A. You mean besides her legs. Seriously—I notice whether she's a regular—a down-to-earth nice person like Mary Astor, Barbara Stanwyck and Annie Sheridan, not a silly dame who twitches and gives those so-called feminine charms an awful beating.

Q. How do you rate as a dancer?

A. Fred Astaire will never have to worry. I just hang on and pray.

Q. Do you like to argue?

A. Certainly. I like to argue about politics providing it's with someone who knows what he's talking about and I can learn something. I'll always argue about the cheap chiselers and petty racketeers you find in every walk of life. I'll always argue about guys who pull fast ones and are protected because "it's for the good of the industry." I always say it's coming to them—so let 'em have it.

Q. What is your best quality as a husband?

A. If I were sure Mrs. Bogart wasn't going to read this, I'd say my devastating charm, my angelic disposition, my sweet, simple love of life and living! However, I think Mrs. B. could answer this one better—and her statement wouldn't be the same as mine.

Q. What is your worst fault as a husband?

A. I eat walnuts in the living room.

Q. What improvement would you suggest in women's make-up?

A. I could do without those shiny-faced dames who look like they've just had a mayonnaise massage.

Q. Now that you're a screen lover, do you like doing love scenes?

A. I hate 'em. Most of them look phony—nine times out of ten the lady in question is thinking about her best angle or whether her lipstick is getting smeared. When you remember there are about five dozen people on the set who are either bored or amused at your "technique" it ceases to be a personal pleasure or privilege.

Q. What type of actors, whom you've known, give you the greatest pain?

A. The creeps who have to get into a "mood" before they can play a scene. You know, they tell you they don't quite "feel" it.

Q. What is your favorite form of entertainment or fun?

A. To sit around with a congenial group of good story tellers. Writers and newspaper reporters usually have wonderful yarns to spin. I enjoy this especially if I don't have to keep an eye on the time because I have an early call.

Q. Did you ever wish you were handsomer?

A. What? And be deprived of hearing a producer say, "Bogey, I've got just the part for you. The guy you play looks and acts like a mug!"

Q. What is your disposition when you get up in the morning?

A. It all depends on what my dissipation has been the night before.

Q. If you weren't an actor, at what sort of work would you be happiest?

A. Just being on a boat—in any capacity.

Q. Do you worry about what people think of you?

A. Long ago I stopped it. I learned you can please some of the people some of the time and none of the people all of the time. I want people to like me, of course. But the thing that's most important is not what people think of me—but what I think of myself.

Q. What nicknames or terms of endearment do you and your wife call each other?

A. I've always called Mayo "Sluggy." My Scotty is called "Sluggy." So is my boat. Anything I love is "Sluggy." Mayo just calls me Bogey.

Q. Have you ever grown a moustache?

A. Just once. Mayo said it tickled. I shaved it off.

Q. On what subject do you consider yourself most un-informed?

A. On several: How to do the Samba; what the well-dressed gentleman should wear; how to pluck a duck; babies—just babies.

Q. What do you think is the most desirable quality in a wife?

A. A sense of humor and, brother, she'd need one if she married me. Companionship—the right kind of companionship is a wonderful thing and especially in the picture business where a girl must understand the peculiar and irregular demands of a career.

Q. Do you carry much money on you?

A. Just a reasonable amount. I try to stick to a weekly allowance.

Q. What one word would you choose to describe your personality?

A. Somnolent.

Q. What's the most usual bone of contention at home?

A. Politics—but don't let's go into that. Mayo and I have yet to agree on a political point. It makes for fights, but home life would be awfully dull without them.

Q. How are you least like the tough guys you play on the screen?

A. The only rod I carry is the one I use on my boat for fishing. Instead of raising the roof, I raise canaries. So far I've never bumped off any helpless ladies or strangled any of the neighbor's kiddies. However, there's a young man up the street from us who plays Rosie the Riveter all night long!!!!

Q. Who does most of the talking at the dinner table?

A. When we have guests it's every man for himself. There never is too much talking because we don't "dine." In fact, we don't like a dining room and ours is just a small nook by a window. When we're alone it's about fifty-fifty. Being an actress herself, Mayo knows what it means to have to talk for eight hours a day so she'll carry the conversation when I feel like relaxing.

Q. Have you ever heard any unflattering remarks about yourself?

A. Not only have I heard them, but when I've read them I've cut them out and collected them. Recently I was given a new seven-year contract by Warner Brothers. When Jack Warner signed it, he said, "You know, it's unusual for us to sign an actor to a straight seven years. The reason we're doing it with you is—nothing could happen to that face that would hurt it."

Q. Can you do any household jobs?

A. Certainly. I'm the best fixer-upper in these here parts. What I can do to a broken down vacuum cleaner shouldn't happen to Hitler. On second thought—it *should*!

Q. What unbecoming personal mannerism have you had to overcome?

A. I have a habit of frowning. Sometimes I do it when people talk to me which gives the impression that I'm annoyed. I'm gradually overcoming it.

Q. Do you like to have your wife visit you on the set?

A. Of course. She's an excellent actress and often makes very helpful suggestions.

Q. Are you an easy mark?

A. And how! The times I've been played for a sucker are too often—and too painful to recall. I've fallen for everything except buying the Brooklyn Bridge.

Q. In what ways are you lazy?

A. Wherever it involves work.

Q. What sort of card player are you?

A. I'm a chess and gin rummy boy myself. I've been carrying on a chess game with the boys, via the mail, and getting a terrific bang out of it. I'd rather play chess than do anything else I know. Well—almost.

Q. What bad habit have you which annoys your friends?

A. To me it isn't a bad habit. I speak my mind. If the shoe happens to fit I can't help it.

Q. Are you addicted to any nervous habits?

A. I do an awful lot of pacing up and down and I smoke too many cigarettes. I do it to keep from getting nervous—but that's what it probably does to others.

Q. What is your main idiosyncrasy?

A. I hate to wear shoes. No, I don't walk around like the barefoot boy, but I go for moccasins and the soft, easy things that couldn't possibly be called shoes. Mayo says she hasn't been able to get shoes on me since we've been married. Now don't all ask for my number eighteen [ration] coupon! It's been promised.

Q. What bores you most?

A. Jerks who talk about themselves and enjoy it. People who change their names and forget that you can't change a background.

Q. What type of clothes do you like best on a woman?

A. Tailored clothes—the kind that leave a little to your *own* imagination.

Q. Do you take vitamin pills?

A. I do *not*. That wouldn't be a crack, by any chance?

Q. What is your favorite way of loafing?

A. Not wearing shoes—living on my boat—talking about everything—and in general doing anything *but* make movies.

Q. Of what personal accomplishment are you most proud?

A. Now *really*!

Q. What type of food do you like best?

A. Plain food and none of this business of hiding it under gravy or sauces. I want to see what I eat. And thumbs down on those fancy desserts that look like Mae West on a spree. Mayo refuses, at times, to have any part of me at mealtimes. Says she can't look at the same dish night after night, so she threatens to eat alone or in some other part of the house. I have no imagination in food. For lunch it's always bacon and eggs and toast. Sometimes I make up my mind I'm going to have something different—but noontime comes and it's bacon and eggs and toast. The waiter doesn't even ask for my order any more. He sees me coming and that's it.

Q. What don't you like about acting?

A. Getting up at dawn. This awful morning rising kills me. Mayo has to prop me up after breakfast or I'd go back to sleep. Another thing I could be happier without in the business are some of the people you meet. Like the balloon-headed type, for instance, who believe their own publicity and don't realize they have bathrooms in their homes the same as everyone else.

Q. What is your sore spot?

A. When it's pointed out to me that something isn't "the right thing to do." By whose standard is a thing right or wrong?

Q. What gives you the jitters?

A. A little thing like a sugar bowl, believe it or not. I can't even sit at a table that holds a sugar bowl simply because the sound of sugar grating drives me wild.

Q. What was one of the biggest boners you ever pulled?

A. I was on location shooting some war stuff. Next to me stood a very nice young soldier. We started to talk. Suddenly over the hill came a general heading toward us. "Well, here comes a nice fat brass hat," I said to the soldier. For a moment there was dead silence. Then the soldier answered, "Yes, he is. He's my father."

Q. What is your favorite off-screen attire?

A. Something that should happen only to a beachcomber. Dirty dungarees, sweat shirt, yachting cap and old sneakers.

Q. What three people would you choose to be with if you were marooned on a desert island?

A. I'm a married man, so let's skip this one!

Q. Are you temperamental?

A. Temperamental—no. Temper—yes. But only after I have exhausted every means of trying to keep peace. Then I let it fly. I always try first to be sure that my reason is justified. The one thing I don't do is carry a grudge. I believe in getting things off my chest and forgetting about it.

Q. Who makes the decisions in the family—you or Mayo?

A. I usually make the decisions as far as my studio life is concerned. Mayo keeps the home fires burning and an excellent job she does, so that's her province.

Q. What actresses do you think have the most sex appeal?

A. Margaret O'Brien and Ouspenskaya.

Q. In what ways don't you resemble an actor?

A. In almost every way. No station wagon. No berets. No boyish bob with a careless lock on my manly forehead. How my memoirs will smell!

Q. What do you do when you have insomnia?

A. A good murder mystery will have me sleeping like a baby. I can't even keep my eyes open long enough to find out if the butler did it.

Q. What is your most modest quality?

A. I dislike talking as much about myself as I'm forced to do in this article!

Copyright: *Motion Picture* December 1943

"Bogart on Hollywood: An Old Pro Tells Some Young Hopefuls How to Make Good in the Movie World"
Look 20 (August 21, 1956): 96–98, 100–101
Produced by William Attwood

People who meet Humphrey Bogart for the first time are occasionally affronted but seldom disappointed. He is the kind of Hollywood personality who can, and often does, live up to his public reputation. He snarls at strangers; he needles guests who take themselves seriously; he makes irreverent remarks about the Industry; he drinks. Unlike some stars whose fans expect them to behave like the boy next door, Bogart can afford to behave as he pleases and when he pleases.

The reason, of course, is that Bogart is as securely established as any actor in Hollywood. At 56, he is a real pro who is respected in the industry for what he can do in front of a camera. He made his reputation, as an actor, the hard, professional way—by practicing his trade for 13 years on Broadway and 22 in Hollywood. But not everybody knows how much he cares about his craft.

Not long ago, six young actors were invited to his house for an evening of shop talk and advice. Their names were Janet Lake, Gerry Gaylor, Dennis Hopper, Bob Benevedes, Tom Laughlin and Jerry Frank, and their ages ranged from 19 to 25. Some had studio contracts; others were studying in drama school; all were ambitious.

Bogart greeted his guests one at a time while his wife, Betty—who also answers to the name of Lauren Bacall—got some cups and poured coffee. After mixing himself a highball, Bogart settled back in his favorite armchair, with the warning that "I don't want to answer a lot of idiotic questions about glamour and stuff like that."

Somebody asked him how many pictures he'd made, and Bogart replied, "I think about 75. Anyway, I claim one more than Spencer Tracy. But that doesn't make me an authority out here. I just have my opinions." He sipped his drink and bared his teeth. "Having said that—well, go ahead."

Frank: Do they really want new faces in Hollywood?

Bogart: You're damned right! The real beef is not that they're tired of us, but that we cost too much. They'd love to get a new Gary Cooper for a tenth of the money.

Frank: But aren't the big stars today all personalities?

Bogart: Sure they are. I happen to be one of them. It took ten to fifteen years to make us personalities. Gable or Cooper can do anything in a picture, and nobody cares. Gable could murder everybody in a picture, and people would say, "Oh, that's just good old Clark."

Benevedes: Who are your favorites among the younger actors?

Bogart: Well, we had Jimmy Dean. And there's Arthur Kennedy—a very fine actor. And Marlon Brando—a good actor, but first a personality. He's the same in every part he plays.

Gaylor: You've been around a long time . . .

Bogart: You're telling me!

Gaylor: What would you say was most important for a newcomer with talent and looks—I mean, to achieve success in acting?

Bogart: You've got to be lucky. Be in the right place at the right time. Of course, a girl can be discovered sitting on a stool at a soda fountain, but it's not so easy for a young man.

Benevedes: What is the thing for us to do then?

Bogart: Keep working. Never be "available." Keep playing in the theater or TV, anywhere, as often as you can. Eventually, if you're any good, somebody will see you. Of course, the best way to get into the picture business is to go on the stage first.

Bacall: (leaning on the back of Bogey's chair) You learn more on the stage.

Bogart: I know you don't learn a damned thing in pictures! But live television—that's good practice—almost like the stage.

Hopper: Most people in Hollywood can't act anyway.

Bogart: You're right, if you mean the so-called young personality boys.

Bacall: They're the ones who try to imitate Brando, for instance.

Bogart: They don't last long.

Hopper: But there's always another one, right behind him.

Bogart: Sure—and that's why talent should have a showcase. By the way, has anybody here studied the Stanislavsky method?

Laughlin: Yes.

Bogart: Can you tell me what the hell it is?

Laughlin: (haltingly) Stanislavsky claims that real interpretation comes from the subconscious... We can't touch it or control it. But if we use all our will power—we can release the flow from our subconscious.

Bogart: If you'll pardon the expression, you've got me completely screwed up. But I know this: The audience is always a little ahead of you. If a guy points a gun at you, the audience knows you're afraid. You don't have to make faces. You just have to believe that you are the person you're playing and what is happening is happening to you.

Hopper: (abruptly) Most people in their private lives, especially in Hollywood, have no sense of truth. They're affected.

Bogart: Wait a minute! You can't say most people in Hollywood. You don't know most people in Hollywood.

Hopper: What I'm trying to say is—without a sense of truth in their own lives, how can they have it in front of the camera?

Bogart: Did it ever occur to you that nobody can be a good actor without a sense of truth, of right and wrong?

Laughlin: I don't think there is nearly so much hypocrisy here in Hollywood as in a small town.

Bogart: You're so right! And if you want to be an actor, be honest with yourself; don't let them push you around. When you believe in something, you fight for it even though you may suffer for it. The actors are better judges than any studio as to what is good for us. As soon as your name gets known and you feel you can say, "I won't do this," if you think the part isn't right—go ahead, say it. In the long run, it will pay off... Just remember to put some dough aside for the times you're suspended.

Frank: What made you come to Hollywood?

Bogart: There was more money out here.

Laughlin: Did you have some purpose in becoming an actor?

Bogart: What's yours? Why do you want to be an actor?

Laughlin: It sounds conceited—but I believe I have something to give.

Hopper: With me, it's a lot of things. To do something in life, to be somebody—but be better.

Bogart: Why acting? Why not farming? Or something else?

Hopper: I'm best suited for acting . . . I want . . . I don't know the urge to be better . . .

Bogart: (smiling) Yes, all right. Go on.

Hopper: . . . to be better than the other guy . . . I don't know.

Bogart: To get out of the millions?

Hopper: Yes.

Bogart: You're O.K., kid.

Lake: I really didn't want to until some people pushed me. Acting makes me feel good.

Bogart: Well, it's more fun than any other kind of work.

Gaylor: I think the highest point is the applause.

Bogart: Sure it is. It's wonderful. It has nothing to do with vanity. It's the satisfaction—like telling a joke and having everybody laugh. (Turns around as Frank Sinatra comes in.) Hiya, kid. We're talking about acting. What do you know about acting? Ever hear of the Stanislavsky method?

Sinatra: I use the Sinatra method myself.

Bogart: Mix yourself a drink. (To the group) Go on.

Lake: Is it harder to break into pictures today than it was 20 years ago?

Bogart: I don't think so. It's tough as hell starting from out here, but through the theater, it's not so tough. Sinatra there started singing for a band. I came from New York with a contract, so I never had to try.

Gaylor: What do you think of the older stars still getting all the good parts?

Bogart: There is a very good financial reason for that. If you have $1,200,000 invested in a picture, Gary Cooper will get your money back. It's too bad, because the movies need new people. We're getting very tired.

Benevedes: And we're out of work.

Bogart: Youth always wants to get there very quick. Take it easy. You have plenty of time.

Bacall: (dryly) *Men* have, you mean.

Bogart: No—girls, too—if you're an actress. As I said before, somebody will find you, if you've got talent.

Gaylor: Should you go to parties to meet the "right people"?

Bogart: NO!

Sinatra: That way, you meet all the wrong people.

Frank: Don't you have to put up with a lot from reporters?

Bogart: A star has to accept a certain invasion of privacy. If you get loaded in a bar, well, you can't get mad if it's printed.

Lake: How do you feel about the star system in the studios?

Bogart: I'm against it.

Sinatra: Watch it, Bogey!

Bogart: Quiet boy. What I mean is—pictures used to be "vehicles" for stars. Now they get better stories because they don't always write with a star in mind. Good stories *make* stars.

Frank: What movies do you like best?

Bogart: I don't like to go to the movies. Most of them are not very good.

Benevedes: What gratification do you get from working in the movies? Don't you miss the applause you get on the stage?

Bogart: I have a charming wife, two beautiful kids, a gorgeous home, a yacht—and I've had the applause. But I'll be damned if I know why I work so hard. Sinatra and I were talking about it the other day. Working is therapy, I guess—it keeps us on the wagon. This is a very bad town to be out of work in. After a week or so not working, you're so bored you don't know what the hell to do.

Laughlin: Many people say there should be an actors' lab out here. Why doesn't somebody do something about it?

Bogart: The answer to your question is—they don't know what acting is in Hollywood. They think it's easy to act. They think actors are a necessary evil. But if you still want to be an actor, don't say "I want to be a star"—just concentrate on acting, learn your trade. You've got to develop confidence if you're to play a scene right and confidence comes from knowing the ropes. Personally, I think you're all in a hell of a mess—wanting to be actors. But keep trying. Keep trying, and it may happen.

Bacall: You mean they may turn out like you? God forbid!

Bogart: Pay no attention to Miss Bacall.

Sinatra: Pay no attention to Mr. Bogart.

Interview: Director Vincent Sherman on Bogart and Filmmaking

Vincent Sherman, who was raised in south Georgia, was in Jacksonville, Florida, as a special guest of the annual Jacksonville Film Festival. This interview took place on August 5, 1990, at the Jacksonville Jewish Center, one of several locations hosting festival events. Sherman has recently published an autobiography, *Studio Affairs: My Life as a Film Director* (University Press of Kentucky, 1996), which discusses his background in the theater, his writing and directing, his personal life, and his impressions of the movie industry at the height of the studio system.

Gerald Duchovnay: Your first relation with Humphrey Bogart was when you were working on *Crime School*. How did that come about?

Vincent Sherman: Yes, that's right. I had been at the studio about two or three months, I think, on the first six-month deal. What happened was that Brynie Foy [who was in charge of B pictures at Warners] called me and said, "Look, I've just been given the Dead End Kids." (They were under contract to the studio.) "We're gonna do a picture called *Crime School* and Humphrey Bogart is gonna play another villain—he's going to play the lead. He said, "Get two scripts. Take the first part of *Mayor of Hell* and the second part of *San Quentin* and put the two together." That was called a "switch." This was Thursday. And he said, "I'll need a script by Monday." "Well, Jesus Christ," I said. "My God. OK, OK." And as I was walking back to my office I said, "God, it's going to take that long to read it and think about how to put the two scripts together." By the time I got to the office, he called and said, "Look you're new at this. I'm gonna get Crane Wilbur, an old hand. He's gonna do a first draft and you can take it and polish it because you know these kids and so forth." So I said, "Fine." On Monday, Crane Wilbur delivered the script—just changed the names. And I read it—it seemed to read all right, but the second part didn't quite mesh with the first part. So I went to the director and I said, "Lew [Lewis Seiler], I don't think that this seems to work here." And I told him what I thought was wrong and how I thought we could fix it, and he said, "Good." He said, "You fix it, because I've got to look for sets.... You get the changes." In those days it didn't take long to prepare on a B picture. I think the picture cost $186,000—the whole movie. So I went to my office and I made the changes. I gave them to the producer, Foy; he looked over them, just glanced through them because if they were all right with the director it was OK [with] him—[and he] put the thing through. And then he said to me, "You go down on the picture as dialogue director." So on *Crime School* I'm listed as dialogue director and screenplay.

At the end of it we had 120 blue pages. I had rewritten the whole damn thing. Now the irony of that story... Well, what happened was this. I saw the first two or three days' work. That was the first time I had ever been on a movie set except when I was an actor a few days with Barrymore. And the scene seemed pretty good, but they were lifeless. Each guy spoke and had his own line, and I said, "Lew, I think the scenes are good, but they don't have the sparkle that these kids usually have. And I think it's because we have given them separate lines and they don't sound spontaneous, [or] improvisational." So he said, "Yeah, you may be right." So I said, "Well, I tell you what. Why don't you rehearse them in the morning the way you want to set the scene up where the camera is going to be where your cuts are going to be and let me take them outside and work with them." He said, "You do that." So I took them outside and said, "Boys, you know what the scene is about. Now forget the lines that are written in the script, but adlib." We said adlib, not improvise in those days. I said, "So adlib the things you feel like saying." And I would listen to the scene, and I sat down with a pad and I scribbled down what their best lines were. Then I said, "OK." Then we'd do it again and I'd preserve those lines. Then I'd go in and make a copy. Do you see? Then give it to the director and the boys knew the scene. And it came to life. Well, we were about two or three days behind schedule and with about a week or ten days before we finished the picture. And the night before the director said to me, "Gee, this scene we have to do in the morning is not very good. I wish to hell we could think of what to do with it." And I said, "Gee Lew, I don't know. I'm tired. I've been working very hard, but let me think about it and see. You're right." So I went home that night and thought about it and around ten o'clock I got an idea and I called him. And I said, "Lew how would it be if we did this, and this, and this?" He said, "Great. Write it and bring it in in the morning." I said, "I'm tired tonight, but I'll come in early in the morning and type it up and give it to you." He said, "Great."

I came in the morning (in those days we started shooting at nine o'clock), around eight o'clock, and I was typing away and I came across a little snag, and you know how it is—you stop to figure out how to clean that up and at nine o'clock he was starting to rehearse with the boys. And I said, "I'm not quite finished, but I will be in ten, fifteen minutes." He said, "OK, keep on. Keep on, I'll vamp." You know how musicians vamp? He's faking rehearsing. So he'd start shooting at nine, anyway. He's down there and I'm typing away in my dressing room and the door flung open and the production manager [is there]—a guy named Tenney Wright—a tough guy. He said, "What the hell are you doing?" I said, "I'm trying to fix this scene Mr. Wright, for the director." "Goddamn it," he said, "that's why this picture's three days behind schedule. You're rewriting; you're a dialogue director. You got no right to be rewriting this picture. I'm gonna tell Mr. Warner that it's your fault we're three days behind." And I just started, making $200 a week, and I was very independent. And I said, "Mr. Wright, I've been working ten, eleven hours every night, you know, and if you and Mr. Warner don't like what I'm doing you and Mr. Warner can take this job and shove it!" He slammed the door in my face and he ran out.

Now the picture opened in New York as an A picture, not a B picture. It got four stars, and was doing tremendous business. It cost $186,000 and grossed over 2 million that year. It was the biggest money-maker Warner's had ever—that and *Robin Hood* were the two big money-makers of the year. And *Crime School* was the bigger money-maker based upon the cost and the percentage. Well, because I was blamed for everything during the making of the picture, I got the lion's share of the credit when the picture was over. Listen to what this kid did, he's the one that was responsible. Well, everybody pitched. Bogie pitched in, the Dead End Kids pitched in, the director—everybody contributed, but I got the lion's share of the credit. And that's the irony of the picture business.

GD: Did you work with Bogart or was your focus on the Dead End Kids?

VS: Well, no. Bogie was in it and helped very much, but we became very friendly. Also, he knew that I had played the same part in the play that he had played (Baby-Face Martin, the gangster in *Dead End*). I played it on the road, and we ended up in California, in Los Angeles, at the Biltmore Theater. He came to the theater too. There was that kind of communion.

GD: Was *Crime School* your first encounter with Bogart?

VS: That was my first experience with Bogart. And then after that, Foy said I had a write up working on a picture for Kay Francis. Kay Francis had been a big star. In order to get rid of her, Warner said, "You're gonna make pictures for Foy." Well, most actors and actresses, if you said to them you're gonna make pictures for Foy, they just refused to do it. Kay Francis was one of the highest paid actresses in Hollywood. Warner was sure that she was gonna say, "I wouldn't think of it" and walk out on her contract. You wouldn't have to pay her a thing—they were paying her $5,000 a week in those days. It was a lot of money. You're talking like $100,000 to $200,000 a week today. She said, "As long as they pay my salary, I'll sweep the stage if they give me a broom." So Foy said to me, "I've got a writer. He's working on a script for Kay Francis. She's gonna do—we're gonna do a remake of Paul Muni's *Dr. Socrates*. I said, "Jesus Christ, how can they put Kay Francis in a part that Paul Muni's played?" But it worked. And then he said, "But this writer is not giving me what I want. I wish you'd take it over." So I went down, and a guy named Joey Bricker and I took over, and rewrote the script. I went down on the set as dialogue director and they made a picture called *King of the Underworld*. And Bogart was in that. He played the villain. When it was first done with Muni, Barton MacLane was the villain, a gangster. And now in this one, Bogart is a gangster. And so that was the second time I worked with him. And the next time I worked with him was, of course, when I became a director.

GD: What was the catalyst for that change?

VS: Foy called me to the office. Now, I had been down on the set on three of the pictures that I had worked on as a writer and been there as a dialogue director. So, he called one day and he said, "Vince, Warner wants to make some new directors and I recommended you." And he said, "What do you think?" And I said, "Well, I think I know how to handle actors and I think I know how to tell a story, but I'm not sure that I know much about the camera and cutting." And McKay said, "Oh the hell with that, you'll pick that up later—the mechanics. I'll give you Sidney Hickcox as cameraman; he's been in the business twenty years. He'll help you and go ahead." And that's it. He had two stories—a comedy and a little mystery/horror picture, and I said, "I'll take the mystery/horror picture." And sure enough, I had Dennis Morgan in one part and Wayne Morris in another part, and that's when Warner said, "Look, I'm going to give you this guy Bogart to play that guy that was hanged and brought back to life, and for Christ sakes see if you can get him to do something else besides Duke Mantee!" So, that's how I got Bogart in the first picture I ever directed.

GD: What was your reaction when you saw the script for *Return of Dr. X*?

VS: I thought it was all right. It was a cornball little mystery. By the way, the reason I took it was I knew I wasn't going to get Cary Grant, and at that time they'd given me some of the B pictures. And I knew that I wasn't dependent on cast for *Return of Dr. X*. When you're doing a mystery/horror picture they come to see the mystery/horror picture and not to see who's in that. I felt that I had a greater chance commercially with a mystery/horror film than I did making a comedy. They were going to do a remake of *Kid Galahad*. I said I'd rather do the mystery/horror picture. There was another guy, George Army, who had been the cutter. He chose *Kid Galahad*. He didn't make it. And I did that picture, which was successful at that time for a B picture. And I continued.

GD: You made an anti-Nazi film, *All Through the Night*, also with Bogart. Both, *Return of Dr. X* and *All Through the Night* are in many ways against character for Bogart.

VS: Yes, that's right.

GD: How was it working with him on those films? On the set, was he complaining about *The Return of Dr. X* and why he was doing it?

VS: No, no. The funny thing was this. When we were doing *Dr. X*, he was just doing one villain after another. Now Bogie came from the theater as I did, and even if it was a cornball, crappy part, you tried to do the best you could with it. So he and I sat and talked seriously about what to do with it. And I said, "Well, you know what would be nice—you should have a white streak in [your] hair because that's when he was electrocuted." That's right, he was electrocuted and not hanged. And I got the idea of him walking around with a rabbit and stroking it because that was life—that was blood. We gave him that pasty look because he had been executed and then brought to life. So, we went out and said, "What can we do to make it interesting?" We weren't laughing. Sure it was corn, but because we both came from the theater you did the best you could. And you say, "How can we make it better? How can we make it as good as possible?" It's what I was trying to say when I said you tell a story with the script as a guideline. "How can I dress this up? How can I make this laugh work? How can I build the suspense here? How can I create the mood that is necessary here?" Those are all elements that go into directing a film.

GD: In that particular film and *All Through the Night* was there a great deal of collaboration or did much of it come from him?

VS: Oh, no. He was fine. It worked very well. Well, he pulled a very funny prank. A guy had worked on the screenplay who was gay, but a very nice man. And Bogie said to me once, "Jesus Christ, who wrote this fucking dialogue? Oh, for Christ sake. I wouldn't say a thing like that; that's stamp your foot dialogue." I said, "What do you feel?" He said, "Why don't I just say so and so?" I said, "Well, why don't you just say so and so?" He'd say, "Yeah, yeah, that's better." He was grousing a lot in that film. You know why? Because he was being underpaid; he wasn't making very much money. I don't think he was making more than $400 a week at that time and I was making $250—no, maybe in *All Through the Night* he was making a little bit more. But I can only tell you at that time nobody would ever have thought that he would have been a great leading man or would have played Ingrid Bergman's lover. Every director, every producer on the lot thought he was great as a villain, but never as . . .

GD: And yet he played juveniles and young lovers in the theater.

VS: Why sure. In theater—absolutely. Absolutely. See, in those days too, you were working. That was the first place. And you were being paid a weekly check, and that was better than sitting around in New York and waiting for something to happen. The life of the average actor in New York in those days, if he got 20 weeks of work out of the year he was lucky. So, with the exception of maybe half a dozen stars it was a tough way to make a living. So pictures came as a welcome relief because when you went under contract you got paid every week.

GD: Was there any difficulty with him because of the personal problems he was having at home?

VS: Yeah. He was married to Mayo Methot when I was working with him. He came in one morning (I've got this in the book) . . . He came in one morning looking terrible, and I said, "Jesus Christ, What's the matter with you?" "Oh," he said, "I got home last night late and I've been drinking and that bitch locked me out. I slept on the front lawn." They had terrible, terrible battles. He settled down after he married Bacall and then he began going up the ladder too, but for a long time he had a rough time—he played nothing but villains at the studio.

One night I was shooting late on Saturday night; in those days we shot six days a week. And we always shot Saturday night because you had to give actors twelve hours between calls, but if we shot Saturday night they could use Sunday as the twelve hour period. If you had night work, you always did it on Saturday night. And we'd work until midnight, one or two o'clock. So we're working on Saturday night and my assistant came to me and said, "Vince, Mayo is in Bogie's dressing room. She's crying and she wants to talk to you." So I went in and they both used to get roaring drunk at times and she got up and she put her arms around me and she's sobbing and crying and saying,

"Vince, he don't love me any more. You got to talk to him. He don't love me any more." You know a drunk. And I said, "Oh, Mayo, of course he loves you. Don't worry about him." "Well, you've got to talk to him." I said, "Sure, sure." I went out looking for Bogie. He was at a snack stand having a cup of coffee with Bill Dennis. I said, "Bogie, Mayo's in the dressing room crying, saying you don't love her any more. Why don't you go and talk to her." He says, "Oh, fuck her. I'm so goddamn fed up with these frustrated actresses. That's all I hear morning, noon and night. Get me a job. Why don't you get me a part?" And oh, they used to have some knock outs.... She was a talented actress. And when she was sober she was very nice. There were a lot of people who drank—a lot of women who drank—in those days and she was one of those. And of course Bogie drank and he used to smoke incessantly on *All Through the Night*—puff one cigarette after another. And sometimes he would cough, hacking coughs, and you thought he was going to tear his guts out. You didn't know enough in those days to say, "For Christ sake, stop smoking."

GD: Did the relationship with Mayo cause him to not be on the set?

VS: Only one time. He came in and we had to wait until he got cleaned up—shave and everything.

GD: Very professional?

VS: He was a real pro. Came from the theater.

Clark Gable by the way was a wonderful guy to work with. You never had to call him but once. At nine o'clock he walked on the set. He was dressed. Ready. Made-up. Knew his lines. Never came in like so many young actors do and say, "Jesus Christ, who wrote this pile of crap?" or "Who wrote these lousy lines?" Gable would study it as it was written and be prepared to do it as it was written. And you'd have to watch him in rehearsal and see if you could sense when something bothered him. And I'd go up to him and ask, "Clark, does that line bother you?" And he said, "Yeah, that doesn't feel quite right." I said, "What do you feel like saying?" And he said, "Well, could I say?" And there's the man who was the "king," asking, "could I say?" Now I've worked with young actors in television—they didn't have that kind of discipline or respect, but he came from the theater where there was a certain respect for the written material. Of course, in the theater it was different thing because the dialogue is the medium of conveyance whereas in pictures it's imagery.

GD: Now was Bogart like that also?

VS: Oh yeah.

GD: If he didn't feel a line was right did he . . . ?

VS: Oh yeah, yeah. By the way, his rise was very slow and very gradual. Just before he had done two pictures that really got him sort of away from just the villain picture. *High Sierra* was a very good story and a very good script in my opinion. They had offered it to George Raft and they offered it to Paul Muni. Both of them turned it down. So throw it to Bogie. There was a guy starving, a guy on the run. So they gave it to him. Picture turned out very well. Then John Huston decided he wanted as his first picture to do a remake of *The Maltese Falcon*. Which had been done twice before, but not as Dash Hammett wrote it. And so he got Bogart for it. And that got marvelous reviews in New York. Now that was followed by *All Through the Night*. And those three things in a row made Bogie acceptable as a leading man. Those three pictures. The first was done by

Raoul Walsh, written by John Huston. The second was written and directed by Huston, and the third one was *All Through the Night*.

GD: All of them different.

VS: Yeah, all different stories, but they began to move Bogart into a different class. He got the girl. When you get the girl, that means you're now a leading man.

GD: Were there specific things about his acting that distinguished him? I've heard often people find it very difficult to describe whether it was his mannerisms or just various aspects of his acting. You described him as a professional.

VS: Yeah. That's right. Bogie had, I guess as a result of his experiences in life . . . he had a kind of cynicism which came through in his work. And that's the reason I think he's more popular today than Cagney because he expresses the feeling of the 70s and 80s—of young people. Bogie would say, "Oh, cut the . . ." Once a guy said something to me about Bogart and I said, "You know something, if Bogie knew that he had become a god, you know, for the modern generation of young people, he would have said, 'Oh, cut the crap.' " That was the kind of guy he was—the beauty of his character which I think has made him so liked by modern audiences. You had a feeling he was down to earth, basic, no nonsense, no sentimentality. Very realistic and somewhat cynical.

GD: All Through the Night was different because of the humor. Nobody really talks about Bogart as a comedian.

VS: Yeah. That's right. But he knew how to throw away a line and get a laugh with it.

GD: Did he take to it naturally? He was working with Phil Silvers, Jackie Gleason, and Will Demarest.

VS: Yeah. He was a good actor, you see. He had this kind of wry, cynical quality which is great for certain kinds of comedy. It was the kind of picture too, that allowed for improvisation a lot, to add things. Of course, I had such a marvelous cast in it. I got a call from Warners just before I started the picture—now because *Underground* was a success (which was a stock melodrama) but it was an anti-Nazi film. That's how I was given *All Through the Night*. One was a stock melodrama and the other was a comedy, a satirical comedy. That's what studios do. If you are successful with one type of picture, they give you another type. He's done a good anti-Nazi film, let him make this one. That's why I was given *All Through the Night*.

So, I got a call from Warner and he said, "Listen Sherman, I got comics I want you to put in the picture." I said, "Mr. Warner, I've already got two or three comedians. I've got Frank McHugh playing a part. I've Bill Demarest who is Bogart's sidekick and a comedian. I think I had Wally Ford. I don't think I have any parts for these." And he said, "Well, make some parts." And I said, "Well, who are the two comedians." He says, "There's one guy named Phil Silvers and there's a fat guy named Jackie Gleason." And I knew they were on the lot; I hadn't met them. I said, "Oh. I don't have anything for them." He said, "Make something for them Vince. Goddamn it, I'm tired of paying these guys money to sit on their ass." They were getting $200 a week. So that's how I got the two guys in. I asked them to meet me in Jerry Wald's office and I said, "Look fellas, this is the situation. Bring me in some jokes and we'll try to work them in." Jackie Gleason brought me in a page of jokes. Phil Silvers brought me in seventeen pages; I could have made an hour out of those jokes. So, Phil played a waiter and he had a few lines at the start. Then Jackie became one of Bogart's henchmen. And that's how the thing was done.

GD: You worked with Bogart on a segment of *Across the Pacific*. What was the story?

VS: Oh boy. Everyone wants to know that story. John tells the story as though he deliberately got Bogart tied up into such knots that nobody could unravel him. Well, it wasn't quite the way it happened. What happened was that I got a call from Warner and he said, "Vince, I want you to go down tomorrow and take over *Across the Pacific*. Huston has to go . . ." I said, "What's the matter with John?" He said, "Well, he has to go into the army." I said, "J. L. You can't tell me the army wouldn't let him finish the picture for Christ sake. He's not going onto the front line—he's not a general." "Well," he said, "it's not only that, but his wife is walking out of one door and Olivia de Havilland is walking in the other door. And the poor son-of-a-bitch doesn't know what the fuck is going on. For Christ sake, get down there and finish the goddamn movie."

So I went down to the set the next day and I see Sidney Greenstreet, Bogart, Mary Astor and one other character. They are walking around with white cockleshell papers in their hand. And I know that stuff has been rewritten the night before. They're walking around, it's about 10:30 the next morning, and I knew the cameraman (Arthur Edeson) and Lee Cass was the assistant. So I said, "What the hell's going on?" He said, "Well, we got new pages and we're just rehearsing the scene." So John saw me and I said, "No, I'll come back later. I want to let them get the master shot in it."

So I left. I came back at four o'clock in the afternoon. They're still walking around with the pages—they haven't made a shot. So I said to Lee, "What the hell's going on?" And he said, "They haven't made a shot yet." They didn't make a shot that day and at five o'clock they said, "Well, let's break. Vince, why don't you pick it up in the morning and you start with the master scene." So I came in. Yeah, it was complex, but I read the script and there was just a kind of mechanical denouement. It wasn't terribly good, but I said to the producer Jerry Wald and to Warner, "Well, the picture's pretty good up to here, but this is just an ordinary finish to the thing." Warner said, "Vince, I don't want to spend any more money on the goddamn thing. Get through with the goddamn picture." Sets were built, the machine gun was in place, the plane was sitting in the jungle—it was all there. So, I shot the best I could and did it big. So, when John talks about it, it was all a big joke the way he set it up. But not quite the way it was.

That was a quality that John had which I had great admiration for but I couldn't be that way. John had the ability—he had great charisma—he had the ability to seem above everything. He didn't do a hell of a lot of directing, strangely enough. If you read Katherine Hepburn's story about the *African Queen*, she said the main thing that he said to her was when she said, "How am I going to play that?" he said, "Well, think about Mrs. Roosevelt." And that's what she remembered about his direction. I think personally he was a much better writer than he was a director. And there were certain kinds of pictures he could do very well and certain kinds he couldn't. He didn't do too well in *In This Our Life* with Bette Davis. But offbeat things he was very good at. There's no question that he was a talented man and he was a good actor too. But he had that quality of being aloof from it . . . you had [about him] a feeling of superiority and a feeling that he always knew much more than he was saying. I invited him once to come down to a place where I was giving some lectures on motion picture direction. It was the dullest lecture I had ever heard. The audience went to sleep. But he was very clever and certainly made some great pictures. But it wasn't quite the way he wrote.

GD: As a director, with your background in writing, were there times when you wanted to put your hand in?

VS: I did in every picture. The only two scripts that were actually almost perfect, so far as I'm concerned—one was *Mr. Skeffington* and *Old Acquaintance*. And *Saturday's Children* was very nice too—a good script. But every other one I was in there with the writing. On *All Through the Night*, I did a lot of work and *Underground*, especially. Also, with the exception of three or four films at the most, I was in on the writing all the time, but I never took credit. Once I became a director, I said that's part of my job—to interpret the script. As I say, the script is a guideline and you try to improvise on that scene and how to build it and make it more effective.

GD: You're known in part as an actor's director. Were there things with Bogart that stood out?

VS: As I say, he had a very realistic approach. He had a kind of cynical attitude. I think he must have had that about life itself. Wonderful guy to work with, strangely enough. Very simple, very realistic, very . . . the thing about Bogie was his reality. If you came in with a lot of horseshit and bullshit with him, he'd detect it right away. It wouldn't work with him. You could be civil, you could be honest with him. And I know, very often I would say, "Bogie, it's a crappy thing, but what the hell. Let's make the best of it." And he would do that. He kept working on it. And he became very friendly with Peter Lorre, who was another wonderful guy—wonderful actor.

Peter, by the way, was a very cultured man—very few people know. Peter came from the German theater. He was a friend of Brecht. He was a friend of Hans Heisler. He worked in a workers theater group in Berlin and he left. And I think that the sad thing (some guy called me once who was doing a book about Peter and he asked me about him) and I said, "Well, the sad thing was that after Peter had originally come to this country after *M*, he did a very serious picture called *Crime and Punishment* based on the Dostoevsky novel. And it flopped. And subsequently he was hired, just as he said, "[to] make faces." And he was very cynical. But it was a means of making money. He did those *Mr. Motto* films. And he used to say, "Well, brother Vince, what do we do today? Do you know? Do we make faces today?" I said, "Yes, Peter we make faces." But it was all a racket.

I had a wonderful cast in *All Through the Night*. I had Conrad Veidt, Judith Anderson—who is a marvelous actress. There was a scene where Bogart and Demarest had gone into an office in the Nazi headquarters, the Bund headquarters and Peter comes down the hallway with a gun. He shoots at the lock, and Judith comes running down and says, "Vas is loos? Vas is loos?" And he said something in German and I cut the scene. And I was going to say "print" but I thought maybe I could get a little something better. And I hesitated for a minute before I said "print" and Peter says, "That's all, brother Vince. I can only do this kind of crap once a day. Besides, it is six o'clock. Time to go home." I said, "Don't give me that Peter. Don't talk about this crap. How'd the hell did you do all those *Mr. Motto*'s?" He said, "I took dope." Everybody laughed. They thought it was a joke. A year later I was at the house of Rudy Fehr, the editor of the film, and I'm telling this as a joke. He says, "But he did." I said, "What do you mean?" He said, "He was taking dope." Years later, he divorced his wife of many years and he married a girl that he met on *All Through the Night*, Kaaren Verne.

GD: Do you think film can have an impact on how we view others?

VS: I think film can. And we're learning more and more all the time as people get better educated and [there is] better communication.

GD: Thanks for your time and observations.

VS: You're welcome.

ARTICLES AND INTERVIEWS BY BOGART

The entries are in chronological order.

Bogart, Humphrey. "Why Hollywood Hates Me." *Screen Book* (January 1940): 66, 68–69.

Bogart Humphrey. "Censorship." *Hollywood Reporter*, 11th Anniversary Issue (October 31, 1941). In *The Hollywood Reporter: The Golden Years*. Ed. Tichi Wilkerson and Marcia Borie. New York: Coward-McCann, 1984. 140–141.

Bogart, Humphrey, as told to Kay Proctor. "Women I'd Like to Bump Off." *Screen Guide* (August 1942): 34, 43.

"Bogart: Neuroses: Methot." *Herald Express*. c. 1942 (Cited in Jeffrey Meyers, *Bogart: A Life in Hollywood* (Boston: Houghton Mifflin, 1997): 354.

Bogart, Humphrey, as told to Sarah Hamilton. "Bogie on the Spot." *Photoplay* 21 (September 1942): 64–65, 88–89.

———. "Things I Don't Like About Myself." *Photoplay*. c. 1942. (Cited in Meyers.)

Bogart, Humphrey, as told to Dorothy B. Haas. "Sister Annie." *Silver Screen* (March 1943): 26–27, 64–65.

Bogart, Humphrey, as told to Jack Holland. "How to Keep Your Marriage Alive." *Silver Screen* (November 1943): 30–31, 68–70.

Bogart, Humphrey. "The Romance I Can't Forget." *Photoplay* 24 (March 1944): 55.

Bogart, Humphrey. "Medal from Hitler: Here's How to Get One." *Photoplay* (January 1945): 28, 87.

Bogart, Humphrey. "I Stuck My Neck Out." *Saturday Evening Post* (February 10, 1945): 19, 87–88.

Bogart, Humphrey, as told to Gladys Hall. "Listen, Kreep." *Silver Screen* 15 (June 1945): 22, 68–69.

Bogart, Humphrey. "Humphrey Bogart Cleans House." *Screen Guide* (July 1945): 28–29.

Bogart, Humphrey. "People I'd Like to Kill." *Motion Picture* 70.1 (August 1945): 52–53, 75.

Bogart, Humphrey. "Think! Before You Say That." *Motion Picture* 70.2 (September 1945): 88.

Bogart, Humphrey. "In Defense of My Wife." *Photoplay* 29 (June 1946): 38–39, 99–100.

Bogart, Humphrey. "My Unlucky Break." *Screen Stars* (October 1946): 10, 68.

Bogart, Humphrey. "The Role I Liked Best . . ." *Saturday Evening Post* (December 14, 1946): 136.

Bogart, Humphrey. "This Is What I Believe." *Screenland* (February 1947): 36, 90–92.

Bogart, Humphrey. "Locationing in Mexico." *Hollywood Reporter* 95.33 (September

1947). In *The Hollywood Reporter: The Golden Years*. Ed. Tichi Wilkerson and Marcia Borie. New York: Coward-McCann, 1984. 205–206.

Bogart, Humphrey. "The Santana and I." *Modern Screen* (1947): 48–50. In *Hollywood in the 1940s: The Stars' Own Stories*. Ed. Ivy Crane Wilson. New York: Ungar, 1980: 33–37.

Bogart, Humphrey. "I'm No Communist." *Photoplay* 32 (March 1948): 52–53, 86. In *Photoplay Treasury*. Ed. Barbara Gelman. New York: Crown, 1972. 356–358.

Bogart, Humphrey, as told to Jerry Asher. "You . . . You . . . You." *Movie Stars Parade* (August 1948): 50, 82–83.

Bogart, Humphrey. "Bogart Balks at Bogey." *New York Times* (November 28, 1948): II:5.

Bogart, Humphrey. "Imagine Me a Father!" *Silver Screen* (May 1949): 24–25, 55.

Bogart, Humphrey. "Safety Pin Expert Tells of His Diaper Troubles." *Los Angeles News*, (June 21, 1949).

Bogart, Humphrey, as told to K. Holliday. "My Mother: I Never Really Loved Her." *McCall's* 103 (April 1976): 41–42. Reprint *McCall's*, "I Can't Say I Loved Her" (July 1949): 8, 30, 32, 34.

Bogart, Humphrey. "The Most Unforgivable Character I've Met." *Photoplay* 36 (July 1949): 48–49, 94.

Bogart, Humphrey. "The Keys to the Keelson." *Los Angeles News* (August 16, 1949).

Bogart, Humphrey. "Listen to Me, Kid." *Photoplay* (September 1949): 34–35, 83–84.

Bogart, Humphrey. "I'm a Christmas Kid." *Screenland* (December 1949): 29, 65–66.

Bogart, Humphrey. " 'Baby' Has Changed." *Screen Guide* (January 1950): 28–29, 88–89.

Bogart, Humphrey. "The Oscar Myth." *Cosmopolitan* 129 (March 1950): 31, 165.

Bogart, Humphrey. "What Do I Owe My Wife?" *Movieland* (March 1950): 52–55, 94.

Bogart, Humphrey. "Sayings." *Preview* (n.d.): 8–9.

Bogart, Humphrey. "Love Begins at 40." *New York Herald Tribune* (October 7, 1951): 17, 27.

Bogart, Humphrey. "Humphrey Bogart Tells the Truth About Hepburn." *Coronet* 31 (April 1952): 139–140, 142, 144, 146, 148, 150.

Bogart, Humphrey. "African Adventure." *American Weekly* (August 31, 1952): 11.

Bogart, Humphrey. "Beat the Devil." *Look* 17 (September 22, 1953): 128–129, 131–133.

Bogart, Humphrey, as told to Joe Hyams. "Movie Making Beats the Devil." *Cue* (November 28, 1953): 14–15.

Bogart, Humphrey. "Around the World in 80 Reels." *This Week Magazine, LA Times* (March 21, 1954): 14–15.

Bogart, Humphrey. "The Way I See Queeg." *American Weekly* (June 27, 1954): 9.

Bogart, Humphrey. "Bogart on Hollywood." *Look* 20 (August 21, 1956): 96–98, 100–101.

4

BIBLIOGRAPHICAL ESSAY

BIOGRAPHIES AND CAREER OVERVIEWS

The facts of Humphrey Bogart's life have been documented with varying degrees of accuracy. Early biographies by Nathaniel Benchley, Ezra Goodman, Joe Hyams, and David Hanna relied on friendship, interviews, or professional connections. The results were only partial views. The most detailed presentation of the last twelve years of his life is found in Lauren Bacall's *By Myself* (1978), supplemented by additional comments in her more recent *Now* (1994). In *By Myself* Bacall gives the public and personal details of their life together: the battles and joys of filmmaking, their friends, politics, and Bogart's battle with cancer. Thoroughly researched, but not documented, she includes materials from numerous interviews and newspaper articles. Unfortunately, not all of the facts are accurate, as when, for example, she says that Mayo Methot went to Reno for divorce (it was Las Vegas), but *By Myself* is appealing for its intimate portrait of their life together and, though one-sided in her appreciation of Bogart, is the most detailed account of the years they spent together until the Meyers and Sperber and Lax biographies of 1997. Bacall's more recent *Now* focuses on her feelings about the events and people in her life, including Bogart, but does not give much information that was not included in the earlier autobiography.

Stephen Humphrey Bogart was only eight years old when his father died. *Bogart: In Search of My Father* (1995) details his search to find out who this person was whom Mike Romanoff described as a "first-class person with an obsessive compulsion to act like a second-class person." Young Bogart scoured articles and spoke with friends to come to terms with his own identity and reconcile himself to a father and a name that have haunted his every action. His view of his father is more pragmatic and less idolatrous than his mother's accounts, and he is willing to see and name flaws. In an interview in *Parade Magazine* he says of his mother's view, "She sees him in a different light.... He was her great love, her mentor, a father figure."[1] For all his research, the published sources go uncited.

Ezra Goodman's uncredited "The Survivor," a cover story for *Time* magazine, appeared shortly before *The Caine Mutiny* opened. In the piece Goodman synthesizes hours of interviews, giving an overview of Bogart's early life and career in the theater. To Goodman, Bogart "may bait and bully his betters, but he can act, and he is reliable" (67). Seen as more mellow since his marriage to Bacall, Bogart is described as a faithful husband who likes to sail, drink, play practical jokes, and speak out on "practically any subject." In addition to remarks on maternal love, whiskey, women, money, exercise, fatherhood, manners, politics, and bad movies, Bogart says of acting: "You can't just make faces. If you make yourself feel the way the character would feel, your face will express the right things—if you're an actor" (68).[2] Because of the proximity to the opening of *The Caine Mutiny*, Goodman gives a brief analysis of Bogart as Queeg: "He brings the hollow, driven, tyrannical character of Captain Queeg to full and invidious life, yet seldom fails to maintain a bond of sympathy with his audience. He deliberately gives Queeg the mannerisms and appearance of an officer of sternness and decision, and then gradually discloses him as a man who is bottling up a scream" (67). Goodman sees Bogart playing Bogart in all his roles; nonetheless, he "manages to achieve surprising range and depth while still remaining the familiar figure with whom millions expect to renew an acquaintance when they pay at the box office to see a Bogart film" (66).

Goodman's *Bogey: The Good-Bad Guy* was the result of the many interviews he conducted in late 1953 and early 1954 for the *Time* magazine article. Sent to Hollywood to interview Bogart and his associates for what was to become the cover story for June 7, 1954, Goodman, a press agent at Warner Brothers in the 1940s, was not a fan of the actor. He sets the tone for many of his own comments when he says, "I had been around Hollywood too long to believe that there were any heroes, particularly off-screen" (11). The book is divided into twenty-seven short chapters. The first two and half are on his own background. Of his own early publicity piece "Exit the 'Bogey'-Man" reprinted in the book, Goodman says, "In retrospect, I wonder if Bogart actually said some of these things or if I thought he may have said them through a gin and vermouth haze" (17). There are three and one-half chapters of "Bogart on Bogart," followed by two chapters of comments by Bacall, and then a series of chapters with comments from Mike Romanoff, Michael Curtiz, Peter Lorre, Clifton Webb, Morgan Maree (Bogart's business manager), Stanley Kramer, Nunnally Johnson, Richard Brooks, and Jerry Wald. Two chapters of "odds and ends" are quotations from a variety of individuals, peppered with Goodman's own cynical remarks. Goodman went back to some of the people he had interviewed previously (Brooks, Kramer) and added Henry Blanke, Pat O'Brien, and Mervyn LeRoy to "update" the material; their comments make up the remaining chapters. The subtitle carries the thesis: the kind of roles Bogart had in the films carried over into his real life, an idea attributed in most accounts to Mike Romanoff. Goodman's love-hate relationship with Hollywood runs throughout the sidebars with his various interviewees. He enjoys being able to interview them, questions how much is typical Hollywood malarky, but presents to the readers everything he was told. He does not edit or correct. Curtiz, for example, says he directed Bogart in *The Santa Fe Trail*, and Jerry Wald says he worked with Bogart on *Background to Danger*. When he does comment on Bogart, Goodman gives him high marks for his dedication to his craft but finds Bogart often nasty and generally not very nice. He attributes the Bogart look to a monumental hangover and says that Bogart had a tendency to bully "little people" at the studio.

While accepting that Bogart was well loved by many and a sentimentalist at heart, Goodman "had some decided reservations about Bogart—partly as an actor and more as a man. He protested too much. And he tried maybe a little too hard to be clever and smart-alecky" (55). On the occasions throughout the book when Goodman recounts his "impressions" of a particular experience or event, he leans toward virulent criticisms. Ironically, the person he most respected (Nunnally Johnson) and the one he was most in awe of (Morgan Maree) had nothing negative to say about Bogart. Goodman's emphasis, then, is on anecdotes and gossip and some mention of Bogart's cult appeal. Much of what Bogart says about himself has appeared in earlier works, but the comments of others frequently appear in subsequent studies. Unfortunately, the book does not have a table of contents, index, illustrations, or bibliography.

Richard Gehman's friendship with Bogart began in 1955, after Gehman called the actor at the suggestion of literary agent "Swifty" Lazar about a story for *Woman's Home Companion*. In writing one of the earliest biographies of the actor, Gehman, like Goodman, does not present an objective account: "I was terribly fond of Bogart as an actor and human being, the latter more than the former." Divided into twenty-nine brief chapters, *Bogart: An Intimate Biography* is compiled from newspaper and magazine articles and interviews with Stuart Rose (Bogart's brother-in-law for a time), Nathaniel Benchley, and an assortment of others, ranging from students to popular culture scholars. He borrows extensively from works by Cameron Shipp, George Frazier, Ezra Goodman, the *New York Times* and *New York Herald Tribune* clipping files, columnists, and friends of the actor. The section on the Holmby Hills Rat Pack (Sinatra, Bogart, Bacall, and others) is a rehash of what appeared in Gehman's earlier *Sinatra and His Rat Pack*. Most of the chapters are snapshots of aspects of Bogart's life: his drinking, his attitude toward certain actors, and his presentation of "Skippy" awards to animals.

Of the four chapters with extended discussions, the first focuses on Bogart's appeal. Gehman quotes extensively from students, critics (Pauline Kael), scholars of popular culture (Leslie Fiedler), and newspaper accounts of Bogart festivals. Chapter 25 is the most thorough of the early presentations of Bogart's career at school and his first work on Broadway. Gehman spoke with teachers, administrators, and fellow classmates and had access to grades and correspondence relating to Bogart's time at Trinity and Phillips Andover. He quotes from a letter Bogart wrote requesting information about his room and board at Andover and from exchanges between Dr. Bogart and administrators at the school on his son's progress. In this same chapter Gehman includes extensive comments from Stuart Rose as to how Bogart got his start in the theater. Gehman mentions the various plays with an occasional comment from theater critics, a strategy employed later by Nathaniel Benchley. The penultimate chapter is a filmography, with a list of seventy-five titles and a selective list of cast members or a comment or two. Gehman's lack of knowledge of film history comes across when he says that other than the one moment in Jean-Luc Godard's *Breathless* when Jean Paul Belmondo is standing before the Bogart poster trying to emulate "Bogie," the film is "of no value itself" (110). He does, though, give a succinct description of how Bogart honed his mannerisms: "Bogart was a cool, knowing craftsman, continually working on mannerisms of speech and exposition, which he regarded as tools; when he found one of either that worked well in his hand or mouth, he put it in his bag and hauled it out to use whenever the time seemed appropriate. Sometimes he used one or another of those tools to parody his original use of it. He did this with a commanding consciousness" (109). Based on secondary sources, primarily the writing of Joe Hyams, the final chapter deals with Bogart's illness and last days. There are numerous stills, no index, and a bibliography in the form of an overview of sources and thanks to those who gave him material.

Joe Hyams's *Bogie: The Biography of Humphrey Bogart* (1966) was heralded as the "authorized" biography when it appeared. A friend of Bogart with an entrée that others lacked,[3] Hyams had been a reporter for the *Herald Tribune* when he came to California, and was one of the first to use tape recorders for accuracy. Bogart liked the *Herald Tribune* because it was the paper he read when he lived in New York in the 1920s and 1930s, and he followed Hyams's writing and eventually brought him in as his voice to the public. Hyams was approached within the first year after Bogart's death by a publisher seeking a biography, but after checking with Bacall who did not want one, he declined the offer. Only after she approved did he agree to write it. That approval also gave him entrée to more than one hundred friends, classmates, and family members. Hyams synthesizes the many pieces on Bogart that he wrote over the years, other published accounts, photos, and interviews with friends and associates as he paints a portrait of the actor's friendships, brawls, studio battles, and climb to stardom. Hyams is clearly enamored of his subject. Although he claims to have written it for readers, not Bacall, she claims he gave her the galleys and she corrected mistakes. She also hoped for a more personal account: "I wish he had told more of the effect that Bogie had on him, the man, the writer."[4] Because of Hyams's friendship there is little that is critical of the actor, and some inaccuracies, such as stating that Bruce Bennett is the killer in *Dark Pas-*

sage, but the portrait is the closest we get to the actor until Lauren Bacall's *By Myself*. There is little analysis of the films, no index, no filmography, and no bibliography, and many of the illustrations appear in Gehman's book.

Nathaniel Benchley's *Humphrey Bogart* is an effort to "bring life to what is rapidly becoming a legend, and to show the subject as he lived and breathed." A friend of Bogart and Bacall (Bogart was good friends with Benchley's father) and a frequent guest, Benchley tries to get at the complexity of Bogart's character by tracing his life in a linear fashion from his birth to his funeral. He divides the book into untitled sections. The factual material is sprinkled with anecdotes, letters and notes, quotations from friends (as best remembered), and numerous photos of the public and private Bogart. Benchley gives a good overview of Bogart's theatrical history, basing his remarks on published reviews and interviews with some of the principals. According to Benchley, what Bogart gained in New York, aside from the needed experience, was the attitude that he was a professional: "He devoted himself to learning his business, and he did it with a professional, no-nonsense approach that made his eventual success all but inevitable. . . . There are some who don't buy the mystique that has built up around him, and there are some who claim that his acting was more a trick and a manipulation of his voice, but there are none who will try to say that he wasn't a professional" (45). This attitude, his respect for his profession, and his knowledge that the theater did not pay are what kept him afloat during his difficult times in Hollywood. Benchley's discussion of Bogart's film career is mostly anecdotal, including six pages on *Casablanca*, plus photos. We learn that Bogart, often ill at ease in love scenes, was advised by a friend, "This is the first time you've ever played the romantic lead against a major star. You stand still, and always make her come to you" (104).

Benchley briefly analyzes the role of Bogart's domineering mother and ineffectual father, his hesitancy to marry Helen Menken and then Mayo Methot, his dependency on Mary Philips and to some extent Lauren Bacall, his savagery when drunk, and various theories about ambition, sexuality, and his Dr. Jekyll–Mr. Hyde personalities. He concludes that Bogart "was simply never really in love on any of the first three occasions" and that after his marriage to Bacall, he became "the antithesis of everything he'd been before" (68–71, 81–88). To Benchley, Bogart is a puritan at heart (never mind the brawls, cursing, and early libertine ways) who embodies "true class," which he achieved "through his integrity and his devotion to what he thought was right, and if there were those who either didn't agree or who saw it in another light, that was their business. He believed in being direct, simple, and honest, all on his own terms, and this ruffled some people and endeared him to others. He couldn't have cared less" (232). He lived his life for sailing, acting, his family, and chess. Some of the dates Benchley gives are in general terms (e.g., "early" in the year); occasionally his dates are wrong: Santana Pictures Corporation was set up in April 1948, not 1947. The strength of the book, which lacks an index and bibliography, is its early section on Bogart in New York and the use of letters, notes, and photos not readily available elsewhere.

Influenced no doubt by French filmmaking and jump cuts in particular, Jonah Ruddy and Jonathan Hill interviewed coworkers and friends to paint a very favorable picture of the actor for the paperback *Bogey: The Man, the Actor, the Legend* (1965). The British version, published under the title *The Bogey Man: Portrait of a Legend* (Souvenir Press, 1965), contains additional material, including a contents page, twenty-nine illustrations, and a notice of a Permanent Charities Committee Auction of antique and period furniture sponsored by Bacall. Misstatements are not corrected or commented on. For example, when Bogart is quoted about working with Barbara Stanwyck, he calls the film *Conflict*, rather than *The Two Mrs. Carrolls*. The authors include a filmography, but there is no index to either the British or American version.

David Hanna's "The Humphrey Bogart I Knew" served as the basis for a longer biography, in which Hanna emphasizes that Bogart liked to stir things up and also liked to make money. Advertised as a "confidential biography," Hanna admits deep in the text that he and Bogart had only a "nodding acquaintance" and that he "seldom had reason to sit down and interview him" (139). He "knew him" through his seventeen years as a reporter for the *Los Angeles Daily News* and the *Hollywood Reporter*. As a result, what he presents is an impressionistic view of Bogart's moods and contradictions, based on what others said about Bogart, but often without giving any more information other than who said what. Hanna claims to have known the Bradys and gives background on them, how Bogart got his first job, and how he drifted from stage managing into acting. Of Bogart's early theater work he says, "One account of his career, published in 1924, reveals the extraordinary amount of work Bogart actually did on the stage—so much of it glossed over in accounts of his life" (41), but Hanna never discusses the source and mentions plays selectively, sometimes omitting plays key to Bogart's career at the moment. When discussing Bogart's film career, Hanna notes that once he began to make it at Warner Bros. and started to challenge Jack Warner, "subtle changes appeared in his characterizations, as his bad men began to look more like troubled human beings than sinister gangsters" (80). Although he laments that the previous biographies do not permit us to know what Bogart is really like, Hanna himself paraphrases or quotes freely from them. He claims the key to understanding Bogart is to "understand his drinking" (15). Bacall's only comment on his drinking is that it was triggered by a sense of emotional and financial insecurity that later in life (after his marriage to her) was no longer needed as a crutch (16).

A "gifted conversationalist" (18), with "impeccable manners" (18), and a "belief in an old-fashioned morality" (46), Bogart's pride was centered in "his craftsmanship, his popularity with the public and the good relationship he maintained with most of the press" (23). As others have noted, fatherhood changed him. He was still outspoken, still a needler, but "no less severe on himself. He never put a halo over his head and pretended to be either a saint, a wise man, even a good man. He was just an ordinary slob who did acting for a living and struggled through life as best he could'' (111). The most extensive commentary in the biography is on *The Barefoot Contessa* (140–170), because Hanna was one of the film's publicists. Hanna's highest praise for the actor is that he was a professional when it came to his job (155). He ends the work with a discussion of Bogart's appeal on college campuses and some "Bogartisms"—one-liners that he finds memorable. Symptomatic of the suspect nature of his presentation is that Hanna gives Bogart's birthdate as December 25, 1899, based on Bacall's remarks (18), but shortly thereafter presents it as a decade earlier, January 23, 1889 (29), and later on says it became Christmas Day when he joined Warner Bros. Hanna's work does not include a table of contents, bibliography, or index.

Except for some personal observations and comments on Bogart and his campaigning for Stevenson, most of the biographical and career assessment that appears in Alistair Cooke's *Six Men* is found in "Epitaph for a Tough Guy" and "Bogart and the Age of Violence: An Idealist in Hollywood." British broadcaster, author, and essayist Cooke first met Bacall and the actor "with the curious animal magnetism" (186) on the Adlai Stevenson presidential campaign train in the fall of 1952 and got to know him fairly well over the next four years. Tentative and reserved, Bogart was very much out of his element on the campaign trail. When Bogart, who considered fidelity "a married man's duty" (202), learned that the Democrats were going to make public a letter about Eisenhower's infidelities if Joe McCarthy delivered a planned speech in Chicago, Cooke found the actor "genuinely shocked" by the charge of adultery. "That moment of shock on the train was the first hint I had that what we were dealing with here were two characters, one fictional, the other private" (187).

Cooke sees Bogart as a "complex private man" (188). Although he incorrectly claims that Bogart said, "Tennis, anyone?" and "Drop the gun, Looey," he pinpoints the coming of sound as the key event that saved Bogart's career. As an aging juvenile, he was not doing much in the theater. Only because of some Hollywood roles and an opportunity in the mid-1930s to do *The Petrified Forest* did Bogart move beyond being cast as a featured player to having the opportunity of playing gangster or antihero roles. To Cooke, *The Petrified Forest*, while an "appalling film to see today," suggested "subtleties inside him itching to get out" (192), which is what critic Otis Ferguson saw in *Black Legion* and *Kid Galahad* and which Cooke considers a sign of an "actor who didn't seem to act but *behaved*" (193).

Not one to discuss "artistry," Bogart saw his acting as a trade and expected others to be professional in what they did (194). While recognizing his being seen as the outsider by French critics, Bogart "packed the more explosive social threat of the Insider gone sour, all the more convincing because the disillusion grew from his own background and the unknown cause of his protest against it" (196). His presence on the screen was so powerful due to "coincidence of the fictional character with what was repressed or socially impermissible in his own" (199). He was seen from two extremes: a "moody drunk" who liked to needle others tastelessly and was disdained by some, and the nineteenth-century gentleman who was "gentle, gallant, modest, full of an indulgent or rueful humor, courteous with strangers, quietly and acutely sensitive to the plight of guests who were shy or being left out" (201). To Cooke, "His iconoclasm was ... the rather gaudy mask of a conservatism that embarrassed him" (201). He had "pedestrian old-school virtues: loyalty to friends, respect for the old, a distaste for conspicuous wealth, for gossip, for boasting" (202), a hatred of pomp, cant, dirty stories, and was "impatient of compliments and perfunctory praise" (203). His secret was "being an incurable puritan, gentle at bottom and afraid to say so" (205). Cooke found him "a much more intelligent man than most of his trade, or several others, a touchy man who found the world more corrupt than he hoped; a man with a tough shell hiding a fine core. He had transmuted his own character into a film persona and imposed it on a world impatient of men more obviously good" (205).

Jonathan Coe, who writes for the *Guardian* and the *London Review* of *Books*, presents a glossy but challenging perspective in *Humphrey Bogart: Take It and Like It*. At first glance Coe's work appears to be another coffee table book, with lots of illustrations (some not published before) and accompanying text. The six chapters follow a chronological arrangement, beginning with an overview of Bogart's early life, theatrical career, and early films, followed by chapters for key periods: 1935–1941, 1941–1943, 1943–1948, 1948–1953, and 1953–1957. What Coe does, however, is bring to play some of the more recent approaches to film criticism combined with some of the standard tropes to get us to focus on those who helped shape Bogart's career (directors, producers, wives), the impact of the studio system on his roles, and the "randomness and chance element in a life that in some ways got luckier as he got older" (11). Bogart's appeal is not between "toughness and vulnerability" but between "power and powerlessness." A cult figure whose time has passed, he cites Huston's remarks on Connery and Caine: "The casting of Connery and Caine [in *The Man Who Would Be King*] is indicative of the great changes, thank heavens, which have taken place in the star system and movie-making in general. They bring a reality to it that the old stars, much as I loved Gable and Bogart, could not do.... Today they would seem synthetic" (188).

The subtitle of the book, taken from *The Maltese Falcon*, emphasizes Bogart's constant battle against studio forces and his ability to maintain a self against the power brokers. The battle, with which Coe believes all of us can identify, was fought with the help of talented writers, directors, and producers—most notably Howard Hawks, John Huston, Nicholas Ray, and Hal Wallis—and his wives and alcohol. Certainly these are not new ideas, but they are presented in a pithy, challenging fashion. Well researched, but not documented, Coe's book should kindle a look at some slighted films (e.g., *The Harder They Fall*), others just now getting attention (*In a Lonely Place*), his acting ability, and his suppressed violence.

It was not until forty years after his death that Humphrey Bogart became the subject of two biographies that have given us a much fuller portrait of the actor and the man. The work of A. M. Sperber and Eric Lax is a collaboration born out of sadness. For seven years Sperber gathered information from published sources, the major and some of the minor archives with Bogart-related materials, and interviews with over 200 individuals who knew the actor. After Sperber's untimely death, Eric Lax synthesized the material into its current narrative; he also interviewed additional subjects and spoke to some who had already been interviewed. The result, *Bogart*, includes extensive commentary from those who knew the actor, including such minutiae as an evaluation of his mood by one of the stewardesses on the flight to Washington in 1947. Sperber was able to track down details about the actor's birth from an Ontario newspaper, but surprisingly, the authors misdate Bogart's funeral by a day, say that Claude Rains won for best supporting actor for *Casablanca* (Charles Coburn was the winner), and contend that the scar on Bogart's lip was not a result of shrapnel injury during the war or a prisoner slashing at him with his handcuffs, but was most likely the result of a free-for-all with friends. Some items are in conflict with Meyers and others biographers (e.g., the date of his divorce from Mary Philips), and for all their research and interviewing, very little is said by Sperber and Lax of his reputed lengthy liaison with Verita Thompson, his hairdresser. Interesting little bits not mentioned in other biographies include his visits for comfort and advice to Helen Menken at critical times in his life and Bogart's spin at being a director for the trailers of *The Big Sleep*. There is only surface presentation and limited analysis of the deep-seated hostilities and psychological motivations for many of his life choices, but this account is more even-handed than any of the previous full-length biographies and will be the starting place for future research. The book's documentation is extensive, including a filmography, listing of plays, notes, bibliography, and detailed index. There is, however, little reference to any of the academic scholarship on Bogart, and only occasional mention of the extensive fan magazine material. This synthesis of opinions and facts gives the most rounded picture of Humphrey Bogart's life and his career in Hollywood.

Appearing almost simultaneously with the Sperber-Lax biography was Jeffrey Meyers's *Bogart: A Life in Hollywood*, which tries to place Bogart in a cultural setting. Early on Meyers links him with subjects of his previous books: Hemingway, Fitzgerald, and Lawrence. He synthesizes and mines the comments from articles, newspaper stories, and earlier biographies and complements these with a number of interviews with Ernest Lehman, Billy Wilder, Verita Thompson, Arthur Miller, and Ted Eden (the current owner of the *Santana*). He also has researched some of the basic archives, including those at UCLA, Columbia, Boston University, and Andover, but he is not as thorough or as inclusive as Sperber and Lax. This work is more focused than other biographies in its attention to Maud Humphrey, the political background of the HUAC hearings, and the holdings in the Herrick Library at the Academy of Motion Picture Arts and Sciences, which others have overlooked or omitted discussing (e.g., Gladys

Hall's papers). Occasionally there are errors with dates. For example, he gives February 29, 1956, as the date for Bogart's operation for cancer of the esophagus, which was actually the day he entered the hospital; the operation was performed the next day. The documentation, including the filmography (no credits), may be frustrating for those who want to track down sources. Meyers often gives quotations, but the footnote for the quotation may be a paragraph or even a page later, and then the footnote may cover several items. Some quotations lack any documentation. The films are divided into "best," "important," "good," and "poor," but there is no discussion of the criteria, and Meyers omits the recent references (begun in Coe) to *The Dancing Town*.

In addition to biographies and articles from which book-length studies germinated, numerous essays have tried to piece together aspects of Humphrey Bogart's life, with varying degrees of success. Stephan Talty's "Young Bogart" visits the sites where Bogart grew up, the schools he attended, the Gramercy Park Hotel where he married Helen Menken, and the actor's stage career through *The Petrified Forest*. Talty believes that by examining Bogart's formative years and the places he frequented, one might find "revelations of himself and his inner codes" (40). Emphasizing Bogart's affluent background, Talty notes how in traveling through "drawing-room dramas, tales of the aristocracy, society farces and murder mysteries that dominated popular Broadway at the time" (44), his characters were those he was familiar with from his social milieu. According to Talty, having to spend time with an overprotective and unloving mother and being forced to serve as a model for the bright, happy children in her illustrations led Bogart to a hatred of his mother and a "lifetime hatred of impostors and of pretty facades over hard natures. . . . He himself had been the famous model for a kind of lie" (44). And although the young boy preferred to spend time boating and fishing with his father, Talty claims Bogart Senior did not know his son very well. When his father died in 1934, Bogart was devastated and was ready for a new life when he was cast in *The Petrified Forest*. Most of the material in this overview is derived from previously published material (his parents, his experiences in school, his friendship with the Bradys), and there is little that is new in this analysis of Bogart's character.

A brief piece in the *New York Times* on February 19, 1939, examines how Bogart fit into the Warner Bros. "rogues' gallery," his pleasure in playing those roles, how *Oklahoma Kid* is the same kind of film with a western motif, and how his character changed from the "harmless collegiate" of his stage roles to snarling triggerman in films. Three months later Elmer T. Peterson's short profile (combined with ones on Boris Karloff and Pat O'Brien) appeared in *Better Homes and Gardens*. Not unlike some of the fluff found in fan magazines, the article asks readers if they "hate" Bogart, and then goes on to show how he is unlike his screen image. Supposedly interviewed at a time when he was making *Unlawful* with Frances Farmer, Bogart was enthusiastic about his petunias and animals. Peterson finds Bogart's chief characteristics to be "his keen sense of humor, his likable personality, and his obvious devotion to the pleasure of quiet home life'' (22).

Like Peterson's profile, Kirtley Baskette's 1943 fanzine-type article presents the "trigger-man" as a "rather nice-looking" 5'8," 150-pound actor who likes chess and to piddle around his home, which he named "Liberty Hall" (43). Later called "Sluggy Hollow," this was "his fortress against Hollywood honey," a place where Bogart could live away from Hollywood hype. Readers learn that his friends are Louis Bromfield, Robert Benchley, Jefferson Machamer, James Thurber, and Hoagy Carmichael, that he plays golf, wears shoe lifts while acting, spends lots of money on his boat, serves as a member of the Coast Guard Auxiliary, and defends the downtrodden or put upon. (He was late for the interview because he was at city hall fighting and then paying for an inspection tax for his laundress's son's dog.) The article also includes an overview of his life that combines fact with fiction: born at Sloan Maternity Hospital on December 25, 1899; kicked out of Andover because of demerits and for pushing an instructor into a pond; joined the navy at age seventeen; splintered his lip as a result of a U-boat shell; and never took a suspension or went on strike, or turned down a part (64).

Reflecting on her costar in a 1967 piece for the *New York Times*, Mary Astor says Bogart worked hard at his profession and knew about the world. At a time when movies were in black and white, she found his characters to be reflections of that either-or categorizing. His looks, rather than actions such as kissing, conveyed his feelings to the audience. In real life, he wanted to trust and believe in others, eschewed hypocrisy, and wanted others to be themselves when around him.

George Frazier's close-up "Humphrey Bogart" came at a time when he was at the height of his popularity and supposedly happily married to Mayo Methot. Frazier sees Bogart as "a realist" who is candid in his own self-appraisal and of actors who take themselves too seriously. In a summary that appears in later commentaries, Frazier recalls how in his first thirty-four pictures for Warner Bros., he "was a jailbird in nine, electrocuted or hanged in eight and riddled by bullets in a dozen." His star began to rise with *High Sierra*, shone more brightly with the *Maltese Falcon*, and was at its brightest with *Casablanca* (57). Although he had an "uncontrollable tic above his left eye, the lip drawn taut over his open mouth, the vaguely oriental cast of his eyebrows, the hangover-gray pallor, the square jaw and the short hair," it was a "face that many women cannot resist" (56). Away from the studio, there were trips to New York to visit the 21 Club or to places frequented by newspapermen such as Bleeck's Artists and Writers Bar or Tim Costello's; there was drinking, and there were marital battles. While incorrect in his claim that Bogart had a happy marriage, Frazier finds the actor's candor and lack of restraint make him an appealing figure: "His private life has remained untouched by snide gossip simply because, by concealing absolutely nothing, he has robbed the columnists of any chance for idle speculation" (55). In a comment about Bogart that is repeated frequently,

Frazier says he acted and spoke in public like his screen image. Frazier's *The One with the Mustache Is Costello* (1947) contains much of the same information as his 1944 article, with some additional information on Bogart's theatrical career and his more recent career moves. Other portraits in the book are of Errol Flynn, Mark Hellinger, and Peter Lorre, figures Frazier had written about for *Life, True, Collier's, Coronet, Go*, and the *Boston Herald*.

Cameron Shipp's "The Adventures of Humphrey Bogart," which appeared in the *Saturday Evening Post* in 1952, was another favorable overview of the actor's first fifty-two years, and how Bogart was trying to break down the image that all actors are wonderful at home. Shipp portrays an actor who "toiled to re-establish the more interesting belief that actors are not necessarily wholesome, meantime making forty-six pictures [sic] getting famous, piling up a fortune, having a whale of a good time, and proving to his satisfaction that he is as tough as the gray-faced gunmen he plays on the screen" (32). As a guest, he was also an "answer to Dale Carnegie" (33). Of his many battles with Mayo, Shipp says that they were often funny but "tasteless" and avoids recounting them. Following in Frazier's footsteps, he notes that Bogart had few friends who were actors, but when he was not sailing, he especially liked to be around writers. He ended his article quoting two oft-repeated lines about Bogart by Dave Chasen that are sometimes attributed to Mike Romanoff: "He's a hell of a guy until eleven-thirty" and "The only trouble with Bogart is, he thinks he's Bogart" (57).

Columnist Earl Wilson includes a chapter on Bogart and Bacall in *The Show Business Nobody Knows*. He begins by recounting in detail the night of January 29, 1945, his big scoop, when Bogart announced to Wilson, and subsequently everyone else at the 21 Club, that he would marry Bacall as soon as his divorce was finalized. Bogart was a columnist's dream: he always made good copy except when he was drunk, and he "was never known to engage in publicity frauds. He lived the year around in a world of make-believe, false faces, and toupees, but he remained a realist who could stare you down and say, 'Now let's cut the crap and have a drink' " (265). Wilson recounts a number of humorous events surrounding his experience with Bogart, finding him refreshing and a part of "the most amusing phase of New York show business history" (266). Summing up his subject's character, Wilson says he was "irreverent, iconoclastic, disrespectful toward people on pedestals; he was civilized, urbane, intelligent; he couldn't tolerate the platitudinous, and I don't think he could do anything caddish or ungentlemanly—except during his moments of extreme overindulgence, and, of course, there were such moments. They were the only times that Bogart was ever boring" (269–270). Wilson does recount a meeting with Verita Thompson when Bogart introduced her first as his mistress and then explained that she was a "kind of secretary and hairdresser" (281).

In one of those Hollywood tell-alls, Verita Thompson claims in *Bogie and Me* that for fifteen years (1942–1957), during his marriages to Mayo Methot and Lauren Bacall, she was Bogart's confidante, hair stylist, and lover. After being introduced to Bogart by Ann Sheridan at a wrap party for *King's Row*, Bogart called the next day and invited her to lunch, and then propositioned her. Although married, she agreed. During the last years of his marriage to Mayo Methot, Thompson claims he escaped to her arms and eventually proposed to her, but she turned him down. After his marriage to Bacall, Thompson claims Bogart described his new wife as a social climber who loved to spend money. In 1949 he put Thompson on his payroll as an "executive secretary." For a time the Bogart and Bacall fan club considered Thompson a *persona non grata*. Reviewers have found the book curious and hurtful, and one that if true, smashes the supposedly idyllic image of the Bogart-Bacall marriage.

James Bacon, a Hollywood columnist who got to know Bogart because of the actor's penchant for working with those who could keep his name before the public—"Bogie was his own best press agent" (90)—has a section, "My Friend Bogie," in *Made in Hollywood* in which he gives background on Bogart's life and cult status, how he campaigned for his Oscar by browbeating voters, his battle with cancer, and his filmmaking. The section is more fiction than fact. Bacon claims that Bogart did say, "Tennis anyone?" (a line Bogart forever denied saying), that he considered his favorite film to be *Beat the Devil* (94), and that he was the most honest person he knew, especially in his discussion of his cancer.

Howard Greenberger's *Bogey's Baby* is yet another undocumented account of the Bacall-Bogart romance, starting with Bacall's arrival in Hollywood. There are sections on her life after Bogart, but most of the book deals with Bacall and her years with Bogart. It is this part of his life that seems to have the greatest appeal to readers and may account for why *Vanity Fair* published an excerpt from Sperber and Lax's *Bogart* on "Bogart and Bacall." This selection includes some photographs that are not found in other books or articles, background material relating to Bacall's early modeling career, comments from colleagues and friends, and some additional names and dates not often cited before connected to the couple's activities.

BIOGRAPHICAL SNAPSHOTS

In the 1942 issue of *Current Biography*, readers are told that Humphrey Bogart was born on January 23, 1899, and that he was notable for his appearance, suggesting that he had made it as a somewhat important figure. The article gives an overview of his theatrical and film background, saying that few remember much that he did before *The Petrified Forest*. We are told that directors found him to be a "steady untemperamental actor" who came to the set knowing his lines (8). His string of hobbies—bridge, golf, sailing, sketching, painting, playing bull fiddle, and making chessmen out of ivory—sound like a studio publicist's list.

Peter Barnes's "Gunman No. 1" is a brief career overview that claims Bogart was one of the few film actors whose last three films (*The Barefoot Contessa*,

Sabrina, and *The Caine Mutiny*) were outstanding for being sympathetic (*Barefoot*), dry and detached (*Sabrina*), and paranoic (*Caine*).

David Shipman says "Bogart took all sorts of characteristics and varying situations, and made them fit the Bogart persona" (71). Although he was wiry and not handsome, women found him attractive, even as he was both contemptuous and courteous; he seldom smiled, but had a "mirthless chuckle which he used mostly for scoffing at authority" (71). Against phonies, he "could be avaricious and mean but stubbornly heroic" (71). After recognizing that accounts differ, Shipman gives a birth date of around 1900, and then gives a few details of his life. Most of the article, except for the opening paragraphs on his screen presence, summarizes and comments on his films.

Hollywood and the Great Stars contains a brief overview of Bogart's life, giving his birthdate as either December 23 or December 25, describes his lip injury as caused by a U-boat shelling, and echoes the comments of others on his various films and how *High Sierra* brought him to the brink of stardom. His image conveyed a sense of "self-possessed arrogance," "at one with his own masculinity," and "he could do more with a cigarette than most actors could do with a machine gun" (7). The essay talks about him as a star, actor, and man and includes a filmography but is good primarily for its "sound bites."

Roger Manvell's brief entry in the *International Dictionary of Films and Filmmakers: Actors and Actresses* includes a short biography, a filmography, publications about Bogart, and a career overview. There is some misinformation about Bogart's attending college and the lip injury's coming from a shelling. To Manvell the career-making films are *The Petrified Forest, Dead End*, and *High Sierra*; the legend-making ones are *The Maltese Falcon* and *Casablanca*; and *The Treasure of the Sierra Madre, Key Largo, The African Queen, In a Lonely Place, Deadline—U.S.A.*, and *The Caine Mutiny* are roles that stretched him as an actor.

A collection of brief essays, including comments on his early life, marriages, Bogie and Bacall, rise to stardom, Hepburn and *The African Queen*, Bogart's pals, women in his films, a filmography, and a trivia quiz appear in volume 3 of *Screen Greats*. Lacking in substance, this is a collector's item for those interested in memorabilia or fan magazine commentary. A segment on his early life sides with those who say he was born on January 23, 1899, and that the studio hyped him as a Christmas baby to get mileage out of his gangster image. Overall this is a general synthesis of comments made by others on the topics discussed.

Alan Frank's book on the actor is part of a series on "Screen Greats," and as such falls into the pattern of the series: an overview of Bogart's life and career, brief comments on a variety of topics, snippets from newspaper reviews integrated into a commentary on the films, numerous illustrations, and a filmography but no index. This work is a more visual than textual pleasure and lacks insightful commentary.

From the title *Boating with Bogart*, by Gloria Stuart, one might expect a personal commentary on Bogart and his love of the sea from someone he knew. This strange little volume, only 100 copies of which were published, includes a few abstract drawings and a kind of verse printed on blue paper that talks about trying to sail with Bogart one day and hoisting a few during cocktail time. It is an oddity that is not readily available but is held in the rare book collection at the Library of Congress.

Twenty-two years after the appearance of the picture book *Bogart's Face*, Marie Cahill published an oversized book of Bogart images. The text accompanying the stills is basic information. In *Bullets and Ballots*, for example, he played a heavy who never gets the girl and will be killed or wounded in his film roles for the next few years. This 112-page book is designed for anyone who wants luxurious black and white publicity stills and an occasional impromptu shot of Bogart. Cahill has produced similar books on *Casablanca* and *The Maltese Falcon*. As the title of Dan Carlinsky's *The Great Bogart Trivia Book* implies, this is a series of quizzes on Bogart roles, character names, lines from films, who said what to whom, photographs, crossword puzzles, locales for films, and the like.

Immediately after Bogart's death, Robert Williams published a five-part biography of the actor in the *New York Post*, beginning January 15, 1957. Detailing some of the controversial things Bogart said and did, Williams brings together a compendium of his opinions and his headline-catching activities that paint him as a tough guy. In subsequent installments he discusses the newsmaking aspects of his life, including some of the apocryphal stories.

APPEAL AND CULT

In 1964, before the extensive publicity on Bogart's cult following at Harvard, Peter Bogdanovich had wanted to write about Bogart as "An American Hero." Because of Norman Mailer's serialization of his novel *An American Dream*, Bogdanovich changed the title of his piece. The essay synthesizes a series of quotations from people who knew and worked with Bogart (Benchley, Capote, Chester Morris, Bazin, Mankiewicz, Bacall, Cukor, Sid Luft, Peter Ustinov, and others) as he assesses the cult and legend. Bogdanovich finds Bogart's appeal to be based on many different factors: clothes, gestures (the snarl, the way he held a gun or a cigarette), his isolation, his ability to overcome great odds by himself, "the right blend of malice, gleeful anticipation and the promise of certain doom," his professionalism, and his avoidance of causes until won over. Part of the appeal is how Bogart represents a "portrait of a patriot, a man interested in the landscape of America" (83–84).

Using ideas of Robert Warshow from *The Immediate Experience* and genre studies, Harris Dienstfrey says that actors and genres together give many movies their power. Using *High Sierra, To Have and Have Not,* and *Casablanca* as examples, Dienstfrey acknowledges the director's stamp on each of these films and the importance of genre (*Casablanca* is described as a "displaced American" genre), but sees them more as embodiments of how an actor supplies "a film's basic orchestration," (36) actor as auteur. Audiences do not see the films again for their interest in themes; they see them because of the actors, in this case Bogart: "a presence simultaneously laconic, self-sufficient, innocent, vulnerable, and courageous—that these pictures acquire their primary force and the meanings, whatever they may be, that speak to us still" (36).

Eugene Archer discusses Bogart as a modern antihero who by 1965 had eclipsed Gable and Cooper. His "Hemingway-oriented directors" understood him as a character who lived by his own rules. "Bogart took nothing from nobody. He liked his women, but he expected nothing from them, and he treated them rough. He was small and arrestingly ugly, his drooping face creased into a permanent cynical sadness. The world, his expression seemed to say, is no damn good, and there's not a thing you can do about it. He wasted no time trying to communicate. Unless he had something to say, he just shut up" (9). To Archer, Bogart's appeal in 1965 was linked to how "in a world without values, he operated under a code of primitive self-interest. Yet he was instinctively loyal too, and there was always something gallant about his defeat" (9). Archer does not consider him a great actor, but notes that Bogart "always brought out the best" in Bergman, Bacall, Lupino, Gardner, Hepburn, and Astor.

In 1965, Richard Gehman published two essays on the Bogart cult, one in *True* and the other in *Cavalier*, and later in his biography of the actor. Gehman finds the core of Bogart's appeal in the attitude he conveyed and his voice. He quotes one New York exhibitor as saying that seventy of seventy-five of his films are box office gold, an obvious hyperbole since many of the earlier films were not available for screening. An NBC spokesperson says, "I can't account for it. . . . All we know is that it's there. We can show one of his oldest ones, and still they tune in. They can't seem to get enough of him" (SB 33). Bogart became a figure of American folklore as the public fascination focused on his drinking, his health, the company he was keeping, and his outlook on life. While Bacall thinks of him as "just a man" and that Bogart would laugh at how he has been canonized, Gehman notes that "the demand of movie and TV audiences all over the country has taken on the quality of a liturgical chant. The transfiguration of a hard-working professional actor, dead these eight years, into the living incarnation of Existential Man answers the need of the kids for a hero America can't, at the moment, give them in any other way." But what about the adults? He appeals to them as well and comes across as "tough, jaded, world-weary, a trifle sentimental without being sloppy, and above all ready for everything that life could throw at him: a fight, a battle, a lost cause, a storm, a woman" (SB 32–33).

Screenwriter (and later director) Robert Towne examines the appeal of Belmondo through his homage to Bogart in *Breathless*. He finds that Bogart, unlike the character Belmondo plays, was never bored. Belmondo's character and his actions are meaningless, the character gains no knowledge. Although he may live the moment with great energy, there is nothing inside. In contrast, what

Bogart's characters had experienced in their past made them what they were and gave some kind of meaning to their lives. With Bogart we see how human feelings and a sense of responsibility are evoked.

In an unsigned article for *Newsweek* in 1965, Joseph Morgenstern says that notwithstanding the apparent cult appeal and various film festivals, Humphrey Bogart was not a great actor (Archer and others have said the same thing) and certainly not as good as Cagney, but he was "marvelously tough and direct. He comes on hip and existential. . . . He also has that drifting quality. No occupation, no connection with family, community or country. He has terrific charisma!" (94A).

Bosley Crowther's "The Career and the Cult" attempts to define the appeal of the Bogart cult. Noting that theaters throughout the country were having Bogart revivals, Crowther compares his appeal to that of contemporary stars such as Connery and Belmondo. Tracing Bogart's appeal to the "style, his manner of being hard-boiled and contemptuous in a nice, dry, sardonic way" (112) that first attracted audiences at the Brattle Theater's showing of *Beat the Devil* in 1956, Crowther contends that when management saw the appeal of *Casablanca* the next year, they began to book his films "singly and then in groups of several over a two-week period" (112).

In assessing the myth or mystique, Crowther says it "has accumulated around a character that is part fictitious and part historical" (112). The fictitious is "the disillusioned, disenchanted individual moving through what is generally an alien world. And the historical part is the image of Bogey as a Hollywood personality of great independence, coolness, candor and disdain for the brass and all the manifestations of smugness and hypocrisy that are shown by the Establishment" (112, 158). The marriage of screen and historical character results from a blending by writers and directors "who created roles for Bogey that conformed to the shape his image took" (158). To Crowther the myth is made up of many elements: the character of Rick in *Casablanca* ("lonesomest loner of them all"); stories of the Holmby Hills Rat Pack; the stringent character of Sam Spade; distant echoes of romance with Baby; and the haunting history of a slow death by cancer endured with courage. "The total myth is far from a reflection of the man that Bogart was. Yet Bogart himself was not really the man he appeared to be—the man he ultimately acted in real life, just as devotedly and sincerely as the one he acted on the screen" (158).

Part of his appeal to the young of the 1960s, says Crowther, was Bogart's belief in certain values that he did not show, such as personal valor, compassion, nobility of spirit, and obeying the Golden Rule. Style, not moral behavior, was important to this group, and Bogart's style spoke to them in his gestures such as how he held a cigarette and he hitched his pants. Young men were attracted to his "firm contempt and cool aplomb" and young women saw him "as an image of masculine self-assurance and command" (160). Unlike James Bond, Bogart was "realistic, down to earth, selective and cool. He makes calculated decisions in situations that are credible. And he is excessively cautious and economical in his relations with women. He is wise to the phonies and the tricksters. It isn't often that he gets hooked. And chance seldom intercedes for Bogey. More often it knocks him around'' (160).

Crowther also observes that Bogart's life paralleled the main events of this century and that his films fit into the spirit of such major events as World War I, the Lost Generation of the 1920s, the Great Depression, the "disturbing Thirties," and World War II. For example, Roy Earle is "an outlaw, a cold and ruthless thug, assumedly unworthy of anyone's sympathy. But the way Bogey plays him, in his customary dry, hard style and with the distinctive white-wall haircut of his memorable Duke Mantee, he becomes a strangely sad and lonely symbol of a vanishing America" (160). In *The Maltese Falcon* he has the traits of the gangster but the guise of an okay Joe: "hip to the techniques of crime, so knowledgeable about and handy with guns, so disreputable in appearance, so cynical in his approach." *The Maltese Falcon* serves as the transition from phase one to phase two of his career, with Rick Blaine being a "smoother Sam Spade." By the time of *To Have and Have Not*, "The juncture was appropriate, for Hemingway's type of man, who is brave, laconic, disillusioned and a strong looker-out for himself, [and this] was pretty much the type that Bogey had come to represent." *The Big Sleep* is the end of the second phase, and the third and last phase begins with *The Treasure of the Sierra Madre*. In this film, which Crowther sees as Bogart's best, he was a "frightening representation of civilized man in a terminal stage" where "material things destroy his soul." In his subsequent roles he played "a succession of older, tireder, run-down men, fellows who have just about had it and are not expecting much more out of life" (161–162).

His romantic roles are "more by implication and innuendo than by the evidence of sexy scenes. . . . There is a conspicuous diffusion of sex drive and energy in his films. You get the peculiar impression that Bogey would rather play chess" (164). Of his professionalism, "He remained, as always, a real professional in his approach to his work. Directors and those who worked with him invariably remember him as the most punctilious and reliable performer they ever knew in Hollywood. He prided himself on being a 'theater actor,' which was his idea of tops" (164).

Kenneth Tynan's "Here's Looking at You Kid: The Man and the Myth," which appeared in the same issue of *Playboy* as Crowther's piece, has been republished under two different titles, with no significant change of content.[5] Tynan, like some of the earlier biographers, knew Bogart from afar, having met him only once. After having read eighty-three accounts of aspects of his life, Tynan noted the differences in such things as dates cited for his birthday, phrases attributed to him ("Drop the gun, Louie"), the accounts of verbal and physical abuse of his "guests," and his fondness for newspapermen and certain taverns in New York (198). As an actor, Tynan liked the " 'great famished wolf' " (196), who first attracted his attention (and his first published writing) in *The Petrified Forest*. Always a fan of the actor, Tynan notes that his darkest day was when Bogart withdrew support for those who he felt "used him" on the ill-fated trip to Washington in support of the First Amendment. Tynan concludes his essay with two ideas already promulgated by André Bazin—Bogart is a stoic, and he represents death on the screen. Tynan links Bogart and his image to comments Seneca wrote to Lucilius: " 'To be the slave of nothing, of no necessity, of no accident, and to make fortune face you on the level.' Therefore, live close to trouble and care nothing" (202). Bogart's appeal to Tynan is found in these traits and in his integrity and his ability to survive hangings, electrocutions, and shootings: "We trusted this antihero because he was a wary loner who belonged to nobody, had personal honour . . . and would therefore survive. Compared with many of his Hollywood colleagues, he seemed an island of integrity, not perhaps very lovable but at least unbought" (202).

Like our contemporary cultural icon the Energizer bunny, Bogart kept on going and going. What Tynan and others do not really focus on is how Bogart, though born of wealth, struggled for fourteen years before he got an important break. How many culturally important actors needed such a lengthy apprenticeship before making it big? But even then, it took almost another decade until he climbed to the top ranks of a studio that constantly treated its actors like chattel.

Exploring the cult at a time when several books had just been published on Bogart, Gerald Weales combines an assessment of the books that celebrate primarily the Bogart of the 1940s with a look at the man and his films. Using the name "Bogey" is anathema to Weales, who finds its use "culty." While the various publications split on whether Bogart was handsome or ugly, Weales finds that his heavy eyebrows and "a kind of vulnerability about the lower lip and chin" give him the "toughness" felt by viewers (665). Then the roles came that married the physical to the screen image, roles that were suggested in *San Quentin* and especially, to Weales, *All Through the Night* (665–666). As an actor, he had limited range and operated within the studio-defined range and within the confines of his own personality. In the last ten years of his film career, though, Bogart created characters "only distantly related to the personality that is now called 'Bogey' " (664).

In a valentine for Humphrey Bogart, Andrew Sarris looks back over the twenty years following the actor's death to consider the image and the appeal (at his peak in the 1940s, "rediscovered" in the 1960s). After glances at the French and Woody Allen's "cheerful image of Bogart" and the commercials that parody his voice and lip, Sarris reviews his career from the slow start in the 1930s to the 1940s. Sarris, like Cooke and Schickel, cites Otis Ferguson as one critic who began to see "the subtle villainies" in his performances (139). Sarris notes that "Bogart, unlike Cagney, was never directly wired to the streets; he was more the loner, the aloof nonconformist" (139). Influenced by *Dead End*, Sarris asks his students, "How could anyone love a man who had been so scarred by suffering that he became inordinately bitter and suspicious?" (139). In so many of his assembly-line films, he did not get the girl; it was not until *High Sierra* that people began to take notice. Then he did *The Maltese Falcon*, and "When he talked, people listened. When he listened, people chose their words with care" (140). *High Sierra* and *The Maltese Falcon* made him a star, but *Casablanca* made him a myth (140).

To Sarris, Bacall was able to rejuvenate Bogart's career because she gave a fifty year old a love that the audience wanted to see (141). Two subsequent roles, *The Treasure of the Sierra Madre* and *The African Queen*, were "showy performances for the actor, two costly self-revelations for the star" (141). But of all his scenes, Sarris chooses one from *The Big Sleep*, the one where Bogart is alone in a room, as the touchstone image. He is in a sinister room, where the atmosphere "drips with evil" and the camera is at a distance as Bogart looks for the clue. He is not just a "deductive detective; he has staked his whole life on the solution to the mystery." In so doing, he brings to the screen "his own very personal gravity. That is why he has proven to be irreplaceable in the past twenty years" (142).

In another thoughtful analysis of the Bogart persona, Joan Mellen says that "Bogart, more than any other screen hero, played the male who has learned that standing for truth, justice, and compassion does not come cheap—physically or materially" (225). The roles of the 1940s and 1950s create the image of the "man of feeling and the man of power and effectiveness." The "quintessential hero of *film noir*," he knew that we live in a world of evil and corruption, but with his code and integrity he was able to stay afloat (no mean accomplishment) in a world of "myriad dishonesties" (222). Unlike other commentators who analyze his misogynistic roles, Mellon sees a respect and high regard for women, more so than in the roles of Sean Connery and Clint Eastwood: "He enjoys their companionship. He empathizes with their plight and appreciates the guile with which they must move through a world in which they are always at a disadvantage" (224). He can walk away from women but does not find particular relief in that, as shown in *Dark Passage* (224). Mellen concludes that "Bogart's appeal was realized through the relinquishment of his freedom in favor of the right goal. It is this dramatization of existential choice that is at the core of his romanticism and may be the most important reason for the enduring attractiveness of his screen image" (225).

Molly Haskell's article in *Gentleman's Quarterly* examines the Bogart legend and its continued appeal over the decades. Very much of the 1940s, he has been rediscovered every decade since the 1960s, as we remember certain films and forget others in our selective memories. Summing up his appeal, Haskell says that he represents "a sexual icon to Woody Allen. A rebel to each new generation of undergraduates. An existential hero to the French, who 'discovered' him and first defined his mystique as one haunted by the 'angel of death.' To conservatives, he's a man in coat and tie who believed in hard work and traditional values and made honest women of his lady loves; to liberals, an idealist who stuck his head out for left-of-center causes and candidates and refused to be controlled by the studios. To men, he's a man's man, tough and undemonstrative; to women, a lover who combines the rock-hard reliability of the 'real' man with the attentiveness of the non-narcissist, an old-fashioned gentleman hiding behind the pose of the cynic'' (160).

There are substantive differences between Bogart's appeal on campuses as a romantic, inarticulate, doomed idealist and Haskell's vision of him as a talker and lover. The women (the "dames") in his films were attracted to him. Louise Brooks first commented on his sex appeal, and this was bolstered by Woody Allen's homage to a man who can get along without them but is also interested in them intellectually and physically (161). Haskell finds him relatively uninteresting in his earlier roles as a young juvenile, but by the 1940s, "time, drink, high living, snarling underworld roles and a mildly disfiguring accident to his upper lip, all combined to give another, uglier and far more interestingly beautiful face." Bogart was attractive not in a narcissistic way, but with a "creased look that never dates." And in later films, "he was a passionate and inward-looking man, without being ostentatiously so" (190). His sex appeal rests in characters with a softer center: "Out of his dark, disillusioned eyes there radiated an appeal that was irresistible to a woman: that of redeeming a man from his own cynicism. The lure of the reprobate, the lost soul—in its modern form, it's the diabolical appeal of Jack Nicholson. But with Nicholson, it's a lost cause.'' His relations with women "were modern" because he applied his code to men and women equally—"no special allowances." For all his "anti-heroic qualities, [Bogart] is essentially a moral force. He lives in an oral world of his own devising—in which loyalty occasionally takes precedence over the law—and he expects women to behave honorably, too'' (191).

François Truffaut's essay, "Portrait d'Humphrey Bogart," written under the pseudonym of Robert Lachenay in 1958, contends that early on he was bad at everything, until eventually "the best film writers and scriptwriters did their best work to order for him. It is thus possible to speak of the 'written work' of Humphrey Bogart'' (293). Truffaut believes his finest work was done with Nicholas Ray, who made him an "appealing hero" (294), but he recommends *Deadline—U.S.A.* and *Battle Circus* as good roles that have gone unrecognized. He concludes, "If Bogart's appearance was modern, his morality [or spirit] was classical. . . . He knew that causes are worth less than beautiful deeds, and that every act is pure so long as it goes by the rules'' (295). Truffaut repeats these same ideas in a subsequent essay for *Saturday Review*. Amplifying some of his earlier remarks, Truffaut notes how *In a Lonely Place* "made Bogart into something larger and better than an actor: an eloquent hero'' (32). Of the actor's mannerisms, gestures, way of speaking, and smile of death, Truffaut says that "the things Bogart did, he did better than the others. He could act longer than anyone else without saying a word, and he could threaten like no one else. When he sweated, you could wring it out of his shirts'' (32).

Shortly after Bogart's death, André Bazin, the guiding spirit of *Cahiers du Cinéma*, says of Bogart's impact and modernity that he was a hero more missed by men than women, a "hero with whom one identifies [rather] than the hero one loves." Bogart was a survivor, one who kept death at bay, as he "for a long time had internalized death," until proven mortal. In comparing him with the French actor and legend Jean Gabin, Bazin notes that Bogart was not a physical star. Much of his power was placed in words and how he said those words. The gun in his hands became an "almost intellectual weapon. . . . Doubtless the genius of this actor who knew how to make us love and admire in him the very image of our decomposition will never be sufficiently admired" (99). For the time 1940–1955 Bogart was "typically the actor/myth of the war and post-war period" (99), whose true character was revealed in his *noir* films. Bogart was very different from prewar heroes such as Gary Cooper and Clark Gable who were "handsome, strong, noble, expressing much more the optimism and efficiency of a civilization than its anxiety" (100). Bazin, who elsewhere develops his ideas of realism in cinema, remarks that three things came together in 1941: "the end of the pre-war period, the arrival of a certain novelistic style in cinematographic *écriture*, and, through Bogart, the triumph of the interiorization and of ambiguity" (100). Contrasting Bogart's acting style to that of the Actor's Studio (Kazin and Brando and Dean), he regards Bogart as a stoic and finds "the permanence of the character lies beyond his roles" as a man who "is not defined by his accidental respect, or his contempt, for bourgeois virtues, by his courage or his cowardice, but above all by this existential maturity which gradually transforms life into a stubborn irony at the expense of death" (101).

Scholars and film critics are not the only ones who have written about Bogart's appeal. In an article for *Seventeen*, sixteen-year-old Debbi Berson says she liked Bogart because he was able to come through "anything," and his slow chuckle, sharp wit, and unique voice made him "hip." Unlike Debbi Berson, eighteen-year-old Eugene Roseman had difficulty with the Bogart cult. While some of his peers viewed Bogart as an Andy Hardy type and others saw him as a complicated, existential hero, Roseman prefers James Cagney or beach party movies with Frankie and Annette that do not isolate Roseman from some of his contemporaries.

John Carlyle's essay on Bogart includes an assessment of the legend and career, a summary of his life, a filmography, and illustrations. A few of the dates, such as when he formed Santana and when he ended his ties with Warner Bros., are incorrect, but the strength of Carlyle's remarks lies in his discussions of Bogart's place in time and his special rapport with a particular generation. Although it took Bogart years to achieve success, he always remembered the advice of Holbrook Blinn, who, when asked how to achieve a reputation, told Bogart to "just keep working. . . . If you keep working, and people keep seeing you, people are going to begin to think you must be pretty good" (15). Bogart's cynicism and reserved sentimentality appealed to the rebels of the 1960s, many of whom simply referred to him as "H." But in "his own lifetime, Humphrey Bogart became an imposing star because his image of toughness and total self-reliance appealed to men, while women were drawn to his seeming loneliness, his weary state of too-knowledgeable bachelorhood due to a series of soured love affairs'' (6). As Berson noted in her piece in *Seventeen*, physical traits are important to an audience. Carlyle catalogs his grizzly appearance, receding hairline, faintly lisping gravel voice, scarred upper lip, and hard-boiled demeanor as traits that made him "immensely likeable" (7).

John Kobal's "Humphrey Bogart," in his oversized, spiral-bound volume *50 Super Stars*, includes a brief biography, a filmography, and general comments and pictures. Kobal finds Bogart the least likely to become a romantic superstar and echoes Dave Chasen's comment about how "he was Bogart, whatever he played, but the persona was not just a part; Bogart believed in things in his private life (which had its ups and downs), and stood up for his beliefs in public, even at the risk of his popularity. This sense of personal involvement came across on the screen with a power and intensity that no one else was ever able to equal" (18). Kobal says only three women were his match on the screen: Bergman in *Casablanca*, Bacall in *The Big Sleep*, and Hepburn in the *The African Queen* (18).

In 1970 Christopher Hart and Douglas Kenny discuss the Cambridge film festivals and the "real" and romantic images of Bogart in an interview with Lauren Bacall and Thomas Thompson of *Movie*. Hart and Kenny, avowed Bogart cultists, explain how some see similarities between Bogart and Mersault, Camus's existential hero in *The Stranger*, who faces the world without emotion. Some see Bogart as the embodiment of Hemingway's "grace under pressure," while to others he is a "tough guy with a heart of gold." Always very human, he has energy and a psychic force that prevents him from being taken in and comes across as a "stud" in his relations with women. Throughout the interview Bacall tries to convey the sense that while many may consider the screen image to be the man, Bogart was an actor playing parts: "I don't think there was one definitive role that was him. I'd say there was a little of him in a lot of parts" (M35). She says that "he belonged to himself more than anyone I've ever known. That to me was his attraction. He seemed to be indestructible because he believed so strongly in what he was doing and in a way of life and a way of dealing with people that permeated every role he played. . . . He was old fashioned about living" (M33). When pressed to name the role that came closest to him in real life, she contends that it was "Sam Spade in a way. . . . He never sold himself down the river. Bogie would never sell himself down the river, either" (M35). Even when others might want to run off, he would never do it because of his integrity and honor. That is why he fought Jack Warner about wretched scripts: "He fought a lot but there comes a point in your life when you have to make a living. He recognized life as it was but he did not compromise himself" (M36).

While many people were idolizing Bogart as a "cinematic saint" in the 1960s, Louise Brooks worked to set the record straight. In a piece that originally appeared in the French film journal *Positif*, later in *Sight and Sound*, and then *Lulu in Hollywood*, Brooks talks about the Bogart she knew from 1924 to 1943, his changes of fortune, his appeal to women, and how good acting adds "eccentricities and mystery to naturalness." For Bogart his mouth and his speech were those eccentricities (22). Of his stage work she remarks, "To be mentioned at all in any review amounted to praise for Bogart. On the stage he was as formless as an impression lost through lack of meditation, as blurred as a name inked on blotting paper" (20). In Hollywood, with all the control the studios had over their employees, the actors had to choose whether they wanted to be "loners" (on suspension or without contract) or employed. After a time in Hollywood, Bogart learned the game and cunningly solicited publicity: "Having rightly ascribed much of his previous failure in the theatre and films to a lack of publicity value, from the moment Bogart settled at Warner Brothers in 1936, all his time not spent before the camera was spent with journalists and columnists who invented for him the private character of Bogey" (19). As he created his persona, so too did he cunningly contrive a voice and lisp that did not exist in the theater.

Never a fan of Bogart, Brooks claims that his training in the theater put him at odds with words, to the point that he was afraid of them. That fear combined with a "fundamental inertia" that was overcome only by a desire for stardom. Brooks considers *In a Lonely Place* a film title that "perfectly defined Humphrey's own isolation among people. *In a Lonely Place* gave him a role that he could play with complexity because the film character's, the screenwriter's, pride in his art, his selfishness, his drunkenness, his lack of energy stabbed with lightning strokes of violence, were shared equally by the real Bogart" (21). His finest role, though, was *The Treasure of the Sierra Madre*, where the agony of Dobbs about to drag himself to the waterhole conveys "the face of my St. Bogart" (23). Unfortunately, in his last ten years, he "allowed himself to be formed into a coarse and drunken bully, a puppet Iago who fomented evil without a motive" (19).

Richard Griffith says even his name separates Bogart from other actors. Who would retain the name *Humphrey* if he wanted to be a star? So begins Griffith's analysis of "that maddening kind of actor who stands where he is told to stand, reads the lines he has memorized with the proper inflection, reacts correctly and on cue—and who seems to give absolutely nothing to a part or a picture beyond the bare essentials. . . . We all know such actors, we even sometimes remember their names" (270). But Bogart was different. He first came to Hollywood to be an actor, wound up a voice coach, then headed back to Broadway after some less-than-challenging roles in eight pictures in two years. A few years later, there he was, sitting in a chair with a machine gun in tow, creating a stir by his presence—the focus of everyone's attention—even though he said little—what Griffith describes as "menace through its very ambiguity" (272). The typecasting—on Broadway as a juvenile and in films as a gangster—resulted in "a lack" that was first touched on in *Black Legion*, which Griffith considers Bogart's "one purely intellectual feat of acting, a portrait which must have been drawn from observation, since there was nothing in his own upper-class background which could have furnished the details" (273). The link between this role and later as Rick Blaine is that "the adventures of the later Bogart are the daydreams of the Bogart of *Black Legion*, put together and served up with that blend of sophistication and infantilism which is the unique characteristic of the mass arts" (273).

Bogart's appeal stemmed in part from his ordinariness—speech, manner, and clothes—yet there was a confidence in his behavior and a sense of ease about living that conveyed a sense of how he could move about in mutually exclusive worlds—working in a factory or dining at the Ritz—that bound him to his audiences (273–274). Rejecting the phoniness and glitz of Hollywood, the one thing that he did latch onto was publicity: "Actors have press agents because what they say on their own is mostly either dull or damaging. Somebody has to write dialogue for them that will make them sound like themselves—i.e., their exciting screen selves. Bogart astounded the Warner publicity department by producing, on call and with ease, quotes that sounded more like him than anything the writers of his screenplays had been able to dream up" (274). His choice of a third wife was in keeping with his screen character. As his screen persona developed from *The Maltese Falcon* on, audiences began to sense "a man who seemed to have decided against a number of things in life. To conventions and manners, social and military usages, all the minutiae of getting through life, he gave a smiling lip service which shatteringly signalled that he had rejected them all. . . . His speech and manner of speaking were so patently insincere that when, as sometimes happened in his pictures, he had to express a genuine feeling or conviction, he was immediately in difficulties. . . . What he said was sardonic persiflage; what he thought you could only guess; it was what he did that you watched for. He was his own objective correlative" (275–276). Bogart created a beat-up Holden Caulfield who would meet things only on his own, self-alienated terms (276).

OTHER CRITICAL STUDIES

David Thomson's entry for Humphrey Bogart in *A Biographical Dictionary of Film* was originally published in 1976 and subsequently revised with brief edits of his earlier comments about his "Tennis, anyone?" roles and the addition of a quotation by Louise Brooks. Although Thomson does not have a high regard for Bogart's craft, he gives a substantive and thoughtful analysis and raises issues that have yet to be addressed in assessments of Bogart. Thomson begins with the cult and the fans in France who in seeing *Breathless* linked the "anarchist, behaviorist hero of the 1960s" to Bogart of the 1940s (71). He attributes the appeal to events of the time, such as the assassination of a president, the "cold war, international conspiracy, man-made pollution, the remorseless spread of corruption, and the ever darker threat of man's aptitude for self-destruction claimed for itself the sardonic pessimism, the neutrality, and the unfailing honor of the Bogart character" (71). He concludes by noting that "underlying everything was the idea that Bogart had been honest, truthful, and that he looked chaos in the eye, that he knew the odds and was the only reliable companion in the night." He finds this "nonsense and probably only possible if Bogart took something like the same view of his work in the cinema. It is time for a reappraisal, and while Bogart is often very close to the illusory heart of the movies, by the highest standards—Grant, Stewart, Mitchum—he is a limited actor, not quite honest with himself" (71).

Thomson dismisses most of his films save four (*High Sierra, To Have and Have Not, The Big Sleep,* and *In a Lonely Place*) and counters much of the praise of his work with Huston. He sees Bogart sharing, to some degree, the illusion of moviegoers that he becomes his screen characters—the "greatest test of stars in the cinema and Bogart falls heavily into it" (72). In an illusory way he is true to himself, is able to maintain grace under pressure, is stylish and elegant in his behavior, and remains detached. After an overview of his early stage career, Thomson says his big break was nothing more than an "ossified play," the film was "appalling," and "Bogart is dreadful in it. . . . Bogart was incapable of bringing character or conviction to such a part," whereas actors like Cagney and Robinson were "vivid and credible" (72). A classic failure is *The Roaring Twenties*, where his cringing and howling were "embarrassingly inept." His "sheer technical limitation" was seen in *Dark Victory* and countless other films (72). Only with *High Sierra* was there a turning point, because he was able to convey how "the outsider was confronted with all the hostile and inhumane forces of the world; crime was offered as an existential gesture." Here Bogart "was detached from everything except his own standards and his reluctant feelings for Ida Lupino. In part, he expressed the stoicism with which a frightened man might equip himself for war. But, most richly, the part pushed Bogart back on his own resources and brought out wit, a greater gentleness, and a grudging humanity—it was as if the world had at last recognized the person he always believed himself to be" (72).

Thomson claims that *The Maltese Falcon* owed most to Hammett, not Huston, and that *Casablanca* was "a wet dream," and "a woman's picture for men and the sort of unblinking tosh, set deep in never-never land, that is the essence of Hollywood" (73). Bogart needed Curtiz "to help him rise above the level of maudlin resentment" (73) in the drunken scene. "It is to Bogart's credit that he seems not only aware of the trick but a prime agent in it. Thus, they work on two levels: as beautiful fantasies and as commentaries by the participants on their very absurdity" (73). *Dead Reckoning* was the "first parody of the Bogart manner" (73), and the three films that pushed Bogart to "a deliberate inspection of his own divided personality" were *The Treasure of the Sierra Madre, The Caine Mutiny,* and *In a Lonely Place*. The first two are "glib." But *In a Lonely Place* "penetrates the toughness that Bogart so often assumed and reaches an intractable malevolence that is more frightening than any of his gangsters" (73). Bogart failed in "a variety of parts outside the narrow range he saw fit for himself. But within that range he had the impact of Garbo or James Dean. Like them, he was a great Romantic. It is harder to see him as such because of the efforts he made to appear anti-Romantic. The implications of his work—as a comment on self-dramatization—are rather more daunting and disturbing than he ever realized'' (73).

Alan Barbour's *Humphrey Bogart* is part of the Pyramid Illustrated History of the Movies series that focuses on key figures in motion picture history. Barbour divides his work into six segments, giving a quick overview of Bogart's life, followed by five chapters on his film career and a short concluding chapter on the Bogart legend. Profusely illustrated, this work has a short bibliography, a filmography that includes unbilled appearances, and an index. Bogart's career is divided into the three standard threads: learning his craft (to *The Petrified Forest*), working on his skills (to *The Maltese Falcon*), and his peak and final years. Barbour, like others before him, finds that Bogart's appeal defies easy analysis because it is based on his multiple screen personae: brash, romantic, insulting, and clever. He is the "ideal lover," a gangster, a hero, and an antihero. The young are attracted to a "somewhat Bohemian image," a man who speaks his mind on behalf of the victimized, an independent spirit, and an individual who makes mistakes. These traits and his looks make him more believable than other screen giants. Women find him attractive because he is intelligent, maintains a posture of superiority, and blends compassion with savagery (137–138). Others see him as an embodiment of an era that has passed. But he appeals to all groups in part because "he always managed to adhere to a particular code of decency and honor that was exemplary" (139). Barbour's book is a good entry-level overview of the career, but does not offer any keen insights.

Along with Goodman, Louise Brooks, and Thomson, James M. Purcell makes one of a few virulent attacks on Bogart the actor and person. Based on personal opinions and incorrect facts (Bogart died in 1956, and *Touch of Evil* is the source for *Psycho*), Purcell says, "There are no Bogart film classics. He was a good, but limited actor; and . . . his starring image . . . had no greater psychic range than the image of Wallace Berry or Will Rogers" (6). Attacking Bogart because his films lack "political guts," are misogynistic, and have been "totally disastrous" as cultural influences (6), Purcell divides Bogart's career into types (Forgotten Bogart, 1930–1932; Contract Player, 1936–1940; Star Career, 1941–1948; and Star-Character-Actor, 1949–1956). He is incorrect in suggesting that up to the time of his essay, no one had done an analysis of Bogart as an actor (Louise Brooks and David Thomson had). While the last thirty years have seen numerous books and articles on film acting and stardom, except for Hanners, Virginia Wright Wexman, Louise Brooks, Richard Thomson, Richard Schickel, and a few other brief commentaries, there is very little on Bogart as an actor.

Instead of analyzing his acting, Purcell says Bogart was not as good as everyone claims because his films were not the top grossers for the year. He considers Bogart's fifteen-year contract to be a "holdup contract" (n. 7:16). Based on his definition of a "classic" (technical innovations, early mutation of a genre film, or absorption of all the technical developments of the time), Bogart's films do not fit the mold. Purcell dismisses *Casablanca* as "a (thin) romance with a

Macguffin plot about a Vichy passport at a frontier town'' (11). The wartime Bogart was used for government purposes and became an A-star without taking any career risks. Purcell totally ignores the studio system, how Bogart was assigned scripts, and the years of apprenticeship. He also finds Bogart's screen character "inseparable from the sex war of his period in our power class as were his private marital experiences" (16).

In an almost point-by-point refutation of Purcell's commentary, Brian Garfield shows how, while complaining about the lack of standards used to review Bogart's acting, Purcell does nothing himself to substantiate his low opinions of Bogart and his films: "He seems to have no standard at all; he simply takes potshots at his target from all possible directions at once" (186). Garfield rightly notes that at one point, Purcell complains that Bogart was part of the studio system, but then complains that his choice of roles was poor. Purcell's denigration of the films shown at film festivals had nothing to do with the financial success of the films when they opened, and *Virginia City* was definitely not one of Bogart's best performances. In his attempt to demythologize Bogart, Purcell dismisses Bogart's films, especially those of the 1940s, while Garfield strongly disagrees.

John Hanners's comments on Bogart's acting are based on a series of highly selective quotations from others. Relying primarily on Louise Brooks (negative), Billy Wilder (negative), Stephen Bogart (positive), and Rod Steiger (positive), Hanners reviews Bogart's theater career ("desultory, and ultimately mediocre") and his transition to film. Much of the essay examines Bogart as stage actor between 1922 and 1935 and how he "transferred his stylized, external technique to film, using creative energy in short bursts to create scenic effects." Using only a fraction of the early commentaries on Bogart as an actor, Hanners zeroes in on his hatred of memorization, his discipline, and his avoidance of any theory of acting: "He knew he had a feel for elements of the actor's craft—recognizable character, timing developed through years of playing comedy, the pre-1930s fear of over analyzing a role, [and] control of external physical features." To Hanners the camera's attraction to his "artificial acting technique" and physical self led to his appeal.

In "The Death of Sam Spade," Joe Goldberg describes Bogart's character as taciturn, resourceful, courageous, solitary, and of few words. He sees Bogart's attitude toward acting (and the many horrid roles) as not unlike Sam Spade—a professional who has a job to do (107). When Goldberg asks himself why Bogart is a symbol of his times, he considers Raymond Chandler's analysis of Philip Marlowe: "He must be a complete man and a common man and yet an unusual man. He must be . . . a man of honor, by instinct, by inevitability, without thought of it, and certainly without saying it. He must be the best man in his world and a good enough man for any world. I do not care much about his private life. . . . If he is a man of honor in one thing, he is that in all things" (108). Goldberg sees Bogart as the embodiment of a personal code, one that the existentialists described as "definition through action" (109). André Gide notes that Hammett's dialogues convey how every character is trying to deceive others. A fine actor, but "not a great one," Bogart was Spade—"a cynical idealist, a romantic gone sour" (110). "Neither the on-screen nor the off-screen Bogart postured or preached, but kept to himself, ambiguous, his privacy unapproachable, until his private ethic told him it was time to act. And then, he did not speak; he *acted*" (112).

When asked about actors, William Faulkner replied that "Humphrey Bogart is the one I've worked with best" in *To Have and Have Not* and *The Big Sleep* (114). Bogart liked to work with Huston because he was "never dull" and permitted actors to concentrate on acting rather than "business" (114). Goldberg considers *The Treasure of the Sierra Madre* to be Bogart's best work and three films with Huston as screen classics: *Maltese*, *Treasure*, and *Beat the Devil*: "The Huston trilogy of murder for riches . . . are the best films Bogart ever made, and contain his best work; significantly, Huston has never attempted to duplicate them with another actor" (115). Within five years after Bogart's death, Hammett, Chandler, Hemingway, and Camus died. "And on the screen Bogart embodied them all, not because he was a great man, a great rebel, or a great actor, but because it was his job" (116).

Allen Eyles's *Bogart* gives a biographical overview, including apocryphal stories, but is mostly an appreciation of the actor. He claims his work provides the first "comprehensive and detailed survey" of the films, as he discusses Bogart's appeal, his dedication to his craft, and his life off screen. We should remember him not for the legend but for being a "fine and sensitive actor." His appeal is based on the luck of certain roles, his stoic heroism, his "neurotic touchiness," a "clammed up aloofness," a "profound disillusionment and disenchantment," and a "craving for emotional honesty and deep commitment" (7–9). Eyles's is one of the few commentaries on Bogart's self-conscious use of gestures and devices that contributed to his screen presence and screen magnetism (13). He presents a good summary and limited but substantive analysis of the films, as he links earlier versions of films, remakes, and the development of Bogart's persona. Profusely illustrated, the volume includes a filmography and highly selective bibliography.

The program director of the London Film Festival and National Film Theatre since 1969 and editor of an international film journal, Ken Wlaschin chose 400 stars to analyze for their importance, reputations, and values. He sees Bogart as being made a star-actor by Walsh, Huston, Curtiz, and Hawks and notes that these directors inverted Bogart's gangster image to become the "epitome of the disillusioned antihero": the "black knight, himself honest in a dishonest world" (51). He says that Walsh added the humor through the wisecracks in *The Roaring Twenties*, a cynical sense of humor in *They Drive by Night*, and a portrait of a gangster with integrity in *High Sierra*; Huston made him an antihero, disenchanted but perceptive; in *Casablanca* Curtiz made him an existential hero who moved beyond his cynical facade; and Hawks created the apotheosis of the new image—more humanity than Spade, but less cynical, with an awareness of his limitations and his environment (51).

In an impressionistic review of Hollywood stardom in *The Stars*, Richard Schickel includes Bogart in his chapter on five heroes, along with Cooper, Gable, Tracy, and Stewart. He places Bogart in the background of the studio system and notes how he worked through roles that reinforced an idea—"a strong, previously well-defined personality" (183)—that was already there in film audiences. Central to Bogart's existence is how his toughness and knowledge of the urban environment helped him to survive a loneliness "based on suspicion of everyone's motives" (190–192). Those traits, combined with "the rightness of setting, mood and dialogue" (190), made him a spectator favorite.

Richard Schickel's 1986 article in *Film Comment*, which served as a preview for the book-length *Legends: Humphrey Bogart*, regrettably never published, is one of the two or three most substantive analyses of Humphrey Bogart's appeal and how his screen roles grew out of his "real" life. Although Raymond Chandler was right that Bogart was the "genuine article" and although Bogart's image as a tough guy remained, "perhaps *the* essential element—in his persona" (34), he had the rare gift of blending real and fictional to the point where "neither the performer nor the audience is entirely aware of where the one ends and the other begins" (34).

Of his roles before *Casablanca*, Schickel finds little in *The Petrified Forest* except Bogart's "trapped-animal seething," which got him a contract at Warner Bros. Two later films, *Black Legion* and *Dead End*, convey a "mutual alienation between himself and society" that found its way into his later roles (37). Miscast in his films between 1937 and 1940, Bogart presented "unredeemable badness" in his films with Cagney, while his counterpart conveyed "vulnerable charm." Was Bogart "trying too hard to make an impression" or could he "make no emotional connection with these supporting roles, could [he] not find a way to inhabit them" (37)? With only limited success and token recognition at the studio, he consoled himself by sailing, playing chess, reading, and entertaining writers such Mark Hellinger, Robert Benchley, John O'Hara, Louis Bromfield, Nunnally Johnson, Quentin Reynolds, and Dorothy Parker at his modest home on Horn Avenue or in New York (38). But *High Sierra* led to a reconsideration of his value to the studio and among critics. As Roy Earle, a man trying to adjust to a new world who would sooner die than adjust to it, Bogart "for the first time in a movie, gave a full and touching performance." But it was not until *The Maltese Falcon* that "he was truly hypnotizing, and unambiguously attractive, on the screen" (39). After this film, he was a star and "a genre unto himself." In *Maltese* and *High Sierra* "his romantic appeal had been couched in essentially masculine terms," but in *Casablanca* "he was permitted to display his emotions, thus doubling his audience by showing himself to have qualities to which women could readily respond" (40).

Although *Casablanca* was not his best role, Schickel notes how it provided him with a role in which "Bogart, the actor, is easeful . . . , instinctively at home with his character in a way that he only rarely had been before, and never as fully as this" (34). Rick embodies the kinds of conflicts that Bogart and so many of us have when "personal desire" is pitted against "traditional moral imperatives and public need," and when memories of the past take us in one direction and thoughts about the future in another. To some, especially the French critics, Bogart "found an objective correlative in Rick" (35). Others may have championed him as a tough guy or an existential hero, but what his characters personified in this and other films are the "general principles of conventional morality or traditional masculine ethics" (35). Bogart frequently said his value system came out of the nineteenth century, and Schickel reminds us that "Rick was but a minor variation on the role he had himself been playing most of his adult life." Bogart-Rick was a "man of breeding and privilege who found himself far from his native haunts, among people of rather less quality, rather fewer standards morally, socially, intellectually, than he had been raised to expect to find among his acquaintances." As a "young man of good family, made restless by their pieties, cautions, and hypocrisies, [he rebelled] against them, ultimately exercising that rebellious spirit in dangerous and romantic ways" (35–36). There is an affinity with Rick, but the key to Schickel is not what he came from but his loss of that which made him what he was. His roles as a juvenile were close to his background, but it was only with time that he developed "the air of rue, of unspoken regret for unnameable things" (36).

After some comparisons with Fred C. Dobbs, Schickel says that as Rick, Bogart portrayed "a man of breeding, education, and social grace—who has been at one of society's centers and is now falling away from it as the result of this thing [mental distress] that has taken possession of him" (43). Bogart's performance synthesizes "all his solitaries of the past decade but draining them of all romance. . . . He simply is" (43). To Schickel, *Casablanca* is the high point and the end of his screen career in that nothing else he does is really new. Bogart achieves legendary status "in the most pleasing possible way, for he had transcended not by transforming himself, not by trying to be something he was not, but by finding within himself certain universal, or at least universally recognizable and appealing, traits. And then by finding, after his arduous apprenticeship, a way of projecting them, without strain, without self-consciousness" (46). But because there were characters he played that were not from himself, characters based on "observation and insight," then he was more than a star, he was "an actor in the fullest sense of the word" (46).

The most recent extended study of Bogart is Robert Sklar's thoughtful and insightful *City Boys: Cagney, Bogart, Garfield*, a study of "film performance in its cultural, social, and political dimensions, through combined professional biographies" of the three actors (xii). The term *city boy* brings together motivating factors in the studio system, genre and production conventions, and ideology (9). Using recent critical approaches to film, including star and cultural studies, combined with historical, biographical, and political perspectives, Sklar examines how Cagney, Bogart, and Garfield embody the urban experience for film audiences, how they used and were used by the studio system, and the impact of the HUAC hearings on their personal and professional lives. Sklar traces Bogart's difficult years, his lackluster theatrical career, and his turbulent relationships with women and studio hierarchy as they connect to each of his films. Always ready to work for top billing and professional recognition, Bogart endured one of the longest apprenticeships in studio history, but as Sklar notes, "It seems quite possible that the delay in Bogart's stardom was due not entirely to the obtuseness of Warner's executives, but also to his own deficiencies as a negotiator or in presenting himself as a performer deserving special attention" (120). Sklar concludes that Bogart's low point came in the little-discussed accounts of his 1947–1948 imbroglio with HUAC and the First Amendment Committee. Turning from his friends and tough guy image because his "will to survive was greater than his courage," Bogart and his screen image hide "a more interesting and complex figure, Humphrey Bogart, the man and the actor" (251).

FILMOGRAPHIES

Clifford McCarty's *Bogey: The Films of Humphrey Bogart* has been considered the standard filmography since its publication. The text builds on an article that appeared in *Films in Review*. McCarty opens the article with a brief biography, followed by apocryphal stories, including how Bogart dunked a teacher at Phillips Academy, a supposed failure at directing a movie for Bill Brady called *Life*, his stint as a road show manager, and how his desire "to get ahead" led to his acting. He spells Helen Menken's name with a "c" and Mary Philips's with two "l's." The article discusses material covered by others: that Bogart liked to help young actors, his appeal to men because of his toughness and to women because of his awareness of their wiles, and a general appeal to the "cynicism of our age" (200). McCarty believes that central to our understanding of his roles and his character is Louis Bromfield's comment to Bogart about the "man in struggle, not the man arrived, holds the interest of an audience, and that people are absorbed with how men get out of difficulties, singled-handed and alone, if possible" (200–201). Typos or misspellings in the credits mar the longer filmography, which includes summaries, photos, and credits for Bogart's seventy-five films and citations for some shorts and cameos. Unlike some of the later books in this particular series, which have analytical essays or discussions of the reception of the films, McCarty provides only brief comments on each of the films.

Other filmographies include those by Terrence Pettigrew (1977) and Wolfgang Fuchs (1987) and a listing by David Badder in *Film Dope*. Badder's filmography adds nothing to previous publications and merely provides the titles of the films. Similar to McCarty's filmography but somewhat more inclusive is Fuchs's volume, which has sections on Bogart's life and times, plot summaries and credits for the films, television appearances, discs, a brief discussion of the cult, selected quotations, and numerous illustrations. Pettigrew gives a general overview of Bogart's films, grouping them by types ("Echoes of Rick," "King Rat," and "Lighter Side") and providing summaries and snippets of film reviews, especially from England. While Bogart films collected four of the top twelve slots in a survey of the *London Sunday Times* around the time Pettigrew was writing the book (5), he believes there is no one answer to Bogart's screen appeal. Still, he claims that the "backbone of Bogart's appeal lies in his dour refusal to accept anyone except on his own terms or to auction his integrity" (6). Much in the study is based on McCarty's book, with filmography (and its inaccuracies) taken from there, and a listing of some of his theater work taken from Bernard Eisenschitz's study that was published in France. Other inaccuracies include his claim that Bogart attended college and was in the navy until 1920. In assessing how Bogart played with the press to his advantage, Pettigrew notes that while we have a history of his activities, the "columnist-biographers" do not give us a sense of the man (10). Some of this material is recast in Pettigrew's *Raising Hell: The Rebel in the Movies*, which is primarily summaries of the films and some brief commentary on each. *All Through the Night*, for example, is a "curious mix of gangland spoof and sober warning about enemy infiltration" (52), *Casablanca* is a "clever political allegory" (53), *Action in the North Atlantic* is "an eloquent tribute to the US merchant marine service" (55), *Sahara* is a hooray for multinational troops (57), *Passage to Marseille* is a paean to our freedoms (59), and *To Have and Have Not* is "a slice of contemporary propaganda" (60).

Paul Michael's *Humphrey Bogart: The Man and His Films* claims to present a close-up view of the actor and his legend. It is profusely illustrated (including a few pictures rarely seen in other books) and contains a short biographical chapter, sprinkled with quotations from those who worked with him or interviews (all undocumented), summaries of each of his films, abbreviated credit and cast lists, and an index. Michael, following a claim made originally by Louise Brooks, says that Bogart had his father operate on his lip when he received a contract from Fox. Like others, Michael sees *The Petrified Forest* as the role that gave him life but *High Sierra* as the real turning point (18). Although there is an attempt at some analysis of Bogart's screen persona in the biographical section, the bulk of the commentary is a description of the plots of the films. Michael does give release dates, not found in McCarty's filmography, but they are not always accurate. *The African Queen*, for example, is listed for March 1952, about the time Bogart was winning the Oscar for it, and the credits are not presented in chronological order, nor are they as inclusive as, for example, those found in McCarty.

For someone who has received so much attention in books and articles, by 1982 Harvey Elliott found a surprisingly limited number of Bogart films on video and disc. In addition to finding his honest, uncompromising character, and strength in the face of adversity to be "fresh and honest and contemporary" (101), Elliott is baffled by the absence of Bogart tapes because "Bogart really started this whole thing—watching old movies again and again" (67). Fifteen years later, except for some of the films from the thirties, most of Bogart's films are available on video.

FILMS

Humphrey Bogart's importance in the history of movies and popular culture of the United States is unquestioned. His frequent appearance as a character actor in the 1930s, his role in major films of the 1940s and early 1950s, his participation in numerous radio broadcasts, and his cult status in the past forty years suggest that his work in films would be the subject of many studies. Not surprisingly, fan magazines always found Bogart good copy, and articles about him appeared frequently, starting in the late 1930s. Since his death in 1957, and especially as a result of Bogart film festivals that began shortly after, interest in Bogart has not abated. Articles and books published overseas began appearing in the 1950s and mushroomed in the 1960s as the Bogart cult spread and audiences, most notably those in France, looked with new enthusiasm at American films of the previous three decades. In the United States, there are countless references to Humphrey Bogart in popular weeklies and monthlies, in surveys of the history of movies, star and director biographies, and studies of cult films, movie genres, and *film noir*, but most of the scholarly work has focused on a handful of his films.

During his career, Humphrey Bogart acted in seventy-five films, one Vitaphone short, spoke in three wartime shorts, and appeared in cameo roles in several films. Most popular and scholarly attention in the United States has been focused on *The African Queen, The Big Sleep, Casablanca, High Sierra, The Maltese Falcon*, and *The Treasure of the Sierra Madre*. Recently, with a profusion of articles and books on *film noir*, greater emphasis on film history and cultural studies, and momentary attention to films of deceased actors with whom Bogart starred, a few of Bogart's other films, including *Black Legion, Dark Passage, In a Lonely Place, Marked Woman*, and *Sabrina*, have begun to receive critical attention. Critics and viewers in other countries seem never to tire of Bogart.

One of the main problems confronting those who want to research Bogart's work is the lack of a comprehensive bibliography. No one source fully lists the articles and books about the actor and his films, and material on the Internet is incomplete and often inaccurate. This section focuses on books or articles with substantive remarks on the films, the actor, or books about professionals who worked with Bogart on particular films and whose commentaries help us to understand his performances, a particular film, or a key aspect of his career better. To include every title with a reference to Humphrey Bogart would be impossible, since references to books about a single actor (e.g., Bette Davis), a studio (e.g., Warner Bros.), a decade (e.g., the 1940s), a director (e.g., John Huston), novels into film (e.g., Chandler, or Faulkner, or Hemingway), genres (e.g., Dashiell Hammett and detective fiction), or reviewers (e.g., James Agee) would extend this study well beyond its focus, but selected titles are included. Similarly, passing mention of Bogart or his films by reviewers such as James Agee, Pauline Kael, Stanley Kauffmann, and Bosley Crowther are generally excluded unless the commentary adds substantively to discussions of Bogart or his persona.

Occasionally, I cite reprints or duplicate listings—for example: an unattributed commentary on *The Maltese Falcon* in *Cinema: The Novel into Film*, the same entry in *Magill's Survey of Cinema*, and once again in *Magill's American Film Guide*, where, finally, author attribution is given. Discussed and listed elsewhere are filmographies that give credits and plot summaries.

I have tried to examine as many of the items cited as possible. Many non-English-language books and articles published overseas are not indexed, and some of those that are were not readily available to me. As a result, I have focused my documentation on English-language publications. Not discussed but available widely are the countless newspaper reviews and film summaries that are accompanied by film credits. The pressbooks are available in the Warner Bros. archives at the State Historical Society of Wisconsin in Madison. Within these parameters, while I have tried to be as inclusive as possible, I am certain that there are articles or books that I have missed. I would like to hear from readers who can recommend additions, corrections, or emendations to this bibliographical material.

According to Jonathan Coe, Bogart's film career began in 1928, when he made the two-reeler *The Dancing Town* with Helen Hayes. Nothing has been written on this film, and Coe and subsequent writers have listed it without any commentary. The New York Public Library (Lincoln Center, Billy Rose Theatre) at one time had a folder in its Universal collection by that title, but the material is missing and I could find no other record or discussion of the film. Clips of Bogart's "next" two-reeler, *A Devil with Women* (1930), have been shown in documentaries of the actor, but nothing substantive has been written about that film or *Up the River, Body and Soul, Bad Sister* (Bogart's first role as a heavy), *Women of All Nations, A Holy Terror, Love Affair, Three on a Match*, or *Midnight* (a.k.a. *Call It Murder*). While there are film summaries and occasionally a picture or two from these films in fan or movie magazines, critics and scholars for the most part began to pay attention to Bogart's performances only starting with *The Petrified Forest*. Between *The Petrified Forest* and *The Harder They Fall*, besides an occasional reference in a studio history, career overview, histories or biographies of other actors, or genre history, no substantive attention has been given to the thirty-five films cited at the end of the checklist (p. 274).

The Petrified Forest

The earliest work of Humphrey Bogart to receive critical attention is *The Petrified Forest*. Carlos Clarens finds the film and others like it to be "loaded with ambition and sociopoetic significance" (142). Joseph Wood Krutch calls it a "melodramatic farce with a moral." Focusing on the disillusionment of the post–World War I era, this film is credited with establishing Bogart in Hollywood. Yet for all its supposed importance in Bogart's career, except for histories of the gangster film, very little has been written about it. Timothy Johnson's overview in *Magill's American Film Guide* provides a summary of the plot, a brief discussion of why the basics of the play were not "opened up," and the existential nature of the film. Paul Trent finds the film "little more than so much pseudo-poetic, semi-sophomoric philosophizing about one remarkably shoddy notion: that a depressed poet and a crazed killer can make a worthwhile contribution to the the world" (108). Even though he received fifth billing, Bogart walked off with the picture as "his terrifying, cold-blooded Mantee . . . salvages the film and invests it with a semblance of reality" (108). In bringing Bogart back to Hollywood, this film is the first salvo in establishing him as "the number-one villain and tough guy in films" (108).

Bullets or Ballots

One of the oft-cited but little discussed gangster films is *Bullets or Ballots*. Lukow and Ricci examine it along with three others (*Little Caesar, Public Enemy*, and *The Roaring Twenties*) in the light of a "relay" of intertextualities at work on the subject (audiences) and the object (text). They see shifts in the presentation of gangsters, the role of the public in fighting them, and "reorientation of spectatorship within the genre" by 1939 (36). With its opening newsreel serving as a catalyst for the violence presented in the film and with gangsters watching gangsters in the newsreel, *Bullets and Ballots* "represents a greater, more direct involvement in the fight against crime by the *medium of film itself*" (32) and is an example of how a film can stress the public's role as it relates to the gangster.

Black Legion

One of many Warner Bros. social commentary films was *Black Legion*, in which Bogart as Frank Taylor loses his promotion to someone who is foreign born. Given all the attention to the Klan and other subversive organizations in this country, it is surprising how little has been written about this film. Reviewers such as Graham Greene found it "intelligent" because "the director and the script-writer know where the real horror lies," but they were unable to capture the true horrors: that people we know act immaturely when they wear robes and hoods, that we romanticize guns, and that the membership takes on a businesslike matter-of-factness. After its release, the film was used in schools to teach about differences, and the Progressive Education Association, as part of a series produced by the Commission on Human Relations Progressive Education Association in New York City, published a thirty-five-page document summarizing the sequences of violence in the film, suggesting questions for discussion, including contemporary newspaper headlines related to Klan and Black Legion violence, and offering other source materials and a bibliography for student use.

Marked Woman

The earliest substantive and most frequently cited article on *Marked Woman* is by Charles Eckert, who gives background on "Lucky" Luciano's trial in 1936 and an extensive summary of how the material was molded into the film. The heart of Eckert's analysis, which uses Marxist, Freudian, and structuralist approaches, is divided into sections on the film's structure and ethos and its place in the gangster genre. To Eckert, Hollywood's film production practices muted the class conflict central to the film. By analyzing the presentation of proletarian women in a gangster film and how gangsters and vice are represented as big business against the backdrop of the Depression, Eckert explains that the filmmakers present and audiences receive the conflicts in the film on an "existential rather than political or economic" level through an elaborate "secondary structure" (11). On one hand there is the gangster and his downfall, and on the other there are the dilemmas the women face in their everyday lives and as victims of Vanning, the Luciano figure. While most socially conscious films of the 1930s and early 1940s often give background information that explains or exonerates the behavior, there is usually a shift to melodrama. Not so in *Marked Woman*, where the "real conditions" of apathy, alienation, and confusion dominate. Even with Vanning out of the way, the women do not escape to a better life (17). As a result, the filmmakers "mitigated some of the worst effects of the melodramatic form" by focusing on women who will not be sentimentalized (24). Bill Nichols notes that Eckert's article "remains one of the most lucid applications of structuralist Marxist and Freudian concepts to film criticism that we have" (407).

Following the lead of Eckert are articles by Mary Beth Haralovich, Haralovich and Cathy Root Klaprat, and Theodora Price. In an examination of a number of films of the 1930s that deal with how women fared under patriarchal capitalism, Haralovich discusses "oppositional meanings in the entertainment film" (172) and how *Our Blushing Brides* (1930) and *Marked Woman*, one film that appears before and one after the introduction of the 1930 Motion Picture Production Code, which dictated what could not be shown, deal with issues of gender, power, and economics, as well as censorship and studio production (182) in "complex and contradictory discourses" (176). Building on Eckert's essay, Haralovich discusses how even though the audience has knowledge through published accounts of the economic advantages of prostitution and the case of Lucky Luciano, both matters are suppressed in the film. Linking the pressbook advertising for Bette Davis, her return to acting after a one-year battle with the studio, and the merchandising of products associated with Davis, Haralovich contends that "the women's costumes, used to demonstrate the economic and sexual exploitation of the women by gangsters, also demonstrate studio production values and the star system as they are offered as fashions and spectacle to the female spectator" (186). Thus, in *Marked Woman*, we see that "censorship works in concert with other conditions of Hollywood film production, notably the star system and merchandising, to displace concerns about morally difficult meanings circulating through the film" (187).

Haralovich and Klaprat examine how narrative and ideology work differently in ninety-second trailers that establish tension, while the full feature presents an expository causal order. "Hermeneutics are much more strongly marked in trailers than in films. . . . Trailers, are in fact, constructed by a series of ruptures to an implied narrative homogeneity by subverting the linearity of causality" (66). They discuss uses of wipes, titles (contextualizes the scenes, withholds information, presents traits relating to the star's persona), and clothing. These trailers show how "expectations and codes" are used to present Bette Davis and dangerous woman roles as they articulate "narrative enigmas, star and genre expectations" (72).

After briefly giving some of the background to the film, Karyn Kay gives an extensive textual reading of the film to support her contention that *Marked Woman* is "one of the best films about women (and, therefore, *for* women) ever to come out of Hollywood" because it defies stereotypes typical of the films of the period (48), presents an "accurate" analysis of the business of prostitution, and deals with "the more advanced philosophical concerns of the women's movement of 1972" (52). The film's closure shows how Hollywood's conventional happy ending is adjusted to "a statement of ultimate respect to all the anonymous women who walk the streets" (52).

Comparing the generic and narrative differences of *Marked Woman* (1937) and *Craig's Wife* (1936) within the context of "woman's work," Marjorie Baumgarten discusses household management and prostitution and that *Marked Woman* gives a voice to the prostitutes and presents their friendship in a positive way (25). Lottie Da and Jan Alexander's history, *Bad Girls on the Silver Screen*, surveys some two thousand films, including *Marked Woman*. Their brief comments on this film remind viewers that *Marked Woman* is based on the life of Lucky Luciano and that Bogart's role is modeled on Thomas E. Dewey. Dismissing the apparent social and historical context and after passing references to Kay and Eckert, Theodora Price condescendingly announces that previous critics have missed "the truth" of what the film is all about: "a thinly disguised political allegory of the Stalinist Popular Front program—enunciated in 1934–1935, and in full political swing by the time the film was made" (25). Price gives a brief overview of the political situation in the 1930s, with a focus on the Popular Front, and then with the widest of possible brushes links screenwriter Robert Rossen's interest in these international events to this political parable. She makes sweeping comments about Robinson and Bogart's being "more or less active in Hollywood Popular Front activities in the '30s" and others (Garfield, for one) involved in the HUAC hearings (28–29). Beyond a "guilt by association" approach, with a good bit of name dropping and a weak, generalized history of other parables of fascism into the early 1940s, Price's essay raises a possible reading of the film that she avoids applying in the essay.

Although he plays a significant role in a culturally important film, other than a mention that his role is modeled on Thomas E. Dewey, Bogart gets short shrift in the commentaries.

Kid Galahad

Roy Kinnard and R. J. Vitone focus on *Kid Galahad* as "an excellent example of Warner Bros. talent pool" (42), noting that this is Bette Davis's fifth (and next-to-last) film with Curtiz, and the first for Bogart. As "Turkey" Morgan, a fight manager, he "becomes a cold, malevolent hood" after he loses a lot of money on a fight.

Dead End

Joan Cohen's overview of *Dead End*, which was nominated for four Oscars—best picture, best supporting actress, best direction, and best art direction—describes the Warner Bros. documentary spirit that resulted in an overtheatrical treatment of poverty and injustice. Both Cohen and Charles and Mirella Affron stress the importance of the sets built on the back lot by designer Richard Day. To the Affrons, the set can stand for the "whole" of the narrative, and the sets "determine character and action and represent the work's ideology" (176).

Cohen says "Bogart was still relatively new to films and in *Dead End* he was able to build his first complete character since his role as the psychopath Duke Mantee" (850). In his study of William Wyler, Michael Anderegg declares, "Although not yet an important star, Bogart could already project an intense neuroticism, giving dimension to a role which might have proved routine in someone else's hands." Much of the impact of *Dead End* is a result of Bogart's performance as a psychotic-neurotic killer (63). Graham Greene considers this "the finest performance that Bogart has ever given—the ruthless sentimentalist who has melodramatized himself from the start (the start is there before your eyes in the juvenile gangsters) up against the truth, and the fine flexible direction supplies a background of beetle-ridden staircases and mud and mist" (181). Most memorable to Greene "is the gangster, the man who in a sentimental moment returns to the old home" only to have us watch how "sentimentality turns savage on him," especially when he sees his mother and his girl (181).

Because of polar opposites of good and evil, Cohen sees the film as "a bit dated," but with a number of strong moments (e.g., Sidney pushing her hair back to show bruises from standing in a union picket line). He notes that the *New York Post* had an editorial suggesting that those who voted against the Wagner Housing Act should see the film. In his general commentary on Bogart's films, Paul Trent considers *Dead End* the beginning of a new film genre, social drama, with its grim portrayal of tenement life, the contrast between rich and poor, the appeal of crime and wealth to the city poor, and as a sample of how poverty breeds crime.

Stand-In

Christopher Ames sees *Stand-In* as one of a few films (along with *The Bad and the Beautiful*) that focuses on the business of filmmaking: "For all its madcap silliness, *Stand-In* is a rich and provocative film, touching on the relations between Hollywood studios and New York financial control, on the struggles between labor and management, and on financial conspiracies to bankrupt studios for essentially hostile takeovers" (138). While being based on events of the 1930s, when efficiency experts influenced studio production and labor disputes permeated the country, *Stand-In* still focuses on the "creative and visionary" (140). Ames considers Bogart's strongest scene to be when he (as Douglas Quintain) gets angry with Thelma (Marla Shelton) for betraying him (with Koslofski's assistance). The scene is not only a "concession to Bogart's tough image," but one that deals with key ideas of movies about Hollywood: "the corrupting influence of fame, the gap between fame and talent, the loss of self-respect in making films you know are inferior" and "a virulent misogyny" in an industry dominated by female stars and male management (146).

In his preview of *Stand-In* for the AMC cable channel, Larry O'Toole considers the film an overlooked jewel satirizing the Hollywood scene, as it teams once again Leslie Howard and Bogart, but this time in a comedy. O'Toole puts it in the same league with *Bombshell*, *Sullivan's Travels*, and *The Player*, and applauds its presentation of those behind the camera. The role is a radical change for Bogart, who plays a director who is always drinking, but comes through in time to edit out the female lead's key scenes in order to make a gorilla the star. The resulting comedy saves Colossal Studios and serves as a send-up for those in Hollywood front offices. Bogart's Hollywood playfulness will appear again in a brief bit in *Thank Your Lucky Stars* and in a much more serious and powerful role as Dix Steele, in Nicholas Ray's *In a Lonely Place*.

Angels with Dirty Faces

The only extended discussion of *Angels with Dirty Faces* is Gregory Mank's overview, in which he gives high praise to a film that brings together Cagney, O'Brien, Bogart, Ann Sheridan, the Dead End Kids, and Michael Curtiz in "one of the most fondly remembered and most frequently revived movies of the 1930's" (138). Mank focuses on Cagney's performance and his mannerisms— "hitching his pants, twitching his neck and shoulders, jabbing his finger to make a point, and cracking 'What do you hear? What do you say?' "—rather than on Bogart.

The Oklahoma Kid

The Oklahoma Kid has received only snippets of commentary in the various histories of the western. Graham Greene sees it as a "good specimen of new-style Western," because it is "more refined than the old silent ones with their rapes and hair-breadth escapes" and it is "typical of a certain intellectuality nowadays that the only rescuers here arrive too late" (221).

Dark Victory

The fullest examination of *Dark Victory* is found in the volume prepared by Bernard Dick as part of the Wisconsin/Warner Bros. Screenplay Series. Dick presents the screenplay, an extended introduction that analyzes the changes made to the stage version (addition of Ann as alter ego), the Davis persona and the film in the context of her career and relationship with Warner Bros., production history, why Casey Robinson instead of director Edmund Goulding shot the stable scenes, how the music works with the narrative, how the narrative anticipates "with interesting variations" (36) Kübler-Ross's five stages of death and dying (the focus of Rita TheBerge's analysis), how death and dying have been presented in American movies, and why *Dark Victory* does not follow the formula of a "woman's film." Of the stable scene, with its "smoldering eroticism that burns out into repentance," Dick notes that "Bogart had the right kind of sullen masculinity for Michael, but it smelled of the street, not the stables, and the Irish accent only made the character seem quaint." Throughout the scene, Davis seemed to be trying to find the source of Bogart's sexual energy so she could connect with it, only to discover that it was flowing into the camera and not into her. To Dick the scene is important because it shows Judith Traherne's "moral center beneath the frivolous facade" (29–30).

A screenwriter for Warner Bros., Casey Robinson has been described by Richard Corliss (*Talking Pictures*, 284–290) as a chameleon. Robinson worked on a variety of scripts, including *Captain Blood* (1935), *All This and Heaven Too* (1940), *Now Voyager* (1942), and *Passage to Marseille* (1944). In an introduction to a commentary by Robinson published in the *Australian Journal of Screen Theory*, Tom Ryan notes that a number of screenwriters' works are "rich with invention and containing a sublimation of desire provoking (albeit unintentionally) a recognition of the frustrations which lie at the heart of a bourgeois culture of the twentieth century." Ryan continues, "The lack, which constructs the gap between desire and fulfillment is a key factor within the Hollywood romantic melodrama" (5). Robinson describes restructuring the screenplay to stress the universal notion of courage, and his preference for scenes in which while one thing is being talked about (love), there is another below it (death) (6). Edmund Goulding, the director, had a story conference with Robinson and explained how they were going to turn words into strips of film. During their conversation and later, Goulding said he did not like the scene between Bogart's character and Bette Davis in the stable. Robinson liked it; Hal Wallis, whom he argued with, liked it; and Davis liked it. When it was time to film the scene, Goulding walked off the set in protest, leaving Robinson to shoot it (7–8). Joel Greenberg repeats this information in his piece in *Focus on Film*.

After a four-page analysis of melodrama and its place in contemporary film criticism, Valentin Almendarez describes *Dark Victory* as an advocate for "informed struggle," rather than "passivity" (59) and a "paradigm for the '30s bourgeois melodrama" (56). Rita TheBerge uses Kübler-Ross's five stages of dying to discuss the film, finding that even with its depressing ending, the film was more successful than the play because of its ability to "depict sexual energy between Humphrey Bogart and Bette Davis" and "the reality of the grief process" (73). In the course of a plot summary of the film, Julie Johnson offers the opinion that Davis gave an especially strong performance, but Bogart was miscast (821). Robert Rosterman is part of a minority who believes Bogart "managed his Irish brogue very well." Rosterman sees this film as giving Bogart "one of his first attention-getting roles" (19). Looking at this and two other films (*Now Voyager* and *The Great Lie*) from a feminine perspective, Deborah Holdstein considers them in terms of life's goals from Sartre's psychological drama as presented in *Nausea*, Molly Haskell's comments in *From Reverence to Rape: The Treatment of Women in the Movies*, on standard presentations of women in melodramatic film, and Holdstein's three-part critical model of "periodic moments," "delayed moments" and "almost moments," which "sum up the aesthetic-emotional strategy" of each film (22). She considers *Dark Victory* "an exemplary film in the 'almost-moment' category," as it "illustrates what becomes of women who seek individuality beyond home and child" (23). Appropriate womanhood is being submissive to the man-doctor-lover, played by George Brent, and inappropriate womanhood is her interaction with the horse trainer, played by Bogart.

The Roaring Twenties

Ellen Draper believes *The Roaring Twenties* is one of Walsh's overlooked films. With its sociopolitical context and use of the FBI and juvenile delinquent films for its moral framework (32), it is an "elegy for the more vicious gangster films of the early Thirties" (30). Carolyn Perkins focuses on the production history of the film and its influence on nostalgia (music, clothes) for the 1920s. In a special issue of *Movietone News* devoted to Raoul Walsh, Peter Hogue analyzes *The Roaring Twenties, High Sierra*, and *White Heat*. Of the three, Hogue most appreciates *The Roaring Twenties*, which he valorizes for Cagney's portrayal of Eddie Bartlett (energy and unglamorous portrait of New York) and the richness of emotion and the "flair for lowlife and violence" that Walsh conveys (17). To Hogue, the Bogart-Cagney scenes (especially the one where the two bootleggers initiate their partnership—Bogart tastes the whiskey, Cagney rubs it in his hands) portray the "quintessential comparison" of the two as actors (16). Jack Shadoian also briefly compares *The Roaring Twenties*, which he sees as "an attempt at an old-style gangster film," and *High Sierra*, which is a "culmination of the first phase of the gangster genre."

Gregory Lukow and Gregory and Steven Ricci examine four gangster films (*Little Caesar, Public Enemy, Bullets or Ballots*, and *The Roaring Twenties*) in the light of a "relay" of intertextualities at work on subject (audiences) and object (text) (29). They consider this the last classic gangster film. Its presentation of history past, present, and future and the way it links current events to the film's action allows it to "sew the film into the genre's heritage while at the same time distancing it from that genre" (34). In an essay that is mostly plot summary, Dan Scapperotti emphasizes the Warner Bros. semidocumentary style, how the film brings together Bogart and Cagney for the last time, and the use of technology to convey passages of time, from the early use of a crystal set to radio news.

The Return of Doctor X

One might expect in books such as Carlos Clarens's *Illustrated History of Horror Films* an extended discussion of Humphrey Bogart's one horror film. Maybe because it was so preposterous, or maybe because few people have anything to say about the film, Clarens and others exclude any discussion of the film in his examination of the horror genre. Don Miller does mention the film in *"B" Movies*, but only long enough to say that Bogart was made to pay penance for his arguments with Jack Warner by playing in this film, Vincent Sherman's directorial debut. (For Sherman's comments on this film, see Chapter 3 in this book.)

They Drive by Night

Peter Hogue's "Boys at Work" is a review-summary of how *They Drive by Night* and *Manpower* tell us something about work, even though Walsh places greater emphasis on comedy than social problems (21). Hogue gives brief comments on the characters and plot, and cites Otis Ferguson's review that deals with "errant plotting." Hogue finds the secondary character of Ed Carlsen (Arthur Hale) the "most interesting" of those in the film and says nothing of note about Bogart.

High Sierra

With *High Sierra*, critics begin to examine with some seriousness Bogart's acting and his place in the history of American cinema. Depending on which accounts of Bogart's career one reads, either this film or *The Petrified Forest* serves as the turning point in the actor's career. Both are important, but for different reasons. If it had not been for Leslie Howard's insistence on casting

Bogart and the critical reception he received to the filmed version of *The Petrified Forest*, Bogart most likely would have languished as a "designated replacement" and character actor for the rest of his career. *High Sierra*, however, was the catalyst for the beginning of the end of his apprenticeship at Warner Bros. With its success, followed shortly by *The Maltese Falcon*, Bogart's career took off. Studies of *High Sierra* have dealt with the film's production, its remakes (*Colorado Territory* in 1949 and *I Died a Thousand Times* in 1955), the director, how the film alters the gangster genre, how the film reflected changing attitudes in American culture and history, and Bogart's acting.

Douglas Gomery's *High Sierra*, part of the Wisconsin/Warner Bros. Screenplay Series, presented for the first time the revised shooting script and an extended introduction that analyzes the production of the film, compares the novel with the various versions of the script, and surveys previous critics on the film to explain its significance to film history and genre studies. Gomery details how the novel focuses on Earle's psychological adjustment, while the film turns the study into more traditional genre fare by focusing on Earle's efforts to adjust to his new environment. Even so, the film is crucial in the history of gangster films for its emphasis on the impact of society on the gangster and as a character study. Lawrence Grobel, John Huston's biographer, focuses on how Huston liked Burnett's work, how the book itself was a treatment, how he was writing a script for Wallis, and the pressures on producer Mark Hellinger to get the script from Huston to Jack Warner so that he could give it to Raft (who turned it down) and then Paul Muni (who turned it down twice), then Cagney, Robinson, Garfield, and finally Bogart. Grobel quotes Huston's oft-repeated statement that *High Sierra* "established" Bogart (211). As Gomery and other critics have noted, what makes this gangster film different from others is the portrayal of Roy Earle: "We had seen bad guys, hundreds, maybe thousands of them, before, but the bad guy Bogart played was a decent man. He had a sense of loyalty, a code of ethics. He could feel sorry for a neglected dog or a crippled girl and go out of his way to help them. He was essentially a loner, a man up against a system, and even though he knew how to use a machine gun and was on the wrong side of the law, he was likable. The way Bogart played him, you couldn't help rooting for Roy Earle" (212). Quoting Otto Friedrich, Grobel tells us that this was the first role for Bogart that gave him a chance "at playing a fugitive convict who could become a romantic hero" (212).

Tom Shales contends that Bogart "conveys the sense of futility in Roy Earle without making him pitiful" (103). In comparing Earle's fall from the top of the mountain to the fall of King Kong, Shales links this fall to the end of the gangster genre of the 1930s. The romantic hero of these films is "a kind of existential errant knight roaming the empty plains of the Depression and managing to survive through brute force and clear daring" (100). When Earle is willing to "settle for Marie," we see the decline and fall of an American lifestyle. Kenneth Alley agrees. He reads the film as a farewell to a bygone era, embodied by Roy Earle. After trying to recapture his pre-Depression childhood by visiting what was once his family farm and then courting and being rejected by Velma, Earle realizes that his dreams for a new life are impossible. A professional with a code of honor, he is forced to work with "twerps, soda jerkers and jitterbugs." Seeking a new world but trapped by his past, the only way Earle can escape is to "crash out." To Alley, Earle is "a hero of universal significance, betrayed like us all by his past, by his fellow human beings, by his judgement, and by his choices" (261).

In his study of three Hollywood directors, Kingsley Canham also believes the film portrays the end of gangster films because of wartime patriotism and national morale (100). He says that in *High Sierra*, Bogart's "performance summed up . . . all the qualities of range and style that had been slowly maturing in his previous ten years' acting experience" (99). No longer the loud punk, he has integrity and spirit—the beginning of the existential hero who has a soft spot for a dog and a woman (99). Carlos Clarens and Jack Shadoian add to the litany of those who see the film as the end of the gangster film. Clarens describes it as "the most memorable of the twilight-of-the-gangster pictures" (168). If played by Raft or Muni, it would have had "a political awareness" (1678), but with Bogart it has "an edgy, weary imitation of mortality that was totally apolitical; Earle knows that there is no hope for himself and very little for the rest of us; he could hardly be a security risk in a nation heading for war and welfare" (169). Earle is "a man done in by time and history, in mourning for himself," and his trip to the West mirrors a "national decline," a mourning for a country that has "grown too civilized and too corrupt" (169).

Not only does the film change the direction of gangster films as it gets into the character of Earle, it also serves as a parable of the American experience to that time. Roy represents the old order of dreams and illusions, and the flawed, impure, unattainable Velma represents the "new myth of America" (73). But more important to Shadoian is how the film inverts Earle's rise and fall to show his death as noble and how in it Earle achieves the freedom that he sought. In so doing, Earle and the gangster film "transcended the world and the judgments of morality" (82).

On the casting of the film, Ken Mate and Pat McGilligan explain how, unlike what others say, Raft did not take the role because Bogart talked him out of it, telling him the part didn't fit him, "Which it didn't" (63). In their discussion with W. R. Burnett, the screenwriter (see Corliss for Burnett's filmography), they learned that the genesis of the idea of traveling across country was not new, since Burnett had used it in *Dark Hazard*. In a background piece on Burnett several months earlier, Mate recounts how Burnett portrayed Earle as a "sympathetic hoodlum" and a "symbolic country boy . . . who represents lost America in the midst of what we're in now, which is pretty bad. A desire to return to simpler ways" (34). She told Mate and McGilligan that Roy Earle and Dillinger represented "a reversion to the Western bandit. They had nothing in common with the hoodlums in Chicago. An entirely different breed." Earle is "a man who is out of his element" and symbolic of "Old America, rural America, and of simpler time" (63). Mate and McGilligan also tell us that Mark Hellinger, Bogart's friend and the associate producer on this film, argued with Burnett about having Velma turn on Roy Earle, but Hellinger lost the argument (63). In an interview with director Walsh in 1974 that appeared in *The Velvet Light Trap*, McGilligan, Weiner, and Bruce include Walsh's view that Bogart did not like the long hours and retakes of filmmaking, but he did like the money. Walsh wanted the film to end with Earle, Marie, and the dog escaping, but the Production Code would not permit any form of villainy to be rewarded (43). Unlike Peck, Gable, or Cooper, audiences and exhibitors permitted only Bogart and Cagney to be killed off at the end (44).

After some brief comments on how Bogart got the role because other "gangsters" at Warner Bros. supposedly did not want it, Michael Shepler notes that the part was a "major step forward in his career" (1448), as Walsh, an outstanding director with an "unpretentious, uncluttered style," and Huston combined to make this "fitting denouement to a decade of gangster films" (1450). No mention is made of W. R. Burnett's contributions. Ann Laemmle sees the strength of *High Sierra* to be the "moral complexity and insecurities" of Roy Earle and Walsh's use of lighting to convey visually the film's thematic ideas, while Julie Kirgo believes that *High Sierra* may be Walsh's "most powerful expression of the individual's quest for freedom, a fact that in some ways seems to divorce it from the *noir* cycle" (126). Walsh's presentation of how the beauty and splendor of the natural world is set in contrast to man's miserable state and insignificance and "cruel, inexorable fate" does, however, give it elements of *noir*.

Shepler finds *High Sierra* "the first true 'Bogart picture,' elevating him to stardom and providing him with the opportunity to prove that he could play highly sensitive roles with skill and even brilliance" (1450). His character is developed with little dialogue as he uses his eyes and ears to appreciate his new freedom. In Henry Random's look at movies of the 1930s and 1940s seen through the eyes of a young boy growing up in the Bronx, we learn that Bogart was to him the "champ of champs" among the Warner Bros. performers (88). Early on he remembers him as the henchman who always died, but as he thinks about Bogart, he recalls how Bogart died every possible way: "He did it so well, so inventively, so plaintively. He died with *brio*, sometimes even with a kind of *elan*" (89). After not seeing him in a movie for some time, the young Random had "vague feelings of uneasiness" (92). Then he appeared in *High Sierra*: "It was a movie that seemed to appeal to all kinds of people.... It was as if he had been a newcomer, just beginning in the movies, instead of having one of the longest and most durable and even monotonous track records of anyone in the motion picture business" (93). He especially liked the "aging lion" aspect of his portrayal (95). This film gave him the status that *The Petrified Forest* never did, but it was not until *The Maltese Falcon* that he "clinched" his star status (97).

After discussing the casting, Bernard Dick calls *High Sierra* "a movie about existential freedom, that freedom to which a human being is condemned" (123). Bogart became an existential cult hero because he "projected the image of a figure living in the present, striving for freedom, and performing meaningful actions to achieve it." Bogart understood the "existential implications of 'crashing out,' " and his face was "extraordinary and fittingly existential" and "not a neighborhood face, nor was it especially handsome. It was a face that knew the mixed blessings of life; a face that did not slacken with age but grew tauter, the eyes retreating into their sockets until by the end of his career they had settled into omniscience" (124). This discussion of Bogart is part of a section in which Dick discusses "Iconic Associations"—"shared features or similarities between (1) the actor's screen image and the character the actor is portraying . . . (2) an actor's screen image and a historical figure or traditional type . . . and, (3) an actor's performance style and that of another actor who is not in the film but whose iconic presence is clearly felt" (122). He places Bogart and Hepburn in category 1.

Peter Hogue believes that *High Sierra* has its moments, but its failed "innovation" and "strained seriousness" misfire, and Bogart's presentation of "Roy Earle's mixture of battle-scarred toughness and misguided sentimentality never quite comes into focus, since Bogart seems to lack the kind of range that permitted Cagney to make some sense of Eddie Bartlett's contradictions in *The Roaring Twenties*. Bogart seems too hard-edged and intelligent to get all wrapped up in a sweet young thing like Velma (Joan Leslie) and too urban and nocturnal to yearn for any 'Indiana farm' " (17–18). Rick Hermann's discussion of myth focuses on the cinematic illusion of place and myth and how, for example, a picturesque scene of mountains and a dude ranch foreshadows the irony of a supposedly safe haven that becomes the location of the mythic Earle's death. Hermann also traces patterns of circularity—actions, places, and characters—that comment on "the illusion of freedom" and entrapment found throughout the film (35). Tom Conley's *Film Hieroglyphs* focuses on how writing, rather than images, works on ideology and history as presented in film. His remarks on *High Sierra* are part of a longer chapter, "Decoding Film Noir." Conley says that Burnett, using real names, gives a sense of immediacy and also presents an "allegory of destiny," as certain shots, such as Bogart's looking into a mirror, bind "writing, history, and filmic transposition" (167). To Conley *High Sierra* "seems to advise viewers duplicitously about how to live, doing so at the conclusion by combining elements of myth, occularity, self-reflexivity, and feminism" (174).

The Maltese Falcon

There have been studies of *The Maltese Falcon*'s production, director, screenwriters, actors, genre, *film noir*, cultural values, character studies, psychology and film, film and literature, and intertextuality. One of the most valuable studies of the film's production history is Rudy Behlmer's essay in *America's Favorite*

Movies. Behlmer starts with background on Hammett's publication of the work in *Black Mask* in 1929, the studio's purchase of the rights for $8,500 shortly after publication in 1930 and its two previous versions, and how Huston did some editing to adapt it before submitting the script to Jack Warner. Behlmer recounts the various changes required by the Production Code Administration that related to Spade's relationships with Iva and Brigid, Cairo's homosexuality, the language, and Spade's body search of Brigid for the $1,000 bill (137–138). In this essay and in *Inside Warner Bros.*, Behlmer presents correspondence that focuses on the casting of *The Maltese Falcon*, including the possible use of Geraldine Fitzgerald in the Mary Astor role, Raft's refusal to do it, the intra-studio squabbles that led to Bogart's being assigned to *The Maltese Falcon* after a two-month suspension for refusing to do *Bad Men of Missouri*, and Hal Wallis's review of the dailies and his desire that Huston quicken the pace of the "tempo and delivery," especially of Bogart's dialogue. Other correspondence discusses the costs of the picture, finishing a few days ahead of schedule, the need to cut the ending (in Spade's office), retakes, the need to redo the opening to avoid audience confusion as a result of preview responses, and the idea of having Hammett do a Spade sequel. The film was completed in thirty-four days, wrapping two days ahead of schedule on July 18, 1941, with some additional scenes in the next month, an added prologue for clarity (at Jack Warner's request), and a retake of the opening scene, also for clarity, after previews on September 5. Using studio documents, Behlmer indicates that the picture, which opened to good reviews, cost $381,000.

Hal Wallis and Charles Higham present some of the standard background found in Behlmer and elsewhere on how Huston got to make *The Maltese Falcon*, casting, how Huston took the cast to lunch every day to create a sense of intimacy, and the importance of the rushes and Hal Wallis's suggestions for changes. Ted Sennett repeats how Huston got to direct, Henry Blanke's advice to shoot it as if each scene were the most important, the importance of focusing on details, how Huston prepared sketches for every shot, how the merry pranksters on the set played games on tourists, and Huston's battle against calling it *The Gent from San Francisco*. In comparing the earlier versions to Huston's, Sennett says that a version can be "true to its source and yet remain inferior in every way to a later, equally faithful version" (58). Screenwriter Allen Rivkin and Laura Kerr tell how the novel came to be filmed for a third time and how the secretary typed the book in basic shots and scenes and dialogue. This tale is repeated again in Stuart Kaminsky's *John Huston: Maker of Magic*, where Kaminsky examines how Huston and Allen Rivkin were assigned the task of writing the screenplay, their instructions to their secretary to type by setting it up in screenplay format with shots, scenes, and dialogue, how she followed standard operating procedures and gave a copy to Warner, and how he, not knowing the details of the "scriptwriting," liked it and told Huston to shoot it.

Based on interviews with John Huston, Gerald Pratley also gives background as to how Huston got the project; its cost, casting, and actors; and how Huston believed that Bogart could not be a "conventional leading man" because "he didn't have the countenance or the physique for that, to be a competitor with Errol Flynn" (42). Pratley considers this a "text-book movie in terms of economy, pace, and direction" (48). Lawrence Grobel, in his biography of John Huston, contends that his subject was one of very few writers, Preston Sturges being another, who was able to move from writing to directing. Huston owed the transition to a clause in his contract and the goodwill of the studio hierarchy. Grobel notes that the novel was congenial to Huston's personality, his impact on the casting of Lorre and Greenstreet, Henry Blanke's advice to "shoot each scene as if it was the most important scene in the film," the careful framing of each shot, and how Bogart came up with the last line of the movie (222).

Allen Eyles gives production credits; plot outline; biographical details for Huston, Arthur Edeson, Bogart, Greenstreet, Lorre, and Astor; a few brief quotations from reviews of the film; and a reevaluation. Although not everyone will agree with his positions, Eyles gives more analysis and information in a few pages than many others give in chapters of books. He sees Hammett as the author of the film, even though some of Huston's changes would benefit the novel. Huston's major contributions were putting on film the atmosphere of the novel and his work with the actors and especially how they related to the camera. Of the former Eyles says: "The film is (partly by its deletions) more compact and unified; and where Huston displays a rare talent for the film medium is in his exact manipulation of his actors, cameraman, set designer, and others, to capture such a rich, near flawlessly correct mood, not just at moments and scenes but throughout the length of the film" (49).

Eyles finds fault with three aspects of the film: the casting of Gladys George as Archer's wife, the way the police are handled after the battle between Cairo and Brigid, and Spade's rage in Gutman's apartment. And he is uncertain about Astor's "curious performance," never quite being the exotic figure one might imagine, but always being fascinating to watch (50). In her autobiography, Mary Astor talks about her role as the congenital liar, slightly psychopathic Brigid, and how there was no improvisation because Huston knew what he wanted and had it all on paper; this kept them ahead of schedule and gave them time to enjoy long lunches and enjoy each other's company. One time Bogart and the others pounced on her as part of their ritual of testing the mettle of others, and after she broke down, his advice was to "be yourself." For Astor, being Bogart meant being "a hardworking guy, a good craftsman" (166). She liked him, but recognized that "when he got drunk he was bitter and smilingly sarcastic and thoroughly unpleasant" (167).

R. T. Jameson, Alan Downer, James Naremore, Danny Peary, Eugene Archer, and Ted Sennett disagree with Eyles, giving most of the credit to Hammett. Jameson notes, for example, that everything of that first scene was written by Hammett, but "the sassy, self-confident personality of Sam Spade [in the opening scene] is the personality of Huston's first film" in its "cheerfully sardonic view of things" (27). At the same time, "this is an exemplary John Huston scene. The sense of an eye cocked always at a slightly unexpected yet appropriate angle, the way rhythms of delivery, nervous gestures, and the various oblique views of characters and their movements are sprung against one another to create a volatile yet disciplined complex of tensions—these are at once the hallmarks of a style and testimony to the distinctiveness of the existential terrain we are privileged to glimpse'' (28). Central to Alan S. Downer's concept of viewing movies is the "monitor image," or the "inward eye of the creative film-maker" (16). Although "scene for scene, character for character, speech for speech, and often gesture for gesture, Huston is rigorously faithful to Hammett" (20), the success of the film is not a result of the fiction of Hammett per se or the performance of Bogart, but Huston's visualization and expression of the work.

James Naremore's 1973 essay, reprinted with slight modifications in 1993, takes issue with Andrew Sarris's much-noted assessment of Huston's contributions to the film as voiced in *The American Cinema: Directors and Directions*. Although Naremore concedes that the casting was important for the film's success, the actors' physical appearances were often very unlike those described by Hammett, and in the case of Astor went against the grain (239). He does see Huston taking most of the words from Hammett, but condensing and economizing the text (241). Taking issue with Agee, who describes Huston's directorial approach as spontaneous and casual, Naremore notes that everything, from the actor's movements and the camera set-ups to the editing, seems planned. Huston's "somewhat stylized quality," (248), his focus on a male world, with its "greed, . . . treachery . . . and sometimes the loyalty of characters" (242) and the drama of his camera work define Huston's temperament and his moviemaking. Jameson observes that there is a link between Spade, Huston, and Bogart from a biographical point of view: all three "move in a world where the put-on is not only a form of self-amusement but also, frequently, a way to hang onto mobility and personal authority, however spurious from time to time—a means of survival" (29).

In his study of cult films, Danny Peary comments that little is original in Huston's version when compared with what came before, but what makes it "so special, a true masterpiece, is the style, the impeccable casting, and the stressing of the various characters' peculiarities" (220). In addition to discussing the editing, camera angles, aspects of *noir* lighting, and how the film established screen personas for its actors, Peary considers the film's major strength to be its characterization created through the ensemble cast of Greenstreet, Lorre, and Cook, and Bogart's Sam Spade, who is filled with ambiguity and contradictions (222).

The *Maltese Falcon* is one of five key Huston films to Eugene Archer. The others are *The African Queen, The Asphalt Jungle, The Treasure of the Sierra Madre,* and *Moby Dick*. Archer says *The Maltese Falcon* fits into Huston's melodramatic mode, and to his credit the film keeps the humor and irony of the original. Although Archer believes that Huston rendered a "completely faithful cinematic transcription of the novel, with a singleness of purpose which adds to its force," he finds each actor to be a perfect fit for the individual roles. This is an "actor's film, depending for its effect on a series of internal tensions accruing from character conflicts and interlocking personalities" (79–80).

Ted Sennett also sees the interaction of characters, not its rather straightforward plot, as its key element. The casting of Lorre and Greenstreet is superior to any of the earlier versions, and a major difference between the 1931 and 1941 versions is the final scene with Wonderly. The 1931 version is "coarsened" by Wonderly's parting remark and Spade's visit to her in prison and his remark to the matron to take good care of her. The "behavioral interplay" is what interests us viewing after viewing, since all the roles, even the minor ones, are well cast. Bogart's performance is "finely judged and the culmination of his years of apprenticeship" (69). In a few brief sentences, Allen Eyles synthesizes how Bogart's "complex qualities of small-time resignation, seedy opportunism and mistrustful cynicism mix with Bogart's wry good-humour and steely integrity to create a Sam Spade more sympathetic and alive than Hammett's original. Bogart's worn features, dark spaniel eyes and moist voice make him seem vulnerable behind his toughness, and a line of aggressive feminine women . . . served to put him on his mettle, brought out the measure of his manly resources" (47). Spade is not the hero in this tale, even though we see things from his point of view, because "there is no one principled character for an audience to associate with" (50).

Joe Goldberg, in one of the best commentaries on Bogart's character in this film and as an influence in our culture, finds Spade taciturn, resourceful, courageous, solitary, and of few words (in a "flat, sardonic voice"). These traits reflect not only Spade but Bogart's attitude toward acting and the many horrid roles he took because as a professional he had a job to do (107). When Goldberg asks himself why Bogart was a symbol of his times, he repeats Raymond Chandler's analysis of Philip Marlowe: " 'He must be a complete man and a common man and yet an unusual man. He must be . . . a man of honor, by instinct, by inevitability, without thought of it, and certainly without saying it. He must be the best man in his world and a good enough man for any world. I do not care much about his private life. . . . If he is a man of honor in one thing, he is that in all things' " (108). Goldberg sees Bogart as the embodiment of a personal code, one that the existentialists described as "definition through action" (109). Goldberg quotes André Gide on how Hammett's dialogue conveys the duplicitous nature of each character. A fine actor, but "not a great one," Bogart was Spade—"a cynical idealist, a romantic gone sour" (110). "Neither the on-screen nor the off-screen Bogart postured or preached, but kept to himself, ambiguous, his privacy unapproachable, until his private ethic told him it was time to act. And then, he did not speak; he *acted*" (112). Goldberg also quotes Faulkner who, when asked about actors, said, "Humphrey Bogart is the one I've worked with best" in *To Have and Have Not* and *The Big Sleep*. Bogart, who called Huston "The Monster," liked to work with him because he was "never dull," and he let him concentrate on his acting rather than "business" (114).

As Bogart himself said in an interview quoted in Kaminsky's book on the director, Huston was " 'stimulating. Offbeat kind of mind. Off center. He's brilliant and unpredictable. Never dull. When I work with John, I think about acting' " (26). Goldberg considers *Treasure* to be Bogart's best work, while other Huston-Bogart films—*The Maltese Falcon* and *Beat the Devil*—are screen classics because "the Huston trilogy of murder for riches . . . are the best films Bogart ever made, and contain his best work; significantly, Huston has never attempted to duplicate them with another actor" (115). Huston, in commenting on Bogart's dislike of traveling, notes that he "took Bogey to many places in the world and some of them were hardships. Well Bogey didn't like that at all. Bogey gave the air of being an adventurer, but really he loved being at home. But he was wonderful to be with. . . . He would never know his lines when he came to the set and in rehearsals he would learn them, and they would have a spontaneity that was remarkable" (Kaminsky 23–24). But an era was ending. Within five years of Bogart's death, Hammett, Chandler, Hemingway, and Camus also died: "And on the screen Bogart embodied them all, not because he was a great man, a great rebel, or a great actor, but because it was his job" (116). David Zinman sees the various Bogart roles up to *The Maltese Falcon* as basically one-dimensional and uses some of the standard phrases in describing his persona as "wry, detached, anti-establishment, a man with the sure masculinity of whiskey straight"; he is "unflinching, outspoken, cynical and a realist: a tough guy in a trenchcoat, a man's man" (33).

As William Everson notes in *The Detective in Film*, *The Maltese Falcon* is essential to the history of the genre. To Everson, who provides an excellent discussion of the three versions of *The Maltese Falcon*, "although Bogart's Spade is a far cry from the traditional movie detective hero of the period, at the same time, as subtly reshaped by Huston, it is a different and more admirable Spade than Hammett's: more honorable and less petty, and certainly with a greater sense of humor and an actor's ability to confuse and outguess his opponents" (41). Building on and considerably expanding Everson's discussion, Virginia Wright Wexman analyzes at length the 1931 and 1936 versions of *The Maltese Falcon*, finding the earlier one to be an "overly-toned down approach" and the latter having an "excessively flamboyant style" (49). Only with Huston's version, which "reinforced the mystery and suspense centering on the quest for the falcon by innovative lighting, sets, photography, sound, and editing," do we have a film that captures the "tough spirit" of Hammett's work. Of all aspects of Huston's version, Wexman agrees with Jameson, Downer, Naremore, Eyles, and others that the casting, especially of Bogart, was the most important ingredient. Bogart's physical appearance—his height, "dark coloring and heavy features" that "gave a suggestion of ethnicity," his "wiry build," his acting style and nervous energy, and his "lisping, nasal edge" (54)—gives us the Sam Spade that fits Hammett's style.

In his textbook *Beyond Formula*, Stanley Solomon declares this film as the defining example of the detective film genre in its mapping out of "the crucial moral terrain" (215). Describing what he perceives to be some of the key traits of the hero (moral awareness, cynicism, mannerisms of the criminal, inner isolation, self-sacrifice, commitment), Solomon presents Spade as an intensely preoccupied moralist (211) who represents the medieval knight errant (218) in his search for the truth. According to Thomas Schatz, Sam Spade is the "prototype for Hollywood's urban private eye" and the "narrative and perceptual center of the film, the organizing sensibility who observes, influences, and ultimately defines the seamy urban world he inhabits" as he serves as a "vulnerable moralist and a man of uncompromising integrity" (127–128). This film establishes the plot and characters for the "hard-boiled" formula. Douglas McVay sees *The Maltese Falcon* as essentially "a peacetime detective story," a melodrama, and "a Hollywood crime thriller." McVay contends that Bogart, the female lead, and the cinematography create "an objective correlative to Hammett's descriptions" (6). James F. Maxfield sees two myths that permeate the novel (and the film): the myth of the falcon itself and the myth of the tarnished knight who is tempted by the femme fatale. Disagreeing with Schatz and Solomon, who see Spade as hard on the outside and soft on the inside, a sentimental moralist, Maxfield finds him "more directly motivated by greed and sadism than by a disinterested concern for truth and justice" (254–255). He wants to dominate everyone with whom he comes in contact.

In *Tough Guys and Gals of the Movies*, Edward Edelson begins his book with the film that many regard as "best detective movie ever made" (1) because it contains a cross-section of traditional toughs in movies: Sam Spade, the cops who use their badges for protection, Joel Cairo (pretensions to toughness), the gunman (Wilmer), the refined and cultivated (Casper Gutman, the fat man), and the femme fatale, who may appear soft on the outside but is tough (Brigid). In his study of the dectective on film, Jon Tuska considers the novel as a parable on greed and its impact on characters. Spade is not a hero; he is just smarter than the others. He gives an overview of the various filmed versions and claims that Huston "humanized" the character for Bogart (182) as he translates the novel's emphasis on character to film. Huston told Tuska, counter to what Huston says in later interviews, that he really did want George Raft: "I thought Raft would be perfect as Spade. If . . . the lines didn't prove too long for him" (185). To Tuska if this was not Bogart's best role, then it "certainly [was] one of his most endurable" (185).

Contrary to most other views, Tuska says that *The Maltese Falcon* is not *noir* because Huston made Spade a hero (340). Agreeing with Tuska, Ted Sennett sees this as *noir* only "in the dark and desperate activities of its characters" (66). Sennett discusses the film for what it lacks: no rain-swept streets, little of the city at night, little action, and no sudden bursts of brutality except when

Wilmer kicks Spade. To Sennett, this is a melodrama of character, not *film noir*. Performing a balancing act on this issue is Stephen Gale, who, instead of using various studies of melodrama and *film noir* as his foundation, uses definitions of melodrama found in the *Oxford English Dictionary*, a companion to the theater, two dictionaries of literary terms, a dictionary of film terms, and two film textbooks for his definition of *film noir*. The brief essay claims that the opening ninety seconds of *The Maltese Falcon* establish why the film "is delayed" after Gutman, Cairo, Brigid, and Sam learn that the falcon is a fake and closes with Sam's turning Brigid over to the police. (Gale misidentifies the actor who plays Miles Archer.) He says that in melodrama, issues relating to the social fabric are not important, whereas conflict over an object with little value is. So to Gale, on one level the film is melodrama. At the same time, he considers *noir* a genre and claims that "the definition of the film noir genre, with its dark emphasis on imperfect human characters confronted with the corrupting nature of greed, lust, and evil, yet salvaged by individual moral strength, can be traced to the very first images seen in *The Maltese Falcon*" (147).

Taking the other side is Marc Vernet, a student of Barthes, who uses a combination of Propp, Freud, and Lévi-Strauss as he positions himself as a viewer of the opening of six films, including *The Maltese Falcon*, to examine the "setup" (*mise-en-place*), the enigma (*pot au noir*), and disjunction and contiguity. As the translator of the essay remarks in a headnote, "Vernet's essay may finally be understood as a contribution to the metapsychology of spectatorship similar to that of Metz, Kuntzel, Bellour, and others.... The noir is considered to be a limit-text in which the structure of fear and suspense, the sudden contrasts and contradictions of story development, and the relations of intrigue and betrayal among the characters, are considered to replay the conditions of fantasy and desire discovered by Freud" (3). In a less dense analysis, William H. Brown, Jr., after giving a sketch of Huston's background and a plot summary and brief analysis of the film, examines aspects of Spade's code and the quest motif. To Brown, the film is initiating, if not presaging, *film noir*, especially through the motivation and characterization of Spade (299–300). Except for Spade, all the characters are on a quest for wealth. To Brown the Bogart figure is detached from the decadence because he embodies "professional integrity" and "broad social responsibilities" (301) as he follows professional ethics through a dark underworld in his quest to find the truth and restore order to the "normal world" (301).

In chapters on "Medium and Metaphor," "From Censor to Teacher," and "From Teacher to Learner," Richard Blake uses a religious perspective to show how film has been a social force in the United States. Blake focuses on the development of Hollywood genre films of the 1930s and 1940s in chapters on *It Happened One Night, Scarface, Stagecoach, Frankenstein*, and *The Maltese Falcon* to "reveal something about the society that produced them" (102). The chapter on *The Maltese Falcon* includes ten pages of background on Huston as auteur, another ten on the historical and literary background of the detective story genre and *film noir*, seven pages of plot summary, and then a commentary and bibliography. The section on the history of the genre notes how God's questioning of Adam and Eve in the Garden of Eden presents the "primal detective" and "prototype of the classical detective" (215–216). His analysis focuses on the murky world of the characters, the inability of the police to impose order on this chaotic world, Huston's recurrent theme of how greed leads to disaster, and how the film's "elusive morality and convoluted motivation" (236) are enhanced by Huston's visual style. Blake sees Huston's vision as marking a "new horizon in American film" as its "cynicism bordered on despair and the visual style gave a generation an image of its own moral quandaries" (238).

Parker Tyler, a major critic of film and culture, considers Sam Spade, like Welles's Kane and Chaplin's Dictator, to be a "good villain" attempting to be "bad hero" (121), especially because of his austerity. In examining gangster films, Tyler notes that "the sociological dictum that ignorance produces crime is socially true but dramatically and esthetically defective" (108). Spade cannot detach himself from a kind of masochism or emotional self-denial, because he stands between a profession and doing a job; as a result, he too is a victim because he has a hard time keeping himself human (130–135).

A number of Bogart's films have been the subject of psychological interpretations. *The Maltese Falcon* is no exception. Three practicing psychiatrists (Bauer, Balter, and Hunt) use fiction (and film) to examine the private detective as a "prototypical American hero" as well as cultural responses to "unconscious fantasy" as they try to "advance our understanding of Western society's increasing narcissistic preoccupations" (275). After distinguishing between American and European detective stories, the authors focus on how the detective is not unlike a psychoanalyst (both ask questions, and both deal with underworlds) and the mythic dimensions and "unconscious fantasy-wishes" (281) of the novel and film versions of *The Maltese Falcon*. The American detective (outcast, loner, shabby, morally ambiguous) differs from his European counterpart (aristocratic of the mind) in part because of the immigrant and frontier experiences that had few traditions. The oedipal conflicts were channeled more to mobility, competence, and power rather than sex and honor (288). With the "lack of development of a well defined and well integrated superego," which results from the disruption of traditional father-son relationships in the "genesis of our American heroes," the worldwide Western phenomenon of traditional expectability has been cynically sacrificed (293–294). This explains to the authors why Bogart, who in working outside traditional authority, embodies heroic iconoclasm and represents a cultural hero for the 1960s: "Bogart, as Spade, presents a mythopoetic struggle. Ultimately meaningfulness is achieved by him through finding and accepting the truth" (294).

Harvey Greenberg agrees with the ideas of Dr. Leo Bellak that readers are able to identify with the criminal who embodies primitive aggression and sexual impulses and the detective whose "inner voice of conscience" represents law and order and "superhuman intelligence" (54). Shifting from the English to the American pulp detective, Greenberg finds Spade to be a "analyst *manqué*" as both seek the truth but submerge their personalities (56). In commenting on the action of the film, Greenberg says, "Spade contends successfully with a series of hostile father surrogates, gains the mother in Brigid, then recoils from her clutches" (76). Thus, "during his quest for the Falcon, Spade eschews friendship, flirts with and rejects both homosexual and heterosexual entanglements. His career must be his sole sustenance, a profession that validates his misanthropy, mistrust, and withdrawal" (77).

Ilsa Bick, like others, sees Flitcraft's abandonment of one life for a very similar new life as the central theme of the novel. In comparing the three versions of the film, she finds that a "historical progression emerges" in which the two earlier films "highlight Spade's strained and adroit heterosexuality and his aggressive seduction of others," whereas Huston's text is "more *re*strained and *con*strained, and most of its overt sexuality goes, almost literally, underground" (183). Bick's analysis focuses on the men and women in the films and the "sociocultural and historical events" that present a shift from "a sexuality that is raucous, bawdy, madcap, and unrestrained (yet nonetheless threatening) to one which is nefarious, duplicitous, secretive, mutedly erotic, and seductive, but substantially less central (yet nonetheless threatening)" (183–184).

According to James F. Maxfield, who uses ideas presented by Bernard Paris, Sam Spade is a prototype of Karen Horney's "arrogant-vindictive" neurotic, who "trusts no one, avoids emotional involvement, and seeks to exploit others in order to enhance his own feelings of mastery" (254). Spade's sense of mastery and need for self-sufficiency, Maxfield claims, are why he has to turn Brigid over to the police. Of his reasons for doing so—professional, pragmatic, and psychological—the last is the root cause because she will forever be a threat to his power and cause him to "experience a fall from dominant self-sufficiency to submissive dependency" (255).

A good deal of criticism of *The Maltese Falcon* has focused on how well Huston adapted Hammett's work to the screen. Pauline Kael, for example, considers *The Maltese Falcon* "an almost perfect visualization" of Hammett's work, but she finds the music to be a minor flaw and is less than enthusiastic about Huston's softening the ending of the film by omitting Effie's view of Spade in order to keep him "a romantic figure," though not too far from Fred C. Dobbs (*5001 Nights* 355). In his study of Huston, Stuart Kaminsky examines differences between the novel and the film, including the time (1928–1929 versus 1940) and, like Kael, the ending, where Spade has his arms around Effie's waist, only to have her pull away from him knowing there is still Archer's wife (20). Kaminsky says that while the 1931 story and dialogue are not that different from Huston's or Hammett's original, the difference is "how each director imagined the same dialogue and story and brought them to the screen. Huston's tough version emphasizes the marginal existence of Spade, his cynicism, commitment to principle, near-madness, and enjoyment of irony. Huston further suggests an admiration for those who can accept defeat'' and "his emphasis on the world of lies and masks through which Spade must move, masks that Spade must penetrate to get to the truth while he himself is proving to be a master at deception" (21). Kaminsky also discusses Huston's working method—"drawings of every set-up" (21), framing shots "like canvases of paintings" with characters in the foreground (25)—and situations that would repeat in later films such as an "obsessed professional, a man who will adhere to pride and dedication to principle unto death," and women who "are a threat, temptations that can only sway the hero from his professional commitment." It is these women who "may . . . be the unwitting cause of the protagonist's defeat or near defeat" (25). Kaminsky repeats some of the same ideas about Huston's painterly style of framing, the different time periods, character changes, and altered ending from the novel in his essay on Huston in the *International Dictionary of Films and Filmmakers*. Kaminsky thus takes issue with those who see the film as a faithful adaptation. Jimmie Reeves, following other critics, examines the various narrative strategies used to present hard-boiled fiction on the screen such as flashback versus linear plot lines without voice-overs and excessive reliance on subjective camera. Like so many other commentators, he sees this film as Bogart's "coming of age" as a star, with Spade serving as a model for his character in *Casablanca* and *The Big Sleep*.

In discussing Hammett's ability to "turn the crime story into literature" (xxviii), Stephen Marcus traces his introduction to Hammett to Bogart's performance in *The Maltese Falcon*. While Huston takes dialogue directly from the novel, he omitted the central moment from the novel—Flitcraft's story—which takes us directly to Hammett's "imagination of the world" (xv) and his sense of ethical and metaphysical contradiction (xviii). (Cooper describes similar aspects in his section on Flitcraft and Hammett; see below.) In describing the work of the unglamorous detective—the Continental Op—who works in the realm of international intrigue and moral ambiguity "to deconstruct, decompose, deploy and defictionalize [a] 'reality' and to construct or reconstruct out of it a true fiction, i.e., an account of what 'really' happened" (xix)—Marcus sees a relationship between the Op and the writer, both of whom create a world, but one that is not necessarily rational (xxi). This is a very rational world to Stanley Solomon, who in *The Film Idea* claims the novel is one of "moral redemption" (214), whereas integrity is the key to Bogart's appeal in the film version. The dialogue becomes more important than the environment, and it is Bogart who brings both elements together as he sacrifices all for his code.

Using a few critics on the film and adaptation, such as Eyles and Naremore as a starting point, Kevin Boon reexamines what others have said about Huston and the adaptation process for this film: Huston used "good sense" and judgment when retaining much of the dialogue and story of the twenty chapters into 125 scenes, and this directorial decision is underrated. The scenes cut from the novel include those that relate to Brigid and Spade and Cairo's homosexuality (106–112). This film is important because it sets "the standard for *film noir* and the hard-boiled detective film, launched Huston's career as a director, and helped to establish Humphrey Bogart as a major screen talent" (101). In sum, *The Maltese Falcon*'s screenplay "is primarily a matter of possessing the creative judgment to conserve the novel's text" (114).

By focusing on what is missing from the novel ("adaptation's negative space") in his essay on Flitcraft and Spade, Stephen Cooper paints Huston as being more faithful to the novel than noted by others because of his deletion of the part about Flitcraft: "As Hammett's novel teaches John Huston to re-tell its story more compactly on film, so does Huston's film teach us how to reread the novel for the double story of what is present on screen but also (faithfully) absent" (119). Citing Freud and Hemingway, Cooper notes that "whatever is obliterated remains indelible" (128). The deletion of the story helps us better to understand Spade, who is Flitcraft's "mirror image." Since everyone has something to hide in Spade's world, Cooper reasons that "every concealment is a story in the process of being told with its difference unfolding because every telling is always a re-telling" (128).

Leslie Abramson sees the novel and film as self-conscious texts that probe the "methods and values of storytelling repeatedly" (112). Spade's world is one of stories that he must decipher. While the book and film are "spiritual allies," the film is faster paced, uses visual images (light and dark, body movements, etc.), and does not permit us to learn of Spade's reactions to events because of camera placement. What holds the plot together are the strong cast and especially "Bogart's presence" (117). As he compares William Dieterle's *Satan Met a Lady* (1936) with Huston's film, Gordon Gow sees the novel as a resilient work. After giving brief summaries of each film, Gow compares the tone (semicomic in *Satan*) and the casting of the various roles. "Bogart's Spade, like Hammett's, rings true for his era" (58); Warren Williams, however, is "flamboyant," "a bit showy," and a "slick rogue" (58); Gutman's role becomes Madame Barabbas (Alison Skipworth), who voices some of the same sentiments as the fat man; and Peter Lorre's Cairo is a "comically villainous" Arthur Treacher.

After discussing the literary roots of the film, Lionel Godfrey focuses on the Brigid–Sam Spade relationship. He claims she is "throwing stardust in his eyes" and he is a "loner and a loser" who "retains his self-respect" (12). While physically tough, he is no superman and is primarily a detective of the heart rather than the head. In *Analyzing Films*, William H. Phillips presents a student paper by Susan Watkins that focuses on the issue of fidelity to the source as it presents Brigid as basically the same character (amoral, self-concerned, and greedy) in the novel and the film, but with changes in age (younger in novel) and physical appearance (tall and slender in the novel). In a far more complex essay, Benaquist uses Roland Barthes's ideas of function and index to discuss narrative in order to find a suitable grammar to discuss this film. Benaquist notes that certain actions pertaining to the quest for the falcon and the relationship between Brigid and Spade become matters of irony through reversal and discovery. Mixing heavy jargon to reflect his use of Barthes, Benaquist presents some questionable examples and terminology from the film. For example, from the time that Archer is killed, Brigid becomes "more functional and less indexical" until Spade becomes involved in the search for the falcon (47). To Benaquist, Brigid, like the falcon, is an object of a quest. Maxfield in his essay refutes this position (259). Comparing courtship conventions and performance styles in *The Big Sleep* and *The Maltese Falcon*, Virginia Wright Wexman examines how Bogart became a romantic hero as he moved from a screen image that focused on class, power, and control, to one that addressed sexual issues and romantic partnerships (*Creating* 26–27, 34).

W. Johnson focuses on how "the interplay between what is seen and heard and how it is seen and heard is the basis for any full understanding of film" (33). This interplay is often marked by tension or disparity. One example of tension between "detached image" ("the images contain very little action") and "urgent sound" ("a profusion of speech") is found in *The Maltese Falcon* (26). To Johnson there are numerous structural similarities between that film and *The Big Sleep*:—Bogart as private eye, its source in detective fiction, character types and double crosses, rapid dialogue—but while both have "copious dialogue," the far greater variety of settings in *The Big Sleep* and a dialogue shared by a bigger cast make *The Big Sleep* a more complex film (27). Mirella and Charles Affron approach the film from its set design, and they contend there is no special coding to the sets. We see what we expect of Spade's office or the living quarters of Brigid and Gutman. Carl Richardson analyzes how Huston's "dark sensibility" and the use of sets that allude to real locations "broadened the canvas of cinematic realism" (68).

Jeanine Basinger's history of American cinema contains a short, tight analysis of differences in production values of studio styles of MGM and Warner Bros. by analyzing components such as casting, sets, cinematography, and tone in two films made from Dashiell Hammett novels: *The Thin Man* (1934) and *The Maltese Falcon* (1941). As in the previous editions of their college textbook *Film Art*, David Bordwell and Kristin Thompson analyze Huston's use of shot and reverse-shot patterns, eyeline matches, and spatial consistency in the opening shots of the film to show how space is used to convey narrative continuity. William Luhr explores ideas of classical narrative organization as developed by Bordwell (*Narration in the Fiction Film*, 1985) and Bordwell, Staiger, and Thompson (*The Classical Hollywood Cinema*, 1985) in *Tracking The Maltese Falcon: Classical Hollywood Narration and Sam Spade*. The film follows a linear pattern, but its "complexity and aesthetic value" are shown in how Huston "organizes formal motifs, explores narrative alternatives and manipulations, and develops subtextual implications of foreignness and deviant sexuality to give the mystery and danger its specificity" (11).

The Maltese Falcon and other Bogart films reverberate in the history of our culture. Some of this is made apparent in articles about the film's sources or impact on other texts. William Bottiggi notes how in Polanski's *Chinatown*, an homage to *The Maltese Falcon*, Jake Gittes, the detective, lacks the vision and perception of Sam Spade. Throughout the Huston film, there are references to "C" (part of an address inside one of Brigid's hats, Gutman lives in suite 12-C, the post office station where Spade mails the package) that alert us and Sam about the importance of clear vision. Similar references appear in *Chinatown*, but Gittes's inability to see clearly is his Achilles heel; he is not able to extricate himself from his nightmare world of lies and half-truths. The comparison with *Chinatown* is found in many of the reviews of the film. For example, Hollis Alpert starts with a reference to *The Maltese Falcon* and ends by noting differences in the amount of sex and violence, but saying otherwise "the script might easily have borne the signature of Dashiell Hammett" (46).[6]

George Wood compares and contrasts aspects of style and content (time, protagonist, relationships with the police and women) in *Chinatown* and *The Maltese Falcon* and concludes that *The Maltese Falcon* shows us something of man's darker side, while *Chinatown* forces us to look at our own actions and society. Stephen Cooper's essay, "Sex/Knowledge/Power in the Detective Genre," examines how women withhold knowledge sought by men, especially in this film, *The Big Heat, Chinatown*, and *Angel Heart*. For him the corrupting tendencies in the detective's acquisition of knowledge leads to power, which in turn leads to corruption; this is seen especially in how the detective victimizes women. As a result, there is an unraveling of the genre as there is a "disillusioned recognition of the detective's own self" (25). In an essay on the initial reception of *Blues in the Night* in *Films in Review*, William Everson briefly compares the plot and character to *The Maltese Falcon*. Pauline Kael's review of Robert Altman's *The Long Goodbye* is one of several reviews that compare and contrast Gould and Bogart and Chandler and Hammett.

Given his importance in the history of American movies, there has been surprisingly little written about Humphrey Bogart's acting. One exception is Virginia Wright Wexman's "Kinesics and Film Acting: Humphrey Bogart in *The Maltese Falcon* and *The Big Sleep*." Borrowing from ideas developed in her earlier essay in *Library Quarterly* on the adaptations of *The Maltese Falcon*, Wexman examines Bogart's "controlled acting techniques" in the two films as related to body language. Unlike earlier, overdrawn acting in *The Petrified Forest*, by the time of *The Maltese Falcon* he was using his delivery, wiry frame, height, ethnic appearance, and gestures to convey a sense of dominance. In *The Maltese Falcon* Bogart's Spade "represented an ideal coming together of actor and character. Tough, cynical, independent, volatile, wryly humorous, and at last alone with his own integrity, the character of Sam Spade merged irrevocably with the star-persona of Bogart in Huston's film" (54).

In an interview on NBC radio in 1957, quoted in Kaminsky's *John Huston: Maker of Magic*, John Huston said of Bogart, "The better I got to know him, the more I admired him. He was a very serious man about his work. He took great pride in being an actor. The face that he presented to the world was quite a different one than the one that those who knew him truly well knew. In society, at Hollywood parties, he assumed the role of gadfly and tormentor of the fat cats. This gave a misunderstanding to those who only saw him on those occasions. They thought of him as a rowdy, bawdy and gaudy. In truth, he was a very sincere, deeply humble and faithful man, faithful to his work, his friends, and finally, his family'' (23).

Not everyone liked Bogart or his films. In Silver and Ward's *Film Noir*, Julie Kirgo finds *The Maltese Falcon* artificial and cold, a "caricature" rather than a motion picture, with "textbook camerawork," and "contemptuous misanthropy" (181–182). The characters are all one-dimensional: "Bogart is the tough guy with the soft heart; Mary Astor, the lying bitch of innocent demeanor; Sidney Greenstreet the threatening, chortling Fat Man[;] Peter Lorre, the mincing menace; Elisha Cook, Jr., the twitchy, stupid little punk." We do not feel anything for Spade at the end when he must decide between love and justice: "With Huston's Spade, the viewer is getting a thrill out of sending Brigid over." In a slight concession, she notes that the best things about the film are its "crisp dialogue and the bravura performances of the principals" (181–182). After an extended discussion of "bothering" (giving victims a hard time, abuse or annoyance), Henry Random presents reflections on why he was not attracted to Bogart (mostly not in "likable parts") and skipped *The Maltese Falcon* when it first opened. What he finally saw was "a movie which showed life as it really was, the real raw stuff, instead of that cloying sweetness-and-light romantic drivel most movies were about" (113). In her examination of films of the 1940s, Barbara Deming gives mostly summary of what happens in film and how it relates to a "tough boy," wandering hero, who, vulnerable and desirous of not being hurt, still "takes the hopeless case, enters the deadly embrace, to prove to himself that he can emerge intact," that he can endure (152).

John Russell Taylor says that what makes the film "special" is "its extreme tightness: everything follows from what has gone before, there are no gaps, no pauses, no chance to dwell on atmosphere or character as something apart from the story" (70). In his collection of great Hollywood films, *New York Times* film critic Bosley Crowther sees Sam Spade's character as being very much a reflection of both the time it was made and the attitude of the youth of the 1960s: "It is a character that subtly communicates the attitude of an age—skeptical, disillusioned, resistant to commitment, detached. Underneath its *demimondain* surface, it states the feelings of many who were disabused of pious idealism by the outbreak of the Second World War within a decade of the Depression. And it continues, unto this day, to satisfy the youngsters who are doubtful of the society in which they live" (158).

William Luhr's edited volume on *The Maltese Falcon*, part of the Rutgers Films in Print Series, includes an introductory discussion of the movie's initial reception ("a major success") and subsequent critical reputation, Dashiell Hammett and detective fiction, the detective film and *film noir*, and a cultural examination of *noir*. There is also a shot-by-shot continuity script and essays on the film's production and the literary and film traditions it drew on. The volume includes reviews and articles by Behlmer, Agee, Naremore, Jean-Loup Bourget, and Ilsa Bick, and a filmography and bibliography.

In *The Maltese Falcon*, Richard Anobile presents the first book in a series on popular feature films. He includes every scene in over 1,400 frame blow-ups, plus all the dialogue. In the course of praising Huston for his intercuts and mobile camera, Anobile explains that he hopes his book will "give the serious film student a rare opportunity to closely examine the work of some of our finest directors" (5). What could only be done with professional equipment in the 1970s was superseded by the advent of freeze frame and slow motion on VCRs. Still, this book and others in the series, including *Casablanca*, remain valuable references for the study of the film. For those interested in a luxurious, oversized black and white picture book accompanied by general commentary on the making of the film, its plot, and a brief career overviews of the actors, Marie Cahill's *Hollywood Classic: The Maltese Falcon* is worth having.

Across the Pacific

Ted Sennett's assessment of *Across the Pacific* as a "minor but entertaining melodrama" of international intrigue is a fairly common view. In his study of two "masters of menace," he focuses on Greenstreet's persona in *The Maltese Falcon*—"urbane, cultivated man of intellect whose capacity for cruelty and violence was cleverly concealed by his refined manner" (111). Not unlike other movie heroes, Greenstreet's man of intellect usually loses out to the man of action. *Across the Pacific*, as a follow-up to *The Maltese Falcon*, uses some of the same cast and similar kinds of dialogue (especially between Bogart and Mary Astor) in an effort to recapture the ethos of the previous film. Sennett gives good marks to Huston for "his skillful handling of atmospheric detail and his artful use of close-ups" (110), and he commends Mary Astor for her performance. In her biography, Astor speaks of the pleasure of working again with Bogart and Greenstreet, the tenseness caused by the bombing of Pearl Harbor and how it required rewriting the script, and her feeling that the results were something less than successful. Alan Downer takes a more focused view in his discussion of Huston's use of the "monitor image" and how he creates "deliberate ambiguity" by letting Bogart play himself. This forces the audience to guess whether he is a renegade, gangster, or hero.

Casablanca

Of all of Bogart's films, no other has received more print coverage than *Casablanca*, and the articles are as diverse as their authors and the film's audience. Charles Francisco traces the making of film from a tattered memo of December 1941 to its critical reception and spinoffs, and discusses the film's place in American folklore, its romance, political intrigue, timeliness of world events, and colorful background and characters. Francisco's overview includes a discussion of the original play, profiles of the cast, the contributions of Hal Wallis, Michael Curtiz, the Epsteins, Howard Koch, and Max Steiner, the scripting of the film, and its influence on contemporary culture. Worked into the narrative is a biography of Bogart's life based on prior, and sometimes erroneous, accounts. Francisco includes illustrations and an extensive index, but no bibliography.

Rudy Behlmer's "George Raft in *Casablanca*?" gives a brief history of the making of the film, including costs (approximately $950,000) and budget ($878,000) and casting—how Raft was suggested by Warner and Wallis but Curtiz said no, the oft-quoted notion of how Ann Sheridan, Ronald Reagan, and Dennis Morgan were possibilities for the leads, and how Hazel Scott and Clarence Muse were considered for the role that went to Dooley Wilson. What would the film have been like if there was an epilogue with Rick and Louis's escaping Casablanca? We will never know because when David O. Selznick saw the film, he liked it as it was. Scheduled for release in June 1943, the studio decided that with Allies landing in North Africa in November 1942, an immediate release would be more propitious. The film opened in limited release on November 26, with a general release on January 23, 1943, during the Roosevelt, Stalin, Churchill conference, and a day that many have considered Bogart's birthday. Looking at the film through history and linking the film's scenario to actual events is Richard E. Osborne's *The* Casablanca *Companion* (1997). Not to be confused with Jeff Siegel's work of the same title, this work examines the relations between Vichy France and Germany and places and events in 1941. The subtitle—*The Movie Classic and Its Place in History*—suggests Osborne's approach. To Behlmer, on the other hand, *Casablanca* is a film with "colorful characters involved in what is essentially a love story, an exotic locale, first-rate supporting players, melodramatic incidents, tough, humorous, cynical repartee, sentimental interludes, and idealism and heroic commitment to a cause" (154). Behlmer's retelling is fuller than Ron Haver's discussion of the film's history and its mystique. Haver believes *Casablanca* "provides tangible evidence of not necessarily the way we were, but more important, the way we wanted to be. It is this sense of the more positive beliefs and virtues of another time that gives the film its timelessness" (*Finally* 16).

Without question, the best scholarly book on the film's production is Aljean Harmetz's *Round Up the Usual Suspects: The Making of* Casablanca—*Bogart, Bergman, and World War II*. Harmetz's full account of the impact of the Hollywood studio system on the making of the film goes well beyond previous works by Francisco, Haver, Behlmer, Lebo, and Siegel. Harmetz relies on archival material, extensive interviews, and a thorough examination of secondary scholarship to convey the definitive history of the making and initial reception of *Casablanca*. Through detailed analysis and extensive documentation, she explains why there was "never any chance" that Ronald Reagan and Ann Sheridan would costar in the film, and how the studio planted a false story to hype the release of *Kings Row* (73–74). Of Bogart, Harmetz says he was "concerned about the script, the love scenes, his marriage, and what he felt to be self-pity at the core of his character—stirred up by a whirlpool. There are few actors about whom opinions are so divided.... It was not that people saw him differently but that they reacted to the same stimuli—his needling, his verbal defiance, his irascibility—with either admiration or disgust. Bogart was almost a Rorschach test'' (197).

Harlan Lebo's *Casablanca: Behind the Scenes* is based on archival material and the use of two independent sources, supplemented by newspaper articles from 1941 to 1943 and books on Bogart, Bergman, Henreid, and other studio personnel. The volume is strong in its factual presentation of material, and includes an interview with Julius Epstein, a compendium of contemporary film reviews, a history of the evolution of the film and its casting, a commentary on Orry-Kelly's costumes, and a career overview for Bogart (45–64). Of Bogart's being chosen for *Casablanca*, Lebo remarks, "It's difficult to imagine that the actor's unique style and on-screen personality could have been questioned. But at the time, in spite of years of patient grooming, Bogart remained an unlikely—and risky—romantic screen prospect'' (63).

Peter van Gelder's "Casablanca" is another overview that discusses how Warner Bros. was just waking up to Bogart as a major star after *The Maltese Falcon*, the costs of the rights to the play, and some of the actors' salaries. While many hands contributed to the script, Howard Koch was present on the set "most of the time." Bogart's contributions included "Here's looking at you, kid" and "Of all the *gin joints* . . ." van Gelder notes that Elliot Carpenter plays the piano for Dooley Wilson, whom he says was a drummer; repeats how Max Steiner tried to veto "As Time Goes By" for one of his own compositions; notes that the opening sequence is by Don Siegel; cites the mistake in the credits of S. Z. (not "K") Sakall; and points out inconsistencies in the film such as fog and rain in North Africa, de Gaulle's having signed the Vichy letters of transit, and the unlikely notion that Rick could have such a famous gin joint within two years of his departure from Paris (47).

In *The Casablanca Companion*, one of several books that appeared on the fiftieth anniversary of the film, Jeff Siegel gives standard coverage to the story, players, writers, responses, and the influences on other works. He sees *Casablanca* as a morality play, and the one movie that defines what we want to think of ourselves: "cynical yet idealistic, independent yet romantic, worldly yet naive" (1). Painting with the broadest of strokes, he claims that everyone in this country sees Rick's behavior as "sensible, logical, and morally correct" (3). There are comments on Bogart's professionalism, his conflicts with Mayo Methot, cast salaries, trivia "interludes," and general background information. Of Bogart's influence Siegel says, "He not only made the trench coat and fedora the uniform of the bitter, disaffected hero, but he made that bitter, disaffected hero part of film lore" (42). Frank Miller's *Casablanca: As Time Goes By* is a lavishly illustrated celebration of the film's golden anniversary, with commentary, stills, and discussion of principles involved, legends, and facts. Miller, like

Sklar, Harmetz, and Lebo, uses the Warner Bros. archives at USC, correspondence, and newspaper articles to present a lively account of how, as Sarris, Harmetz, and others have noted, *Casablanca* was "a series of lucky accidents [that] brought together the perfect script, director, and stars to create the definitive romantic thriller" (10). It is also an "icon for lost love, devotion to a cause, and a simpler time when right and wrong could be drawn in bold strokes of black and white" (11). Although less analytical than Sklar and with fewer details than Harmetz, Miller's text is buoyed by the numerous stills that serve as a pictorial review of the film and its reception, and brief career overviews for all the major principals in the film. The discussion of Bogart says, as others have, that Hal Wallis never really wanted George Raft for the part and that this role made Bogart: "The image that made him a star was that of a loner shrouded in a haze of liquor and cigarette smoke, the man whose isolation stemmed either from romantic loss or the shattering ideals in some long-ago youth. On screen, he explored variations on cynical detachment. Off-screen, he carefully projected the image of the sardonic iconoclast" (171). In *Starmaker*, Wallis (and Higham) present memos related to the productions of *Casablanca* and brief discussions of the producer's contributions to other films with Bogart.[7]

As part of a series of eight books intended to present literal translations of film to paper, Richard Anobile has published a shot-by-shot presentation of *Casablanca* and an accompanying interview with Ingrid Bergman that gives little insight into the film. If Anobile's book or the video or laserdisc is not at hand, you might want to gaze at Marie Cahill's *Hollywood Classics*: Casablanca, an oversized picture book that tries to portray the "drama and romance of *Casablanca*" through publicity stills and candid shots of the cast and crew. The text gives snippets of background on the making of the film and a fair amount of description of the pictures. This volume is primarily for collectors of *Casablanca* memorabilia.

The script and its source have been debated, both in and out of court. Joan Alison and Murray Burnett, for example, sued Bogart biographer Nathaniel Benchley for defamation of character, seeking $5 million from Benchley and $1.5 million from Little, Brown, claiming that Benchley's book says that the film was in no way based on the play. Bernard Dick in *Anatomy of Film* gives a brief plot summary of "Everybody Comes to Rick's," and explains how much the film is liked "because there is a solid mythic foundation beneath a rickety plot" (203). In "Lose it Again, Sam," *Variety* reports that Judge Saypol dismissed the suit because Benchley's statement that the play "died" before reaching Broadway is a common metaphor and was not libelous. Burnett also sued Howard Koch for $6.5 million after he wrote an article in 1973 claiming that the play had very little of what was in the film. Burnett also sued Warner Bros. to get back the rights to his characters. He lost all the suits. Harmetz discusses the conflict in her book (36–37) and was asked to write Burnett's recent obituary for the *New York Times*. In the notice she again says that Burnett was "the unsung author of the play on which one of America's iconic movies . . . was based," Burnett having supplied the "spine of 'Casablanca' and a few of the famous lines" (C23).[8]

In 1979 Casey Robinson told Joel Greenberg that he worked on the screenplay and helped rewrite the love relationship between Rick and Ilsa to Bogart's satisfaction. According to the screenwriter, Bogart wanted a great love story and walked from the role until Robinson, who had written him in as romantic trainer in *Dark Victory*, returned to work on the script. Hal Wallis wanted Robinson to get screen credit, but Robinson refused because there were three other writers on the project. He later regretted his decision because of the recognition afforded the credited screenwriters after they received an Oscar for their efforts. On the ending, Robinson says that "there was, incidentally, never any question about the way the story would end, whether Bogart would go with her or the husband: this was clear as far as I was concerned, and as far as Hal was concerned, once I was on the picture. We never discussed it" (16). In recalling events and personal contributions, sometimes memory is faulty. In her analysis of the making of the film, Harmetz discusses Robinson's contribution, but also points out his selective or inaccurate memory in some cases, such as when he dismissed *Everybody Comes to Rick's* as almost irrelevant to the movie (178). In a discussion of the film in 1975, Richard Corliss notes the script's resemblance to Casey Robinson's *It's Love I'm After* (1937), and the "reconciling of opposites: comradeship and love, realism and idealism, war and resistance to warmakers" (105).

In an interview with Harry Haun, Julius Epstein, an Academy Award winner for his work on the script, recounts that it was great to write for Warner Bros. character actors and that he and his twin brother, Philip, were dispatched to David O. Selznick's office to pitch the nonexistent story line for *Casablanca* in an effort to get Ingrid Bergman. After going on for about thirty minutes without mentioning Bergman's character, he said to Selznick, " 'Aw, it's going to be a lot of crap like *Algiers*.' Selznick nodded, and we got Bergman" (520). In an interview with B. Case that appeared in 1992, screenwriter Julius Epstein said that he was at a loss to explain the film's enduring popularity, yet years before, in *Sound and the Cinema: The Coming of Sound to American Film*, he said *Casablanca* was one of his least favorite films while giving as one reason for its success the Bogart cult (105). Like Edward Edelson, Epstein finds it a phony romance, in which even the key letters of transit are phony. He much prefers *Light in the Piazza, Pete 'n Tillie*, and *Take a Giant Step* to *Casablanca*. In *America in the Dark: Hollywood and the Gift of Unreality*, David Thomson calls the film maudlin—nowhere more so than with Bogart hunched over the table, with whiskey bottle at hand. This, to Thomson, is "but the replica of the woman torturing herself over a lost love" [in women's pictures] (208).

Howard Koch's *Casablanca: Script and Legend* (1973) is one of the most-referred-to sources relating to the study of the film. The introduction discusses the original play and the making of the film, how the Epsteins sold Selznick on the film for Bergman, Koch's collaboration with the Epsteins and their falling out, how Koch pieced the script together, Curtiz's solicitation of other opinions—"Mike leaned strongly on the romantic elements of the story while I was more interested in the characterizations and the political intrigues" (10)—the last hectic weeks of shooting, and the unexpected reception of the film (mysticism, nostalgia, idealism disguised as cynicism). Koch also presents the script (14–161), cast credits, Richard Corliss's "Analysis of the Film," reviews by Howard Barnes and Bosley Crowther, and his own essay: "In Conclusion: What Happened to the Story in Contemporary Film?" Koch gives himself too much credit for his work and downplays Burnett's contributions. In a subsequent edition of this book (1992), Koch emends his comments and apologizes to Burnett.

Other versions of the script are available, including the one found in *Best Film Plays of 1943–1944*, edited by John Gassner and Dudley Nichols. This script is collated with dialogue and continuity material that did not appear in the final film. A more recent collection of twelve screenplays, edited by Sam Thomas, a creative writing instructor at UCLA, includes *Casablanca* in *Best American Screenplays*.

For all its stature in American culture, Chuck Ross demonstrated in 1982 how agents are not always familiar with touchstones of our culture. His article in *Film Comment* describes how he sent slightly doctored *Casablanca* scripts (Sam becomes Dooley, and the title becomes *Everybody Comes to Rick's*) to 217 agents to see if they had an interest in this property. Even with its top-ten listing in the *LA Times* readers' poll (1967 and 1978), its listing as one of the top three films of all time in the American Film Institute 1977 poll, and its ranking as the most popular and frequently shown film on television (*TV Guide*, 1977), not all readers saw the hoax. Ninety agents would not read it, seven never responded, and eighteen claimed it may have gotten lost in the mail. Of the others, thirty-three recognized it, three wanted to represent him on it, eight noticed similarities, one wanted to turn it into a novel, and thirty-eight rejected it. In a note in the same issue of *Film Comment*, Richard Corliss claims that the script would not be accepted or filmed in today's market because the sex is by innuendo, there is only one teenager (and Belgian at that), the chase lasts only a few seconds, there is only one punch in the climactic fight scene, and there is more talking than action.

Of all the actors, Paul Henreid's performance is the one most often criticized, but Frank Miller defends his "simplicity and quiet strength" (194) and his ability to lead people through words on paper (195). Aljean Harmetz finds the least appealing figure in the film to be Victor Laszlo, because he lacks the essential ingredient of the film's staying power: ambiguity (*Round Up* 353). Unlike Roger Ebert, who dislikes Victor Laszlo because he "has no humor and no resilience," "hardly deserves Ilsa," and is blind to the love between Rick and Ilsa (842) and Harmetz, Miller says that Henreid's ability to give an emotional performance is amply demonstrated in *Joan of Paris* (1942), but he offers little to support his performance in *Casablanca*.

Another very strong defender of Henreid is Mary Beth Crain, who in two publications in 1976 defends her hero's honor. Crain laments that Bogart and Bergman get all the publicity for *Casablanca*, when to her, Henreid (as Laszlo) represents "the symbol of Allied victory and integrity. . . . He is the embodiment of both the message of the film and Rick's political moral conscience" (12). At the end of the film, Rick "is enough aware of Laszlo's inner struggle to choose to administer to his needs, in the end, rather than Ilsa's" (12). To Crain, the focus of the film is not a love affair but Rick's personal transformation "away from personal isolationism and toward political activism" (14). In an extended interview with Crain, Henreid discussed the blacklists, *Casablanca*, his life and career, directing, and why he signed with Warner Bros. against his better judgment. (He did not want to be detained as a foreigner.) His dislike for *Casablanca* was intense: "I hated the script, I hated the story, I disliked everything about it and I was absolutely right because it started to be written continuously"; above all he hated the idea of the white suit (19–20). Henreid described the character of Laszlo as a "tortured," complex person. Of Bogart he said, "Nobody in the lifetime of Bogey ever talked about him as a brilliant actor. He was a personality, Bogey, and he was actually very limited in what he could do." With *The Treasure of the Sierra Madre* he became "great," though his "greatest performance" was *The Caine Mutiny* (19–20). What annoyed Henreid the most about Bogart had little to do with his acting. As a member on the Committee for the First Amendment, Henreid traveled with Bogart to Washington to defend what later became known as the Hollywood Ten. Henreid himself was blacklisted and found reprehensible Bogart's subsequent apology that he (Bogart) was "misguided." To Henreid, Bogart's action "was very embarrassing for all his friends, it really was shocking" (23).

Ingrid Bergman's *Ingrid Bergman: My Story* includes a few general comments on Bogart and *Casablanca*, but offers no insights into her performance or the film. Laurence Leamer's *As Time Goes By: The Life of Ingrid Bergman* deals in passing with the making of *Casablanca* and Bergman's preparation for the role of Ilsa. Bergman found Bogart professional on the set, but her most-quoted line about him is, "I kissed him but I never knew him" (87). Of Bogart, Leamer writes, "No romantic star had ever had a face like Bogart's. He did for ordinary-looking men what Perrier did for water" (86). Leamer quotes Bogart as saying, "I didn't do anything I've never done before. . . . But when the camera moves in on that Bergman face, and she's saying she loves you, it would make anybody look romantic" (87). Bergman does say in her autobiography that the audience "acts" for her in *Casablanca* by reading into her face what they desired (473). Using secondary sources, Leamer tells us that Bogart followed the advice of Mel Baker: "This is the first time you've ever played the romantic lead against a major star. You stand still, and always make her come to you. Mike probably won't notice it, and if she complains you can tell her it's tacit in the script. You've got something she wants, so she has to come to you" (88). Like Mary Beth Crain, Leamer finds Rick Blaine to be "a man struggling with his own personal isolation, a metaphor for America herself in the days before Pearl Harbor'' (90).

John J. Croft stresses Bergman's intuitive understatement, deep emotions, delicate gentility, and radiant countenance that were enhanced by cinematographer Arthur Edeson, who was never given adequate credit for his work. Melva Baker analyzes the character of Ilsa as part of a larger study of the woman refugee in *Casablanca* and how her character ties in with women's roles in top-grossing films from 1941 to 1945. Baker says Ilsa has ''uncommon qualities'' of loyalty, courage, and beauty, but is a woman ''primarily concerned with human relationships and her part in them'' (53). William Hamilton later disagrees with this view of Ilsa, finding her weak and needing to be controlled by Rick.

Leonid Kinskey, who plays Sascha the Russian bartender in the film, looks back after thirty years and attributes its appeal to ''unusual personalities . . . the concert of outstanding soloists'' (132) and nostalgia for these actors. Bergman saw herself as an outsider, and at times Bogart and his cronies did not help the situation, using off-color language with which she was not familiar. Kinskey claims that Bogart tried to be something of a big brother to her, was ''ever-obliging, cut no-nonsense,'' was easy to work with, and was ''manly, honest in his acting, and never created a problem'' with the crew or director (127). As an actor, ''Bogie seemingly never worked on his part. He always had time for the usual chitchat between rehearsals or 'takes,' but anybody who led himself to believe that Bogie never worked on his parts was terribly mistaken. He never did any role without serious thinking about every phase of the character he played: the gamut of his emotions, the entire pattern of his psychological behavior. In other words, he lived his characters, and to do that, an actor has to put in a great deal of work'' (128).

Richard Corliss's analysis of the film and a later, slightly revised essay are among the better textual discussions of the film. Corliss briefly examines Bogart as an ''existential hero-in-spite-of-himself''; how the film might work as political allegory; the elements of repressed homosexual fantasy (Rick and Renault ''want companionship more than they need love''); and how particular scenes and dialogue (e.g., with Yvonne) capture the Bogart essence of no wasted motions, actions, or dialogue. What is open for interpretation are the enigmatic ambiguity of his partner Renault (171), Ilsa's platitudes, and Rick's ''Here's looking at you.'' It is by preserving illusions that Rick saves lives at the end. The multiplicity of meanings as allegory, popular myth, and romantic melodrama, in combination with its script, pacing, casting, and sheer entertainment value, establishes its power in our culture.

The auteur approach, looking at the film as a Michael Curtiz film, finds its way into much of the commentary. Sidney Rosenzweig's Casablanca *and Other Major Films of Michael Curtiz* is a detailed study of Curtiz's importance at Warner Bros., his ''directorial prerogatives,'' how by the late 1940s he was able to form his own production unit at the studio, and critical perspectives on *Cas-*

ablanca. Using Robin Wood's idea that genres are dealing with the same conflicts but with different strategies, Rosenzweig gives a brief overview of other critical studies, including Donelly's use of Leslie Fiedler to show how the Rick-Sam-Renault relationships demonstrate "repressed homosexuality"; Greenberg's Freudian reading of Rick's Oedipal complex, with Ilsa the mother and Laszlo the father figure; Corliss and others on the importance of the minor figures and how they become a "hall of mirrors" of Rick's character; and the attraction and mythological appeal of Rick's isolation and self-sacrifice as presented by Michael Wood (78–81).

Two other auteur studies are James Robertson's *The Casablanca Man* and William Meyer's work on Warner Bros. directors. Robertson explores Curtiz's European and U.S. work, his visual style, his work in various genres, and his work on screenplays, with information from financial documents and archives. After some misinformation about casting related to Ronald Reagan and Ann Sheridan, Meyer tells us that Curtiz had talent but lacked genius (75), and that above all, he will be remembered for *Casablanca*. To Meyer the pace of the film gives a glimpse of everything and a series of "opposed emotional tones," but its true greatness "lies in the commitment made by those of vastly different character to further the Allied cause. Romantic to be sure, propagandistic to be certain, very possibly silly, but such traits are revealed in exotic Casablanca, where one can meet all kinds of people" (96).

D. McVay also discusses the atmosphere and visual composition of the film, finding the close-up a key element of this film, especially when Ilsa listens to the song, when she reacts to Rick's arrival, and when he "murmurs his salute to her for the last time" (6). Even so, McVay would not use the label of auteur for Curtiz. The three chief themes in the film are Rick's place as "escapist cocoon and political microcosm which springboards the narrative"; "ideologies" (as seen in the singing of "La Marseillaise"); and the love of Rick and Ilsa.

Dan Ackerman analyzes Curtiz's "intricate" visual compositions as it relates to character and also discusses the scripting of the film, its similarity to *Captain Blood*, and how the individual contributions created the "dynamic qualities" of the film (33). Jerry Tillotson's "Cry for *Casablanca*" is a lament for the 1940s that focuses on Curtiz's visuals. To Tillotson, no television series could capture the ambience of *Casablanca*, which with its actors, music, studio, and facial and body gestures is the "essence of Forties film-making" (21). A key difference between filmmakers of the 1980s and the 1940s is that recent filmmakers want to make their films look real through costumes and look, while the films of the 1940s with their low-key lighting, "glossy camera work," and dreamlike quality are made to look like movies (21). Barry Day also speaks to the director's visual flair and finds the struggle ("synergism") between Koch's concern for politics and the contemporary struggle against fascism combine with Curtiz's stress on romance to add power to the film. Day contends that Curtiz's use of flashbacks in the Paris sequence helps to relieve the tension, proves Rick's softer side, and allows for greater audience identification (23). Maureen Turim also analyzes how the flashbacks let us in on Rick and Ilsa's personal memories of their time in Paris. With "its retrospective assimilation" the use of flashback "clears their love of recrimination and self doubt" (127) and evokes in the American audience an additional kind of memory as a result of Pearl Harbor.

To Robert B. Ray *Casablanca* is the culmination of "Classic Hollywood" moviemaking and allegory of U.S. military intervention, while also reworking many of the motifs in Twain's *Huckleberry Finn*. With Rick and Laszlo, we reduce "national ideological tensions to the manageable size of outlaw hero–official hero conflicts" (91), seen as an outgrowth of frontier mythology—"two strains of American culture" (102) put into wartime film, transposing "propaganda into melodrama" (89). Part of a larger study of ideology and classical narrative cinema, Ray says we cannot say with certainty whether *Casablanca* reflected the tastes of its audience or imposed them, but the film does tell its audience that solutions are found within the individual (363–364). With very little documentation of his reading of the film and its reception, but greatly influential in certain quarters (see, for example, Gabbard and Gabbard, "Play It"), Ray says it "reverberates with echoes of films coming before and after it," including Rhett Butler in *Gone with the Wind* and Hans Solo in *Star Wars* (4). Umberto Eco presents a more detailed discussion of how the film brings together patterns from other films and genres.

Roy Kinnard and R. J. Vitone's "*Casablanca*" gives high marks to "a wonderful ensemble," but considers *Casablanca* a director's film. They claim Walsh and Huston were responsible for Bogart's screen persona, but it was Curtiz who smoothed over "the remaining rough edges" and added the "final touches" to the "quintessential Bogie," which is the "tough, world-weary, cynical man, self-governed by a private code of honor and susceptible to a vulnerable romanticism." Curtiz emphasizes Rick's "romantic torment" rather than his apolitical stance, and they see Renault functioning as Rick's conscience. They mistakenly believe that Bogart was offered the role because he "made very high marks with the studio hierarchy" for accepting almost everything sent his way (82–84).

Casablanca is very much a product of the Hollywood studio system of the 1940s. In his high praise for the film, Roger Ebert (*Video Companion*) compliments Curtiz on his use of the grammar of film established by Griffith: establishing shots, movement, medium shots, alternating close-ups, point-of-view shots, and reactions. Stephen Hanson says that Curtiz emphasizes characterization and atmosphere in a film that works both as anti-Nazi propaganda and a love story (606). Dana Polan develops the idea of the importance of the tenor of the times when he talks about *Casablanca* as an example of a "conversion narrative," in which the internal (or external) forces that are resistant to "unity," "unambiguous reciprocity and community" (74) are converted to "a new and proper set of values and beliefs" (75), combined with an "oedipal narrative" (155). Even though the battle may be on the fringes to Polan, "a space outside the official representation of the struggle" (155), his conversion is a "private, existential struggle" that while "unrepresentable" when Rick walks off into the fog in the last scene (156), is a "complete, total, . . . all-consuming adoption of a prescribed way of being" (76).

Richard Maltby's *Harmless Entertainment: Hollywood and the Ideology of Consensus* examines cinematic mechanisms (physical relationships, use of close-ups, medium shots, etc.) and the relationship between audience and film to argue that when a film uses fixed conventions in what he calls "consensual cinema," then the text is realistic, "regardless of what perceptional systems it operates" (193). Maltby examines *Casablanca*, with glances at *Citizen Kane, Since You Went Away, The Wizard of Oz, The Searchers*, and *The Man Who Shot Liberty Valance*. The narrative of *Casablanca* is "constructed to support and clarify the story of the film, aiming at a coherence in the revelation of the plot in order to concentrate attention on the story as it is revealed" (193). Each scene advances the plot and adds information. In the treatment of time and space, Curtiz has the actors unite real life with screen image, especially Bogart and Bergman: "Bogart the crumpled isolationist whose verbal cynicism imperfectly conceals his honorable sentimentality, Bergman the mysterious insecure woman wary of her own passion." Film realism is "not a perceptual system, but rather an idiomatic tendency" that is created through its use of "codes of behavior" familiar to film audiences (201–205).

Gary L. Green's "The Happiest of Happy Accidents? A Reevaluation of *Casablanca*" claims that although there are many stories on how this film is an accidental masterpiece, "at the heart of *Casablanca* is a visual style that the script and actors complement but in no way completely define; that style is the work of Michael Curtiz" (4). The film, with Curtiz's influences, is a mood piece as seen in a visual style that deals with treachery, corruption, and decadence found in other films by Curtiz (5). Key to Green is how Curtiz blends "form and content in a visual style defined by triangular constructions [especially of characters] that mirror the narrative triangles, which in turn are constantly seeking resolution; and in the chiaroscuro lighting the tensions within the triangle are mirrored" (13). Accident or not, Edward Edelson contends that if "viewed logically, *Casablanca* is sentimental trash. Every character in the film is, in one way or another, a cliché" (10–11). Stephen Hanson's overview in *Magill's American Film Guide* sketches some of the difficulties in putting the film together, but how with its tightly constructed plot, well-balanced cast, superb cinematography and music, and studio team it was a "successful fusion of the major qualities of the Hollywood romantic melodrama at its finest" (606).

More than anything else, commentators on *Casablanca* discuss Rick's character. Robert Sklar remarks that Bogart, for the first time in his career, was "taking charge of his own screen persona" (142), a character whom the Epstein brothers created as "intense, somewhat repressed, and whose strength initially was declared by the powerful reaction of others" (138). Dan Ackerman considers Rick a complex force who makes decisions hinged to a morality based on a "search for authenticity into a political context: Finding the validity in a political cause is equated with finding the validity in oneself and others" (36). Kingsley Canham gives Curtiz the credit for molding Bogart as the loner who controls his own destiny. Claiming that Bogart's various gestures and mannerisms suggest confidence, Canham gives Bogart little credit for shaping his character, but maintains that the primary reasons for the film's popularity are Bogart, his existential characterization, and the high quality of the entire cast (39). In the second chapter of her book on the impact of movies on the 1940s, Barbara Deming analyzes Bogart as a war hero as embodied in *Casablanca* (and also *Passage to Marseille*). At the end, the dream of his relationship with Ilsa, which is still in Rick's heart (and ours), has caused a transformation as he regains his "lost faith" (21). Rick's faith to the cause is defined analogously: "Just because he wears the aspect of utter cynicism, one can be sure that he is the real man of faith" (22). In the dark, as we dream, we become believers, because *Casablanca* is a portrait of ourselves.

Although screenwriters Julius Epstein and Edward Edelson find little reason for the film's success, others do not have such a hard time explaining its appeal. Thomas Cripps claims that a liberal agenda toward civil rights in Hollywood and the use of Dooley Wilson in *Casablanca* helped to advance the cause of "conscience-liberalism," a kind of political action found in some movies of the time. Lenny Rubinstein stresses that the film is a political allegory of U.S. participation in World War II: "a melodrama compounded of romance and wartime intrigues that has molded the sensibilities of at least two generations of film-goers" (35). In "*Casablanca* and United States Foreign Policy," Richard Raskin presents a reassessment of *Casablanca*'s political stance toward Vichy and Free French forces as related to official U.S. policy. The film "contributed to a blurring of public awareness of the essentially anti–Free French orientation of U.S. policy and of American support of Vichy leaders in North Africa" (161). Raskin questions why astute commentators of the time did not use the film to attack Roosevelt's policies toward the French (161).

In a commentary in *Time* on the film's lasting appeal on the occasion of its fortieth anniversary, L. Morrow considers the casting, the dialogue, the sentimentality, and the politics: "*Casablanca* is, among other things, a fable of citizenship and idealism, the duties of the private self in the dangerous public world. It is a thoroughly escapist myth about getting politically involved" (76). But through it all, "there clings a quality of lovely, urgent innocence. Those who cherish the movie may be nostalgic for moral clarity, for a war in which good and evil were obvious and choices tenable. They may be nostalgic for a long-lost connection between the private conscience and the public world" (76). Sidney Rosenzweig's analysis of *Casablanca* focuses on how the film's "thematic and structural base, the conflict between love and politics, becomes associated with a number of other oppositions, all contained within its two worlds of Paris and Casablanca" (78) and the conflict between private feelings and public duty. In this analysis, he briefly discusses Donnelly and Corliss's allegorical reading of the film as a reflection of contemporary politics, with Rick as FDR and living in *casa blanca* ("white house") and how Rick's decisions parallel FDR's shift from neutrality to action (79).

Michael Wood in *America in the Movies* comments on the ever-present image of Bogart sitting at a table, cigarette in hand and drink in front of him as the image of both "romantic introspection" (24) and a "portrait of a mood that goes well beyond *Casablanca* and beyond Bogart" (25). In a discussion of isolationism, Bogart, and the United States, Wood notes that Bogart embodies a concern about the kinds of demands by friends and allies that are put on heroes and their liberty *after* the battles are won and the decisions have been made (29–30).

Peter Hogue's "I Bet They're Asleep All over America" is a reassessment of the film's "troubling aspects" such as the elegant appearances of Laszlo and Ilsa and Rick's character. In a city of refugees, the one who seems to be suffering the most is Rick, and that pain is connected to a broken love affair. Rick is "most loved" by audiences because he is everything to everyone, which suggests "in matters of character and identity, to be everything is to be nothing." We are to accept that even with his prior commitments (on the Nazis' enemies list, helped antifascist causes, etc.), he wallows in self-pity and is broken by a love affair gone sour. Rick's character and dialogue satisfy the needs of adolescents: Rick's control over characters is "wish-fulfillment of the sort that endorses the child's fantasy in which one is the center of the world and the world responds accordingly." Renault is corrupt, yet we are made to like this "profoundly unreliable character." Both Rick and Renault are "saved" by their sentimentality. The film is thus pleasing even though audiences ignore its "painful realities" (25–26). Hogue claims that Bogart has better roles in films such as *To Have and Have Not, The Big Sleep, The Maltese Falcon*, and *In a Lonely Place*, where he avoids the "sentimental pitfalls" of *Casablanca*.

Stanley Solomon sees Rick as "perhaps the most admired personality ever portrayed in the American cinema." On Bogart's image, he writes, "He seems entirely conscious of his image, which is the deliberate creation of a man who wants to appear a certain way both to preserve his privacy and to establish his public facade." Rick Blaine is "charming, detached, mysterious, and amiable even in his alienation." Rick is a romantic, an exile, who finds his way back "into the community of civilized men through an emotional appeal to his essentially romantic nature" (278). John Kobal disagrees with those who see Bogart as a romantic. He says that Bogart, like Raft, Garfield, Ladd, and Holden, is not a romantic hero and does not belong in romantic cinema. They all are "tough softies." With regard to *Casablanca*'s appeal, Kobal contends that it stems from the doubt surrounding the film, the exotic location, the encroaching danger, beautiful women, dangerous men, patriotism and cowardice, indecision, and love, duty, and honor. Bogart is a cynical, embittered character who is juxtaposed to an idealistic, rapturous Bergman. What binds them together in an air of unpredictability is "As Time Goes By." In *Retakes: Behind the Scenes of 500 Classic Movies*, John Eastman recalls that music director Max Steiner wanted to edit out the song "As Time Goes By," but because Bergman had already had her hair cut for *For Whom the Bell Tolls*, they could not reshoot certain scenes (54). In "Finally, the Truth About *Casablanca*," Ron Haver presents an overview of various influences on the film and script, from Hal Wallis, to Julius and Philip Epstein, Max Steiner, and Bogart, but sees the score as tying "the disparate elements of the film together with a romantic patina" (16).

Although the patriotism, sexism, and romanticism of the film grow more and more dated, Jimmie L. Reeves sees the "*crystalized* ambivalence" of Bogart as the "incarnation of the complex bundle of contradictions called modern man" as the strongest element of the film. The continuing popularity of *Casablanca* "is a function of our fascination with the Bogart persona." It is Bogart, not Curtiz, whom Reeves finds to be the "primary creative force," or auteur, for this film (62).

William Hamilton, in "*Amor-Vincit-Omnia*, a Meditation on *Casablanca*," considers Camus's remark that there are only victims and executioners, and this movie "is one of the last texts expressing the atmosphere of moral lucidity, when to know the right and to do it was fairly easy" (179). He finds lots of problems with the film, including Henreid's clothes, uneven acting, so-so sets and dialogue, but the films tells us about ourselves, where we were at that time in relation to World War II, and especially "about morality and moral choice" (172). Stretching to include an Augustinian reading of the film (Creation, Fall, Redemption, Life, Final Fulfillment), this essay's primary focus is on the relation between Rick and Ilsa and Renault. He repeats the standard bromides: one rejects Ilsa, another is cynical and tries to remain neutral, and the third is politically committed. She is "a weak, boring, and neurotic woman" (177) who asks Rick to think for her. In his rejection of Ilsa, Rick "held her to a higher moral standard than she thought she was capable of, and helped her to achieve it" (179). This idea about Ilsa was stated originally by Casey Robinson, who said that when Rick sends Ilsa off with Laszlo, "He is not just solving a love triangle. He is forcing the girl to live up to the idealism of her nature, forcing her to carry on with the work that in these days is far more important than the love of two little people" (Harmetz 178).

If the characters and actors make this film, as many contend, then their psychological makeup tells us about them and about us as spectators. In *Psychiatry and the Cinema*, Krin and Glen O. Gabbard use Michael Wood's reading of American movie myths (*America at the Movies*) and Robert B. Ray's argument (*A Certain Tendency of the Hollywood Cinema, 1930–1980*) about the outlaw hero versus the official hero as key ideas in their work. In *Casablanca*, for example, a world conflict becomes the subject of melodrama, as Rick, who could be considered the outlaw hero in contrast to Laszlo, the official hero, struggles with his personal conflicts. *Casablanca*, with Rick working out the conflict himself, presents a pattern of reconciliation that is soon to fade from the screen. In an article that appeared after their book, the Gabbards explore the narrative of *Casablanca* through a psychoanalytical reading that focuses on Oedipal parallels and Lacanian theory, and how these readings lend themselves to *Casablanca* as a cult film. Robert Lapsley and Michael Westlake's "From *Casablanca* to *Pretty Woman*: The Politics of Romance" also uses Lacanian theory to discuss how even romantic love cannot make good the lack: "Romantic love seen from the outside is fraught with illusion, that lovers' estimation of what their life together will be like is deeply unrealistic, that their mutual valuation is absurdly inflated, and that in representing their love they are pretending something that exists that really does not" (29). Lapsley and Westlake mention *Casablanca* only in passing, while looking at many films, most particularly *Pretty Woman*.

Carl Goldberg's "The Role of Passion in the Transformation of Anti-Heroes," originally presented at a meeting of the American Psychological Association, says that current sentiments against romatic love are rooted in harmful Freudian ideas of sublimation: "The bifurcation of passion—exalting Platonic love and altruism at the cost of denigrating romantic yearning has had a devastating effect on self-esteem and purposive action" (4). He considers Rick Blaine to be an existential antihero—a possessor of "courageous defiance" and "integrity" (5)—who, through a psychological process, comes to terms with romantic passion and is thus able to become "a resolute and committed man of principle and action" (6).

William Grimes's "Buried Themes: Psychoanalyzing Movies" also comes at the film from a psychological approach, discussing how Bruce Sklarew, co-chair of the Forum for the Psychoanalytic Study of Film, finds the farewell scene in *Casablanca* a successful resolution of Rick's Oedipal complex. Harvey R. Greenberg, a practicing psychiatrist, says our fantasies are realized in film: "The movies, like waking dreams, interpret every aspect of our lives—the unique past, the troubled present, our anxious premonitions of the future, our neurotic conflicts and our inspired gropings towards the light" (3). While many see aesthetic problems in the movie, they still are moved by it. Greenberg asks, "Why?" Bogart's power comes from more than the violent men he has played; in *Casablanca* he becomes "more accessible" (81). After an extended discussion of the events of the film, Greenberg tells us that Rick has landed in Casablanca "on a misguided quest to cure melancholy with solitude" (86). Unlike Dobbs and Sam Spade, Rick's paranoia is less apparent as he distances himself from all around him. Rick's problem is Oedipal: "If Laszlo and Rick are unconscious reflections of Ilsa's fathers, she in turn appears to be his unconscious as a mother-surrogate" (98–99). Rick's willingness to let Ilsa go with Laszlo demonstrates how he overcomes those murderous feelings, reversing the events in Paris (but here with an explanation), in a way similar, according to Greenberg, to Sam Spade's giving up Brigid O'Shaughnessy. Greenberg finds the idea of Rick being a homosexual to be a "lunatic" idea, but he does not deny Rick's greater sense of ease with men and his misogyny and fear of women. In giving up Ilsa, he gets back a part of himself.

The countless showings of *Casablanca* at film festivals on college campuses and on television, combined with the Bogart cult, helped to establish *Casablanca* as one of the most popular cult films. Danny Peary includes the credits, a synopsis, and a discussion of the film's cult status in the first of three volumes on the topic. Peary talks about the film as a touchstone of the 1940s, with its "action, adventure, bravery, danger, espionage, exotic locale, friendship, gunplay, humor, intrigue, love triangle, masculine hero, mysterious heroine, patriotism, politics (without being too political), romance, sentimentality, theme song, time factor, venomous villain, and war.'' He also discusses briefly how the Bogart cult developed at the Brattle Theatre in the 1960s (47). Not unlike the later *Sahara*, this film is peopled with a kind of mini-UN. Because Warner Bros. made only films that supported the war effort, Rick had to change from noncommitted to committed. Peary sees Rick and Ilsa as opposites: "His face is hard, dark, stubbly even after a shave, ugly; hers is soft, glowing, warm, beautiful. His eyes are cold, suspicious, narrow, introspective; her eyes sparkle, are trusting, generous, caring. He is demanding, critical, secretive; she is comforting, loving, open-armed. Rick and Ilsa are a couple who are not meant to be despite the great love they have for one another'' (50).

In "Confessions of a *Casablanca* Cultist: An Enthusiast Meets the Myth and Its Flaws,'' James Card, himself a Bogart and *Casablanca* cultist, admires the film even though it raises lots of questions for the noncultist. For example, what is one to make of the dazzling clothes Laszlo and Ilsa wear while on the run? Much of Card's article deflates the various myths surrounding the making of the film: Ronald Reagan, Ann Sheridan, and Dennis Morgan were to star in it; Hedy Lamarr was to play Bergman's role; the film's final lines were completed after the film was done; Ilsa could have stayed with Rick (not so because of the Production Code); who wrote the script (Epstein brothers, Howard Koch, Casey Robinson); the film is based on a very bad play; and that everything related to the making of the film was coincidental.

To Barry Day *Casablanca* retains its cult status because of its "immutable values'': "lost heritage ... tremendous sense of patriotism ... an emotion we are starved for ... the kind of film that makes a radical feel he's part of the mainstream'' with Stanford University students. He sees Bogart's character as holding the "narrative and psychological threads together.'' Recalling Crain's position on Laszlo, Day finds the patriot to be an embodiment of Rick with "his convictions still intact and his ideals undefiled, priggishly so'' (21). The attack on Rick, from Renault to Laszlo (idealism) to Ilsa (emotions), "really reduces the how to when'' in a dramatic structure not unlike a Jacobean or Elizabethan drama. This "tidiness of construction'' is also one of the film's appeals (23). Day commends Curtiz for his use of shadow and visual flair to support the narrative. For actors Bogart, Lorre, and Greenstreet, this film "crystalised'' their roles (and persona) for "the rest of their careers'' (23). A topical thriller to some, an allegory of Roosevelt being forced to take sides to others, to Day Bogart represents a Hamlet who "did make his mind up, did find a solution that was worth a sacrifice and gave an expression for idealism" (24).

William Donnelly sees *Casablanca* as a "mildly campy sacred text" that is a filmed play with wit, cynicism, political allegory, and a "renunciation of sexual maturity for a life of action" (107) for Rick and Renault that echoes ideas about male bonding and homosexuality as expressed by Leslie Fiedler in *Love and Death in the American Novel* (1960). Using Corrigan's idea that cult films have "seemingly conflicting visions" and Eco's view that *Casablanca* is a collage that allows us to look back to earlier movies (and experiences) and to the future, Larry Vonalt examines how the film's visual style, with its blending of aspects of the American dream as seen in part through the glamorous clothes of the players, lets us understand their personality traits. At the same time, there is a dark side to their appearances and actions and moods in Rick's place, which lead to betrayals by Rick, Renault, Strasser, and others. This duplicity and ambiguity, found in *film noir*, is the other side of glamour.

In discussing the appeal of the film, Paul Hendrickson details how there were riots in a Mexican expatriate's artist colony when 1,000 people wanted to get in to an auditorium that held 250. Why here and elsewhere around the world? Because *Casablanca* has "graspable values . . . : Love and honor and courage and all the old verities that it's somehow not cool to talk about anymore. Things you learn with your heart, not your glands" (B1). In speaking at an American Film Institute meeting attended by Paul Hendrickson, Howard Koch claims *Casablanca* is therapeutic in that it helps us "to find out what is worth celebrating" (B1). At the AFI screening, Koch continued the bromides that Jack Warner wanted George Raft and Hedy Lamarr, then Dennis Morgan and Ann Sheridan, and for a time Ronald Reagan for Laszlo's role. In talking about his own life, Koch recalls that he was blacklisted for working for democratic labor unions and was told that if he recanted and paid a certain sum he would be removed from the blacklist. He refused. All this material is covered in his memoirs, *As Time Goes By* (1979).

In *As Time Goes By* Koch presents an overview of aspects of *Casablanca* covered in his earlier book. In a survey administered to Stanford University students, whom Koch finds "fairly typical of their age group and [providing] some indication of the personal and social context in which the film is viewed" (186), he sees "a latent idealism under the protective mask of cynicism, much like the tough-tender stance of Bogart's Rick in the film" (83). To Koch one student best summed up the appeal: "*Casablanca* shows you things you really long for. There are all those graspable values floating around in the film. It's full of lost heritage that we can't live. Life is no longer like that" (84). The film's appeal can be seen in its continuing popularity, the number of articles written about it, the various products and places named after it, Woody Allen's play, *Play It Again, Sam* (1969), and how it has become a part of our cultural language. On today's movies Koch says, "They can impress us with their photographic beauty. Titillate us with their sensuality, and shock us with their creepy horrors, but rarely do they enlist our feelings.... The images flash across our screens and we look at them from an emotional distance. The eye is sated, the glands stimulated, but the heart is left hungry'' (218).

Richard Schickel's "Some Nights in Casablanca" sees the film as "a somewhat better-than-average example of what the American studio system could do when it was at its most stable and powerful, with the anxieties occasioned by consolidation, the coming of sound and the depression behind it" (115). He gives high marks to actors and how they play off one another, but claims that too much has been made of Rick's renunciation of Ilsa: "Damage has already been done to Bogart posthumously by trying to make an existential hero out of the screen character he created when nothing so fancy—or self-conscious—had been intended" (122). To Schickel, *Casablanca* stands up against many of the war films of the time because it "berated nothing and promised nothing" (123). This is his favorite film in part because of when he saw it, but also because it balances heart and belief and that "one may still be given the chance to serve love, decency and a good abstract ideal in a single grand gesture" (125). John Weisman's essay, "60 Minutes Correspondents Pick ... Their Finest Hours," focuses on the synergism that occurred during the film's creation, its resultant pleasure to viewers and why, of his nearly thirteen hundred stories, Harry Reasoner chose "*Casablanca*—The Best Movie Ever Made?" (air date, November 15, 1981) as his favorite piece.

On the occasion of the fiftieth anniversary of *Casablanca*, and its re-release in Dallas, Russell Smith, Jane Sumner, and Philip Wuntch, three film critics from the *Dallas Morning News*, contend the film's lasting appeal is attributable to "the singing of 'La Marseillaise' and 'As Time Goes By,' the screenplay's cynical wit and soft heart, Mr. Bogart's hard-boiled panache, and Ms. Bergman's eternal radiance" (5C)—all this for a film that after it opened in Dallas ranked twenty-second in revenues for 1943 (10C). David Middleton's "*Casablanca*: The Function of Myth in a Popular Classic" follows the early box office success of the film and sets out to answer why, as late as 1986, *Casablanca* "shows no sign of losing its appeal or flagging in its ability to stir its viewers at their deepest levels" (11). Middleton claims that the appeal is based on the film's use of a monomyth: the hero's journey through "his physical and psychic life" (11) as he retreats for a time, only to reemerge regenerated. In addition to the mythical element that Middleton sees as central to the film's appeal, he describes how narrative, theme, and film "icons" create a "mystical" film that derives its power from the audience's "close, intense identification" with their own subjective experiences (12–13). Also writing at the time of the film's anniversary, Abigail McCarthy questions its appeal in the 1960s when students were cynical and disillusioned and concludes that they found "some vestige of belief in cause and country" (10). Thinking about heroes today, McCarthy concludes we have "spontaneous heroes," but no leaders "who embody values and a vision worth serving with heroism" (11).

"We'll Always Have *Casablanca*" is L. Morrow's commentary on the film's lasting appeal on its fortieth anniversary. After mentioning the basics, such as the cast, dialogue, and sentimentality, Morrow claims that "*Casablanca* is, among other things, a fable of citizenship and idealism, the duties of the private self in the dangerous public world. It is a thoroughly escapist myth about getting politically involved" (76). Of the many perspectives one might take to view the film, including semiotics (myth of sacrifice), Freudian, anthropological, Rick as the American Adam, cigarettes and alcohol, rationalization and sublimation of adultery, and Oedipal and Jungian archetypes, Morrow finds that through them all, "there clings a quality of lovely, urgent innocence. Those who cherish the movie may be nostalgic for moral clarity, for a war in which good and evil were obvious and choices tenable. They may be nostalgic for a long-lost connection between the private conscience and the public world" (76).

Some critics analyze particular images or scenes to get at the essence of the film. In *American Cinema: One Hundred Years of Filmmaking*, Jeanine Basinger analyzes the opening eight minutes, explaining that this film "perfectly defines classic Hollywood style" (70), and introduces, except for Laszlo and Ilsa, conflicting worlds and a cast of primary and secondary characters. Marshall Deutelbaum focuses on "The Visual Design Program of Casablanca." After claiming that the cult status of the film resides in two traditions—the "failure of romantic love" and its resulting retreat into cynical disdain and to a French "Poetic Realism" that "invariably leads to death" (36)—Deutelbaum uses the film's "design program" of decor, lighting, and arrangement of costuming to suggest another reason for the film's appeal—the chess motif suggests the "political and romantic ambiguities" of the film (45). In a textbook designed for film history classes, Stephen Prince includes an examination of selected continuity editing codes such as the use of master shot, matching shots to master, short reverse shot with eyeline match, and the 180-degree rule.

Umberto Eco analyzes the intertextual frames and archetypes of the opening twenty minutes of *Casablanca* to show that the film pulls together principal archetypes on a grand scale. It is "a cult movie precisely because all the archetypes are there, because each actor repeats a part played on other occasions, and because the characters live not the 'real' life of human beings, but a life as stereotypically portrayed by previous films" (10). This film is not a single film: "It is 'the movies' " (10), and was created unintentionally, whereas current filmmakers (he uses Spielberg and Lucas as examples) are "semiotically nourished authors working for a culture of instinctive semioticians" (12).

J. P. Telotte's "*Casablanca* and the Larcenous Cult Film," a revised version of which is found in *The Cult Film Experience*, builds on and disagrees with Eco's trivializing of the public's perception of *Casablanca* and sees the film as unified in its use of Joseph Campbell's journey of the hero (retreat and quest phases) and especially in its use of thievery as applied to archetypal and contemporary themes. He also sees similarities to Poe's "Purloined Letter." With the thieves as the "true heroes," Telotte contends that part of its appeal to a wide audience is that "we are allowed to embrace an identity that is at once dangerous and safe, revolutionary and conservative, outlawed and lawabiding" (367).

J. Hoberman's essay "On Casablanca" in Howard Koch's fiftieth anniversary edition of *Casablanca: Script and Legend*, contends that "*Casablanca* was the culture of the West, everything we were fighting for in World War II, brought together in one neat package" (270). Building on Eco's idea that it is all movies, Hoberman says that each generation makes it own version, whether it be Dennis Hopper's *The Last Movie* (1971), or Spielberg's *Raiders of the Lost Ark* (1981), or Pollack's *Havana* (1990). Also using Eco's notion of intertextuality, Colin McArthur's *The Casablanca File* traces *Casablanca*'s appearance in advertisements and images worldwide and demonstrates that the film is "the most prolific generator of secondary texts in the field of popular culture." He reviews television and magazine advertisements, film and television plays, names of night clubs, bars, and restaurants for their intertextuality in this profusely illustrated text.

There have been a number of articles that discuss how *Casablanca* was influenced by or influenced other movies or literature. E. Sorel and others have noted that Warner Bros. wanted to make a film like *Algiers*. In *To Have and Have Not* Bruce Kawin points out that Hawks was not consciously trying to imitate *Casablanca* and finds it "so superficially similar to and so profoundly different [especially in its tone] from the earlier melodrama" (47). John Stickney's "Last Word on *Last Tango* and *Casablanca*" presents analogies between the two films, specifically the characters and the differing styles of romantic love. He considers *Last Tango* less revolutionary than critics made it out to be when it is compared with *Casablanca* and its mystery and search for true identities of the lovers. *Last Tango* is an example of how "carnality triumphs over love; duty is neglected" (129), and how the characters in Bertolucci's film have "lost sight of standards" as they "grope in the dark" (150).

Peter F. Parshall's "East Meets West: *Casablanca* vs. *The Seven Samurai*" deals with the reluctant hero and how *Casablanca* "represents the ideal solution to the individual/collective conflict" found so often in westerns. Parshall uses *Casablanca* because of its representativeness, as the baseline for a discussion of Kurosawa's *The Seven Samurai* with regard to ideology, and its cinematic strategies such as the restricted locale of *Casablanca*. Most of *Casablanca* takes place in Rick's Café, which "represents the introspection and concern for self which the film lauds" (276). Quoting Ray, Parshall claims that *Casablanca* turns political, sociological, and economic matters into personal melodrama, as Rick changes his mind not for the cause but because of his love for Ilsa (278).

In an item in the *Shakepeare-on-Film Newsletter*, Robert F. Willson, Jr., says the scene where Ilsa pulls the gun on Rick for the letters of transit and his subsequent desire to work through the problem is possibly from *Richard III*, although both Richard and Rick are "quite different characters." While aware that the scene has "become a stage and film cliché," Willson says that not only are the outlines of the scene and the goal the same ("to dominate and control the women"), but even more important to him is that "the climax in each sequence comes with the release of the weapon, transforming stage business into symbolic action" (4). Steve Kellman's somewhat strained "Everybody Comes to Roquentin's: *La Nausée* and *Casablanca*" discusses the many similarities in locale and character (especially the absence of commitment) between *Casablanca* and Sartre's *La Nausée* (1938). Howard Koch, for one, said he never read Sartre's work.

In *Cineliteracy: Film among the Arts*, Charles Eidsvik presents *Casablanca* as an examination of caricature (characters as "perfect embodiments of social types"), setting, audience assumptions, technical aspects (actors, dramatic structure, music, cinematography), and the "what-if" aspects of narrative. As much a touchstone of our culture as any other American film, the film and its characters have come in for its share of kidding. Robert Coover's short story "You Must Remember This" is a playful, fictional account of the sexual gaps in Ilsa and Rick's encounter in his apartment in Casablanca when she enters seeking the letters of transit. In discussing this story and its critical reception, Joel Black, expecting audiences and critics to decry the send-up, finds instead praise for Coover's "unmasking the inauthenticity of Hollywood's products and conventions" (84), as he intertextually interpolates a sexually explicit scene for the fade-out. To Black the emphasis on "this" in the song is a reference to their sexual relationship that represents their "private erotic world" rather than the "public world of ethical conduct" (88). There is even an altered version of the film. After giving a brief overview of the film's appeal, how the Germans banned it until after the war, and the results of the British Film Institute poll and *TV Guide* survey on its popularity, Susan Sackett notes that in 1987, Joao Luiz Albuquerque "re-edited a print and changed the ending to show Ingrid Bergman . . . coming back into the arms of Bogey" (41).

After fifty years, Charles Champlin still loves the film and considers it "the apotheosis of the Hollywood romantic melodrama" for its memories of his youth, "rich frosting of personal associations and a sweet melancholy, born of the intimations of mortality" (231). David Zinman lists it in his *50 Classic Motion Pictures* and, after a summary of the film, notes that to many this picture captures the Bogart mystique of the outwardly cynical, uncommitted, self-centered Rick who inwardly is "an idealist, a sentimentalist motivated by a deep-seated honesty. Although he puts on the cool front, he's really a good guy committed to doing the right thing in the end" (275). To Bernard Dick the subtext of the film is the myth of regeneration. If Rick can change, there is hope for all of us. With Bogart and Bergman we have "a coinciding of persona and character results" (204).

Bosley Crowther finds "its interest and remarkable achievement were its buildup of an overpowering sense of modest people in the shadow of grave perils doing gallant, self-sacrificial things" (66). Bogart's character serves as a metaphor for youth in his completely self-confident style and casual mannerisms. He is a "cool existential individual in full control of virtually everything," but in the end he does something real for humanity (67). J. H. Davis echoes the views of others, when he focuses on three aspects of the final scene of *Casablanca* to explain its enduring popularity: Rick's character as an "ambiguous archetype" (124) who is "at times tough and tender, cynical and sentimental, skeptical and idealistic, selfish and generous" (125); the enduring nature of the song, "still the same old story"; and the open-ended script that lets the viewers finish the film. In an addendum to an earlier article in *Literature/Film Quarterly*, Davis analyzes the paradoxical nature of Rick's commitment. On one hand there is a "toughness, cynicism, and selfishness," and on the other there is a "tenderness, kindness, or generosity" (277). To Davis the repeated use of these conflicts suggests that "one is not to be alone" (276).

In his section "Revivals and Restoration" in the 1996 edition of *Roger Ebert's Video Companion*, Ebert says that while this movie may not be the best or the most profound, it is the one that has touched more moviegoers than any other and has "transcended categories" (841). Ebert discusses the fiftieth anniversary release of the film by the Turner movie division and the laserdisc found in the Criterion Collection. To Ebert this is one of those rare films that improves with each viewing. We see the film for the first time; then "the next time we see it, every word between Ilsa and Rick, every nuance, every look or averted glance, has a poignant meaning" as we consider the "infinite gradations of poignancy to be found behind every look, and overheard in every line" (842). The film, like most other Hollywood romances that matter to us, is not about love but about nobility and self-sacrifice, and letting the higher good win out over love. Bogart's scene with the bottle and cigarette and his comments to Ilsa are examples of masochistic self-pity; Rick is opening old wounds, the pain of which Ilsa does not comprehend since she is "a beat behind what is really happening" (842). Ebert considers the story that the actors did not know the ending to be a myth because the conventions of the Production Code with regard to sexual liaisons outside of marriage and the "moral undercurrent" of the film dictated that Rick give up Ilsa (842). The Production Code, revised periodically after 1930, outlined what filmmakers could not put on the screen with regard to language, plot, and intimacies. In another item that appeared in Howard Koch's book on the film, Ebert says that there are no great shots in this film about nobility and self-sacrifice (not love), because nothing calls attention to itself. Still, the pivotal scene of Ilsa's entrance into Rick's place is more effective with each viewing.

During the course of Ted Sennett's discussion of Peter Lorre and Sydney Greenstreet, Sennett praises the film for its "lushly romantic screenplay, the effortless direction by Curtiz, the superb camera work of Arthur Edeson, and the Max Steiner score, but concludes that the film has "passed beyond criticism into the realm of legend" (77). For all the ink spent on *Casablanca*, P. Matthews's "You Must Remember This" celebrates the film and may well summarize the thoughts of many viewers when he contends that although there have been numerous readings of the film, its life beyond the critical analyses of auteur theory, deconstruction, and other types of readings makes it the definitive Hollywood film.

Action in the North Atlantic

Stephen Hanson considers *Action in the North Atlantic* a strong action and adventure film saluting the men of the U.S. Merchant Marine. With the ethnic mix of the characters and the stress on action over plot, Hanson claims the film's power holds its own against more recent actions films such as *Superman II* and *Raiders of the Lost Ark*. Aljean Harmetz and Bernard Dick focus on the film as a reflection of a particular moment in history. To Harmetz, the film was part of the war effort of the studio and fit in well with the aims of the Office of War Information. Harmetz says that the action scenes were well done, as were most of the propaganda segments. For Bogart this film led to rumors that he was going to join the Merchant Marine, and a later notation in his FBI file that he played in a film favorable to Russia that was written by John Howard Lawson, one of the Hollywood Ten. Dick's emphasis is on the propaganda aspects of the film and how it was influenced by Soviet filmmaking, specifically its emphasis on montage. He also explains that Lawson borrowed the structural outline from *Potemkin*: the torpedoing (opening of *Potemkin*), the homecoming (seaman and singer meet), the gathering of ships (opening of part three of *Potemkin*), and the U-boat attack (related to the massacre on the Odessa steppes). In his view the "merchant seaman's union was Communist controlled" (223) and this film was more political than *Sahara* because of its view of labor and the war. It was "Soviet propaganda at its most artful" (225).

Thank Your Lucky Stars

Warren Spector's "Thank Your Lucky Stars" (1943) summarizes the standard wartime staple of an all-star revue that follows in the footsteps of those produced by Paramount and MGM. In this one, Bogart parodies his own image. What makes it a bit different to Spector is how the film presents Hollywood as "a town of images" (39) and its attempt to have a "coherent narrative to tie the sketches and musical numbers together" (37), even though he admits as the film progresses the narrative gets lost (39).

Sahara

Remade in 1995 with Jim Belushi playing Bogart's role, the 1943 *Sahara* (not to be confused with the 1984 film of the same name but based on *Perils of Pauline*), is one of hundreds of movies about World War II. Considered by some commentators as an excellent presentation of the American soldier, others see it as good entertainment but preposterous melodrama. The film's emphasis is on characterization within type, with the only female part belonging to the tank, Lulubelle. Lawrence Suid stresses the film's focus on stereotypes, with actors representing various nationalities and races. To Suid, the film is another example of Hollywood's anti-Nazi posture; its action, drama, and message "stimulate patriotism and the war effort at home" (50). Jeanine Basinger uses *Sahara* as one of five war films (the others are *Bataan, Guadalcanal Diary, Destination Tokyo,* and *Air Force*) to define the recurring traits of character, setting, narrative structure, cultural attitudes, and language (film language and dialogue) found in the World War II combat film. Like Suid and others, she notes how *Sahara* uses men to create a mini-UN, whereas so many of the other war films focus on Americans (70).

Bernard Dick discusses how scriptwriter John Howard Lawson was influenced by the Russian film *The Thirteen* (1937). In bringing together comrades from different countries, the film is "dialectic rendered as narrative" (223), with a synthesized ending that is a miracle in the same way that brotherhood would be a miracle. Thomas O. Kelly is less charitable in his analysis of the racism in the film. In "Race and Racism in the American World War II Film: The Negro, the Nazi, and the 'Jap' in *Bataan* and *Sahara*," Kelly examines the racist attitudes of Americans and how those attitudes were reflected in films made in Hollywood. Attitudes toward Germans were not as racist as those toward Japanese, and presentations of African Americans suggested tokenism (571). Kelly gives some background on the various offices (propaganda and censorship) created by the government and the Bureau of Motion Pictures' work with them to try to create certain type of images, including emphasis on an ethnically complex "team" (574). While discussing the plot similarities with John Ford's 1934 *The Lost Patrol* (working for the good of the cause, trying to establish delaying strategies, confronting superior numbers, struggling to survive attrition of the team), Kelly compares and contrasts the didacticism in each film, and how blacks, Germans, and Japanese are presented. In *Sahara* the Germans "are more real and less essentially malevolent," and they are "much more fully realized" (575). The death of Tambul (the black) is heroic and ironic in that he kills a Nazi pilot face to face and prevents the Nazi from conveying the truth about his comrades' weak position and their lack of water. While stating that the extremely negative attitude toward the Japanese and the less hostile presentation of the Germans reflected "American attitudes of the day," Kelly never relies on documentation to prove his generalizations.

Theodore Kornweibel's examination of the movie focuses on two aspects of the film: "the process of government pressure on movie studios to ensure that the 'approved' war aims were presented" and the "possibilities for artfully harnessing wartime patriotism to cherished American values of individual self-reliance, self-sacrifice, and the nation's role as beacon of hope and right to a benighted world" (5–6). He finds the film's propaganda "an archetypally American vision" (15) that plays on standard stereotypes of cruel Germans and confused Italians. Presenting a dignified portrait of the American soldier and his allies, Kornweibel contends that *Sahara* used cowboy-frontier imagery to manipulate emotions about the war effort.

Passage to Marseille

Is *Passage to Marseille* a soppy romance, an attempt to capitalize on the success of *Casablanca*, a political treatise, or just another studio production by Michael Curtiz? Critics are divided. To Barbara Deming this is another 1940s film with Bogart as a war hero, not unlike his persona in *Casablanca*. Ted Sennett considers *Passage* a typical wartime melodrama, "bursting its seams with patriotic fervor to the point of delirium" (84). It is a good mix of director, actors, cinematographer, but a poor sceenplay, with too many flashbacks within flashbacks. Something akin to *Casablanca*, with a "disillusioned man restored to his former ideals" (85), there are some well-done scenes on Devil's Island and a "strong and intense performance" by Bogart, who is convincing in the shift from misanthrope to "impassioned partisan" (86). To Robert Sklar, other than the "Chinese boxes series of flashbacks, the most remarkable aspect . . . is its representation of Hollywood's ideological consensus on the war" (165–166).

Aljean Harmetz finds it "a hymn of praise to de Gaulle's Free French warriors" but an "awful movie, soggy with patriotism, soupy with sentimentality" (303), and unduly influenced by the success of *Casablanca* and the Office of War Information. Roy Kinnard and R. J. Vitone disagree with Deming and Harmetz and argue that this film owes nothing to any predecessors, including *Casablanca*, but instead "offered both Humphrey Bogart and Michael Curtiz interesting challenges" (86). Rather than being the star, Bogart is part of an ensemble, and his story is the foundation for the others. They consider La Belle France to be the leading lady of the film (88). Bogart plays Matrac with "powerful grace"; as a "peaceful man driven by injustice and outrage to fight for his country, he virtually explodes during scenes" (87). Going against the commonplace opinion that this is one of Curtiz's less important works, Kinnard and Vitone consider Curtiz to be at his best here in taking a good story and elevating it into a "great film" (88). Kenneth D. Alley takes exception to Harmetz and other critics who find the film structurally flawed because of its use of flashbacks. Alley contends that although the patriotic tenor might raise eyebrows today, for its time it appealed to the filmgoing public. And the flashbacks are suitable, artistic, and "remarkable" in their clarity and contribution to a structure whose "balance, harmony, and rhythm" make *Passage to Marseille* "quite unique for its time" (203).

Mary McCarthy considers the film a good "allegory of the French political dilemma" until "the romanticists in Hollywood could not stomach this, and they threw in Humphrey Bogart and a ridiculous story about a crusading French editor who was framed for murder and sent to Guiana because of his opposition to Daladier and Munich. This and other war movies do not make the war "real" but "only familiar" (34). Mjagkij examines how the French are presented in the film. Because of French collaboration with the Vichy government, there were no *Why We Fight* films focusing on France. Instead, Hollywood focused on making films about the French Resistance. Although this was not a major film, Mjagkij quotes Bernard Dick's comment in *The Star Spangled Banner* to the effect that *Passage to Marseille* is a "rousing tribute to the Free French [and the] most vehemently anti-Vichy film made during World War II" (37). While noting the Nazi collaboration of some and the country's colonial stance, *Passage* demonstrated "the spirit of democracy was alive in the resistance" and that the French government "had no popular support" because it "used its colonial possessions as a means to subdue dissidents and opponents" (38). Mjagkij continues with a reading of narrative elements of the film as confirmation of these points, and how "the French government fell to the Nazis because it was already corrupt prior to the German invasion" (43). Mostly a narrative summary of the film, the essay concludes with the idea that this film was as much a propaganda piece as any of the "factual" *Know Your Ally* or *Know Your Enemy* films produced by the U.S. Office of War Information.

Using an auteur approach and Robin Wood's idea that genres are dealing with the same conflicts but with different strategies, Sidney Rosenzweig links similarities of *Passage* to *To Have and Have Not* and to *Casablanca*, claiming that "Bogart again represents isolationist America playing the tough, cynical, worldly-wise adventurer determined to keep his private life free from political and romantic involvement" (98). He claims that the visual styles are different and that Hawks was not making a personal film but Curtiz was. The "significant difference between the films is not quality but dramatic form" (100). *Casablanca* is melodrama rather than tragedy; *To Have and Have Not* comes closest to comedy (101), and *Passage* is an adventure-melodrama that comes as close to tragedy as *To Have and Have Not* comes to comedy (108). *Passage* can be summarized briefly: "A group of convicts escape from Devil's Island to a ship bound for Europe; they fight Vichy officials who attempt to commandeer it and join a Free French unit in England" (102). What Rosenzweig details at length is the film's structure and how the story is told. Playing off the comments of Robin Wood and Michael Wood, Rosenzweig finds *Passage* lacking "*Casablanca*'s central opposition between romance and politics, love and duty" (103); it can be viewed as "an exercise in mood [somber] and atmosphere [suffocating]" (106).

To Have and Have Not

James Agee, in his review of October 1944, says *To Have and Have Not* is "a kind of romance which the movies have all but forgotten about" (354), and as such makes it a worthy successor to *Casablanca*. Agee gives high marks to Bacall for her delivery of lines, her character, her singing, and a personality that combines Dietrich, West, Garbo, Davis, Harlow, and Glenda Farrell. In a subsequent commentary appearing in the *Nation*, he finds the film to be "an unusually happy exhibition of teamwork, and concentrates on character and atmosphere rather than plot" (121), as it conveys a sense of improvisation and relaxation. Agee's comments on the film's characters, its connection to *Casablanca*, and the influence of Hemingway's novel have been touchstones for much of the subsquent criticism on the film. Except for articles on Hawks as auteur, little has been written about the film except in the context of these issues until Bruce Kawin's extended study of the history and critical reception of *To Have and Have Not*.

Kawin brings together illustrations, screenplay, notes, production credits, cast, and substantial commentaries on the film in articles and reviews as part of his introduction to the screenplay, one of the titles in the Wisconsin/Warner Bros. Screenplay Series. He provides detailed discussions of changes from novel to script, rewrites by Hawks, Jules Furthman, and William Faulkner, and the temporary screenplay available in case Bacall was not up to the role. In another book of his, *Faulkner and Film*, Kawin says that by the time the film was finished, it was only marginally something by Faulkner. It was instead a Hawks and Bogart and Bacall vehicle, with much of the script reworked for the pair. Faulkner's contributions are most visible in the themes of patriotism and fear and the characters of the resistance fighters. Kawin considers the focus of the novel to be one person's battle against hostile forces, which becomes a demonstration of that person's power in battling fascist forces. The relationships between the actors and the director became the central element in the filmmaking process, since Hawks was most interested in having fun, and got the actors to trust him as they worked to create a film that "makes its audience happy" in its "completely satisfying balance between good and evil, fun and melodrama, light wit and tough words, healthy sexuality and clear politics, and even between impotence . . . and the redeeming power of love" (*To Have and Have Not* 47). Included in Kawin's analysis is a detailed comparison of this film and *Casablanca*. While both deal with love and political commitment, the tone differs in that "*Casablanca* is romantic, but *To Have and Have Not* is a romance" (48). Kawin's study is the place to start, since he synthesizes and extends the studies of most of the other critics who deal in one way or another with the adaptation process, the film's links with *Casablanca*, or Hawks as auteur.

Frank Laurence, Gene Phillips, Gerald Mast, and Thomas Hemmeter and Kevin Sweeney examine the film's literary links. Laurence's study of *To Have and Have Not* in *Hemingway and the Movies* argues that Hawks's filmed version of this novel and other Hemingway works helped establish the Hemingway persona by reaching the moviegoing audience. Steve Blackburn also deals with this idea when he explains that the films boosted Hemingway's popularity, even if they were loose adaptations. To Laurence many of Hemingway's works became "simple love stories" (82), but this one was "cynical and tough" (82). From the start Hawks wanted the property for Bogart and paid Howard Hughes $80,000 for it after Hughes had initially paid $10,000 for the rights. The Hawks film contains little from the novel, but Hawks claimed in an interview that after discussing the novel with Hemingway on a hunting trip, he returned to Hollywood and told William Faulkner and Jules Furthman, who were collaborating on the film, the ideas to work into the script. Hawks moved away from the novel's proletarian aspects and away from using Cuba as the locale. This was the time when the new Good Neighbor Policy, and possible threats from the Office of Censorship, could have prevented the studio from receiving an export license, which would have significantly affected the film's foreign distribution and would have created a political problem for the studio. Laurence finds those scenes that Agee describes as a "series of leisurely mating duels" between Morgan (Bogart) and Marie (Bacall) as the best parts of the script.

In *Hemingway and Film*, Gene Phillips says we should not expect detailed fidelity to the novels or short stories, but should consider them as re-creations of archetypal encounters. He repeats some of the information found in Kawin on the history of the making of the film and sees the film as Bogart's embodiment of the Hemingway hero with a code of courage, loyalty, and duty. Marshall Deutelbaum disagrees with Phillips's claim that the film only recreates archetypal encounters. He believes that Hemingway's terse style is conveyed in cinematic terms through the film's *mise-en-scène*. Even though Harry Morgan, for example, may not articulate his commitment to Marie and the Free French cause, Hawks's visual style complements or supersedes the dialogue and is integral to the developing relationship between Marie and Harry, and this is what leads to Morgan's political action.

In his study of William Faulkner and film, Phillips repeats the accounts of how Hawks told Hemingway he could make a film out of his worst novel; how Jules Furthman crafted the initial draft; and how Fulkner joined them in February 1944, often working with director and actors to smooth over dialogue and other concerns. To Phillips, this film and *The Big Sleep* are "the peak of Faulkner and Hawks's collaborative efforts" (48). Treading much of the same ground, William Rothman in "To Have and Have Not Adapted a Novel" describes how Hawks worked with adapting Hemingway's novel and how the film "differs in perspective and position from the novel, indeed constitutes a critique of it" (108). He sees the Bogart-Bacall relationship as central to the film, and that the antifascism owes more to the *Casablanca* influence. The film lacks the intense emotionalism of the novel in one of Hawks's "most easygoing, pleasurable films" (109). Rothman goes on to discuss plot design, theme, and narrative technique, especially how Hawks breaks certain conventional reaction shots by having them after sequences to show how Bogart "continues to act, marshaling his theatricality in an attempt to deceive himself about his own nature" (114). This, to Rothman, forces Bogart "to acknowledge the inadequacy of his own conception of himself" (115). Daniel Shaw also compares *To Have and Have Not* and *Casablanca* and how Hawks's film is more clearly an "expression of the American democratic ideology" of "good citizenship" (73). Rita TheBerge examines differences in the novel and film and shows briefly that the film is a reflection of Hawks's universe and his affirmation of individual independence and his special brand of male-female relationships.

Using Christopher Orr's idea that more could be gained by examining the ideology of the original with the filmed versions rather than a point-for-point examination of novel and film, Thomas Hemmeter and Kevin W. Sweeney apply a dialogic method to examine the novel and three filmed versions: *To Have and Have Not* (1943), *The Breaking Point* (1953), and *The Gun Runners* (1957). They see parallel movements in Harry Morgan's willingness to commit to Marie—"the other half of a compatible union" (67)—and his subsequent willingness to assist the Free French cause in Hawks's version. To them, "The film establishes a direct connection between Harry's committing himself to Marie and his joining the forces fighting the oppressive Vichy government" (68).[9]

Like Kawin and others, Gerald Mast compares the various scripts and the novel to the film. Mast finds resemblances primarily in the names, the character of Johnson, and the first four chapters of the novel, and he analyzes the narrative pattern, the "spiritual unity," dialogue, music, and directorial acumen of Hawks. Mast, along with Laurence, Steve Blackburn and Julie Barker, sees links with *Casablanca* but notes that the "unity of personal, moral, and vocational commitments" makes this a Hawks film and not a remake of *Casablanca* (250). To Mast, the personal and public morality are reflected in the locales for the action, with much of it taking place in private places (257). Laurence sees links with *Casablanca* in such things as the opening with its map (Europe for one, Caribbean for the other), internal warfare, hotel and nightclub, the piano player, the political mood, and how both Morgan and Rick are tough and cynical and have suffered lost loves. In both there are issues of documents that will allow safe conduct, and in *To Have and Have Not* there is a Captain Renard, whereas in *Casablanca* we have Captain Renault. Helene, though attracted to Morgan, stays with her husband, who is the leader of the resistance, and Ilsa stays with Laszlo. Differences include Morgan's only renting a room, whereas Rick owns the place, and Rick's wearing a tuxedo, while Morgan wears khakis. When Jerry Wald produced and Huston directed the Warner Bros. adaptation of Maxwell Anderson's play *Key Largo* in 1948, they used the gunfight on the boat from Hemingway's novel. And elements of the filmed versions of *Casablanca* and *To Have and Have Not*—political intrigue, a gambling club in Damascus, an apolitical Harry Smith who becomes involved with a woman who needs to escape Damascus—can be found in *Sirocco* as well.

Peter Bogdanovich, as one might expect, approaches film criticism from an auteur perspective. He combines interviews with a commentary on how Hawks developed the Bacall character to match Bogart's insolence by having her walk out on him in each scene, but at the same time playing her as a "warmer version of Dietrich" (25). Hawks says that Bogart was an underrated actor, whose mannerisms due to his cut lip and his patience with Bacall made him Hawks's "kind of actor" (24). Richard T. Jameson finds Hawks' "stylish collaboration" with Bogart and Bacall not unlike what we find in the work of Truffaut and Renoir, as Hawks brings together Bacall and Bogart on screen to translate their real-life mating dance to film (15). Using Hemingway's novel as a vehicle, he plies the material to develop basic themes in his filmmaking: people needing other people, proving one's worth, and surviving with class. Julie Barker also takes an auteur approach, claiming this may be a better movie than *The Big Sleep*, as Hawks reunites his key players and manipulates Hemingway's novel to try to create another *Casablanca*. Barker finds Bogart's character to be more appealing than *The Big Sleep*—"a loner, not an outlaw. He makes his own decisions out of choice, not because he is pursued. . . . It adds a new dimension to the Bogart persona. He is softened and given humor, without losing any of his strength" (3408).

In a study of Hawks published in 1968, Robin Wood challenges the perception that *The Big Sleep* is central to a study of the director's films; rather, he sees *To Have and Have Not* as central to an understanding of Hawks, and as a rich, emotional work for Bogart and Bacall. For some, the film could be seen as antifascist, but Wood presents it in more global terms as he analyzes how the "protest is against any authoritarian interference with the rights of the individual." Bogart's sympathies, not unlike what we find in *Casablanca*, are based on personal choices: commitment when it suits him, based on "respect and *personal* allegiance." Wood sees the presentation of Bogart's Harry Morgan—tough on the outside but with a "spontaneous-intuitive centre" as the most complete presentation of his screen image and of the Hawks hero (26–29).

Five years after his book on Hawks, Wood, in an article in *Film Comment*, modulated his views. After noting the film's indebtedness to *Morocco, Casablanca*, and *Across the Pacific*, he goes on to explain how the film is a test case of the auteur theory. Hawks took the material and molded its "spirit, tone, ethos, characterization, [and] values" through his personal vision (31). *Casablanca*, for example, deals with the past and is sentimental, but Hawks's film never uses flashbacks and focuses on the here and now and the spontaneity of the characters (34). Of the writers, Wood finds Faulkner an "able and intelligent executant rather than . . . an independent creative force" (31), and Jules Furthman a significant contributor to Hawks's films, but the exact contributions of his authorship are hard to determine given the "sheer complexity of the interconnections" (32). In Joseph McBride's *Hawks on Hawks*, the director discusses that he knew Bacall was going to be funny from the first minutes of the preview, his preference for certain lines that convey "frankness and honesty," his writing of the famous line about Steve's not having to do anything but whistle, and that he told Hemingway he could make a movie out of his worst novel. Later he irritated Hemingway by telling him he paid $10,000 for the rights to make the movie and he (Hawks) made more than $1 million from it.

Molly Haskell finds Bacall and Bogart as representative of relationships that "bring to the screen the kind of morally and socially 'pedagogic' relationship that Lionel Trilling finds in Jane Austen's characters, the 'intelligent love' in which the two partners instruct, inform, educate, and influence each other in the continuous college of love" (26). Bacall, as "Slim," holds her own and embodies traits found in Emma Woodhouse: intelligence, sensuality, pride, and submission (211). Using strategies not unlike those found in Jane Austen novels, Hawks, according to Joseph Rosenbaum in *Moving Places*, notes that the war is forever present in the background of the film, but like Austen, Hawks makes his audience forget the "outside world" (6). Daniel Shaw, however, says that the outside world is very present in the film's intertextuality; Warner Bros. and Hawks embody an American ideology that suggests a "transition from isolationism to involvement" (73).

As an embodiment of "late romanticism," *To Have and Have Not* is very different from *Casablanca* in its presentation of love. Using Robert Ray's remarks on *Casablanca* in *A Certain Tendency of the Hollywood Cinema, 1930–1980*, especially his notion of how Curtiz's film embodies "the avoidance of choice between autonomy and commitment" as a foil, Shaw contends that *Casablanca* uses "great sacrifice and ultimate separation" along with "a nebulous political apathy," while *To Have and Have Not* is an "optimistic vision of the future" (78). Frederick Jameson's "People Who Need People" (1975) is a celebration of filmmaking and the re-release of the film after being in copyright limbo for the better part of a decade. In a note to the article, Jameson talks about François Truffaut's interpretation of Hawks's *Hatari!* as a film about filmmaking. While Jameson sees *Only Angels Have Wings* as the most representative of Hawks's allegories of the filmmaking process, he translates that approach to this Bogart-Bacall vehicle.

Two different approaches to the film are found in the writings of John L. Fell and David Thomson. Fell uses Vladimir Propp's methodology in his analysis of Russian fairytales, specifically "plot constituents" that Propp called "functions," and applies it to narrative in genre films. When applied to films that deviate somewhat from idioms of a genre, films such as *To Have and Have Not*, *Rio Bravo*, and *Underworld*, Fell finds that the "Proppian highway becomes narrower and steeper" (23). When motives become complex, when conflicts are not acted out, when personalities divide, when incidents do not evolve from character, when thought and words are not identical to the action, then the Proppian system, while adaptable, may not always be systematic in application. Thomson sees this film as being a new genre—*film gris*—in which we find "unhindered fancy of happy endings may be redeemed by a hardboiled tone" (13). There is a happy ending in *To Have and Have Not*, but it is a film that tries to "be rid of all the solemn genres," and as a result it wears better than other American movies (17).

Conflict

In *Masters of Menace: Greenstreet and Lorre*, Ted Sennett focuses on Greenstreet and how he is less interesting in roles that favor "justice and morality." The plot in *Conflict* comes across as a "routine melodramatic exercise," but the murder itself is to Sennett "the film's only highlight" (122). Although there are many other films based on the plot of a murderer tricked into confession, this one lacks "colorful" secondary characters, and Bogart is "reduced to being a glum nonentity, grimly going about his nefarious deed, then turning overwrought as the web tightens around him" (123).

The Big Sleep

In early 1997, the original version of *The Big Sleep*, which was discovered a few years ago by Bob Gitt of the UCLA Film and Television Archive, made its way onto the big screen. Because of Hawks's desire to play up the Bogart-Bacall relationship, he cut one scene of about nine minutes that includes an overview of the case for the district attorney and police detective. Other changes include a conversation with Bacall, rather than the butler, when Bogart returns with Carmen in his arms; Eddie Mars's wife is played by Peggy Knudsen in the revised version and by Patricia Clarke in the original; and other scenes were reshot to heighten Bacall's screen presence. The existence of an alternate version of the film has been known since the 1940s, although only with Gitt's discovery did a print surface. In 1971 Paxton Davis shared personal reminiscences with the readers of *Film Journal* about seeing the film numerous times in 1944 while he was a soldier overseas and his surprise at the version shown in the United States in 1946. While others have played Marlowe, Davis sees Bogart so dominating the role "that one winds up adjusting Marlowe to him rather than the other way round" (3). In the same year George Garrett and two colleagues published the film script written by Leigh Brackett and William Faulkner but rejected by the censors; this, though, is not the final, emended shooting script.

There have been numerous studies of the changes made from Chandler's work, the many hands that contributed to the script, and its production history. Leigh Brackett, one of the principals, explains that Hawks liked her dialogue, and thus she got paid $125 a week and that William Faulkner agreed to write alternate chapters. In a piece in *Take One* and a subsequent interview with S. Swires, Brackett discusses her view of her craft and that she found the "tough, incorruptible, good-bad man who worked for justice by his own hard unsentimental light, still fresh and exciting" (27), and in remarks to Jon Tuska, Brackett says that Bogart "projected an inner power into the Marlowe character" and related to people in ways that were lacking in the novels (318–319). John Blades agrees that much depends on Bogart's being right for the role. Some of the appeal to today's audience is nostalgia, but to others it is "straightforward, bareknuckled, without any fanciness, and with just the right note of self-mockery" (10). While there is a sense of the audience's being kidded, Blades does not see the kind of exploitation or contemptuousness he finds in films like *Tony Rome* or *Point Blank*. "Bogart was one of the great tongue-in-cheek talents of all time, and the reason he was so attractive was that he never seemed to take himself, or his role, seriously. He was putting us on and we knew it—and *he* knew we knew it. Too puny for the part, Bogart nevertheless atoned for it with his tough, sardonic cool'' (11), making it a better private-eye movie than *The Maltese Falcon*, which is a "cinematic classic," because of its "cerebral qualities" (12). The best thing about *The Big Sleep* is Bogart as Philip Marlowe.

In an interview with Peter Bogdanovich, the often-elusive Hawks says the film's title probably refers to death and that he was not concerned about clarity in the plot but wanted to make "good" scenes and entertain. It "disarmed the critics because they were trying to be as smart as the fellow in the picture and they ended up being no smarter" (25). Of the bookstore scene, Hawks says that Bogart improvised the sunglasses, the movement with the hat brim, the effeminate character, and that he, Hawks, added new dialogue. Joseph McBride's interview with Hawks casts some light on how he set the tone of his relationship with Bogart ("don't get tough with me") and how Bogart was "one of the best actors" he had worked with—willing to take a chance (bookstore scene), take criticism, and, with Hawks's approval, be part of the creative process. While Hawks claims to have created the scene in the bookstore, McBride, like Jensen, notes that the idea was in the novel.

P. Jensen, who follows the various versions of the script, from the one printed in *Film Scripts One* to the Theatre Research Collection script at Lincoln Center, to the 1946 film, agrees with McBride about the bookstore scene, except for the gesture of turning up the hat brim, which is new. Jensen tells how the *Film Scripts One* version leaves out some material from the film, as each version puts more and more emphasis on Vivian. Jensen reports that while Hawks may claim credit for the bookstore scene, except to David Thomson that scene is exemplary of how the film is comic and how early illusion and absurdity meet: "The most camp element in *The Big Sleep* is the mounting calm with which the detective story becomes only a pretext for self-conscious artifice" (123). In his shot-by-shot analysis of the Acme Bookshop that appeared in *Sight and Sound*, Thomson argues that the film is "a seemingly infinite realization of male fantasies"and that Hawks was "adolescent, randy, and irresponsible" (125).

To Bruce Kawin *The Big Sleep* is historically the most important film William Faulkner was ever associated with. While the hero is a throwback to characters who valued professionalism, honor, and integrity, the film's ending reflected a kind of paradigm shift in how audiences approached film—moving away from following a film for its plot or structure to a willingness to follow action for action's sake (115–116). Kawin's book-length study *Faulkner and Film* examines changes in the novel, how the ending is a "fast curve" (116), and how the censors would not permit Carmen's death by Eddie Mars. To Kawin, although this movie has some perversity and amorality, it is not "dark" because Hawks is more interested in the relationships and the violent "fun."

Others too have examined differences between the novel and the film and matters of plotting. In a thin discussion, Gene Phillips reviews the collaboration of Faulkner and Leigh Brackett and says that Chandler liked the first half of the film, which is primarily the work of Brackett and Faulkner. In analyzing the confusion of the plot, Ronald Librach tells us that while Marlowe believes he knows who killed Owen Taylor (Joe Brody) and Shawn Reagan (Eddie Mars), he cannot confirm his beliefs. As a result, "Hawks endorses his hero's belief, passing and executing sentence on both transgressors with the stern sobriety of a narratively omniscient judge" (174). In so doing, Hawks imposes closure. In *Howard Hawks*, Robin Wood finds the director's indifference to plot a strength, not a weakness: "One respects him [Hawks] for conceiving the film primarily in terms of the Bogart-Bacall relationship, and of Bogart's moral relationship to the background and general atmosphere" (170). Philip D. Castille explains that Faulkner drew on *The Sound and the Fury*, converting Chandler's Carmen "into a version of Caddy Thompson's rebellious daughter" (55). Peter Lev presents an overview of how the many principals involved in the film contributed to and shared the film's "authorship," starting with the original source and moving through script, filming, and postproduction. He also looks at contractual and personnel matters tied to the filmmaking in this exhaustive examination of behind-the-scenes matters.

As parts of book-length studies, Stephen Pendo and William Luhr examine Chandler's work on film. Luhr discusses the Bacall-Bogart relationship, homosexuality, Marlowe and women, and how this film differs from other *noir* films because it has no retrospective narration, no flashbacks, no sense of a haunted, lonely, or vulnerable central character, no black widow, no off-balance or unexpected camera angles, little harsh lighting or murky shadows, and a protagonist who lives and works in the dark world but has no physical or psychic scars and is thus able to remain above the fray (136–137). At the end of his study Pendo charts a comparison of novel, script, and film and discusses Chandler's novel, the protagonist's character traits, the critical reception of the film (criticized for its violence and incoherence), and censorship matters. Of the latter, he contends that what was censored remained, but the actual things—Geiger's pornography shop, the homosexual relationship between Geiger and Lundgren, and Carmen's nudity—were cut (45).

John Blades believes *The Big Sleep*, in its "relentless, simple-minded and amoral, smart-alacky and kinetic" way, is never unfaithful to its source (12). It is "a great piece of pulp art," with Bogart as "the apotheosis of all pulp actors" (8). To Gerald Mast *The Big Sleep* is a response to *The Maltese Falcon*. He disagrees with Blades that the film is faithful to the text: "The Bogart character can synthesize the demands of love and honor because the woman he confronts becomes a woman with whom he can work—for she, too, has a personal code of integrity and honor." The film is not about confusing sequences but how Vivian and Marlowe discover one another (275–276). There are lots of details (e.g., fog imagery) that are not explained, and so left to the viewer to infer their meanings. The stylish elements reinforce unity of narration and relate to the search for meaning and value through personal integrity, vocational honor, and emotional fulfillment (294).

Peter Hogue examines and catalogs changes, including omissions and variations between film and novel, Hawks's presentation of atmosphere and violence, and the more sympathetic treatment of females, in particular Vivian. To Hogue, the changes and the omissions make the film "less misogynistic, less socially aware, and less despairing than the novel" (13), and they make the "question of risk-taking a far greater moral issue than it was in the book" (14). He sees the changes in the movie and its resulting confusion "a virtue" as they move it "closer to nightmare and myth" (14). To Hogue, "Chandler and Hawks are part of a generation of storytellers whose works reflect the disillusionment of World War I and the cynicism of Prohibition while dramatizing a very modern and perhaps unprecedented reliance on personal style and integrity" (16). After an extensive discussion of adaptation process, Jimmie L. Reeves examines the compromises involved in getting it on the screen, especially the Production Code and the audience. Reeves concludes that police corruption, crime, and sordid aspects of novel are downplayed in the film. With changes to Vivian's character for the film, Marlowe is able to be more sexually active, and thus we move closer to the Hawksian macho hero than Chandler's celibate knight (69–70).

James F. Maxfield sees Hawks as changing the novel's emphasis from "mystery, mortality, and morality to a primary focus on the love relationship," as the film takes the Hollywood turn away from Chandler's emphasis on "the inevitability of death" and "the unavoidability of moral corruption" (11). Unlike Robin Wood, who finds the convoluted plot a plus, Maxfield asks how successful a mystery can be if it "doesn't adequately solve the problems it presents to its audience" and omits details that make scenes comprehensible (14). Maxfield agrees with others that the movie suggests Brody killed Taylor (16) and considers Eddie Mars as the "ultimate source of evil" (20).

Gill Davies moves away from the literature versus film approach to an examination of how realistic elements are used in a narrative text. Using semiotics and structuralism as they relate to literature and film, most notably *Written on the Wind, Citizen Kane*, and *The Big Sleep*, Davies finds that in studying literature, one can limit the terms of the study, but with film the "ideological operations" require a "wider range of analytic devices" (66). The second half of the article considers the ideas of V. Propp (less useful) and Claude Lévi-Strauss (greater flexibility in four-part homology) in a structuralist reading of *The Big Sleep*, which "has become a certain sort of myth" in both its formal properties and function in society (69). Davies demonstrates that the "film articulates a passage into the family and out of it by Marlowe" (71). It is these domestic relationships, rather than criminal activities, that Davies finds central to the film: "As the paradigmatic structure reveals, the film is a deeply conventional celebration of all-American, heterosexual family life" (75), and "a crisis in American society in the post-war period, especially in relation to the central institution, the family" (75). Raymond Bellour presents a semiological analysis of Metz's scene and segment in two scenes: one in Eddie Mars's garage and the other in Geiger's house at the end. To Bellour, "Eddie Mars's death brings the open series of enigma and peripeteia to a close and sets the seal on the emergence of a couple'' (7).

The importance of the greenhouse and woman as spectacle are discussed by Judith Mayne in "The Limits of Spectacle." Building on Bellour's analysis, Mayne examines the opening of the film (seen as a "matrix") and how the male authority is diverted by a woman. She sees the greenhouse as taking on various forms in the film, as "woman becomes spectacle in *The Big Sleep* to facilitate the private detective's access to the various re-presentations of the father's greenhouse." To Mayne, "Spectacle is indeed the fixing of the image of the woman, with the accompanying narrative movement of getting to the father's room" (6). In the light of this film, Mayne moves back in time to consider primitive films, their "primal scenes," and nineteenth-century photographs by Arthur Munby of working women. She concludes that viewers are attracted to images by a desire to possess, but also by a desire to be separated from the image.

Annette Kuhn studies the text-intertext-history relation in the film, using a psychoanalytical analysis in which repressed themes are conveyed via *mise-en-scène*. Her analysis attempts to demonstrate how the second part of film does not answer questions of the first part by "displacing and condensing them," but contends that there is "a high degree of closure" in the film's narrative (4). She focuses on the *mise-en-scène* of Geiger's house and Sternwood's hothouse, which "may be read as censored and distorted representations of a series of implied degeneracies, representations mapped onto and expressed in the form of the two incomplete or perverse 'families' of the first part of the narrative" (11). Kuhn's dense essay is reworked and expanded in *The Power of the Image*, in which she combines textual and contextual analysis to examine "social, historical, and industrial contexts" (74). Using ideas of Russian formalist Vladimir Propp's "moves," Kuhn sees *The Big Sleep* as being produced by "various institutional conditions of production" (84) and structured by "textual effect[s]" based on the "contexts and intertexts" of censorship (79).

Christopher Orr also uses a psychological approach in "The Trouble with Harry: On the Hawks Version of *The Big Sleep*," in which he presents a strained ideological interpretation of Harry Jones, or Jonesie, as Marlowe's double. Orr says that Jones dies "to justify Marlowe's subsequent killing of Canino" (67) and that Jones represents the passive, female side of the protagonist's nature (70). Orr disagrees with Monaco's attitude that women are relatively autonomous (74–75). Solomon also sees an important relationship between Bogart's character and Jones, but not to the point of linking the two as doubles. Lionel Godfrey focuses on the private eye image in the film, but contends that the traits found in *The Maltese Falcon*—sardonic humor, earthiness, frank sensuality, and compassion that results from the death of Harry Jones—are fully developed in *The Big Sleep*.

The issue of the film's misogyny and that of its director are discussed by Brian Gallagher, Molly Haskell, Annette Kuhn, Judith Mayne, Vibeke Pedersen,

Janey Place, and Rita TheBerge. Haskell examines Hawks's view and presentation of women in his films and how the competition between men and women is uniquely American. She believes the "interests of melodrama and comedy are perfectly fused in the sexually pregnant atmosphere of *The Big Sleep*" (38). Haksell notes that Bacall is the only actress Hawks used more than once, gravitating more toward her because "she pulls her own weight—verbally, professionally, sexually—to a much greater degree than most movie heroines" (36). She was also under contract to Hawks. Annette Kuhn finds a dual attitude toward women that is not uncommon in Hawks's films: the female is dangerous and morally inferior and must be rejected, or if there is acceptance of the female, it is based on male standards. In *Creating the Couple*, an extensive study of Hollywood's presentation of courtship, marriage, and monogamy through the aspects of star persona, performance, and cinematic narrative, Virginia Wright Wexman demonstrates the shift from Bogart's persona of "male supremacy" and the "tough-guy hero" in Huston's *The Maltese Falcon* to the "Hawksian theme of male camaraderie adapted to emphasize the creation of the modern companionate couple" in *The Big Sleep* (35–36).

Pedersen considers how female pleasure comes from four kinds of spectator positions described by Laura Mulvey and Mary Ann Doane, and compares Carmen and Vivian and how the latter "can be recuperated into the symbolic order" as she is "integrated in the patriarchial order as a sexual object." Carmen, by her various actions and comments, presents herself as an active sexual object, but Marlowe's gaze is "almost from the beginning the voyeuristic gaze of the detective, the devaluating, punishing gaze." Carmen "is represented like a phallic woman in the way she speaks and dresses in trousers and priest-like dress" (106–107).

After giving background on the existential motifs in Camus and Sartre, Rita TheBerge analyzes why, in Marlowe's battle with the absurdity of crime on one side and a corrupt legal system on the other (14), Vivian is his "ideal companion in his existential search. She is intelligent and gutsy; she drinks 'like a man,'" and is "willing to play his silly sex games" but she is "as aggressive and suggestive as he is." What we have is a confrontation then between "existential man and his equal" (15–16). The idea of a verbal battle between the sexes, not unlike what we find in Restoration drama, is developed by Keith Price, who says that all the characters and actions are defined by "games." Price claims that "almost all the characters in *The Big Sleep* are defined in terms of games and how they play them" (4). Hawks had Bogart and Bacall "fight with their mouths, but love with their bodies" (3). The director created tension between Marlowe and Vivian by keeping them in the same frame, thereby not undercutting their emotional interplay: "Hawks is interested in what they are finding out about each other, not in what they are trying to find out about the blackmail or murder" (3). To James Monaco, this film has a "gallery of women who are just as 'insolent,' just as competent and often just as sublimely amoral as any of the men in the film, which makes it something of a high-water mark for women's roles in Hollywood'' (38).

In discussing the film in 1968, Robin Wood considers it almost a failure. Attacked when it opened for its violence and amorality (see Houseman), Wood sees its appeal in the late 1960s due to those same traits: "violence, cynicism, tough attitudes, 'black humor,' " the appeal of Bogart, and "style and method" (Hawks 168). There is no visual equivalent in Hawks for Chandler's subjective narrative that presents characters in Marlowe's terms: "cynical arrested adolescence, insisting tiresomelessly on smartness" (169). Yes, every scene begins and ends with Bogart, and we see what he sees, but we do not think or know what he knows: "what we have is not so much Bogart acting Marlowe as Marlowe becoming Bogart" (169). In his correspondence (edited by Frank MacShane), Chandler comments that Bogart "is also so much better than any other tough-guy actor that he makes bums of the Ladds and the Powells.... Bogart can be tough without a gun. Also, he has a sense of humor that contains that grating undertone of contempt." To Chandler Bogart dominates any scene he enters. Wood disagrees, and along with Penelope Houston and Henry Random, finds Dick Powell's performance in *Farewell My Lovely* closer to an ideal Marlowe. Nevertheless, what is positive about the film to Wood is that we connect with Bogart and the "sense of positive, sympathetic relationships" not found in the book. In the scenes where the language is "tough and cynical, the acting [between Bogart and Bacall] conveys a mutual sympathetic awareness" (170). Hawks's indifference to plot is a strength: "One respects him [Hawks] for conceiving the film primarily in terms of the Bogart-Bacall relationship, and of Bogart's moral relationship to the background and general atmosphere" (170). In his book on Hawks published by the British Film Institute (1983), Wood notes the charm and tenderness in the film, and attributes it to Hawks.

With all that has been written about Humphrey Bogart, there is suprisingly little discussion of Bogart as an actor. Many of the articles about this or his other touchstone films mention what he does, but few give extended analysis of his craft. Lionel Godfrey, for one, discusses briefly Bacall's performance and its seeds in Nora Charles in *The Thin Man* and says that Bogart's only comparable performance to *The Big Sleep* is *In a Lonely Place* (13), but little more is said about Bogart the actor. Robin Wood and Virginia Wright Wexman do discuss his performances. According to Wood, to evaluate actors requires placing them in a context of particular codes, "of particular directors and genres, [and] in relation to particular traditions," including differences between stage and film performances, as well as abilities and personalities of the stars, the relationships between star and director and star and audience, and acting style as related to values and themes (23–24). Surprises in the theatre can be attributed to the actor; on film, they are attributed to the director, the theme of the film, or some other influence (20). Wood uses Bogart's role in *The Big Sleep*, particularly the opening scene, to show how it "is partly dependent on the accumulation of previous roles'' (21) and how particular codes influence our views of acting and reception of a particular film.

Wexman is much more focused on Bogart's "controlled acting techniques" related to body language. She demonstrates that this role is unlike his overdrawn acting in *The Petrified Forest*. By the time of *The Maltese Falcon*, Bogart was using his delivery, wiry frame, height, ethnic appearance, and gestures to convey a sense of dominance. In *The Big Sleep*, with a different director and different sensibilities at work on the film, his acting focused more on "cooperation rather than competition" (50). Instead of approaching each other head on, the various characters circle each other; this can be seen in the circling motif throughout the film. There are fewer close-ups, which according to Wexman lessen the ethnic emphasis (never defined), and there is greater relaxation and less control in Marlowe's character as he uses numerous mannerisms or gestures not present in the combative and aggressive Sam Spade of *The Maltese Falcon*.

The fullest analysis of Bogart's character and appeal in this film as it connects to Bogart's acting is Joe Goldberg's "The Death of Sam Spade." Taciturn, resourceful, courageous, solitary, and presenting his character in a "flat, sardonic voice,'' Bogart conveys in Sam Spade an attitude toward acting and the many horrid roles he had to take on as a professional with a job to do (107). When Goldberg asks himself why Bogart is a symbol of his times, he considers Raymond Chandler's analysis of Philip Marlowe: " 'He must be a complete man and a common man and yet an unusual man. He must be . . . a man of honor, by instinct, by inevitability, without thought of it, and certainly without saying it. He must be the best man in his world and a good enough man for any world. I do not care much about his private life. . . . If he is a man of honor in one thing, he is that in all things' '' (108). Goldberg sees Bogart as an embodiment of a personal code, one that the existentialists described as "definition through action'' (109). In keeping with this existential persona, "Neither the on-screen nor the off-screen Bogart postured or preached, but kept to himself, ambiguous, his privacy unapproachable, until his private ethic told him it was time to act. And then, he did not speak; he *acted*'' (112). Goldberg quotes Faulkner, who when asked about actors said, "Humphrey Bogart is the one I've worked with best'' (114). To Goldberg, Bogart was a fine actor, but "not a great one.'' As Spade he was "a cynical idealist, a romantic gone sour'' (110). He considers *Treasure* Bogart's best work ("grimly comic film'' 115), and the three films with Huston as screen classics. "Huston has never attempted to duplicate them with another actor'' because Bogart embodied the type of characters and ideas expressed in the works of Hammett, Chandler, Hemingway, and Camus, "not because he was a great man, a great rebel, or a great actor, but because it was his job'' (115–116).

In his famous and oft-quoted essay "The Simple Art of Murder,'' Chandler says his hero is a man of honor, who is "everything,'' walking down mean streets, taking "no man's money dishonestly and no man's insolence without a due and passionate revenge'' (59). John Houseman takes issue with the kind of hero presented in *The Big Sleep* and what it says to our culture. Using the film as his prime example, Houseman sees the "tough" movie as having no "moral energy" and one that might represent the "neurotic personality" of the United States at the time. These tough dramas, the whodunits and thrillers, are "without personal solution or catharsis of any kind" (163). Houseman contends, "In all history I doubt there has been a hero whose life was so unenviable and whose aspirations had so low a ceiling" (161). He sees the novel as a dramatization and the film as "basically romantic" because a male star makes love to a "rising and very lovely female star" (161–162). What Houseman finds repugnant in these films is not their violence ("a basic element of American life") but "their absolute lack of moral energy, their listless, fatalistic despair," a direct contrast to the gangster films of the 1930s that always had energy and morality. "It almost looks as if the American people, turning from the anxiety and shock of war, were afraid to face their personal problems and the painful situations of their national life" (163). In talking about gangster films in general, with only a passing reference to this film, Wheeler Dixon says the film is one of many that reflects the ethos of the age and how gangster films romanticize and mythologize gangsters. John Blades defends the film against attacks on its immorality, savagery, and cynicism, finding it entertaining, but not of any intellectual import. Without doing much analysis of audience reception, Blades attributes the criticism to the prevailing ethos at the time of its release. "Despite all its unsavory elements—and it is virtually a casebook of sin and violence, laced with murder, bestiality, blackmail, nymphomania and undercurrents of homosexuality—it seems no more unwholesome today than a Tom and Jerry cartoon" (13).

In her cultural analysis of the 1940s through film, Barbara Deming emphasizes that the appeal of Bogart's character is a result of how the hero is tested. Without being tested, and in this case it is Brigid who embodies all the tests he must go through to prove himself, he is nothing and nowhere. Gwen Rowling also examines the film's cultural context, focusing on the changes that came over America after the war and the shifts in pulp crime fiction away from the rationale of the classical detectives (Poe and Holmes) to a stress on human behavior and the characteristics of the hard-boiled detective who lives in a city, is a creature of the night, smokes cigarettes, maintains a shabby office with the neon light of the neighborhood bar reflecting on its window, lives and works alone in a dark world, and tries to establish some semblance of order and civilization, but rejects the values of his society (69). In this world of "ever-changing alliances and deceptive appearances, his integrity is the only stable moral center; however, it too is constantly threatened" (69). A realist, he knows that greed and corruption are ever present, and love is a commodity that, along with respect, is demonstrated through commitment and loyalty (73).

Brian Gallagher touches on a variety of matters related to the film, such as the Production Code, box office considerations (Bacall and Bogart), and the novel, but he sees the changes to the film and the additions as contributing to a reading of the subtext as a parable of loss and recovery related to the war years and the "nature of the postwar American family," a family that in its "hostile, competitive environment" "must learn to defend its interests and aggrandize itself, even at the cost of abandoning some of the older, more benevolent views of family life and the responsibility of the family to society" (88–89). To Gallagher the film contains matters easily identifiable to returning servicemen: "aggression, violence, sex, and domestic arrangements" (79), and he says that Hawks's Marlowe, unlike Chandler's hero who avoids sexual liaisons, is a "sexual opportunist" (79), a very sexual creature "willing to take his pleasures, sexual and otherwise" (81). Examples in the film include the woman cab driver who is willing to spend evenings with him, the coffeeshop waitress who gives him the eye, the hostess and the cigarette girl at Eddie Mars's casino who are interested in him, and Vivian (81). Gallagher also sees a parallel to Bogart's persona in *To Have and Have Not* and *Casabalanca*, where he "abandons an isolationist posture for a committed and involved one" (80). As a "citizen-soldier" rather than a "knight-errant," Marlowe battles his professional foes, but also presents a darker side: "licentiousness, opportunism, even momentary cowardice" (81). Vivian is his ideal mate: "a complementary degree of toughness, realism, and unabashed sexuality, without being, like the psychotic Carmen, naturally treacherous or murderous. And she is also willing to be subservient and compliant, circumstances permitting" (87). In a note to the article in which he talks about coded allusion to homosexuality, Gallagher remarks that "oddly, but explicably, Bogart's momentary impersonation of a homosexual [in Geiger's bookstore] is the only action fully marked as homosexual in the film. It is a measure of the film's audacity, its heterosexual audacity, that it allows Bogart (whose slight lisp might already be considered of a suspicious nature sexually) to parody himself—and still remain unquestionably and completely heterosexual" (91).

Roger Shatzkin believes Marlowe's "vacillating relationship with Vivian [is] the film's deep structure and raison d'être" (92). He sees the attraction-repulsion as key to leading to their fate together and that Regan is Marlowe's doppelgänger. To Shatzkin, the novel is not so much a quest for a solution to a puzzle, but finding a double or doppelgänger (87). Confusion and inpenetrability are at the center of both the film and novel. What is central is not the logic of the plot, but the emotional logic: we come to respect them through their verbal battles, coping with hostile environment, and compatibility (94). In *America in the Dark*, David Thomson says something along the same lines when he contends that the "real confusion can never be unraveled: The honorable man can only try to stay sane. That now seems the point of *The Big Sleep*, and the companionship of Bogart and Bacall is its assertion of human values" (176). Like Charles Gregory, Frank McConnell deals with the idea of the knightly test in his *Storytelling and Mythmaking*. By focusing on one scene from the novel, an exchange between Marlowe and Carmen Sternwood and how he was undergoing a knightly test, McConnell contends that Chandler is "the most consummately aware of the mythic overtones of his stories" (146). As a twentieth-century heir of the knight, Marlowe is caught up in that which he is trying to prevent and is thus "deformed" in his way.

Linked to the presentation of women in this film is its genre, Janey Place locates *The Big Sleep* as central to the classic of the detective genre, where no one cares about plot gyrations. After quoting Chandler on Bogart's being "the genuine article" and "tough-yet-romantic" as Marlowe, Place talks about the fictional Marlowe, always in control, "above all pure" and untainted by those he comes into contact with and always looking for the woman worthy of him (346–347). A misogynist, in the novel he is "uncontaminated by women" (347). To Place, sexual fear is at center of the characterizations, but in her discussion of the film, she focuses on the use of space and how physical space defines power relationships. For example, Vivian occupies more space when she is in control, but as Marlowe begins to take over, her space is reduced as she loses her power and falls in love with him. "By the end of *The Big Sleep* she has been visually immobilized and confined and verbally reduced to a second-rate assistant for Marlowe, in sharp contrast to the aggressive, witty, and tough fighter she was in the beginning, and the independent, provocative woman she was in Eddie Mars's gambling club" (348).

Thomas Schatz discusses the film in the context of the hard-boiled detective genre's postwar development, being one of a number of films in response to the success of *Murder, My Sweet* and *Double Indemnity*; but like Thomson and Shatzkin, Schatz notes that Hawks wanted to capitalize on the Bogart-Bacall chemistry, and thus mixed action and violence with repartee. William Everson considers this a commercially successful detective film, but its cult appeal is primarily due to Bogart's combining with director Hawks and the "thundering" score (231). One dissertation, by Robert B. Hairston, examines the nonverbal communication in three *noir* films, including *The Big Sleep* and its remakes. Focusing on whether the originals and remakes could be classified as genre films, subgenres, or something else, Hairston concludes that these *noir* films are in fact a film genre. In his textbook study of genre films, Stanley Solomon contends that Hawks places a premium on style in this film that, although it is more brutal and violent than others, the hero has the typical traits: coolness, professionalism, absolute bravery, and wit. David Bordwell, in his critically well-received *Narration in the Fiction Film*, uses *The Big Sleep* and *Murder My Sweet* to show how his principles of narration work as he explains how a "syuzhet,"—a system that arranges the components of plot according to specific principles—is constructed and how style works in relation to it. In particular he focuses on omniscience, restrictions on it, and self-consciousness in these films and how the viewers as a result get information in the mystery genre.

In their encyclopedia of *film noir*, James Paris, Julie Kirgo, and Alain Silver explain how Chandler made this a "series of journeys across a mythical landscape of darkened bungalows, decaying office buildings, and sinister nightspots" and the impact of the substitution of Los Angeles for other *noir* cities (34). The motivations are reflected in "the stylistic analogue of the dark streets and lonely houses the movie Marlowe explores." The movie stresses "characterization and visual style" rather than story line in which a "series of character encounters in which the drama of trust tendered, trust betrayed, and trust restored is played out" (34). The Marlowes of both film and fiction are outsiders with a strong belief in "right conduct," but "the interpretation of Marlowe and Vivian by Bogart and Bacall is full of nonverbal expressions of sympathy that quickly undermine the initial antagonism of the characters" (34). They conclude that the film is "ultimately" "faithful to the noir vision" because of the irony of the final image and the impact of the experience on the protagonists, but the film "romanticizes" the novel (34). Marc Vernet, a student of Barthes, also uses Propp, as well as Freud and Lévi-Strauss, as he positions himself as a viewer of the opening of this and five other *noir* films, in order to examine the "set-up" (*mise-en-place*), the enigma (*pot au noir*), and disjunction and contiguity.

Discussion of *The Big Sleep* as *noir* is of little import to Robert Sklar. He finds with the passage of time that the film wears best as a romance: *"The Big Sleep* is a noir film only by broadest definition; its ties to the dark vision of its source novel are equally tenuous. Some four decades after its creation it appears more a romance than a murder mystery; or, to put it from a spectator's perspective, after the mystery wears off its aspect as a romantic comedy emerges" (174). While falling back on some of his old screen mannerisms or gestures, the film works for Sklar as Bogart's "most complete screen persona to date" (176).

In his study of Hawks and *film noir*, Michael Walker says there are many ways in to this film: as a Bogart-Bacall vehicle, as an adaptation, as a classic private eye *film noir* or a complex narrative, as a gloss on contemporary ideological tensions and fears, or as a Howard Hawks movie; but he sees *The Big Sleep* as a movie about Hollywood. As a Hawks film, it is "economical, fluid, smoothly functional, with no unusual camera angles, no 'expressionistic' effects" (191). One of the major structuring devices is how Hawks's use of parallel scenes permits Marlowe to gain "control over the *noir* world" (192). After briefly discussing aspects of adaption (close) and the Production Code, and a psychoanalytical analysis of shots (especially condensation and displacement), Walker says that unlike other *noir* films, this ending has a hero and heroine who still need to be rescued from the dark and violent place. Unlike other Hawks adventure films, "the hero has no best friend and he is not a member of a group." What male friendships Marlowe may have had are treated as if they were a "loss" in the past (194–195), and thus with this lack (of a best friend) there is "sexual ambiguity" throughout the movie (197). The idea that Carmen and Vivian are "threats," a sexual subtext for both Lundgren and Mars who are "ambiguously desired figures" (202), and issues of homosexuality (especially in Geiger's house, which Marlowe returns to explore) pervade the film as the ambiguity of a number of shots and scenes question the hero's sexual identity

(198). This uneasiness about Marlowe's sexuality is compensated for by Hawks by women who are easy pickups for Marlowe. Bogart-Marlowe stands in for Hawks's alter ego, and thus the film reveals more about Hawks than he would admit (202).

Occasional discussions of the characters of Philip Marlowe include changes in character as presented by other directors and actors. Of Robert Altman's *The Long Goodbye* (1973) Pauline Kael says that Elliott Gould is so unlike Bogart that he does not "propel" the action. Charles Gregory focuses on Altman's *The Long Goodbye* and how in casting Gould he changes Marlowe's character to the point where Marlowe's integrity is "limited, suspect, even dangerous" (156). The admiration for the Hawks film is based on the Bogart-Bacall pairing and the interest in Hawks.

In a thirty-year retrospective of the film and its reception, James Monaco sees renewed interest in private eye films and compares *The Long Goodbye, Chinatown,* and *The Big Sleep.* He sees *The Big Sleep* as one of the seminal films in Bogart's career, "the Hollywood icon of that Forties's existential hero," the central focus of the career of Hawks, and "a meeting place for many other talents, trends, styles and attitudes" (35). Monaco considers it a summation of twenty years of Hollywood filmmaking and also its future because of its tone, downbeat visual style, and dark images. He laments Hawks's omission of the political (the corruption of the police) and his capitulation to the Production Code and its staff who recommended a violent rather than a political ending, but still "because it is a second-generation screwball comedy; because it is the ultimate Bogart-Bacall film; because it has some relatively advanced sexual politics; because it is a classic private-eye film; because it prefigures the *film noir* of the next decade; and because it is a concentrated model of Howard Hawks stylish storytelling, *The Big Sleep* is a landmark film" (38). The film captures the mood of the "seedy, decaying, slow and hot" setting, and human relationships that are "superficial, abrupt and eventually seen as incontrovertible evidence of a pervasive and deep-rooted corruption of the spirit" (35). To Monaco, "If Chandler's protagonist has symbolic value today, part of the reason is because Humphrey Bogart played him—and gave him life.... He, alone, was the Hollywood icon of that Forties' existential hero that Chandler described in his prose" (35). Monaco sees this film as a "summary of [Hawks's] world which depends equally on the wit and tone of the earlier [screwball] comedies and the harsh, existential mood of the gangster films, and which seems to balance them dialectically" (35). The existential hero of the 1940s is pitted against the "orgasmic, simplistic violence of Clint Eastwood and Charles Bronson" of the 1970s (37). To Monaco the film is quintessential Hawks: sharp and economical editing of scenes; efficient composition of frames, organized around action; precision and richness of dialogue and rapid-fire delivery; use of good screenwriters; and collaboration with actors to refine the dialogue (37).

David Thomson has written more about this film than any other critic. In one article he notes that while we are accustomed to giving credit to directors, composers, and cinematographers, the production design and art direction of the first ten minutes of *The Big Sleep* establish all that follows. In discussing other films from Warner Bros., Twentieth Century-Fox, and RKO, Thomson notes that few directors, now or then, influence the designs for film (16). More recently Thomson was commissioned by the British Film Institute to write about *The Big Sleep* as part of its series on film classics. In this work Thomson traces the cultural and historical background of Chandler and his novel, Hawks's fantasies, his relations with women and their influence on casting and scripts, and the differences between the novel and the film. Thomson finds an "exhilarating ease and pleasure" in the film (63) and likes Bogart's wryness and embodiment of "Marlowe's laconic humour" and the way he handles himself (17). He finds the elaborately crafted sets a reflection of the ideas in the film, which is "both radical and decadent as it relates to the history of the narrative movie" (46). *The Big Sleep* "affected an indifference to narrative consequence that was startling" (63); it is a "movie about movies, about movie-ness" (64). Reflecting on the increased role for Bacall as the film progressed, Thomson notes that there seems to have been much more excellent work by Martha Vickers (as the nymphomaniac Carmen), but that Vickers had to be "reined in" so as not to take away from Bacall. Thomson finds Bogart and Bacall " 'legendary,' secure against fact" (60). Of the film itself, he concludes, "*The Big Sleep* inaugurates a post-modern, camp, satirical view of movies being about other movies that extends to the New Wave and *Pulp Fiction*" (67).

Dead Reckoning

Much of the critical commentary on *Dead Reckoning* focuses on aspects of genre, the place of the film at Columbia, and Bogart as a *noir* hero. Bernard Dick, for example, sees this film as Columbia's entry into *noir*, although most assign it to *My Name Is Julia Ross* (156). To Dick it is "an example of the system's creative ventriloquism; it resonates with echoes of Columbia's films and those of other studios. An amalgam of motifs created at Paramount, Warners, and MGM, it also continues along the lines of *Gilda*" (157), which is discussed related to *noir*. Dick claims that Harry Cohn wanted Bogart at Columbia because a Bogart film conveyed a Bogart persona: "As an icon, Bogart was never just a character, but the habituation of character. The character—whether it was Sam Spade, Roy Earle, or Philip Marlowe—was the endoskeleton. It was not what was within that mattered, but what happens when the camera finds the point where actor, character, and myth converge. Bogart required a script that was not only tailored to his persona but also followed the conventions of the lethal lady/hardboiled detective movie" (160). In addition, Bogart had made *Sahara* for Columbia, and Bogart and Cohn worked together professionally on Bogart's Santana Productions.

Also taking a studio approach, J. P. Telotte examines how Columbia, seeing the success of larger studios with *noir* films, soon became "one of the most prolific and consistent producers" of these films (107). In several of his *noir* films, including *Dead Reckoning* for Columbia, Bogart is "bringing with him his nearly mythic image of the alienated yet unfailingly moral loner" (108). With this film Columbia brings together the various patterns and elements in *noir* in such a way as to make it the prototypical *noir* to that time, and also a most disturbing film in how it capitalizes on "the darker, disturbing upwellings in our culture" (109). To Telotte *Dead Reckoning, The Dark Past, The Lady from Shanghai*, and *In a Lonely Place* "played at the margins of conventional cinematic practices" (116), at a time "when the conventional formulas would no longer hold" (112).

Frank Krutnik puts *Dead Reckoning* in a category of the " 'tough' thriller" and discusses how Rip (Bogart), an ex-military figure, represents "male discourse and male comradeship" (173). In trying to find out the truth about and clear the name of his buddy Johnny, his motives become confused when he meets Coral, the woman in Johnny's life. As Rip tries to work through the events, he must deal with "conflicting allegiances," and as a result "has difficulty in his mission because of this lack of a stable and regimented framework of masculine authority in normal social life" (176). Once he accepts Coral as a guilty object, he is able to overcome and regulate his feelings for her and thus cling to "an idealised and impossible fantasy of 'tough' masculinity" in order to overcome conflicts in "potentialities and desires" (180). Carl Macek demonstrates that Bogart is a "noir icon of a man who is at once hunted and the hunter" (86). Macek finds this "noir vision of love" by John Cromwell to be "sometimes brutal yet oddly sensitive" and an "example of the *femme fatale*'s inability to transcend the limitation of her persona (86). Dick touches on some of these topics as well when he discusses bonding between men and the dress of women (Coral in black), use of voice-over, and echoes of other *noir* and Bogart films (158–159). In *The Detective in Hollywood*, Jon Tuska claims that Bogart is at his best in this film (308), and that this film and *film noir* are "the closest the American cinema had dared come in re-creating in the collective consciousness of the audience the emotional traumas and sensations men experience when the key breaks and the door cannot be shut again" (340).

The Two Mrs. Carrolls

Jeanine Basinger analyzes the scene in *The Two Mrs. Carrolls* where Bogart tries to murder his second wife (Barbara Stanwyck) by poisoning her with a glass of milk. Upon failing and realizing that his wife knows what he is about, he decides to strangle her and make it appear as if she is the victim of a strangler who is stalking local women. Basinger notes that the audience gains knowledge about characters and action through technical tricks, such as editing, cutting, and camera angles.

Dark Passage

While Barbara Deming discusses the role of the wandering hero in film and its impact on the culture of the United States in the 1940s, much of the attention paid to *Dark Passage* has focused on *film noir* and the use of the subjective camera. To Bernard F. Dick, this film is an example of how the subjective camera "should be restricted to specific scenes or sequences" and how camera movements "express the presence's emotional state." Eileen McGarry says the film carries its "basic visual premise too far" by showing only a shadow of the protagonist in the first thirty minutes and not allowing the audience to see his face until an hour into the film. The audience knows it is Bogart because of the voice; using someone else "might have been better suited to this visual premise." While the film has the "innocent man framed by a villainous 'spider-woman type,' stalked by a vulturous punk, and the police," this is not typical *noir* because the "causality is external." The protagonist does not suffer "fear, guilt, and legal retribution" and the film "lacks much of the internal structure of human weakness and fatalism central to the complete *film noir*" (83–84).

In "Blind Insights and Dark Passages: The Problems of Placement in Forties Films" and in a reworking of the article for *Power and Paranoia*, Dana Polan shows that change and conflict were both accepted and rejected in the 1940s, and *Dark Passage*, through its use of first-person camera style in which "narrative and the image come apart, refusing to provide any but the most meager of certainties and centerings" (*Power* 195), is a "mutation" of the visual and narrative style in *Pride of the Marines* and other classical narratives of the 1940s. In addition this film reflects certain changes that were taking place in the political arena, as Truman's "force of narrative" and his often "contradictory or arbitrary... assertive determination" differed substantially from Roosevelt's. Polan sees *Dark Passage* as a commentary on the political history of film narrative and notes that this film and *Pride of the Marines* show that "different historical stituations demonstrate different narrative, textual, and ideological practices" (27). In *Dark Passage* "the narrative and the image come apart, refusing to provide any but the most meager of certainties and centerings" (30), thus lacking the centering subjects of postwar *noir* film (32).

J. P. Telotte also examines the subjective camera in *noir* and how in this film the human gaze is "a measure of isolation and alienation" (26) caused by "cultural conditioning and circumstance" (24). Although "free" from prison, Vincent Parry (Bogart) remains imprisoned by how others see him and how he sees himself (19). In a reply to Polan, Telotte contends that *Dark Passage* offers a different stylistic approach from other *noir* films and has a different kind of centering, which resides in the shifting subjective perspective of "the gaze itself" (21). In a revision of this article in his book *Voices in the Dark*, Telotte shows how the subjective point of view, the film's examination of "the nature of identity" (121), and how this most disturbing *noir* film (124), with its "sense of fragmentation and alienation" (127), ties together "how we see the *world* with how *we* are perceived" (120). By using the subjective camera, we may see too clearly that "our seeing is conditioned and channeled by our nature and our culture" (132). For all the discussions of subjective camera, Robert Sklar finds the film little more than a "curiosity" (193).

The Treasure of the Sierra Madre

Part of the Wisconsin/Warner Bros. Sceenplay Series, James Naremore's *The Treasure of the Sierra Madre* contains Huston's screenplay, frame enlargements that illustrate points in the analysis, and a lengthy introduction that compares the screenplay and film, Huston's influence on the film, and his system of working. Naremore stresses that Huston lessens the Marxist influence in the original work by Traven and turns it instead into character studies of the three men and what the quest for gold does to them. Bogart is a paradoxical blend of greed, ingenuity, and resilience. Naremore also reviews the impact of the studio system and Huston's variation from procedure: the use of location shooting instead of back lots, the lack of glamour, and the absence of romantic interests and a happy ending. Naremore finds Huston both unorthodox and traditional (31) and notes that Bogart conveys a "Nixonesque fellow who was generated by an exact reversal of the heroic pattern: outwardly a dedicated member of a community and a would-be idealist, he ultimately betrays the group out of a selfishness, fear, and neurosis" (23–24). Working with Huston, Bogart is able to make the character "as much a victim as a villain" (24).

Olive Graham, writing for *Texas Cinema Notes*, gives a brief background on Huston's making of the film, the absence of women and a hero, and the pursuit of the American dream. Much of the general commentary on the film deals with the presentation of greed. Bosley Crowther discusses the impact of the idolatry of money and how the film's moralistic bent portrays man's primitive nature when greed replaces generosity. Eugene Archer sees defects in the film, but considers it successful in part because of its being shot on location—with the environment serving as a catalyst for the actions of the characters (81)—and its "large theme" of lust for gold and its impact on men (71). Alan Downer, stressing Huston's visual style, compares *The Maltese Falcon* and *Treasure* and finds that in their "simplest terms" they are the "same story seen through different lenses" because both deal with frustrated quests, characters outside the law, a misogynistic attitude, and a hero who is "equivocal, though his ultimate object is unequivocally money" (24–25). The last idea is not validated in *The Maltese Falcon* because Spade is not after money. Leslie Taubman sees this film as "one of the most masculine in style ever made and displays a strikingly true cinematic understanding of character and men" (3442).

The search for gold and the desire for money get at the psyche of the individuals involved. Harvey R. Greenberg focuses on a Freudian reading of *Treasure* as something that goes well beyond "a clinical vignette of a diseased personality driven mad by gold" (34). It is about a "young man's coming of age, of an aging man's search for his last resting place," as well as "a rousing adventure tale, a subtle commentary on the capitalist mentality, and a document of cultural collision more vivid than most anthropology texts" (35). Gerald Pratley finds the film "profound in its study of human nature" (68).

Some critics are most concerned with the search for the identity of B. Traven, the author of the novel on which the film is based. Will Wyatt's *The Secret of the Sierra Madre: The Man Who Was B. Traven* gives an account of how he traced the identity of Traven to Otto Wienecke, a German actor, writer, and radical politician. Lawrence Grobel says that Huston was less concerned about the identity of Traven than in the successful shooting of a film on location and scheduling problems caused by fears that the film would portray Mexico in a negative light. These concerns were repeated in other on-location films shot by Huston, including *The African Queen*. Huston knew that Bogart was unhappy with location shooting, and the two had several disagreements, but after Huston physically abused Bogart, he received fewer complaints (294). Morris Beja also discusses matters relating to Traven's identity (170), but the bulk of his piece is a series of quotations and questions suitable for classroom discussion.

John Engell, in an article in *Literature/Film Quarterly*, claims that Huston is relatively faithful to his source, but that as he shifts from a verbal to a visual medium, he shifts the ideology of the text and focuses on the three characters rather than society (245). After sketching in the ideological background of the "radical intellectual anarchist tradition" of this work, Engell argues that the anarchist tradition is replaced in Traven by a communal myth found in the noble Indian and that it is through a kind of "mythic agrarianism" that the characters find their freedom (246). As Huston works with the text, he uses the myth in the character of Curtin, who embodies "the agrarian citizen-owner" representative of the "typical American" (251). Stuart Kaminsky in "Gold Hat, Gold Fever, Silver Screen," and its later incarnation in *American Film Genres*, examines differences between the film and the novel (setting, plot, narrative technique, characters and characterization, denouement) with a focus on Dobbs's character. Like Traven and Huston, Dobbs is full of contradictions. A "moral brute" and "madman," he is also generous and helpful until he succumbs to gold and regresses to animalism. Two other studies of the differences between fiction and film are Stuart McDougal's essay in *Made into Movies: From Literature to Film* and Gabriel Miller's essay in *Screening the Novel: Rediscovered American Fiction in Film*. McDougal gives a brief overview of the film, its reception, *mise-en-scène*, and lighting before analyzing how Huston gutted the novel's historical background and social commentary to focus on the inner conflicts of the three men who are parts of a whole. To McDougal, Huston shows the positive aspects of Dobbs's character that are not found in the novel in order to emphasize his subsequent breakdown. By expanding one or two other roles, such as that of the bandit, Huston universalizes the themes of growth and fulfillment and disintegration and destruction (124). Miller discusses the novel in the light of how Traven deals with death and discovery or disintegration of the self (88). To Miller, Huston's men are "less complex" than Traven's, and they "diverge sharply into clear-cut character types, acting and reacting predictably according to the contrastive psychological patterns established early in the film" (106).

Peg Masterson's comments in *Texas Cinema Program Notes* focus on background to the novel and the conflict between the Old World's social order and the New World's raw and primitive state. Building on Miller's idea of Dobbs-Bogart's being a Conradian figure who has been up the river, seen hell, and can only laugh in its face, Masterson places *Treasure* in the western genre and explains how it "has adopted the classic American theme of the class between innocence and nature . . . and cultivation on the other." She sees the film as "Fred Dobbs' tragedy" because he has "adopted his own society's values" (75), and the film as "an indictment of the society it portrays" (74). A reading different from most others, although certainly touching on Miller's notion of Dobbs's reaction after seeing hell, is Barbara Deming's view of the film as a comedy. She compares the film to other comedies of the decade in which all that was given was taken away. She takes great pleasure in seeing what is "frantically sought, and sometimes almost grasped, elude the searcher" (188).

In evaluating Huston as a director, Alan Downer stresses his handling of three matters: the fresh way of dealing with an old story line, conveying the emotional rather than the intellectual, and avoiding the lure of making the film an allegory (26–27). Above all is Huston's visual skill in every scene (27). Probably no other writer on Huston as director or auteur is more quoted than Agee, who became Huston's collaborator for a time. Agee's two reviews (January 31, 1948, and February 2, 1948) praise Huston for his superlative filmmaking, ranking his directorial acumen second only to Chaplin. He calls *Treasure* rich in "themes, semi-symbols, possible implications, and potentialities as a movie," and praises Huston for his "practically invisible" and "virile" style. Richard T. Jameson sees Agee's "criticism" as offering little of substance. When Huston was attacked or denied auteurist status by Sarris and others, Agee's remarks were of little support because they lacked specifics. To Jameson, an auteur revisits themes, has an interest in certain subjects, or has a "recognizably evolving style," and Huston thematically focuses on failed quests, cockeyed fatality, found-and-lost prizes, and accidental partnerships (34). Jameson moves away from literary comparisons to discuss the "angles, textures, tones, movements, compositional balance or imbalance" in *Treasure*, which is "seemlessly expressionistic" through its use of mirrors, reflections, and doppelgänger, and its opening frames set up much of what is to follow, including character, the feel of Tampico, and the resonance of images and themes (34–36). Jameson concludes by contending that *The Treasure of the Sierra Madre* has influenced *McCabe and Mrs. Miller, California Split, The Long Goodbye, The Wild Bunch, The Ballad of Cable Hogue*, and *Bring Me the Head of Alfredo Garcia* (37).

To James Agee, the most significant weakness in *The Treasure of the Sierra Madre* is the character played by Bogart. Agee commends Bogart for his acting, considering this better than anything he had done before, but says he cannot forget that he is Bogart, who is "so fantastically undisciplined and troublesome that it is impossible to demonstrate or even to hint at the real depth of the problem, with him on hand." What Bogart is doing is "putting on an unbelievably good act" (293). Leslie Taubman find the film's major strengths to be the directing of Huston and the acting (against persona) of Bogart and Walter Huston. Harvey R. Greenberg, somewhat in agreement with Agee, says the Bogart character was in keeping with earlier roles as Rick Blaine and Philip Marlowe, men with tough outward appearances but sensitive inside. Weakness, vulnerability, and paranoia are elements of Bogart portrayals in this and other films (52).

Although audiences found the film too depressing, Bogart got a fair amount of good press for his performance when the film opened. Bosley Crowther, for example, remarks that Bogart "combines perfidy and ferocity of some of his gangsters with the cool detachment and self-serving of Sam Spade." His portrait of Dobbs "could be Spade after several turns of hard luck and financial setbacks" (190). To Robert Sklar if Bogart wanted to remain a star or "screen presence" rather than an actor, the role of Dobbs might not have been a good choice. But in it he is able to mix the " 'acid and comedy' " of his earlier roles in this somewhat allegorical presentation of a capitalistic society in search of its moral spine at a time of the HUAC hearings (194).

Key Largo

In a brief overview of *Key Largo*, Lawrence Fargo, Jr., discusses how Maxwell Anderson is not much performed or much remembered today. John Huston and Richard Brooks rewrote the material to make this a "director's film" (1736) as they worked through the disillusionment of a returning veteran and his desire to establish roots. Lawrence Grobel discusses how Huston, familiar with the stage version starring Paul Muni as a disillusioned veteran of the Spanish Civil War, did not want to film it, even with Bogart. Huston told Richard Brooks he would consider doing it only if the story was better. When Brooks came up with the idea of a Little Caesar from Cuba, Huston was hooked (297). On the set, even though Bogart had top billing, he always deferred to Edward G. Robinson (313). Grobel quotes Bacall as saying that Huston was able to keep Bogart "fresh" by getting him to "do things that he would never have done. Bogie wasn't one to analyze parts, but John certainly knew what he wanted and would make that clear" (314). Except for the ending, which Fargo finds flawed because of its "sentimental conclusion" (blanket of sunlight), he sees it very much in keeping with Huston's ideas in other films, and with Bogart's giving a "strong performance" without the usual "overdone heroics" (1739). Kristin Laskas finds *Key Largo*, of Huston's many adaptations, to be the one least true to its source, and as such "gives evidence of [his] direct thematic interpretation and manipulation of the gangster genre" (104).

Nina Nichols says that *Key Largo* was not one of the better texts Huston worked with, yet the film serves as a mix of "*noir* disillusionment with a swan song for the gangster hero," as both Bogart and Robinson use "earlier performances to help build a character of substantial depth" (31–32). Carlos Clarens contends that Bogart played his familiar role of "cynic forced to fight for ideals he professes to have renounced," but notes that some of Bogart's remarks about the "aimless and political corruption of postwar America [sound] suspiciously close to John Birch" (224). Thomas Schatz sees this film and *White Heat* as embodying the end of the classic gangster-hero film with the death of the protagonists. This hybrid film of gangster and detective "presents a fascinating example of how stars and genres themselves evolve and intermingle" (106). Joan Cohen finds Robinson and his hoods to be "relics of an old order that has passed" (151). Robinson is a "complete antiromantic" and "a sadist and a misogynist," while Bogart is a "disillusioned veteran" and Bacall an "embittered widow" (151). Robert Sklar finds little to cheer about in this "subdued" performance, to which Bogart is "unable to give much personality to a poorly conceived character" (229).

Knock on Any Door

Bogart and Nicholas Ray first joined forces on the Santana production of *Knock on Any Door*. Bernard Eisenschitz, who has done major studies on both Ray and Bogart, focuses on Ray, with side glances at Bogart as entrepreneur and actor. *Knock on Any Door* was Bogart's first film away from Warner Bros., but in choosing a powerful, socially conscious novel to adapt, he was following in the studio's tradition. Bogart chose a director, though, who avoided studio formulas and who was simpatico with him in regard to the studio system, work, alcoholism, and young wives. Ray, noted for his work with young actors, played a key role in the casting and trying to break Bogart of his "professional habits" (116). Robert Sklar finds Bogart regressing to his "atavistic mannerisms" (231), unable to make much of his character, but finally playing the first role "for himself." Geoff Andrew notes that this film permits Ray to deal with some of the same ideas and approaches in the "lyrical and mythic" *They Live by Night*, but also allows him to explore Chicago of the 1930s, capital punishment, and the role of the underdog. A transition film between *They Live by Night* and *Rebel Without a Cause*, it is "too stridently explicit in its social meaning," especially as a result of his uses of flashback and "social-realist veneer." Andrew finds that "Ray's symbolic use of décor and composition transcends genre, and is characteristic of his own very special precision in the creation of mood and meaning" (42–43). Morton's denunciation of poverty, prejudice, neglect, and inequality has Bogart bring the "full moral weight of his heroic screen persona" to the film (46) and embodies Ray's "romantic pessimism" and his themes dealing with the pressures of society, the desire for the American dream, and the realities of poverty, inequality, and complacency (16). Although there are some notable pluses, Andrew finds problems with Emma's "unblemished, near-angelic" character and the script's heavy didacticism (45). Blake Lucas agrees that the social commentary works against the film, which "suffers from the explicitness of its social consciousness" (influence of environment on character) and the "simplification of Nick Romano's character" (162). In addition, Lucas believes that Bogart's character contributes little to the plot. What *noir* elements there are occur in the flashbacks, with the "evocation of city streets, pool halls, and impoverished flats; and in the close-ups and dissolves of Nick following Emma's death" (162). What most remember from the film is Nick's line, "Live fast, die young and have a good-looking corpse."

In a Lonely Place

Bernard Eisenschitz considers *In a Lonely Place* one of the finest films ever made about Hollywood. Hollywood outsiders Bogart and Ray became close friends as a result of their collaboration on this film. Eisenschitz discusses Ray's choice of Grahame for the role, quotes from a number of participants on their memory of specific scenes, and presents a close textual analysis with a discussion of professional constraints, Hollywood friendships, violence, and jealousy. He traces the writing and filming of the script, the *Kammerspiel* effect that influences Ray's intimate style (138), and how the components come together in a film that verges on pyschodrama (144).

Using comments by Dana Polan on Bogart's confrontation with two women over stuffed pandas at the El Morocco night club, differences between novel and film, and James W. Palmer on Hollywood and blacklisting, Christopher Ames discusses the use of locations, the depiction of screenwriters and writing, the resistance to narrative formulas, the blacklist, and Bogart's persona. He finds screenwriter Dixon Steele an "alienated intellectual" who embodies "essential loneliness" and "explosive qualities" (172) in a film that contains elements of the detective story, murder mystery, *film noir*, female gothics, screwball comedies, and Hollywood narratives (181), with echoes of Hollywood's complicity in the dark days of blacklisting. While the original screenplay had parallels between the "Althea Bruce" narrative and the Dix-Laurel relationship, Ray altered the film's complexities to avoid neatness and add to the film's "essential ambiguity" (191). In his retrospective and paean to Ray, David Thomson notes that *In a Lonely Place*, filled with "confessional melancholy," was the "most personal of Ray's films and one that looks more austere as years pass, and less and less like a Hollywood picture" (218).

In "*Film Noir* and the Dangers of Discourse," J. P. Telotte comments on changes from the novel that said little about the film industry. As a commentary on Hollywood, the film speaks to the dangers of discourse—speech and images—at a time when paranoia was ever-present in Hollywood. The adaptation, with a third-person point of view, "turns style into subject" (190). Ray examines the world of screenwriter Dixon Steele, who must rely on communication, but is often inarticulate and given to rage and violence. He embodies "a basic discrepancy between the public and private" discourse. While following the pattern of classical film narrative, *In a Lonely Place* suggests that we are often unable fully to understand "truth" as presented in public discourse, including the movies, and it also questions "how much we can rely on any public discourse" to get at truth (194).

Using an auteur approach, Geoff Andrew sees this work as one of Ray's "most achingly romantic and thematically dense" (55). It permitted Ray to deal with themes he was much concerned with, including Hollywood's being a lonely place, causes of violence, society's influence on a love affair, the relationship between the environment and emotion, and the "painful vulnerability of lonely and hypersensitive" people (56). Shepler agrees that Ray is thematically consistent with his other films that deal with "protagonists who are confused and tortured men, often at odds with the society around them" (1581). Andrew finds Dix and Laurel as "archetypal Ray creations, in that they are prone to the same romantic impulses and dreams and to many of the same confusions as their younger counterparts" (56). Dix's problem is one of repression, and when he does let go of emotions, "they are extreme and obsessive"—a "fundamental lack of control and balance in his personality that he is forever on the brink of cracking up" (57). "Because she diverts his attention away from the success ethic and social hierarchy of Hollywood which are partly the reason for his paranoia and violence," Laurel offers him escape through "salvation and redemption" (57–58). Seeing and being seen are central to Ray's theme and method, as invasion of privacy becomes to Ray an invasion of space (58–59). Space and visibility are important in a film that is a product of its time (the McCarthy era) and typical of Ray's films in which "destruction of an idealistic romance between lonely outsiders, by the harsh realities of the world around them" is foremost (61). Andrew considers this one of the best Bogart films because it strips away "the insolence of so many of his roles to explore the insecurity, the romanticism and the repression that lay beneath a macho, violent facade" (61).

In his examination of cult films, Danny Peary considers this "the sleeper among Humphrey Bogart's best films" (113), and one of a number of films of the 1940s and 1950s that deal with neurotic characters. His tough demeanor and name (Steele) are a front for his insecurity and insanity (113). Peary quotes Palmer on how Steele's attitude toward Hollywood phonies, his defense of his friends, and his high professional standards reflect Bogart's own personality. He also agrees with Palmer's assessment of Steele's contradictory nature (sentimental and sadistic, playful and paranoid, gentle and combative) as two sides of Bogart (114). In addition, the film is about the HUAC witch-hunts and how hunter criminals are not unlike screenwriters pursued by HUAC. Peary, following Ames, Telotte, and others, compares the film with its source (the novel by Dorothy B. Hughes) and notes that the novel is an examination of assassins, serial killers, and other sociopaths. Peary disagrees with those who find the ending "reactionary because it justifies the police's hounding of Dix, in that it got him to reveal his true colors" (116). Rather, he sees it as showing that "everyone is capable of violence (and insanity) if pushed too far" (116).

Echoing Ames, Peary, and others, V. F. Perkins says that while the film is based on a murder mystery, Ray's film uses Hollywood for its social environment to examine "sordid realities" through "intimacy and detail" of a "psychological and social portraiture" (222–223). He builds on Palmer's ideas, well established even when the film opened, that it was a commentary on the HUAC hearings, as it develops a parallel between the off-screen lives of Bogart and Ray (225). Even if Joe Hyams claims that Bogart did not like the film because of its evocation of the witch-hunts in Hollywood, Perkins sees this as one of Bogart's best roles: "One of his and the film's triumphs is to render the violence in his instability of mood and purpose with full force, taking it to the edge of absurdity without loss of conviction" (226). After a close reading of the film, Perkins says that the film embodies "an eloquence and spontaneity of gesture unsurpassed in Ray's work" (231).

At a time when much was being said about *Fatal Attraction* and *Sammy and Rosie Get Laid*, Judith Williamson offers brief comments in the *New Statesman* on two re-releases of Ray films: one about sexual mistrust (*In a Lonely Place*) and the other about social corruption (*The Big Heat*). Williamson notes that Ray's films were made "on the brink of another era of return to family values, after the upheaval immediately following the war" (27). Nevertheless, much of the film's sexual meanings come through Gloria Grahame's "good lines," "strong visual presence," and her point of view. The film's "economy" and "naturalism" are enhancements to the intensity of both films. To Williamson the theme of *In a Lonely Place* is "fear and suspicion in sexual relations" (27). Bogart is an exemplum of an *homme fatale*. As we move from Bogart's point of view to Grahame's, Williamson suggests that the lonely place of the title is "the self—the distance between the lovers taking the graphic form of the kind of no-person's land between their neighboring apartments." Ray, who studied with Frank Lloyd Wright, uses cinematic space for meaning as he places "characters in terms of their relative power and significance," and wastes nothing (27–28).

Ellen Draper sees the film as a refinement of the "dark themes and excessive stylization of earlier *noir* cinema into a perfectly balanced, self-critical film" (62). Julie Kirgo and Alain Silver find this "a peculiar kind of film noir" that is "strange, sad, and hauntingly romantic" (145). This film brings together a "harsh murder mystery," a "sleazy milieu with a colorful, semi-hard-boiled cast of characters" with typical Ray subject matter of "alienation, effort, failure, and loss" (145). Steele is a "fallen romantic" with "destructive impulses" (145), a "noir hero trapped in a compulsive role; caught, almost frozen, between the dark past and a bleak future, he is unable to see a continuum that valorizes the present except through Laurel. Hence Steele is literally and figuratively in a lonely place" (146). Dix Steele's lines quoted by Laurel at the film's end are a few of the most famous in *film noir*: "I was born when you kissed me. I died when you left me. I lived a few weeks while you loved me."

In "The Displaced Voice in *In a Lonely Place*," J. P. Telotte discusses the narrative voice in the film and its narrative source. He sees the film as working in the classical tradition described by Bordwell, Staiger, and Thompson but also exemplifies "*noir* revisionism" (1) as it "undermines much of its conventional seeming" (source, character focus, use of major star, conventional point of view) by a shift in point of view and its focus on the film industry (1–2). What distinguishes this film from others to Telotte is that it "turns style into subject, displacing the novel's internal human voice in favor of an external cultural voice, that of the movies; and in the process it insinuates a far more subversive 'why' than we would expect in a classical film narrative" (4). He sees Palmer's emphasis on the historical as missing a key point: "how the inner human voice might be drowned out or displaced by a powerful and suggestive popular voice—including one that speaks against any possible subversion" (5). In examining differences from the novel, Telotte notes that the shift to the movie industry "becomes both the context for nearly every action in the film and a chief motivating force," as Dix Steele battles his inner voice of integrity and the voice of the film industry (7–8). In a note to this article, Telotte links the Bogart persona in this and his other *noir* films with a "kind of free-floating existential angst and world weariness" (12); while maybe he was not the dangerous psychotic of the novel, both *The Caine Mutiny* and *The Treasure of the Sierra Madre* suggest the "dark potential in the isolated, self-certain, but also implicitly dangerous character that Bogart had sketched out in the previous decade's roles" (12).

Nicholas McVay sees "the core of the film's force and fascination" to be Bogart, "whose presentation of Dix Steele is "probably the most psychologically complicated and disturbing portrait of his entire career" (6). McVay summarizes and analyzes the main characters and notes that the work "operates and succeeds on many levels: the public and private, the specific and universal, the cerebral and the visceral, the bitter and the sweet" (7). He considers the film less a comment on Hollywood than *A Star Is Born*, *Sunset Boulevard*, *The Bad and the Beautiful*, or *The Last Tycoon*, but more of a study of a flawed character in Hollywood, not unlike *The Goddess* (7). Robert Sklar, after noting that many critics take an auteur approach, finds this "a Bogart film" that brings together aspects of some of his violent screen roles and those in which he plays romantic leads: "Bogart did not rid himself of violence, but transformed it into socially acceptable forms—as a private eye or man at war—as his romantic image developed" (236). As one of his "great performances," Bogart as Dix Steele "shares most of the characteristics of his classic performances except that the tie between the killer and the lover is laid bare, without romanticism, the genre conventions, or the political ideology" (236).

James W. Palmer talks about flawed characters and the film's emphasis on historical context, as it serves as a critique of Hollywood's complicity and paranoia regarding the HUAC hearings. To Palmer, the film's success lies in its portrayal of Hollywood paranoia (200). He compares Dorothy B. Hughes's novel with its maniacal killer to the Ray film with its violent and haunted protagonist who "tries and fails to renounce violence" (203), and he takes issue with Peter Biskind's oversimplification of the film as an attack on what happens when one is not normal or average.[10] To Palmer, the film champions toleration and trust at a time of conspiracies and suspicion as it presents a self-destructive protagonist typical of a Nicholas Ray film and a Bogart persona not out of keeping with the duality of the star's image (204–205).

The best single study of the film is Dana Polan's volume for the British Film Institute. Polan synthesizes much of what has been written about the film, focusing on the film's autobiographical aspects (Ray and Grahame and Bogart's life); how the film mixes elements of screwball comedy and *film noir* as it portrays changes in the old Hollywood, disintegrating romances, and the mixing of violence and romance; the differences between Dorothy Hughes's novel and the film; and its reception when it opened. As in *noir* and screwball comedy, Polan finds that the film "offer[s] meditations on romance in which it is made clear that whatever love is achieved comes at great cost, is fragile, could easily have flipped into its cynical opposite" (18).

The Enforcer

Marc Vernet, as he has done with *The Maltese Falcon* and three other films, looks at the opening of *The Enforcer* to examine its *mise-en-place* and *pot au noir* as ways of understanding spectatorship and *film noir*, but does not extend our understanding of this film in any significant way.

The African Queen

Since Humphrey Bogart won his only Oscar for *The African Queen*, one might expect a number of studies of Bogart's acting in the film, but most of the attention has focused on the process of adaptation and various accounts by the principals considered for or involved in the making of the film. David Niven, for example, relates that as early as 1938, he was going to play Charlie, opposite Bette Davis. Warner Bros. had purchased the Forester novel as a Davis vehicle, but the project fell through because of one of her contretemps. From late 1942 to 1948 James Agee was movie reviewer for *Time* and wrote for the *Nation*. His reviews of Huston's films and his long piece on Huston for *Life* in 1950 brought them together as collaborators. Lawrence Grobel, Huston's biographer, synthesizes many of the discussions of the film in his summary of the work of Agee and Huston on the screenplay; Huston's response to Agee's symbolic reading of the story; how Allnut is a reflection of Agee's character; Huston's preference for location shooting (first of eight films in ten years on location and away from the United States and his family); Bogart's deferred payment of

$125,000 plus 30 percent interest in profits and the rest of the production costs; the problems with the script; Huston's penchant for hunting elephants; his direction of Hepburn; the living conditions (food, red ants, disease); the conflicts between Sam Spiegel and Huston; and the final weeks of shooting in England. For a brief overview of the actual production process, Andrew Sinclair's work on Sam Spiegel covers the commissioning, shooting, and success of *The African Queen*, as well as the initial agreements with the actors and director, some of the renegotiations, Spiegel's falling out with Huston, and the eventual box office success of the film.

While most discussions of the screenplay focus on Huston and Agee, with an occasional nod to Peter Viertel, Tom Milne reminds us that John Collier also had a hand in the work, and only with the publication of a Collier Reader in the mid-1970s did his work become available again. James Fultz studies the relationship of the two creative spirits and examines the additions, deletions, and modifications that turned the novel into a film. His discussion of Agee's contribution to the script and his work with Huston is based on original documents and the two versions of the novel (1935 and 1940, with original ending). Much of Agee's work came in the first one hundred pages, with Huston contributing the last sixty, but Milne reminds us that John Collier and Peter Viertel had a hand in it, even though "Agee shows the visual imagination of a novelist or of a director-on-paper who is in absolute control of every finely-shaded detail even in the recording of violent action" (14). Agee's most important contributions are the first three scenes, which are not in the novel: (1) natives worshipping; (2) Charlie at tea, which "sets whatever is natural and vital and unseemly because spontaneous and alive against whatever is artificial and merely conventional and essentially dead" (16), thus establishing thematic opposites; and (3) the German raid. To Fultz, these scenes, while written by Agee, belong very much to Huston's camera angles, tight framing, *mise-en-scène*, dialogue, and emphasis on Charlie's social discomfort and suffocation. Building on Huston's own comments about the Bogart-Hepburn collaboration, Fultz sees some of the humorous dialogue developing from the Bogart-Hepburn interaction. This "element of comedy" was not in the novel: Hepburn sips tea as if she is in a Victorian parlor, and Allnut is garrulous, respectful, but a teaser who is able to loosen her up (17). "Both were cast against type, but they could go only so far in violating their public's expectations of them. Hepburn had specialized in tongue-in-cheek comedy, and Bogart could not be seen too seriously as weak and vacillating" (18). While the collaboration radiated in several directions, the most important modifications were changes in Rose and Charlie that met the needs of Bogart and Hepburn.

Lillian Ross also discusses some of the creative differences and debates Agee and Huston had over symbolism in fiction and film, Huston's indifference to how Rose's trip down the river signified "the act of love," and his visual concern that movies have to show ("demonstrate") everything. On the additions to the script, Huston told Ross that a key change was the comedic element that came out of the Bogart-Hepburn collaboration: "This situation had never happened to me before, although I had worked with Bogie on four other films. Katie and he were just funny together, one calling forth that quality in the other, and the combination of their two characterizations brought out the humor of dramatic situations which, originally, none of us thought existed. Basically, the humor underlies the story, for it's a case of the little worm of a man who turns or the prim spinster suddenly becoming the captain of the ship. But it doesn't come out of the printed page. It was the surprising combination of Hepburn and Bogart which enabled the comedy to emerge" (92).

Huston gives his own take on the adventure in *An Open Book*, recounting the character and craft of James Agee, his work with Hepburn and Bogart, and his hunting expeditions. Repeating what he told Gerald Pratley, Huston says, "With Bogie, it wasn't so much where you acted but how you acted, and he'd just as soon have been at home. He liked the London or Paris night-life scene, but when it came to acting, he saw no reason why it couldn't be done in comfort in the studio" (203). Huston says that Bogart did not especially like the character of Allnut, but he grew into the character as Huston "slowly got him into it, showing him by expression and gesture what I [Huston] thought Alnut should be like. He first imitated me, then all at once he got under the skin of that wretched, sleazy, absurd, brave little man" (203).

At the time of the making of the film, *Life* magazine covered the shoot for its readers. In her autobiography, Lauren Bacall recounts how adjusting to the hardships caused by bugs, food, sickness, and rain led to lifetime friendships. To Bacall, Huston always sought fantasy (this time, big game hunting) and Bogart was always after reality, wanting to make the film and get out. To get a better understanding of the characters involved in this film, Pauline Kael and others have recommended Peter Viertel's fictionalized account of the making of the film, *White Hunter, Black Heart*, which was later turned into a movie of the same name starring Clint Eastwood (1990). In response to remarks by Rudy Behlmer, Viertel says that the "novel does... lean heavily on the actual happenings, although the talk and the confrontations were eighty percent invention" (250). Hepburn's best-seller on the making of the film highlights "some happenings you can't forget": her travels to the Belgian Congo; her life in a bamboo bungalow situated somewhat away from the rest of the group; surviving for a time on pineapple slices and tinned biscuits; her outhouse encounter with a poisonous black mamba and her battles with ants, dysentery, and the cast and crew of *The African Queen*; her frustrations that the script was not complete; and her shifting views and developing friendships with Bogart, Bacall, and Huston. The book does not offer much to our understanding of the filmmaking process or claims that the film might be viewed as "a comic allegory on the war of the sexes" (49); rather, its light, conversational tone reads like a friend talking about friends. In *Me* Hepburn adds little to our understanding of this film.

Gerald Pratley includes Huston's account of his work with Agee, the trip to

Africa, how they used rafts for the shooting, his fondness for Hepburn's "great energy and dedication" and her willingness to accompany him on his hunting expeditions, and that Bogart "liked the comforts of Beverly Hills" but fortunately had Bacall with him (91). Alex Masden bases his account on the printed materials of others and says, inaccurately, that Huston used real leeches on Bogart (123). Jeffrey Meyers quotes an occasional newspaper account as he rehashes what has been covered by Hepburn and others, offering no new insights into the trip or the making of the film. Fuller and more substantive in his background analysis than the others, Rudy Behlmer explains that this was only the third film shot on location in Africa; the casting choices over the years; John Collier's involvement as scriptwriter and his repurchasing the script from Warner Bros.; the plot's similarities to Maugham's short story "The Vessel of Wrath"; and Viertel's work on the ending. Of the last, Behlmer says, "Other than the ending, the narrative line of John Collier's script and the Agee-Huston-Viertel versions are the same as Forester's. The differences are in tone, dialogue, and detail" (243). He also details the complex financing of film, the shift in tone to comedy as a result of the Bogart-Hepburn pairing, and the difficulties of working in Africa. Behlmer attributes the success of the film to the "comedy of character. Hepburn and Bogart are superb together, with each presenting new and interesting aspects of their acting reserves as well as extensions and variations of their personalities" (252). Robert Sklar reiterates the importance of the comic in Bogart's screen roles when he notes that "comedy was an essential complement both to his tough and romantic side; indeed, without the comic leavening the romantic Bogart had been less than convincing" (241).

Stuart Kaminsky claims that Huston's "anti-German attitude is evident" and that he continued to polish his visual style, focusing on "the placement of characters in a frame so that their size and position reflect what they are saying and doing" (89). He considers Charlie very much removed from the earlier "Bogart/Huston liars" when he joins Rosie in her plan to destroy the German boat. Of the critical biographies on Huston, Kaminsky gives the fullest analysis of Huston as a filmmaker.

Where this film fits into Huston's work and its importance are the subject of articles by Lesley Brill, Eugene Archer, R. T. Jameson, and Ellen Snyder. Snyder offers a broad overview, detailing an adventure and implausible love affair with low humor that developed from the collaboration of the actors. Snyder joins the chorus when she concludes the characters are more important than the setting, with "Bogart's Charlie . . . a masterpiece of comic characterization" (41). To Jameson, the key to our understanding of Huston's first overt comedy and first color film is the director's "contact with the evocative undertow of myth so indispensable to the earlier Bogart triumphs" (40). Allnut is an "unreconstructed boor and godless Christian, [who] enters the film like a nonavuncular version of Old Howard, fanned by native boys, a glass of gin and riverwater at hand; this benign version of Fred C. Dobbs" (41). But "Huston's God reverses the Eden process and sanctifies the sinners" (42). The Bogart-

Hepburn pairing made Huston rethink his use of unsuccessful endings and the tone; here, unlike the characters in the novel and the earlier Huston-Agee version, the protagonists succeed, and, unlike the novel, these two characters are more into middle age.

Archer also focuses on the Bogart-Hepburn collaboration as he discusses Huston, Hemingway, and other literary figures. He finds *The African Queen* "a testament to human endurance and natural instinct against the worst that man and nature can provide" (88). It is funniest when it brings us closest to tears, but its real strength is Bogart's "magnificent *tour de force*" that complements Hepburn's performance (91). Lesley Brill's analysis includes a study of the characters' identities, the influence of foreign cultures and "cultural construction," courtship and lovemaking, and how the water and fire imagery suggest "overcoming of obstacles" (16–18). While Brill sees the lack of complications as somewhat different from other Huston films, his shots, themes, dialogue, rhythm of editing and actions, and use of fantastic adventure are common to his other films and, other critics notwithstanding, demonstrate why he is an auteur.

Deadline—U.S.A.

For all his love of newspapermen and writing, nothing of substance has been written about Bogart's role in *Deadline—U.S.A.* In a study of François Truffaut, Wheeler Dixon gives the director's brief comments on the film (called *Deadline*, or *Bas les Masques*), focusing on the screenplay by Brooks and his knowledge that "cinematography is the art of petty details that do not strike one" (22). In his commentary, Truffaut asks, "Isn't the task of a work of art to solve the drama rather than expose it?"

Beat the Devil

John Huston's cult film *Beat the Devil* was little understood by the actors during the filming or the many who attended its early screenings. Over the years, it has grown to be appreciated by some as a satirical, somewhat absurd film. Some see in it a link to Hitchcock's use of a "MacGuffin," the key but often meaningless element in a suspense story that serves only as a catalyst for the characters' actions. Charles Champlin considers it a "fast and disciplined comedy," his favorite Huston film, with great lines about time. Ed Hulse views it as a black comedy–caper film that was ahead of its time, a satire on *The Maltese Falcon*. Others see it as mostly fluff. Joe Hyams details how Huston first showed Bogart the book, his interest in doing it because the author was impoverished, how Bogart bought it for Santana Productions, the stress created by a wretched script, and the hiring of Truman Capote to doctor it (132–136). In an interview in 1984, John Huston said he found it originally "a very poor excuse for a script," but by the end it was an "amusing, good picture" (71). There were problems with the cast, production crews, communication problems with cast and crew, a car accident with Huston and Bogart, and shenanigans on the set, including arm wrestling between Bogart and Capote. Olive Graham notes that it was for its time an "expensive exercise in off-beat thrillers," cynical in tone, with a nonrealistic visual style, and an Italian Riviera background that contributed to the $600,000 it cost Bogart and Santana Productions to make. Lawrence Grobel adds information about the Jennifer Jones and David Selznick connection, Bogart's problem with Production Code because of the film's original treatment of adultery, and how this shaggy dog story has become a cult favorite. Two scholarly articles that focus on the film as a cult classic are by R. T. Jameson and T. J. Ross, and two that are geared more for mass consumption are by Ted Sennett and Danny Peary.

Peary includes a synopsis of the film and its credits and synopsis, plus a discussion of "the fifties' most peculiar A-budget film," its production difficulties, and its negative reception by general audiences. To Peary, the film's great joys are that the characters go against type and their misbegotten adventure. Unlike other Bogart films, this has a "distinctly Continental flavor: open air cafés, villas, balconies that look over town squares, hotel rooms warmed by sea breezes, statues along Mediterranean cliffs, characters lounging in house robes, and most important, characters with manners (bad manners perhaps, but manners nevertheless)" (15–16). Sennett says to call it a cult film is "unwarranted" (176) because it is a satire on the "den-of-thieves" subgenre started in *The Maltese Falcon* (176). Reporting on the actors' thoughts about the film, Sennett says that Lorre saw it as a "sardonic comedy, meant for art houses," that Bogart "looks baffled and uneasy" both on screen and as its producer, and that Jennifer Jones was "painfully miscast." Disagreeing with Huston's later comments, Bogart early on said only "phonies" would like it and that the film was a "mess" (177–179).

For R. T. Jameson the film does not work as a tale of romance or intrigue. In this "comically grotesque" *Falcon*, Huston "has perversely lent the film a manic drive at the same time he clearly regards the matter and the outcome of the scenario to be of surpassing irrelevance" (43). Not unlike other Huston movies, this one is hostile to women, but Jameson is uncertain as to whether this came from Capote, Huston, or both. In a film that continually reminds us that "there is no exit," Jameson concludes that "it is hard to watch *Beat the Devil* without feeling that Bogart is dying before your eyes" (44–45).

Less harsh in his analysis of the film, T. J. Ross finds *Beat the Devil* a "prototypical cult film," conscious of itself as cult film as it "evokes the very tradition in which it works" by moving away from the traditional, linear, cause-effect narrative that has verisimilitude and pyschologically defined and goal-oriented characters. Ross finds the film a modernist text of sorts because of the "difficulty" in style and characterization (79–81). Trying to place the film in larger historical context, Ross notes that the film's "perspective on romantic love combined with its persistent reflexive turns," although done on a surface level, can be seen as a preview of such films as *L'Avventura*, without "the psychological and sociological speculation" (87). By undermining objectivity and observed truth, disrupting the classical narrative pattern, and presenting an uncomfortable Bogart who has no code on which to guide his character, Ross sees this as holding narrative possibilities for Bogart's character, and thus keeps the viewer forever alert (82).

The Caine Mutiny

One of Bogart's strongest performances near the end of his life was as Captain Queeg in *The Caine Mutiny*. This was a role he wanted so badly that he was willing to receive less than his usual fee. Two overviews of the film are by William H. Brown, Jr., and Donald Spoto. Brown discusses the navy's objections to making the film (because a commander is in charge of the ship and the use of *mutiny* in the title), and the use of Edward Dmytryk as director. Dmytryk had previously directed such classics as *Crossfire* (1947) and *Murder, My Sweet* (1944), but was one of the Hollywood Ten. Spoto examines the conditions under which the film came to be made, the importance of casting to Kramer, the film's length (it needs to be longer), and the importance of the shift in tone as it moves from the story of a psychopath (anti-navy) to the concluding "cheer for the navy." Of the latter, Gabbard and Gabbard note that the psychiatrist is viciously attacked in the novel, but in the film "is shown indirectly to have been correct." With the changes caused by the war, exalting a "neurotic hero" at the end is no longer possible: "In many ways, the idealization of psychiatry that was about to become entrenched in American movies can be understood as a somewhat desperate means of preserving Hollywood's consoling paradigms for an American public that was increasingly unlikely to believe in them" (81).

In *American Weekly* Bogart says that Queeg has small victories, but he is a sick man with many frustrations and insecurities. To Spoto, Bogart gives a "virtuoso performance," but wonders aloud why Queeg could have advanced so far in the military career without being seen for what he is, and Brown does not find the characterization to be as strong as Dobbs in *The Treasure of the Sierra Madre*. Robert Sklar agrees, noting that while *The Caine Mutiny* may well resonate with audiences because of recent cultured concerns about authority, loyalty, and power, *Treasure* is a "more imaginatively complex film" (244–245). In one of his early critical essays, François Truffaut examines Queeg's developing neurosis, finds the casting to be uneven, and identifies the storm scene and Bogart's testimony as the two scenes that make the movie worth watching. He also finds the film representative of Hollywood's effort to intellectualize best-sellers by making Wouk's 1951 Pulitzer Prize winner into a "popular" movie. Brown, on the other hand, while agreeing that the story's "diffused nature" undermines its power, discusses *The Caine Mutiny* in terms of other powerful films dealing with military hierarchy such as Robert Aldrich's *Attack!* (1956) and Stanley Kubrick's *Paths of Glory* (1957).

Sabrina

Remade in 1995 by Sydney Pollack and starring Julia Ormand, Harrison Ford, and Greg Kinnear, *Sabrina* is the Cinderella story of a chauffeur's daughter being wooed by a playboy and a stodgy tycoon, who happen to be the two sons of her father's employer. With the remake, especially with Harrison Ford in the Bogart role and the friendship between Wilder and Pollack, essays comparing the original and the remake may well follow. Other than mentions in books on the director or other actors in the original film, and a brief summary and commentary by Leslie Donaldson for the Magill series, very little has been written about *Sabrina*. Maurice Zolotow's *Billy Wilder in Hollywood* includes a brief discussion based on earlier reports of the well-known hostility on the set between Bogart and Holden, Hepburn, and Wilder. Bogart told a correspondent for *Time* magazine that *Sabrina* was "a crock of shit" and he disliked working with Wilder, even though Wilder was one of the few "acceptable" directors he agreed to work with when he signed his contract in 1946. Robert Sklar suggests that Wilder may have chosen Bogart "for the elements of surprise and cognitive dissonance he brought to the film" (245).

Leslie Donaldson comments on how Wilder twists the cliché of the poor waif who falls for a good-looking, wealthy bachelor to take her out of her poverty. The resolution of the plot is unsettling to audiences because, while there is a happy ending, its foundation is fragile. In a discussion of the transformation of women to "feminine ideal," as their social class and "literacy" change, Lisa Starks notes that Sabrina's "metamorphosis does not seem to extend much beyond a new look and self-confidence in her physical attractiveness.... What Paris has taught her is... how to wear her hair, how to shop, and how to accessorize to project the image of a sophisticated, elegant woman of leisure. ... [A] growth in her intellect and maturity would most likely have impeded her success" (51).

The Barefoot Contessa

The few articles on and the brief reviews of *The Barefoot Contessa* by Louis Marks, Pauline Kael, Penelope Houston, and others tend to focus on the plot and the contributions of Joseph L. Mankiewicz. Pauline Kael finds *Contessa* "a trash masterpiece: a Cinderella story in which the prince turns out to be impotent. It's hard to believe Mankiewicz ever spent an hour in Hollywood; the alternative supposition is that he spent too many hours there" (235). To Henry Hart, the film is a "lively pastiche," in which the unnecessary voice-over is used as a vehicle for Mankiewicz's commentary. François Truffaut, enthralled by Mankiewicz's *A Letter to Three Wives*, finds *Contessa* a strange film. There is "total sincerity, novelty, daring, and fascination," and a clear attack on vulgarity, but Truffaut wants to know what we are left with. The film attacks Hollywood, raises the issue of impotence, and presents a guide to the Riviera and to "one of the most beautiful portraits of woman ever filmed" (130), but it is to Truffaut a film either to accept or reject, but not to evaluate. He accepts it for "its freshness, intelligence, and beauty" (131).

Hollis Alpert sees the film as being part of Mankiewicz's period of "doubt and uncertain success." He finds the film too long, unfocused, and "obscure" as it attempts to both satirize and romanticize (154–155). Mankiewicz admitted that the film did not have the focus he wanted; instead of zeroing in on the empty lives of the jet set, he combined it with a portrait of a self-destructive and masochistic movie star. Richard Corliss stresses the "grace of his films' monologues" and that *Contessa* is close to Albert Lewin's *Pandora and the Flying Dutchman*, and he tries to place the film with *A Letter to Three Wives* and *All About Eve*. But Mankiewicz, like other screenwriters who went to Europe to direct and escape Hollywood pressures, wound up without tension: "When the tension of the Hollywood hothouse evaporated, so did the dramatic tension these writers were capable of injecting into their films." With "testament" films like *Contessa*, audiences were no longer willing to sit through "a series of monologues," no matter who the star was, and "Mankiewicz's attempts, especially in the lead-footed *Contessa*, to bring Shavian dialogues to Hollywood films was a failure" (246).

We're No Angels

Robert Sklar makes the only comments of note on *We're No Angels*. He finds little credit given to Bogart in this "deliberately stagey performance" in which Bogart is "probably the closest he came on-screen to the way he must have appeared as a romantic boy back on Broadway in the 1920s" (248).

The Desperate Hours

Michael Cimino's remake of *Desperate Hours* (1990), starring Mickey Rourke and Kelly Lynch, ignores the conflict in the 1955 version between the criminal, haunted by his relationship with his father, and the father of the family. As Philip Wuntch notes, "Several years from now, everyone involved with the movie will change the subject whenever the title *Desperate Hours* is mentioned" (6C). Michael Anderegg sees the original as capturing the "essential paranoia" of the United States in the 1950s (180). Because of the casting of Richard Eyer as a "strident brat" and Frederic March as the father (a role intended for Spencer Tracy), the dysfunctional nature of the family created an unsympathetic response in audiences (180). "Tired and gray, his illness add[ing] a grim edge of desperation to his role," Bogart's Glen Griffin faces death with "a moment of resigned, suicidal bravado" and reminds us of Baby Face Martin and Duke Mantee (183–184).

Julie Barker gives high marks to Bogart's performance. Although he had played social outcasts and deviates before, "he gave the part much more than just a walk-through" with a "blood-chilling" performance of a "squint-eyed, dry-mouthed... criminal awaiting his chance for revenge." Like some of his other outstanding roles, the power of this performance is demonstrated in Bogart's ability to keep everything "just below the surface, always on the verge of exploding" (886). By using deep focus instead of rapid cutting, "Wyler's technique is less manipulative," and he uses power also in blocking, lighting, and camera angles to create conflict (889).

In using *The Desperate Hours* and *Teen Age Crime Wave* as two examples of a number of recent films in which "a family or community... is imprisoned or besieged by criminals" (39), Martin Dworkin examines how one might judge and recognize gratuitous violence and "the effects violent films have upon us" so that we will better understand how, through analogy, these films affect how we deal with local, national, and international problems (40). With little regard or patience for *Teen Age Crime Wave* and seeing *The Desperate Hours* as "perhaps the outstanding film of its kind" (41), Dworkin examines how both create "a situation of primordial challenge" that justifies the use of violence, as "decency is not only vexed and incited to act, but forced to preserve itself" (41). The power of *The Desperate Hours*, in addition to its screenplay and directing, is the use of two actors (March and Bogart) whose "dramatic presence... can vivify and dominate the screen" (41) and who serve as "the protagonists of decency and of evil in the traditional single combat of the conventional melodrama" (43). Robert Sklar finds this to be Bogart's "most brutal role of his career" and one that makes little effort to situate "Griffin's criminality in a social context" (249). To Dworkin what makes this film's ending different from others of its type and what makes it a "critical point in the course of film entertainment during the past ten years" is that March does not use the typical "heroic violence... on the side of right"; he does not shoot Bogart—the embodiment of "heroicized malevolence," but instead the film shows that violence "is no better than an expedient," and the audience, which identifies with March, "is made responsible for its acts" (44–48).

The Harder They Fall

The Harder They Fall is Humphrey Bogart's last film. Surprisingly, little has been written about it, or his final performance, although Robert Sklar calls it among his "least distinguished—both in characterization and performance" (250). Blake Lucas categorizes *The Harder They Fall* as a typical fight film like *Rocky* in that the fighter is "more spectacle than man" (1389). He believes that Mark Robson's experience as film editor helped with the short scenes and claims screenwriter Philip Yordan (*The Big Combo* and *The Naked Jungle*) has a "gift for subtly poeticizing his material" (1391). By this time, Bogart had "established an image in most of his classic films... of the hard-shelled idealist who ultimately turns out to be a white knight in black armor." In this his last film, "Bogart looks more world-weary than ever (perhaps the result of his illness) and the film's responsiveness to the audience's faith in his essential integrity adds much feeling to the final sequences. This is an excellent example of the idolization of a star adding dimension and meaning to a film'' (1390).

NOTES

1. Walter Scott, "Personality Parade," *Parade Magazine* (December 10, 1995): 2.
2. Bogart takes this idea from his friend Peter Lorre, who said acting was making faces.
3. David Hanna calls him "Bogart's Boswell" (131).
4. H. Frankel, "The Tough Guy and the Jet Set," *Saturday Review* (September 24, 1965): 33.
5. I am using references to the *Profiles* reprint, which might be easier to access.
6. *Saturday Review World* July 27, 1974: 46.
7. *Marked Woman, Kid Galahad, Swing Your Lady, Dark Victory, The Roaring Twenties, Invisible Stripes, It All Came True, They Drive by Night, The Wagons Roll at Night, The Maltese Falcon, High Sierra,* and *Passage to Marseille.*
8. "Murray Burnett, 86, Writer of Play Behind 'Casabalanca,' " *New York Times* (September 29, 1997): C23.
9. Hemmeter and Sweeney note that the novel was made into several other films, including *The Breaking Point* (1950), with John Garfield and Patricia Neal and directed by Michael Curtiz; *The Gun Runners* (1958), with Audie Murphy, Eddie Albert, and Patricia Owens, and directed by Don Siegel; and *Girls! Girls! Girls!* (1962) with Elvis Presley and Stella Stevens. A part of *Islands in the Stream* (1977) also uses material from *To Have and Have Not* (110).
10. Peter Biskind, *Seeing Is Believing: How Hollywood Taught Us to Stop Worrying and Love the Fifties* (New York: Pantheon, 1983), 37.

5
BIBLIOGRAPHICAL CHECKLISTS OF HUMPHREY BOGART SOURCES

BIOGRAPHICAL AND CRITICAL STUDIES

Archer, Eugene. "Bogart: Man and Superman." *New York Times* (January 3, 1965): X:9.
"Art of Mr. Bogart, The." *New York Times* (February 19, 1939): IX:4.
"As Time Goes By: Humphrey Bogart, Hollywood's Most Enduring Legend." *American Movie Classics Magazine* (June 1990): 12–13.
Astor, Mary. " 'Bogie Was for Real.' " *New York Times* (April 23, 1967): II:D21.
Bacall, Lauren. *Now.* New York: Knopf, 1994.
———. *Lauren Bacall By Myself.* New York: Knopf, 1978.
———. "Lauren Bacall Talks About Bogart, Sinatra and Her New Life." *McCall's* 93 (July 1966): 24, 116.
Bacon, James. *Made in Hollywood.* New York: Warner 1977.
Badder, David. "Humphrey Bogart." *Film Dope* 4 (March 1974): 17–18.
Barbour, Alan D. *Humphrey Bogart.* New York: Pyramid, 1973. Rpt. Galahad, 1974.
Barnes, Peter. "Gunman No. 1." *Films and Filming* 1.12 (September 1955): 12.
Baskette, Kirtley. "Hollywood's Trigger Man." *American Magazine* 135 (June 1943): 43, 63–64.
Bazin, André. "Mort d'Humphrey Bogart." *Cahiers du Cinéma* 68 (February 1957). Trans. Phillip Drummond. Rpt. in *Cahiers du Cinéma: The 1950s: Neo-Realism, Hollywood, New Wave.* Ed. Jim Hillier. Cambridge. Mass.: Harvard University Press, 1985. 98–101.
Benchley, Nathaniel. "Here's Looking at You Kid: Humphrey Bogart." *Atlantic* 235 (February 1975): 39–48, 81–84.
———. *Humphrey Bogart.* Boston: Little, Brown, 1975.
Berson, Debbi. "Bogie Really Had Cool." *Seventeen* (January 1967): 16.
"Bogart." *Screen Greats.* Vol. 3. New York: Starlog, 1980.
"Bogart, Humphrey." *Current Biography* (May 1942): 7–8.

"Bogart, Humphrey." *International Motion Picture Almanac* (1941–1942).
"Bogart, Humphrey." *American Annual, 1953* (1953): 73.
"Bogart, Humphrey." *Collier's Yearbook, 1953* (1953): 85.
"Bogart, Humphrey." *National Cyclopedia of American Biography* 45 (1962): 558.
Bogart, Stephen Humphrey. *Bogart: In Search of My Father.* New York: Dutton, 1995.
"Bogart Seeks New Talents for Indie." *Hollywood Reporter* 99 (July 28, 1948): 1.
Bogart's Face. Los Angeles: Stanyan, 1970.
"Bogart's Regret." *Newsweek* 30 (December 15, 1947): 23.
"Bogart's Venture." *Newsweek* (April 9, 1951): 48.
Bogdanovich, Peter. "Bogie in Excelsis." *Esquire* 62 (September 1964): 108–109. Rpt. in *Pieces of Time: Peter Bogdanovich on the Movies.* New York: Arbor House/ Esquire Book, 1973. 82–98.
"Bogie." In *Hollywood and the Great Stars.* Ed. Jeremy Pascall. New York: Crescent, 1976. 5–10.
"Bogie's Moroccan Campaign." *Newsweek* (October 10, 1949): 22.
Bromfield, Louis. "Bogie." *Photoplay* 18 (March 1941): 22–23, 94–95.
Brooks, Louise. "Humphrey and Bogey." Trans. *Positif* 81. *Sight and Sound* 36.1 (winter 1966–1967): 18–23. Rpt. in *Lulu in Hollywood.* New York: Knopf, 1982. 57–69.
Cahill, Marie. *Humphrey Bogart: A Hollywood Portrait.* New York: Smithmark, 1992.
Carlinsky, Dan. *The Great Bogart Trivia Book.* New York: Fawcett, 1980.
Carlyle, John. "Bogart: The Legend Inspires a Cult." *Hollywood Legends: The Life and Films of Humphrey Bogart and Greta Garbo* 1.1 (1967): 1–35.
Chesnick, Davis. "Humphrey Bogart: The Man Behind the Pith." *Washington Star* (January 9, 1977): F1, 7.
Coe, Jonathan. *Humphrey Bogart: Take It and Like It.* New York: Grove Weidenfeld, 1991.
Cooke, Alistair. "Humphrey Bogart: Epitaph for a Tough Guy." In *Six Men.* New York: Knopf, 1977.
Crowther, Bosley. "The Career and the Cult." *Playboy* 13.6 (June 1966): 110–111, 158, 160–162, 164–167.
[Darrach, Brad]. "Bogey Worship." *Time* (February 7, 1964): 80.
Dawson, Warren J. "Letters: 'Bogart-Mania.' " *Films in Review* 17 (June–July 1966): 391.
Dienstfrey, Harris. "Hitch Your Genre to a Star." *Film Culture* 34 (fall 1964): 35–37.
Eisenschitz, Bernard. *Humphrey Bogart.* Paris: Le Terrain Vague, 1967.
Elliott, Harvey. "Here's Looking at You, Bogie." *Video* (March 1982): 67–68, 98–101.
Eyles, Allen. *Bogart.* New York: Doubleday, 1975.
Frank, Alan. *Humphrey Bogart.* London and New York: Optimum, 1982.
Frazier, George. "Humphrey Bogart: He Has a Hard, Unhappy Face, and a Hard and Happy Life." *Life* (June 12, 1944): 55–60.
———. *The One with the Mustache Is Costello.* New York: Random House, 1947: 21–31.
Friedrich, Otto. *City of Nets: A Portrait of Hollywood in the 1940's.* New York: Harper & Row, 1986.
Fuchs, Wolfgang J. *Humphrey Bogart: Cult Star, A Documentation.* Trans. Richard Leigh. Berlin: Taco Verlagsgesellschaft und Agenture, 1987.
Garfield, Brian. "Garfield for the Defense: Purcell vs. Bogart." *Armchair Detective* 11.2 (1978): 186–188.

Gehman, Richard. *Bogart: An Intimate Biography*. Greenwich, Conn.: Gold Medal Books, 1965.
———. "Bogart: A Cool Cult Warms Up to an Old Hero." *True* (September 1965): 50–54, 107–121.
———. "Saint Bogart and His Cult." *Cavalier: The New Magazine for the New Man* (November 1965): 32–34, 56, 58–59.
"Ghosts in the Commercials." *Time* (December 23, 1991): 56.
"Ghoulish New Diet Coke Commercial." *TV Guide* (December 28, 1991): 23.
Glass, Madeline. "Strong, But Not Silent." *Screenland* (January 1937): 70, 92–93.
Goldberg, Joe. "The Death of Sam Spade." *Evergreen Review* 7.28 (January–February 1963): 107–116.
[Goodman, Ezra]. "The Survivor." *Time* 63 (June 7, 1954): 66–72.
———. *Bogey: The Good-Bad Guy*. New York: Lyle Stuart, 1965.
Greenberger, Howard. *Bogey's Baby*. New York: St. Martin's Press, 1978.
Griffith, Richard. "Humphrey Bogart." In *The Movie Stars*. Garden City, N.Y.: Doubleday, 1970. 264–276.
Hamill, Pete. "The Rebels: Humphrey Bogart." *New York Post Magazine* (August 12, 1963): 2.
Hanna, David. "The Humphrey Bogart I Knew." *Coronet* (June 1964): 34–38.
———. *Bogart*. New York: Leisure Books, 1976.
Hanners, John. "From 'Goggle-Eyed' to 'Bogie': The Evolution of Humphrey Bogart's (1899–1957) Stage and Film Personae." *Theatre Southwest* 24 (forthcoming).
Hart, Christopher, and Douglas Kenny. "The Bogie Gap." *Movie* (January 23, 1970): M32–36.
Haskell, Molly. "Here's Looking at You Kid! The Legend of Humphrey Bogart Endures . . . As Time Goes By." *GQ* (January 1988): 160–161, 190–192.
———. *From Reverence to Rape: The Treatment of Women in the Movies*. New York: Holt, Rinehart and Winston, 1974.
Hoberman, J., and J. Rosenbaum. "Curse of the Cult People." *Film Comment* 27.1 (January–February 1991): 18–21.
Holland, Jack. "Mellow Merchant of Menace." *Movie Show* (June 1947): 32–33, 77–79.
Hopper, Hedda. "Bogart's Still Bouncing at 52!" *Chicago Sunday Tribune* (February 3, 1952): 9, 15.
Huston, John. "At Bogart's Death, a Eulogy for a Tough Guy." *Life* (January 28, 1957): 44.
Hyams, Joe. *Bogart and Bacall*. New York: McKay, 1975.
———. *Bogie: The Biography of Humphrey Bogart*. New York: New American Library, 1966.
———. "How His Widow and Friends Remember Him: The Last Days of Humphrey Bogart." *Good Housekeeping* 162 (January 1966): 54–57, 171, 177–185.
———. *Mislaid in Hollywood*. New York: Peter H. Wyden, 1973.
Iachetta, Michael. "Big Bogart Boom." *New York Sunday News* (April 25, 1965): 19.
Kobal, John. "Humphrey Bogart." In *50 Super Stars*. New York: Bounty, 1974. 18.
———. *Hollywood Color Portraits*. New York: Morrow, 1981.
Lowry, Cynthia. "Bogart's Family Life Elegantly Casual Save That He Frets When Not Acting." *Washington Sunday Star* (May 1, 1955): E1.
Manvell, Roger. "Humphrey Bogart." In *Actors and Actresses. The International Dic-*

tionary of Films and Filmmakers. Ed. James Vinson. Chicago: St. James Press, 1986. 3:80–82.
Marlowe, Don. "The Man, Bogie." *Classic Film Collector* 30 (spring 1971): 31.
McCarty, Clifford. "Humphrey Bogart." *Films in Review* 8.5 (May 1957): 193–204.
———. *Bogey: The Films of Humphrey Bogart.* New York: Citadel Press, 1965.
Mellen, Joan. "Humphrey Bogart: Moral Tough Guy." In *Close-Ups: Intimate Profiles of Movie Stars.* Ed. Danny Peary. New York: Workman, 1978. 222–227.
Meyers, Jeffrey. *Bogart: A Life in Hollywood.* Boston: Houghton Mifflin, 1997.
Michael, Paul. *Humphrey Bogart: The Man and His Films.* New York: Bonanza, 1965.
[Morgenstern, Joseph.] "The Bogey Boom." *Newsweek* (November 1, 1965): 94, 94A, 94C.
Moshier, W. Franklyn. "Ruth Etting Today." *Film Fan Monthly* 159 (September 1974): 19–25.
"Night Life of the Gods." *Time* (October 10, 1949): 27.
Peterson, Elmer T. "The Human Side of Hollywood He-Men." *Better Homes and Gardens* (May 1939): 22–23.
Pettigrew, Terence. *The Bogart File.* London: Golden Eagle, 1977. Rpt. as *Bogart: A Definitive Study of His Film Career.* London and New York: Proteus, 1981.
———. *Raising Hell: The Rebel in the Movies.* New York: St. Martin's Press, 1986.
Polan, Dana. *In a Lonely Place.* London: British Film Institute, 1993.
Purcell, J[ames] M[ark]. "Humphrey Bogart: Some Comments on the Canonization Process." *Armchair Detective* 11.1 (1978): 6–16.
Roseman, Eugene. "In My Opinion." *Seventeen* (February 1967): 268.
Ruddy, Jonah, and Jonathan Hill. *Bogey.* New York: Tower, 1965.
Sarris, Andrew. "Here's Looking at You, Bogie." *Village Voice* (February 14, 1977): 44–45. Rpt. as "Humphrey Bogart." In *The Movie Star (The National Society of Film Critics on the Movie Star).* Ed. Elisabeth Weis. New York: Penguin, 1981. 137–142.
Schickel, Richard. "Humphrey Bogart." In *The Stars.* New York: Dial, 1962. 190–195.
———. "Bogart." *Film Comment* 22.3 (May–June 1986): 33–44, 46.
Schmidt, M. A. "Battling Bogart's Saga: Or an Appraisal of Humphrey Bogart's Rebellious Climb Up the Ladder." *New York Times* (September 6, 1953): 2:5.
Shearer, Lloyd. "Bogart and Bacall: Here's How They Fooled Hollywood." *Parade* (January 29, 1956): 16–18.
Shipman, David. "Humphrey Bogart." In *The Great Movie Stars: The Golden Years.* New York: Bonanza, 1970. 71–75.
Shipp, Cameron. "The Adventures of Humphrey Bogart." *Saturday Evening Post* (August 2, 1952): 32–33, 54, 57.
Silke, James R., and Peter Bogdanovich. "Bogart: The Image." *Movies International* (Hollywood) 1.2 (December 1965): n.p.
Sklar, Robert. *City Boys: Cagney, Bogart, Garfield.* Princeton University Press, 1992.
Sperber, A. M., and Eric Lax. "Bogart and Bacall." *Vanity Fair* 438 (February 1997): 122–140.
———. *Bogart.* New York: Morrow, 1997.
Steinberg, Cobbett S. *Film Facts.* New York: Facts on File, 1980.
Stuart. Gloria. *Boating with Bogart.* Los Angeles: Imprenta Glorias, 1993.
Talty, Stephan. "Young Bogart." *American Film* 16.4 (April 1991): 40–45.

Thompson, Verita, and Donald Shepherd. *Bogie and Me*. New York: St. Martin's Press, 1982.
Thomson, David. *A Biographical Dictionary of Film*. 3rd ed. New York: Knopf, 1994.
Towne, Robert. "Bogart and Belmondo." *Cinema* (Los Angeles) 3.1 (December 1965): 4–7.
Truffaut, François. "Truffaut on Bogart." *Saturday Review of the Arts* 1 (March 1973): 31–32.
———. "Portrait d'Humphrey Bogart." *Cahiers du Cinema* 52 (November 1955). Trans. in revised version as "A Portrait of Humphrey Bogart." In *The Films in My Life*. Trans. Leonard Mayhew. New York: Simon & Schuster, 1978. 292–295.
Tynan, Kenneth. "Here's Looking at You Kid: The Man and the Myth." *Playboy* (June 1966): 110–111, 168–170, 172.
———. "The Bogart I Never Knew." In *Tynan: Right and Left*. New York: Atheneum, 1967. 341–349.
———. "Humphrey Bogart." In *Profiles: Kenneth Tynan*. Ed. Kathleen Tynan and Ernie Eban. New York: Harper, 1990. 196–203.
Weales, Gerald. "The Bogart Vogue: Character and Cult." *Commonweal* (March 11, 1966): 664–666.
Williams, Robert. "The Bogart Story." *New York Post* (January 15–19, 1957).
Wilson, Earl. *The Show Business Nobody Knows*. New York: Cowles, 1971; Bantam, 1973. 263–292.
Wlaschin, Ken. "Humphrey Bogart." In *The Illustrated Encyclopedia of the World's Greatest Movie Stars and Their Films*. New York: Harmony Books, 1979. 51–52.

FILMS

Across the Pacific (1942)

Astor, Mary. *A Life on Film*. New York: Delacorte, 1971.
Downer, Alan S. "The Monitor Image." In *Man and the Movies*. Ed. W. R. Robinson. Baton Rouge: Louisiana State University Press, 1967. Rpt. New York: Penguin, 1969. 13–30.
Sennett, Ted. *Masters of Menace: Greenstreet and Lorre*. New York: Dutton, 1979. 109–111.

Action in the North Atlantic (1943)

Dick, Bernard F. The *Star-Spangled Screen: The American World War II Film*. Lexington, KY: University Press of Kentucky, 1985. 223–225.
Hanson, Stephen L. "Action in the North Atlantic." In *Magill's American Film Guide*. 5 vols. Ed. Frank N. Magill. Englewood Cliffs, N.J.: Salem, 1983. 1:9–12.
Harmetz, Aljean. *Round Up the Usual Suspects: The Making of* Casablanca—*Bogart, Bergman, and World War II*. New York: Hyperion, 1992. 298–300.

The African Queen (1951)

Agee, James. *Agee on Film: Five Film Scripts by James Agee.* New York: McDowell, Oblesnky, 1960. Rpt. New York: Grosset & Dunlap, 1969. 2:149–259.
Archer, Eugene. "John Huston—The Hemingway Tradition in American Film." *Film Culture* 19 (1959): 66–101.
———. "Taking Life Seriously: Part I, 'A Touch of Hemingway.' " *Films and Filming* 5.12 (September 1959): 13–14, 28, 33.
———. "Small People in a Big World, Part 2, 'A Touch of Melville.' " *Films and Filming* 6.1 (October 1959): 9–10, 25, 34.
Bacall, Lauren. "Hollywood vs. Africa." *Los Angeles Mirror* (March 31–April 2, 1952).
———. *Lauren Bacall By Myself.* New York: Knopf, 1979. 201–212.
Behlmer, Rudy. " 'Remember Eleanor Roosevelt's Serene Smile': *The African Queen*." In *America's Favorite Movies: Behind the Scenes.* New York: Ungar, 1982. 234–252.
Brill, Lesley. *"The African Queen* and John Huston's Filmmaking." *Cinema Journal* 34.2 (winter 1995): 3–21.
Fultz, James. "A Classic Case of Collaboration . . . *The African Queen." Literature/Film Quarterly* 10.1 (1982): 13–24.
Grobel, Lawrence. *The Hustons.* New York: Avon, 1989. 362–382.
Hepburn, Katharine. *The Making of The African Queen, or How I Went to Africa with Bogart, Bacall, and Huston and Almost Lost My Mind.* New York: Knopf, 1987.
———. *Me.* New York: Knopf, 1991. 247–250.
Huston, John. *"African Queen*: Behind-the-Scenes Story." *Theatre Arts* 36 (February 1952): 48–49, 92.
———. *An Open Book.* New York: Knopf, 1980. 187–204.
Jameson, R. T. "John Huston." *Film Comment* 16 (May–June 1980): 25–56.
Kaminsky, Stuart. *John Huston: Maker of Magic.* Boston: Houghton Mifflin, 1978. 83–90.
"Life Goes on Location in Africa: *African Queen." Life* (September 17, 1951): 172–176.
Masden, Alex. *John Huston: A Biography.* New York: Doubleday, 1978. 112–123.
Mathews, Tom. "Kate." *Newsweek* (August 31, 1987): 48–52.
Meyers, Jeffrey. "Bogie in Africa." *American Scholar* (spring 1997): 237–250.
Milne, Tom. "The Elusive John Collier." *Sight and Sound* 45.2 (spring 1976): 104–108.
Niven, David. *Bring on the Empty Horses.* New York: Putnam, 1975. 337–338.
Pratley, Gerald. *The Cinema of John Huston.* South Brunswick and New York: A. S. Barnes, 1977. 88–94.
Ross, Lillian. *Picture.* New York: Rinehart, 1952. 146–147.
Sinclair, Andrew. *Spiegel: The Man Behind the Pictures.* Boston: Little, Brown, 1987. 55–62.
Sklar, Robert. *City Boys: Cagney, Bogart, Garfield.* Princeton: Princeton University Press, 1992. 239–242.
Snyder, Ellen J. *"The African Queen."* In *Magill's American Film Guide.* 5 vols. Ed. Frank N. Magill. Englewood Cliffs, N.J.: Salem, 1983. 1:38–41.
———. "The African Queen." In *Cinema: Great Directors.* Ed. Frank Magill. Pasadena, Calif.: Salem Softbacks, 1981. 265–268.

Thompson, Howard. "An Independent Operator Takes Inventory." *New York Times* (March 2, 1952): II:5.
Viertel, Peter. *White Hunter, Black Heart*. Garden City, N.Y.: Doubleday, 1953.

Angels with Dirty Faces (1938)

Mank, Gregory William. *"Angels with Dirty Faces."* In *Magill's American Film Guide*, 5 vols. Ed. Frank N. Magill. Englewood Cliffs, N.J.: Salem, 1983. 1:138–140.

The Barefoot Contessa (1954)

Alpert, Hollis. *The Dreams and the Dreamers*. New York: Macmillan, 1962. 154–155.
Corliss, Richard. "Joseph L. Mankiewicz." In *Talking Pictures: Screenwriters in American Cinema*. New York: Penguin, 1975. 236–246.
Hart, Henry. "The Barefoot Contessa." *Films in Review* 5.8 (October 1954): 430–432.
Houston, Penelope. "The Barefoot Contessa." *Sight and Sound* 24.3 (January–March 1954): 146.
Kael, Pauline. *Kiss Kiss Bang Bang*. Boston: Atlantic Monthly Press, 1968. 234–235.
Marks, Louis. "The Barefoot Contessa." *Films and Filming* 1.3 (December 1954): 18.
Truffaut, François. "Joseph Mankiewicz: *The Barefoot Contessa*." In *The Films in My Life*. Trans. Leonard Mayhew. New York: Simon & Schuster, 1978. 129–132.
Ward, L. E. "The Great Films: *The Barefoot Contessa*." *Classic* 135 (September 1986): 32–33.

Beat the Devil (1954)

"Beat the Devil." *Sight and Sound* (October–December 1953): 77.
"Beat the Devil." *Look* (September 22, 1953): 128–129, 131–133.
Bogart, Humphrey, as told to Joe Hyams. "Movie Making Beats the Devil." *Cue* (November 28, 1953): 14.
Champlin, Charles. "Look Back: John Huston's *Beat the Devil*." *Millimeter* 3.12 (December 1975): 56–57.
Graham, Olive. "Beat the Devil." *Cinema Texas Program Notes* (September 2, 1980): 1–5.
Grobel, Lawrence. *The Hustons*. New York: Avon, 1989. 382–383, 401–416.
Hulse, Ed. "Beat the Devil." In *Magill's American Film Guide*. 5 vols. Ed. Frank N. Magill. Englewood Cliffs, N.J.: Salem, 1983. 1:281–283.
Huston, John. "Stalling for Time." *American Film* 5 (September 1980): 45.
Hyams, Joe. *Bogie: The Biography of Humphrey Bogart*. New York: New American Library, 1966.
Jameson, R. T. "John Huston." *Film Comment* 16 (May–June 1980): 25–56.
"John Huston: Dialogue on Film" *Film Comment* 9.4 (January–February 1984): 19, 22, 70–71.
Peary, Danny. "Beat the Devil." In *Cult Movies 2*. New York: Dell, 1983. 15–18.
Ross, T. J. "The Cult Send-Up: *Beat the Devil* or Goodbye, *Casablanca*." In *The Cult Film Experience: Beyond all Reason*. Ed. J. P. Telotte. Austin: University of Texas Press, 1991. 79–89.

Sennett, Ted. *Masters of Menace: Greenstreet and Lorre.* New York: Dutton, 1979. 175–179.

The Big Sleep (1946)

Bellour, Raymond. "The Obvious and the Code." *Screen* 15.4 (winter 1974–1975): 7–17. Trans. from *Cinéma: Théorie and Lectures*, a special issue of *Revue D'Esthetique.* Paris: Klincksieck, 1973.
"The Big Sleep" (script). In *Film Scripts One.* Ed. George P. Garrett, O. B. Hardison, Jr., and Jane R. Gelfman. New York: Appleton-Century-Crofts, 1971. 137–239.
Blades, John. "The Big Sleep." *Film Heritage* 5.4 (summer 1970): 7–15.
Bogdanovich, Peter. "The Big Sleep." In *The Cinema of Howard Hawks.* New York: Film Library of the Museum of Modern Art, 1962. 25–26.
Bordwell, David. *Narration in the Fiction Film.* Madison: University of Wisconsin Press, 1985. 63–70, 126–128, passim.
Brackett, Leigh. "From *The Big Sleep* to *The Long Goodbye* and More or Less How We Got There." *Take One* 4.1 (January 1974): 26–28.
Brackett, Leigh, William Faulkner, and Jules Furthman. *The Big Sleep: Film Scripts One.* Ed. George P. Garrett, O. B. Hardison, and Jane R. Gelfman. New York: Appleton, 1971. 137–329.
Castille, Philip Dubuisson. "Compson and Sternwood: William Faulkner's 'Appendix' and *The Big Sleep.*" *Post Script* 13.3 (summer 1994): 54–61.
Chandler, Raymond. "The Simple Art of Murder." *Atlantic Monthly* 174.6 (December 1944): 53–59.
Davies, Gill. "Teaching About Narrative." *Screen Education* 29 (winter 1978–1979): 56–76.
Davis, Paxton. "Bogart, Hawks, and *The Big Sleep* Revisited Frequently." *Film Journal* 1.2 (summer 1971): 2–9.
Deming, Barbara. *Running Away from Myself: A Dream Portrait Drawn from the Films of the Forties.* New York: Grossman, 1969. 144–154.
Dixon, Wheeler. "The Romance of Crime." In *Crime in Motion Pictures. Proceedings of Fourth Annual International Film Conference.* Kent, Ohio: Kent State University Press, 1986. 70–73.
Everson, William K. *The Detective in Film.* Secaucus, N.J.: Citadel Press, 1972.
Gallagher, Brian. "Howard Hawks's *The Big Sleep*: A Paradigm for the Postwar American Family." *North Dakota Quarterly* 51.3 (summer 1983): 78–91.
Godfrey, Lionel. "Martinis Without Olives." *Films and Filming* 14.7 (April 1968): 10–14.
Goldberg, Joe. "The Death of Sam Spade." *Evergreen Review* 7.28 (January–February 1963): 107–116.
Goodwin, Michael, and Naomi Wise. "An Interview with Howard Hawks." *Take One* 3 (November–December 1971): 19–25.
Gregory, Charles. "Knight Without Meaning? Marlowe on the Screen." *Sight and Sound* 42.3 (summer 1973): 155–159.
Grimes, William. "Original 'Big Sleep' Has Less Bacall." *Dallas Morning News* (February 18, 1997): C2.
Hairston, Robert B. "An Examination of the Nonverbal Communication in Three Noir

Films: *The Postman Always Rings Twice, The Big Sleep*, and *Murder My Sweet* in the Original and Remake Versions." *Dissertation Abstracts International* 50 (June 1990): 3770A.
Haskell, Molly. "Howard Hawks—Masculine Feminine." *Film Comment* 10.2 (March–April 1974): 34–39.
"Hazards of Humphrey Bogart." *Newsweek* (September 2, 1946): 77–78. (Review of *The Big Sleep*.)
Hicks, J. "Raymond Chandler Movies." *Hollywood Studio* 20.12 (1987): 12–15+.
Hogue, Peter. "Hawks, Chandler, and *The Big Sleep*." *Movietone News* 57 (February 1978): 12–16.
Houseman, John. "Today's Hero: A Review." *Hollywood Quarterly* 2.2 (January 1947): 161–163. (Followed by responses by Lester Asheim 2.4 (July 1947): 414–416 and Houseman 3.1 (fall 1947): 89–90.) Rpt. in *Entertainers and the Entertained*. New York: Simon & Schuster, 1986. 134–139.
Houston, Penelope. "The Private Eye." *Sight and Sound* 26.1 (summer 1956): 22–23, 55.
Jensen, P. "From Fiction to Fantasy with Howard Hawks." *Film Comment* 10.6 (November–December 1974): 23.
Kael, Pauline. "Movieland—The Bums' Paradise." *Reeling*. New York: Atlantic Monthly/Little, Brown, 1976. 182–190.
Kawin, Bruce. *Faulkner and Film*. New York: Ungar, 1977.
———. "Hawks and Faulkner." In *Howard Hawks: American Artist*. Ed. Jim Hillier and Peter Wollen. London: British Film Institute, 1996. 144–151.
Kuhn, Annette. "*The Big Sleep*: A Disturbance in the Sphere of Sexuality." *Wide Angle* 4.3 (1980): 4–11.
———. "*The Big Sleep*: Censorship, Film Text, and Sexuality." In *The Power of the Image: Essays on Representation and Sexuality*. London: Routledge, 1985. 74–95, 136–137.
Lev, Peter. "*The Big Sleep*: Production History and Authorship." *Canadian Review of American Studies* 19.1 (1988): 1–21.
Librach, Ronald S. "Adaptation and Ontology: The Impulse Towards Closure in Howard Hawks's Version of *The Big Sleep*." *Literature/Film Quarterly* 19.3 (1991): 164–175.
Luhr, William. *Raymond Chandler and Film*. New York: Ungar, 1972. 121–137. 2nd ed. Tallahassee: Florida State University Press, 1991.
MacShane, Frank, ed. *Selected Letters of Raymond Chandler*. New York: Columbia University Press, 1981.
———. "Raymond Chandler and Hollywood." *American Film* 1.6/7 (April 1976): 62–69; part 2, *American Film* 1.7 (May 1976): 54–60.
Mast, Gerald. "Hemingway and Chandler into Bogart-Bacall and Hawks: *To Have and Have Not* and *The Big Sleep*." In *Howard Hawks, Storyteller*. New York: Oxford University Press, 1982. 243–295.
Maxfield, James F. "Love in the Dark: Howard Hawks's Film Version of *The Big Sleep*." *Clues* 14.1 (spring–summer 1993): 11–20.
Mayne, Judith. "The Limits of Spectacle." *Wide Angle* 6.3 (1984): 4–15.
McBride, Joseph. "Bogart and *The Big Sleep*." In *Hawks on Hawks*. Berkeley: University of California Press, 1982. 102–106.
———, ed. *Focus on Howard Hawks*. Englewood Cliffs, N.J.: Prentice Hall, 1972.

McConnell, Frank. *Storytelling and Mythmaking: Images from Film and Literature.* New York: Oxford University Press, 1979. 144–150.

McCullough, J. "Pedagogy in the Perverse Text." *Cineaction!* 19/20 (winter–spring 1990): 74–83.

Monaco, James. "Notes on *The Big Sleep* Thirty Years After." *Sight and Sound* 44.1 (winter 1974–1975): 34–38.

Orr, Christopher. "The Trouble with Harry: On the Hawks Version of *The Big Sleep*." *Wide Angle* 5.2 (1982): 66–71.

Paris, James, Julie Kirgo, and Alain Silver. "The Big Sleep." In *Film Noir.* Ed. Alain Silver and Elizabeth Ward. Woodstock, N.Y.: Overlook, 1979. 33–34.

Pedersen, Vibeke. "Male and Female Spectator Positions in *The Big Sleep* (Hawks 1946)." *Nordic Cinema Studies* 1–2 (1988): 105–107.

Pendo, Stephen. *Raymond Chandler on Screen: His Novels into Film.* Metuchen, N.J.: Scarecrow Press, 1976. 38–62.

Phillips, Gene D. "*The Big Sleep*." In *Fiction, Film, and Faulkner: The Art of Adaptation.* Knoxville: University of Tennessee Press, 1988. 48–50.

Place, Janey. "*The Big Sleep*." In *Magill's American Film Guide.* 5 vols. Ed. Frank N. Magill. Englewood Cliffs, N.J.: Salem, 1983. 1:346–348.

[———]. "Big Sleep." In *Cinema: Great Directors.* Ed. Frank Magill. Pasadena, Calif.: Salem Softbacks, 1981. 167–169.

Ponder, Anne. "*The Big Sleep*: Romance Rather Than Detective Fiction." *Armchair Detective* 17.2 (spring 1984): 171–174.

Price, Keith. "The Big Sleep (1946)." *Cinema Texas Program Notes* (April 1, 1975): 1–5.

Random, Henry. "Real Private Eyes, and the Kind You See in the Movies." In *Memoirs of a Moviegoer.* San Francisco: Editorial Service Bureau, 1975. 98–133.

Reeves, Jimmie L. "The Big Sleep (1946)." *Cinema Texas Program Notes* (October 14, 1981): 63–72.

Rowling, Gwen. "The Big Sleep (1946)." *Cinema Texas Program Notes* (February 16, 1981): 67–77.

Schatz, Thomas. *Hollywood Genres: Formulas, Filmmaking, and the Studio System.* New York: Random House, 1981. 136–138.

Shatzkin, Roger. "Who Cares Who Killed Owen Taylor." In *The Modern American Novel and the Movies.* Ed. Gerald Peary and Rogert Shatzkin. New York: Ungar, 1978. 80–94.

Sklar, Robert. *City Boys: Cagney, Bogart, Garfield.* Princeton: Princeton University Press, 1992. 172–176.

Solomon, Stanley. *Beyond Formula: American Film Genres.* New York: Harcourt Brace, 1976. 219–222.

Swires, S. "Grab What You Can Get: The Screenwriter as Journeyman Plumber; A Conversation with Leigh Brackett." *Films in Review* 27 (August–September 1976): 413–421.

TheBerge, Rita. "The Big Sleep (1946)." *Cinema Texas Program Notes* (March 24, 1977): 13–18.

Thomson, David. "At the Acme Bookshop." *Sight and Sound* 50 (spring 1981): 122–125.

———. "The Art of the Art Director." *American Film* (February 1977): 12–20.

———. *America in the Dark: Hollywood and the Gift of Unreality*. New York: Morrow, 1977. 175–177.
———. *The Big Sleep*. London: BFI, 1997.
Tuska, Jon. *The Detective in Hollywood*. Garden City, N.Y.: Doubleday, 1978.
Van Wert, William. "Philip Marlowe: Hardboiled to Softboiled to Poached." *Jump Cut* 3 (1974): 10–13. (Review of screen images of Marlowe.)
Vernet, Marc. "The Filmic Transaction: On the Openings of Film Noirs." *Velvet Light Trap* 210 (summer 1983): 2–9.
Walker, Michael. "*The Big Sleep*: Hawks and *Film Noir*." *Cineaction!* 13/14 (summer 1988): 29–39. Rpt. in *The Movie Book of Film Noir*. Ed. Ian Cameron. London: Studio Vista, 1992. 191–202.
Wexman, Virginia Wright. "Kinesics and Film Acting: Humphrey Bogart in *The Maltese Falcon* and *The Big Sleep*." *Journal of Popular Film and Television* 7.1 (1978): 42–55.
———. "Courtship Conventions and Performance Styles: Humphrey Bogart in *The Maltese Falcon* and *The Big Sleep*." *Creating the Couple: Love, Marriage, and Hollywood Performance*. Princeton: Princeton University Press, 1993. 25–36.
Willis, Donald C. *The Films of Howard Hawks*. Metuchen, N.J.: Scarecrow Press, 1975.
Wood, Robin. "Acting Up." *Film Comment* 12 (March–April 1976): 20–25.
———. *Howard Hawks*. Garden City, N.Y.: Doubleday, 1968. 168–170. (Additional information in ed. London: Secker and Warburg, 1968.)
———. *Howard Hawks*. London: BFI, 1981.

Black Legion (1937)

Greene, Graham. "Black Legion." In *Graham Greene on Film: Collected Film Criticism 1935–1940*. Ed. John Russell Taylor. New York: Simon & Schuster, 1972. 151–154.
Study Guide to Black Legion. New York: Progressive Education Association, 1939.

Bullets or Ballots (1936)

Lukow, G., and S. Ricci. "The Audience Goes Public: Inter-Textuality, Genre, and the Responsibilities of Film Literacy." *On Film* 12 (spring 1984): 29–36.

The Caine Mutiny (1954)

Bogart, Humphrey. "The Way I See Queeg." *American Weekly* (June 27, 1954): 9.
Brown, William H., Jr. "*The Caine Mutiny*." In *Magill's American Film Guide*. 5 vols. Ed. Frank N. Magill. Englewood Cliffs, N.J.: Salem, 1983. 1:557–561.
Gabbard, Krin, and Glen O. Gabbard. *Psychiatry and Cinema*. Chicago: University of Chicago Press, 1987. 80–81.
Miller, A. L. "The Caine Mutiny." *F News* (summer 1980): 36–37.
Sklar, Robert. *City Boys: Cagney, Bogart, Garfield*. Princeton: Princeton University Press, 1992. 244–245.
Spoto, Donald. "Bargaining for Battleships—*The Caine Mutiny*, 1954." In *Stanley Kramer: Film Maker*. New York: Putnam's, 1978. 167–178.

Truffaut, François. "Ouragan sur le Caine." In Wheeler W. Dixon, *The Early Film Criticism of François Truffaut*. Bloomington: Indiana University Press, 1993. 143–144.

Casablanca (1942)

Ackerman, Dan. "Casablanca (1942)." *Cinema Texas Notes* (January 17, 1977): 31–38. Rpt. from *Cinema Texas Notes* (January 7, 1976) and (September 5, 1978): 31–38.
Allen, J. C. *Conrad Veidt: From Caligari to Casablanca*. Pacific Grove, Calif.: Boxwood Press, 1987. 201–215.
Altman, R. "Dickens, Griffith, and Film Theory Today." *SAQ* 88.2 (1989): 321–359.
Anobile, Richard, Ed. *Casablanca*. New York: Avon, 1974.
Arkadin. "Film Clips." *Sight and Sound* 37 (autumn 1968): 210–211.
Baker, Melva Joyce. *Images of Women in Film: The War Years, 1941–1945*. Ann Arbor: UMI Research, 1981. 47–56.
Bart, P. "Fundamental Things." *Variety* (September 21, 1992): 3+.
Basinger, Jeanine. *American Cinema: One Hundred Years of Filmmaking*. New York: Rizzoli, 1994. 70–73.
Behlmer, Rudy. "George Raft in *Casablanca*?" In *America's Favorite Movies: Behind the Scenes*. New York: Ungar, 1982. 154–176.
Bergman, Ingrid, and Alan Burgess. *Ingrid Bergman: My Story*. New York: Delacorte, 1980.
Black, Joel. " 'You Must Remember This': The Intimate and the Obscene in Filmic Narrative." *Yearbook of Comparative and General Literature* 40 (1992): 83–89.
Bok [B. Knight]. "Casablanca." *Variety* (April 13, 1983): 56.
Bourgnet, Jean-Loup. "Romantic Dramas of the Forties: An Analysis." *Film Comment* 10 (January 1974): 46–51, esp. 48–49.
Burkhart, Jeff, and Bruce Stuart. *Hollywood's First Choices: (Or Why Groucho Marx Never Played Rhett Butler): How the Greatest Casting Decisions Were Made*. New York: Crown, 1994.
"Burnett Alison Sue Nathaniel Benchley on Alleged Slur." *Variety* (October 15, 1975): 3, 38.
Cahill, Marie. *Hollywood Classics: Casablanca*. New York: Smithmark Publishers, 1991.
Canham, Kingsley. *The Hollywood Professionals*. Vol. 1: *Michael Curtiz, Raoul Walsh, Henry Hathaway*. New York: A&S Barnes, 1973. 32–39.
Card, James. "Confessions of a Casablanca Cultist: An Enthusiast Meets the Myth and Its Flaws." In *The Cult Film Experience: Beyond All Reason*. Ed. J. P. Telotte. Austin: University of Texas Press, 1991. 66–78.
"Casablanca." *Hollywood Studio* 17.2 (1984): 20–21.
Case, B. "As Time Goes By." *Time Out* (London) (July 1, 1992): 65.
Champlin, Charles. "Thoughts on Casablanca." In *Casablanca: Script and Legend. The 50th Anniversary Edition*. Ed. Howard Koch. Woodstock, N.Y.: Overlook, 1992. 231–232.
Cooke, B. "100 Questions on Casablanca." *Hollywood Studio* 17.2 (1984): 8–10.
Coover, Robert. "You Must Remember This." In *A Night at the Movies*. New York: Simon & Schuster, 1987. Rpt. Normal, Ill.: Dalkey Archive, 1992. 156–187.

Corliss, Richard. "Analysis of the Film: [*Casablanca.*]" In Howard Koch, *Casablanca: Script and Legend*. Woodstock, N.Y.: Overlook Press, 1973. 163–178. Rpt. *Casablanca: Script and Legend. The 50th Anniversary Edition*. Ed. Howard Koch. Woodstock, N.Y.: Overlook, 1992. 233–247.

———. "Howard Koch." *Talking Pictures: Screenwriters in American Cinema*. New York: Penguin, 1975. 102–122.

———. "Who'd Look at You Now, Kid." *Film Comment* 18.6 (November–December 1982): 19.

Craft, J. J. "*Casablanca* Revisited." *Classic Film Collector* 42 (spring 1974): 43.

Crain, Mary Beth. "*Casablanca*: In Defense of What's His Name." *Media Montage*. 1.1 (1976): 12–17.

———. "*Casablanca's* Unsung Hero: A Conversation with Paul Henreid." *Media Montage* 1.1 (1976): 18–24.

Cripps, Thomas. "*Casablanca, Tennessee Johnson*, and the Negro Soldier—Hollywood Liberals and World War II." In *Feature Films as History*. Ed. K. R. M. Short. Knoxville: University of Tennessee Press, 1981. 138–156.

Croft, John J. "*Casablanca* Revisited: It Has Survived Its Directors." *Classic Film Collector* 42 (spring 1974): 43.

Crowther, Bosley. *Vintage Films*. New York: Putnam, 1977. 64–67.

Davis, J. H. " 'Still the Same Old Story': The Refusal of Time to Go By in *Casablanca*." *Literature/Film Quarterly* 18.2 (1990): 122–127.

———. "Additions and Corrections to 18.2: American Commitment in *Casablanca*." *Literature/Film Quarterly* 18.4 (1990): 275–276.

Day, Barry. "The Cult Movies: *Casablanca*." *Films and Filming* 20 (August 1974): 20–24.

Deming, Barbara. *Running Away from Myself: A Dream Portrait of America Drawn from Films of the Forties*. New York: Grossman, 1969.

Deutelbaum, Marshall. "The Visual Design Program of *Casablanca*." *Post Script* 9.3 (summer 1990): 36–48.

Dick, Bernard. *Anatomy of Film*. 2nd ed. New York: St. Martin's Press, 1990. 202–204.

Donnelly, William. "Love and Death in *Casablanca*." In *Persistence of Vision: A Collection of Film Criticism*. Ed. Joseph McBride (Madison: Wisconsin Film Society Press, 1968). 103–107.

Eastman, John. *Retakes: Behind the Scenes of 500 Classic Movies*. New York: Ballantine, 1989. 53–54.

Ebert, Roger. "Casablanca." In *Roger Ebert's Video Companion, 1996 Edition*. Kansas City: Andrews and McMeel, 1995. 841–842.

———. "Casablanca at Fifty." In *Casablanca: Script and Legend. The 50th Anniversary Edition*. Ed. Howard Koch. Woodstock, N.Y.: Overlook, 1992. 249–251.

Eco, Umberto. "*Casablanca*: Cult Movies and Intertextual Collage." *SubStance* 47 (1985): 3–12.

Edelson, Edward. *Tough Guys and Gals of the Movies*. Garden City, N.Y.: Doubleday, 1978.

Eidsvik, Charles. *Cineliteracy: Film Among the Arts*. New York: Random House, 1978. 6–7, 86–87 passim.

Ferguson, K. "Casablanca 50 Years Young." *Film Monthly* 4 (July 1992): 12–13.

Francisco, Charles. *You Must Remember This: The Filming of Casablanca*. Englewood Cliffs, N.J.: Prentice Hall, 1980.

Gabbard, Krin, and Glen O. Gabbard. "Play It Again, Sigmund: Psychoanalysis and the Classical Hollywood Text." *Journal of Popular Film and Television* 18 (spring 1990): 7–17.

———. *Psychiatry and the Cinema*. Chicago: University of Chicago Press, 1987.

Gassner, John, and Dudley Nichols, eds. *Best Film Plays of 1943–1944*. New York: Crown, 1945. 631–694.

Goldberg, Carl. "The Role of Passion in the Transformation of Anti-Heroes." *Journal of Evolutionary Psychology* (Pittsburgh) 9.1–2 (March 1989): 2–16.

Green, Gary L. "The Happiest of Happy Accidents? A Reevaluation of *Casablanca*." *Smithsonian Studies in American Art* 1.2 (fall 1987): 3–13.

Greenberg, Harvey R. "Casablanca: If It's So Schmaltzy, Why Am I Weeping?" In *The Movies on Your Mind*. New York: Saturday Review Press and E. P. Dutton, 1975. 79–105. Chapter on *Casablanca*; later reprinted with additional comments as "Cult Cinema: *Casablanca*—If It's So Schmaltzy, Why Am I Weeping?" Rpt. in *Screen Memories: Hollywood Cinema on the Psychoanalytic Couch*. New York: Columbia University Press, 1993. 39–66.

Greenberg, Joel. "Casey Robinson." Beverly Hills: American Film Institute Oral History Project, 1974.

———. "Writing for the Movies: Interview with Casey Robinson." *Focus on Film* 32.7 (April 1979): 7–24.

Grimes, William. "Buried Themes: Psychoanalyzing Movies." *New York Times* (December 23, 1991): C11.

Hamilton, William. "*Amor-Vincit-Omnia*, a Meditation on *Casablanca*." *Religious Humanism* 28.4 (1994): 171–179.

Hanson, Stephen L. "*Casablanca*." In *Magill's American Film Guide*. 5 vols. Ed. Frank N. Magill. Englewood Cliffs, N.J.: Salem, 1983. 1:606–608.

Harmetz, Aljean. *Round Up the Usual Suspects: The Making of Casablanca—Bogart, Bergman, and World War II*. New York: Hyperion, 1992.

———. "Round Up the Usual Suspects." In *Casablanca: Script and Legend. The 50th Anniversary Edition*. Ed. Howard Koch. Woodstock, N.Y.: Overlook, 1992. 267–268.

Haun, Harry. "The Man from *Casablanca* (Julius J. Epstein)." *Films in Review* 35.9 (November 1984): 514–525.

———. "Beyond *Casablanca*: Screenwriter Julius Epstein." *Horizon* 27.6 (July–August 1984): 54–57.

Haver, Ron. "Finally, the Truth About *Casablanca*." *American Film* 1.8 (June 1976): 10–16.

———. "*Casablanca* Revisited: Three Comments." *American Film* 2 (October 1976): 3–4.

Hendrickson, Paul. "For 'Casablanca'—Here's Looking at You, Howard Koch."*Washington Post* (September 29, 1979): B1–2.

Henreid, Paul, with Julius Fast. *Ladies Man*. New York: St. Martin's Press, 1984.

Hoberman, J. "On Casablanca." In *Casablanca: Script and Legend. The 50th Anniversary Edition*. Ed. Howard Koch. Woodstock, N.Y.: Overlook, 1992. 269–270.

Hogue, Peter. "I Bet They're Asleep All over America." *Film Comment* 27 (May–June 1991): 24–26.

Italie, H. "Casablanca." *Classic* 203 (May 1992): 26+.

Jennings, D. "Letters." *Films in Review* 40 (March 1989): 190–191.

"Julius J. Epstein, Screenwriter." In *Sound and the Cinema: The Coming of Sound to American Film*. Ed. Evan William Cameron. Pleasantville, N.Y.: Redgrave, 1980. 104–106.

Kawin, Bruce. *To Have and Have Not*. Madison: University of Wisconsin Press, 1980.

Kellman, Steve. "Everybody Comes to Roquentin's: *La Nausée* and *Casablanca*." *Mosaic* 16.1–2 (winter–spring 1983): 103–112.

Kinnard, Roy, and R. J. Vitone. "Casablanca." In *The American Films of Michael Curtiz*. Metuchen, N.J.: Scarecrow Press, 1986. 81–86.

Kinskey, Leonid. "*Casablanca*: Why It Lingers Deliciously in Memory 'As Time Goes By.'" *Movie Digest* 1.5 (September 1972): 118–133.

Kobal, John. *Romance and the Cinema*. London: Vista, 1973.

Koch, Howard. "Notes on the Production of *Casablanca*." In *Persistence of Vision: A Collection of Film Criticism*. Ed. Joseph McBride. Madison: Wisconsin Film Society Press, 1968. 93–95.

———. "Excerpts from the Original Treatment." In *Persistence of Vision: A Collection of Film Criticism*. Ed. Joseph McBride. Madison: Wisconsin Film Society Press, 1968. 97–100.

———. *Casablanca: Script and Legend*. Woodstock, N.Y.: Overlook Press, 1973.

———. "In Conclusion: What Happened to the Story in Contemporary Film?" In *Casablanca: Script and Legend*. Woodstock, N.Y.: Overlook Press, 1973. 187–204.

———. "The Making of America's Favorite Movie: Here's Looking at You, *Casablanca*." *New York* (April 30, 1973): 74–78.

———. *As Time Goes By: Memoirs of a Writer*. New York: Harcourt Brace Jovanovich, 1979. 76–84.

———. "*Casablanca*? They'll Play it Forever, Sam." *Screen Actor* 25.1 (1986): 31.

Lapsley, Robert, and Michael Westlake. "From *Casablanca* to *Pretty Woman*: The Politics of Romance." *Screen* 33.1 (spring 1992): 27–49.

Leamer, Laurence. *As Time Goes By: The Life of Ingrid Bergman*. New York: Harper & Row, 1986. 81–91.

Lebo, Harlan. *Casablanca: Behind the Scenes*. New York: Simon & Schuster, 1992.

Leiva, Steven Paul. "Richard J. Anobile Blowing Up in Hollywood." *Cinephile* (Anaheim, Calif.) 1.9 (February 1977): 1, 6, 9, 11.

Lindstrom, Pia, as told to George Christy. "My Mother, Ingrid Bergman." *Good Housekeeping* (October 1964): 80+.

"Lose it Again, Sam: *Casablanca* Libel Suit Again Kayoed." *Variety* 284 (September 8, 1976): 5, 24.

Maltby, Richard. *Harmless Entertainment: Hollywood and the Ideology of Consensus*. Metuchen, N.J.: Scarecrow, 1983. 192–217.

Margolick, D. "Writer Who Created Rick's Cafe Battles in Court to Play It Again." *New York Times* (October 10, 1985): B1+.

Matthews, P. "You Must Remember This." *Modern Review* (London) 1.4 (summer 1992): 32.

McArthur, Colin. *The Casablanca File*. London: Half Brick Images, 1992.

McBride, Joseph. *Persistence of Vision: A Collection of Film Criticism*. Madison: Wisconsin Film Society Press, 1968.

McCarthy, Abigail. "Of All the Gin Joints." *Commonweal* (June 5, 1992): 10–11.

McVay, D. "Revival: *The Maltese Falcon* and *Casablanca*." *Focus on Film* 30 (June 1978): 4–7.

Meyer, William R. "Curtiz, Michael." In *Warner Brothers Directors: The Hard Boiled, the Comic, and the Weepers*. New Rochelle, N.Y.: Arlington House, 1978. 74–107.

Middleton, David. "*Casablanca*: The Function of Myth in a Popular Classic." *New Orleans Review* 13.1 (1986): 11–18.

Miller, Frank. *Casablanca: As Time Goes By*. Atlanta: Turner Publishing, 1992.

Morrison, Rachela. "*Casablanca* Meets Star Wars: The Blakean Dialectics of Blade Runner." *Literature/Film Quarterly* 18.1 (1990): 2–10.

Morrow, L. "Essay: We'll Always Have *Casablanca*." *Time* (December 27, 1982): 76.

Osborne, Richard E. *The* Casablanca *Companion: The Movie Classic and Its Place in History*. Indianapolis: Riebel Roque, 1997.

Parshall, Peter F. "East Meets West: *Casablanca* vs. *The Seven Samurai*." *Literature / Film Quarterly* 17.4 (1989): 274–280.

Peary, Danny. "Casablanca." In *Cult Movies: The Classics, the Sleepers, the Weird, and the Wonderful*. New York: Dell, 1981. 47–50.

Polan, Dana. *Power and Paranoia: History, Narrative and the American Cinema, 1940–1950*. New York: Columbia University Press, 1986. 74–76, 155–156 passim.

Polunsky, B. "Flicker Footnotes." *Classic Film Collector* 56 (fall 1977): 25.

Prince, Stephen. "The Codes of Continuity Editing." In *Movies and Mean: An Introduction to Film*. Boston: Allyn and Bacon, 1997. 122–127.

Raskin, Richard. "*Casablanca* and United States Foreign Policy." *Film History* 4.2 (1990): 153–161.

Ray, Robert B. *A Certain Tendency of the Hollywood Cinema, 1930–1980*. Princeton: Princeton University Press, 1985. 89–112.

Reeves, Jimmie L. "Casablanca (1942)." *Cinema Texas Notes* (October 12, 1981): 57–62.

Robertson, James C. *The Casablanca Man: The Cinema of Michael Curtiz*. London and New York: Routledge, 1993.

Rosenzweig, Sidney. Casablanca *and Other Major Films of Michael Curtiz*. Ann Arbor: UMI Research Press, 1982. 77–95.

Ross, Chuck. "The Great Script Tease." *Film Comment* 18.6 (November–December 1982): 15–19.

Rubinstein, Lenny. "A Second Look: *Casablanca*." *Cineaste* 8 (summer 1977): 34–35.

Sackett, Susan. "Casablanca." In *The Hollywood Reporter Book of Box Office Hits*. New York: Billboard Books, 1990. 41.

Sakall, Szoke. *The Story of Cuddles*. Trans. Paul Tabori. London: Cassell, 1954.

Sakowski, S. "Casablanca." *Cinema* 36 (February 1982): 35–36.

Sarris, Andrew. *The American Cinema*. New York: Dutton, 1968. 176.

Schickel, Richard. "Some Nights in Casablanca." In *Favorite Movies: Critics' Choice*. Ed. Philip Nobile. New York: Macmillan, 1973. 114–125.

Sennett, Ted. *Masters of Menace: Greenstreet and Lorre*. New York: Dutton, 1979. 77–81.

Sherman, Eric. "Howard Koch." Beverly Hills: American Film Institute Oral History Project, 1974.

Siegel, Jeff. *The Casablanca Companion: The Movie and More*. Dallas: Taylor Publishing, 1992.

Sklar, Robert. *City Boys: Cagney, Bogart, Garfield*. Princeton: Princeton University Press, 1992. 137–143.

Smith, J. "Keats on Casablanca." *Poetry Review* 84.2 (1994): 86.

Smith, Russell, Jane Sumner, and Philip Wuntch. "The Return of Casablanca." *Dallas Morning News* (April 11, 1992): 5C, 10C.

Solomon, Stanley. "Casablanca." In *Beyond Formula: American Film Genres*. New York: Harcourt Brace Jovanovich, 1976. 278–281.

Sorel, E. "Movie Classics." Casablanca. *Esquire* 94 (November 1980): 130.

Steele, Joseph Henry. *Ingrid Bergman: An Intimate Portrait*. New York: McKay, 1959.

Stickney, John. "Last Word on *Last Tango* and *Casablanca*." *Mademoiselle* 77 (July 1973): 128–129, 150–151.

Telotte, J. P. "*Casablanca* and the Larcenous Cult Film." *Michigan Quarterly Review* 26.2 (1987): 357–368. Rev. in *The Cult Film Experience: Beyond All Reason*. Ed. J. P. Telotte. Austin: University Texas Press, 1991. 43–54.

———. *The Cult Film Experience*. Austin: University Texas Press, 1991. (Reprints with some changes to the previous item and includes articles by Larry Vonalt, James Card, and T. J. Ross.)

Thomas, Sam, ed. *Best American Screenplays*. New York: Crown, 1986.

Thomson, David. *America in the Dark: Hollywood and the Gift of Unreality*. New York: Morrow, 1977.

Tillotson, Jerry. "Cry for *Casablanca*." *Hollywood Studio* 17.2 (1984): 20–21.

Turim, Maureen. *Flashbacks in Film: Memory and History*. New York and London: Routledge, 1989. 126–127.

van Gelder, Peter. "Casablanca." In *That's Hollywood: A Behind-the-Scenes Look at 60 of the Greatest Films of all Time*. New York: Harper, 1990. 43–47.

Vonalt, Larry. "Looking Both Ways in Casablanca." In *The Cult Film Experience: Beyond All Reason*. Ed. J. P. Telotte. Austin: University Texas Press, 1991. 55–64.

Wallis, Hal, with Charles Higham. *Starmaker*. New York: Macmillan, 1980. 83–92.

Weisman, John. "60 Minutes Correspondents Pick . . . Their Finest Hours." *TV Guide* (February 25, 1981): 4–7, 9.

Willson, Robert F., Jr. "Disarming Scenes in *Richard III* and *Casablanca*." *Shakepeare-on-Film Newsletter* 10.1 (December 1985): 4.

Wood, Michael. *America in the Movies: or "Santa Maria, It Had Slipped My Mind."* New York: Basic Books, 1975. 24–29 passim.

Wright, J. "Casablanca (Though the Facts Don't Fit)." *Poetry Australia* 77 (1981): 22–23.

Youngking, Stephen D., James Bigwood, and Raymond G. Cabana, Jr. *The Films of Peter Lorre*. Secaucus, N.J.: Citadel, 1982.

Zinman, David. "Casablanca." In *50 Classic Motion Pictures: The Stuff That Dreams Are Made Of*. New York: Crown, 1970. 275–278.

Conflict (1945)

Sennett, Ted. *Masters of Menace: Greenstreet and Lorre*. New York: Dutton, 1979. 118–124.

Dark Passage (1947)

Deming, Barbara. *Running Away from Myself: A Dream Portrait Drawn from the Films of the Forties.* New York: Grossman, 1969.
Dick, Bernard F. "Dark Passage." In *Anatomy of Film.* 2nd ed. New York: St. Martin's Press, 1990. 37–38.
McGarry, Eileen. "Dark Passage." In *Film Noir.* Ed. Alain Silver and Elizabeth Ward. Woodstock, N.Y.: Overlook, 1979. 83–84.
Polan, Dana. "Blind Insights and Dark Passages: The Problems of Placement in Forties Films." *Velvet Light Trap* 20 (1983): 27–33.
———. "Blind Insights and Dark Passages: The Problems of Placement." In *Power and Paranoia: History, Narrative, and the American Cinema, 1940–1950.* New York: Columbia University Press, 1986. 193–202 passim.
Sklar, Robert. *City Boys: Cagney, Bogart, Garfield.* Princeton: Princeton University Press, 1992. 192–193.
Telotte, J. P. "Seeing in a *Dark Passage.*" *Film Criticism* 9.2 (winter 1984–1985):15–27.
———. "Seeing in a *Dark Passage.*" In *Voices in the Dark: The Narrative Patterns of Film Noir.* Urbana and Champaign: University of Illinois Press, 1989. 117–118, 120–133.

Dark Victory (1939)

Almendarez, Valentin. "Dark Victory (1939)." *Cinema Texas Program Notes* (February 2, 1976): 51–60.
Dick, Bernard F. *Dark Victory.* Madison: University of Wisconsin Press, 1981.
Greenberg, Joel. "Writing for the Movies: Casey Robinson." *Focus on Film* 32 (April 1979): 11–12.
Haskell, Molly. *From Reverence to Rape: The Treatment of Women in the Movies.* New York: Holt, Rinehart and Winston, 1974.
Holdstein, D. H. "Women's Pictures: The Perfect Moment." *Jump Cut* 32 (April 1986): 22–24.
Johnson, Julie. "Dark Victory." In *Magill's American Film Guide*, 5 vols. Ed. Frank N. Magill. Englewood Cliffs, N.J.: Salem, 1983. 2:819–821.
Philbert, B. "Dark Victory." *Cinematographe* 80 (July–August 1982): 60–61.
Robinson, Casey. "Dark Victory." *Australian Journal of Screen Theory* 4 (1978): 5–10.
Rosterman, Robert. "Another Great Film from 1939." *Hollywood Studio* 22.3 (1989): 18–19.
TheBerge, Rita. "Dark Victory (1939)." *Cinema Texas Program Notes* (September 27, 1979): 69–74.

Dead End (1937)

Affron, Charles, and Mirella Jona Affron. *Sets in Motion.* New Brunswick, N.J.: Rutgers University Press, 1995. 173–177.
Anderegg, Michael. *William Wyler.* Boston: Twayne, 1979.

Cohen, Joan. "*Dead End.*" In *Magill's American Film Guide*. 5 vols. Ed. Frank N. Magill. Englewood Cliffs, N.J.: Salem, 1983. 2:849–851.
Greene, Graham. "Dead End." In *Graham Greene on Film: Collected Film Criticism 1935–1940*. Ed. John Russell Taylor. New York: Simon & Schuster, 1972. 180–181.
Trent, Paul. *The Thirties: Those Fabulous Movie Years*. Barre, Mass.: Barre Publishing, 1975.

Deadline—U.S.A. (1952)

Dixon, W. W. *The Early Film Criticism of François Truffaut*. Bloomington: Indiana University Press, 1993. 22. (The seeds for this book appeared as an article by the same name in the *New Orleans Review* 16.1 [1989]: 5–32.)

Dead Reckoning (1947)

Dick, Bernard. "Columbia's Dark Ladies and the Femmes Fatales of *Film Noir*." *Literature/Film Quarterly* 23.3 (1995): 155–162.
Krutnik, Frank. "A Problem in 'Algebra': *Dead Reckoning* and the Regimentation of the Masculine." In *In a Lonely Street: Film Noir, Genre, Masculinity*. London: Routledge, 1991. 164–181.
Macek, Carl. "Dead Reckoning." In *Film Noir*. Ed. Alain Silver and Elizabeth Ward. Woodstock, N.Y.: Overlook, 1979. 85–86.
Telotte, J. P. "*Film Noir* at Columbia: Fashion and Innovation." In *Columbia Pictures: Portrait of a Studio*. Ed. Bernard F. Dick. Lexington: University Press of Kentucky, 1992. 106–117.
Tuska, Jon. *The Detective in Hollywood*. Garden City, N.Y.: Doubleday, 1978.

The Desperate Hours (1955)

Anderegg, Michael. *William Wyler*. Boston: Twayne, 1979.
Barker, Julie. "*Desperate Hours*." In *Magill's American Film Guide*. 5 vols. Ed. Frank N. Magill. Englewood Cliffs, N.J.: Salem, 1983. 2:886–889.
Dworkin, Martin. "The Desperate Hours and the Violent Screen." *Shenandoah* 11 (1960): 39–48.
Sklar, Robert. *City Boys: Cagney, Bogart, Garfield*. Princeton: Princeton University Press, 1992. 248–249.
Wuntch, Philip. "Pretty Desperate." *Dallas Morning News* 8 (October 1990): 5–6C.

The Enforcer (1951)

"Bogey Sides the Laws in *The Enforcer*." *Cue* (December 2, 1950): 16.
Vernet, M. "The Filmic Transaction: On the Opening of Film Noirs." *Velvet Light Trap* 20 (summer 1983): 2–9.

The Harder They Fall (1956)

Lucas, Blake. "The Harder They Fall." In *Magill's American Film Guide*. 5 vols. Ed. Frank N. Magill. Englewood Cliffs, N.J.: Salem, 1983. 2:1389–1391.

Sklar, Robert. *City Boys: Cagney, Bogart, Garfield*. Princeton: Princeton University Press, 1992. 250.

High Sierra (1941)

Alley, Kenneth. "High Sierra—Swan Song for an Era." *Journal of Popular Film* 5.3–4 (1976): 248–262.

Canham, Kingsley. *The Hollywood Professionals*. Vol. 1: *Michael Curtiz, Raoul Walsh, Henry Hathaway*. New York: A&S Barnes, 1973.

Clarens, Carlos. *Crime Movies: From Griffith to the Godfather and Beyond*. New York: Norton, 1980. 168–171.

Conley, Tom. *Film Hieroglyphs: Ruptures in Classical Cinema*. Minneapolis: University of Minnesota Press, 1991. 167–177.

Corliss, Richard. *The Hollywood Screenwriters*. New York: Avon, 1972. 297–298.

Dick, Bernard. *Anatomy of Film*. 2nd ed. New York: St. Martin's Press, 1990. 123–124.

Druxman, Michael B. *Make It Again, Sam*. South Brunswick, N.J.: A&S Barnes, 1975. 69–74.

Godfrey, T. "TAD at the Movies." *Armchair Detective* 17.1 (1984): 69–72.

Gomery, Douglas, ed. *High Sierra*. Madison: University of Wisconsin Press, 1979.

Grobel, Lawrence. *The Hustons*. New York: Avon, 1989. 209–212.

Hermann, Rick. "He's from Back Home": Man and Myth in *High Sierra*." *Movietone News* 45 (November 1975): 34–37.

Hogue, Peter. "Big Shots." *Movietone News* 45 (November 1975): 14–21.

Kirgo, Julie. "High Sierra." In *Film Noir*. Ed. Alain Silver and Elizabeth Ward. Woodstock, N.Y.: Overlook, 1979. 125–126.

Laemmle, Ann. "High Sierra (1941)." *Cinema Texas Program Notes* (April 5, 1979): 97–102.

Mate, Ken. "Memories, Success . . . and Anonymity." *Calendar, Los Angeles Times* (April 11, 1982): 31–34.

———, and Pat McGilligan. "Burnett." *Film Comment* 19.1 (January–February 1983): 58–68.

McGilligan, Patrick, Debra Weiner, and Dix Bruce. "Raoul Walsh Remembers Warners." *Velvet Light Trap* 15 (fall 1975): 42–49.

Random, Henry. "The Simple Art of Dying, Humphrey Bogart Style." In *Memoirs of a Moviegoer*. San Francisco: Editorial Service Bureau, 1975. 88–97.

Sarris, Andrew. "Notes on the Auteur Theory in 1962." In *The Primal Screen*. New York: Simon & Schuster, 1973. 53.

Shadoian, Jack. "High Sierra." In *Dreams and Dead-Ends: The American Gangster/Crime Film*. Cambridge, Mass.: MIT Press, 1977. 67–82.

Shales, Tom. *The American Film Heritage: Impressions from the American Film Archives*. Washington: Acropolis Books, 1972. 100–103.

Shepler, Michael. "*High Sierra*." In *Magill's American Film Guide*. 5 vols. Ed. Frank N. Magill. Englewood Cliffs, N.J.: Salem, 1983. 2:1448–1450.

Simons, John L. "Henry on Bogie: Reality and Romance in 'Dream Song No. 9' and *High Sierra*." *Literature/Film Quarterly* 5.3 (summer 1977): 269–271.

In a Lonely Place (1950)

Ames, Christopher. *Movies About the Movies: Hollywood Reflected*. Lexington: University Press of Kentucky, 1997. 164–192.
Andrew, Geoff. *The Films of Nicholas Ray: The Poet of Nightfall*. London: Letts, 1991. 55–61.
Dick, Bernard. "Columbia's Dark Ladies and the Femmes Fatales of *Film Noir*." *Literature/Film Quarterly* 23.3 (1995): 155–162.
Draper, Ellen. "In a Lonely Place." *Cinema Texas Program Notes* (April 21, 1980): 61–65.
Eisenschitz, Bernard. *Nicholas Ray: An American Journey*. Trans. Tom Milne. London and Boston: Faber and Faber, 1993. 133–146. Originally published in 1990 as *Roman Américain: Les vies de Nicholas Ray*. Christian Bourgois Editeur & Longue Distance.
Kirgo, Julie, and Alain Silver. "In a Lonely Place." In *Film Noir*. Ed. Alain Silver and Elizabeth Ward. Woodstock, N.Y.: Overlook, 1979. 144–146.
Langlois, G. "Nicholas Ray (1911–1979)." *Avant-Scene* (May 1, 1981): 209–240.
McVay, Nicholas. "Outcast State: Nicholas Ray's *In a Lonely Place*." *Bright Lights* 7 (1978): 4–7.
Palmer, James W. "*In a Lonely Place*: Paranoia in the Dream Factory." *Literature/Film Quarterly* 13.3 (1985): 200–207.
Peary, Danny. "In a Lonely Place." In *Cult Movies* 3. New York: Fireside, 1988. 113–116.
Perkins, V. F. "In a Lonely Place." In *The Movie Book of* Film Noir. Ed. Ian Cameron. London: Studio Vista, 1992. 222–231.
Polan, Dana. *In a Lonely Place*. London: British Film Institute, 1993.
Shepler, Michael. "*In a Lonely Place*." In *Magill's American Film Guide*. 5 vols. Ed. Frank N. Magill. Englewood Cliffs, N.J.: Salem, 1983. 3:1581–1583.
Sklar, Robert. *City Boys: Cagney, Bogart, Garfield*. Princeton: Princeton University Press, 1992. 233–238.
Telotte, J. P. "*Film Noir* and the Dangers of Discourse." *Quarterly Review of Film Studies* 9.2 (1984): 101–112. Rpt. with changes in *Voices in the Dark: The Narrative Patterns of Film Noir*. Urbana: University of Illinois Press, 1989. 189–194.
———. "The Displaced Voice in *In a Lonely Place*." *South Atlantic Review* 54.1 (1989): 1–12.
Thomson, David. "In a Lonely Place." *Sight and Sound* 48.4 (autumn 1979): 215–220.
Williamson, Judith. "Lean Cuts." *New Statesman* (January 22, 1988): 27–28.

Key Largo (1948)

Clarens, Carlos. *Crime Movies: From Griffith to The Godfather and Beyond*. New York: Norton, 1980. 224.
Cohen, Joan. "Key Largo." In *Film Noir*. Ed. Alain Silver and Elizabeth Ward. Woodstock, N.Y.: Overlook, 1979. 150–151.

Fargo, Lawrence, Jr. "*Key Largo.*" In *Magill's American Film Guide*. 5 vols. Ed. Frank N. Magill. Englewood Cliffs, N.J.: Salem, 1983. 3:1736–1739.
———. "Key Largo." In *Cinema: Great Directors*. Ed. Frank Magill. Pasadena, Calif.: Salem Softbacks, 1981. 269–272.
Grobel, Lawrence. *The Hustons*. New York: Avon, 1989. 295–297, 305–317.
Laskas, Kristin. "Key Largo (1948)." *Cinema Texas Program Notes* (April 13, 1976): 103–108.
Nichols, Nina. "Key Largo (1948)." *Cinema Texas Program Notes* (October 22, 1979): 29–34.
Schatz, Thomas. "*Key Largo* and *White Heat*: The Gangster's Epitaph." In *Hollywood Genres: Formulas, Filmmaking, and the Studio System*. New York: Random House, 1981. 104–110.
Sklar, Robert. *City Boys: Cagney, Bogart, Garfield*. Princeton: Princeton University Press, 1992. 228–229.
Ward, L. E. "The Great Films: *Key Largo* (1948)." *Classic* 144 (June 1987): 46–47.

Kid Galahad (1937)

Kinnard, Roy, and R. J. Vitone. "Kid Galahad." In *The American Films of Michael Curtiz*. Metuchen, N.J.: Scarecrow Press, 1986. 41–42.

King of the Underworld (1939)

Calanquin, L. "Best of the B's: King of the Underworld." *Classic* 120 (June 1985): 9+.
Nielsen, R. "Ray's Way: Vincent Sherman and King of the Underworld." *Classic* 156 (June 1988): 56.

Knock on Any Door (1949)

Andrew, Geoff. *The Films of Nicholas Ray: The Poet of Nightfall*. London: Letts, 1991. 41–48.
Eisenschitz, Bernard. "Knock on Any Door." In *Nicholas Ray: An American Journey*. Trans. Tom Milne. London and Boston: Faber and Faber, 1993. 111–118. Originally published 1990.
Lucas, Blake. "Knock on Any Door." In *Film Noir*. Ed. Alain Silver and Elizabeth Ward. Woodstock, N.Y.: Overlook, 1979. 161–162.
Sklar, Robert. *City Boys: Cagney, Bogart, Garfield*. Princeton: Princeton University Press, 1992. 230–231.
Wilmington, Michael. "Nicholas Ray: The Years at RKO." *Velvet Light Trap* 10 (fall 1973): 46–53.

The Maltese Falcon (1941)

Abramson, Leslie H. "Two Birds of a Feather: Hammett's and Huston's *The Maltese Falcon*." *Literature/Film Quarterly* 16.2 (1988): 112–118.

Affron, Charles, and Mirella Jona Affron. *Sets in Motion*. New Brunswick, N.J.: Rutgers University Press, 1995. 46–48.

Anobile, Richard J., ed. *The Maltese Falcon*. New York: Flare Books, 1974.

Archer, Eugene. "John Huston—The Hemingway Tradition in American Film." *Film Culture* 19 (1959): 66–101.

———. "Taking Life Seriously." *Films and Filming* 5.12 (September 1959): 13–14, 28, 35.

———. "Small People in a Big World." *Films and Filming* 6.1 (October 1959): 9–10, 25, 34.

Astor, Mary. *A Life on Film*. New York: Delacorte, 1971. 159–166.

Basinger, Jeanine. *American Cinema: One Hundred Years of Filmmaking*. New York: Rizzoli, 1994. 209–215.

Bauer, Stephen F., Leon Balter, and Winslow Hunt. "The Detective Film as Myth: *The Maltese Falcon* and Sam Spade." *Am Imago* 35.3 (1978): 275–296.

Behlmer, Rudy. "The Stuff That Dreams Are Made Of." In *The Maltese Falcon. America's Favorite Movies: Behind the Scenes*. New York: Ungar, 1982. 135–153.

———. *Inside Warner Bros. (1935–1951)*. New York: Simon & Schuster, 1985. 149–159.

Benaquist, Lawrence. "Function and Index in Huston's *The Maltese Falcon*." *Film Criticism* 6.2 (1982): 45–50.

Bick, Ilsa J. "The Beam That Fell and Other Crises in *The Maltese Falcon*." In *The Maltese Falcon, John Huston, Director*. Ed. William Luhr. New Brunswick, N.J.: Rutgers University Press, 1995. 181–199.

Blake, Richard A. "The Detective Story: *The Maltese Falcon*." In *Screening America: Reflections on Five Classic Films*. New York: Paulist Press, 1991. 205–239.

Boon, Kevin. "In Debt to Dashiell: John Huston's Adaptation of *The Maltese Falcon*." *Creative Screenwriting* 4.2 (summer 1997): 99–115.

Bordwell, David, and Kristin Thompson. *Film Art: An Introduction*. 5th ed. New York: McGraw-Hill, 1997. 288–293.

Bottiggi, William D. "The Importance of 'C—ing' in Earnest: A Comparison of *The Maltese Falcon* and *Chinatown*." *Armchair Detective* 14.1 (winter 1981): 86–87.

Brown, William H., Jr. "*The Maltese Falcon*." In *Cinema: The Novel into Film*. Ed. Frank N. Magill. Pasadena, CA: Salem Softbacks, 1980. 299–302.

———. "*The Maltese Falcon*." In *Magill's American Film Guide*. 5 vols. Ed. Frank N. Magill. Englewood Cliffs, N.J.: Salem, 1983. 3:2050–2053.

———. "Maltese Falcon." *Cinema: Great Directors*. Ed. Frank Magill. Pasadena, Calif.: Salem Softbacks, 1981. 273–276.

Cahill, Marie. *Hollywood Classics*: The Maltese Falcon. New York: Smithmark, 1991.

Collins, G. "Falcons as Fake as the Real Thing." *New York Times* (November 1, 1988): C17.

Cooper, Stephen. "Sex/Knowledge/Power in the Detective Genre." *Film Quarterly* 42.3 (1989): 23–31.

———. "Flitcraft, Spade, and *The Maltese Falcon*: John Huston's Adaptation." In *Perspectives on John Huston*. Ed. Stephen Cooper. New York: G. K. Hall, 1994. 117–132.

Crowther, Bosley. "*The Maltese Falcon*." In *The Great Films: Fifty Golden Years of Motion Pictures*. New York: G. P. Putnam, 1967. 153–158.

Deming, Barbara. *Running Away from Myself: A Dream Portrait Drawn from the Films of the Forties*. New York: Grossman, 1969. 144–154.
Downer, Alan S. "The Monitor Image." In *Man and the Movies*. Ed. W. R. Robinson. Baton Rouge: Louisiana State University Press, 1967. Rpt. New York: Penguin, 1969. 13–30.
Druxman, Michael B. *Make It Again, Sam*. South Brunswick, NJ: A&S Barnes, 1975. 114–119.
Edelson, Edward. *Tough Guys and Gals of the Movies*. New York: Doubleday, 1978. 1–5 passim.
Everson, William K. *The Detective in Film*. Secaucus, N.J.: Citadel Press, 1972. 39–46.
———. "Rediscovery: *Blues in the Night*." *Films in Review* 31.3 (March 1980): 160–162.
Eyles, Allen. "Great Films of the Century: *The Maltese Falcon*." *Films and Filming* 11.2 (November 1964): 45–50.
Flint, Peter B. "Mary Astor, 81, Is Dead, Star of *The Maltese Falcon*." *New York Times* (September 26, 1987): 34.
Friedrich, Otto. "The Stuff Dreams Are Made Of: How Chance Created a Classic." *Washington Post* (June 14, 1987): H1.
Gale, Stephen. "*The Maltese Falcon*: Melodrama or Film Noir?" *Literature/Film Quarterly* 24.2 (1996): 145–147.
Giannetti, Louis. "Roughing It: The Cinema of John Huston." In *Masters of the American Cinema*. Englewood Cliffs, N.J.: Prentice-Hall, 1981. 247–266.
Godfrey, Lionel. "Martinis Without Olives." *Films and Filming* (April 1968): 10–14.
Goldberg, Joe. "The Death of Sam Spade." *Evergreen Review* 7.28 (January–February 1963): 107–116.
Gow, Gordon. "Pursuit of the Falcon." *Films and Filming* 20.6 (March 1974): 56–58.
Greenberg, Harvey R. *The Movies on Your Mind*. New York: Saturday Review Press and E. P. Dutton, 1975. 53–78. Reprinted with additional comments as "The Detective Film: *The Maltese Falcon*—Even Paranoids Have Enemies." In *Screen Memories: Hollywood Cinema on the Psychoanalytic Couch*. New York: Columbia University Press, 1993. 67–92.
Grobel, Lawrence. *The Hustons*. New York: Avon, 1989. 212–223.
Jameson, R. T. "John Huston." *Film Comment* 16 (May–June 1980): 25–56.
Johnson, W. "Sound and Image." *Film Quarterly* 43.1 (1989): 24–35.
Kael, Pauline. "The Maltese Falcon." In *Kiss Kiss Bang Bang*. Boston: Little, Brown, 1968.
———. "Movieland—The Bums' Paradise." In *Reeling*. New York: Atlantic Monthly/Little, Brown, 1976. 182–190.
———. *5001 Nights at the Movies*. New York: Holt, Rinehart and Winston, 1982.
Kaminsky, Stuart. *John Huston: Maker of Magic*. Boston: Houghton Mifflin, 1978. 19–26.
———. "The Maltese Falcon." In *International Dictionary of Films and Filmmakers. Films*. Ed. Christopher Lyon and Susan Doll. Chicago: St. James Press, 1984. 1: 276.
Kirgo, Julie. "The Maltese Falcon." In *Film Noir*. Ed. Alain Silver and Elizabeth Ward. Woodstock, N.Y.: Overlook, 1979. 181–182.
Krutnik, Frank. *In a Lonely Street: Film Noir, Genre, Masculinity*. London: Routledge, 1991. 93–95 passim.

Luhr, William. "Tracking *The Maltese Falcon*: Classical Hollywood Narration and Sam Spade." In *Close Viewings: An Anthology of New Film Criticism*. Ed. Peter Lehman. Tallahassee: Florida State University Press, 1990. 7–22.

———, ed. *The Maltese Falcon: John Huston, Director*. New Brunswick, N.J.: Rutgers University Press, 1995.

Marcus, Stephen. Introduction to *The Continental Op*. New York: Vintage, 1974, 1992.

Maxfield, James F. "La Belle Dame Sans Merci and the Neurotic Knight: Characterization in *The Maltese Falcon*." *Literature/Film Quarterly* 17.4 (1989): 253–260.

McVay, Douglas. "*The Maltese Falcon* and *Casablanca*." *Focus on Film* 30 (June 1978): 4–7.

Naremore, James. "John Huston and *The Maltese Falcon*." In *Reflections in a Male Eye: John Huston and the American Experience*. Ed. Gaylyn Studlar and David Desser. Washington, D.C.: Smithsonian, 1993. 119–135.

———. "John Huston and *The Maltese Falcon*." *Literature/Film Quarterly* 1.3 (July 1973): 239–249.

Nolan, William F. *John Huston: King Rebel*. Los Angeles: Sherbourne Press, 1965.

———. *Dashiel Hammett: A Casebook*. Santa Barbara, Calif.: McNally and Loftin, 1969. 102–105.

Peary, Danny. "The Maltese Falcon." In *Cult Movies: The Classics, the Sleepers, the Weird, and the Wonderful*. New York: Dell, 1981. 219–222.

Phillips, William H. *Analyzing Films: A Practical Guide*. New York: Holt, Rinehart and Winston, 1985.

Pratley, Gerald. *The Cinema of John Huston*. South Brunswick, N.J.: A&S Barnes, 1977. 38–48.

Random, Henry. "Real Private Eyes, and the Kind You See in the Movies." In *Memoirs of a Moviegoer*. San Francisco: Editorial Service Bureau, 1975. 98–133.

Reeves, Jimmie L. "The Maltese Falcon (1941)." *Cinema Texas Program Notes* (October 20, 1981): 73–78.

Richardson, Carl. "Film Noir in the Studio: *The Maltese Falcon*." *Autopsy: An Element of Realism in Film Noir*. Metuchen, N.J., & London: Scarecrow, 1992. 37–75.

Rivkin, Allen, and Laura Kerr. *Hello Hollywood!* New York: Doubleday, 1962.

Sarris, Andrew. *The American Cinema: Directors and Directions, 1929–1968*. New York: E. P. Dutton, 1968.

Schatz, Thomas. "The Hardboiled Prototype: Huston's *The Maltese Falcon*." In *Hollywood Genres: Formulas, Filmmaking, and the Studio System*. New York: Random House, 1981. 126–130.

Sennett, Ted. *Masters of Menace: Greenstreet and Lorre*. New York: Dutton, 1979. 52–74.

Solomon, Stanley. "The Private Eye Genre: Huston's *The Maltese Falcon*." In *The Film Idea*. New York: Harcourt Brace Jovanovich, 1972. 210–221.

———. "The Maltese Falcon." In *Beyond Formula: American Film Genres*. New York: Harcourt Brace Jovanovich, 1976. 215–218.

Steinberg, Barry. "Henry Blanke." Beverly Hills: University of California/AFI Oral History Project, 1969.

Taylor, John Russell. "John Huston and the Figure in the Carpet." *Sight and Sound* 38.2 (spring 1969): 70–73.

Tuska, Jon. *The Detective in Hollywood*. Garden City, N.Y.: Doubleday, 1978.

Tyler, Parker. *The Hollywood Hallucination.* New York: Simon & Schuster, 1970. 128–136. Originally published in 1944.

van Gelder, Peter. "The Maltese Falcon." In *That's Hollywood: A Behind-the-Scenes Look at 60 of the Greatest Films of All Time.* New York: Harper, 1990. 182–186.

Vernet, Marc. "The Filmic Transaction: On the Openings of Film Noirs." Trans. David Rodowick. *Velvet Light Trap* 20 (Summer 1983): 2–9.

Wallis, Hal, with Charles Higham. *Starmaker.* New York: Macmillan, 1980. 109–111.

Watkins, Susan. "Brigid in the Book and 1941 Film Version of *The Maltese Falcon.*" In William H. Phillips, *Analyzing Films: A Practical Guide.* New York: Holt, Rinehart and Winston, 1985. 151–153.

Wexman, Virginia Wright. "The Transfer from One Medium to Another: *The Maltese Falcon* from Fiction to Film." *Library Quarterly* 15.1 (January 1975): 46–55.

———. "Kinesics and Film Acting: Humphrey Bogart in *The Maltese Falcon* and *The Big Sleep.*" *Journal of Popular Film and Television* 7.1 (1978): 42–55.

———. "Courtship Conventions and Performance Styles: Humphrey Bogart in *The Maltese Falcon* and *The Big Sleep.*" *Creating the Couple: Love, Marriage, and Hollywood Performance.* Princeton: Princeton University Press, 1993. 25–36.

Wood, George. "A New Look at an Old Genre." *Journal of the University Film Association* 27.2 (1975): 39, 46.

Zinman, David. *50 Classic Motion Pictures: The Stuff That Dreams Are Made Of.* New York: Crown, 1970. 33–34.

Marked Woman (1937)

Baumgarten, Marjorie. "Women Working: A Thirties Double Feature." *Texas Cinema Program Notes* (October 18, 1978): 19–25.

Da, Lottie, and Jan Alexander. *Bad Girls of the Silver Screen.* New York: Carroll and Graf, 1989.

Eckert, Charles W. "The Anatomy of a Proletarian Film: Warner's *Marked Woman.*" *Film Quarterly* 17.2 (winter 1973–1974): 10–24. Rpt. in *Movies and Methods.* Ed. Bill Nichols. Berkeley: University of California Press. 2:407–425.

Haralovich, Mary Beth. "The Proletarian Woman's Film of the 1930s: Contending with Censorship and Entertainment." *Screen* 31.2 (1990): 172–187.

———, and Cathy Root Klaprat. "*Marked Woman* and *Jezebel*: The Spectator-in-the-Trailer." *Enclitic* 5/6.1/2 (1981–1982): 66–74.

Kay, Karyn. "Sisters of the Night." *Velvet Light Trap* 17 (winter 1977): 48–52. Rpt. from *Velvet Light Trap* 6 (Fall 1972) and in *Movies and Methods.* Ed. Bill Nichols. Berkeley: University of California Press, 1976. 1:185–194.

Neilsen, R. "Ray's Way: Ben Welden and *Marked Woman.*" *Classic* 112 (October 1984): 41+.

Price, Theodora. "The Truth About the Bette Davis 1937 Gangster Movie *Marked Woman.*" In *Crime in Movies. Proceedings of Fourth Annual International Film Conference.* Ed. Radcliff, Umstead, and Douglas. Kent, Ohio: Kent State University Press, 1986. 24–32.

The Oklahoma Kid (1939)

Greene, Graham. "Oklahoma Kid/The Lone Ranger." In *Graham Greene on Film: Collected Film Criticism 1935–1940*. Ed. John Russell Taylor. New York: Simon & Schuster, 1972. 221–222.

Passage to Marseille (1944)

Alley, Kenneth D. "*Passage to Marseille*: A Case of Unjust Neglect." *Literature/Film Quarterly* 25.3 (1997): 198–203.
Crowther, Bosley. "Passage to Marseille: A Heavy Action Drama in Which Free Frenchmen Figure, with Bogart, at the Hollywood." *New York Times* (February 17, 1944): 12:5.
Deming, Barbara. *Running Away from Myself: A Dream Portrait of America Drawn from Films of the Forties*. New York: Grossman, 1969.
Harmetz, Aljean. *Round Up the Usual Suspects: The Making of Casablanca—Bogart, Bergman, and World War II*. New York: Hyperion, 1992. 302–306.
Kinnard, Roy, and R. J. Vitone. "Passage to Marseilles." In *The American Films of Michael Curtiz*. Metuchen, N.J.: Scarecrow Press, 1986. 86–88.
McCarthy, M. "Mary McCarthy Goes to the Movies." *Film Comment* 12 (January–February 1976): 32–34.
Mjagkij, N. "Know Your Occupied Ally: The Image of France in *Passage to Marseille*." *Film and History* 20.2 (1990): 37–43.
Rosenzweig, Sidney. "In the Shadows of *Casablanca*: Hawks's *To Have and Have Not* and Curtiz's *Passage to Marseille*." In *Casablanca and Other Major Films of Michael Curtiz*. Ann Arbor: UMI Research Press, 1982. 97–108.
Sennett, Ted. *Masters of Menace: Greenstreet and Lorre*. New York: Dutton, 1979. 84–87.
Sklar, Robert. *City Boys: Cagney, Bogart, Garfield*. Princeton: Princeton University Press, 1992. 165–167.

The Petrified Forest (1936)

Clarens, Carlos. *Crime Movies*. New York: Norton, 1980. 142–145.
Johnson, Timothy. "The Petrified Forest." In *Magill's American Film Guide*. 5 vols. Ed. Frank N. Magill. Englewood Cliffs, N.J.: Salem, 1983. 4:2571–2574.
Trent, Paul. *The Thirties: Those Fabulous Movie Years*. Barre, Mass.: Barre Publishing, 1975.

The Return of Dr. X (1939)

Clarens, Carlos. *Illustrated History of Horror Films*. New York: Putnam, 1967.
Miller, Don. *"B" Movies*. New York: Curtis Books, 1973.

The Roaring Twenties (1939)

Draper, Ellen. "The Roaring Twenties (1939)." *Cinema Texas Program Notes* (September 17, 1979): 29–35.

Hogue, Peter. "Big Shots." *Movietone News* 45 (November 1975): 14–21.
Lukow, Gregory, and Steven Ricci. "The Audience Goes Public: Inter-Textuality, Genre, and the Responsibility of Film Literacy." *On Film* 1.2 (spring 1984): 29–36.
Nielsen, R. "Ray's Way: Jeffrey Lynn in *The Roaring Twenties.*" *Classic* 203 (May 1992): 38.
Perkins, Carolyn. "The Roaring Twenties (1939)." *Cinema Texas Program Notes* (March 18, 1975): 1–7.
Scapperotti, Dan. "*The Roaring Twenties.*" In *Magill's American Film Guide.* 5 vols. Ed. Frank N. Magill. Englewood Cliffs, N.J.: Salem, 1983. 4:2806–2809.
Shadoian, Jack. *Dreams and Dead-Ends: The American Gangster/Crime Film.* Cambridge, Mass.: MIT Press, 1977. 81–82.

Sabrina (1954)

Donaldson, Leslie. "*Sabrina.*" In *Magill's American Film Guide*, 5 vols. Ed. Frank N. Magill. Englewood Cliffs, N.J.: Salem, 1983. 4:2860–2862.
———. "Sabrina." In *Cinema: Great Directors*. Ed. Frank Magill. Pasadena, Calif.: Salem Softbacks, 1981. 367–369.
Sklar, Robert. *City Boys: Cagney, Bogart, Garfield*. Princeton: Princeton University Press, 1992. 245–246.
Starks, Lisa. "Educating Eliza: Fashioning the Model Woman in the 'Pygmalion' Film." *Post Script* 16.2 (winter–spring 1997): 44–55.
Zolotow, Maurice. *Billy Wilder in Hollywood*. New York: Putnam's, 1977.

Sahara (1943)

Basinger, Jeanine. *The World War II Combat Film: Anatomy of a Genre*. New York: Columbia University Press, 1986.
Dick, Bernard F. *The Star-Spangled Screen: The American World War II Film*. Lexington, Ky.: University Press of Kentucky, 1985. 222–223.
Kelly, Thomas O. "Race and Racism in the American World War II Film: The Negro, the Nazi, and the 'Jap' in *Bataan* and *Sahara.*" *Michigan Academician* 24.4 (1992): 571–583.
Kornweibel, Theodore, Jr. "Humphrey Bogart's *Sahara*: Propaganda, Cinema and the American Character in World War II." *American Studies* 22.1 (1981): 5–19.
Shindler, Colin. *Hollywood Goes to War: Films and American Society, 1939–1952*. London: Routledge and Kegan Paul, 1979.
Suid, Lawrence H. *Guts and Glory: Great American War Movies*. Reading, Mass.: Addison-Wesley, 1978. 47–51.

Stand In (1937)

Ames, Christopher. *Movies about the Movies: Hollywood Reflected*. Lexington: University Press of Kentucky, 1997. 137–150.
O'Toole, Larry. "Hollywood Player? Or Stand-in?" *American Movie Classics* (March 1994): 10–11.

Thank Your Lucky Stars (1943)

Spector, Warren. "Thank Your Lucky Stars (1943)." *Cinema Texas Program Notes* (April 19, 1979): 35–40.

They Drive by Night (1940)

Hogue, Peter. "Boys at Work." *Movietone News* 45 (November 1975): 21–24.

To Have and Have Not (1945)

Agee, James. "*To Have and Have Not*." *Time* (October 23, 1944). Rpt. In *Agee on Film*. New York: Grosset & Dunlap, 1969. 1:353–355. *Howard Hawks: American Artist*. Ed. Jim Hillier and Peter Wollen. London: British Film Institute, 1996. 21–23.
———. [*To Have and Have Not*]. *Nation* (November 4, 1944). Rpt. In *Agee on Film*. New York: Grosset & Dunlap, 1969. 1:121–122.
Barker, Julie. "*To Have and Have Not*." In *Magill's American Film Guide*. 5 vols. Ed. Frank N. Magill. Englewood Cliffs, N.J.: Salem, 1983. 5:3405–3408.
———. "To Have and Have Not." In *Cinema: Great Directors*. Ed. Frank Magill. Pasadena, Calif.: Salem Softbacks, 1981. 196–199.
Blackburn, Steve. "To Have and Have Not (1944)." *Cinema Texas Program Notes* (February 19, 1983): 37–42.
Bogdanovich, Peter. "To Have and Have Not." In *Cinema of Howard Hawks*. New York: Film Library of the Museum of Modern Art, 1962. 23–25.
Deutelbaum, Marshall. "Showing the Strings That Don't Show: Mise-en-Scène and Meaning in *To Have and Have Not*." *North Dakota Quarterly* 51.3 (summer 1983): 61–77.
Fadiman, R. K. "Of Hemingway and Hollywood." *Quarterly Review of Film Studies* 7.2 (1982): 185–189.
Fawell, J. "The Musicality of the Filmscript." *Literature/Film Quarterly* 17.1 (1989): 44–49.
Fell, John L. "Vladimir Propp in Hollywood." *Film Quarterly* 30.3 (spring 1977): 19–28.
Godard, Jean-Luc. *Godard on Godard*. Ed. Jean Narboni and Tom Milne. New York: Viking, 1972. 28–30.
Haskell, Molly. *From Reverence to Rape: The Treatment of Women in the Movies*. 2nd ed. Chicago: University of Chicago Press, 1987. 25–26, 211–213, passim.
Hemmeter, Thomas, and Kevin W. Sweeney. "Marriage as Moral Community: Cinematic Critiques of Hemingway's *To Have and Have Not*." In *A Moving Picture Feast: The Filmgoer's Hemingway*. Ed. Charles M. Oliver. New York: Praeger, 1989. 64–75.
Jameson, Richard T. "People Who Need People: [To Have and Have Not]." *Movietone News* (April 13, 1975): 11–15.
Kawin, Bruce. *Faulkner and Film*. New York: Ungar, 1977. 109–113, 153–155, passim.
———. *To Have and Have Not*. Madison: University of Wisconsin Press, 1980.

Laurence, Frank M. "Action Adventure: *To Have and Have Not*." In *Hemingway and the Movies*. Jackson: University Press of Mississippi, 1981. 82–113.
Mast, Gerald. "Hemingway and Chandler into Bogart-Bacall and Hawks: *To Have and Have Not* and *The Big Sleep*." In *Howard Hawks, Storyteller*. New York: Oxford University Press, 1982. 243–295.
McBride, Joseph. *Hawks on Hawks*. Berkeley: University of California Press, 1982. 28–29, 78–79, 94–95, 107–108, passim.
Oliver, Charles M. *A Moving Picture Feast: The Filmgoer's Hemingway*. New York: Praeger, 1989.
Phillips, Gene D. *Hemingway and Film*. New York: Ungar, 1980. 48–60.
———. "To Have and Have Not." In *Fiction, Film, and Faulkner: The Art of Adaptation*. Knoxville: University of Tennessee Press, 1988. 42–48.
Rosenbaum, Joseph. *Moving Places: A Life at the Movies*. New York: Harper & Row, 1980. 5–6.
Rothman, William. "To Have and Have Not Adapted a Novel." In *The Modern American Novel and the Movies*. Ed. Gerald Peary and Roger Shatzkin. New York: Ungar, 1978. 70–79. Rpt. in William Rothman. *The "I" of the Camera: Essays in Film Criticism, History, and Aesthetics*. Cambridge: Cambridge University Press, 1988. 108–116.
Shaw, Daniel G. "Individual Commitment in *To Have and Have Not* (1944)." *Film and History* 27.1–4 (1997): 72–79.
Sklar, Robert. *City Boys: Cagney, Bogart, Garfield*. Princeton: Princeton University Press, 1992. 167–172.
TheBerge, Rita. "To Have and Have Not (1944)." *Cinema Texas Program Notes* (April 12, 1977): 63–68.
Thomson, David. "The End of the American Hero." *Film Comment* 17 (July–August 1981):13–17.
Wood, Robin. "To Have (Written) and Have Not (Directed)." *Film Comment* 9.3 (May–June 1973): 30–35.
———. *Howard Hawks*. Garden City, N.Y.: Doubleday, 1968. 25–32.

The Treasure of the Sierra Madre (1948)

Agee, James. *Agee on Film*. New York: Grosset & Dunlap, 1969. 1:290–293, 398–401.
Archer, Eugene. "John Huston—The Hemingway Tradition in American Film." *Film Culture* 19 (1959): 66–101, esp. 81–83.
Beja, Morris. "The Treasure of the Sierra Madre." In *Film and Literature*. New York: Longman, 1979. 168–174.
Claro, J., and M. Stern. "Letters: Huston and the Man Who Might Be Traven." *New York Times* (July 27, 1987): A18.
Crowther, Bosley. *The Great Films: Fifty Golden Years of Motion Pictures*. New York: Putnam, 1967. 189–192.
Deming, Barbara. *Running Away from Myself: A Dream Portrait Drawn from the Films of the Forties*. New York: Grossman, 1969. 187–200.
Downer, Alan S. "The Monitor Image." In *Man and the Movies*. Ed. W. R. Robinson. Baton Rouge: Louisiana State University Press, 1967. Rpt. New York: Penguin, 1969. 13–30.

Engell, John. "*The Treasure of the Sierra Madre*: B. Traven, John Huston and Ideology in Film Adaptation." *Literature/Film Quarterly* 17.4 (1989): 245–252.

———. "Traven, Huston, and the Textual Treasures of the Sierra Madre." In *Reflections in a Male Eye: John Huston and the American Experience*. Ed. Gaylyn Studlar and David Desser. Washington, D.C.: Smithsonian, 1993. 79–95.

Graham, Olive. "Treasure of the Sierra Madre (1948)." *Texas Cinema Program Notes* (May 3, 1979): 85–88.

Greenberg, Harvey R. "*The Treasure of the Sierra Madre*—There's Success Phobia in Them Thar Hills." In *The Movies on Your Mind*. New York: Saturday Review Press and E. P. Dutton, 1975. 33–52.

Grobel, Lawrence. *The Hustons*. New York: Avon, 1989. 287–298, 310–311.

Jameson, Richard T. "John Huston." *Film Comment* 16 (May–June 1980): 25–56.

Kaminsky, Stuart M. "Gold Hat, Gold Fever, Silver Screen." In *The Modern American Novel and the Movies*. Ed. Gerald Peary and Roger Shatzkin. New York: Ungar, 1978. 53–62.

———. *American Film Genres*. 2nd ed. Chicago: Nelson-Hall, 1985. 97–105.

Majdalany, Fred. "Viewing Report: *Treasure of the Sierra Madre*." *Screen Education* (London) (March–April 1965): n.p.

Masterson, Peg. "Treasure of the Sierra Madre (1948)." *Texas Cinema Program Notes* (November 9, 1976): 73–76.

McDougal, Stuart Y. "The Treasure of the Sierra Madre." In *Made into Movies: From Literature to Film*. New York: Holt, Rinehart, Winston, 1985. 118–125.

Miller, Gabriel. "The Wages of Sin: *The Treasure of the Sierra Madre*." In *Screening the Novel: Rediscovered American Fiction in Film*. New York: Ungar, 1980. 99–115.

Naremore, James. Ed., *The Treasure of the Sierra Madre*. Madison, Wis.: University of Wisconsin Press, 1979.

Nolan, William F. *John Huston: King Rebel*. Los Angeles: Sherbourne Press, 1965.

Overton, R. "The Treasure of the Sierra Madre." *Literature Film/Quarterly* 1.2 (1973): 166.

Pratley, Gerald. *The Cinema of John Huston*. South Brunswick and New York: A. S. Barnes, 1977. 66–68.

Sklar, Robert. *City Boys: Cagney, Bogart, Garfield*. Princeton: Princeton University Press, 1992. 193–197.

Taubman, Leslie. "The Treasure of the Sierra Madre." In *Magill's American Film Guide*. 5 vols. Ed. Frank N. Magill. Englewood Cliffs, N.J.: Salem, 1983. 5:3439–3442.

———. "The Treasure of the Sierra Madre." In *Cinema: Great Directors*. Ed. Frank Magill. Pasadena, Calif.: Salem Softbacks, 1981. 290–293.

Traven, B. *The Treasure of the Sierra Madre*. Trans. Erich Sutton. New York: Knopf, 1935. Rpt. New York: New American Library, 1968.

Wyatt, Will. *The Secret of the Sierra Madre: The Man Who Was B. Traven*. New York: Doubleday, 1980.

The Two Mrs. Carrolls (1947)

Basinger, Jeanine. *American Cinema: One Hundred Years of Filmmaking*. New York: Rizzoli, 1994. 25–27.

The Wagons Roll at Night (1941)

Nielsen, R. "Ray's Way: Eddie Albert and *Wagons Roll at Night*." *Classic* 142 (April 1987): 10–11.

We're No Angels (1955)

Sklar, Robert. *City Boys: Cagney, Bogart, Garfield*. Princeton: Princeton University Press, 1992. 248.

There is little or no substantive commentary on the following films: *All Through the Night*, 1942; *The Amazing Dr. Clitterhouse*, 1938; *Battle Circus*, 1953; *Big City Blues*, 1932; *The Big Shot*, 1942; *Brother Orchid*, 1940; *Chain Lightning*, 1950; *China Clipper*, 1936; *Crime School*, 1938; *The Dancing Town*, 1928; *A Devil with Women*, 1930; *The Great O'Malley*, 1937; *A Holy Terror*, 1931; *Invisible Stripes*, 1939; *Isle of Fury*, 1936; *It All Came True*, 1940; *Kid Galahad*, 1937; *King of the Underworld*, 1939; *The Left Hand of God*, 1955; *Love Affair*, 1932; *Men Are Such Fools*, 1938; *Midnight* [aka *Call It Murder*], 1934; *Racket Busters*, 1938; *The Return of Dr. X*, 1939; *San Quentin*, 1937; *Sirocco*, 1951; *Swing Your Lady*, 1938; *Three on a Match*, 1932; *Tokyo Joe*, 1949; *Two Against the World* (aka *Case Against Mrs. Pembrook*), 1936; *Up the River*, 1930; *Virginia City*, 1940; *Wagons Roll at Night*, 1941; *We're No Angels*, 1955; *Women of All Nations*, 1931; *You Can't Get Away with Murder*, 1939.

APPENDIXES

I

CHRONOLOGICAL BIOGRAPHY

December 25, 1899	Birth of Humphrey Bogart in New York City
September 1906	Enters Delancey School
September 1909	Enters Episcopal Trinity School
September 1917	Enters Phillips Andover Academy
June 1918	Enlists in U.S. Navy
June 1919	Honorably discharged from the navy
1920	Variety of jobs, including road manager for *Experience* (with Alice Brady)
January 2, 1922	*Drifting*
March 3, 1922	*Up the Ladder*
October 16, 1922	*Swifty*
November 26, 1923	*Meet the Wife*
September 1, 1924	*Nerves* (with Mary Philips)
January 26, 1925	*Hell's Bells*
September 7, 1925	*Cradle Snatchers*
May 20, 1926	Marries Helen Menken after four-year engagement; marriage dissolved eighteen months later
January 26, 1927	*Saturday's Children* (Bogart replaces actor after the run begins)
June 9, 1927	*Baby Mine*
November 18, 1927	Menken and Bogart divorce
1928	*The Dancing Town* (first movie, two-reeler for, supposedly, Paramount, with Helen Hayes)

April 3, 1928	Marries Mary Philips in Hartford, Connecticut
November 26, 1928	*A Most Immoral Lady* (replaces actor)
January 11, 1929	*The Skyrocket*
August 6, 1929	*It's a Wise Child*
1930	*Broadway's Like That*
October 1930	*A Devil with Women*
	Up the River
March 1931	*Body and Soul*
	Bad Sister (Bogart's first role as a heavy)
May 1931	*Women of All Nations*
July 1931	*A Holy Terror*
December 3, 1931	*After All*
1932	Returns to New York (makes film *Midnight*, released 1934)
March 1932	*Love Affair*
May 29, 1932	*The Mad Hopes* (Los Angeles)
September 1932	*Big City Blues*
October 1932	*Three on a Match*
October 11, 1932	*I Loved You Wednesday*
November 15, 1932	*Chrysalis*
March 2, 1933	*Our Wife*
May 8, 1933	*The Mask and the Face*
March 1934	*Midnight*
May 17, 1934	*Invitation to a Murder*
September 8, 1934	Death of Dr. Belmont DeForest Bogart
January 7, 1935	*The Petrified Forest*; runs 181 performances
July 30, 1935	*The Stag at Bay* (Skowhegan, Maine), *Ceiling Zero* (Skowhegan, Maine)
August 27, 1935	*Rain* (Skowhegan, Maine)
December 10, 1935	Warner Bros. contract for twenty-six weeks at $550 per week with options
January 1936	*The Petrified Forest*
May 1936	*Bullets or Ballots*
June 8, 1936	Twenty-six-week option at $600 per week
July 1936	*Two Against the World*
August 1936	*China Clipper*
October 1936	*Isle of Fury*
December 9, 1936	Twenty-six-week extension at $650 per week

Chronological Biography 279

January 1937	*Black Legion*
January 25, 1937	Parts from Mary Philips
February 1937	*The Great O'Malley*
March 1937	Catherine (Kay) Bogart dies
April 1937	*Marked Woman*
May 1937	*Kid Galahad* (a.k.a. *The Battling Bellhop*)
June 9, 1937	Studio extends option
July 21, 1937	Mary Philips awarded interlocutory decree; not executed until 1938
August 1937	*San Quentin*
	Dead End
October 1937	*Stand-In*
November 30, 1937	Option extended, fifty-two weeks at $850 per week; renegotiated for $1,110 per week as of December 31, 1937
January 1938	*Swing Your Lady*
May 1938	*Crime School*
June 1938	*Men Are Such Fools*
July 1938	*The Amazing Dr. Clitterhouse*
August 1938	*Racket Busters*
	Mary Philips executes interlocutory decree; marries Kenneth McKenna
August 20, 1938	Marries Mayo Methot
November 1938	*Angels with Dirty Faces*
January 1939	*King of the Underworld*
March 1939	*The Oklahoma Kid*
April 1939	*Dark Victory*
May 1939	*You Can't Get Away with Murder*
October 1939	*The Roaring Twenties*
December 1939	*The Return of Dr. X*
	Invisible Stripes
March 1940	*Virginia City*
April 1940	*It All Came True*
June 1940	*Brother Orchid*
August 1940	*They Drive by Night*
August 16, 1940	Dies Committee hearings
November 23, 1940	Maud Humphrey dies
January 1941	*High Sierra*

280 Appendix I

April 1941	*The Wagons Roll at Night*
October 1941	*The Maltese Falcon*
December 29, 1941	Fourth extension of contract (December 31, 1937), 52 weeks at $1,850 per week
January 3, 1942	Renegotiates contract, seven years at $2,750 per week
January 1942	*All Through the Night*
1942	*In This Our Life* (cameo appearance)
June 1942	*The Big Shot*
September 1942	*Across the Pacific*
November 1942	*Casablanca* (limited release, New York)
January 1943	*Casablanca* (general release)
June 1943	*Action in the North Atlantic*
September 1943	*Thank Your Lucky Stars*
October 1943	*Sahara*
December 1943	35,000-mile USO tour to Europe and Africa with Mayo
February 1944	Bogarts return from USO tour
March 1944	*Passage to Marseille*
	Report from the Front (short)
May 10, 1944	Completes filming of *To Have and Have Not*
November–December 1944	Divorce negotiations and proceedings begin
January 1945	*To Have and Have Not*
January 12, 1945	Completes filming of *The Big Sleep*
1945	*Hollywood Victory Caravan* (appeal for Victory Loan Bonds)
May 10, 1945	Mayo Methot secures divorce in Las Vegas
May 21, 1945	Marries Betty Bacall at Louis Bromfield's farm in Mansfield, Ohio
	Temporary residence at the Garden of Allah, then on to home in King's Road in Hollywood Hills
June 1945	*Conflict*
December 1945	Bogart buys the *Santana*, a fifty-five-foot yawl, from Dick Powell
1946	Buys home of Hedy Lamar at 2707 Benedict Canyon
August 1946	*Two Guys from Milwaukee*, with cameo appearances by Bogart and Bacall
	The Big Sleep

Chronological Biography   281

August 21, 1946	Puts imprint at Grauman's Chinese Theatre
October 14, 1946	Radio broadcast of *To Have and Have Not*
December 19, 1946	Contract revision, $13,333 per week for every picture, with a minimum of fifteen consecutive weeks; contract commences January 1, 1947, for fifteen years
January 1947	*Dead Reckoning*
May 1947	*The Two Mrs. Carrolls*
September 1947	*Dark Passage*
	Begins treatments for hair loss caused by alopecia areata
October 26, 1947	Bogart and Bacall and friends (Committee for First Amendment Rights) fly to Washington, D.C., to protest actitivities of House Un-American Activities Committee
December 21, 1947	Mark Hellinger dies
January 1948	*Always Together* (unbilled appearance)
January 1948	*The Treasure of the Sierra Madre*
April 7, 1948	Forms Santana Production Company with business manager A. Morgan Maree and Robert Lord, who had been a writer-producer for Warner Bros. Five productions from the company: *Knock on Any Door, In a Lonely Place, Tokyo Joe, Sirocco, Beat the Devil*
July 1948	*Key Largo*
January 6, 1949	Stephen Humphrey Bogart born
April 1949	*Knock on Any Door*
September 25, 1949	El Morocco fracas
September 30, 1949	Robin Roberts's panda lawsuit dismissed
November 1949	*Tokyo Joe*
February 1950	*Chain Lightning*
August 1950	*In a Lonely Place*
1951	Enters into agreement to do "Bold Venture," a radio series
February 1951	*The Enforcer*
June 9, 1951	Death of Mayo Methot
July 1951	*Sirocco*
December 1951	*The African Queen*
1952	Cameo appearance in *The Road to Bali*

March 1952	Wins Academy Award for Best Actor for *The African Queen*
Spring 1952	Moves into new home, 232 South Mapleton, Holmby Hills
May 1952	*Deadline—U.S.A.*
July 1952	U.S. Savings Bond trailer
August 23, 1952	Leslie Bogart born
1953	Cameo appearance in *The Love Lottery*
February 6, 1953	Hurt in car crash with John Huston near Naples
September 21, 1953	Released from Warner Bros. contract
March 1953	*Battle Circus*
	The Love Lottery (unbilled appearance)
March 1954	*Beat the Devil*
June 1954	*The Caine Mutiny*
September 3, 1954	"Person-to-person" interview
	Sabrina
	The Barefoot Contessa
1954	Sells Santana Production Company to Columbia
May 30, 1955	Costars with Bacall in television production of *The Petrified Forest*, with Henry Fonda. Completes stage-to-film-to-TV cycle
July 1955	*We're No Angels*
September 1955	Announces the formation of Mapleton Productions with Allied Artists
	The Left Hand of God
October 1955	*The Desperate Hours*
January 1956	Wardrobe tests for *Melville Goodwin, USA*
March 1, 1956	Surgery for cancer of the esophagus
March 26, 1956	Bogart and Bacall do costume tests for *Melville Goodwin, USA.*
May 1956	*The Harder They Fall*
January 14, 1957	Dies
January 17, 1957	Funeral, All Saints Episcopal Church, Beverly Hills; cremated at Forest Lawn
February 9, 1960	Bogart honored with a star on Hollywood Boulevard
July 31, 1997	U.S. Post Office issues Humphrey Bogart stamp

II

THEATRICAL PERFORMANCES

The Ruined Lady, 1920 on tour

Drifting, January 2, 1922

Up the Ladder, March 1922

Swifty, October 17, 1922

Meet the Wife, November 26, 1923

Nerves, September 1, 1924

Hell's Bells, January 26, 1925

Cradle Snatchers, September 7, 1925

Baby Mine, June 9, 1927

Saturday's Children, April 9, 1928*

A Most Immoral Lady, November 26, 1928

The Skyrocket, January 11, 1929

It's a Wise Child, August 6, 1929

After All, December 3, 1931

The Mad Hopes, May 28, 1932

I Love You Wednesday, October 11, 1932

Chrysalis, November 15, 1932

Our Wife, March 2, 1933

The Mask and the Face, May 8, 1933

*The play opened on January 26, and Bogart joined the cast to replace an actor who became ill. Other plays that Bogart may have been in are *The Teaser, The Nest, Mary the Third*, and *Steve* (in Chicago).

Invitation to a Murder, May 17, 1934
The Petrified Forest, January 7, 1935
Ceiling Zero, Summer 1935
The Stag at Bay, July 30, 1935
Rain, August 27, 1935

III

FILMOGRAPHY

Any material in square brackets indicates information not appearing on film's screen credits but included in other sources.

THE DANCING TOWN (1928?)

Attribution: Uncertain. Paramount. Cast: Helen Hayes, Humphrey Bogart.

BROADWAY'S LIKE THAT (1930)

Vitaphone Varieties No. 960. Produced by the Vitaphone Corporation. Distributed by Warner Bros. Director-in-chief, Murray Roth. Story and dialogue by Stanley Rauh. Musical director, Harold Levey. Running time, 10 minutes. Cast: Ruth Etting, Humphrey Bogart, Joan Blondell.

A DEVIL WITH WOMEN (1930)

A Fox Picture. Directed by Irving Cummings. Associate producer, George Middleton. Screenplay by Dudley Nichols and Henry M. Johnson. Based on novel *Dust and Sun* by Clement Ripley. Director of photography, Arthur L. Todd. Music by Peter Brunelli. Film editor, Jack Murray. Art director, William Darling. Sound recorders, E. Clayton Ward and Harry M. Leonard. Song, "Amor Mio," by James Monaco and Cliff Friend. Running time, 76 minutes. Cast: Victor McLaglen (Jerry Maxton); Mona Maris (Rosita Fernandez); Humphrey Bogart (Tom Standish); Luana Alcaniz (Dolores); Michael Vavitch (Morloff); Soledad Jiminez (Jiminez); Mona Rico (Alicia); John St. Polis (Don Diego); Robert Edeson (General Garcia); Joe De LaCruz (Bandit Chieftan).

286   Appendix III

UP THE RIVER (1930)

A Fox Picture. Directed by John Ford. Original screenplay by Maurine Watkins. Director of photography, Joseph August. Staged by William Collier, Sr. Film editor, Frank Hull. Sound recorder, W. W. Lindsay, Jr. Running time, 92 minutes. Cast: Spencer Tracy (St. Louis); Claire Luce (Judy); Warren Hymer (Dannemora Dan); Humphrey Bogart (Steve); William Collier, Sr. (Pop); Joan Marie Lawes (Jean); George MacFarlane (Jessup); Gaylord Pendleton (Morris); Sharon Lynn (Edith LaVerne); Noel Francis (Sophie); Goodee Montgomery (Kit); Robert Burns (Slim); John Swor (Clem); Bert E. O'Connor (The Warden); Louise MacIntosh (Mrs. Massey); Richard Keene (Dick); Johnny Walker (Happy); Pat Somerset (Beauchamp); Morgan Wallace (Frosby); Edythe Champman (Mrs. Jordan); Althea Henly (Cynthia); Keating Sisters (May and June); Joe Brown (Deputy Warden); Wilbur Mack (Whiteley); Harvey Clark (Nash); Carol Wines (Daisy Elmore); Adele Windsor (Minnie); Mildred Vincent (Annie).

BODY AND SOUL (1931)

A Fox Picture. Directed by Alfred Santell. Screenplay by Jules Furthman. From the play *Squadrons* by A. E. Thomas, based on the story "Big Eyes and Little Mouth" by Elliott White Springs. Director of photography, Glen MacWilliams. Music by Peter Brunelli. Film editor, Paul Weatherwax. Art director, Anton Grot. Special effects by Ralph Hammeras. Sound recorder, Donald Flick. Technical adviser, Bogart Rogers. Running time, 70 minutes. Cast: Charles Farrell (Mal Andrews); Elissa Landi (Carla); Humphrey Bogart (Jim Watson); Myrna Loy (Alice Lester); Donald Dillaway (Tap Johnson); Craufurd Kent (Major Burke); Pat Somerset (Major Knowls); Ian MacLaren (General Trafford-Jones); Dennis D'Auburn (Lieutenant Meggs); Douglas Dray (Zane); Hardold Kinney (Young); Bruce Warren (Sam Douglas).

BAD SISTER (1931)

A Universal Picture. Directed by Hobart Henley. Produced by Carl Laemmle, Jr. Screenplay by Raymond L. Schrock and Tom Reed. Dialogue by Edwin Knoft. Based on the story "The Flirt" by Booth Tarkington. Director of photography, Karl Freund. Film editor, Ted Kent. Sound recorder, C. Roy Hunter. Running time, 73 minutes. Cast: Conrad Nagel (Dick Lindley); Sidney Fox (Marianne Madison); Bette Davis (Laura Madison); ZaSu Pitts (Minnie); Slim Summerville (Sam); Charles Winninger (Mr. Madison); Emma Dunn (Mrs. Madison); Humphrey Bogart (Valentine Corliss); Bert Roach (Wade Trumbull); David Durand (Hedrick Madison).

WOMEN OF ALL NATIONS (1931)

A Fox Picture. Directed by Raoul Walsh. Original screenplay by Barry Connors. Based on the characters created by Laurence Stallings and Maxwell Anderson. Director of photography, Lucien Androit. Music by Reginald H. Bassett. Film editor, Jack Dennis. Art director, David Hall. Sound recorder, George Leverett. Musical director, Carli D. Elinor. Production manager, Archibald Buchanan. Running time, 72 minutes. Cast: Victor McLaglen (Sergeant Flagg); Edmund Lowe (Sergeant Quirt); Greta Nissen (Elsa); El

Brendel (Olsen); Fifi Dorsay (Fifi); Marjorie White (Pee Wee); T. Roy Barnes (Captain of Marines); Bela Lugosi (Prince Hassan); Humphrey Bogart (Stone); Joyce Compton (Kiki); Jesse DeVorska (Izzie); Charles Judels (Leon); Marion Lessing (Gretchen); Ruth Warren (Ruth).

A HOLY TERROR (1931)

A Fox Picture. Directed by Irving Cummings. Associate producer, Edmund Grainger. Scenario by Ralph Block. Dialogue by Alfred A. Cohn and Myron Fagan. Based on the novel *Trailin'* by Max Brand. Director of photography, George Schneiderman. Film editor, Ralph Dixon. Sound recorder, Donald Flick. Running time, 53 minutes. Cast: George O'Brien (Tony Bard); Sally Eilers (Jerry Foster); Rita LaRoy (Kitty Carroll); Humphrey Bogart (Steve Nash); James Kirkwood (William Drew); Stanley Fields (Butch Morgan); Robert Warwick (Thomas Woodbury); Richard Tucker (Tom Hedges); Earl Pingree (Jim Lawler).

LOVE AFFAIR (1932)

A Columbia Picture. Directed by Thornton Freeland. Adaptation and dialogue by Jo Swerling and Dorothy Howell. Continuity by Dorothy Howell. Based on the *College Humor* story by Ursula Parrott. Director of photography, Ted Tetzlaff. Film editor, Jack Dennis. Sound recorder, Charles Noyes. Running time, 68 minutes. Cast: Dorothy Mackaill (Carol Owen); Humphrey Bogart (Jim Leonard); Jack Kennedy (Gilligan); Barbara Leonard (Felice); Astrid Allwyn (Linda Lee); Bradley Page (Georgie); Halliwell Hobbes (Kibbee); Hale Hamilton (Bruce Hardy); Harold Minjir (Antone).

BIG CITY BLUES (1932)

A Warner Bros. Picture. Directed by Mervyn LeRoy. Screenplay by Ward Morehouse and Lillie Hayward. Based on the play *New York Town* by Ward Morehouse. Director of photography, James Van Trees. Film editor, Ray Curtiss. Art director, Anton Grot. Music and arrangements by Ray Heindorf and Bernhard Kaun. Musical director, Leo F. Forbstein. Running time, 65 minutes. Cast: Joan Blondell (Vida); Eric Linden (Bud); Inez Courtney (Faun); Evalyn Knapp (Jo-Jo); Guy Kibbee (Hummell); Lyle Talbot (Sully); Gloria Shea (Agnes); Walter Catlett (Cousin Gibboney); Jobyna Howland (Mrs. Cartlich); Humphrey Bogart (Adkins); Josephine Dunn (Jackie); Grant Mitchell (Station Agent); Thomas Jackson (Quelkin); Ned Sparks (Mr. Stackhouse); Sheila Terry (Lorna); Tom Dugan (Red); Betty Gillette (Mabel); Edward McWade (Baggage Master).

THREE ON A MATCH (1932)

A First National Picture for Warner Bros. Directed by Mervyn LeRoy. Scenario by Lucien Hubbard. Dialogue by Kubec Glasmon and John Bright. Based on a story by Kubec Glasmon and John Bright. Director of photography, Sol Polito. Film editor, Ray Curtiss. Art director, Robert Haas. Orchestral arrangements by Ray Heindorf. Musical director of Vitaphone Orchestra, Leo F. Forbstein. Gowns by Orry-Kelly. Running time,

64 minutes. Cast: Joan Blondell (Mary Keaton); Warren William (Henry Kirkwood); Ann Dvorak (Vivian Revere); Bette Davis (Ruth Westcott); Lyle Talbot (Mike Loftus); Humphrey Bogart (Harve); Patricia Ellis (Linda); Sheila Terry (Naomi); Grant Mitchell (Principal of School, Mr. Gilmou); Glenda Farrell (Vivian's Chum); Frankie Darro (Bobby); Clara Blandick (Mrs. Keaton); Hale Hamilton (Defense Attorney); Dick Brandon (Horace); Junior Johnson (Max); Dawn O'Day (Vivian Revere as a child); Virginia Davis (Mary Keaton as a child); Betty Carse (Ruth Westcott as a child); Buster Phelps (Junior); Allen Jenkins (Dick); Edward Arnold (Ace).

MIDNIGHT (1934)

An All-Star Production. Released by Universal. Produced and directed by Chester Erskine. Screenplay by Chester Erskine. Based on the play by Paul and Claire Sifton. Running time, 80 minutes. Cast: Sidney Fox (Stella Weldon); O. P. Heggie (Edward Weldon); Henry Hull (Nolan); Margaret Wycherly (Mrs. Weldon); Lynne Overman (Joe Biggers); Katherine Wilson (Ada Biggers); Richard Whorf (Arthur Weldon); Humphrey Bogart (Garboni); Granville Bates (Henry McGrath); Cora Witherspoon (Elizabeth McGrath); Moffat Johnson (District Attorney Plunket); Henry O'Neill (Ingersoll); Helen Flint (Ethel Saxon).

THE PETRIFIED FOREST (1936)

A Warner Bros. Picture. Directed by Archie Mayo. Associate producer, Henry Blanke. Screenplay by Charles Kenyon and Delmer Daves. Based on the play by Robert E. Sherwood. Director of photography, Sol Polito. Music by Bernhard Kaun. Film editor, Owen Marks. Assistant director, Dick Mayberry. Art director, John Hughes. Gowns by Orry-Kelly. Special effects by Warren E. Lynch, Fred Jackman and Willard Van Enger. Sound recorder, Charles Lang. Running time, 83 minutes. Cast: Leslie Howard (Alan Squier); Bette Davis (Gabrielle Maple); Genevieve Tobin (Mrs. Chisholm); Dick Foran (Boze Hertzlinger); Humphrey Bogart (Duke Mantee); Joseph Sawyer (Jackie); Porter Hall (Jason Maple); Charley Grapewin (Gramp Maple); Paul Harvey (Mr. Chisholm); Eddie Acuff (Lineman); Adrian Morris (Ruby); Nina Campana (Paula); Slim Thompson (Slim); John Alexander (Joseph).

BULLETS OR BALLOTS (1936)

A First National Picture for Warner Bros. Directed by William Keighley. Associate producer, Louis F. Edelman. Screenplay by Seton I. Miller. Based on an original story by Martin Mooney and Seton I. Miller. Director of photography, Hal Mohr. Music by Heinz Roemheld. Film editor, Jack Killifer. Assistant director, Chuck Hansen. Art director, Carl Jules Weyl. Special effects by Fred Jackman, Fred Jackman, Jr., and Warren E. Lynch. Sound recorder, Oliver S. Garretson. Running time, 81 minutes. Cast: Edward G. Robinson (Johnny Blake); Joan Blondell (Lee Morgan); Barton MacLane (Al Kruger); Humphrey Bogart (Nick ''Bugs'' Fenner); Frank McHugh (Herman); Joseph King (Captain Dan McLaren); Richard Purcell (Driscoll); George E. Stone (Wires); Joseph Crehan (Grand Jury Spokesman); Henry O'Neill (Bryant); Henry Kolker (Hollister); Gilbert Emery (Thorndyke); Herbert Rawlinson (Caldwell); Louise Beavers (Nellie); Norman Willis (Vinci); William Pawley (Crail); Ralph Remley (Kelly); Frank Faylen (Gatley).

TWO AGAINST THE WORLD (1936)

A First National Picture for Warner Bros. Directed by William McGann. Associate producer, Bryan Foy. Screenplay by Michel Jacoby. Based on the play *Five Star Final* by Louis Weitzenkorn. Director of photography, Sid Hickox. Music by Heinz Roemheld. Film editor, Frank McGee. Dialogue director, Irving Rapper. Assistant director, Carrol Sax. Art director, Esdras Hartley. Special effects by Fred Jackman, Jr., and Rex Wimpy. Sound recorder, C. A. Riggs. Running time, 64 minutes. Cast: Humphrey Bogart (Sherry Scott); Beverly Roberts (Alma Ross); Helen McKellar (Martha Carstairs); Henry O'Neill (Jim Carstairs); Linda Perry (Edith Carstairs); Carlisle Moore, Jr. (Malcolm Sims, Jr.); Virginia Brissac (Mrs. Marion Sims); Robert Middlemass (Bertram C. Reynolds); Clay Clement (Mr. Banning); Harry Hayden (Martin Leavenworth); Claire Dodd (Cora Latimer); Hobart Cavanaugh (Tippy Mantus); Douglas Wood (Malcolm Sims); Bobby Gordon (Herman O'Reilly); Paula Stone (Miss Symonds); Frank Orth (Tommy); Howard Hickman (Dr. McGuire); Ferdinand Schumann-Heink (Sound Mixer).

CHINA CLIPPER (1936)

A First National Picture for Warner Bros. Directed by Ray Enright. Associate producer, Louis F. Edelman. Original screenplay by Frank Wead. Director of photography, Arthur Edeson. Music by Bernhard Kaun and W. Franke Harling. Film editor, Owen Marks. Dialogue director, Gene Lewis. Assistant director, Lee Katz. Art director, Max Parker. Gowns by Orry-Kelly. Aerial photography by Elmer G. Dyer and H. F. Koenekamp. Special photographic effects by Fred Jackman, [Willard Van Enger and H. F. Koenekamp]. Sound recorder, Everett A. Brown. Technical adviser, William I. Van Dusen, Pan-American Airways. Musical director, Leo F. Forbstein. Running time, 85 minutes. Cast: Pat O'Brien (Dave Logan); Beverly Roberts (Jean Logan); Ross Alexander (Tom Collins); Humphrey Bogart (Hap Stuart); Marie Wilson (Sunny Avery); Henry B. Walthall (Dad Brunn); Joseph Crehan (Jim Horn); Joseph King (Mr. Pierson); Addison Richards (B. C. Hill); Ruth Robinson (Mother Brunn); Carlyle Moore, Jr. (Radio Operator on Clipper); Dennis Moore (Engineer on Clipper); Wayne Morris (Navigator on Clipper); Alexander Cross (Bill Andrews); William Wright (Pilot); Kenneth Harlan (Department of Commerce Inspector); Anne Nagel (Secretary); Marjorie Weaver (Secretary); Milburn Stone (Radio Operator); Owen King (Radio Operator).

ISLE OF FURY (1936)

A Warner Bros. Picture. Directed by Frank McDonald. Associate producer, Bryan Foy. Screenplay by Robert Andrews and William Jacobs. Based on the novel *The Narrow Corner* by W. Somerset Maugham. Director of photography, Frank Good. Music by Howard Jackson. Film editor, Warren Low. Assistant director, Frank Heath. Art director, Esdras Hartley. Gowns by Orry-Kelly. Special effects by Fred Jackman, Willard Van Enger, and H. F. Koenekamp. Sound recorder, Charles Lang. Dialogue director, Jerry Morse. Running time, 60 minutes. Cast: Humphrey Bogart (Val Stevens); Margaret Lindsay (Lucille Gordon); Donald Woods (Eric Blake); Paul Graetz (Captain Deever); Gordon Hart (Anderson); E. E. Clive (Dr. Hardy); George Regas (Otar); Sidney Bracey (Sam); Tetsu Komai (Kim Lee); Miki Morita (Oh Kay); Houseley Stevenson, Sr. (The Rector); Frank Lackteen (Old Native).

BLACK LEGION (1937)

A Warner Bros. Picture. Directed by Archie Mayo. Associate producer, Robert Lord. Screenplay by Abem Finkel and William Wister Haines. Based on an original story by Robert Lord. Director of photography, George Barnes. Music by Bernhard Kaun. Film editor, Owen Marks. Assistant director, Jack Sullivan. Art director, Robert Haas. Gowns by Milo Anderson. Special effects by Fred Jackman, Jr., and H. F. Koenekamp. Sound recorder, C. A. Riggs. Running time, 83 minutes. Cast: Humphrey Bogart (Frank Taylor); Dick Foran (Ed Jackson); Erin O'Brien-Moore (Ruth Taylor); Ann Sheridan (Betty Grogan); Robert Barrat (Brown); Helen Flint (Pearl Davis); Joseph Sawyer (Cliff Moore); Addison Richards (Prosecuting Attorney); Eddie Acuff (Metcalf); Clifford Soubier (Mike Grogan); Paul Harvey (Billings); Samuel Hinds (Judge); John Litel (Tommy Smith); Alonzo Price (Alf Hargrave); Dickie Jones (Buddy Taylor); Dorothy Vaughan (Mrs. Grogan); Henry Brandon (Joe Dombrowski); Charles Halton (Osgood); Pat C. Flick (Nick Strumpas); Francis Sayles (Charlie); Paul Stanton (Barham); Harry Hayden (Jones); Egon Brecher (Dombrowski, Sr.).

THE GREAT O'MALLEY (1937)

A Warner Bros. Picture. Directed by William Dieterle. Associate producer, Harry Joe Brown. Screenplay by Milton Krims and Tom Reed. Based on the story "The Making of O'Malley" by Gerald Beaumont. Director of photography, Ernest Haller. Music by Heinz Roemheld. Film editor, Warren Low. Dialogue director, Irving Rapper. Assistant director, Frank Shaw. Art director, Hugh Reticker. Gowns by Milo Anderson. Special effects by James Gibbons, Fred Jackman, Jr., and H. F. Koenekamp. Sound recorder, Francis J. Scheid. Orchestrations by Hugo Friedhofer. Running time, 71 minutes. Cast: Pat O'Brien (James Aloysius O'Malley); Sybil Jason (Barbara Phillips); Humphrey Bogart (John Phillips); Ann Sheridan (Judy Nolan); Frieda Inescort (Mrs. Phillips); Donald Crisp (Captain Cromwell); Henry O'Neill (Defense Attorney); Craig Reynolds (Motorist); Hobart Cavanaugh (Pinky Holden); Gordon Hart (Doctor); Mary Gordon (Mrs. O'Malley); Mabel Colcord (Mrs. Flaherty); Frank Sheridan (Father Patrick); Lillian Harmer (Miss Taylor); Delmar Watson (Tubby); Frank Reicher (Dr. Larson).

MARKED WOMAN (1937)

A First National Picture for Warner Bros. Directed by Lloyd Bacon. Associate producer, Louis F. Edelman. Original screenplay by Robert Rossen and Abem Finkel. Director of photography, George Barnes. Music by Bernhard Kaun and Heinz Roemheld. Film editor, Jack Killifer. Assistant director, Dick Mayberry. Art director, Max Parker. Gowns by Orry-Kelly. Special effects by James Gibbons and Robert Burks. Sound recorder, Everett A. Brown. Songs: "My Silver Dollar Man" by Harry Warren and Al Dubin; "Mr. and Mrs. Doaks" by M. K. Jerome and Jack Scholl. Musical director, Leo F. Forbstein.

Running time, 96 minutes. Cast: Bette Davis (Mary Dwight); Humphrey Bogart (David Graham); Lola Lane (Gabby Marvin); Isabel Jewell (Emmy Lou Egan); Eduardo Cianelli (Johnny Vanning); Rosalind Marquis (Florrie Liggett); Mayo Methot (Estelle Porter); Jane Bryan (Betty Strauber); Allen Jenkins (Louie); John Litel (Gordon); Ben Welden (Charlie); Damian O'Flynn (Ralph Krawford); Henry O'Neill (Arthur Sheldon); Raymond Hatton (Lawyer at Jail); Carlos San Martin (Headwaiter); William B. Davidson (Bob Crandall); Kenneth Harlan (Eddie); Robert Strange (George Beler); James Robbins (Bell Captain); Arthur Aylesworth (John Truble); John Sheehan (Vincent); Sam Wren (Mac); Edwin Stanley (Ferguson); Alan Davis (Henchman); Allen Mathews (Henchman); Guy Usher (Detective Ferguson); Gordon Hart (Judge at First Trial); Pierre Watkin (Judge at Second Trial); Herman Marks (Joe).

KID GALAHAD (1937)

A Warner Bros. Picture. Directed by Michael Curtiz. Associate producer, Samuel Bischoff. Screenplay by Seton I. Miller. Based on the novel by Francis Wallace. Director of photography, Tony Gaudio. Music by Heinz Roemheld and Max Steiner. Film editor, George Amy. Dialogue director, Irving Rapper. Assistant Director, Jack Sullivan. Art director, Carl Jules Weyl. Gowns by Orry-Kelly. Special effects by James Gibbons and Edwin B. DuPar. Sound recorder, Charles Lang. Orchestrations by Hugo Friedhofer. Song, "The Moon Is in Tears Tonight," by M. K. Jerome and Jack Scholl. Running time, 101 minutes. Cast: Edward G. Robinson (Nick Donati); Bette Davis (Fluff); Humphrey Bogart (Turkey Morgan); Wayne Morris (Ward Guisenberry); Jane Bryan (Marie Donati); Harry Carey (Silver Jackson); William Haade (Chuck McGraw); Soledad Jiminez (Mrs. Donati); Joe Cunningham (Joe Taylor); Ben Welden (Buzz Barett); Joseph Crehen (Brady); Veda Ann Borg (The Redhead); Frank Faylen (Barney); Harland Tucker (Gunman); Bob Evans (Sam); Hank Hankinson (Burke); Bob Nestell (O'Brien); Jack Kranz (Denbaugh); George Blake (Referee).

SAN QUENTIN (1937)

A First National Picture for Warner Bros. Directed by Lloyd Bacon. Associate producer, Samuel Bischoff. Screenplay by Peter Milne and Humphrey Cobb. Story by Robert Tasker and John Bright. Director of photography, Sid Hickox. Music by Heinz Roemheld, Charles Maxwell, and David Raksin. Film editor, William Holmes. Assistant director, Dick Mayberry. Art director, Esdras Hartley. Gowns by Howard Shoup. Special effects by James Gibbons and H. F. Koenekamp. Sound recorder, Everett A. Brown. Orchestrations by Joseph Nussbaum and Ray Heindorf. Song, "How Could You?" by Harry Warren and Al Dubin. Musical director, Leo F. Forbstein. Running time, 70 minutes. Cast: Pat O'Brien (Capt. Stephen Jameson); Humphrey Bogart (Joe "Red" Kennedy); Ann Sheridan (May Kennedy); Barton MacLane (Lieut. Druggin); Joseph Sawyer ("Sailor Boy" Hansen); Veda Ann Borg (Helen); James Robbins (Mickey Callahan); Joseph King (Warden Taylor); Gordon Oliver (Captain); Garry Owen (Dopey); Marc Lawrence (Venetti); Emmett Vogan (Lieutenant); William Pawley (Convict); Al Hill (Convict); Max Wagner (Prison Runner); George Lloyd (Convict); Ernie Adams (Fink).

DEAD END (1937)

A Samuel Goldwyn Production. Released through United Artists. Directed by William Wyler. Produced by Samuel Goldwyn. Associate producer, Merritt Hulburd. Screenplay by Lillian Hellman. Based on the play by Sidney Kingsley. Director of photography, Gregg Toland. Film editor, Daniel Mandell. Dialogue director, Edward P. Goodnow. Assistant director, Eddie Bernoudy. Art director, Richard Day. Set decorations by Julia Heron. Costumes by Omar Kiam. Special effects by James Basevi. Sound recorder, Frank Maher. Musical director, Alfred Newman. Running time, 93 minutes. Cast: Sylvia Sidney (Drina); Joel McCrea (Dave Connell); Humphrey Bogart (Baby Face Martin); Wendy Barrie (Kay Burton); Claire Trevor (Francey); Allen Jenkins (Hunk); Marjorie Main (Mrs. Martin); Billy Halop (Tommy); Huntz Hall (Dippy); Bobby Jordan (Angel); Leo Gorcey (Spit); Gabriel Dell (T. B.); Bernard Punsley (Milty); Charles Peck (Philip Griswold); Minor Watson (Mr. Griswold); James Burke (Officer Mulligan); Ward Bond (Doorman); Elisabeth Risdon (Mrs. Connell); Esther Dale (Mrs. Fenner); George Humbert (Mr. Pascagli); Marcelle Corday (Governess); Charles Halton (Whitey).

STAND-IN (1937)

A Walter Wanger Production. Released through United Artists. Directed by Tay Garnett. Produced by Walter Wanger. Screenplay by Gene Towne and Graham Baker. Based on the *Saturday Evening Post* serial by Clarence Budington Kelland. Director of photography, Charles Clarke. Music by Heinz Roemheld. Film editors, Otho Lovering and Dorothy Spencer. Assistant director, Charles Kerr. Art director, Alexander Toluboff; associate, Wade Rubottom. Costumes by Helen Taylor. Sound recorder, Paul Neal. Musical director, Rox Rommel. Running time, 90 minutes. Cast: Leslie Howard (Atterbury Dodd); Joan Blondell (Lester Plum); Humphrey Bogart (Douglas Quintain); Alan Mowbray (Koslofski); Marla Shelton (Thelma Cheri); C. Henry Gordon (Ivor Nassau); Jack Carson (Potts); Tully Marshall (Pennypacker, Sr.); J. C. Nugent (Pennypacker, Jr.); William V. Mong (Pennypacker).

SWING YOUR LADY (1938)

A Warner Bros. Picture. Directed by Ray Enright. Associate producer, Samuel Bischoff. Screenplay by Joseph Schrank and Maurice Leo. Based on the play by Kenyon Nicholson and Charles Robinson. Director of photography, Arthur Edeson. Music by Adolph Deutsch. Film editor, Jack Killifer. Dialogue director, Jo Graham. Assistant director, Jesse Hibbs. Art director, Esdras Hartley. Gowns by Howard Shoup. Sound recorder, Charles Lang. Orchestrations by Hugo Friedhofer. Musical numbers created and directed by Bobby Connolly. Songs: "Mountain Swingaroo," "Hillbilly from Tenth Avenue," "The Old Apple Tree," "Swing Your Lady," and "Dig Me a Grave in Missouri" by M. K. Jerome and Jack Scholl. Musical director, Leo F. Forbstein. Running time, 79 minutes. Cast: Humphrey Bogart (Ed Hatch); Frank McHugh (Popeye Bronson); Louise Fazenda (Sadie Horn); Nat Pendleton (Joe "Hercules" Skopapoulos); Penny Singleton (Cookie Shannon); Allen Jenkins (Shiner Ward); Leon Weaver (Waldo Davis); Frank Weaver (Ollie Davis); Elviry Weaver (Mrs. Davis); Ronald Reagan (Jack Miller); Daniel

Boone Savage (Noah Webster); Hugh O'Connell (Humpty Smith, Referee); Tommy Bupp (Rufe Horn); Sunny Bupp (Len Horn); Joan Howard (Mattie Horn); Sue Moore (Mabel); Olin Howland (Hotel Proprietor); Sammy White (Specialty Number).

CRIME SCHOOL (1938)

A First National Picture for Warner Bros. Directed by Lewis Seiler. Associate producer, Bryan Foy. Screenplay by Crane Wilbur and Vincent Sherman. Based on an original story by Crane Wilbur. Director of photography, Arthur Todd. Music by Max Steiner. Film editor, Terry Morse. Dialogue director, Vincent Sherman. Assistant director, Fred Tyler. Art director, Charles Novi. Gowns by N'Was McKenzie. Sound recorder, Francis J. Scheid. Orchestrations by Hugo Friedhofer and George Parrish. Running time, 86 minutes. Cast: Humphrey Bogart (Mark Braden); Gale Page (Sue Warren); Billy Halop (Frankie Warren); Bobby Jordan (Squirt); Huntz Hall (Goofy); Leo Gorcey (Spike Hawkins); Bernard Punsley (Fats Papadopolo); Gabriel Dell (Bugs Burke); George Offerman, Jr. (Red); Weldon Heyburn (Cooper); Cy Kendall (Morgan); Charles Trowbridge (Judge Clinton); Spencer Charters (Old Doctor); Donald Briggs (New Doctor); Frank Jaquet (Commissioner); Helen MacKellar (Mrs. Burke); Al Bridge (Mr. Burke); Sibyl Harris (Mrs. Hawkins); Paul Porcasi (Nick Papadopolos); Frank Ott (Junkie); Ed Gargan (Officer Hogan); James B. Carson (Schwartz).

MEN ARE SUCH FOOLS (1938)

A Warner Bros. Picture. Directed by Busby Berkeley. Associate producer, David Lewis. Screenplay by Norman Reilly Raine and Horace Jackson. Based on the *Saturday Evening Post* story by Faith Baldwin. Director of photography, Sid Hickox. Music by Heinz Roemheld. Film editor, Jack Killifer. Dialogue director, Jo Graham. Assistant director, Chuck Hansen. Art director, Max Parker. Gowns by Howard Shoup. Sound recorder, Stanley Jones. Musical director, Leo F. Forbstein. Orchestrations by Ray Heindorf. Running time, 70 minutes. Cast: Wayne Morris (Jimmy Hall); Priscilla Lane (Linda Lawrence); Humphrey Bogart (Harry Galleon); Hugh Herbert (Harvey Bates); Penny Singleton (Nancy); Johnnie Davis (Tad); Mona Barrie (Beatrice Harris); Marcia Ralston (Wanda Townsend); Gene Lockhart (Bill Dalton); Kathleen Lockhart (Mrs. Dalton); Donald Briggs (George Onslow); Renie Riano (Mrs. Pinkel); Claude Allister (Rudolf); Nedda Harrigan (Mrs. Nelson); Eric Stanley (Mr. Nelson); James Nolan (Bill Collyer); Carole Landis (June Cooper).

THE AMAZING DR. CLITTERHOUSE (1938)

A First National Picture for Warner Bros. Directed by Anatole Litvak. Associate producer, Robert Lord. Screenplay by John Wexley and John Huston. Based on the play by Barré Lyndon. Director of photography, Tony Gaudio. Music by Max Steiner. Film editor, Warren Low. Dialogue director, Jo Graham. Assistant director, Jack Sullivan. Art director, Carl Jules Weyl. Wardrobe by Milo Anderson. Sound recorder, C. A. Riggs. Orchestrations by George Parrish. Technical adviser, Dr. Leo Schulman. Musical director, Leo F. Forbstein. Running time, 87 minutes. Cast: Edward G. Robinson (Dr. Clitterhouse); Claire Trevor (Jo Keller); Humphrey Bogart (''Rocks'' Valentine); Allen Jenkins

(Okay); Donald Crisp (Inspector Lane); Gale Page (Nurse Randolph); Henry O'Neill (Judge); John Litel (Prosecuting Attorney); Thurston Hall (Grant); Maxie Rosenbloom (Butch); Bert Hanlon (Pal); Curt Bois (Rabbit); Ward Bond (Tug); Vladimir Sokoloff (Popus); Billy Wayne (Candy); Robert Homans (Lieutenant Johnson); Irving Bacon (Foreman of the Jury).

RACKET BUSTERS (1938)

A Warner Bros. Picture. A Cosmopolitan Production. Directed by Lloyd Bacon. Associate producer, Samuel Bischoff. Original screenplay by Robert Rossen and Leonardo Bercovici. Director of photography, Arthur Edeson. Music by Adolph Deutsch. Film editor, James Gibbon. Assistant director, Dick Mayberry. Art director, Esdras Hartley. Gowns by Howard Shoup. Sound recorder, Robert B. Lee. Orchestrations by Hugo Friedhofer. Musical director, Leo F. Forbstein. Running time, 71 minutes. Cast: Humphrey Bogart (Pete Martin); George Brent (Denny Jordan); Gloria Dickson (Nora Jordan); Allen Jenkins ("Skeets" Wilson); Walter Abel (Allison); Henry O'Neill (Governor); Penny Singleton (Gladys); Anthony Averill (Crane); Oscar O'Shea (Pop Wilson); Elliott Sullivan (Charlie Smith); Fay Helm (Mrs. Smith); Joe Downing (Joe); Norman Willis (Gus); Don Rowan (Kimball).

ANGELS WITH DIRTY FACES (1938)

A First National Picture for Warner Bros. Directed by Michael Curtiz. Associate producer, Samuel Bischoff. Screenplay by John Wexley and Warren Duff. Based on an original story by Rowland Brown. Director of photography, Sol Polito. Music by Max Steiner. Film editor, Owen Marks. Dialogue director, Jo Graham. Assistant director, Sherry Shourds. Art director, Robert Haas. Gowns by Orry-Kelly. Sound recorder, Everett A. Brown. Orchestrations by Hugo Friedhofer. Technical adviser, Father J. J. Devlin. Running time, 97 minutes. Cast: James Cagney (Rocky Sullivan); Pat O'Brien (Jerry Connolly); Humphrey Bogart (James Frazier); Ann Sheridan (Laury Ferguson); George Bancroft (Mac Keefer); Billy Halop (Soapy); Bobby Jordan (Swing); Leo Gorcey (Bim); Gabriel Dell (Pasty); Huntz Hall (Crab); Bernard Punsley (Hunky); Joseph Downing (Steve); Edward Pawley (Edwards); Adrian Morris (Blackie); Frankie Burke (Rocky as a boy); William Tracy (Jerry as a boy); Marilyn Knowlden (Laury as a child); St. Brendan's Church Choir.

KING OF THE UNDERWORLD (1939)

A Warner Bros. Picture. Directed by Lewis Seiler. Associate producer, Bryan Foy. Screenplay by George Bricker and Vincent Sherman. Based on the *Liberty Magazine* serial *Dr. Socrates* by W. R. Burnett. Director of photography, Sid Hickox. Music by Heinz Roemheld. Film editor, Frank Dewar. Dialogue director, Vincent Sherman. Assistant director, Frank Heath. Art director, Charles Novi. Gowns by Orry-Kelly. Sound recorder, E. A. Brown. Technical adviser, Dr. Leo Schulman. Musical director, Leo F. Forbstein. Running time, 69 minutes. Cast: Humphrey Bogart (Joe Gurney); Kay Francis (Carol Nelson); James Stephenson (Bill Stevens); John Eldredge (Niles Nelson); Jessie Busley (Aunt Josephine); Arthur Aylesworth (Dr. Sanders); Raymond Brown (Sheriff);

Harland Tucker (Mr. Ames); Ralph Remley (Mr. Robert); Charley Foy (Slick); Murray Alper (Eddie); Joe Devlin (Porky); Elliott Sullivan (Mugsy); Alan Davis (Pete); John Harmon (Slats); John Ridgely (Jerry); Richard Bond (Interne); Pierre Watkin (District Attorney); Charles Trowbridge (Dr. Ryan); Edwin Stanley (Dr. Jacobs).

THE OKLAHOMA KID (1939)

A Warner Bros. Picture. Directed by Lloyd Bacon. Associate producer, Samuel Bischoff. Screenplay by Warren Duff, Robert Buckner, and Edward E. Paramore. Based on an original story by Edward E. Paramore and Wally Klein. Director of photography, James Wong Howe. Music by Max Steiner. Film editor, Owen Marks. Assistant director, Dick Mayberry. Art director, Esdras Hartley. Gowns by Orry-Kelly. Sound recorder, Stanley Jones. Orchestral arrangements by Hugo Friedhofer and Adolph Deutsch. Technical adviser, Al Jennings. Musical director, Leo F. Forbstein. Running time, 80 minutes. Cast: James Cagney (Jim Kincaid); Humphrey Bogart (Whip McCord); Rosemary Lane (Jane Hardwick); Donald Crisp (Judge Hardwick); Harvey Stephens (Ned Kincaid); Hugh Sothern (John Kincaid); Charles Middleton (Alec Martin); Edward Pawley (Doolin); Ward Bond (Wes Handley); Lew Harvey (Curley); Trevor Bardette (Indian Jack Pasco); John Miljan (Ringo); Arthur Aylesworth (Judge Morgan); Irving Bacon (Hotel Clerk); Joe Devlin (Keely); Wade Boteler (Sheriff Abe Collins).

DARK VICTORY (1939)

A First National Picture for Warner Bros. Directed by Edmund Goulding. Associate producer, David Lewis. Screenplay by Casey Robinson. Based on the play by George Emerson Brewer, Jr., and Bertram Bloch. Director of photography, Ernest Haller. Music by Max Steiner. Film editor, William Holmes. Assistant director, Frank Heath. Art director, Robert Haas. Gowns by Orry-Kelly. Sound recorder, Robert B. Lee. Orchestrations by Hugo Friedhofer. Song, "Oh, Give Me Time for Tenderness," by Elsie Janis and Edmund Goulding. Technical adviser, Dr. Leo Schulman. Executive Producer, Hal B. Wallis. Associate producer, David Lewis. Musical director, Leo F. Forbstein. Running time, 106 minutes. Cast: Bette Davis (Judith Traherne); George Brent (Dr. Frederick Steele); Humphrey Bogart (Michael O'Leary); Geraldine Fitzgerald (Ann King); Ronald Reagan (Alec Hamm); Henry Travers (Dr. Parsons); Cora Witherspoon (Carrie Spottswood); Dorothy Peterson (Miss Wainwright); Virginia Brissac (Martha); Charles Richman (Colonel Mantle); Herbert Rawlinson (Dr. Carter); Leonard Mudie (Dr. Driscoll); Fay Helm (Miss Dodd); Lottie Williams (Lucy).

YOU CAN'T GET AWAY WITH MURDER (1939)

A First National Picture for Warner Bros. Directed by Lewis Seiler. Associate producer, Samuel Bischoff. Screenplay by Robert Buckner, Don Ryan, and Kenneth Gamet. Based on the play *Chalked Out* by Warden Lewis E. Lawes and Jonathan Finn. Director of photography, Sol Polito. Music by Heinz Roemheld. Film editor, James Gibbon. Dialogue director, Jo Graham. Assistant director, William Kissel. Art director, Hugh Reticker. Gowns by Milo Anderson. Sound recorder, Francis J. Scheid. Orchestrations by Hugo Friedhofer, Arthur Kay, and Rudolph Kopp. Musical director, Leo F. Forbstein.

Running time, 78 minutes. Cast: Humphrey Bogart (Frank Wilson); Billy Halop (Johnnie Stone); Gale Page (Madge Stone); John Litel (Attorney Carey); Henry Travers (Pop); Harvey Stephens (Fred Burke); Harold Huber (Scappa); Joe Sawyer (Red); Joe Downing (Smitty); George E. Stone (Toad); Joseph King (Principal Keeper); Joseph Crehan (Warden); John Ridgely (Gas Station Attendant); Herbert Rawlinson (District Attorney).

THE ROARING TWENTIES (1939)

A Warner Bros.–First National Picture. Directed by Raoul Walsh. Executive producer, Hal B. Wallis. Screenplay by Jerry Wald, Richard Macaulay, and Robert Rossen. Based on an original story by Mark Hellinger. Director of photography, Ernest Haller. Music by Heinz Roemheld and Ray Heindorf. Film editor, Jack Killifer. Dialogue director, Hugh Cummings. Assistant director, Dick Mayberry. Art director, Max Parker. Wardrobe by Milo Anderson. Makeup artist, Perc Westmore. Special effects by Byron Haskin and Edwin B. DuPar. Sound recorder, Everett A. Brown. Songs: "My Melancholy Baby" by Ernie Burnett and George A. Norton; "I'm Just Wild About Harry" by Eubie Blake and Noble Sissle; "It Had to Be You" by Isham Jones and Gus Kahn; "In a Shanty in Old Shanty Town" by Jack Little, Joseph Young, and John Siras. Orchestral arrangements by Ray Heindorf. Narrated by John Deering. Running time, 106 minutes. Cast: James Cagney (Eddie Bartlett); Priscilla Lane (Jean Sherman); Humphrey Bogart (George Hally); Gladys George (Panama Smith); Jeffrey Lynn (Lloyd Hart); Frank McHugh (Danny Green); Paul Kelly (Nick Brown); Elisabeth Risdon (Mrs. Sherman); Edward Keane (Pete Henderson); Joseph Sawyer (Sergeant Pete Jones); Joseph Crehan (Mr. Fletcher); George Meeker (Masters); John Hamilton (Judge); Robert Elliott (First Detective); Eddie Chandler (Second Detective); Abner Biberman (Lefty); Vera Lewis (Mrs. Gray); Elliott Sullivan (Eddie's Cellmate); Bert Hanlon (Piano Accompanist); Murray Alper (First Mechanic); Dick Wessel (Second Mechanic); George Humbert (Restaurant Proprietor); Ben Welden (Tavern Proprietor).

THE RETURN OF DOCTOR X (1939)

A First National Picture for Warner Bros. Directed by Vincent Sherman. Associate producer, Bryan Foy. Screenplay by Lee Katz. Based on the story "The Doctor's Secret" by William J. Makin. Director of photography, Sid Hickox. Music by Bernhard Kaun. Film editor, Thomas Pratt. Dialogue director, John Langan. Assistant director, Dick Mayberry. Art director, Esdras Hartley. Gowns by Milo Anderson. Makeup artist, Perc Westmore. Sound recorder, Charles Lang. Technical adviser, Dr. Leo Schulman. Running time, 62 minutes. Cast: Wayne Morris (Walter Barnett); Rosemary Lane (Joan Vance); Humphrey Bogart (Marshall Quesne); Dennis Morgan (Michael Rhodes); John Litel (Dr. Francis Flegg); Lya Lys (Angela Merrova); Huntz Hall (Pink); Charles Wilson (Detective Ray Kincaid); Vera Lewis (Miss Sweetman); Howard Hickman (Chairman); Olin Howland (Undertaker); Arthur Aylesworth (Guide); Cliff Saum (Detective Sgt. Moran); Creighton Hale (Hotel Manager); John Ridgely (Rodgers); Joseph Crehan (Editor); Glen Langan (Interne); DeWolf Hopper (Interne).

INVISIBLE STRIPES (1939)

A Warner Bros.–First National Picture. Directed by Lloyd Bacon. Executive producer, Hal B. Wallis. Associate producer, Louis F. Edelman. Screenplay by Warren Duff. From an original story by Jonathan Finn, based on the book by Warden Lewis E. Lawes. Director of photography, Ernest Haller. Music by Heinz Roemheld. Film editor, James Gibbon. Dialogue director, Irving Rapper. Assistant director, Elmer Decker. Art director, Max Parker. Gowns by Milo Anderson. Makeup artist, Perc Westmore. Special effects by Byron Haskin. Sound recorder, Dolph Thomas. Orchestrations by Ray Heindorf. Running time, 82 minutes. Cast: George Raft (Cliff Taylor); Jane Bryan (Peggy); William Holden (Tim Taylor); Humphrey Bogart (Chuck Martin); Flora Robson (Mrs. Taylor); Paul Kelly (Ed Kruger); Lee Patrick (Molly); Henry O'Neill (Parole Officer Masters); Frankie Thomas (Tommy); Moroni Olsen (Warden); Margot Stevenson (Sue); Marc Lawrence (Lefty); Joseph Downing (Johnny); Leo Gorcey (Jimmy); William Haade (Shrank); Tully Marshall (Old Peter).

VIRGINIA CITY (1940)

A Warner Bros.–First National Picture. Directed by Michael Curtiz. Executive producer, Hal B. Wallis. Associate producer, Robert Fellows. Original screenplay by Robert Buckner. Director of photography, Sol Polito. Music by Max Steiner. Film editor, George Amy. Dialogue director, Jo Graham. [Assistant director, Sherry Shourds]. Art director, Ted Smith. Makeup artist, Perc Westmore. Special effects by H. F. Koenekamp. Sound recorders, Oliver S. Garretson and Francis J. Scheid. Orchestrations by Hugo Friedhofer. Music director, Leo F. Forbstein. Running time, 121 minutes. Cast: Errol Flynn (Kerry Bradford); Miriam Hopkins (Julia Hayne); Randolph Scott (Vance Irby); Humphrey Bogart (John Murrell); Frank McHugh (Mr. Upjohn); Alan Hale (Olaf Swenson); Guinn "Big Boy" Williams (Marblehead); John Litel (Marshall); Douglass Dumbrille (Major Drewery); Moroni Olsen ([Dr.] Cameron); Russell Hicks (Armistead); Dickie Jones (Cobby, young boy); Frank Wilcox (Union Soldier); Russell Simpson (Gaylord); Victor Kilian (Abraham Lincoln); Charles Middleton (Jefferson Davis).

IT ALL CAME TRUE (1940)

A Warner Bros.–First National Picture. Directed by Lewis Seiler. [Executive producer, Hal B. Wallis]. Producer, Mark Hellinger. Screenplay by Michael Fessier and Lawrence Kimble. Based on the story "Better Than Life" by Louis Bromfield. Director of photography, Ernie Haller. [Music by Heinz Roemheld]. Film editor, Thomas Richards. Dialogue director, Robert Foulk. [Assistant director, Russ Saunders]. Art director, Max Parker. Gowns by Howard Shoup. Makeup artist, Perc Westmore. [Special effects by Byron Haskins and Edwin B. DuPar. Sound recorder, Dolph Thomas]. Dance director, Dave Gould. [Songs: "Angel in Disguise" by Kim Gannon, Stephan Weiss, and Paul Mann; "The Gaucho Serenade" by James Cavanaugh, John Redmond and Nat Simon]. Orchestral arrangements by Ray Heindorf and Frank Perkins. Musical director, Leo F. Forbstein. Running time, 97 minutes. Cast: Ann Sheridan (Sarah Jane Ryan); Jeffrey Lynn (Tommy Taylor); Humphrey Bogart (Grasselli [Chips Maguire]); ZaSu Pitts (Miss Flint); Una O'Connor (Maggie Ryan); Jessie Busley (Mrs. [Norah] Taylor); John Litel

(Mr. Roberts); Grant Mitchel (Rene Salmon); Felix Bressart (The Great Boldini); Charles Judels (Henri Pepi de Bordeaux); Brandon Tynan (Mr. Van Diver); Howard Hickman (Mr. Prendergast); Herbert Vigran (Monks); Tommy Reilly, the Elderbloom Chorus, Bender and Daum, White and Stanley, The Lady Killers' Quartet.

BROTHER ORCHID (1940)

A Warner Bros.–First National Picture. Directed by Lloyd Bacon. Executive producer, Hal B. Wallis. Associate producer, Mark Hellinger. Screenplay by Earl Baldwin. Based on the *Collier's* magazine story by Richard Connell. Director of photography, Tony Gaudio. Music by Heinz Roemheld. Film editor, William Holmes. Dialogue director, Hugh Cummings. [Assistant director, Dick Mayberry]. Art director, Max Parker. Gowns by Howard Shoup. Makeup artist, Perc Westmore. Special effects by Byron Haskin, Willard Van Enger, [and Edwin B. DuPar]. Montages by Don Siegel and Robert Burks. Sound, C. A. Riggs. Orchestral arrangements by Ray Heindorf. Musical director, Leo F. Forbstein. Running time, 91 minutes. Cast: Edward G. Robinson (Little John Sarto); Ann Sothern (Flo Addams); Humphrey Bogart (Jack Buck); Donald Crisp (Brother Superior); Ralph Bellamy (Clarence Fletcher); Allen Jenkins (Willie the Knife); Charles D. Brown (Brother Wren); Cecil Kellaway (Brother Goodwin); Morgan Conway (Philadelphia Powell); Richard Lane (Mugsy O'Day); Paul Guilfoyle (Red Martin); John Ridgely (Texas Pearson); Joseph Crehan (Brother MacEwen); Wilfred Lucas (Brother MacDonald); Tom Tyler (Curley Matthews); Dick Wessel (Buffalo Burns); Granville Bates (Pattonsville Supt.); Paul Phillips (Al Muller); Nanette Vallon (Fifi); Tim Ryan (Turkey Malone); Joe Caites (Handsome Harry); Pat Gleason (Dopey Perkins); Tommy Baker (Joseph).

THEY DRIVE BY NIGHT (1940) [ROAD TO FRISCO IN GREAT BRITAIN]

A Warner Bros.–First National Picture. Directed by Raoul Walsh. Executive producer, Hal B. Wallis. Associate producer, Mark Hellinger. Screenplay by Jerry Wald and Richard Macaulay. Based on the novel *Long Haul* by A. I. Bezzerides. Director of photography, Arthur Edeson. Music by Adolph Deutsch. Film editor, Thomas Richards. Dialogue director, Hugh MacMullen. Assistant director, Elmer Decker. Art director, John Hughes. Gowns by Milo Anderson. Makeup artist, Perc Westmore. Special effects by Byron Haskin, H. F. Koenekamp [James Gibbons, John Holden, and Edwin B. DuPar]. [Montages by Don Siegel and Robert Burks]. Sound by Oliver S. Garretson. Orchestrations by Arthur Lange. Music by Adolph Deutsch. Musical director, Leo F. Forbstein. Running time, 93 minutes. Cast: George Raft (Joe Fabrini); Ann Sheridan (Cassie Hartley); Ida Lupino (Lana Carlsen); Humphrey Bogart (Paul Fabrini); Gale Page (Pearl Fabrini); Alan Hale (Ed Carlson); Roscoe Karns (Irish McGurn); John Litel (Harry McNamara); George Tobias (George Rondolos); Henry O'Neill (District Attorney); Charles Halton (Farnsworth); Paul Hurst (Pete Haig); John Ridgely (Hank Dawson); George Lloyd (Barney); Joyce Compton (Sue Carter); Charles Wilson (Mike Williams); Pedro Regas (McNamara's Helper); Norman Willis (Neves); Joe Devlin (Fatso); William Haade (Driver); Vera Lewis (Landlady); John Hamilton (Defense Attorney).

HIGH SIERRA (1941)

A Warner Bros.–First National Picture. Directed by Raoul Walsh. Executive producer, Hal B. Wallis. Associate producer, Mark Hellinger. Screenplay by John Huston and W. R. Burnett. Based on the novel by W. R. Burnett. Director of photography, Tony Gaudio. Music by Adolph Deutsch. Film editor, Jack Killifer. Dialogue director, Irving Rapper. Art director, Ted Smith. Gowns by Milo Anderson. Makeup artist, Perc Westmore. Special effects by Byron Haskin and H. F. Koenekamp. Sound recorder, Dolph Thomas. Orchestrations by Arthur Lange. Running time, 100 minutes. Cast: Ida Lupino (Marie Garson); Humphrey Bogart (Roy Earle); Alan Curtis (Babe Kozak); Arthur Kennedy (Red Hattery); Joan Leslie (Velma); Henry Hull (Doc Banton); Henry Travers (Pa Goodhue); Jerome Cowan (Healy); Minna Gombell (Mrs. Baughman); Barton MacLane (Jake Kranmer); Elisabeth Risdon (Ma Goodhue); Cornel Wilde (Louis Mendoza); Donald MacBride (Big Mac); Paul Harvey (Mr. Baughman); Isabel Jewell (Blonde); Willie Best (Algernon); Spencer Charters (Ed); George Meeker (Pfiffer); Robert Strange (Art); John Eldredge (Lon Preiser); Sam Hayes (Announcer).

THE WAGONS ROLL AT NIGHT (1941)

A Warner Bros.–First National picture. Directed by Ray Enright. Associate producer, Harlan Thompson. Screenplay by Fred Niblo, Jr., and Barry Trivers. Based on the novel *Kid Galahad* by Francis Wallace. Director of photography, Sid Hickox. Music by Heinz Roemheld. Film editor, Frederick Richards. Assistant director, Jesse Hibbs. Art director, Hugh Reticker. Special effects by Byron Haskin and H. F. Koenekamp. Orchestrations by Ray Heindorf. Running time, 84 minutes. Cast: Humphrey Bogart (Nick Coster); Sylvia Sidney (Flo Lorraine); Eddie Albert (Matt Varney); Joan Leslie (Mary Coster); Sig Rumann (Hoffman the Great); Cliff Clark (Doc); Charley Foy (Snapper); Frank Wilcox (Tex); John Ridgely (Arch); Clara Blandick (Mrs. Williams); Aldrich Bowker (Mr. Williams); Garry Owen (Gus); Jack Mower (Bundy); Frank Mayo (Wally).

THE MALTESE FALCON (1941)

A Warner Bros.–First National Picture. Directed by John Huston. Executive producer, Hal B. Wallis. Associate producer, Henry Blanke. Screenplay by John Huston. Based on the novel by Dashiell Hammett. Director of photography, Arthur Edeson. Music by Adolph Deutsch. Film editor, Thomas Richards. Dialogue director, Robert Foulk. [Assistant director, Claude Archer.] Art director, Robert Haas. Gowns by Orry-Kelly. Makeup artist, Perc Westmore. Sound recorder, Oliver S. Garretson. [Orchestrations by Arthur Lange.] Musical director, Leo F. Forbstein. Running time, 100 minutes. Cast: Humphrey Bogart (Sam [Samuel] Spade); Mary Astor (Brigid O'Shaughnessy); Gladys George (Iva Archer); Peter Lorre (Joel Cairo); Barton MacLane (Lieutenant of Detectives Dundy); Lee Patrick (Effie Perine); Sydney Greenstreet (Kasper Gutman); Ward Bond (Detective Tom Polhaus); Jerome Cowan (Miles Archer); Elisha Cook, Jr. (Wilmer Cook); James Burke (Luke); Murray Alper (Frank); John Hamilton (District Attorney Bryan); Unbilled: Emory Parnell (Mate of the *La Paloma*); and Walter Huston (Captain Jacobi).

300   Appendix III

ALL THROUGH THE NIGHT (1942)

A Warner Bros.–First National Picture. Directed by Vincent Sherman. Associate producer, Jerry Wald. Screenplay by Leonard Spigelgass and Edwin Gilbert. Based on a story by Leonard Q. Rodd (Leo Rosten) and Leonard Spigelgass. Director of photography, Sid Hickox. Music by Adolph Deutsch. Film editor, Rudi Fehr. [Assistant director, William Kissel.] Art director, Max Parker. Special effects by Edwin B. DuPar. Sound recorder, Oliver S. Garretson. Orchestrations by Frank Perkins. Song, "All Through the Night," lyrics by Johnny Mercer, and music by Arthur Schwartz. Makeup by Perc Westmore. Musical director, Leo F. Forbstein. Running time, 107 minutes. Cast: Humphrey Bogart (Gloves Donahue); Conrad Veidt (Hall Ebbing); Kaaren Verne (Leda Hamilton); Jane Darwell (Mrs. [Ma] Donahue); Frank McHugh (Barney); Peter Lorre (Pepi); Judith Anderson (Madame); William Demarest (Sunshine); Jackie C. Gleason (Starchy); Phil Silvers (Waiter); Wally Ford (Spats Hunter); Barton MacLane (Marty Callahan); Edward Brophy (Joe Denning); Martin Kosleck (Steindorff); Jean Ames (Annabelle); Ludwig Stossel (Mr. Miller); Irene Seidner (Mrs. Miller); James Burke (Forbes); Ben Welden (Smitty); Hans Schumm (Anton); Frank Sully (Sage); Charles Cane (Spence); Sam McDaniel (Deacon).

THE BIG SHOT (1942)

A Warner Bros.–First National Picture. Directed by Lewis Seiler. Produced by Walter MacEwen. Original screenplay by Bertram Millhauser, Abem Finkel, and Daniel Fuchs. Director of photography, Sid Hickox. Music by Adolph Deutsch. Film editor, Jack Killifer. Dialogue director, Harold Winston. Assistant director, Art Lueker. Art director, John Hughes. Gowns by Milo Anderson. Makeup artist, Perc Westmore. Sound recorder, Stanley Jones. Orchestrations by Jerome Moross. Musical director, Leo F. Forbstein. Running time, 82 minutes. Cast: Humphrey Bogart (Duke Berne); Irene Manning (Lorna Fleming); Richard Travis (George Anderson); Susan Peters (Ruth Carter); Stanley Ridges (Martin Fleming); Minor Watson (Warden Booth); Chick Chandler (Dancer); Joseph Downing (Frenchy); Howard da Silva (Sandor); Murray Alper (Quinto); Roland Drew (Faye); John Ridgely (Tim); Joseph King (Toohey); John Hamilton (Judge); Virginia Brissac (Mrs. Booth); William Edmunds (Sarto); Virginia Sale (Mrs. Miggs); Ken Christy (Kat); Wallace Scott (Rusty).

ACROSS THE PACIFIC (1942)

A Warner Bros.–First National Picture. Directed by John Huston. Produced by Jerry Wald and Jack Saper. Screenplay by Richard Macaulay. Based on the *Saturday Evening Post* serial "Aloha Means Goodbye" by Robert Carson. Director of photography, Arthur Edeson. Music by Adolph Deutsch. Film editor, Frank Magee. Dialogue director, Edward Blatt. [Assistant director, Lee Katz.] Art directors, Robert Haas and Hugh Reticker. Gowns by Milo Anderson. Makeup artist, Perc Westmore. Special effects by Byron Haskin and Willard Van Enger. Montages by Don Siegel. Sound recorder, Everett A. Brown. Musical director, Leo F. Forbstein. [Orchestrations by Clifford Vaughan.] Running time, 97 minutes. Cast: Humphrey Bogart (Rick Leland); Mary Astor (Alberta Marlow); Sydney Greenstreet (Dr. Lorenz); Charles Halton (A. V. Smith); Sen Yung (Joe

Totsuiko); Roland Got (Sugi); Lee Tung Foo (Sam Wing On); Frank Wilcox (Captain Morrison); Paul Stanton (Colonel Hart); Lester Matthews (Canadian Major); John Hamilton (Court-martial President); Tom Stevenson (unidentified man); Roland Drew (Captain Harkness); Monte Blue (Dan Morton); Chester Gan (Captain Higoto); Richard Loo (First Officer Miyuma); Keye Luke (Steamship Office Clerk); Kam Tong ([T. Oki] Prince—Emperor's son); Spencer Chan (Chief Engineer Mitsuko); Rudy Robles (Filipino Assassin).

CASABLANCA (1943)

A Warner Bros.–First National Picture. Directed by Michael Curtiz. Produced by Hal B. Wallis. Screenplay by Julius J. and Philip G. Epstein and Howard Koch. Based on the play *Everybody Comes to Rick's* by Murray Burnett and Joan Alison. Director of photography, Arthur Edeson. Music by Max Steiner. Film editor, Owen Marks. Dialogue director, Hugh MacMullen. Assistant director, Lee Katz. Art director, Carl Jules Weyl. Set decorations by George James Hopkins. Gowns by Orry-Kelly. Makeup artist, Perc Westmore. Special effects by Lawrence Butler and Willard Van Enger. Montages by Don Siegel and James Leicester. Sound recorder, Francis J. Scheid. Orchestrations by Hugo Friedhofer. Songs: "As Time Goes By" by Herman Hupfeld; "Knock on Wood" by M. K. Jerome and Jack Scholl. Technical adviser, Robert Aisner. Narrated by Lou Marcelle. Running time, 102 minutes. Cast: Humphrey Bogart (Rick); Ingrid Bergman (Ilsa); Paul Henreid (Victor Laszlo); Claude Rains (Captain Louis Renault); Conrad Veidt (Major Strasser); Sydney Greenstreet (Senor Farrari); Peter Lorre (Ugarte); S. Z. Sakall (Carl); Madeleine LeBeau (Yvonne); Dooley Wilson (Sam); Joy Page (Annina Brandel); John Qualen (Berger); Leonid Kinsky (Sascha); Helmut Dantine (Jan Brandel); Curt Bois (Pickpocket); Marcel Dalio (Croupier); Corinna Mura (Singer); Ludwig Stossel (Mr. Leuchtag); Ilka Gruning (Mrs. Leuchtag); Charles La Torre (Italian Officer Tonelli); Frank Puglia (Arab Vendor); Dan Seymour (Abdul).

ACTION IN THE NORTH ATLANTIC (1943)

A Warner Bros.–First National Picture. Directed by Lloyd Bacon. Produced by Jerry Wald. Screenplay by John Howard Lawson. Based on the story by Guy Gilpatric (additional dialogue by A. I. Bezzerides and W. R. Burnett). Director of photography, Ted McCord. Music by Adolph Deutsch. Film editor, George Amy. Dialogue director, Harold Winston. [Assistant director, Reggie Callow.] Art director, Ted Smith. Set decorations by Clarence I. Steensen. Makeup artist, Perc Westmore. Special effects by Jack Cosgrove, and Director, Edwin B. DuPar. Montages by Don Siegel and James Leicester. Sound recorder, C. A. Riggs. Orchestrations by Jerome Moross. Musical director, Leo F. Forbstein. Running time, 127 minutes. Cast: Humphrey Bogart (Joe Rossi); Raymond Massey (Captain Steve Jarvis); Alan Hale (Boats O'Hara); Julie Bishop (Pearl); Ruth Gordon (Mrs. Jarvis); Sam Levene (Chips Abrams); Dane Clark (Johnny Pulaski); Peter Whitney (Whitey Lara); Dick Hogan (Cadet Robert Parker); Minor Watson (Rear Admiral Hartridge); J. M. Kerrigan (Caviar Jinks); Kane Richmond (Ensign Wright); William von Brincken (German Sub Captain); Chick Chandler (Goldberg); George Offerman, Jr. (Cecil); Don Douglas (Lieutenant Commander); Art Foster (Peter Larson); Ray Montgomery (Aherne); Glenn Strange (Tex Mathews); Creighton Hale (Sparks); Elliott

Sullivan (Hennessy); Alec Craig (McGonigle); Ludwig Stossel (Captain Ziemer); Dick Wessel (Cherub); Frank Puglia (Captain Carpolis); Iris Adrian (Jenny O'Hara); Irving Bacon (Bartender); James Flavin (Lieutenant Commander).

THANK YOUR LUCKY STARS (1943)

A Warner Bros.–First National Picture. Directed by David Butler. Produced by Mark Hellinger. Screenplay by Norman Panama and Melvin Frank and James V. Kern. Based on an original story by Everett Freeman and Arthur Schwartz. Director of photography, Arthur Edeson. Film editor, Irene Morra. Dialogue director, Herbert Farjean. Assistant director, Phil Quinn. Art directors, Anton Grot and Leo K. Kuter. Set decorations by Walter F. Tilford. Gowns by Milo Anderson. Makeup artist, Perc Westmore. Special effects by H. F. Koenekamp. Sound recorders, Francis J. Scheid and Charles David Forrest. Dance numbers created and staged by Leroy Prinz. Songs by Arthur Schwartz and Frank Loesser. Orchestral arrangements by Ray Heindorf. Vocal arrangements by Dudley Chambers. Musical adaptations by Heinz Roemheld. Orchestrations by Maurice de Packh. Running time, 127 minutes. Cast: Humphrey Bogart (Himself); Eddie Cantor (Himself and Joe Simpson); Bette Davis (Herself); Olivia De Havilland (Herself); Errol Flynn (Himself); John Garfield (Himself); Joan Leslie (Pat Dixon); Ida Lupino (Herself); Dennis Morgan (Tom Randolph); Ann Sheridan (Herself); Dinah Shore (Herself); Alexis Smith (Herself); Jack Carson (Himself); Alan Hale (Himself); George Tobias (Himself); Edward Everett Horton (Farnsworth); S. Z. Sakall (Dr. Schlenna); Hattie McDaniel (Gossip); Ruth Donnelly (Nurse Hamilton); Don Wilson (Announcer); Willie Best (Soldier); Henry Armetta (Angelo); Joyce Reynolds (Girl with a book); Spike Jones and His City Slickers.

SAHARA (1943)

A Columbia Picture. Directed by Zoltan Korda. Produced by Harry Joe Brown. Screenplay by John Howard Lawson and Zoltan Korda. Adaptation by James O'Hanlon. From an original story by Philip MacDonald, based on an incident in the Soviet film *The Thirteen*. Director of photography, Rudolph Maté. Music by Miklos Rozsa. Film editor, Charles Nelson. Assistant director, Abby Berlin. Art director, Lionel Banks; associate, Eugene Lourie. Set decorations by William Kiernan. Sound recorder, Lodge Cunningham. Musical director, Morris Stoloff. Running time, 97 minutes. Cast: Humphrey Bogart (Sergeant Joe Gunn); Bruce Bennett (Waco Hoyt); J. Carrol Naish (Giuseppe); Lloyd Bridges (Fred Clarkson); Rex Ingram (Tambul); Richard Nugent (Capt. Jason Halliday); Dan Duryea (Jimmy Doyle); Carl Harbord (Marty Williams); Patrick O'Moore (Ozzie Bates); Louis Mercier (Jean Leroux); Guy Kingsford (Peter Stegman); Kurt Krueger (Capt. Von Schletow); John Wengraf (Major Von Falken); Hans Schumm (Sergeant Krause).

REPORT FROM THE FRONT (1944)

Red Cross Drive Committee of the Motion Picture Industry. Distributed by National Screen Service. Running time, 3 minutes. Cast: Humphrey Bogart (as himself) and Mayo Methot (as herself).

PASSAGE TO MARSEILLE (1944)

A Warner Bros.–First National Picture. Directed by Michael Curtiz. Produced by Hal B. Wallis. Screenplay by Casey Robinson and Jack Moffitt. Based on the novel *Men Without Country* by Charles Nordhoff and James Norman Hall. Director of photography, James Wong Howe. Music by Max Steiner. Film editor, Owen Marks. Dialogue director, Herschel Daugherty. Assistant director, Frank Heath. Art director, Carl Jules Weyl. Set decorations by George James Hopkins. Gowns by Leah Rhodes. Makeup artist, Perc Westmore. Special effects by Jack Cosgrove, Edwin B. DuPar, [Byron Haskin, E. Roy Davidson, and Rex Wimpy]. Montages by James Leicester. Sound recorder, Everett A. Brown. Orchestrations by Leonid Raab. Song, "Someday I'll Meet You Again," by Max Steiner and Ned Washington. Technical adviser, Sylvain Robert. Running time, 109 minutes. Cast: Humphrey Bogart (Matrac); Claude Rains (Capt. Freycinet); Michele Morgan (Paula); Philip Doran (Renault); Sydney Greenstreet (Major Duval); Peter Lorre (Marius); George Tobias (Petit); Helmut Dantine (Garou); John Loder (Manning); Victor Francen (Capt. Malo); Vladimir Sokoloff (Grandpére); Eduardo Cianelli [Edward Cinnelli] (Chief Engineer); Corinna Mura (Singer); Konstantin Shayne (First Mate); Stephen Richards (Lt. Hastings); Charles La Torre (Lt. Lenoir); Hans Conried (Jourdain); Monte Blue (Second Mate); Billy Roy (Mess Boy); Frederick Brunn (Bijou); Louis Mercier (Second Engineer).

TO HAVE AND HAVE NOT (1945)

A Warner Bros.–First National Picture. Produced and directed by Howard Hawks. Screenplay by Jules Furthman and William Faulkner. Based on the novel by Ernest Hemingway. Director of photography, Sid Hickox. Music by Franz Waxman. Film editor, Christian Nyby. [Assistant director, Jack Sullivan.] Art director, Charles Novi. Set decorations by Casey Roberts. Gowns by Milo Anderson. Makeup artist, Perc Westmore. Special effects by Roy Davidson and Rex Wimpy. Sound recorder, Oliver S. Garretson. Orchestrations by Leonid Raab. Song: "How Little We Know." Music by Hoagy Carmichael and lyrics by Johnny Mercer. Technical adviser, Louis Comien. Musical director, Leo F. Forbstein. Running time, 100 minutes. Cast: Humphrey Bogart (Harry Morgan); Walter Brennan (Eddie); Lauren Bacall (Marie); Dolores Moran (Helene de Brusac); Hoagy Carmichael (Cricket); Walter Molnar (Paul de Brusac); Sheldon Leonard (Lieutenant Coyo); Marcel Dalio (Gerard); Walter Sande (Johnson); Dan Seymour (Captain Renard); Aldo Nadi (Renard's Bodyguard); Paul Marion (Beauclerc); Patricia Shay (Mrs. Beauclerc); Emmett Smith (Bartender); Sir Lancelot (Horatio).

CONFLICT (1945)

A Warner Bros.–First National Picture. Directed by Curtis Bernhardt. Produced by William Jacobs. Screenplay by Arthur T. Horman and Dwight Taylor. Based on an original story by Robert Siodmak and Alfred Neumann. Director of photography, Meritt Gerstad. Music by Frederick Hollander. Film editor, David Weisbart. Dialogue director, James Vincent. Assistant director, Elmer Decker. Art director, Ted Smith. Set decorations by Clarence I. Steensen. Gowns by Milo Anderson. Makeup artist, Perc Westmore. Sound recorder, Oliver S. Garretson. Orchestrations by Jerome Moross. Running time, 86 minutes. Cast: Humphrey Bogart (Richard Mason); Alexis Smith (Evelyn Turner); Sydney Greenstreet (Dr. Mark Hamilton); Rose Hobart (Kathryn Mason); Charles Drake (Prof. Norman Holdsworth); Grant Mitchell (Dr. Grant); Patrick O'Moore (Detective Lt. Egan); Ann Shoemaker (Nora Grant); Frank Wilcox (Robert Freston); Edwin Stanley (Phillips); James Flavin (Detective Lt. Workman); Mary Servoss (Mrs. Allman).

HOLLYWOOD VICTORY CARAVAN (1945)

Produced for the War Activities Committee and the Treasury Department by Paramount Pictures. War Activities Committee release No. 136. Directed by William Russell. Produced by Louis Harris. Supervisor, Bernard Luber. Script by Melville Shavelson. Song, "We've Got Another Bond to Buy," by Jimmy McHugh and Harold Adamson. Running time, 20 minutes. Cast: Robert Benchley, Humphrey Bogart, Joe Carioca, Carmen Cavallero and his orchestra, Bing Crosby, William Demarest, Dona Drake, Bob Hope, Betty Hutton, Alan Ladd, Diana Lynn, Noreen Nash, Franklin Pangborn, Olga San Juan, Barbara Stanwyck, Charles Victor, Marjorie Weaver, Virginia Welles, and the U.S. Maritime Service Training Station Choir.

TWO GUYS FROM MILWAUKEE (1946)

A Warner Bros.–First National Picture. Directed by David Butler. Produced by Alex Gottlieb. Original screenplay by Charles Hoffman and I. A. L. Diamond. Director of photography, Arthur Edeson. Music by Frederick Hollander. Film editor, Irene Morra. Dialogue director, Felix Jacoves. Assistant director, Jesse Hibbs. Art director, Leo K. Kuter. Set decorations by Jack McConaghy. Gowns by Leah Rhodes. Makeup artist, Perc Westmore. Special effects by Harry Barndollar and Edwin B. DuPar. Montages by James Leicester. Sound recorder, Stanley Jones. Orchestrations by Lenoid Raab. Song, "And Her Tears Flowed Like Wine," by Charles Lawrence, Joe Greene, and Stan Kenton. Running time, 90 minutes. Cast: Dennis Morgan (Prince Henry); Jack Carson (Buzz Williams); Joan Leslie (Connie Reed); Janis Paige (Polly); S. Z. Sakall (Count Oswald); Patti Brady (Peggy); Tom D'Andrea (Happy); Rosemary DeCamp (Nan); John Ridgely (Mike Collins); Pat McVey (Johnson); Franklin Pangborn (Theatre Manager); Francis Pierlot (Dr. Bauer); Lauren Bacall (Herself); Humphrey Bogart (Himself).

THE BIG SLEEP (1946)

A Warner Bros.–First National Picture. Produced and directed by Howard Hawks. Screenplay by William Faulkner, Leigh Brackett, and Jules Furthman. Based on the novel by Raymond Chandler. Director of photography, Sid Hickox. Music by Max Steiner. Film editor, Christian Nyby. [Assistant director, Robert Vreeland.] Art director, Carl Jules Weyl. Set decorations by Fred M. MacLean. Wardrobe by Leah Rhodes. Special effects by E. Roy Davidson. Director, Warren E. Lynch, [William McGann, Robert Burks, and Willard Van Enger.] Sound recorder, Robert B. Lee. Orchestrations by Simon Bucharoff. Makeup, Perc Westmore. Musical director, Leo F. Forbstein. Running time, 114 minutes. Cast: Humphrey Bogart (Philip Marlowe); Lauren Bacall (Vivian Rutledge); John Ridgely (Eddie Mars); Martha Vickers (Carmen Sternwood); Dorothy Maline (Bookshop Proprietress); Peggy Knudsen (Mrs. Eddie Mars); Regis Toomey (Bernie Ohls); Charles

Waldron (General Sternwood); Charles D. Brown (Norris); Bob Steele (Canino); Elisha Cook, Jr. (Harry Jones); Louis Jean Heydt (Joe Brody); Sonia Darrin (Agnes); James Flavin (Captain Cronjager); Thomas Jackson (District Attorney Wilde); Dan Wallace (Carol Lundgren); Theodore Von Eltz (Arthur Gwynn Geiger); Joy Barlowe (Taxicab Driver); Tom Fadden (Sidney); Ben Welden (Pete); Trevor Bardette (Art Huck); Joseph Crehan (Medical Examiner).

DEAD RECKONING (1947)

A Columbia Picture. Directed by John Cromwell. Produced by Sidney Biddell. Screenplay by Oliver H. P. Garrett and Steve Fisher. Adaptation by Allen Rivkin. Based on an original story by Gerald Adams and Sidney Biddell. Director of photography, Leo Tover. Music by Marlin Skiles. Assistant director, Seymour Friedman. Art directors, Stephen Goosson and Rudolph Sternad. Set decorations by Louis Diage. Gowns by Jean Louis. Makeup artist, Clay Campbell. Hair styles by Helen Hunt. Sound recorder, Jack Goodrich. Song, "Either It's Love or It Isn't," by Allan Roberts and Doris Fisher. Musical director, Morris Stoloff. Running time, 100 minutes. Cast: Humphrey Bogart (Rip Murdock); Lizabeth Scott (Coral Chandler); Morris Carnovsky (Martinelli); Charles Cane (Lieutenant Kincaid); William Prince (Johnny Drake); Marvin Miller (Krause); Wallace Ford (McGee); James Bell (Father Logan); George Chandler (Louis Ord); William Forrest (Lt. Col. Simpson); Ruby Dandridge (Hyacinth).

THE TWO MRS. CARROLLS (1947)

A Warner Bros.–First National Picture. Directed by Peter Godfrey. Produced by Mark Hellinger. Screenplay by Thomas Job. Based on the play by Martin Vale. Director of photography, Peverell Marley. Music by Franz Waxman. Film editor, Frederick Richards. [Assistant director, Claude Archer.] Art director, Anton Grot. Set decorations by Budd Friend. Wardrobe, Milo Anderson [Ms. Stanwyck's gown by Edith Head.] Makeup artist, Perc Westmore. Special effects by Robert Burks. Sound recorder, C. A. Riggs. Orchestrations by Leonid Raab. Musical director, Leo F. Forbstein. Running time, 99 minutes. Cast: Humphrey Bogart (Geoffrey Carroll); Barbara Stanwyck (Sally Carroll); Alexis Smith (Cecily Latham); Nigel Bruce (Dr. Tuttle); Isobel Elsom (Mrs. Latham); Pat O'Moore (Charles Pennington); Ann Carter (Beatrice Carroll); Anita Bolster (Christine); Barry Bernard (Mr. Blagdon); Colin Campbell (MacGregor); Peter Godfrey (Race Track Tout).

DARK PASSAGE (1947)

A Warner Bros.–First National Picture. Directed by Delmer Daves. Produced by Jerry Wald. Screenplay by Delmer Daves. Based on the novel by David Goodis. Director of photography, Sid Hickox. Music by Franz Waxman. Film editor, David Weisbart. Assistant director, Dick Mayberry. Art director, Charles H. Clarke. Set decorations by William Kuehl. Wardrobe by Bernard Newman. Makeup artist, Perc Westmore. Special effects by H. F. Koenekamp. Sound recorder, Dolph Thomas. Orchestrations by Leonid Raab. Running time, 106 minutes. Cast: Humphrey Bogart (Vincent Parry); Lauren Bacall (Irene Jansen); Bruce Bennett (Bob Rapf); Agnes Moorehead (Madge Rapf); Tom

D'Andrea (Sam); Clifton Young (Baker); Douglas Kennedy (Detective); Rory Mallinson (George Fellsinger); Houseley Stevenson (Dr. Walter Coley).

ALWAYS TOGETHER (1948)

A Warner Bros.–First National Picture. Directed by Frederick de Cordova. Produced by Alex Gottlieb. Original screenplay by Phoebe and Henry Ephron and I. A. L. Diamond. Director of photography, Carl Guthrie. Music by Werner Heymann. Film editor, Folmer Blangsted. Dialogue director, John Maxwell. Assistant director, James McMahon. Art director, Leo K. Kuter. Set decorations by Jack McConaghy. Wardrobe by Travilla. Makeup artist, Perc Westmore. Special effects by William McGann and Edwin B. DuPar. Montages by James Leicester. Sound recorder, C. A. Riggs. Orchestrations by Leonid Raab. Running time, 78 minutes. Cast: Robert Hutton (Donn Masters); Joyce Reynolds (Jane Barker); Cecil Kellaway (Jonathan Turner); Ernest Truex (Mr. Bull); Don McGuire (McIntyre); Ransom Sherman (Judge); Douglas Kennedy (Doberman); Unbilled cameo: Humphrey Bogart.

THE TREASURE OF THE SIERRA MADRE (1948)

A Warner Bros.–First National Picture. Directed by John Huston. Produced by Henry Blanke. Screenplay by John Huston. Based on the novel by B. Traven. Director of photography, Ted McCord. Music by Max Steiner. Film editor, Owen Marks. Assistant director, Dick Mayberry. Art director, John Hughes. Set decorations by Fred M. MacLean. Makeup artist, Perc Westmore. Special effects by William McGann and H. F. Koenekamp. Sound recorder, Robert B. Lee. Orchestrations by Murray Cutter. Musical director, Leo F. Forbstein. Running time, 126 minutes. Cast: Humphrey Bogart (Dobbs); Walter Huston (Howard); Tim Holt (Curtin); Bruce Bennett (Cody); Barton MacLane (McCormick); Alfonso Bedoya (Gold Hat); A. Soto Rangel (Presidente); Manuel Donde (El Jefe); Jose Torvay (Pablo); Margarito Luna (Pancho); Jacqueline Dalya (Flashy Girl); Robert Blake (Mexican Boy); John Huston (White Suit); Jack Holt (Flophouse Bum).

KEY LARGO (1948)

A Warner Bros.–First National Picture. Directed by John Huston. Produced by Jerry Wald. Screenplay by Richard Brooks and John Huston. Based on the play by Maxwell Anderson as produced on the Spoken Stage, by the Playwrights Company. Director of photography, Karl Freund. Music by Max Steiner. Film editor, Rudi Fehr. [Assistant director, Art Lueker.] Art director, Leo K. Kuter. Set decorations by Fred M. MacLean. Wardrobe by Leah Rhodes. Makeup artist, Perc Westmore. Special effects by William McGann, director and Robert Burks. Sound recorder, Dolph Thomas. Orchestrations by Murray Cutter. Song, "Moanin' Low," by Ralph Rainger and Howard Dietz. Running time, 101 minutes. Cast: Humphrey Bogart (Frank McCloud); Edward G. Robinson (Johnny Rocco); Lauren Bacall (Nora Temple); Lionel Barrymore (James Temple); Claire Trevor (Gaye Dawn); Thomas Gomez (Curley Hoff); Harry Lewis (Toots Bass); John Rodney (Deputy Clyde Sawyer); Marc Lawrence (Ziggy); Dan Seymour (Angel Garcia); Monte Blue (Sheriff Ben Wade); William Haade (Ralph Feeney); Jay Silverheels (Tom Osceola); Rodric Redwing (John Osceola).

KNOCK ON ANY DOOR (1949)

A Santana Production. Released by Columbia Pictures. Directed by Nicholas Ray. Produced by Robert Lord. Associate producer, Henry S. Kesler. Screenplay by Daniel Taradash and John Monks, Jr. Based on the novel by Willard Motley. Director of photography, Burnett Guffey. Music by George Antheil. Film editor, Viola Lawrence. Assistant director, Arthur S. Black. Art director, Robert Peterson. Set decorations by William Kiernan. Gowns by Jean Louis. Makeup artist, Clay Campbell. Hair styles by Helen Hunt. Sound recorder, Frank Goodwin. Orchestrations by Ernest Gold. Musical director, Morris Stoloff. Technical advisers, National Probation and Parole Association. Running time, 100 minutes. Cast: Humphrey Bogart (Andrew Morton); John Derek (Nick Romano); George Macready (Kerman); Allene Roberts (Emma); Susan Perry (Adele Morton); Mickey Knox (Vito); Barry Kelley (Judge Drake); Cara Williams (Nelly); Jimmy Conlin (Kid Fingers); Sumner Williams (Jimmy); Sid Melton (Squint); Pepe Hern (Juan); Dewey Martin (Butch); Robert A. Davis (Sunshine); Houseley Stevenson (Junior); Vince Barnett (Bartender); Thomas Sully (Officer Hawkins); Florence Auer (Aunt Lena); Pierre Watkin (Purcell); Gordon Nelson (Corey); Argentina Brunetti (Ma Romano); Dick Sinatra (Julian Romano); Carol Coombs (Ang Romano); Joan Baxter (Maria Romano).

TOKYO JOE (1949)

A Santana Production. Released by Columbia Pictures. Directed by Stuart Heisler. Produced by Robert Lord. Associate producer, Henry S. Kesler. Screenplay by Cyril Hume and Bertram Millhauser. Adaptation by Walter Doniger. Based on a story by Steve Fisher. Director of photography, Charles Lawton, Jr. Music by George Antheil. Film editor, Viola Lawrence. Dialogue director, Jason Lindsey. Assistant director, Wilbur McGaugh. Art director, Robert Peterson. Set decorations by James Crowe. Gowns by Jean Louis. Makeup artist, Clay Campbell. Hair styles by Helen Hunt. Sound recorder, Russell Malmgren. Orchestrations by Ernest Gold. Musical director, Morris Stoloff. Running time, 88 minutes. Cast: Humphrey Bogart (Joe Barrett); Alexander Knox (Mark Landis); Florence Marly (Trina); Sessue Hayakawa (Baron Kimura); Jerome Courtland (Danny); Gordon Jones (Idaho); Teru Shimada (Ito); Hideo Mori (Kanda); Charles Meredith (General Ireton); Rhys Williams (Colonel Dahlgren); Lora Lee Michael (Anya); Kyoko Kamo (Nani-San); Gene Gondo (Kamikaze); Harold Goodwin (Major Loomis); James Cardwell (M. P. Captain); Frank Kumagai (Truck Driver); Tetsu Komai (Takenobu); Otto Han (Hara); Yosan Tsuruta (Goro).

CHAIN LIGHTNING (1950)

A Warner Bros.–First National Picture. Directed by Stuart Heisler. Produced by Anthony Veiller. Screenplay by Liam O'Brien and Vincent Evans. Based on an original story by J. Redmond Prior. Director of photography, Ernest Haller. Music by David Buttolph. Film editor, Thomas Reilly. Assistant director, Don Page. Art director, Leo Kuter. Set decorations by William Wallace. Gowns by Leah Rhodes. Makeup artist, Perc Westmore. Special effects by William McGann, Harry Barndollar, H. F. Koenekamp, and Edwin B. DuPar. Sound recorder, Francis J. Scheid. Orchestrations by Maurice de Packh. Song, "Bless 'Em All," by J. Hughes, Frank Lake, and Al Stillman. Running time, 94 minutes.

Cast: Humphrey Bogart (Matt Brennan); Eleanor Parker (Jo Holloway); Raymond Massey (Leland Willis); Richard Whorf (Carl Troxell); James Brown (Major Hinkle); Roy Roberts (General Hewitt); Morris Ankrum (Ed Bostwick); Fay Baker (Mrs. Willis); Fred Sherman (Jeb Farley).

IN A LONELY PLACE (1950)

A Santana Production. Released by Columbia Pictures. Directed by Nicholas Ray. Produced by Robert Lord. Associate producer, Henry S. Kesler. Screenplay by Andrew Solt. Adaptation by Edmund H. North. Based on the novel by Dorothy B. Hughes. Director of photography, Burnett Guffey. Music by George Antheil. Film editor, Viola Lawrence. Assistant director, Earl Bellamy. Art director, Robert Peterson. Set decorations by William Kiernan. Gowns by Jean Louis. Makeup artist, Clay Campbell. Hair styles by Helen Hunt. Sound recorder, Howard Fogetti. Orchestrations by Ernest Gold. Musical director, Morris Stoloff. Technical adviser, Rodney Amateau. Running time, 94 minutes. Cast: Humphrey Bogart (Dixon Steele); Gloria Grahame (Laurel Gray); Frank Lovejoy (Brub Nicolai); Carl Benton Reid (Captain Lochner); Art Smith (Mel Lippman); Jeff Donnell (Sylvia Nicolai); Martha Stewart (Mildred Atkinson); Robert Warwick (Charlie Waterman); Morris Ankrum (Lloyd Barnes); William Ching (Ted Barton); Steven Geray (Paul); Hadda Brooks (Singer); Alice Talton (Frances Randolph); Jack Reynolds (Henry Kesler); Ruth Warren (Effie); Ruth Gillette (Martha); Guy Beach (Swan); Lewis Howard (Junior).

THE ENFORCER (1951)

A United States Picture for Warner Bros. Directed by Bretaigne Windust. Produced by Milton Sperling. Original screenplay by Martin Rackin. Director of photography, Robert Burks. Music by David Buttolph. Film editor, Fred Allen. Assistant director, Chuck Hansen. Art director, Charles H. Clarke. Set decorations by William Kuehl. Sound recorder, Dolph Thomas. Orchestrations by Maurice de Packh. Running time, 87 minutes. Cast: Humphrey Bogart (Martin Ferguson); Zero Mostel (Big Babe Lazich); Ted De Corsia (Joseph Rico); Everett Sloane (Albert Mendoza); Roy Roberts (Capt. Frank Nelson); Lawrence Tolan (Duke Mallow); King Donovan (Sgt. Whitlow); Bob Steele (Herman); Adelaide Klein (Olga Kirshen); Don Beddoe (Thomas O'Hara); Tito Vuolo (Tony Vetto); John Kellogg (Vince); Jack Lambert (Philadelphia Tom Zaca); Patricia Joiner (Angela Vetto); Susan Cabot (Nina Lombardo); Mario Siletti (Louis the Barber).

SIROCCO (1951)

A Santana Production. Released by Columbia Pictures. Directed by Curtis Bernhardt. Produced by Robert Lord. Associate producer, Henry S. Kesler. Screenplay by A. I. Bezzerides and Hans Jacoby. Based on the novel *Coup de Grâce* by Joseph Kessel. Director of photography, Burnett Guffey. Music by George Antheil. Film editor, Viola Lawrence. Assistant director, Earl Bellamy. Art director, Robert Peterson. Set decorations by Robert Priestley. Makeup artist, Clay Campbell. Hair styles by Helen Hunt. Sound recorder, Lodge Cunningham. Orchestrations by Ernest Gold. Musical director, Morris Stoloff. Running time, 98 minutes. Cast: Humphrey Bogart (Harry Smith); Marta Toren (Violette); Lee J. Cobb (Colonel Feroud); Everett Sloane (General LaSalle); Gerald Mohr

(Major Leon); Zero Mostel (Balukjian); Nick Dennis (Nasir Aboud); Onslow Stevens (Emir Hassan); Ludwig Donath (Flophouse Proprietor); David Bond (Achmet); Vincent Renno (Arthur); Martin Wilkins (Omar); Peter Ortiz (Major Robbinet); Edward Colmans (Colonel Corville); Al Eben (Sergeant); Peter Brocco (Barber); Jay Novello (Hamal); Leonard Penn (Rifat); Harry Guardino (Lieutenant Collet).

THE AFRICAN QUEEN (1951)

A Horizon-Romulus Production. Released through United Artists. Color by Technicolor. Directed by John Huston. Produced by S. P. Eagle [Sam Spiegel]. Screenplay by James Agee and John Huston. Based on the novel by C. S. Forester. Director of photography, Jack Cardiff. Music by Alan Gray, played by the Royal Philharmonic Orchestra conducted by Norman Del Mar. Film editor, Ralph Kemplen. Assistant director, Guy Hamilton. Art director, Wilfred Shingleton; associate, John Hoesli. Production managers, Leigh Aman and T. S. Lyndon-Haynes. Ms. Hepburn's costumes by Doris Langley Moore; other clothes by Connie De Pinna. Makeup artist, George Frost. Second unit photography by Ted Scaife. Special effects by Cliff Richardson. Sound recorder, John Mitchell. Sound editor, Eric Wood. Camera operator, Ted Moore. Hairdresser, Eileen Bates. Wardrobe mistress, Vi Murray. Continuity by Angela Allen. Running time, 105 minutes. Cast: Humphrey Bogart (Charlie Allnut); Katharine Hepburn (Rose Sayer); Robert Morley (Rev. Samuel Sayer, The Brother); Peter Bull (Captain of the Louisa); Theodore Bikel (First Officer (Louisa); Walter Gotell (Second Officer (Louisa); Gerald Onn (Petty Officer (Louisa); Peter Swanwick (First Officer (Shona); Richard Marner (Second Officer (Shona).

DEADLINE—U.S.A. (1952)

A 20th Century-Fox Picture. Directed by Richard Brooks. Produced by Sol C. Siegel. Original screenplay by Richard Brooks. Director of photography, Milton Krasner. Music by Cyril Mockridge and Sol Kaplan. Film editor, William B. Murphy. Assistant director, Dick Mayberry. Art directors, Lyle Wheeler and George Patrick. Set decorations by Thomas Little and Walter M. Scott. Wardrobe direction, Charles Le Maire. Costumes by Eloise Jensen. Makeup artist, Ben Nye. Special effects by Ray Kellogg. Sound recorders, E. Clayton Ward and Harry M. Leonard. Orchestrations by Edward Powell and Bernard Mayers. Musical director, Lionel Newman. Running time, 87 minutes. Cast: Humphrey Bogart (Ed Hutchinson); Ethel Barrymore (Mrs. Garrison); Kim Hunter (Nora); Ed Begley (Frank Allen); Warren Stevens (George Burrows); Paul Stewart (Harry Thompson); Martin Gabel (Tomas Rienzi); Joe De Santis (Herman Schmidt); Joyce MacKenzie (Kitty Garrison Geary); Audrey Christie (Mrs. Willebrandt); Fay Baker (Alice Garrison Courtney); Jim Backus (Jim Cleary); Carleton Young (Crane); Selmer Jackson (Williams); Fay Roope (Judge); Parley Baer (Headwaiter); John Douchette (Hal); Florence Shirley (Miss Barndollar); Kasia Orzazewski (Mrs. Schmidt); Raymond Greenleaf (Lawrence White); Tom Powers (Wharton); Thomas Browne Henry (Fenway); Philip Terry (Lewis Schaefer); Joseph Sawyer (Whitey); Lawrence Dobkin (Larry Hansen); Alex Gerry (Prentiss); Clancy Cooper (Captain Finlay); Willis Bouchey (Henry); Joseph Crehan (White's City Editor).

U.S. SAVINGS BOND TRAILER (1952)

Appeal by Bogart to purchase savings bonds, attached to July 25–26 newsreel releases.

BATTLE CIRCUS (1953)

A Metro-Goldwyn-Mayer Picture. Directed by Richard Brooks. Produced by Pandro S. Berman. Screenplay by Richard Brooks. Based on an original story by Allen Rivkin and Laura Kerr. Director of photography, John Alton. Music by Lennie Hayton. Film editor, George Boemler. Assistant director, Al Jennings. Art directors, Cedric Gibbons and James Basevi. Set decorations by Edwin B. Willis and Alfred E. Spencer. Makeup artist, William Tuttle. Special effects by A. Arnold Gillespie. Recording supervisor, Douglas Shearer. Orchestrations by Robert Franklyn. Technical advisers, Lt. Col. K. E. Van Buskirk and Lt. Mary Couch. Running time, 90 minutes. Cast: Humphrey Bogart (Major Jed Webbe); June Allyson (Lt. Ruth McCara); Keenan Wynn (Sgt. Orvil Statt); Robert Keith (Lt. Col. Hillary Whalters); William Campbell (Capt. John Rustford); Perry Sheehan (Lt. Laurence); Patricia Tiernan (Lt. Rose Ashland); Jonathan Cott (Adjutant); Adele Longmire (Lt. Jane Franklin); Ann Morrison (Lt. Edith Edwards); Helen Winston (Lt. Graciano); Sarah Selby (Capt. Dobbs); Danny Chang (Danny); Philip Ahn (Korean Prisoner); Steve Forrest (Sergeant); Jeff Richards (Lieutenant); Dick Simmons (Capt. Norson).

BEAT THE DEVIL (1954)

A Santana-Romulus Production. Released through United Artists. Directed by John Huston. Associate producer, Jack Clayton. Screenplay by John Huston and Truman Capote. Based on the novel by Claude Cockburn (*London Times* correspondent) [James Helvick, pseudonym]. Director of photography, Oswald Morris. Music by Franco Mannino. Film editor, Ralph Kemplen. Art director, Wilfred Shingleton. Sound recorders, George Stephenson and E. Law. Musical director, Lambert Willamson. Running time, 93 minutes. Cast: Humphrey Bogart (Billy Dannreuther); Jennifer Jones (Gwendolen Chelm); Gina Lollobrigida (Maria Dannreuther); Robert Morley (Petersen); Peter Lorre (O'Hara); Edward Underdown (Harry Chelm); Ivor Barnard (Major Ross); Bernard Lee (C.I.D. Inspector); Marco Tulli (Ravello); Mario Perroni (Purser); Alex Pochet (Hotel Manager); Aldo Silvani (Charles); Guilio Donnini (Administrator); Saro Urzi (Captain); Juan de Landa (Hispano-Suiza Driver); Manuel Serano (Arab Officer); Mimo Poli (Barman).

THE CAINE MUTINY (1954)

A Stanley Kramer Company Production. Released by Columbia Pictures. Color by Technicolor. Directed by Edward Dmytryk. Produced by Stanley Kramer. Screenplay by Stanley Roberts. Additional dialogue by Michael Blankfort. Based on the novel by Herman Wouk. Director of photography, Franz Planer. Music by Max Steiner. Production design by Rudolph Sternad. Film editors, William Lyon and Henry Batista. Assistant director, Carter DeHaven, Jr. Art director, Cary Odell. Set decorations by Frank Tuttle. Gowns by Jean Louis. Makeup artist, Clay Campbell. Hair styles by Helen Hunt. Second unit photography by Ray Cory. Special effects by Lawrence Butler. Sound recorder, Lambert Day. Songs: "I Can't Believe That You're in Love with Me" by Jimmy McHugh and

Clarence Gaskill; "Yellowstain Blues" by Fred Karger and Herman Wouk. Color consultant, Francis Cugat. Technical adviser, Comdr. James C. Shaw, U.S.N. Running time, 125 minutes. Cast: Humphrey Bogart (Captain Queeg); José Ferrer (Lt. Barney Greenwald); Van Johnson (Lt. Steve Maryk); Fred MacMurray (Lt. Tom Keefer); Robert Francis (Ensign Willie Keith); May Wynn (May Wynn); Tom Tully (Captain DeVriess); E. G. Marshall (Lt. Comdr. Challee); Arthur Franz (Lt. Paynter); Lee Marvin (Meatball); Warner Anderson (Captain Blakely); Claude Akins (Horrible); Katharine Warren (Mrs. Keith); Jerry Paris (Ensign Harding); Steve Brodie (Chief Budge); Todd Karns (Stilwell); Whit Bissell (Lt. Comdr. Dickson); James Best (Lt. Jorgensen); Joe Haworth (Ensign Carmody); Guy Anderson (Ensign Rabbit); James Edwards (Whittaker); Don Dubbins (Urban); David Alpert (Engstrand).

SABRINA (1954)

A Paramount Picture. Produced and directed by Billy Wilder. Screenplay by Billy Wilder, Samuel Taylor, and Ernest Lehman. Based on the play *Sabrina Fair* by Samuel Taylor. Director of photography, Charles Lang, Jr. Music by Frederick Hollander. Film editor, Arthur Schmidt. Assistant director, C. C. Coleman, Jr. Art directors, Hal Pereira and Walter Tyler. Set decorations by Sam Comer and Ray Moyer. Costumes by Edith Head. Makeup artist, Wally Westmore. Special effects by John P. Fulton and Farciot Edouart. Sound recorders, Harold Lewis and John Cope. Running time, 113 minutes. Cast: Humphrey Bogart (Linus Larrabee); Audrey Hepburn (Sabrina Fairchild); William Holden (David Larrabee); Walter Hampden (Oliver Larrabee); John Williams (Thomas Fairchild); Martha Hyer (Elizabeth Tyson); Joan Vohs (Gretchen Van Horn); Marcel Dalio (Baron); Marcel Hillaire (The Professor); Nella Walker (Maude Larrabee); Francis X. Bushman (Mr. Tyson); Ellen Corby (Miss McCardle).

THE BAREFOOT CONTESSA (1954)

A Figaro Incorporated Production. Released through United Artists. Color by Technicolor. Directed by Joseph L. Mankiewicz. Original screenplay by Joseph L. Mankiewicz. Production supervisor, Forrest E. Johnston. Production associates, Franco Magli and Michael Waszynski. Director of photography, Jack Cardiff. Music by Mario Nascimbene. Film editor, William Hornbeck. Assistant director, Pietro Mussetta. Art director, Arrigo Equini. Gowns by Fontana. Sound recorder, Charles Knott. Running time, 128 minutes. Cast: Humphrey Bogart (Harry Dawes); Ava Gardner (Maria Vargas); Edmond O'Brien (Oscar Muldoon); Marius Goring (Alberto Bravano); Valentina Cortesa (Eleanora Torlato-Favrini); Rossano Brazzi (Vincenzo Torlato-Favrini); Elizabeth Sellars (Jerry); Warren Stevens (Kirk Edwards); Franco Interlenghi (Pedro); Mari Aldon (Myrna); Bessie Love (Mrs. Eubanks); Diana Decker (J. Montague Brown); Alberto Rabagliati (Night Club Proprietor); Enzo Staiola (Busboy); Haria Zanoli (Maria's Mother); Renato Chiantoni (Maria's Father); John Parrish (Mr. Black); Jim Gerald (Mr. Blue); Riccardo Rioli (Gypsy Dancer); Tonio Selwart (The Pretender); Margaret Anderson (The Pretender's Wife); Gertrude Flynn (Lulu McGee); John Horne (Hector Eubanks); Robert Christopher (Eddie Blake); Anna Maria Paduan (Chambermaid); Carlo Dale (Chauffeur).

WE'RE NO ANGELS (1955)

A Paramount Picture. In VistaVision. Color by Technicolor. Directed by Michael Curtiz. Produced by Pat Duggan. Screenplay by Ranald MacDougall. Based on the play *La Cuisine des Anges* by Albert Husson. Director of photography, Loyal Griggs. Music by Frederick Hollander. Film editor, Arthur Schmidt. Assistant director, John Coonan. Dialogue assistant, Norman Stuart. Art directors, Hal Pereira and Roland Anderson. Set decorations by Sam Comer and Grace Gregory. Costumes by Mary Grant. Makeup artist, Wally Westmore. Special effects by John P. Fulton. Sound recorders, Hugo Grenzbach and John Cope. Songs: "Sentimental Moments" by Frederick Hollander and Ralph Freed; "Ma France Bien-Aimée" by G. Martini and Roger Wagner. Color consultant, Richard Mueller. Running time, 103 minutes. Cast: Humphrey Bogart (Joseph); Aldo Ray (Albert); Peter Ustinov (Jules); Joan Bennett (Amelie Ducotel); Basil Rathbone (André Trochard); Leo G. Carroll (Felix Ducotel); John Baer (Paul Trochard); Gloria Talbott (Isabelle Ducotel); Leo Penman (Madame Parole); John Smith (Arnaud).

THE LEFT HAND OF GOD (1955)

A 20th Century-Fox Picture. CinemaScope. Color by DeLuxe. Directed by Edward Dmytryk. Produced by Buddy Adler. Screenplay by Alfred Hayes. Based on the novel by William E. Barrett. Director of photography, Franz Planer. Music by Victor Young. Film editor, Dorothy Spencer. Assistant director, Ben Kadish. Art directors, Lyle Wheeler and Maurice Ransford. Set decorations by Walter M. Scott and Frank Wade. Wardrobe director, Charles Le Maire. Costumes by Travilla. Makeup artist, Ben Nye. Hair styles by Helen Turpin. Special effects by Ray Kellogg. Sound recorders, Eugene Grossman and Harry M. Leonard. Orchestrations by Leo Shuken and Sidney Cutner. Color consultant, Leonard Doss. Technical adviser, Frank Tang. Running time, 87 minutes. Cast: Humphrey Bogart (Jim Carmody); Gene Tierney (Anne Scott); Lee J. Cobb (Mieh Yang); Agnes Moorehead (Beryl Sigman); E. G. Marshall (Dr. David Sigman); Jean Porter (Mary Yin); Carl Benton Reid (Reverend Cornelius); Victor Sen Yung (John Wong); Philip Ahn (Jan Teng); Benson Fong (Chun Tien); Richard Cutting (Father O'Shea); Leon Lontoc (Pao Ching); Don Forbes (Father Keller); Noel Toy (Woman in Sarong); Peter Chong (Feng Tso Lin); Marie Tsien (Woman in Kimono); Stephen Wong (The Boy); Sophie Chin (Celeste); George Chan (Li Kwan); Walter Soo Hoo (Hospital Orderly); Henry S. Quan (Orderly); Doris Chung (Nurse); Moy Ming (Old Man); George Lee (Mi Lu); Beal Wong (Father); Stella Lynn (Pao Chu); Robert Burton (Reverend Marvin); Soo Yong (Midwife).

THE DESPERATE HOURS (1955)

A Paramount Picture. In VistaVision. Produced and directed by William Wyler. Associate producer, Robert Wyler. Screenplay by Joseph Hayes, based on his novel and play. Director of photography, Lee Garmes. Music by Gail Kubik. Film editor, Robert Swink. Assistant director, C. C. Coleman, Jr. Art directors, Hal Pereira and Joseph MacMillan Johnson. Set decorations by Sam Comer and Grace Gregory. Costumes by Edith Head. Makeup artist, Wally Westmore. Special effects by John P. Fulton and Farciot Edouart. Sound recorders, Hugo Grenzbach and Winston Leverett. Running time, 112 minutes.

Cast: Humphrey Bogart (Glenn Griffin); Fredric March (Dan Hilliard); Arthur Kennedy (Jesse Bard); Martha Scott (Eleanor Hilliard); Dewey Martin (Hal Griffin); Gig Young (Chuck); Mary Murphy (Cindy Hilliard); Richard Eyer (Ralphie Hilliard); Robert Middleton (Sam Kobish); Alan Reed (Detective); Bert Freed (Winston); Ray Collins (Masters); Whit Bissell (Carson); Ray Teal (Fredericks); Michael Moore (Detective); Don Haggerty (Detective); Ric Roman (Sal); Pat Flaherty (Dutch); Beverly Garland (Miss Swift); Louis Lettieri (Bucky Walling); Ann Doran (Mrs. Walling); Walter Baldwin (Patterson).

THE HARDER THEY FALL (1956)

A Columbia Picture. Directed by Mark Robson. Produced by Philip Yordan. Screenplay by Philip Yordan. Based on the novel by Budd Schulberg. Director of photography, Burnett Guffey. Music by Hugo Friedhofer. Film editor, Jerome Thoms. Assistant director, Milton Feldman. Art director, William Flannery. Set decorations by William Kiernan and Alfred E. Spencer. Makeup artist, Clay Campbell. Hair styles by Helen Hunt. Sound recorder, Lambert Day. Orchestrations by Arthur Morton. Musical director, Lionel Newman. Technical adviser, John Indrisano. Running time, 109 minutes. Cast: Humphrey Bogart (Eddie Willis); Rod Steiger (Nick Benko); Jan Sterling (Beth Willis); Mike Lane (Toro Moreno); Max Baer (Buddy Brannen); Jersey Joe Walcott (George); Edward Andrews (Jim Weyerhause); Harold J. Stone (Art Leavitt); Carlos Montalban (Luis Agrandi); Nehemiah Persoff (Leo); Felice Orlandi (Vince Fawcett); Herbie Faye (Max); Rusty Lane (Danny McKeogh); Jack Albertson (Pop); Val Avery (Frank); Tommy Herman (Tommy); Vinnie DeCarlo (Joey); Pat Comiskey (Gus Dundee); Matt Murphy (Sailor Rigazzo); Abel Fernandez (Chief Firebird); Marion Carr (Alice).

IV

RADIO AND TELEVISION APPEARANCES

While living in New York, Bogart did whatever he could to pay the bills. Most likely he worked in radio for a time, but with little recognition. In the article "Strong But Silent," published in January 1937 in *Screenland*, Bogart tells Madelin Glass, "In radio work I got nervous because there is no way of feeling audience reaction" (92). I have not been able to track down any of the titles from those early performances, but I would appreciate any information about those shows for future updates of this listing.

RADIO

Henry IV broadcast, 1937

Rudy Vallee Program, January 27, 1938

Bakers Radio Program, February 13, 1938

Screen Guild Players, *High Sierra*, April 17, 1938

Bing Crosby Show, c. May 19, 1938

Bing Crosby's Kraft Music Hall, January 26, 1939

Chase & Sanborn Radio Program, January 29, 1939

Bing Crosby, *Oklahoma Kid* interview, February 2, 1939

Chase & Sanborn Radio Program, February 5, 1939

Kate Smith Hour, February 23, 1939

Lux Radio Program, Bullets or Ballots with Edward G. Robinson and Mary Astor, April 17, 1939

Chase & Sanborn Radio Program, April 30, 1939

Community Chest, May 10, 1939

Community Chest, May 18, 1939

Gateway to Hollywood Radio Program, June 18, 1939
Gulf Screen Guild Theatre Anthology, "If Only She Could Cook," CBS, c. June 1939
Kraft Radio Show, September 1939
Kraft Music Hall/Bing Crosby Program, January 4, 1940
Screen Actors Guild, *The Petrified Forest*, January 7, 1940
Silver Theatre, March 10, 1940
Bing Crosby Show to plug *Virginia City*, c. March 14, 1940
Kraft Music Hall, March 21, 1940
Help Thy Neighbor radio program, October 13, 1940
Campbell Playhouse Radio Program, November 29, 1940
Eddie Cantor Radio Program, March 5, 1941
Eddie Cantor Presents the March of Dimes, NBC, January 25, 1941
The Humphrey Bogart Show (a.k.a. *Humphrey Bogart Presents*), 1941
March of Dimes Appeal, April 1941
Unknown radio show to plug *Wagons Roll at Night*, April 25, 1941
Kraft Music Hall, May 22, 1941
Kraft Radio Program, October 31, 1941
Al Pearce Radio Program, October 31, 1941
Gulf Screen Guild or Screen Actor's Guild, *The Amazing Dr. Clitterhouse*, November 2, 1941
Bing Crosby Kraft Music Hall, November 27, 1941
Shirley Temple Time, December 26, 1941
Screen Guild Theatre Radio, January 4, 1942
Nobody's Children, January 22, 1942
Silver Theatre Radio Program, January 25, 1942
Silver Theatre, February 1, 1942
Jack Benny Jello Radio Program, February 1, 1942
Rudy Vallee Sealtest Radio Program, February 19, 1942
Phil Baker Program, November 29, 1942
Screen Guild Players Radio Program to plug *Across the Pacific*, January 25, 1943
Screen Guild Players Radio Program, recreating *Casablanca*, April 26, 1943
Third War Loan Drive for Hollywood Victory Committee, September 8, 1943
Chase & Sanborn Radio Program, September 12, 1943
Screen Guild to plug *The Maltese Falcon*, September 20, 1943
Phillip Morris Playhouse, High Sierra, 1942 and 1943
Screen Guild Players Radio Show to plug *High Sierra*, April 17, 1944
American Newspaper Guild Program, June 10, 1944
Democratic National Committee broadcast on behalf of Roosevelt, October 1944

Democratic National Committee broadcast on behalf of Roosevelt, November 6, 1944

Burns and Allen broadcast, December 12, 1944

Milton Berle Show, January 30, 1945

American Jewish Committee, CBS, February 1945

Suspense Theatre, Love's Lovely Counterfeit, March 8, 1945

Lux Radio Theatre, Moontide, April 30, 1945

Theatre of Romance, Conflict, August 11, 1945

Screen Guild Radio Program, *The Valiant*, September 2, 1945

Theatre of Romance, September 11, 1945

The Valiant, September 17, 1945

Cavalcade of Stars radio program, October 18, 1945

Calvacade of America, My Son, John, October 29, 1945

Theatre of Romance radio program, *One Way Passage*, December 18, 1945

Ginny Simms Program, March 22, 1946

Radio request, June 15 or 22, 1946

Academy Award Theatre, The Maltese Falcon, 30 minutes, CBS, July 3, 1946

Lux Radio Theatre, To Have and Have Not, with Lauren Bacall, October 14, 1946

Take It or Leave It to plug *The Big Sleep*, October 20, 1946

Phil Baker, October 20, 1946

Radio broadcast, *To Have and Have Not*, November 1946, December 1946, January 1947

Jack Benny Show, January 5, 1947

Hollywood Fights Back, Part I, ABC, October 26, 1947

Philadelphia guest appearance, WIP Radio, October 29, 1947

Hollywood Fights Back, Part II, ABC, November 2, 1947

Fred Allen Show, November 30, 1947

Louella Parsons, February 1, 1948

Duffy's Tavern, March 17, 1948

The Prudential Hour of Stars, 1948–1949, CBS.

The Treasure of the Sierra Madre, Lux Radio Theatre, April 18, 1949

Bold Venture, 1951–1952, thirty-eight shows, 423 stations. Background is Havana. Exploits of Slate Shannon and Sailor Duval (Slate's ward). He is the owner-operator of a boat called *Bold Adventure* and hotel of same name. Basis for television series.

The African Queen, Lux Radio Theatre, December 15, 1952

TELEVISION APPEARANCES

Adlai Stevenson rally, October 27, 1952, Dumont Network

Jack Benny Show, October 25, 1953, CBS

The Philip Morris Program, 1953—Warner Bros., one-hour live dramatization

Edward R. Murrow interview, *Person to Person*, September 3, 1954, CBS

27th Annual Academy Awards, March 30, 1955, NBC. Bogart presents black and white cinematography award.

Producer's Showcase, The Petrified Forest, May 30, 1955, NBC

V

DISCOGRAPHY

A number of these recordings are included in the Library of Congress records, but some are not available there.

The African Queen. Mark 56 LP668. 1975.
Bold Venture. Command Performance Records LP-4.
———. American Forces Radio and Television Service. RU 52-4, 5B, 1974.
Bullets or Ballots. Center for Cassette Studies, 1978.
Casablanca: *Classic Film Scores for Humphrey Bogart*. Red Seal ARLI0422, 1974. (Some tapes include program notes by Rudy Behlmer.)
Casablanca (abridged), with Screen Guild Players. Radiola MR-1099.
Casablanca. Soundtrack. Rhino, 1997. CD R272911.
Dead Man. Command Performance LP-13.
———. American Forces Radio and Television Service, RU 22-1, 66A, 1970.
The Enforcer. Mark 56 Records 707, 1975.
Henry IV. Murray Hill Records 898667.
High Sierra. American Forces Radio and Television Service RU 31-3, 3B [1973] from Playhouse 25, 1944.
Love's Lovely Counterfeit/The Maltese Falcon. Command Performance LP-1/Radio MR-1061.
The Maltese Falcon on Lady Ester Screen Guild Players and Academy Award Theatre, Radiola MR-1091.
The Maltese Falcon. American Forces Radio and Television Service RU 39-2, 5B, 1972.
The Star of Sheba/The Blue Moon. Command Performance LP-4.
To Have and Have Not. Radiola MR/ME-1007.
———. Mark 56 Records 695, 1976.
The Treasure of the Sierra Madre. Mark 56, LP 610, 1973.

COMPILATION DISCS

Calling All Stars. Star Tone ST-203.
50 Years of Film. Warner Bros. Records 3XX2737.

VI

BROADCASTS AND/OR VIDEOS ABOUT HUMPHREY BOGART

Bacall on Bogart. Dir: David Heeley. A&E, March 11, 1988. Later rebroadcast on PBS. Educational Broadcasting Corp. and Turner Entertainment Co., 1988.
The Best of Bogart. Narrated by Edward G. Robinson, Warner Bros., 1971.
Blacklist: Hollywood on Trial. Dir: Chris Koch. American Movie Classics Special. 1995.
Bogart. Dir: Martin Flamm. ABC, April 22, 1967.
Bogart: The Man Behind the Myth. Dir: Mike Omansky. Worldwide Entertainment Marketing and Cine Productions, 1991. (aka: *Portrait: Humphrey Bogart*, and *Humphrey Bogart and Hollywood's Gangsters*.)
Bogart: The Untold Story. Narrated by Stephen Bogart. TNT, January 1997. Later rebroadcast on TMC and PBS.
Bogie: The Last Hero. Dir: Vincent Sherman. USA Home Video, Charles Fries Productions, 1979. Televised, March 4, 1980.
Breakdowns of 1936 and 1937. Thunderbird, n.d. Outtakes from Warner Bros.
Here's Looking at You, Warner Bros.: The History of the Warner Bros. Studio. Dir: Robert Guenette. Warner Home Video, 1993.
Historical Videos. n.d., n.p. Includes the *Person to Person* interview of September 3, 1954.
Hollywood and the Stars. September 30, 1963, Sept 28, 1964.
Hollywood on Trial. Dir: David Helpern, narrated by John Huston. 1988.
Humphrey Bogart: Behind the Legend. Biography A-to-Z. A&E. September 1995.
Jack Benny Comedy Hour (with *The Funniest Men of Comedy*). Goodtimes Home Video, 1986.
Kisses. Dir: Neil Steinberg and Bruce Cohn. Narrated by Lauren Bacall. TBS Productions, 1991 and Turner Home Entertainment, 1992.
Legends: Humphrey Bogart. Narrated by Richard Basehart. HBO, 1979.
The Man Called Bogart. Hollywood and the Stars. Narrated by Joseph Cotton. United Artists TV, 1963. Broadcast, September 11, 1963.
The Man with Bogart's Face (a.k.a. *Sam Marlowe, Private Eye*). Dir: Robert Day. 1985.

Presidential Blooper Reel. Budget Video, n.d. Outtakes.
The Return of Video Yesterbloop. Video Yesteryear, n.d.
Sex Symbols on the Silver Screen, May 4, 1981.
Showbiz Ballyhoo. Narrated by David Steinberg. T.A.D. Productions, 1983. (Previously available on USA Home Video.)
Tribute to Bogart. January 1972. BBC-TV.

VII

INTERNET

Web sites and their contents change frequently.[1] Various Internet search engines will provide thousands of sites to search. For most search engines, the researcher can reduce the listings by narrowing the topic of the search to, for example, Humphrey Bogart and *The Maltese Falcon*. Of the particular sites, one might start with a few that have links to other particular sites on the Internet:

<http://www.zweb.com/bogart> also accessed through <http://www.sd02.znet.com/bogart/> is at the moment considered the best of the Bogart sites. The creator of the site, Mike Rosenberg, includes pictures, sound bites, filmography, biography, bibliography, games, posters, merchandise, and links to other sites. Those links include "Rick's Café Americain," "Welcome to Cyberblanca," "Bogie and Baby," "Welcome to the Santana," "The Maltese Falcon FAQ," fifteen links to movies in general, and links to actors, actresses, and directors.

<http://www.film100.com/cig/direct.cgi?v.boga> is the usual summary of Bogart's career, and other Internet links.

<http://www.tv-now.com/stars/bogart.html> includes what Bogart films are playing on television.

<http://www.cmgww.com/stars/bogart/bogart.html> is the official Bogart merchandising site, run by CMG, the marketing and licensing agent for the Bogart family. If you are interested in seeing what merchandise has been authorized or approved for sale, this is the site. Sketchy biographical and factual information about Bogart is provided, although for many months after the site went up, it contained incorrect biographical information.

<http://www.us.imdb.com/> is a comprehensive source of information on movies on the Internet.

NOTE

1. I thank Mary Brunz, Michele Lellouche, and Brian Duchovnay for their assistance in searching the various web sites.

INDEX

Abdul, Paula, 72
Abramson, Leslie, 172, 264
Ackerman, Dan, 184, 186–87, 254
Adams, Don, 67
Adams, Douglas, 61
Affron, Charles, 153, 173, 260, 265
Affron, Mirella Jona, 153, 173, 260, 265
Agee, James, 149, 164, 176, 225, 271, 272; *African Queen*, 232, 234–35, 248; *To Have and Have Not*, 201–2
Air Force, 199
Albino Alligator, 66
Albuquerque, Joao Luiz, 196
Alderman, Tom, 70
Aldrich, Robert, 238
Alexander, Jan, 152, 268
Algiers, 180, 195
Alison, Joan, 179
All About Eve, 240
Allen, J. C., 254
Allen, Woody, 6, 64, 71, 72, 80, 133–35
Alley, Kenneth, 62, 158–59, 200, 262, 269
Almendarez, Valentin, 260
Alpert, Hollis, 240, 249
Alphaville, 63
Altman, R., 254
Altman, Robert, 64

Ames, Bobby, 10
Ames, Christopher, 154, 228, 230, 263, 270
Amo, Gary, 73
Anderegg, Michael, 153, 240, 260, 261
Anderson, Judith, 112
Anderson, Maxwell, 204, 226
Andover, Phillips Academy. *See* Bogart, education
Andrew, Geoff, 227–29, 263, 264
Angel Heart, 174
Anger, Kenneth, 22
Animated cartoons, 68–69
Anobile, Richard, 176, 179, 254, 265
Archer, Eugene, 131, 243, 248, 265, 272; *African Queen*, 235–36; Bogart as anti-hero, 130; *The Maltese Falcon*, 163–65; *Treasure of the Sierra Madre*, 223
Arkadin, 254
Armstrong, Louis, 72
Armstrong, Tom, 74
Asphalt Jungle, The, 164
Astaire, Fred, 96
Astor, Mary, 111, 125, 130, 243, 247, 265; *Across the Pacific*, 176; Bogart on, 96; *The Maltese Falcon*: Astor's character, 175, commentaries, 162–64, radio recording, 52

A-Team, 67
Atkinson, Brooks, 12, 15
Attack!, 238
Attwood, Willliam, 100
Austen, Jane, 205–6

Bacall, Lauren, 52, 87, 118, 137, 243, 248; in Africa, 234–35; attitude on movies about Bogart, 72; on Bogart's alleged affair with Verita Thompson, 21, 126–27; on Bogart's birth date, 2; after Bogart's death, 21; on Bogart's influence on, 37, 116, 130; *Bold Venture* (radio), 30; *By Myself*, 115, 119; co-hosting young actors, 101–4; engagement announced, 126; first meeting with Bogart, 20–21; images of, 54–56, 60; influence on Bogart's career, 134; look-alikes/impersonators, on, 71; love and marriage, 22–26, 28–36; on Helen Menken, 10; on Mayo Methot, 16; Nicholas Ray on, 22; *Now*, 115; political activism, 28, 42 n.113, 121; schooling for Stephen Bogart, 4; signing by Howard Hawks, 20, 41 n.73
Bacall films: *The Big Sleep*, 25, 207–20; *Confidential Agent*, 25 *Dark Passage*, 25, 222; *Key Largo*, 25, 226; *The Petrified Forest* (tv), 33; *To Have and Have Not*, 21, 24, 201–6
Bacall to Arms, 68
Bach, Richard, 61
Bacon, James, 127, 243
Bad and the Beautiful, The, 232
Badder, David, 243
Bad Men of Missouri, 20, 162
Bailey, Hal, 69
Baker, Mary, 16
Baker, Melva J., 183, 254
Ball, Lucille, 72
Ballad of Cable Hogue, The, 225
Balter, Leon, 169, 265
Barbour, Alan D., 141, 243
Barb Wire, 66
Barker, Julie, 204–5, 240–41, 261, 271
Barnes, Peter, 127–28, 243
Barrymore, John, and Elaine Barry, 21
Bart, P., 254

Barthes, Roland, 168, 172–73, 218
Basinger, Jeanine, 56; *Casablanca*, 194, 254; *The Maltese Falcon*, 173, 265; *Sahara*, 199, 270; *Two Mrs. Carrolls*, 221, 273
Baskette, Kirtley, 125, 243
Bataan, 199
Battleship Potemkin, 198
Bauer, Stephen F., 169, 265
Baumgarten, Marjorie, 152, 268
Baxt, George, 59
Bazin, André, 129, 133, 135–36, 243
Behlmer, Rudy, 161–62, 177, 234–35, 248, 254, 265
Beja, Morris, 224, 272
Bellak, Leo, 169
Bellour, Raymond, 168, 210–11, 250
Belmondo, Jean-Paul, 63, 73, 118, 130–31
Belushi, Jim, 198
Benaquist, Lawrence, 172–73, 265
Benavedes, Bob, 101–4
Benchley, Nathaniel, 2, 23, 52, 115, 117–20, 179, 243
Benchley, Robert, 16, 125, 129, 144
Benton, Robert, 64
Bergman, Andrew, *Hollywood and LeVine*, 58
Bergman, Ingrid, 16, 56, 62, 254; *Casablanca*, 18, 66, 177–79, 182–83, 186, 188–89, 193; screen presence, 137
Bernstein, Leonard, 23
Berryman, John, "Dream Song 9," 60
Berson, Debbi, 136–37, 243
Bertolucci, Bernardo, 195
Bick, Ilsa J., 170, 176, 265
Big Combo, The, 241
Big Heat, 174, 230
Big Night, 66
Big Sleep, The (Mitchum), 47
Billingsley, Sherman, 28
Birns, Margaret Boe, 60
Biskind, Peter, 232
Black, Joel, 196, 254
Black Bird, The, 64
Blackburn, Steve, 204, 271
Black Mask, 162
Blades, John, 207–9, 215, 250

Blake, Richard A., 168–69, 265
Blanke, Henry, 116, 162, 163
Blinn, Holbrook, 136
Block, Lawrence, 59
Blondell, Joan, 10, 11
Bogart, Belmont DeForest (father), 2, 92, 119; death, 11, 124; love of sea, 3; medical practice, 3; relationship with son, 25; son at school, 118
Bogart, Catherine "Kay" (sister), 2, 11, 13
Bogart, Frances "Pat" (sister), 2, 5, 11, 13, 36. *See also* Rose, Stuart
Bogart, Humphrey DeForest
  actor: acting ability, 7, 9, 12, 213–14; attitude about, 16, 17, 26, 27, 31, 32, 97, 101–4; as career choice, 6–7; acting as a trade, 121, 125–26; freedom of expression of actors, 90–96, 99, 100–104, 106–12, 116; impact on other actors, 130–31; embodiment of ideas of writers, 214
  ancestry, 2, 91–92
  appeal, 117, 122, 127, 129–41
  appearance, 32, 96, 97, 99–100, 125, 128, 129, 130, 135–38
  articles by, 113–14, 249, 253
  baldness, 27, 40 n.63, 96
  businessman, 27, 30
  biographical studies and career overviews, 115–29
  birth: conflicting dates, 1–2, 121, 128; Sloan Maternity Hospital, 1, 125
  Bold Venture, 30
  broadcasts or videos about, 321–22
  CFA activities, 29, 133, 146, 182
  cancer, 26, 33–35, 118
  censorship, 87, 88–90, 91
  character, 35–37, 79, 88, 116; Bogart on Bogart, 18; fan club view, 79; Methot on, 16; affairs, attitude about, 21–24; argumentative, 28, 96; attitude toward children, 89–90; candor, 99, 125–26; complainer, 17; cynical, 110; domestic habits, 16, 26, 83 n.51; drinking, 13, 24, 108, 117, 120, 126, 163; embittered, 23–24; generosity, 19, 36–37, 125; polite, 8, 9, 126; quarrelsome, 16, 28
  chronology, 277–282
  contract with Fox, 147
  contract with Warner Bros., 14, 26, 30, 32, 33; 98
  critics: Agee on 225–26; Julie Barker on, 240–41; Bazin on Bogart's acting style, 136; Benchley on, 119; Louise Brooks on acting, 138; Cooke on, 37; Garfield on, 142; Hanners on, 142; Hawks on, 204; Henreid on, 182; Huston on, 35–36, 226; Kinskey on, 183; Purcell on, 141–42; Schickel on, 144–45; Sennett on, 165; Thomson on, 140
  cult appeal, 117, 122, 127, 129–39
  death, 35, 60, 135–36 166
  directing trailers, 123
  education, 118; Delancy School, 4; Phillips Andover Academy, 4, 9, 92, 118, 125; Trinity School, 4, 9, 38 n.10, 118
  funeral, 35–36
  "F.Y. Fund," 13, 28
  hobbies, 127; chess, 70, 77, 98, 119, 125, 132, 144; golf, 96, 125; sailing, 96, 97, 119, 125, 144
  kinds of roles, 17, 45, 46, 88, 125, 159; comedy, 33, 108, 110, 235–37; detective, 45; gangster, 45, 158; horror, 45, 107–8; love scenes, 21, 88, 96, 119, 182; romantic, 110, 132
  lip injury, 5, 123, 125, 138, 147
  love affair with Lauren Bacall, 20–21, 23
  love affair with Verita Thompson, 19, 21–23
  mannerisms, 98
  marriages, 36, 97; to Lauren Bacall, 25, 26, 119; to Helen Menken, 7, 9–10; to Mayo Methot, 15, 20–21, 24–25, 36; to Mary Philips, 10, 14–15
  money/financial security, 6, 13, 17, 19, 28, 30, 61, 94, 102, 120, 160
  navy service, 5, 92
  Oscars, 31–32, 88, 232
  panda incident, 28, 228

political views, 22, 28, 29, 88, 90–96, 97, 121
popular culture, impact on: animated cartoons, 68–69; cartoons, 74; Casablanca, 181; ceiling fans, 51; dialogue, 75; fan clubs, 77, 79; fashions, 73; film festivals, trends, and popularity, 47–49, 80; image promoted by Maud Humphrey, 3, 4, 46, 55; literary influences, 56–61, 78; look-alikes, 70–73, 76, 79; lounges and restaurants, 49–51, 80; memorabilia, 69–70, 76–79, 128; movies, 62–68; popularity polls, 46, 49, 81 n.14; publications, 46, 78; quotations, 46, 80; records, music, and dance, 51–53; stills and posters, 53–56; television programming, 47–49; U.S. postage stamp, 46, 78; wax museums, 62
public image vs. private life, 13, 16, 26, 28, 88, 97–98, 100–101, 103, 125–26, 137, 165
radio appearances, 315–17
residences: 79 East 56th Street, 11; 103rd St., 11; 245 West 103rd Street, 3; 434 East 52nd St., 11; Benedict Canyon, 78; Beverly Hills Hotel, 24; Garden of Allah, 24–25; Holmby Hills, 30; Horn Avenue, 144; Kings Road, 25; "Sluggy Hollow" (aka "Liberty Hall"), 16, 125
sex, interest in, 8, 22
smoking, advertisements, 71, 61, 99, 109
television appearances, 33, 102, 317–18; Academy Award telecast, 33; Edward R. Murrow, 33; *Jack Benny Show*, 33; *The Petrified Forest*, 33
theater performances, 6, 7, 12, 46, 118, 119, 120, 127; *After All*, 11; *Baby Mine*, 8; *Chrysalis*, 11; *Cradle Snatchers*, 8, 9; *Drifting*, 7; *Hell's Bells*, 8; *I Love You Wednesday*, 11; *Invitation to a Murder*, 12; *It's a Wise Child*, 8; *The Mask and the Face*, 11; *Meet the Wife*, 8–10; *A Most Immoral Lady*, 8; *Nerves*, 8, 10; *Our Wife*, 11; *The Petrifield Forest*, 12, 15; *The Ruined Lady*, 6; *Saturday's Children*, 8–9; *Skyrocket*, 8; *Swifty*, 7–8; minor roles: *Mary the Third*, 7; *The Nest*, 7; *Steve*, 7; *The Teaser*, 7
travels, 166, 224, Africa, 30–31, 235; London, Paris, Rome, 30; USO tour, 20
value system, 8, 20, 119, 120–22; 131–32, 134, 145
voice, 12
Warner, Jack L., 13, 16, 26, 97
women, attitude toward, 21, 96–97, 130, 131–34
work, 102, 125, 136, 163
work habits, 108–12, 125, 132
writers, 26, 125, 144

Bogart films
Across the Pacific, 19, 88, 111, 176, 205
Action in the North Atlantic, 26, 47, 147, 198
The African Queen, 27, 73, 77, 147, 164, 224; boat, 69; commentaries, 232–36; filming, 30–31, 111; music, 51; wax museum image, 62
All Through the Night, 19, 68, 88, 107–10, 112, 133, 147, 274
The Amazing Dr. Clitterhouse, 274
Angels with Dirty Faces, 154
Bad Sister, 10, 149
The Barefoot Contessa, 27, 32, 121, 127–28, 239
Battle Circus, 27, 32, 47, 135, 274
Beat the Devil, 27, 28, 32, 127, 131, 143, 166, 236–38
Big City Blues, 11, 274
The Big Shot, 274
The Big Sleep, 58, 132–33, 140, 143, 171, 173–74, 188, 205; commentaries, 207–20; intertextual references, 63–65; personal turmoil during filming, 24–26
Black Legion, 13–14, 47, 121, 138–39, 144, 150
Body and Soul, 10, 149
Broadway's Like That, 10
Brother Orchid, 274

Bullets or Ballots, 13, 47, 129, 150
The Caine Mutiny, 27, 32, 33, 116, 127–28, 140, 182, 231, 238
Casablanca, 16, 26, 125, 145, 147, 171, 216; appeal and cult, 47–49, 129–32; influence on *Bold Venture*, 30; commentaries, 176–98; ending, 180; influence on making of *Passage to Marseille* and *To Have and Have Not*, 200–204; intertextual references, 49–52, 57–58, 62– 69, 72–80; making of, 19–20; Oscar nomination, 31; personal turmoil, 24–25; relation to other roles, 143–44; script con, 181; as wet dream, 140
Chain Lightning, 27, 47, 274
China Clipper, 13, 274
Conflict, 19, 26, 68, 96, 206–7
Crime School, 88, 104–6, 274
The Dancing Town, 10, 39 n.34, 124, 149, 274
Dark Passage, 27, 65, 68, 134, 222–23
Dark Victory, 140, 155–56
Dead End, 47, 106, 133, 153–54
Deadline—U.S.A., 27, 32, 135, 236
Dead Reckoning, 27, 48, 140, 220–21
The Desperate Hours, 27, 32, 33, 240–41
A Devil with Women, 10, 149, 274
The Enforcer, 27, 32, 51, 232
The Great O'Malley, 13, 274
The Harder They Fall, 27, 32, 33, 241–42
High Sierra, 19, 58, 60, 62, 132, 140; antihero image, 140; commentaries, 157–61; popularity, 47–48; remake, 125; Vincent Sherman on, 109; star recognition for Bogart, 24, 125, 129, 133–34, 147; working conditions, 17
A Holy Terror, 10, 149, 274
In a Lonely Place, 27, 30, 138; B's performance, 33, 140, 188, 213; breaks down genre formulas, 221; commentaries, 228–32; intertextual reference, 65; Thomson on, 58, 140; Truffaut on Bogart image, 135
Invisible Stripes, 274
Isle of Fury, 13, 274

It All Came True, 274
Key Largo, 27, 30, 47, 67, 68, 73, 204, 226–27
Kid Galahad, 107, 121, 153, 274
King of the Underworld, 107, 274
Knock on Any Door, 27, 30, 227–28
The Left Hand of God, 27, 32, 47, 274
Love Affair, 11, 12, 149, 274
The Maltese Falcon, 78, 96, 188; Bogart's appeal, 19; commentaries, 161–76; compared to *The Big Sleep*, 208–9; compared to *The Treasure of the Sierra Madre*, 223; Huston, 109; intertextual references, 51, 58–60, 64–65, 68, 70, 73; popularity, 48; satirized in *Beat the Devil*, 236–37; screen presence, 24, 125, 132, 134, 139, 144, 160, 214; star status, 160
Marked Woman, 13, 15, 150–53
Men are Such Fools, 274
Midnight, 11, 149, 274
The Oklahoma Kid, 17, 70, 124, 155
Passage to Marseille, 20–21, 26, 77, 200–201
The Petrified Forest: acting, 121, 144, 214; body language, 174; career boost, 18, 46, 147, 160; commentaries, 149–50; Leslie Howard's influence, 158; intertextual references, 73
Racket Busters, 24, 274
The Return of Dr. X, 88, 107, 157, 274
The Roaring Twenties, 24, 140, 143, 156–57, 161
Sabrina, 27, 32, 33, 73, 127–28, 239
Sahara, 20, 26, 147, 191, 198–99
San Quentin, 105, 133, 274
Sirocco, 27, 28, 30, 204, 274
Stand-In, 13, 47, 154
Swing Your Lady, 274
Thank Your Lucky Stars, 198
They Drive by Night, 143, 157
Three on a Match, 11, 12, 149, 274
To Have and Have Not, 20, 26, 129, 132, 140, 188, 242 n.9; Bogart's persona compared to *The Big Sleep* and *Casablanca*, 216; commentaries, 201–6; compared to *Casablanca*,

195; Faulkner and, 143; influence on *Bold Venture*, 30; intertextual references, 47–48, 63, 73; Methot on love scenes, 24; as propaganda, 147
Tokyo Joe, 27–28, 274
The Treasure of the Sierra Madre, 27, 30, 132, 238; Bogart's performance, 33, 143, 164, 166, 182; Bogart's persona, 134, 138, 140, 231; commentaries, 223–26; intertextual references, 73, 77; popularity, 48
Two Against the World, 13, 274
The Two Mrs. Carrolls, 25, 27, 221
Up the River, 10, 11, 32, 149, 274
Virginia City, 142, 274
Wagons Roll at Night, 274
We're No Angels, 27, 32, 240
Women of All Nations, 10, 274
You Can't Get Away with Murder, 274
Bogart, Leslie (daughter), 30, 36, 72, 79
Bogart, Maud Humphrey (mother). *See* Humphrey, Maud
Bogart, Neil (Bogats), 52
Bogart, Stephen (son), 31, 36, 87, 244; autobiography, 115–16; birth, 30; commercialization of father's mage, 72, 79; education, 4; father's imperfections, 23; as novelist, 58–59; television documentary on father, 49
Bogart: In Search of My Father (Stephen Bogart), 2, 115–16
Bogart: The Untold Story, 49
Bogart Look-Alikes, 70–73, 76
Bogdanovich, Peter, 129, 204, 208, 244, 250, 271
Bogie (France), 60
Bogie (film), 65, 72, 88
The Bogie Man (Scotland), 60
Bok, B. Knight, 254
Boland, Mary, 8–9
Bold Venture, 30
Bombshell, 154
Boon, Kevin, 171, 265
Booth, Shirley, 9
Bordwell, David, 173, 217, 231, 250, 265
Bottiggi, William D., 173–74, 265
Bourgnet, Jean-Loup, 176, 254
Brackett, Leigh, 35, 64, 207, 250

Brady, Alice, 6, 7
Brady, Bill, Jr., 5, 7
Brady, William A., 6, 32
Brando, Marlon, 31–32, 49, 65, 73, 101
Brandsma, Maynard, 34
Brattle Theatre, 47, 131, 191
Brautigan, Richard, 60
Brazaville, 62
Breaking Point, The, 204
Breathless, 47, 63, 73, 80, 118, 139
Breck, Henry R., 76
Breen Office. *See* Production Code
Briggs, Donald, 14
Brill, Lesley, 235–236, 248
Bring Me the Head of Alfredo Garcia, 225
Bromfield, Louis, 15, 25, 96, 125, 144, 146, 244
Bronson, Charles, 65, 219
Brookins, Gary, 74
Brooks, Geraldine, 29
Brooks, Louise, 8, 22, 135, 137–38, 141, 147, 244
Brooks, Richard, 30, 116, 226, 236
Broun, Heywood Hale, 8, 52
Brown, William H., Jr., 168, 238, 253, 265
Buchwald, Art, 75
Bukowski, Charles, 60
Burgess, Alan, 254
Burke's Peerage, 2
Burkhart, Jeff, 254
Burnett, Murray, 179–81
Burnett, W. R., 158–161
Burrows, Victoria, 68
Buster Keaton Show, 62, 67

Cable, Carol, 74
Caboblanco, 65
Cagney, James, 19, 90, 158; compared to Bogart, 133, 136, 140, 144–46, 156–57; intertextual references, 64, 68, 72; on Warner Bros. treatment of Bogart, 17–18
Cahill, Marie, 129, 176, 179, 244, 254, 265
Caine, Michael, 122
The Caine Mutiny Court Martial, 238

Calanquin, L, 264
California Celebrity Rights Act, 72
California Split, 225
Campbell, Joseph, 194
Camus, Albert, 137, 166, 189, 212, 214
Candy Cabaret, 69
Canham, Kingsley, 159, 187, 254, 262
Capote, Truman, 129, 236–37
Captain Blood, 184
Card, James, 191, 254
Carlinsky, Dan, 244
Carlyle, John, 136–37, 244
Carmichael, Hoagy, 125
Carpenter, Elliot, 178
Carrotblanca, 69
Case, B., 180, 254
Castellanos, Rev. Kermit, 35
Castille, Philip D., 209, 250
Cellini, Benvenuto, 94–95
Champlin, Charles, 196, 236, 249, 254
Chandler, Raymond, 64, 166, 250; *Big Sleep*, 219–20; Bogart's persona, 213–14, 216–17; on Marlowe's character, 142; as novelist, 207–10
Chaplin, Charlie, 46, 169, 225
Chase and Sanborn Coffee Co., 19
Chasen, Dave, 126
Cheap Detective, The, 47, 64
Cheatham, Maude, 21
Chesnick, Davis, 244
Chinatown, 58, 173–74, 219
Chinese Theatre (Grauman's), 26, 76, 78
Churchill, Winston, 95
Cimino, Michael, 240
Citizen Kane, 186, 210
Clarens, Carlos, 149–50, 157, 159, 227, 262, 263, 269
Clarkson, Ben, 69
Claro, J., 272
Clift, Montgomery, 73
Close, John, 57
CMG (Curtis Management Group), licensing agent, 2, 72, 79
Coe, Jonathan, 2, 10, 29, 122–23, 149, 244
Cohen, Joan, 153, 227, 261, 263
Cohen, William E., 75

Cohn, Harry, 11, 27, 34, 35, 43 n.136, 220
Collier, John, 233, 235
Collins, G., 265
Colorado Territory, 158
Columbia Pictures, 11, 27, 220–21
Columbo, 67, 73, 220
Committee for the First Amendment (CFA), 29, 133, 146, 182
Conklin, Betty, 12
Conley, Tom, 161, 262
Connery, Sean, 122, 131, 134
Conspirators, The, 62
Conte, Richard, 29
Cook, Elisha, Jr., 76
Cooke, Alistair, 21–22, 29, 37, 121–22, 244
Cooke, B., 254
Cooper, Gary, 19, 26, 35, 101, 103, 130, 136, 160
Cooper, Stephen, 171–72, 174, 265
Coover, Robert, 58, 196, 254
Copeland, Roger, 62, 63
Corley, Edwin, *Shadows*, 58
Corliss, Richard: *Barefoot Contessa*, 240, 249; Bogart as existential hero, 183–84; Casey Robinson and *Casablanca* script, 180–81; Casey Robinson and *Dark Victory*, 155; *High Sierra*, 262; reading of *Casablanca*, 187–88, 255
Craft, J. J., 255
Crain, Mary Beth, 181–82, 191, 255
Crawford, Broderick, 16
Crime and Punishment (film), 112
Cripps, Thomas, 187, 255
Croft, John J., 183, 255
Cromwell, John, 5, 7, 26, 221
Crosby, Bing, 72
Crossfire, 238
Crowther, Bosley, 149, Bogart's career and cult, 244; *Casablanca*, 255; *Casablanca*, Rick's character, 131, 196–97; *Maltese Falcon*, 175, 265; *Treasure of the Sierra Madre*, 223, 226, 272
Cukor, George, 129
Cumming, Don, 20
Curtiz, Michael, 62, 116–17; *Casablanca*, 177, 181, 183–87, 189, 191, 197; influ-

ence on Bogart, 26, 140, 143, 187; *Passage to Marseille*, 200

Da, Lottie, 152, 268
Daily Worker, The, 29
Dale, Alan, 7
Dalio, Marcel, 67
Dark Hazard, 159
Dark Past, The, 221
Darrach, Brad, 244
Dau's Blue Book, 3
Daves, Delmar, 26
Davies, Gill, 210, 250
Davis, Bette, 10, 26, 59, 68, 111, 201, 232; *Marked Woman*, 151; *Dark Victory*, 156
Davis, J. H., 197, 255
Davis, Ken, and John Stanley, *Bogart '48*, 57
Davis, Paxton, 207, 250
Davis, Sarah, 79
Dawson, Warren J., 244
Day, Barry, 184–85, 191–92, 255
Day, Robert, 80
Dead End Kids, 105–6
Dead Men Don't Wear Plaid, 65
Dean, James, 73, 101, 140
Debrett's Guide to the Aristocracy, 2
DeCarlo, Yvonne, 65
De Havilland, Olivia, 111
Delancy School. *See* Bogart, education
Delehanty, Thornton, 31
Delineator, 3
Demarest, William, 110, 112
Deming, Barbara, 222; *Big Sleep*, 250; Bogart as war hero, 187, 200, 215; *Casablanca*, 255; *Dark Passage*, 260; *Maltese Falcon*, 175, 266; *Passage to Marseille*, 269; *Treasure of the Sierra Madre*, comic aspects of, 225, 272
DeNiro, Robert, 56
Desperate Hours (Cimino), 240
Destination Tokyo, 199
Deutelbaum, Marshall, 194, 203, 255, 271
Deutsch, Armand, 56
Dewey, Thomas E., 94–95
Dick, Bernard: *Action in the North Atlantic* and propaganda, 198, 247; *Casablanca* and myth, 179, 196, 255; *Dark Victory*, 155, 260; *Dead Reckoning*, 220–21, 261; *High Sierra*, 160–61, 262; *In a Lonely Place*, 263; *Passage to Marseille*, 201; *Sahara*, as dialectic, 199, 270
Dienstfrey, Harris, 129, 244
Dies, Martin, 18
Dieterle, William, 172
Dietrich, Marlene, 35, 54, 59, 201, 204
Disney/MGM Studios (Florida), 70
Dixon, Wheeler, 215, 236, 250, 261
Dmytryk, Edward, 238
Doane, Mary Ann, 212
Doctorow, E. L., 61
Dolack, Monte, 53
Donaldson, Leslie, 239, 270
Donnelly, William, 184, 187–88, 192, 255
Double Indemnity, 217
Downer, Alan S., 163–64, 176, 223, 225, 247, 266, 272
Draper, Ellen, 156, 230, 263, 269
Dreyfuss, Richard, 64
Dr. Socrates, 106
Druxman, Michael B., 262, 266
Duchovnay, Gerald, interview with Vincent Sherman, 104–13
Dudley, Larry, 35
Dunne, Philip, 29
Dworkine, Martin, 241, 261
Dynamite Chicken, 64

Earl Theater, 19
Eastman, John, 189, 255
Eastwood, Clint, 64, 81, 134, 219, 234
Easy Rider, 52
Ebert, Roger, 66, 185, 197, 255
Eckert, Charles W., 151–52, 268
Eco, Umberto, 185, 192, 194–95, 255
Edelson, Edward, 167, 180, 186–87, 255, 266
Eden, Ted, 123
Edeson, Arthur, 111, 163, 183, 197
Egen, Maureen, 66
Eidsvik, Charles, 196, 255
8 Ball Bunny, 69
Einfeld, Charles, 24

Eisenhower, Dwight D., 22, 29
Eisenschitz, Bernard, 147, 227–28, 244, 263, 264
Elliott, Harvey, 48, 147–48, 244
El Morocco panda incident, 28, 228
Enforcer, The (Eastwood), 64
Engell, John, 224, 273
English Patient, The, 66
Engstead, John, 55
Epstein, Julius, 177–78, 180, 186–87, 189, 191
Epstein, Philip, 177, 180, 186, 189, 191
Epstein, Randi Hutter, 61
Erskine, Charles, 11
Etting, Ruth, 10
Evans, Larry, 77
Everson, William K., 166, 174, 217, 250, 266
Everybody Comes to Rick's, 179–80
Eyer, Richard, 240
Eyles, Allen, 143, 163, 165, 171, 244, 266

Fadiman, R. K., 271
Falk, Peter, 64, 73
Farewell, My Lovely (film), 64, 213
Fargo, Lawrence, Jr., 226, 264
Farmer, Francis, 124
Farrell, Charles, 10
Farrell, Glenda, 201
Fatal Attraction, 230
Faulkner, William, 20, 45, 143, 165, 202–3, 207–9, 214
Fawell, J., 271
FBI, 2, 18, 198
Feel the Heat, 67
Fehr, Rudy, 112
Fell, John L., 206, 271
Fellus, Elias (Graphics East), 53
Fenady, Andrew, *The Man with Bogart's Face*, 58
Ferguson, K., 255
Ferguson, Otis, 133
Fiedler, Leslie, 117, 184, 192
Fiennes, Ray, 66
Finney, Albert, 63–64
Fitzgerald, Geraldine, 62, 162
Flint, Peter B., 266

Flocos, Nicholas, 60
Flynn, Errol, 26, 62; compared to Bogart, 163
Fonda, Henry, 22, 33
Ford, Harrison, 5–6, 63, 80–81, 239
Ford, John, 1, 10; *Up the River*, 10, 199
Ford, Wally, 110
Forester, C. S., 232
For Whom the Bell Tolls, 189
Foster, Paul, 57
Fox, Sidney, 10, 11
Fox Film Corporation, 10
Foy, Bryan (Brynie), 104–7
Francis, Kay, 106
Francisco, Charles, 47, 176–77, 255
Frank, Alan, 244
Frank, Jerry, 101–4
Frank, Michael, 78
Fraternity of Man, 52
Frazier, George, 117, 125, 244
Frears, Stephen, 63
Freud, Sigmund, 168, 172, 218, 223
Friedrich, Otto, 2, 158, 244, 266
Frueh, Al, 74
Fuchs, Wolfgang, 79, 146–47, 244
Fultz, James, 203, 233, 248
Furthman, Jules, 20, 202–3, 205

Gabbard, Glen, 185, 189–90, 238, 253, 256
Gabbard, Krin, 185, 189–90, 238, 253, 256
Gable, Clark, 72, 75; Bogart on, 101; compared to Bogart, 19, 130, 136, 160; Huston on, 122; recent popularity, 49; Vincent Sherman on, 109
Gale, Stephen, 168, 266
Gallagher, Brian, 211–12, 215–16, 250
Gallico, Paul, 55
Garbo, Greta, 54, 140, 201
Garden of Allah. *See* Bogart, residences
Gardner, Ava, 130
Garfield, Brian, 142, 244
Garfield, John, 19, 152, 158; compared to Bogart, 145–46, 188
Garland, Judy, 30
Garland, Robert, 8, 12
Garrett, Betty, 52

Garrett, George, 207, 250
Garson, Greer, 34
Gassner, John, 181, 256
Gaylor, Gerry, 101–104
Geherin, David, 60
Gehman, Richard, 117–18, 130, 245
Gent from San Francisco, The, 162
George, Gladys, 163
Gersh, Phil, 30
Get Smart, 67
Giannetti, Louis, 266
Gibson, Mel, 81
Gide, André, 142, 165
Giesler, Jerry, 25
Gilda, 220
Gitt, Bob, 207
Glass, Madeline, 245
Gleason, Jackie, 110–11
Glimmer Man, The, 66
Glissements progressifs du plaisir, 64
Godard, Jean-Luc, 47, 63, 80, 130, 271; *Alphaville*, 63; *Breathless*, 47, 63, 130
Goddess, The, 231
Godfrey, Lionel, 172, 213, 250, 266
Godfrey, T., 262
Goldberg, Carl, 190, 256
Goldberg, Joe, 142–43, 165–66, 214, 245, 250, 266
Gomery, Douglas, 158, 262
Gone with the Wind, 185
Goodbye Girl, 64
Goodman, Ezra, 2, 28, 57, 115–17, 245
Good Night My Love, 64
Good Shepherd, The, 34
Goodwin, Michael, 250
Gould, Elliott, 64, 174
Goulding, Edmund, 155–56
Gow, Gordon, 172, 266
Graham, Katharine, 75
Graham, Olive, 223, 237, 249, 273
Graham, Sheilah, 23
Grahame, Gloria, 22, 228–32
Grammer, Kelsey, 78
Grant, Cary, 33, 49, 107
Green, Gary L., 186, 256
Greenberg, Harvey R., 169–70, 184, 190, 223–24, 226, 256, 266, 273
Greenberg, Joel, 180, 256, 260

Greenberger, Howard, 127, 245
Greene, Graham, 150, 153, 155, 253, 261, 269
Greenfield, Jeff, 76
Greenfield, Judge Edward J., 72
Greenstreet, Sydney, 51, 62, 76, 111; *Across the Pacific*, 176; *Casablanca*, 197; *Conflict*, 206–7; *Maltese Falcon*, 76, 163–65, 175
Gregory, Charles, 216, 250
Gremlins 2, 63
Griffith, Richard, 138–39, 245
Grimes, William, 190, 250, 256
Grobel, Lawrence, 158, 163, 224, 226, 232, 237, 248–49, 262, 264, 266, 273
Gruber, Peter, 52
Guadalcanal Diary, 199
Guernsey, Otis L., Jr., 27
Gumshoe, 63
Gun Runners, The, 204
Gurney, Noll, 14

Hairston, Robert B., 217, 250
Halliday, David, 60
Halsman, Philippe, 76
Hamill, Pete, 245
Hamilton, Hale, 7
Hamilton, Neil, 6
Hamilton, William, 183, 189, 256
Hammett, Dashiell, 64, 76, 140, 143, 166, 214; *The Maltese Falcon*, 76, 162–64, 171
Hanna, David, 1, 8, 115, 120–21, 245
Hanners, John, 141–42, 245
Hanson, Stephen L., 185–86, 198, 247, 256
Haralovich, Mary Beth, 151–52, 268
Hark, Ralph, 20
Harlow, Jean, 201
Harmetz, Aljean, 189; *Action in the North Atlantic*, 198, 247; Bogart and popular culture, 50, 58, 70, 76; *Casablanca* 177–81, 256; *Passage to Marseille*, 200, 269
Harold and Maude, 49
Harper, 63
Harper's Bazaar, 20
Hart, Christopher, 22, 137, 245

Hart, Henry, 239, 249
Haskell, Molly: Bogart and Bacall, 205; Bogart and fashions, 73, 245; Bogart's legend and appeal, 22, 134–35; *Dark Victory*, 156, 260; *To Have and Have Not*, 271; Howard Hawks, 251; Hawks, Bogart, and misogyny, 211–12
Hatari!, 206
Haun, Harry, 180, 256
Havana, 195
Haver, Ron, 177, 189, 256
Havoc, June, 29
Hawkes, Dana (Sotheby's), 54
Hawks, Howard, 20, 21, 23, 24, 26, 122, 143, 195; *The Big Sleep*, 24, 207–20; on Bogart, 204, 208; *To Have and Have Not*, 202–6; Hawks-Feldman Productions, 20
Hawks, Nancy "Slim," 20
Hayden, Sterling, 29
Haye, Helen, 11
Hayes, Helen, 10, 149
Hayward, Leland, 35
Hellinger, Mark, 58, 144 Bogart's business dealings with, 27; death of, 27, 29; *High Sierra*, 160
Hemingway, Ernest, 20, 137, 166, 172, 202–5, 214
Hemmeter, Thomas, 202–3, 271
Hendricks, Jim, 69
Hendrickson, Paul, 256
Henreid, Paul, 29, 62, 178, 181–82, 189, 192, 256
Hepburn, Audrey, 239
Hepburn, Katharine: *African Queen*, 30, 31, 35, 49, 62, 111, 233, 235, 248; screen presence, 130, 137, 161
Here's Looking at You, Warner Bros., 63
Hermann, Rick, 161, 262
Hickcox, Sidney, 107
Hicks, J., 251
Higgins, Bertie, 52
Higham, Charles, 162, 268
Hill, George Roy, 80
Hill, Jonathan, 120
Hitchcock, Alfred, 236
Hoberman, J., 195, 245, 256
Hodgins, Eric, 4

Hoffman, Dustin, 31
Hogue, Peter: *Big Sleep*, 209–10, 251; *Casablanca*, 188, 256; *High Sierra*, 161, 262; *Roaring Twenties*, 156, 270; *They Drive by Night*, 157, 271
Holden, William, 188, 239
Holdstein, D. H., 156, 260
Holland, Jack, 20, 27, 34 245
Hollywood Reporter, 88, 120
Hollywood Steps Out, 68
Hollywood Ten, 238
Holmby Hills "Rat Pack," 30, 117, 131
Holmes, Sherlock, 215
Hood, Mike, and John Close, 57
Hoover, J. Edgar, 29
Hopkins, Arthur, 12, 32; *The Petrified Forest* (play), 32
Hopper, Dennis, 101–4, 195
Hopper, Hedda, 245
Horne, Lena, 36
Horney, Karen, 170
House Across the Bay, 24
Houseman, John, 213–15, 251
House Un-American Activities Committee (HUAC), 29, 146, 226, 229–30, 232
Houston, Penelope, 213, 239, 249, 251
Hover, Helen, 87, 88, 96–100
Howard, Leslie, 12–13, 15, 32, 68, 74
Huckleberry Finn, 185
Hughes, Howard, 29
Hulse, Ed, 236, 249
Humphrey Bogart Rumba, 52
Humphrey, Maud: background and career, 2–4, 55, 119; Humphrey Bogart on 3, 92, 124; Bogart's wives' reflection of, 9; care of husband, 11; death from cancer, 34
Hunt, L., 74
Hunt, Marsha, 29
Hunt, Winslow, 169, 265
Hurrell, George, 54
Huston, John: *The African Queen*, 30–31, 111–12, 232–36, 248; *Beat the Devil*, 236–38, 249; on Bogart, 174–75, 234; Bogart on, 26, 165–66; on Bogart's screen persona, 185; CFA, 29; eulogy, 35, 245; film festival, 48; *High Sierra*,

as screenwriter, 158; *Key Largo*, 226–27; *The Maltese Falcon*, 162–75, 214; on new generation of actors, 122; as screenwriter and director, 111–12, 143; Vincent Sherman on, 109–10; *The Treasure of the Sierra Madre*, 223–26

Hyams, Joe: access to Bogart, 115, 118–19; adaptation of biography to film (*Bogie*), 65; *Beat the Devil*, 236, 249; biographies of, 245; Bogart's night life, 8; on fidelity, 23; *In a Lonely Place*, 230; press voice for Bogart and Bacall, 34–35

Iachetta, Michael, 245
I Died a Thousand Times, 62, 158
In This Our Life, 111
Invitation to a Murder, 12
Ira Roberts, Inc., 53
Isenberg, Barbara, 77
Italie, H., 256
I Wonder Who's Killing Her Now, 64

Jack Benny Show, 67, 78
Jaffe, Sam, 19
Jameson, Frederick, 206
Jameson, Richard T.: *African Queen*, 248; *Beat the Devil*, 249; *To Have and Have Not*, 204–5, 225, 271; *Maltese Falcon*, 163–64, 237, 266; *The Treasure of the Sierra Madre*, 235, 273
Jennings, D., 256
Jensen, P., 208, 251
Joan of Arc, 181
Johnson, Don, 73
Johnson, Julie, 156, 260
Johnson, Nunnally, 31, 35, 116–17, 144
Johnson, Timothy, 150, 269
Johnson, W., 173, 266
Johnson, W. Parke, 77
Jones, Jennifer, 35, 237
Jones, John, 34

Kael, Pauline, 117, 149; *African Queen*, 234; *Barefoot Contessa*, 239, 249; *Big Sleep*, 251; *Long Goodbye*, 174, 219; *Maltese Falcon*, 170, 266
Kaminsky, Stuart: *African Queen*, 235, 248; *Bullet for a Star* (fiction), 57–58; Huston on Bogart as actor, 174–75; Huston on Bogart and travel, 166; *Maltese Falcon*, 162, 170–71, 266; *The Treasure of the Sierra Madre*, 224, 273
Kaplan, Ira, 53
Kauffmann, Stanley, 149
Kaufman, Dave, 33
Kawin, Bruce, 195, 202–4, 208, 251, 257, 271
Kay, Karyn, 152, 268
Kaye, Danny, 29, 35
Keaton, Buster, 62
Kelly, Thomas O., 199, 270
Kellman, Steve G., 62, 195, 257
Kennedy, Andrew, *Just Like Humprhey Bogart*, 58
Kennedy, Arthur, 101
Kenny, Douglas, 22, 137, 245
Kerr, Laura, 162, 267
Keyes, John and Evelyn, 29
Kilgallen, Dorothy, 34
King, Rufus, 12
King's Row, 127, 177
Kinnard, Roy, 153, 185, 200, 257, 264, 269
Kinnear, Greg, 239
Kinskey, Leonid, 183, 257
Kirgo, Julie, 160, 175, 217–18, 230, 262, 263, 266
Kisses, 52
Klapart, Cathy Root, 151–52, 268
Know Your Ally, 201
Know Your Enemy, 201
Knudsen, Peggy, 207
Kobal, John, 137, 188, 245, 257
Koch, Howard: *Casablanca*, 177–78, 184, 191–93, 257; essay collection on *Casablanca*, 180–81, 195–96; Oscar sold, 69
Kornweibel, Theodore, Jr., 199–200, 270
Kovner, Irving, 70
Kramer, Stanley, 116, 238
Krüger, Sebastian, 54–55
Krutch, Joseph Wood, 150
Krutnik, Frank, 221, 261, 266
Kuhn, Annette, 211–12, 251
Kurosawa, Akira, 66

LaBro, Philippe, 63
La Cava, Gregory, *My Man Godfrey*, 6
Lacy, Jerry, 70–71
Ladd, Alan, 26, 188, 213
Lady from Shanghai, The, 221
Laemmle, Ann, 160, 262
Lake, Janet, 101–4,
Lamarr, Hedy, 78, 191, 192
Lamond, John M., 15
Lancaster, Elsa, 19
Langlois, G., 263
Lapsley, Robert, 189, 257
Lardner, Ring, Jr., 7
Larson, Gary, 74
Laskas, Kristin, 226, 264
Last Detail, The, 5
Last Man Standing, 66
Last Movie, The, 195
Last Tango in Paris, 195
Last Tycoon, 231
Late Show, The, 64
Laughlin, Tom, 101–4
Laurence, Frank M., 202–4, 272
L'Avventura, 237
Lawson, John Howard, 198–99
Lawton, Richard, 56
Lax, Eric, 2, 5, 23, 33, 123, 127
Lazar, Irving "Swifty," 23, 30, 33, 35, 117
Leamer, Laurence, 182–83, 257
Lebo, Harlan, 177–78, 257
Lee, Pamela Anderson, 66
Leech, John L., 18
Lehman, Ernest, 123
Leiva, Steven Paul, 257
Lemmon, Jack, 63
Leopold, Christopher, 60
Lerner, Alan J., and Frederick Loewe, 56
LeRoy, Mervyn, 116
Leslie, Amy, 9
Leslie, Joan, 161
Letter to Three Wives, A, 239–40
Lev, Peter, 209, 251
Levine, David, 76
Lévi-Strauss, Claude, 168, 210, 218
Lewin, Albert, 240
Lewis, Al, 10
Librach, Ronald S., 209, 251

Life Science (Heath), 60–61
Life with Buster Keaton, 62
Limbo, Sonny, 52
Lindstrom, Pia, 257
Little, Rich, 67
Little Feat, 52
Little Romance, A, 65, 80
Logan, Joshua, 22
Long Goodbye, The, 64, 174, 219, 225
Look, 100
Loos, Anita, 16
Lord, Robert, 27
Lorre, Peter, 62, 76, 112, 116; *Casablanca*, 197; *The Maltese Falcon*, 163–65, 172, 175
Losfeld, Eric, 70
Lost Patrol, The, 199
Love Boat, The, 67
Lowry, Cynthia, 245
Loy, Myrna, 10
Lucas, Blake, 228, 241, 262, 264
Lucas, George, 194
Luft, Sid, 30, 129
Luhr, William, 173, 175–76, 209, 251, 267
Lukow, Gregory, 150, 157, 253, 270
Lupino, Ida, 19, 130

MacDonald, George, *The Light Princess*, 3
Macek, Carl, 221, 261
Machamer, Jefferson, 125
Mack, Grace, 9
McGraw, Charles, 67
MacKaill, Dorothy, 11
MacKenna, Kenneth, 5, 10, 12, 15
MacLane, Barton, 107
MacShane, Frank, 213, 251
Mailer, Norman, 129
Majdalany, Fred, 273
Maltby, Richard, 186, 257
Maltese Bippy, The, 63
Mancuso, Nick, 67
Mank, Chaw, 79
Mank, Gregory W., 154, 249
Mankiewicz, Joseph L., 129, 239–40
Mann, Delbert, 33
Manvell, Roger, 245

Man Who Came Back, The, 10
Man Who Shot Liberty Valance, The, 1, 186
Man Who Would Be King, The, 87, 122
Man with Bogart's Face, The, 65, 71, 80
March, Frederic, 18, 240–41
Marcus, Stephen, 171, 267
Maree, A. Morgan, 27, 116–17
Margolick, D., 257
Marks, Louis, 239, 249
Marlette, Doug, 74
Marlow, Don, 246
Martin, Steve, 65
Marx, Groucho, 62
Marx Brothers, 62
Masden, Alex, 235, 248
Mason, Marsha, 56
Mast, Gerald, 202, 204, 209, 251, 272
Masterson, Peg, 225, 273
Mate, Ken, 159–60, 262
Mathews, Tom, 248
Matthews, P., 197–98, 257
Maugham, W. Somerset, 235
Maurstad, Tom, 80
Maxfield, James F., 167, 170, 210, 251, 267
Mayne, Judith, 211–12, 251
Mayor of Hell, 105
McBride, Joseph, 272
McArthur, Colin, 78, 195, 257
McBride, Joseph, 205, 208, 251, 257
McCabe and Mrs. Miller, 225
McCarthy, Abigail, 193, 257
McCarthy, Joseph, 22
McCarthy, M., 200, 269
McCarty, Clifford, 146, 246
McConnell, Frank, 216–17, 252
McCullough, J., 252
McDougal, Stuart Y., 224, 273
McDowell, Roddy, 54
McGarry, Eileen, 222, 260
McGilligan, Patrick, 159–60, 262
McHugh, Frank, 110
McLaglen, Victor, 10
McLaughlin, Mignon, 56
McPherson, Virginia, 26, 30
McQuarrie, Christopher, 66
McVay, D., 167, 184, 257

McVay, Nicholas, 231, 263, 267
Meade, Glen, 76
Meehan, Thomas, 60
Mellen, Joan, 134, 246
Mellins Baby Food Co., 3, 38 n.7, 46
Melville Goodwin, USA, 34
Memorabilia, 69–70
Menken, Helen: Bogart's hesitancy to marry, 119; character in a play, 57; dalliances, 23; descendant of John Wilkes Booth, 39 n.33; divorce, 9–10; engagement, 7; marriage, 7; relationship after divorce, 123; theater career, 39 n.23
Methot, Mayo, 14, 58, 66, 115, 178; Bogart on, 15, 96; Bogart's hesitancy to marry, 119; Bogart's sense of obligation, 24; Louise Brooks on, 15; character in a play, 57; divorces John M. Lamond, 15; divorces Percy T. Morgan, 25; drinking, 24; early stage career, 15; jealousy, 20, 24, 108–9; marriage, 15, 36; Vincent Sherman on, 108–9; stormy relationship, 20, 23, 26; support of Bogart, 16, 24, 36; Verita Thompson on, 126–27
Metz, Christian, 168, 210
Meyer, William R., 184, 258
Meyers, Jeffrey, 2, 23, 115, 123–24, 235, 246, 248
MGM, 173, 220
Michael, Paul, 147, 246
Middleton, David, 193, 258
Milan, Frank, 12
Milan, Gary, 69
Miller, A. L., 253
Miller, Arthur, 123
Miller, Don, 157, 269
Miller, Frank, 178–79, 181, 258
Miller, Gabriel, 62, 224–25, 273
Miller, Gilbert, 32
Milne, Tom, 233, 248
Mr. Skeffington, 112
Mitchum, Robert, 47, 64, 66
Mjagkij, N., 200–201, 269
Moby Dick (film), 164
Monaco, James, 212, 219, 252
Monroe, Marilyn, 45–46, 49, 72, 75
Mooks, S. R., 28

Moonraker, 65
Moore, Roger, 65
Morgan, Dennis, 107, 177, 191–92
Morgan, Joseph, 3
Morgan, Percy T., Jr., 15
Morgenstern, Joseph, 131, 246
Morocco, 205
Morris, Chester, 129
Morris, Wayne, 107
Morrison, Rachela, 258
Morrow, L., 187, 193–94, 258
Moshier, W. Franklyn, 246
Motion Picture, 96
Muir, Jean, 18
Mulvey, Laura, 212
Munby, Arthur, 211
Muni, Paul, 106–7, 109, 158, 226
Muppet Movie, The, 67
Muppets Go to the Movies, 67
Muppet Show, The, 67
Murder, My Sweet, 217, 238
Murphy, Mary, 23
Murrow, Edward R., *Person to Person*, 87
Muse, Clarence, 177
My Little Chickadee, 24
My Name Is Julia Ross, 220
Myra Breckenridge, 58

Naipaul, V. S., *Miguel Street*, 61
Naked Jungle, The, 241
Naremore, James, 163–64, 171, 176, 223, 267, 273
Nausée, La, 196, 257
Neilsen, R., 268
Never Say Goodbye, 62
Newman, Paul (*The Desperate Hours*), 56, 63
Nichols, Bill, 151, 268
Nichols, Dudley, 181
Nichols, Mike, 56
Nichols, Nina, 227, 264
Nicholson, Jack, 81
Nickolas, Murray, 55
Nielsen, R., 264, 270, 274
Night in Casablanca, A, 62
Nimoy, Leonard, 5–6

Niven, David, 21, 25, 30, 35, 37, 232, 248
Nolan, William F., 267, 273
Northcutt, Jim, 51
Nowland, Robert, and Gwendolyn Nowland, 56

O'Brien, Margaret, 100
O'Brien, Pat, 116, 124
O'Connor, Kevin, 57, 65
Office of War Information, 198, 200–201
O'Hara, John, 144
Old Acquaintance, 112
Oliver, Charles M., 272
Olson, Sidney, 29
Once in Paris, 65
O'Neal, Ryan, 63
Only Angels Have Wings, 206
Ontario County Times, 2
Ormand, Julia, 239
Orr, Christopher, 204, 211, 252
Osborne, Richard E., 177, 258
O'Toole, Larry, 154, 270
Our Blushing Brides, 151
Ouspenskaya, Maria, 100
Out of the Fog, 19
Overdrawn at the Memory Bank, 57
Overton, R., 273

Paderewski, Ignace, 94–95
Palance, Jack, 62
Palmer, Bill, 50
Palmer, James W., 228–29, 231–32, 263
Palmer, Karen, 50
Pandora and the Flying Dutchman, 240
Paramount Studios, 220
Paris, Bernard, 170
Paris, James, 217–18, 252
Parker, Dorothy, 144
Parshall, Peter F., 195, 258
Parsons, Louella, 1, 34
Paths of Glory, 238
Peary, Danny: *Beat the Devil*, 237, 249; *Casablanca*, 191, 258; *In a Lonely Place*, 229–30, 263; *Maltese Falcon* as cult film, 163–64, 267
Peck, Gregory, 35, 160
Pedersen, Vibeke, 211–12, 252

Pendo, Stephen, 209, 252
Penn, Sean, 66
Perils of Pauline, 198
Perkins, Carolyn, 156, 270
Perkins, V. F., 230, 263
Peskett, Hugh, *Debrett's Guide to the Aristocracy*, 2
Peterson, Elmer T., 124, 246
Pettigrew, Terence, 146–47, 246
Philbert, B., 260
Philips, Mary, 2, 10, 14, 16, 119; divorce from Bogart, 14–15; marriage to Bogart, 10
Phillips, Gene, 202–3, 208–9, 252, 272
Phillips, William H., 172, 267
Phillips Academy. *See* Bogart, education
Pintoff, Ernie, 64
Pitts, Zasu, 10
Place, Janey, 212, 212, 217, 252
Player, The, 154
Play It Again, Sam: film, 57, 62, 63, 71, 80; play, 6, 57, 71, 192
Poe, Edgar Allan, 194, 215
Point Blank, 207
Polan, Dana, 27, 185–86, 222, 228, 246, 258, 260, 263
Polanski, Roman, 64
Pollack, Sydney, 239
Polunsky, B., 258
Ponder, Anne, 252
Powell, Dick, 25, 213
Pratley, Gerald, 162–63, 224, 234–35, 248, 267, 273
Prescription: Murder, 67
Presley, Elvis, 45, 46, 48
Pressbooks, 149
Price, Keith, 212, 252
Price, Theodora, 151–52, 268
Pride of the Marines, 222
Prince, Stephen, 194, 258
Pritchett, Florence, 36
Production Code (Production Code Administration), 160, 162, 191, 197, 210, 215, 218, 237
Progressive Education Association, 150
Projectionist, The, 62
Propp, Vladimir, 168, 206, 210–11, 218

Pulp Fiction, 220
Purcell, James M., 141, 246
Pynchon, Thomas, 60

Radio performances, *Bold Venture*, 30
Raft, George, 90, 188; animated cartoon character, 68; Bogart compared to, 19; *Casablanca* casting, 177, 179, 192; refuses *Maltese Falcon*, 109, 162; in spoof (*Man with Bogart's Face*), 65
Raiders of the Lost Ark, 63, 195, 198
Rains, Claude, 75, 123
Ralli, Paul, 25
Randishi, Robert J., 60
Random, Henry, 160, 175, 213, 252, 262, 267
Raskin, Richard, 187, 258
Rat Pack. *See* Holmby Hills "Rat Pack"
Ray, Nicholas, 22, 27, 122, 135, 227–32
Ray, Robert B., 185, 189, 195, 206, 258
Reagan, Ronald, 36–37; *Casablanca* casting, 177, 184, 191
Reasoner, Harry, 193
Rebel Without a Cause, 227
Reed, Carol, 66
Reeve, Fred, 69
Reeves, Jimmie L., 171, 189, 210, 252, 258, 267
Reiner, Carl, 65
Remington Steele, 67
Renoir, Jean, 204
Revson, Charles, 52
Rey, Fernando, 65
Reynolds, Burt, 48
Reynolds, Quentin, 144
Ricci, Steven, 150, 157, 253, 270
Rice, Sean Michael, 56
Richard III (play), 195
Richardson, Carl, 173, 267
Rio Bravo, 206
River School (Conn.), 69
Rivkin, Allen, 162, 267
RKO, 220
Robards, Jason, 65
Robbe-Grillet, Alain, 64
Roberts, Julia, 66
Roberts, Robin, 28
Robertson, James C., 184, 258

Robinson, Casey, 155–56, 180, 189, 191, 260
Robinson, Edward G., 12, 14, 158, 227–28; compared to Bogart 140, 152
Robson, Mark, 241
Rocky, 241
Romanoff, Mike, 30, 35, 115–17, 126; Romanoff's Restaurant, 2, 32, 33, 35
Roosevelt, Franklin Delano, 94–95
Rope of Sand, 62
Rose, Frances Bogart. *See* Bogart, Frances "Pat"
Rose, Stuart, 5, 10, 117–18
Roseman, Eugene, 136, 246
Rosenbaum, Joseph, 206, 245, 272
Rosenzweig, Sidney, 183–84, 187–88, 201, 258, 269
Ross, Chuck, 181, 258
Ross, Herbert, 64
Ross, Lillian, 30, 233–34, 248
Ross, T. J., 237–38, 249
Rossen, Robert, 152
Rosten, Leo, 60
Rosterman, Robert, 156, 260
Rothman, William, 203, 272
Rowling, Gwen, 215, 252
Rubinstein, Lenny, 187, 258
Ruddy, Jonathan, 120, 246
Ryan, Tom, 155

Sabrina (Pollack), 80, 239
Sacchi, Robert, 58, 65, 68, 70–71
Sackett, Susan, 196, 258
Sacks, Frank, 56
Sahara (remake), 80
Sakall, Szoke Z. ("Cuddles"), 178, 258
Sakowski, S., 258
Sammy and Rosalie Get Laid, 230
Samuels, Charles, 26
Sanda, Dominique, 65
Sanders, George and Helen, 70
Santana, 20, 25, 32, 34, 36, 37, 123
Santana Pictures Corporation (aka Santana Productions), 27, 30, 119, 220, 227, 236–37
Sarris, Andrew, 133–34, 164, 179, 225, 246, 258, 262, 267
Sartre, Jean-Paul, 156, 212

Satan Met a Lady, 172
Saturday Evening Post, 90
Saturday's Children, 112
Save the Tiger, 62–63
Scapperotti, Dan, 157, 270
Schatz, Thomas, 167, 217, 227, 252, 264, 267
Schickel, Richard, 6, 20, 141, 144–45, 193, 246, 258
Schmidt, M.A., 246
Schultz, Charles, 74
Scott, Hazel, 177
Seaman, Billy, 28
Searchers, The, 186
Segal, George, 64
Seiler, Lewis, 105
Seligson, Tom, 5
Selznick, David, 35, 62, 177, 180, 237
Seneca Point, 3
Sennett, Ted: *Across the Pacific*, 176, 247; *Beat the Devil*, 250, 267, 269; *Casablanca*, 197, 258; *Conflict*, 206–7, 247, 259; *Maltese Falcon*, 162–65, 167–68, 237, 267; *Passage to Marseille*, 200, 269
Seven Samurai, The, 195
Sewell, J., 60
Seymour, Dan, 67
Shadoian, Jack, 157, 159, 262, 270
Shales, Tom, 158, 262
Shatzkin, Roger, 216–17, 252
Shaw, Daniel G., 203, 206, 272
Shearer, Lloyd, 246
Sheehan, Winnie, 32
Shepler, Michael, 160, 229, 262, 263
Sheridan, Ann, 19, 94, 96, 127; *Casablanca* casting, 177, 184, 191–92
Sherman, Eric, 258
Sherman, Vincent, 88, 104–13
Sherwood, Robert E., 32; *The Petrified Forest*, 12, 32
Shettler, Judge, 25
She Was an Acrobat's Daughter, 68
Shindler, Colin, 270
Shipman, David, 128, 246
Shipp, Cameron, 117, 126, 246
Shoot the Piano Player, 63, 80
Siegel, Don, 178

Siegel, Jeff, 177, 258
Silke, James R., 246
Silver, Alain, 217–18, 230, 263
Silver Screen, 20
Silvers, Phil, 110–11
Simon, Neil, 64
Simons, John L., 263
Sinatra, Frank, 30, 103–4, 117
Since You Went Away, 186
Sinclair, Andrew, 233, 248
Singer, Bryan, 66
Sirocco (1995), 66
Sklar, Robert, 246; *African Queen*, 235, 248; *Big Sleep*, 218, 252; *Caine Mutiny*, 238, 253; *Casablanca*, 179, 186, 259; *City Boys*, 145–46; *Dark Passage*, 260; *Desperate Hours*, 261; *Harder They Fall*, 241, 262; *To Have and Have Not*, 272; *Key Largo*, 227, 264; *In a Lonely Place*, 263; *Passage to Marseille*, 200, 269; *Sabrina*, 239, 270; *Treasure of the Sierra Madre*, 226, 273; *We're No Angels*, 240, 274
Sklarew, Bruce, 190
Sledgehammer, 67
Slick Hare, 68
Slide, Anthony, 53
Sluggy (boat), 16, 25
"Sluggy Hollow" (residence), 16
Smith, J., 258
Smith, Liz, 21, 66
Smith, Russell, 193, 259
Snyder, Ellen J., 235, 248
Solomon, Stanley, 167, 171, 188, 217, 252, 259, 267
Sorel, E., 195, 259
Sotto, Sotto, 65
Soul, David, 67
Sound and the Fury, The, 209
Spacey, Kevin, 66
Spector, Warren, 198, 271
Spencer, Lady Diana, 2
Sperber, A. M., 2, 5, 23, 33, 115, 123, 127, 246
Spiegel, Sam, 233
Spielberg, Steven, 63, 194
Spitting Image, 57
Spoto, Donald, 238, 253

Staiger, Janet, 173, 231
Stanislavsky method, 102–3
Stanley, John, and Ken Davis, *Bogart '48*, 57
Stanwyck, Barbara, 96, 120
A Star Is Born, 231
Starks, Lisa, 239, 270
Star Trek: The Next Generation, 68
Star Wars, 63, 185
Stearns, Alfred E. (Phillips Academy), 4
Steele, Joseph H., 259
Steiger, Rod, 142
Steinberg, Barry, 267
Steinberg, Cobbett S., 246
Steiner, Max, 177–78, 189, 197
Stevenson, Adlai, 22–23, 29
Stewart, Jimmy, 22, 28, 49
Stickney, John, 195, 259
Storer, Doug, 4
Stork Club, 28
Strand Theater, 19
Streisand, Barbra, 63
Strudwick, Sheppard, 29
Stuart, Bruce, 254
Stuart, Gloria, 128–29, 246
Sturges, Preston, 163
Suid, Lawrence H., 199, 270
Sugar, Andy, 64
Sullivan, Ed, 29
Sullivan's Travels, 154
Sumner, Jane, 193, 259
Sunset Boulevard, 231
Superman II, 198
Sussman, Gerald, 60
Sweeney, Kevin W., 202–4
Swift, Jonathan, 34
Swires, S., 207, 252

Taking Off, 65
Talbot, Lyle, 11
Tales from the Crypt, 68
Talma, François Joseph, 95
Talty, Stephan, 124, 46
Taplinger, Robert S., 18
Taradash, Daniel, 65
Taubman, Leslie, 223, 226, 273
Taylor, John Russell, 175, 267
Teenage Crime Wave, 241

Telotte, J. P., *Casablanca* as cult film, 194–195, 259; *Dark Passage*, 222–23, 260; *Dead Reckoning*, 220–21, 261; *In a Lonely Place* 228–29, 231, 263
10, 49
TheBerge, Rita, 155–56, 203, 252, 260, 272
They Live by Night, 227
Thin Man, The, 173, 213
Third Man, The, 66
Thirteen, The, 199
This Gun for Hire, 24
Thomas, Bob, 71
Thomas, J. Parnell, 29
Thomas, Sam, 259
Thompson, Howard, 27, 249
Thompson, Kristin, 173, 231, 265
Thompson, Thomas, 137
Thompson, Verita, 19, 21, 23, 123, 126–27, 247
Thomson, David: *Big Sleep*, 208, 216–17, 219–20, 252; Bogart bio, 247; *Casablanca*, 180, 259; *To Have and Have Not*, 206, 272; *In a Lonely Place*, 228, 263; *The Maltese Falcon*, 139–41; *Suspects* (novel), 58
Thurber, James, 17, 74, 125
Tillotson, Jerry, 184, 259
Tolson, Andrew, 77
Tolson, Clyde (FBI), 29
Tone, Franchot, 18
Tony Rome, 207
Towne, Robert, 130, 247
Trace of Murder, A, 67
Tracy, Spencer, 10, 33, 35, 101, 240
Traven, B., *The Treasure of the Sierra Madre*, 223–26, 273
Trent, Paul, 153–54, 261, 269
Trilling, Lionel, 205
Trilling, Steve, 19
Trinity School. *See* Bogart, education
Truffaut, François, 80, 135, 204, 206, 236, 238, 239–40, 247, 249, 254
Truman, Harry, 87
Turim, Maureen, 185, 259
Turner, Ted, 48, 49, 74
Tuska, Jon, 167, 207, 221, 253, 261, 267
Twentieth Century Fox, 35, 220

Two for the Road, 63
Tyler, Parker, 169, 268
Tynan, Kenneth, 132–33, 247

Underground, 112
Underworld, 206
Universal Studios, 10
USO, 2, 16, 20
USS *Leviathan*, 5
USS *Santa Olivia*, 5
Ustinov, Peter, 129
Usual Suspects, The, 66

Valley of the Giants, 24
Van Gelder, Peter, 178, 259, 268
Van Leeuwen, Jean, 61
VanWert, William, 253
Veidt, Conrad, 112
Verne, Kaaren, 112
Vernet, Marc, 168, 218, 232, 253, 261, 268
Vickers, Martha, 220
Vidal, Gore, 58
Viertel, Peter, 233–35, 249
Vitone, R. J., 153, 185, 200, 257, 264
Vogues of 1938, 22
Vonalt, Larry, 192, 259

Wald, Jerry, 111, 116, 204
Walker, Jimmy, 89
Walker, Michael, 218–19, 253
Wallis, Hal, 62, 122; *Casablanca*, 177, 179, 189, 259; *Dark Victory*, 156; *The Maltese Falcon*, 162, 268
Walsh, Michael, 66
Walsh, Raoul, 6, 10, 17, 110, 143, 156–57, 160, 185
Wanger, Walter, 22
Ward, L. E., 249, 264
Warner, Jack L., Sr., 35; battles with Bogart, 19, 36, 120, 137; casting for *Casablanca*, 192; casting for *The Maltese Falcon*, 162; contracts, 26, 32, 98; politics, 28, 94
Warner Bros., 35, 54, 220, 227; *African Queen*, 232, 235; Basinger on, 173; *Big City Blues*, 11; Bogart's contracts, 13, 14, 144; Bogart's status at, 14, 19,

20, 120, 137, 144, 158; *Carrotblanca*, 69; *Casablanca* and *Algiers*, 195; *Casablanca* remake, 66; *Casablanca* sequel, 62; documentary spirit, 153, 157; ideology at, 90, 191, 206; *Key Largo*, 204; *Petrified Forest*, 12; popularity of Bogart's films, 48; Vincent Sherman at, 104–13; studio history (documentary), 63; sued on rights to *Casablanca*, 179
Warner Brothers Presents, 67
Warshow, Robert, 129
Watkins, Susan, 172, 268
Wax museums, 62
Wayne, John, 46, 48, 49, 72, 75
Weales, Gerald, 47, 133, 247
Webb, Clifton, 116
Webb, Jack, 72
Weisman, John, 193, 259
Wellbourne, Scotty, 76
Welles, Orson, 169
West, Mae, 59
Westlake, Michael, 190, 257
Wexman, Virginia Wright, 141, 166, 173, 174, 212–14, 253, 268
What's Up Doc, 63
When Harry Met Sally, 65
White Heat, 227
White Hunter, Black Heart, 234, 249
Why We Fight, 201
Wilbur, Crane, 105
Wild Bunch, The, 225
Wilder, Billy, 29, 33, 35, 123, 142, 239
Williams, Robert, 129, 247
Williamson, David, *Burke's Peerage*, 2
Williamson, Judith, 230, 263
Willis, Bruce, 66
Willis, Donald C., 253

Willow Brook, 3
Willson, Robert F., Jr., 195–96, 259
Wilmington, Michael, 264
Wilson, Dooley, 69, 177, 187
Wilson, Earl, 21, 126, 247
Wilson, Tom, 74
Wise, Naomi, 250
Without Apparent Motive, 63
Wizard of Oz, 186
Wlaschin, Ken, 143, 247
Wolper, David, 67
Wood, George, 174, 268
Wood, Michael, 189, 201, 259
Wood, Robin, 201; *The Big Sleep*, 209–10, 213–214, 253; *Casablanca*, 184, 188; *To Have and Have Not*, 272; Howard Hawks, 205, 253
Woollcott, Alexander, 7, 8, 9, 87
Wouk, Herman, 238
Wright, Frank Lloyd, 230
Wright, J., 259
Wright, Lloyd, 25
Wright, T. C. (Tenney), 106
Written on the Wind, 210
Wuntch, Philip, 193, 240, 259, 261
Wyatt, Jane, 29
Wyatt, Will, 224, 273
Wyler, William, 29, 241

Yacowar, Maurice, 57
Yojimbo, 66
Yordan, Philip, 241
Young, Roland, 40 n.45
Youngking, Stephen D., 259

Zemeckis, Robert, 68
Zinman, David, 166, 196, 259, 268
Zolotow, Maurice, 33, 239, 270

About the Author

GERALD DUCHOVNAY is a professor of English and head of the Department of Literature and Languages at Texas A&M University—Commerce. A recipient of a Dana Foundation Fellowship at Carnegie Mellon University, NEH summer fellowships at the Johns Hopkins University and the University of North Carolina, and a Modern Media Institute Fellowship, he is the founding and general editor of *Post Script: Essays in Film and the Humanities*, an international film publication.

**Recent Titles in
Popular Culture Bio-Bibliographies**

W. C. Fields: A Bio-Bibliography
Wes D. Gehring

Elvis Presley: A Bio-Bibliography
Patsy Guy Hammontree

Charles A. Lindbergh: A Bio-Bibliography
Perry D. Luckett

The Marx Brothers: A Bio-Bibliography
Wes D. Gehring

Mae West: A Bio-Bibliography
Carol M. Ward

The Beatles: A Bio-Bibliography
William McKeen

Laurel & Hardy: A Bio-Bibliography
Wes D. Gehring

John Wayne: A Bio-Bibliography
Judith M. Riggin

Bob Dylan: A Bio-Bibliography
William McKeen

Walt Disney: A Bio-Bibliography
Kathy Merlock Jackson

Buster Keaton: A Bio-Bibliography
Joanna E. Rapf

Shirley Temple Black: A Bio-Bibliography
Patsy Guy Hammontree